Constraint-Based Reasoning

Special Issues of *Artificial Intelligence: An International Journal*

The titles in this series are paperback, readily accessible editions of the Special Volumes of *Artificial Intelligence: An International Journal*, edited by Daniel G. Bobrow and produced by special agreement with Elsevier Science Publishers B.V.

Qualitative Reasoning about Physical Systems, edited by Daniel G. Bobrow, 1985.

Geometric Reasoning, edited by Deekpak Kapur and Joseph L. Mundy, 1989.

Machine Learning: Paradigms and Methods, edited by Jaime Carbonell, 1990.

Artificial Intelligence and Learning Environments, edited by William J. Clancey and Elliot Soloway, 1990.

Connectionist Symbol Processing, edited by G. E. Hinton, 1991.

Foundations of Artificial Intelligence, edited by David Kirsh, 1992.

Knowledge Representation, edited by Ronald J. Brachman, Hector J. Levesque, and Raymond Reiter, 1992.

Artificial Intelligence in Perspective, edited by Daniel G. Bobrow, 1994.

Constraint-Based Reasoning, edited by Eugene C. Freuder and Alan K. Mackworth, 1994.

Constraint-Based Reasoning

edited by
Eugene C. Freuder and Alan K. Mackworth

A Bradford Book
The MIT Press
Cambridge, Massachusetts
London, England

First MIT Press edition, 1994
© 1992 Elsevier Science Publishers B.V., Amsterdam, the Netherlands

All rights reserved. No part of this book may be reproduced in any form by any electronic or mechanical means (including photocopying, recording, or information storage and retrieval) without permission in writing from the publisher.

Reprinted from *Artificial Intelligence: An International Journal*, Volume 58, Numbers 1–3, 1992. The MIT Press has exclusive license to sell this English-language book edition throughout the world.

Printed and bound in the United States of America. This book is printed on acid-free paper.

Library of Congress Cataloging-in-Publication Data

Constraint-based reasoning / edited by Eugene C. Freuder and Alan K. Mackworth.
    p. cm.
"A Bradford book."
Reprinted from Artificial intelligence, volume 58, numbers 1–3, 1992.
Includes bibliographical references and index.
ISBN 0-262-56075-5
1. Constraints (Artificial intelligence) 2. Reasoning. I. Freuder, Eugene C. II. Mackworth, Alan K.
Q340.C65 1994
006.3—dc20
    93-21600
    CIP

CONTENTS

E.C. Freuder and A.K. Mackworth
Introduction to the Special Volume on Constraint-Based Reasoning [ARTINT 947] — 1

A.K. Mackworth
The logic of constraint satisfaction [ARTINT 948] — 3

E.C. Freuder and R.J. Wallace
Partial constraint satisfaction [ARTINT 949] — 21

E. Hyvönen
Constraint reasoning based on interval arithmetic: the tolerance propagation approach [ARTINT 950] — 71

P. Van Hentenryck, H. Simonis and M. Dincbas
Constraint satisfaction using constraint logic programming [ARTINT 951] — 113

S. Minton, M.D. Johnston, A.B. Philips and P. Laird
Minimizing conflicts: a heuristic repair method for constraint satisfaction and scheduling problems [ARTINT 952] — 161

P.R. Cooper and M.J. Swain
Arc consistency: parallelism and domain dependence [ARTINT 953] — 207

R. Dechter and J. Pearl
Structure identification in relational data [ARTINT 954] — 237

M. Zweben, E. Davis, B. Daun, E. Drascher, M. Deale and M. Eskey
Learning to improve constraint-based scheduling [ARTINT 955] — 271

P. van Beek
Reasoning about qualitative temporal information [ARTINT 956] — 297

G.A. Kramer
A geometric constraint engine [ARTINT 957] — 327

Q. Yang
A theory of conflict resolution in planning [ARTINT 958] — 361

Index — 393

Introduction to the Special Volume on Constraint-Based Reasoning

Eugene C. Freuder
Department of Computer Science, University of New Hampshire, Durham, NH 03824, USA

Alan K. Mackworth
Department of Computer Science, University of British Columbia, Vancouver, BC, Canada V6T 1Z2

Constraint-based reasoning has long been a productive research focus for researchers in artificial intelligence. Richard Fikes, for example, reported an early contribution in the very first issue of this journal. Lately, the subject has enjoyed markedly increased attention. This interest has been influenced by, and in turn influenced, an acceleration of progress on many fronts. This special volume reports new results in three important areas: paradigms, tractability, and applications.

Paradigms

The first paper, by Alan Mackworth, places the standard AI formalization of constraint satisfaction problems within a space of logical representation and reasoning systems. Freuder and Wallace extend standard constraint satisfaction methods to cope with situations in which it is unnecessary or impossible to satisfy all the constraints. Eero Hyvönen presents a new approach to satisfying constraints on intervals. Van Hentenryck, Simonis and Dincbas use constraint logic programming to solve practical problems.

Tractability

Minton, Johnston, Philips and Laird, demonstrate that for some problems it can be very efficient to satisfy constraints by refining an initial imperfect

Correspondence to: E.C. Freuder, Department of Computer Science, University of New Hampshire, Durham, NH 03824, USA. Fax: (603) 862-3775. E-mail: ecf@cs.unh.edu.

0004-3702/92/$05.00 © 1992 — Elsevier Science Publishers B.V. All rights reserved

solution. Cooper and Swain demonstrate how parallelism can speed up constraint satisfaction. Dechter and Pearl discuss identification of computationally tractable structures. Zweben, Davis, Daun, Drascher, Deale and Eskey use a form of explanation-based learning to acquire search control knowledge for constraint-based scheduling.

Applications

Peter van Beek shows how to reason about qualitative temporal constraints. Glenn Kramer describes a geometric constraint engine. Qiang Yang develops a computational theory of conflict resolution in planning using constraint satisfaction techniques.

Of course, this tripartite framework for the volume does not result in mutually exclusive categories. For example, the "tractability" paper by Zweben et al. presents a scheduling application while the "applications" paper of van Beek presents computationally efficient algorithms.

The volume itself has its roots in the Eleventh International Joint Conference on Artificial Intelligence (IJCAI-89) and the Eighth National Conference on Artificial Intelligence (AAAI-90), where interest in constraint-based reasoning blossomed into two workshops and a plethora of excellent conference papers. The editors invited the authors of a selection of these papers to submit new papers with their latest results. Unfortunately, the selection was necessarily limited: many fine papers could not be considered due to a variety of constraints such as limited space, breadth of coverage and availability of the paper. Submissions were sent out for formal review; the revised, accepted papers appear here. We should note that the editors' papers appear first because, although they are intended as research contributions, we hope that each in its own way also serves a tutorial function in this volume: the first in placing constraint-based reasoning in its logical context, the second in reviewing some of the standard constraint satisfaction algorithms.

The most satisfying outcome of bringing this special volume together is the demonstration of the coherence of the constraint-based reasoning paradigm. It provides a fundamental set of theoretical and practical tools that cuts across (and unifies) the traditional division of artificial intelligence into task domains such as perception, language use, reasoning, planning, learning and action. Another outcome is the solidification of the connections of this approach with related developments in areas such as logic programming, numerical computation, algorithm design, complexity theory, operations research, graphics and robotics.

The logic of constraint satisfaction

Alan K. Mackworth*
Department of Computer Science, University of British Columbia, Vancouver, BC, Canada V6T 1W5

Abstract

Mackworth, A.K., The logic of constraint satisfaction, Artificial Intelligence 58 (1992) 3–20.

The constraint satisfaction problem (CSP) formalization has been a productive tool within Artificial Intelligence and related areas. The finite CSP (FCSP) framework is presented here as a restricted logical calculus within a space of logical representation and reasoning systems. FCSP is formulated in a variety of logical settings: theorem proving in first order predicate calculus, propositional theorem proving (and hence SAT), the Prolog and Datalog approaches, constraint network algorithms, a logical interpreter for networks of constraints, the constraint logic programming (CLP) paradigm and propositional model finding (and hence SAT, again). Several standard, and some not-so-standard, logical methods can therefore be used to solve these problems. By doing this we obtain a specification of the semantics of the common approaches. This synthetic treatment also allows algorithms and results from these disparate areas to be imported, and specialized, to FCSP; the special properties of FCSP are exploited to achieve, for example, completeness and to improve efficiency. It also allows export to the related areas. By casting CSP both as a generalization of FCSP and as a specialization of CLP it is observed that some, but not all, FCSP techniques lift to CSP and thereby to CLP. Various new connections are uncovered, in particular between the proof-finding approaches and the alternative model-finding approaches that have arisen in depiction and diagnosis applications.

1. Logical frameworks for constraint satisfaction

Informally, a constraint satisfaction problem (CSP) is posed as follows. Given a set of variables and a set of constraints, each specifying a relation on a particular subset of the variables, find the relation on the set of all the variables which satisfies all the given constraints. Typically, the given unary relation for each variable specifies its domain as a set of possible values; the required solution relation is a subset of the Cartesian product of the variable domains. If

---

Correspondence to: A.K. Mackworth, Department of Computer Science, University of British Columbia, Vancouver, BC, V6T 1W5
* Shell Canada Fellow, Canadian Institute for Advanced Research.

each domain is finite, the CSP is a finite constraint satisfaction problem (FCSP).

The formulation of the CSP paradigm has yielded substantial theoretical and practical results [6, 17]. It is important, though, not to conceive of the CSP paradigm in isolation but to see it in its proper context, namely, as a highly restricted logical calculus with associated properties and algorithms. The purpose of this paper is to place CSPs in that context, to redevise some old results in new, simpler ways, and to establish connections amongst the differing logical views of CSPs. Essentially the paper can be seen as an extended answer to the question, "Does the CSP framework make logical sense?". It can also be seen as a response to a cynical critic who asks, "Is CSP merely old wine in new bottles?". It is intended to lead to answers to the following questions:

- Can FCSP be posed and solved in logical frameworks?
- Can the special properties of FCSP be exploited to get better algorithms?
- Are tractable classes of FCSP revealed?
- What are the relationships among the several logical views of FCSP?
- Can the approaches for FCSP be lifted to CSP?
- Do new results and systems follow from this approach?

2. An FCSP: the Canadian flag problem

To fix the ideas of this paper, a trivial FCSP will be used as an example. Consider the well-known Canadian flag problem. A committee proposed a new design for the Canadian flag, shown in Fig. 1. The problem is to decide how to colour the flag. Only two colours, red and white, should be used; each region should be a different colour from its neighbours, and the maple leaf should, of course, be red. The problem is so trivial that its solution requires little thought, but it serves our purpose here.

Fig. 1. A trivial FCSP: colour the Canadian flag.

3. FCS as theorem proving in FOPC

Solving an FCSP can be formulated as theorem proving in a restricted form of first-order predicate calculus, as follows [1, 16]. The FCSP decision problem is equivalent to determining if *Constraints*⊢*Query* where *Query* has the form

Query:
$$\exists X_1 \exists X_2 \cdots \exists X_n \, QMatrix(X_1, X_2, \ldots, X_n)$$

or

Query:
$$\exists X_1 \exists X_2 \cdots \exists X_n \, p_{X_1}(X_1) \wedge p_{X_2}(X_2) \wedge \cdots \wedge p_{X_n}(X_n) \wedge$$
$$p_{X_1 X_2}(X_1, X_2) \wedge p_{X_1 X_3}(X_1, X_3) \wedge \cdots \wedge$$
$$p_{X_1 X_2 X_3}(X_1, X_2, X_3) \wedge \cdots \wedge$$
$$\vdots$$
$$p_{X_1 X_2 X_3 \cdots X_n}(X_1, X_2, X_3, \ldots, X_n)$$

and *Constraints* is a set of ground atoms specifying the extensions of the predicates

Constraints:
$$\{ p_{X_{i_1} X_{i_2} \cdots X_{i_m}}(c_{i_1}, c_{i_2}, \ldots, c_{i_m}) \mid 1 \leq i_k < i_{k+1} \leq n \}$$

where the c_i are constants. Notice that in this formulation we are only specifying the tuples allowed by a relation, not the tuples forbidden, since *Constraints* consists of positive literals.

4. FCS decision problems

An FCSP is specified by a (*Constraints*, *Query*) pair. A common candidate formulation of the FCS decision problem is to determine if it can be shown that a solution exists or does not exist: *Constraints*⊢*Query*, or *Constraints*⊢¬*Query*. However, given the positive form specified for *Constraints*, it is never possible to establish that *Constraints*⊢¬*Query*, so this candidate formulation is unacceptable. Later, when we consider the completion of *Constraints*, we shall return to a variant of this formulation.

The FCS decision problem (FCSDP) is to determine if it can be shown that a solution exists or if it cannot be shown that a solution exists: *Constraints*⊢*Query* or *Constraints*⊬*Query*.

If the decision problem is posed in the form of FCSDP and the constraints are supplied or discovered incrementally in the form of additional allowed tuples, extending the set *Constraints*, then the answers to FCSDP are monotonic: a "No" may change to "Yes" but not vice versa.

Proposition. *FCSDP is decidable.*

Proof. For an FCSP specified by the pair (*Constraints*, *Query*), a decision algorithm to determine if *Constraints*⊢*Query* or *Constraints*⊬*Query* is required. The Herbrand universe H of the theory *Constraints* ∪ ¬*Query* is

$$H = \{c \mid p_\gamma(\ldots, c, \ldots) \in \textit{Constraints}\}.$$

H is finite.

Consider the following algorithm:

    Decision Algorithm DA:

    Success ← No
    For each tuple $(c_1, c_2, \ldots, c_n) \in H^n$
        If *Constraints*⊢*QMatrix*$(c_1, c_2, \ldots, c_n)$ then
            Success ← Yes
    Report *Success*
    End DA

where *Constraints*⊢*QMatrix*$(c_1, c_2, \ldots, c_n)$ iff for each *Atom* mentioned in *QMatrix*$(c_1, c_2, \ldots, c_n)$ it is the case that *Atom* ∈ *Constraints*.

DA always terminates. It reports "Yes" iff *Constraints*⊢*Query*. It reports "No" iff *Constraints*⊬*Query*. □

The number of predicate evaluations made by DA is

$$(\# \text{ atoms in } \textit{QMatrix}(X_1, X_2, \ldots, X_n)) \times |H|^n.$$

5. Completing the constraints

Consider the completion of *Constraints* with respect to *Query*. Each predicate mentioned in *Query* can be completed, using Reiter's Closed World Assumption [23], in the following sense:

    completion(*Constraints*) =

    Constraints ∪

    $\{\neg p_\gamma(c_1, c_2, \ldots, c_k) \mid c_i \in H, p_\gamma(c_1, c_2, \ldots, c_k) \notin \textit{Constraints}\}.$

In other words, the complete extension of each k-ary predicate over H^k is specified, positively and negatively, in *completion*(*Constraints*).

Notice that $Constraints \vdash Query$ iff $completion(Constraints) \vdash Query$ and $Constraints \not\vdash Query$ iff $completion(Constraints) \vdash \neg Query$. Hence, DA reports "Yes" iff $completion(Constraints) \vdash Query$ and "No" iff $completion(Constraints) \vdash \neg Query$.

We may choose to interpret the answer from DA in the original sense of FCSDP or under the assumption that *Constraints* has been completed. Both interpretations are correct. "Yes" means $Constraints \vdash Query$ and $completion(Constraints) \vdash Query$; on the other hand, "No" means $Constraints \not\vdash Query$ and $completion(Constraints) \vdash \neg Query$.

6. The flag FCSP in FOPC

Using the FCSP formalism presented above we can formulate the flag problem as follows (see Fig. 2):

Query:

$$\exists X \exists Y \exists Z \exists U \; p(X) \wedge q(Y) \wedge s(Z) \wedge t(U) \wedge$$
$$ne(X, Y) \wedge ne(Y, Z) \wedge ne(Y, U) \,.$$

Constraints:

$\{p(r), p(w), q(r), q(w), s(r), s(w), t(r), ne(r, w), ne(w, r)\}$.

$H = \{r, w\}$, where r stands for red and w for white.

$H^4 = \{(r, r, r, r), (r, r, r, w), \ldots, (w, w, w, w)\}$.

On the FCSP (*Query*, *Constraints*), algorithm DA returns "Yes" succeeding on the tuple (r, w, r, r).

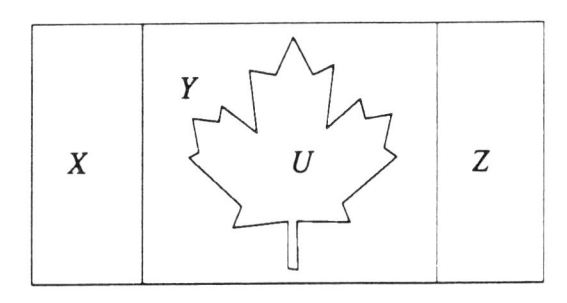

Fig. 2. The Canadian flag problem as an FCSP.

7. Logical representation and reasoning systems

Faced with a problem in representation and reasoning, a wide spectrum of logical representation systems is available to us. In choosing an appropriate system, we can rely on two sets of criteria: descriptive and procedural adequacy criteria [24]. These are often in conflict. The best advice is to use Occam's Razor: choose the simplest system with the level of descriptive adequacy required. Some representation and reasoning systems are shown, organized as a DAG, in Fig. 3. If there is a downward arc from system A to system B, then A's descriptive capabilities are a strict superset of B's. In the previous section, for example, FCS was shown to be equivalent to theorem-proving in a very restricted form of FOPC. Horn FOPC restricts FOPC in only allowing Horn clauses. (Recall that a clause, a disjunction of literals, is Horn if it has at most one positive literal. A Horn clause has one of four forms: a positive unit clause consisting of a single positive literal, a negative clause consisting only of negative literals, a mixed Horn clause consisting of one positive literal and at least one negative literal and, trivially, the empty clause, □. A definite clause has exactly one positive literal; it is either a unit positive clause or a mixed Horn clause.) Definite clause programs (DCP), without predicate completion, restrict Horn FOPC by allowing only one negative clause which serves as the query. Datalog essentially restricts DCP by eliminating function symbols. FCS restricts Datalog by disallowing rules, mixed Horn clauses. There are several further restrictions on FCS possible with correspond-

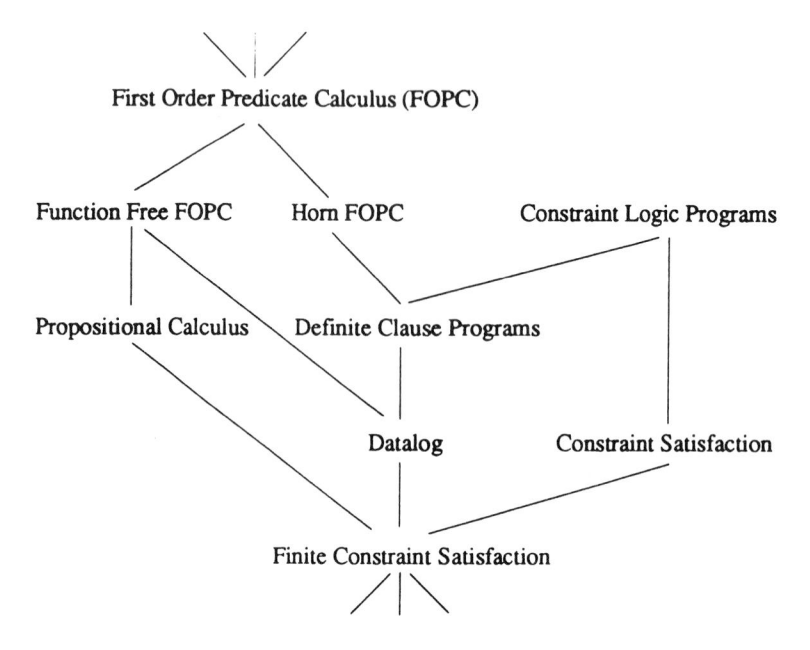

Fig. 3. Some logical representation and reasoning systems.

ing gains in tractability and some generalizations of FCS with gains in expressive power. We shall examine various logical formulations of FCS and investigate some of their interrelationships.

8. FCS as theorem proving in propositional calculus

The algorithm DA can be interpreted as implementing a view of FCS as theorem proving in the propositional calculus. *Query* is a theorem to be proved. If a solution exists, the theory *Constraints* $\cup \neg Query$ leads to a contradiction.

$\neg Query$:

$$\neg \exists X_1 \exists X_2 \cdots \exists X_n \, QMatrix(X_1, \ldots, X_n)$$

$$\forall X_1 \forall X_2 \cdots \forall X_n \, \neg QMatrix(X_1, \ldots, X_n) \, .$$

A solution exists iff *Constraints* $\cup \neg Query$ has no (Herbrand) models. There are no universal quantifiers in *Query* and so there are no existential quantifiers in the theory *Constraints* $\cup \neg Query$. Hence no Skolem functions are introduced when the theory is converted to clausal form. This important restriction guarantees that the Herbrand universe H is finite. This allows us to replace each of the universal quantifiers by the conjunction of the $\neg QMatrix(X_1, X_2, \ldots, X_n)$ clauses instantiated over H^n. This rewritten theory has the same set of Herbrand models as the original theory.

For the flag example the rewritten theory is:

$$\{p(r), p(w), q(r), q(w), s(r), s(w), t(r), ne(r, w), ne(w, r)\}$$

$$\cup$$

$$\{\neg p(r) \vee \neg q(r) \vee \neg s(r) \vee \neg t(r) \vee \neg ne(r, r) \, ,$$

$$\neg p(r) \vee \neg q(r) \vee \neg s(r) \vee \neg t(w) \vee \neg ne(r, r) \vee \neg ne(r, w) \, ,$$

$$\vdots$$

$$\neg p(r) \vee \neg q(w) \vee \neg s(r) \vee \neg t(r) \vee \neg ne(r, w) \vee \neg ne(w, r) \, , \qquad (*)$$

$$\vdots$$

$$\neg p(w) \vee \neg q(w) \vee \neg s(w) \vee \neg t(w) \vee \neg ne(w, w)\} \, .$$

This theory, now a propositional formula in CNF, has a particular restricted form for any FCSP. It consists only of a set of unit positive clauses, arising from the constraints, and a set of negative clauses, from the query. There are no mixed clauses. Note that it is also always Horn. It is unsatisfiable iff the FCSP has a solution. Since it is Horn, SAT is linear time in the size of the formula [8], but, of course, there are $|H|^n$ negative clauses in the formula. Also note that unit resolution alone is complete for this class of formulas. For the flag example, repeated unit resolution on the clause marked (∗) reduces it to the empty clause □, corresponding to the solution $\{X = r, Y = w, Z = r, U = r\}$. For any FCSP, using subsumption (whereby if clauses of the generic form C and $C \vee D$ are both present, $C \vee D$ is deleted) does not affect the completeness result. Iterating unit resolution followed by subsumption leaves invariant the special properties of the formula (only negative and unit positive clauses) and, moreover, only decreases its size. Hence, it terminates (correctly). As, of course, does the linear time HornSAT algorithm. The HornSAT algorithm exactly mimics the algorithm DA. The propositional variable in each unit positive literal is set to T and each negative clause is checked: if any clause has each (negative) literal required to be F then the formula is unsatisfiable otherwise it is satisfiable.

9. FCS as theorem proving in definite theories

The methods discussed so far are not serious candidates for actually solving an FCSP: they simply serve to clarify the semantics and methods of the serious candidates. One such candidate is a Prolog interpreter, which is a theorem prover for theories consisting of definite clauses. Since an FCSP can be seen as a pure Prolog program, SLD-resolution is a sound and complete solution method. A depth-first SLD-resolution strategy may fail to find a proof for a query that is in fact a theorem for an arbitrary definite clause program but will always do so for an FCSP. It is also, generally speaking, more efficient than other resolution methods such as the one embodied in algorithm DA. For the flag example, we can assert the constraints as ground facts in the Prolog database and then define and pose the conjunctive query to Prolog:

```
%prolog
| ?- [user].
| p(r). p(w). q(r). q(w). s(r). s(w). t(r).
| ne(r, w). ne(w, r).
yes
| ?- p(X), q(Y), s(Z), t(U), ne(X, Y), ne(Y, Z), ne(Y, U).
X = Z = U = r,
Y = w
```

In finding the one solution the interpreter essentially checks every possible set of bindings for the variables X, Y, Z and U. By permuting the query one may reduce the size of the search space: a partially completed set of bindings can be rejected by a single failure. For the query

```
| ?- p(x), q(Y), ne(X, Y), s(Z), ne(Y, Z), t(U), ne(Y, U)
```

the search tree is somewhat smaller. Heuristics, such as instantiating the most constrained variable next, can be used to reorder the query dynamically but, on realistic problems, this tactic is doomed. In general, no variable ordering can avoid *thrashing* by repeatedly rediscovering incompatible variable bindings [16].

Just as for the algorithm DA, we may interpret Prolog's failure to find a proof for this class of theories as meaning either *Constraints* ⊬ *Query* or *completion*(*Constraints*) ⊢ ¬ *Query*.

10. FCS as Datalog

Since FCS is a restriction of Datalog, the techniques developed in the relational database community are available [19]. The solution relation is the natural join of the relations for the individual constraints. The consistency techniques discussed below can be interpreted similarly; for example, making an arc consistent in a constraint network can be interpreted as a semi-join. Results that exploit this interpretation can be found in [1, 6, 17, 21, 24, 28].

11. FCS in constraint networks

Consideration of the drawbacks of the SLD-resolution approach mentioned above leads to a view of FCS in *constraint networks*. A constraint network represents each variable in the query as a vertex. The unary constraint $p_X(X)$ establishes the domain of X, and each binary constraint $p_{XY}(X, Y)$ is represented as the edge (X, Y), composed of arc (X, Y) and arc (Y, X). This easily generalizes to k-ary predicates using hypergraphs. The network for the flag problem is shown in Fig. 4.

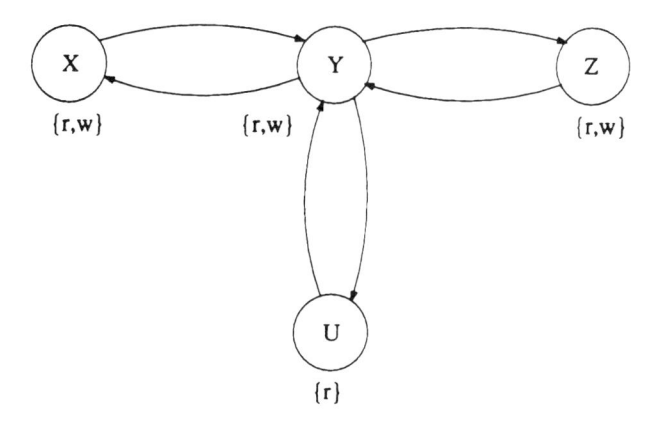

Fig. 4. Constraint network for the flag problem.

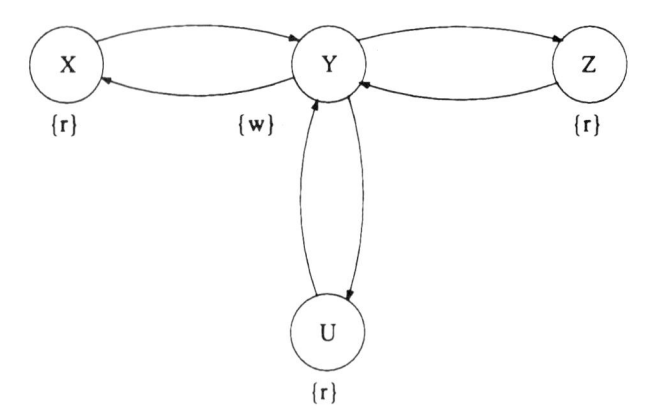

Fig. 5. Arc consistent network for the flag problem.

An arc (X, Y) is *consistent* iff the following metalanguage sentence holds for *Constraints*:

$$\forall X \{ p_X(X) \rightarrow \exists Y [p_Y(Y) \wedge p_{XY}(X, Y)] \} .$$

A network is arc consistent if all its arcs are consistent. An arc (X, Y) may be made consistent without affecting the total set of solutions by deleting the values from the domain of X that are not consistent with some value in Y. The original flag network is not arc consistent because the single arc (Y, U) is inconsistent. Delete r from the domain of Y to make arc (Y, U) consistent. This now makes arcs (X, Y) and (Z, Y) inconsistent. They can be made consistent by deleting w from the domains of both X and Z, making the network arc consistent as shown in Fig. 5.

Arc consistency can be enforced in time linear in the number of binary constraints; moreover, if the constraint graph is a tree, as it is for the flag, then arc consistency alone suffices as a decision procedure for the FCSP [18]. Various other graph-theoretic properties of the constraint network can be used to characterize and solve FCSPs [6, 11, 22].

12. Logical interpreters for FCSP

Using these ideas we can implement an interpreter for FCS [16, 27] which could be called LINC (logical interpreter for a network of constraints). Given

Query: $\exists X \exists Y \exists Z \exists U \; p(X) \wedge q(Y) \wedge s(Z) \wedge t(U) \wedge$

$ne(X, Y) \wedge ne(Y, Z) \wedge ne(Y, U)$

then, following [2], for LINC we choose to complete each predicate in

Constraints and represent it by its *definition*, its necessary and sufficient conditions, so

Constraints:
$$p(X) \leftrightarrow ((X = r) \vee (X = w)),$$
$$q(Y) \leftrightarrow ((Y = r) \vee (Y = w)),$$
$$s(Z) \leftrightarrow ((Z = r) \vee (Z = w)),$$
$$t(U) \leftrightarrow (U = r),$$
$$ne(X, Y) \leftrightarrow (X = r \wedge Y = w) \vee (X = w \wedge Y = r).$$

Restricting LINC to arc consistency, it non-deterministically rewrites *Constraints* using the *AC rewrite rule*:

$$p_X(X) \Leftarrow p_X(X) \wedge \exists Y[p_Y(Y) \wedge p_{XY}(X, Y)].$$

Here:

$$q(Y) \Leftarrow q(Y) \wedge \exists U[t(U) \wedge ne(Y, U)]$$
$$\Leftarrow (Y = r \vee Y = w) \wedge \exists U[U = r \wedge$$
$$(Y = r \wedge U = w \vee Y = w \wedge U = r)]$$
$$\Leftarrow (Y = w).$$

The set of AC rewrite rules, corresponding to the set of arcs in the constraint network, applied to *Constraints* constitutes a production system with the Church–Rosser property. Repeated application of the rules, rewriting the definitions of the unary predicates, eventually reduces *Constraints* to a fixpoint:

$$p(X) \leftrightarrow (X = r),$$
$$q(Y) \leftrightarrow (Y = w),$$
$$s(Z) \leftrightarrow (Z = r),$$
$$t(U) \leftrightarrow (U = r),$$
$$ne(X, Y) \leftrightarrow (X = r \wedge Y = w) \vee (X = w \wedge Y = r).$$

In general, LINC must interleave the AC relaxation with some non-deterministic case analysis or higher-order network consistency.

CHIP [27] is, amongst other things, an implementation of this approach. Similarly, a connection graph theorem prover for full FOPC, as proposed in [15], essentially performs AC relaxation on the possible sets of substitutions for variables in the literals of each clause. Using such a prover with an SLD-resolution strategy on a FCSP query would produce an effect isomorphic to using LINC.

13. CSP and CLP($\mathcal{D}$)

The FCS constraint form is a special case of the CLP($\mathcal{D}$) rule form [12]:

$$p(X, Y, \ldots) \leftarrow a_1(X, Y, \ldots) \wedge a_2(X, Y, \ldots) \wedge \cdots \wedge$$
$$p_1(X, Y, \ldots) \wedge p_2(X, Y, \ldots) \wedge \cdots$$

where $a_i(\cdot)$ is a constraint on its arguments and $p_j(\cdot)$ is a predicate.

In definite clause programs $\mathcal{D} = H$ and the constraints are equalities on terms.

A general constraint satisfaction problem fits the CLP($\mathcal{D}$) scheme. Consider the CSP represented by this CLP($\mathcal{R}$) program:

Constraints:

$$p(X) \leftarrow (1 \leq X) \wedge (X \leq 3),$$
$$q(Y) \leftarrow (0 \leq Y) \wedge (Y \leq 2),$$
$$r(X, Y) \leftarrow X \leq Y$$

and the

Query:

$$\exists X \exists Y [p(X) \wedge q(Y) \wedge r(X, Y)].$$

Using the same AC rewrite rule that LINC used for finite CSP *Constraints* is refined to the fixpoint

Constraints:

$$p(X) \leftarrow (1 \leq X) \wedge (X \leq 2),$$
$$q(Y) \leftarrow (1 \leq Y) \wedge (Y \leq 2),$$
$$r(X, Y) \leftarrow X \leq Y.$$

This demonstrates that these ideas lift from FCSP to CSP and CLP. It is an open research issue to determine the limits of their applicability and their usefulness [3, 26].

14. FCS as model finding in propositional logic

A qualitatively different logical framework for FCS is as model finding in propositional logic [4, 14, 20, 24]. For example, in [24] an account of depiction is presented. An interpretation of an image is defined to be a logical model of a theory describing the image, the scene and the mapping between them. Under certain assumptions this theory reduces to a propositional theory whose models are identified with possible states of the world. Finding those models corresponds directly to solving an FCSP. In [4, 20] the model-finding framework for FCSP is used to elucidate the connection to truth maintenance systems.

In this framework a propositional formula F is constructed for the FCSP such that each model of F corresponds to a solution of the FCSP. Each proposition in F represents a possible binding of a variable to a value. For the flag example, the proposition $X:r$ means that variable X takes the value r. F may be in CNF with a set of clauses representing the fact that each variable must take a value, e.g. $X:r \vee X:w$, the fact that the values are pairwise exclusive, e.g. $\neg X:r \vee \neg X:w$, and the constraints on related variables. The constraints may be encoded as clauses in any suitable fashion. A "negative" encoding [4, 20] represents only the forbidden tuples of the constraints, e.g. $\neg W:r \vee \neg Y:r$. Using that encoding for the flag example, we have

$$F = \{X:r \vee X:w, Y:r \vee Y:w, Z:r \vee Z:w, U:r,$$
$$\neg X:r \vee \neg X:w, \neg Y:r \vee \neg Y:w, \neg Z:r \vee \neg Z:w,$$
$$\neg X:r \vee \neg Y:r, \neg X:w \vee \neg Y:w, \neg Y:r \vee \neg Z:r,$$
$$\neg Y:w \vee \neg Z:w, \neg Y:r \vee \neg U:r\}.$$

In this framework we have a SAT problem again. It is crucial to observe that this approach is *not* the model-theoretic counterpart of the proof-theoretic approach presented earlier. In the propositional proof-finding framework, the FCSP has a solution iff the formula has no models. Under this model-finding framework each solution corresponds to a model of F. To find the models we could use the Davis–Putnam algorithm. But we note that the SAT problem has the same special form again: there are no mixed clauses in this encoding. This can be exploited to simplify the formula before deciding if there are any models. Two inference rules can be used—a specialized form of negative hyperresolution H_2 and a form of unit resolution U.

$$H_2: \quad p \vee q \vee r \vee \cdots \vee u$$
$$\neg p \vee \neg v$$
$$\neg q \vee \neg v$$
$$\neg r \vee \neg v$$
$$\vdots$$
$$\neg u \vee \neg v$$
$$\overline{}$$
$$\neg v$$

$$U: \quad p \vee q \vee r \vee \cdots \vee u$$
$$\neg q$$
$$\overline{}$$
$$p \vee r \vee \cdots \vee u$$

These rules of inference are supplemented with two subsumption rules: S_p and S_n. Given two positive clauses C_1 and C_2 where all the literals in C_1 appear in C_2 then S_p deletes C_2, the subsumed clause. S_n deletes subsumed negative clauses.

Now, we define the *AC-resolution strategy*: $(H_2 S_n^* U S_p)^*$.

A trace of AC-resolution on the flag example as it simplifies F is shown in Fig. 6.

The resultant simplified formula is

$$F_s = \{X:r, Y:w, Z:r, U:r, \neg X:w, \neg Y:r, \neg Z:w\}$$

which obviously has exactly one model, corresponding to the solution.

Notice that resolution and subsumption are used here in a nonstandard way, namely, not to prove a theorem but to find models. It is easy to verify that the AC-resolution strategy has the following properties:

(1) The set of models is invariant under AC-resolution. The models of F are the models of F_s. This follows from the soundness theorem [9]. $F \models F_s$

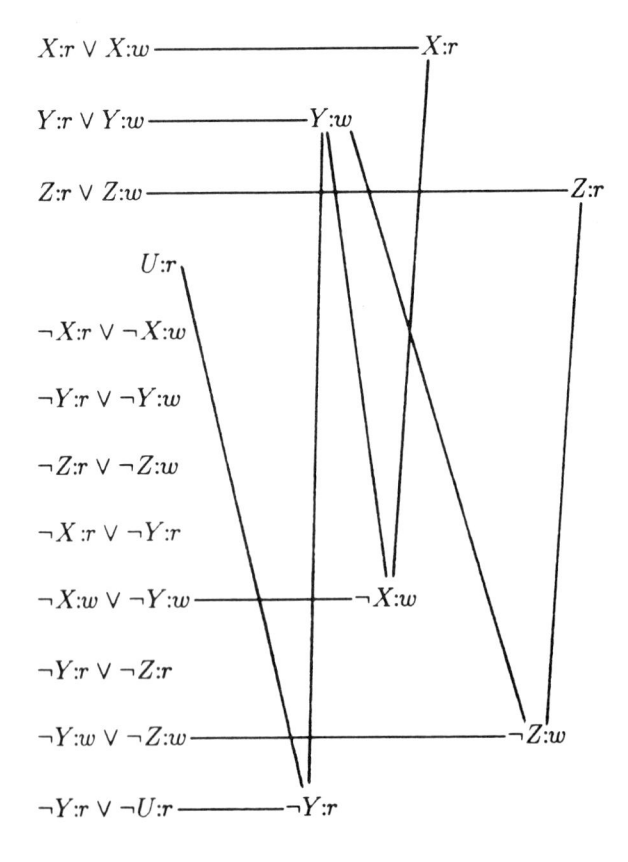

Fig. 6. A trace of AC-resolution on the flag problem.

(every model of F is a model of F_s) because $F \vdash F_s$, and $F_s \models F$ because $F_s \vdash F$.

(2) No mixed clauses are generated so the separation into positive and negative clauses is invariant.

(3) The total number and length of clauses decreases monotonically.

(4) AC-resolution is $O(e)$ where e is the number of constraints [18].

(5) In general, AC-resolution is incomplete in the sense that it does not always terminate with F_s either as the empty clause $\square$ or consisting only of unit literals. It must be interleaved with search, such as assigning a truth value to a proposition, or enforcing higher-order network consistency, which corresponds to other forms of hyperresolution [4], to determine the models of F explicitly.

(6) AC-resolution used for model-finding exactly mimics the behaviour of the LINC interpreter using the AC rewrite rule on FCSP (and the connection graph theorem prover) since each proposition, e.g. $X:r$, reifies a possible substitution for a variable in the FOPC theorem-proving framework.

The model-finding framework shows the relevance of a variety of serial and parallel complexity results on special cases of SAT, such as planar SAT [25], 2-SAT and HornSAT. If the variables in an FCSP have a maximum domain size of 2 and the constraints are only unary or binary (as is the case for the flag problem) then this encoding results in a 2-SAT problem which is $O(e)$ serial time [10] and polylogarithmic parallel time since it is in NC [13, 14].

A mixed encoding of the constraints may well be more appropriate than the negative encoding [24], especially for sparse constraints. Consider directed constraint networks [7] which are a specialization of FCSP. In a directed constraint network, for each constraint some subset of its variables can be considered as input variables to the constraint with the rest considered as output variables. The projection of the constraint relation on the input variables is the universal relation—that is, they are unconstrained. A constraint relation that is functional on the input variables has this form. A directed constraint that is not functional can be made functional by introducing additional input variables to discriminate between the different output values possible for the same values of the original input variables. The topology of the constraint network must respect this distinction between input and output variables.

A suitable mixed encoding of a directed constraint network in the model-finding framework can be arranged as a propositional theory, as follows. First, make each constraint functional as described above. A suitable theory can then be constructed with a positive clause for each variable, specifying that it must have a value in its domain, and a set of negative clauses for each variable, specifying that the values are pairwise exclusive, as before, but there are definite clauses for all the multivariable constraints. Each definite clause has negative literals for all the input variable/value bindings and a positive literal for the resulting output variable/value. If the values for the input variables to the network are known, the theory essentially collapses to become Horn as a modified HornSAT algorithm can determine the entire state of the network in $O(e)$ time [8]. On the other hand, determining the input values required to produce a given output can be much harder. Diagnosis of the internal state of a causal system can also be put in this framework: the states of the components correspond to introduced input variables [5].

15. Conclusions

In summary, the questions posed in Section 1 of this paper have all been answered affirmatively except, of course, the one posed by the cynical critic. The basic approach has been to see finite constraint satisfaction as a restricted logical calculus in a space of logical representation and reasoning systems. The FCSP framework has been formulated in a variety of logical settings: theorem proving in FOPC (which reduces to propositional theorem proving and hence SAT), the Prolog and Datalog approaches, constraint network algorithms, a logical interpreter for networks of constraints, the CLP paradigm and forms of propositional model-finding (and hence SAT, again, but in radically different context). Several standard, and some not-so-standard, logical methods can therefore be used to solve these problems. By doing this we obtain a specification of the semantics of the common approaches.

This synthetic treatment also allows algorithms and results from many of these disparate areas to be imported, and specialized, to FCSP; the special properties of FCSP are exploited to achieve, for example, completeness and to improve efficiency. It also allows export to the related areas. By casting CSP both as a generalization of FCSP and a specialization of CLP it was observed that some, but not all, FCSP techniques lift to CSP and, perhaps, thereby to CLP. Various new connections have been uncovered, in particular between the proof-finding approaches and the alternative model-finding approaches that have arisen in depiction and diagnosis applications.

Acknowledgement

The contents of this paper benefitted from discussions with Johan de Kleer, Alex Kean, Nick Pippenger, David Poole, Ray Reiter, Ron Rensink and Zhang Ying, and from the comments of the referees. This research was supported by the Canadian Institute for Advanced Research, the Natural

Sciences and Engineering Research Council of Canada and the Institute for Robotics and Intelligent Systems Network of Centres of Excellence.

References

[1] W. Bibel, Constraint satisfaction from a deductive viewpoint, *Artif. Intell.* **35** (1988) 401–413.
[2] K.L. Clark, Negation as failure, in: H. Gallaire and J. Minker, eds., *Logic and Databases* (Plenum Press, New York, 1978) 293–322.
[3] E. Davis, Constraint propagation with interval labels, *Artif. Intell.* **32** (1987) 281–331.
[4] J. de Kleer, A comparison of ATMS and CSP techniques, in: *Proceedings IJCAI-89*, Detroit, MI (1989) 290–296.
[5] J. de Kleer, A.K. Mackworth and R. Reiter, Characterizing diagnoses, in: *Proceedings AAAI-90*, Boston, MA (1990) 324–330.
[6] R. Dechter, Constraint networks, in: S.C. Shapiro, ed., *The Encyclopedia of AI* (Wiley, New York, 1992) 276–285.
[7] R. Dechter and J. Pearl, Directed constraint networks, in: *Proceedings IJCAI-91*, Sydney, Australia (1991) 1164–1170.
[8] W.F. Dowling and J.H. Gallier, Linear-time algorithms for testing the satisfiability of propositional Horn formulae, *J. Logic Program.* **3** (1984) 267–284.
[9] H.B. Enderton, *A Mathematical Introduction to Logic* (Academic Press, Orlando, FL, 1972).
[10] S. Even, A. Itai and A. Shamir, On the complexity of timetable and multicommodity flow problems, *SIAM J. Comput.* **5** (4) (1976) 691–703.
[11] E.C. Freuder, Complexity of k-tree structured constraint satisfaction problems, in: *Proceedings AAAI-90*, Boston, MA (1990) 4–9.
[12] J. Jaffar and J.-L. Lassez, Constraint logic programming, in: *Proceedings 14th ACM Principles of Programming Languages Conference*, Munich, Germany (1987) 111–119.
[13] N.D. Jones, Y.E. Lien and W.T. Laaser, New problems complete for nondeterministic log space, *Math. Syst. Theor.* **10** (1976) 1–17.
[14] S. Kasif, Parallel solutions to constraint satisfaction problems, in: *Proceedings First International Conference on Principles of Knowledge Representation and Reasoning*, Toronto, Ont. (1989) 180–188.
[15] R. Kowalski, A proof procedure using connection graphs, *J. ACM* **22** (4) (1975) 572–595.
[16] A.K. Mackworth, Consistency in networks of relations, *Artif. Intell.* **8** (1977) 99–118.
[17] A.K. Mackworth, Constraint satisfaction, in: S.C. Shapiro, ed., *The Encyclopedia of AI* (Wiley, New York, 1992) 285–293.
[18] A.K. Mackworth and E.C. Freuder, The complexity of some polynomial network consistency algorithms for constraint satisfaction problems, *Artif. Intell.* **25** (1985) 65–74.
[19] D. Maier, *The Theory of Relational Databases* (Computer Science Press, Rockville, MD, 1983).
[20] D.A. McAllester, Truth maintenance, in: *Proceedings AAAI-90*, Boston, MA (1990) 1109–1116.
[21] U. Montanari, Networks of constraints: fundamental properties and applications to picture processing, *Inf. Sci.* **7** (1974) 95–132.
[22] U. Montanari and F. Rossi, Constraint relaxation may be perfect, *Artif. Intell.* **48** (2) (1991) 143–170.
[23] R. Reiter, Nonmonotonic reasoning, in: H.E. Shrobe, ed., *Exploring Artificial Intelligence* (Morgan Kaufmann, San Mateo, CA, 1988) 439–482.
[24] R. Reiter and A.K. Mackworth, A logical framework for depiction and image interpretation, *Artif. Intell.* **41** (1989) 125–155.
[25] R. Seidel, A new method for solving constraint satisfaction problems, in: *Proceedings IJCAI-81*, Vancouver, BC (1981) 338–342.

[26] G. Sidebottom and W.S. Havens, Hierarchical arc consistency applied to numeric processing in constraint logic programming, Tech. Rept. CSS-IS TR 91-06, Simon Fraser University, Burnaby, BC (1991).
[27] P. Van Hentenryck, *Constraint Satisfaction in Logic Programming* (MIT Press, Cambridge, MA, 1989).
[28] Y. Zhang and A.K. Mackworth, Parallel and distributed algorithms for constraint satisfaction problems, in: *Proceedings 3rd IEEE Symposium on Parallel and Distributed Processing*, Dallas, TX (1991) 394–397.

Partial constraint satisfaction*

Eugene C. Freuder and Richard J. Wallace
Computer Science Department, Kingsbury Hall, University of New Hampshire, Durham, NH 03824, USA

Abstract

Freuder, E.C. and R.J. Wallace, Partial constraint satisfaction, Artificial Intelligence 58 (1992) 21–70.

A constraint satisfaction problem involves finding values for variables subject to constraints on which combinations of values are allowed. In some cases it may be impossible or impractical to solve these problems completely. We may seek to partially solve the problem, in particular by satisfying a maximal number of constraints. Standard backtracking and local consistency techniques for solving constraint satisfaction problems can be adapted to cope with, and take advantage of, the differences between partial and complete constraint satisfaction. Extensive experimentation on maximal satisfaction problems illuminates the relative and absolute effectiveness of these methods. A general model of partial constraint satisfaction is proposed.

1. Introduction

Constraint satisfaction involves finding values for problem variables subject to constraints on acceptable combinations of values. Constraint satisfaction has wide application in artificial intelligence, in areas ranging from temporal reasoning to machine vision. *Partial constraint satisfaction* involves finding values for a subset of the variables that satisfy a subset of the constraints. Viewed another way, we are willing to "weaken" some of the constraints to permit additional acceptable value combinations. Partial constraint satisfaction problems arise in several contexts:

- The problem is overconstrained and admits of no complete solution.
- The problem is too difficult to solve completely but we are willing to settle for a "good enough" solution.

Correspondence to: E.C. Freuder, Computer Science Department, Kingsbury Hall, University of New Hampshire, Durham, NH 03824, USA. Fax: (603) 862-3775. E-mail: ecf@cs.unh.edu.
* This material is based upon work supported by the National Science Foundation under Grant No. IRI-8913040 and Grant No. IRI-9207633. Part of this work was done while the first author was a Visiting Scientist at the MIT Artificial Intelligence Laboratory.

- We are seeking the best solution obtainable within fixed resource bounds.
- Real time demands require an "anytime algorithm", which can report *some* partial solution almost immediately, improving on it if and when time allows.

The utility of some form of partial constraint satisfaction has been repeatedly recognized. A variety of applications has motivated a variety of approaches. As AI increasingly confronts real world problems, in expert systems and robotics, for example, we are increasingly likely to encounter situations where, rather than searching for a solution to a problem, we must, in a sense, search for a problem we can solve.

Conflicting constraints have arisen in a variety of domains. Descotte and Latombe made "compromises" among antagonist constraints in a planner for machining problems [10]. Borning used constraint "hierarchies" to deal with situations in which a set of requirements and preferences for the graphical display of a physical simulation cannot all be satisfied [2]; these hierarchies have been imbedded in a constraint logic programming language [3]. Hower used "sensitive relaxation" to resolve conflicts in floor planning [21].

Scheduling problems are a natural source of constraint satisfaction problems, and schedule conflicts a natural source of partial satisfaction problems. Fox added the concepts of constraint "relaxation" (the selection of constraint alternatives), "preferences" among relaxations and constraint "importance" to constraint representations, to cope with conflicting constraints in job-shop scheduling [12]. Feldman and Golumbic [11] used "priorities" in looking for optimal student schedules.

Machine vision has also provided motivation for work on partial constraint satisfaction. Shapiro and Haralick [35] treated inexact matching of structural descriptions using an extension of constraint satisfaction that they called the inexact consistent labeling problem, which sought a solution within a given error bound. Mohr and Masini [31] suggested a modification of local consistency processing to deal with errors, permitting values to fail to satisfy some constraints, in order to cope with noise in domains such as computer vision; Cooper [5] defined an alternative generalization of constraint satisfaction with errors.

The related problem of approximate constraint satisfaction, where weights are assigned to individual combinations of values [34, 36] is motivated by machine vision as well. The expression of preferences in database queries is a also a related problem [23]. Note that the concept of optimization can play a role in constraint satisfaction problems even when all constraints are satisfied; there may be an additional criterion to optimize among alternative solutions [5, 7, 37].

Most of this paper will focus on methods for *maximal constraint satisfaction*, where we seek a solution that satisfies as many constraints as possible. We have systematically reviewed the basic backtracking and local consistency methods for constraint satisfaction [28, 29, 32], and developed analogous methods for maximal satisfaction. The maximal satisfaction context has provided new challenges and new opportunities. The algorithms we formulated were subjected to carefully designed experiments that shed light on both relative and absolute performance as a function of basic structural problem parameters.

Our algorithms also allow for *sufficient satisfaction*, where we terminate the search if we find a solution which is sufficiently good, in the sense that the number of constraint violations does not exceed some predetermined bound. Our methods easily extend to *resource-bounded satisfaction*, where we report the best solution in hand when a resource bound has been reached, and naturally support anytime algorithms.

Maximal satisfaction provides a form of optimization. Sufficient satisfaction incorporates a concept of acceptable error. Our methods clearly generalize to the use of more complex metrics to evaluate proposed solutions than a simple count of the number of violated constraints. In this manner, preferences can be introduced to distinguish among conflicting constraints. However, the simple metric of counting constraint violations facilitates the presentation of our algorithms, and provides a suitable context for an initial evaluation of their performance.

At the end of the paper we develop a still more general model of partial constraint satisfaction [14], in which we compare alternative problems rather than alternative solutions. We suggest viewing partial satisfaction of a problem, P, as a search through a space of alternative problems for a solvable problem "close enough" to P. We argue that a full theory of partial satisfaction should consider not merely how a partial solution requires us to violate or vitiate constraints, but how the entire solution set of the problem with these altered constraints differs from the solution set of the problem with which we started.

In this paper we will use for pedagogical purposes a simple, toy problem involving a fashion-conscious robot seeking to choose matching clothes while getting dressed in the morning. (This could be regarded more seriously as a simple version of a configuration problem [30].) The problem is pictured in Fig. 1. Our robot has a minimal wardrobe: sneakers or Cordovans for footwear, a white and a dark green shirt and three pairs of slacks: denim, dress blue, and dress gray. The robot has been told that: the sneakers only go with the denim slacks; the Cordovans only go with the gray slacks and the white shirt; the white shirt will go with either denim or blue slacks; the green shirt only goes with the gray slacks. These are the constraints under which it has to operate.

Section 2 discusses methods for achieving maximal constraint satisfaction. Branch and bound for maximal constraint satisfaction is the natural extension of backtracking for constraint satisfaction. Retrospective and prospective backtrack techniques for constraint satisfaction are shown to have analogues in a branch and bound setting for maximal satisfaction. Local consistency methods

{Cordovans, sneakers}

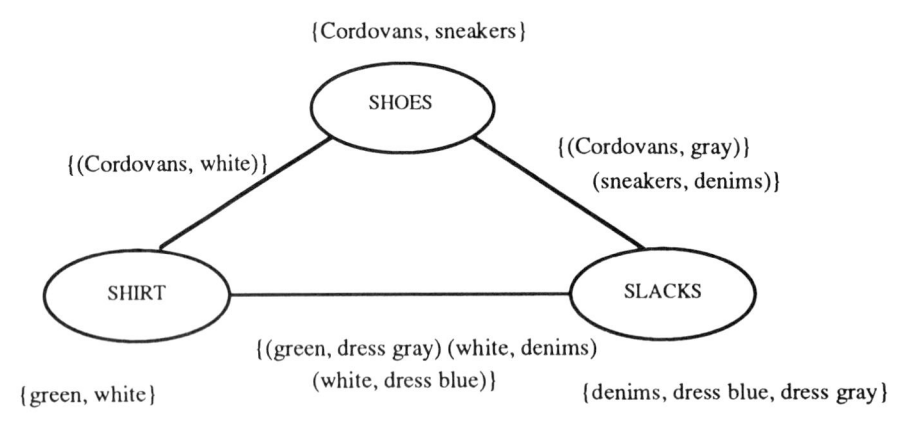

Fig. 1. Robot clothing problem.

for constraint satisfaction have analogues in maximal satisfaction methods. Ordering techniques are if anything likely to be more important for branch and bound than for backtracking.

Section 3 describes extensive testing of maximal constraint satisfaction methods corresponding to several of the most successful constraint satisfaction methods. The results demonstrate the effectiveness of the maximal satisfaction analogues. They also illustrate the importance of taking advantage of the additional information available in the partial satisfaction domain, where the world is not just black and white (consistency or inconsistency), but shades of grey. Furthermore, the experimental design permits insights into the relationship between problem structure and the performance of the different methods.

Section 4 generalizes to other forms of partial satisfaction. Other metrics are briefly discussed. Partially ordered problem spaces are introduced. A partial constraint satisfaction problem is defined as a search through a space of alternative problems. Section 5 contains brief concluding remarks.

2. Methods

2.1. Introduction

A *constraint satisfaction problem* (*CSP*) involves a set of problem *variables*, a *domain* of potential values for each variable, and a set of *constraints*, specifying which combinations of values are acceptable. A *solution* specifies an assignment of a value to each variable that does not violate any of the constraints. We will consider here *binary*, *finite CSPs* where the constraints only involve two variables at a time, and the domains are finite sets of values. A constraint can therefore be represented explicitly as a set of permitted pairs of values. (If all pairs of values are allowed between two variables, then there is effectively no constraint between them; we will say that these variables do not *share* a constraint.)

For our running example: the variables are shoes, slacks, and shirt; the values for shoes are Cordovans and sneakers; the constraint between shoes and shirt specifies that the only allowable combination of values is Cordovans and white shirt. Two values, like Cordovans and white shirt, that satisfy the relevant constraint, are *consistent*. A pair of values that violates a constraint is an *inconsistency*.

For now we define a *partial constraint satisfaction problem* (*PCSP*) as a CSP where we are willing to accept a solution that violates some of the constraints. A more formal approach to PCSPs is developed in Section 4.

Backtracking [18] is the classic algorithm for solving CSPs. A number of variations and refinements of backtracking have been developed. Several algorithms, including classical backtracking itself, utilize *retrospective* techniques, in which a new value selected to try to extend an incomplete solution is tested by "looking back" over the previously chosen values in the incomplete solution, to see if the new value is consistent with the previously chosen values. By "remembering" more about the course of the search process, some variations reduce redundant testing. Other algorithms employ *prospective* strategies. Values are tested against the domains of variables that are not yet represented in the incomplete solution, so that inconsistencies can be dealt with before values from these domains are considered for inclusion. *Ordering* techniques have been used to direct the order in which variables, values, or constraints are considered during search.

Our strategy in studying PCSP algorithms was to look for analogues of successful CSP techniques, focusing on backtrack and its variations. Branch and bound [24, 33, 37] is a widely used optimization technique that may be viewed as a variation on backtracking. Thus it was a natural choice in seeking an analogue of backtracking to find optimal partial solutions for PCSPs.

We begin by applying branch and bound to constraint satisfaction problems. Then we set about finding analogues of various CSP retrospective, prospective, and ordering techniques, for partial, specifically maximal, constraint satisfaction algorithms. Finding appropriate analogues presents both challenges and opportunities. In presenting these algorithms we will generally begin with a review of the CSP version, then move on to the PCSP version, highlighting the differences. We will present examples and discussions as well as the algorithms themselves.

2.2. Retrospective techniques

2.2.1. Basic branch and bound

Branch and bound for maximal constraint satisfaction is the natural analogue of backtracking for constraint satisfaction. First we will briefly review backtrack search in the context of our running example. Backtrack search will find no solutions; the problem is overconstrained. Then we will use a basic branch and bound algorithm to find a way to dress our robot while violating a minimal number of its esthetic requirements.

A depth-first traversal of the tree in Fig. 2 traces the progress of a backtrack search on our running example. First we try Cordovans for shoes, then denims for slacks. According to the given constraints, denim slacks are not consistent with Cordovans, so we try blue slacks. These do not work so we try gray. Gray is good; we can move on to try and find a consistent shirt. The green shirt does not go with the Cordovans so we try the white shirt. It is consistent with the Cordovans but not with the gray slacks (we will assume that consistency is checked "top-down" against the already chosen values). At this point we need to back up. We find that we have tried all the values for slacks, so we back up further to try another value for shoes. Ultimately all possibilities fail.

Backtrack search tries all value combinations exhaustively if necessary, but can avoid considering some combinations, by observing that a subset of values cannot be extended to a full solution, thus pruning a subtree of the search space. A standard measure of effort for CSP algorithms is the number of *constraint checks*. A constraint check occurs every time we ask a basic question of the form: is value a for variable X consistent with value b for variable Y? For example, when we ask whether Cordovans are consistent with denims, that is a constraint check. The total number of constraint checks (cc) accumulated when search has reached each leaf node of the search tree is shown in the figure. In total the search required 11 constraint checks to find that there is no solution.

We will be discussing the way different algorithms work through a search tree like this, and will need a suitable vocabulary. We will talk about the *levels*

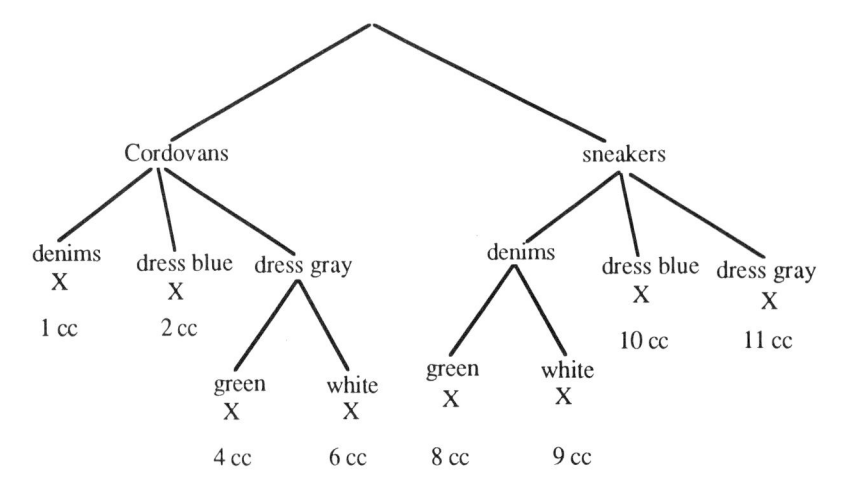

Fig. 2. Backtracking example.

in the search tree; each level in the search tree corresponds to a problem variable. We will assume the levels are numbered from the top down; *higher levels* have smaller numbers. A shirt value will be found at a lower level or *deeper* in the search tree than a slacks value.

The branching corresponds to variable values, e.g. the choice of denim for slacks. The nodes in the search tree represent *assignments* of values to variables during the search. The green shirt value is always considered at the same level; however it is considered twice in this search. The second time the green shirt is encountered, the search has *backed up* in the interim to the shoe level. The set of assigned values along a branch of the tree, from the top down to some level, e.g. (sneakers denims), is a *search path*. The search path leading down to the most recently chosen value is the *current search path*. It represents the current set of *choices* of values for variables. It represents a proposed, *incomplete* solution, unless it includes values for all the variables.

One theme that will recur in deriving our PCSP analogues is the different definition of local *failure* during CSP and PCSP search. A CSP search path fails as soon as a single inconsistency is encountered. A PCSP search path will not fail until enough inconsistencies accumulate to reach a cutoff bound. Retrospective techniques excel at determining the inconsistencies implied by past choices. Prospective techniques excel at estimating the inconsistencies implied by future choices.

Branch and bound operates in a similar fashion to backtracking in a context where we are seeking a *maximal solution*, one which satisfies as many constraints as possible. Branch and bound basically keeps track of the best solution found so far and abandons a line of search when it becomes clear that it cannot lead to a better solution. A version of backtracking that searches for all solutions, rather than the first solution, most naturally compares with the branch and bound extension to find a maximal solution.

Figure 3 traces a branch and bound search for a maximally satisfying solution for our sample problem. Branch and bound is applied in this context by using as an evaluation function a count of the number of violated constraints, or inconsistencies. Where the backtrack search, looking for a *perfect solution*, that violates no constraints, said that denims were inconsistent with Cordovans and preceeded on to blue slacks, branch and bound, looking for a maximal partial solution, observes that any partial solution containing Cordovans and denims will violate at least one constraint, and proceeds to consider shirts.

Specifically it is noted that any partial solution containing Cordovans and denims will be at a distance, d, of (at least) 1 from a perfect solution. *Distance* measures the number of constraints violated by the chosen values. By the time we add a green shirt we have violated three constraints. We say that green shirt is an *extension* of the search path (Cordovans, denims). We will talk about *extending* a search path by adding one or more values, and, in particular, extending a search path to a complete solution that contains a value for each

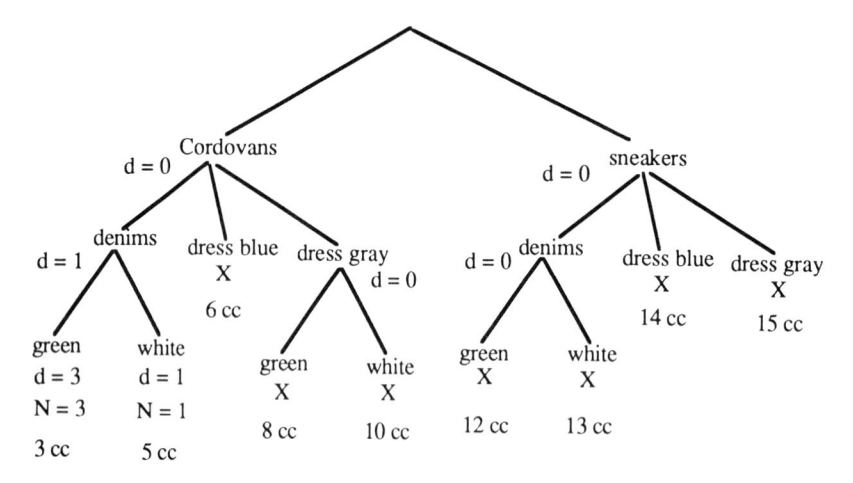

Fig. 3. Branch and bound example.

variable. The search path leading from Cordovans, through denims, to green shirt now contains three inconsistencies, giving it an associated distance (from a perfect solution) of three. The *first inconsistent value* in the search path is denims. It is the first value in the search path to be inconsistent with another value in the search path. The *last inconsistent value* is green shirt.

Cordovans, denims, and a green shirt provide a partial solution at a distance of 3 from a perfect solution. This distance is taken as the value of N. N is used during the search to store the number of inconsistencies in the best solution found up to that point in the search. N is a *necessary bound*, which we will often simply refer to as the *bound*, in the sense that to do better it is necessary to find a solution with fewer inconsistencies.

The necessary bound N can be set initially based on a priori knowledge that a solution is available that violates fewer than N constraints, or an a priori *requirement* that we are not interested in solutions that violate more than $N-1$ constraints. As branch and bound proceeds, if a solution is found that violates $N' < N$ constraints, N is replaced by N'.

As the branch and bound search proceeds in our example, it finds a better partial solution, with a single constraint violation (Cordovans, denims, white shirt). This updates N to be 1. Now when it tries Cordovans and blue slacks (hoping that an even better, in this case perfect, solution is to be found), it recognizes that any solution involving Cordovans and blue slacks can be no better than the solution already found. Thus it does not consider matching a shirt to the Cordovans and blue slacks, but proceeds immediately to try gray slacks. As with backtrack search, the basic idea of recognizing defeat early permits pruning of the search space.

Search concludes when we find a perfect solution, not available in this case, or run out of things to try. We could also quit when we reach a preset *sufficient bound S*, which specifies that we will be satisfied if we find a partial solution that violates no more than *S* constraints. We may know, for example, that no exact solution is possible and thus be able to set *S* to 1. We may be willing to settle for a "close enough" or *sufficient solution*. Obviously the larger we set *S* the easier the problem is likely to be.

Circumstances may also impose resource bounds. In particular, real time processing may require immediate answers that can be refined later if time allows. The branch and bound process is well suited to providing resource-bounded solutions. We can simply report the best solution available when, for example, a time bound is exceeded. The branch and bound process is also clearly well-suited to support an anytime algorithm, which can repeatedly provide a "best-so-far" answer when queried. It can quickly provide *some* answer, with a better one perhaps to follow as time allows.

Figure 4 provides a basic branch and bound algorithm for maximal constraint satisfaction. It also provides for a priori sufficient and necessary bounds, *S* and

```
P-BB(Search-path, Distance, Variables, Values)
    if Variables = nil then {all problem variables have been assigned values
                             in Search-path}
        Best-solution <- Search-path
        N <- Distance
        if N ≤ S then return 'finished'{Best-solution is sufficiently close}
        else return 'keep-searching'
    else if Values = nil then    {tried all values for extending search path}
        return 'keep-searching' {so will back up to see if can try another value for
                                 the last variable assigned a value in Search-path}
    else if Distance = N then    {already extended Search-path to assign values for
                 remaining variables without violating any additional constraints}
        return 'keep-searching' {so will see if can do better by backing up to try
                 another value for the last variable assigned a value in Search-path}
    else {try to extend Search-path}
        Current-value <- first value in Values
        New-distance <- Distance
        try choices in Search-path, from first to last, as long as New-distance < N:
            if choice is inconsistent with Current-value then
                New-distance <- New-distance + 1
        if New-distance < N and
            P-BB(Search-path plus Current-value, New-distance,
                 Variables minus the first variable,
                 values of second variable in Variables)
            = 'finished' then return 'finished'    {Search-path was extended to
                                                    sufficient solution}
        else {will see if can do better with another value}
            return P-BB(Search-path, Distance, Variables,
                 Values minus Current-value)
```

Fig. 4. Branch and bound algorithm.

N, on an acceptable solution. If there are no such a priori bounds, S is initially 0 and N "infinity". The parameters of the P-BB procedure appear in several other algorithms in this paper. The parameter *Search-path* carries the current search path. *Distance* carries the number of constraints already violated by the values on the current search path, the number of inconsistencies in the proposed, incomplete solution. *Variables* carries a list of the variables not assigned values in the current search path, the variables at lower levels in the search tree. *Values* carries a list of the values not previously tried as extensions of the current search path; the first value in *Values* is the next value that can be tried as an instantiation of the first variable in *Variables*.

In this and several subsequent algorithms we will be employing N, S, and *Best-solution* as global variables containing the necessary and sufficient bounds and the best solution found so far. Other variables in all the algorithms are local, with the exception of some backmarking arrays as indicated in Section 2.2.3.

The basic recursive structure of P-BB is also common to many other algorithms in this paper. P-BB works sideways in the search tree by recursing through a set of values for a variable, and deeper into the search tree by recursing through the variables. Backing up is implemented through the unwinding of the recursion.

In this algorithm as in all retrospective procedures, a value being considered for inclusion in the solution is compared with values already chosen, to determine whether constraints between the instantiated variables and the current one are satisfied. Each comparison of two values is a constraint check.

Since the total number of constraint checks is a standard measure of CSP algorithm efficiency, we wish to minimize this quantity. To this end, the new distance is compared with N after *each* constraint failure, so that if the bound is reached, the present value is not checked further. A subtle point involves the test to see if *Distance* is already N before trying a new value, v, for V. (Actually our implementation checked for *Distance* $\geq N$, but an equality test appears sufficient.) One might wonder, if the number of inconsistencies among the already chosen values stored in *Search-path* equals the bound, what is the algorithm doing trying to extend *Search-path* to another variable, V? However, when the algorithm began trying to extend the solution, N may have been larger. A complete assignment of values to variables, extending *Search-path* and requiring only the current N constraint violations, may have been found in the interim, using another value for V, before reaching v.

We have chosen here a depth-first implementation of the branch and bound paradigm. Other branch and bound control structures, notably a best-first approach, are possible. Depth-first is the most direct analogue of backtrack and as such facilitates the development of analogues of backtrack variations. Depth-first also supports an anytime algorithm that will almost immediately have a "best-so-far" solution to report. (Limited experimentation with a best-first approach was not encouraging with respect to its efficiency, but this should not preclude further study.)

In Fig. 3 the total number of constraint checks (cc) accumulated by the time each leaf node of the search tree has been processed is given at the bottom of the figure. Note that, due to our procedures for minimizing constraint checks, some checks are avoided at many points of the search tree, including at some of the lowest-level nodes. In some cases subtrees are pruned; in some cases a value does not need to be checked against the entire preceding search path.

The general worst-case bound for this algorithm is of course exponential. However, it is no worse than that for a backtrack algorithm for finding a perfect solution. Both, in the worst case, will end up trying all possible combinations of values, and testing all the constraints among them. On the other hand, the exponential worst-case bound is bad enough. We want to consider techniques that may help to avoid achieving that bound. As we have indicated, our strategy is to look for analogues of methods which have already proven successful for finding perfect solutions.

2.2.2. Backjumping

Backjumping [17] remembers information about previous failures to reduce the need for redundant constraint checks to rediscover them. Consider what happens when we test shirts in the branch of the backtrack search tree that begins with sneakers and denims (Fig. 2). Both shirts fail immediately upon being tested against sneakers; there is no need to see if they are consistent with denims. Yet classical, so-called "chronological", backtracking blindly backs up and tries dress blue slacks. There is no point in doing so; even if the blue slacks went with the sneakers, we would obviously fail again when we reached the shirt level. Backjumping recognizes this, and after the shirts fail to match the sneakers it immediately backtracks to the shoe level. There it tries to consider another type of shoe; since there is none, search terminates. The final two constraint checks have been avoided. Backjumping generalizes this insight.

We need to recognize that all the values tried for a given variable may not fail against the same previous value. When processing a variable, backjumping remembers the deepest level, l, in the search tree at which any of the values fails. When all the values have been discarded, backtracking can proceed directly to this level. Actually, the algorithm does not "jump" directly to this level. As the recursive calls unwind, they return the depth l; the recursion unwinds until level l is reached before trying to consider any more values. As we extend search paths we ultimately must reach levels where all value choices for extending the search path do fail to be consistent with previous choices, or else we successfully proceed all the way down to a solution. Of course, the deepest level of failure may simply be the previous level, so no real jumping back need result.

In the backjumping analogue for partial constraint satisfaction, failure does

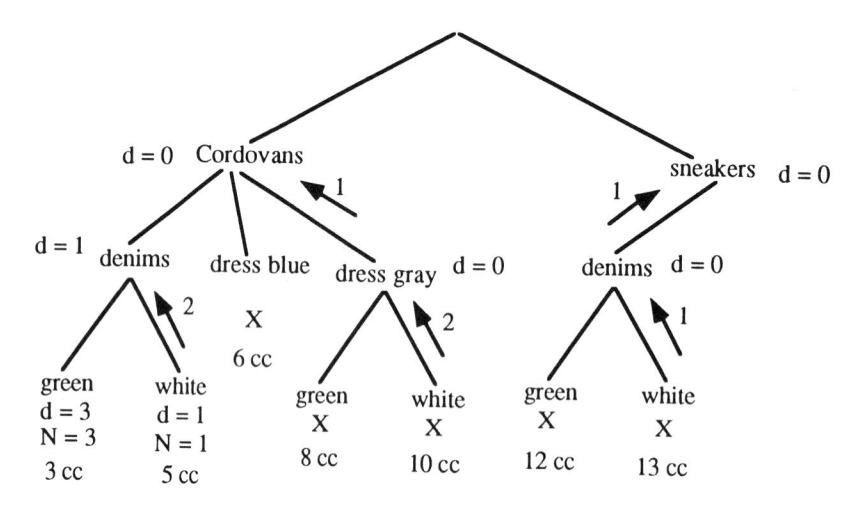

Fig. 5. Backjumping example.

not necessarily occur when an inconsistency is found. Failure occurs only when an inconsistency pushes us too far away from the perfect solution, i.e. when the accumulated number of inconsistencies reaches the necessary bound, N. For example, if search has reached the seventh variable in the sequence, and checking a value of its domain against the value for the fourth variable causes the distance to increase to the bound N, the depth of failure of that variable is 4. Figure 5 shows a trace of backjumping for a maximal solution on our running example. The numbers on the arrows show some of the values returned by P-BJ; notice how the returned depth of 1 at the bottom right of the search tree supports a jump back to the shoes level without considering additional slacks.

Figure 6 contains a backjumping algorithm for partial satisfaction. Aside from the different definition of failure, there is one major difference from the conventional backjumping algorithm. We cannot always jump back all the way to the deepest level of failure. If any values below that level were inconsistent when chosen, i.e. required an increase in *Distance* when they were chosen, we can only jump back to the level, l, of the last, deepest, one of these inconsistent values. Otherwise, minimum distance solutions can be missed that are based on other values yet to be tried at level l. This is because alternative values at level l may involve fewer inconsistencies, adding less to *Distance*, so that search can proceed from this level without encountering the bound at the same point in the search.

As an example of this phenomenon, we adapt the matching clothes problem, supposing that there are other values that were tested before, giving a bound of 2 (Fig. 7). We also change the order in which we examine the variables; the variable search order is indicated by numbers on the nodes. Each domain is checked from left to right, and a vertical line appears to the right of the values

P-BJ(Search-path, Distance, Variables, Values,
      Current-depth, Return-depth, Inconsistency-depth)
  if Variables = nil then {have new best solution}
    Best-solution <- Search-path
    N <- Distance
    if $N \leq S$ then return 'finished' else return Current-depth - 1
  else if Values = nil or Distance = N then
    return Return-depth {may lead to backjumping}
  else {try to extend Search-path}
    Current-value <- first value in Values
    New-distance <- Distance
    try choices in Search-path, first to last, until New-distance = N or tried all:
      if the choice is inconsistent with Current-value then
        New-distance <- New-distance + 1
        Fail-depth1 <- level of the choice
    if New-distance < N then Fail-depth1 <- Current-depth {did not fail}
    if New-distance < N and
      the value, Fail-depth2, of
      P-BJ(Search-path plus Current-value, New-distance,
        Variables minus the first variable,
        values of second variable in Variables,
        Current-depth + 1, 0,
        Current-depth if New-distance $\neq$ Distance else Inconsistency-depth),
      is = 'finished' {found a sufficient solution}
      or < Current-depth {can backjump!}
    then return Fail-depth2 {backup immediately}
  else {try another value}
    return P-BJ(Search-path, Distance, Variables,
      Values minus the first value,
      Current-depth,
      max(Fail-depth1, Return-depth, Inconsistency-depth),
      Inconsistency-depth)

Fig. 6. Backjumping algorithm.

N = 2

slacks   1   ...., dress blue, | dress gray, denims

inconsistency

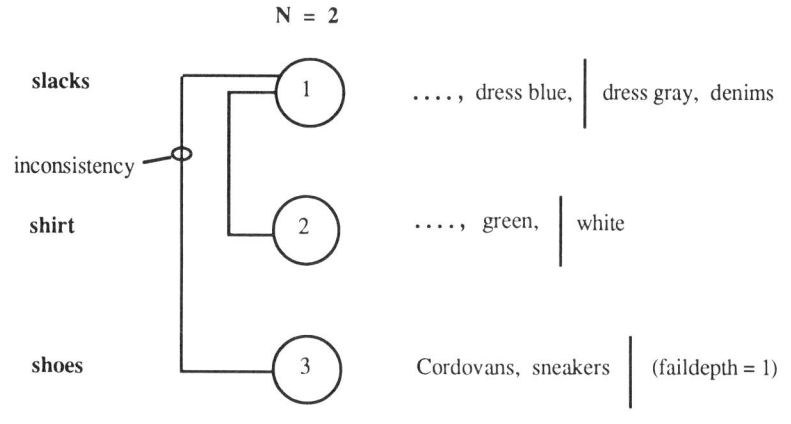

shirt   2   ...., green, | white

shoes   3   Cordovans, sneakers | (faildepth = 1)

Fig. 7. Backjumping to the level of the last inconsistent choice.

currently being considered. Current inconsistencies are indicated by the lines joining two nodes. Search has reached a dead end with the third variable (since the number of inconsistencies equals the bound), with the deepest level of failure (where the total number of inconsistencies became equal to the bound) at the level of variable 1. If this were a CSP, search would now jump back to variable 1 and the next value (gray slacks) would be selected. However, in the present problem the next value associated with variable 2 (white shirt) is compatible with the present value of variable 1 (blue slacks), so in this case no inconsistency is present between variables 1 and 2. Therefore, if search backs up to variable 2, a value can be chosen that leaves the distance at zero. In addition, the Cordovans (at variable 3) are compatible with the white shirt, but not with the blue slacks, so it is possible to find a solution including the blue slacks and white shirt that gives a total distance of 1. Since N is currently 2, this is a better solution. However, it would have been overlooked if we had followed the ordinary backjumping procedure used for CSPs.

To handle this situation, the backjumping analogue must keep track of the deepest level associated with an inconsistency (*Inconsistency-depth*), in addition to tracking the depth of failure. In the present implementation, *Inconsistency-depth* is passed along as search proceeds, and updated to *Current-depth*, the level at which we are currently trying to extend the search path, if there is a failure at this level of testing. Obviously, this addition to the procedure will tend to lessen the efficiency of this form of backjumping.

2.2.3. Backmarking

Backmarking [16] has the potential to avoid some redundant successful constraint checking, as well as some redundant discoveries of inconsistencies. When trying to extend a search path by choosing a value for a variable V, backmarking marks the individual level, *Mark*, in the search tree at which an inconsistency is detected for each value of V. For example, if value b for variable V is consistent with the first value in the search path, but inconsistent with the second value, the *Mark* for value b is 2. (If no inconsistency is detected for a value, its *Mark* is set to the level above the level of the value.) Assuming we cannot successfully extend the search path to a complete solution, and have to back up from V, backmarking also remembers the highest level, *Backto*, to which search has backed up since the last time V was considered. When backmarking next considers a value v, for V, the *Mark* and *Backto* levels can be compared. There are two cases:

(1) *Mark* < *Backto*. If the level at which v failed before is above the level to which we have backtracked, we know, without further constraint checking, that v will fail again. The value it failed against is still there.
(2) *Backto* ≤ *Mark*. If since v last failed we have backed up to or above the level at which v encountered failure, we have to test v; however, we can

start testing values against v at level *Backto*. The values above that level are unchanged since we last—successfully—tested them against v.

Figure 8 contains a backmarking algorithm for partial constraint satisfaction. Again, for partial satisfaction failure for a value, v, does not necessarily occur

```
P-BMK(Search-path, Distance, Variables, Values, Current-depth, Value-index)
    if Variables = nil then
        Best-solution <- Search-path
        N <- distance
        if N ≤ S then return 'finished'
        else return 'keep searching'
    else if Values = nil then
        set array Backto, beginning with current variable, to Current-depth-1
        return 'keep searching'
    else if    (    (Lastmark[Current-depth, Value-index] ≥ Backto[Current-depth]
                    {search has backed up to or above the level of the last inconsistency
                    marked at the previous encounter with the first of Values}
                    and
                    adding to Distance the number of inconsistencies found between the
                    first of Values and previous values in Search-path starting at level
                    min(Backto[Current-depth], Firstmark[Current-depth, Value-index])
                    (updating Arrays appropriately)
                    produces a New-distance < N)
                    {adding the first of Values to the search path
                    will not push the number of inconsistencies to the bound}
                or
                    (Distance + Inconsistencies[Current-depth, Value-index] < N
                    {current distance + recorded inconsistencies is less than the bound}
                    and
                    adding to Distance + Inconsistencies[Current-depth, Value-index]
                    the number of inconsistencies found between the first of Values
                    and previous values in Search-path starting at level
                    Lastmark[Current-depth, Value-index]+1
                    (updating Arrays appropriately)
                    produces a New-distance < N ))
                    {adding the first of Values to the search path
                    will not push the number of inconsistencies to the bound}
            and
                P-BMK(Search-path plus Current-value, New-distance,
                        Variables minus the first variable,
                        values of second variable in Variables, Current-depth+1, 1)
                = 'finished'
            then return 'finished'
        else return P-BMK(Search-path, Distance, Variables,
                        Values minus the first value,
                        Current-depth, Value-index+1)
```

Fig. 8. Backmarking algorithm.

at the first inconsistency. It occurs at a level, *Lastmark*, where the last inconsistency is found, that which causes us to reach the bound that terminates the search path. We call this level *Lastmark*, rather than *Mark*, because, as we shall see in a moment, we also need to keep track of the level *Firstmark* where the first inconsistency with v was found. Thus we mark a range, as opposed to a single failure point. As before we store the level, *Backto*, the highest level to which search has backed up since last trying to assign a value to V. *Firstmark*, *Lastmark*, *Backto*, and *Inconsistencies* are arrays, and are global, with the rows associated with the variables and the columns (except for *Backto*) with values. *Firstmark* elements are initialized to 1, *Lastmark* and *Inconsistencies* to 0, *Backto* to 1.

Again, we have two cases:

(1) *Lastmark* < *Backto*. If the level at which v failed before is above the level to which we have backtracked, we again know, without further testing, that v will fail again. All the values it failed against are still there.

(2) *Backto* ≤ *Lastmark*. If since v last failed we have backed up to or above the level at which v encountered failure, we have to test v. However, we cannot always start the new testing of values against v at level *Backto*, as in the CSP case. In the CSP case we know that there were no inconsistencies above the level of failure. Now we only know that there are no inconsistencies above the level where the first inconsistency was found. Thus there are two further cases:

  (a) *Backto* ≤ *Firstmark*. If we have backed up to or above the level where the first inconsistency was found, we know that the unchanged values above that level are still consistent with v, and we can start the new testing of v at level *Backto*.

  (b) *Firstmark* < *Backto*. Otherwise we need to start testing at the level of the first inconsistency, *Firstmark*. Above that level, the unchanged values will still be consistent with v.

Actually the situation is even a bit subtler and more distinct from CSP backjumping than we have let on. *Lastmark* may not in fact mark a failure point at all. The previous time we considered v, the last inconsistency may not have pushed us over the bound (or as in the CSP case, we may have found no inconsistency at all, in which case *Lastmark* is again set to the level above the level of v). On the other hand, even if the inconsistencies with v did not induce failure before, they may now, since the distance, the current number of other known inconsistencies, as well as the bound N, may have changed in the interim.

Accordingly we save another piece of information, the number of *Inconsistencies* between v and the values in the search path down to level *Lastmark*.

Case (1) above is really:

(1′) *Lastmark* < *Backto*.
  (a) If the current *Distance* plus *Inconsistencies* is not less than N, we know that v will fail again without further testing. The values which produced those inconsistencies before are still present.
  (b) Otherwise, add *Inconsistencies* to the current *Distance*, and commence further testing of v at the level below *Lastmark*. The values which caused the inconsistencies before are still there. (We feel that it may be possible to commence testing at level *Backto*, but subtle bookkeeping issues need to be resolved.)

Several snapshots of the search with the backmarking analogue for the clothes matching problem are shown in Fig. 9. Each copy of the arrays shows the values following the portion of search diagrammed to its left; only changed values are shown. For each array, rows associated with the first level of search are omitted from the figure because their entries never change.

For example, consider the cells associated with the value green shirt after the first portion of the search, which is represented at the far left of Fig. 9. The green shirt value is associated with row three and column one in the arrays. The value of *Firstmark*[3, 1] is 1, since the green shirt does not match the Cordovans at level 1. The value of *Lastmark*[3, 1] is 2, due to the mismatch between the green shirt and the denims. Since there are two mismatches, or constraint failures, associated with the green shirt, *Inconsistencies*[3, 1] is 2.

Note that in the last column of arrays, the cells associated with the green shirt and the white shirt (row three) all have a value of 1, since the comparisons with sneakers at level one resulted in a constraint failure and this was sufficient to attain the bound. In addition, *Backto*[3] has value 2. Suppose when search proceeds to the next value for the variable slacks (dress blue, not shown), there is no failure, so the current distance is zero. However, before the green shirt is

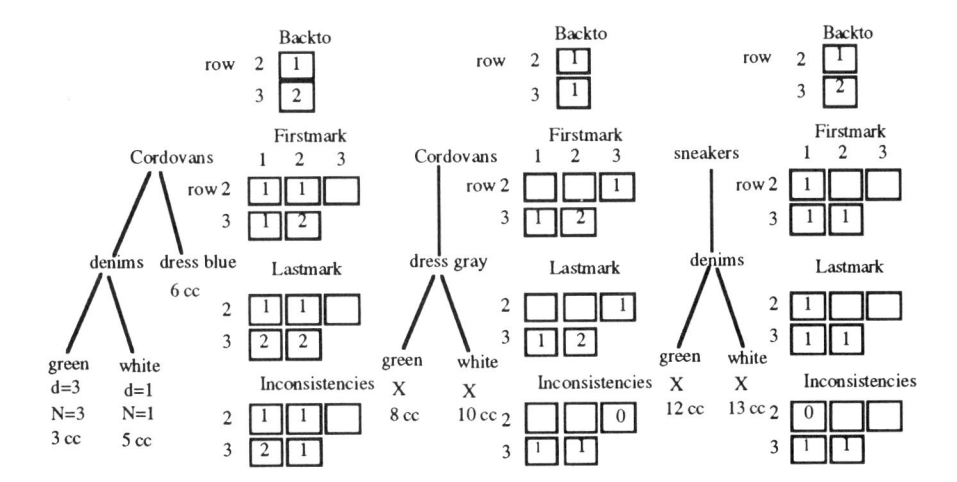

Fig. 9. Backmarking example.

tested again, the value of *Backto*[3] is found to be greater than *Lastmark*[3, 1]—case (1') above—and the value of *Inconsistencies*[3, 1] is 1 while N is also 1, so we are in case (1'a), and green shirt fails without any further constraint checking. The same situation is found with the white shirt. Search returns to level 2, where the gray slacks are tested; these fail to match the sneakers and search ends with a total of 15 constraint checks.

The version of backmarking used in the experiments described in Section 4 used an enhancement to minimize the number of constraint checks (though it turned out not to make much difference). Under the second "else if" of the algorithm as described in Fig. 8, the distance was first checked against N; if N had been reached or exceeded, there was no need for constraint checking. Unfortunately, this tactic entailed further checking after the last "else" and possible revision of the values of *Firstmark*, *Lastmark*, and *Inconsistencies* if the bound had been reached *and* the algorithm had since backed up into the recorded range of constraint failures. For example, if the value in *Backto* was now between the corresponding values in *Firstmark* and *Lastmark*, *Lastmark* was set to *Firstmark* and *Inconsistencies* set to 1.

Various refinements of PCSP backmarking are possible that have not yet been implemented. Observe that in our running example, the second time we encounter the green shirt, while the *Lastmark* and *Inconsistencies* machinery does not help us, the *Firstmark* value could. Since *Firstmark* occurs at level 1, which is above the *Backto* level, and the bound is already down to one at this point, we could infer, without any further constraint checks, that using the green shirt will bring us to the bound. In fact, we could consider storing all levels at which values encountered inconsistencies, and using that additional information for further pruning without further constraint checking.

2.3. Prospective techniques

Prospective techniques "look ahead" to establish some form of local consistency before continuing the search for a global solution. Prospective techniques can prune from consideration values that do not meet local consistency criteria. Consistency techniques can be used as *preprocessing* methods prior to search (in some situations leaving little if any work for subsequent search). They can be interleaved with backtracking to form *hybrid algorithms*. There are also methods of applying local consistency techniques repeatedly to subproblems to achieve global solutions.

The most commonly used form of local consistency is *arc consistency* [25]. A problem is fully arc consistent if every value in the domain of every variable is consistent with, we also say *supported by*, at least one value in every other variable domain. Arc consistency preprocessing eliminates all unsupported values.

The most familiar hybrid algorithm is *forward checking* [19]. In forward checking, each assignment of a value, v, to a variable, V, is followed by a limited amount of arc consistency checking, in which the domains of variables that share a constraint with V are tested against v.

It is a standard branch and bound strategy (often discussed in terms of "lower bounds") to increase pruning by estimating the implications of proceeding on from the current search point. Prospective methods provide a means of implementing this strategy for partial constraint satisfaction. Until now, we have been discontinuing a search path if the number of inconsistencies on that path, the distance D, is not less than the bound N. If we had some way of determining that no matter how we sought to continue that path we would encounter at least D' additional inconsistencies, then we could discontinue the search if $D + D'$ failed to be less than N. Prospective methods permit us to obtain such D' values.

2.3.1. Pruning with arc consistency counts

In the CSP context, arc consistency permits us to eliminate values that arc consistency processing determines cannot participate in any complete solution. In our running example, sneakers can be eliminated because it is not consistent with any shirt. Furthermore the dark green shirt and the dress blue slacks can be eliminated because they are not consistent with any shoes. Notice further that although the denim slacks were originally supported by sneakers, now that sneakers have been eliminated there is no support for denims, and they can be eliminated in turn. Now there is no longer any support for the white shirt. Having eliminated both shirt possibilities arc consistency has, for this problem, discovered that there is no global solution, and no further search is necessary.

In the PCSP context, it is not possible to discard values in this way unless we have an initial value for the necessary bound, N. If we did know, for example, a priori, that there was a solution that violated only one constraint, or that any solution that did violate more than one constraint was unacceptable, we could eliminate a value for a variable that was not consistent with any value for two other variables.

However, it is possible to perform prior calculations regarding the increments in distance associated with specific values. In particular, for each value, the number of domains with no supporting values can be tallied; this number, the *arc consistency count*, is a lower bound on the increment in distance that will be incurred if this value is added to the solution. An algorithm for computing arc consistency counts is given in Fig. 10.

In the course of subsequent search, the arc consistency count for a proposed search path extension, v, can be added to the distance associated with the search path, and this sum compared with the current bound N. If the sum is not less than N, then we know that any complete solution starting with the current search path and involving v will violate too many constraints. We can fail at this point without testing v at all. Of course, v was tested once during

```
P-ACC(Variables, Domains, Counts)
    For all Vi belonging to Variables:
        For all Vj ≠ Vi such that there is a constraint between Vi and Vj:
            For each value, a, in domain of Vi:
                if there is no value, b, in the domain of Vj such that the pair (a, b)
                    is allowed by the constraint between Vi and Vj
                then increment the count for value a
```

Fig. 10. Algorithm for computing arc consistency counts.

the preprocessing; however, we may encounter v many times during subsequent search, and on a number of those occasions the preprocessing may save further testing of v. The forward checking algorithm below uses a similar strategy involving a limited, dynamic form of arc consistency count.

If arc consistency checking is used to tally the number of domains that do not support a value, then one constraint failure may be involved twice, once for each value that does not belong to an acceptable pair. This is not a problem during subsequent search because a consistency count is not incorporated into the distance except to check against the bound when first considering that value for extending the search path. (If the value is accepted, then adjustment of the distance through consistency checking is done in the same way as with basic branch and bound.) Suppose a particular value is included, and another value is considered afterwards whose arc consistency count depends in part on a constraint that also affected the former value's consistency count. Since the current distance is based on retrospective checking, it does not yet include this constraint, so the second count can be used without modification in computing a projected distance to compare with the upper bound.

Arc consistency counts have the advantage that they need only be computed once, before search, and can be done in $O(cd^2)$ time, where c is the number of constraints and d the maximum domain size for the variables. They can then be stored in an appropriate form for testing against the current distance. In contrast, both the retrospective and hybrid techniques require more extensive calculation to retain and update information related to distance for specific values.

Because no values are actually discarded, there is no propagation of failure in the manner of arc consistency algorithms for CSPs (e.g. where the removal of sneakers led in turn to the removal of denim). It may be possible to propagate counts in a manner analogous to ordinary constraint propagation. (Hybrid analogues based on this idea may also be possible and were suggested by Shapiro and Haralick [35] for inexact matching.) This might involve retaining information about the conditions of failure, employing conditional counts that can only be used if the supporting values are *not* used in the solution. In the arc consistency count algorithm, in contrast, which takes one pass through the variables, we are assured that the consistency counts are all unconditional.

2.3.2. Forward checking

Forward checking is a hybrid algorithm that uses a very limited amount of arc consistency checking. Each time a value, v, is assigned to a variable, V, the algorithm looks ahead to all the variables that currently have not been assigned a value, and that share a constraint with V, and removes from the domains of these variables any values inconsistent with v. For example, when Cordovans are proposed for shoes, the denim and dress blue slacks will be removed, and the green shirt.

If later we change our mind about v, the pruned values have to be restored. E.g. when we move on to consider sneakers, the denim and dress blue slacks and the green shirt must reappear. (In an implementation, recursion can handle the bookkeeping for the variable domains during backup.) Of course, since sneakers are not consistent with any shirt, forward checking with sneakers will reduce the shirt domain to the empty set, signaling a failure point.

Notice that despite the fact that it can be viewed as an integration of consistency processing and backtracking, forward checking really is almost the complement of standard backtracking. Standard backtracking checks a value for consistency against previously chosen values. With forward checking, when we propose a value we already know it is consistent with the previously chosen values (or else the consistency processing would already have pruned it away). Now we test it against the domains of the remaining uninstantiated variables.

When used for partial satisfaction, forward checking is based on the same type of looking ahead as ordinary forward checking. However, again, the differing definition of failure comes into play. If there is an inconsistency, a value is not rejected unless the total number of currently chosen values with which it is inconsistent is equal to the bound N. This means that the algorithm must dynamically keep track of the number of times a value has been found to be inconsistent with currently chosen values. This number, a form of dynamic arc consistency count, we will call the *inconsistency count* for a value.

An example of forward checking beginning to operate on the matching clothes problem is shown in Fig. 11. In this figure, counts associated with the values of variables which share a constraint with a variable, V, are shown at the point in the search at which they are calculated. For example, when Cordovans are chosen, the inconsistency count for green shirt becomes one; it increases to two when denims are chosen.

Although we see more constraint checks performed in the early stages of this example than we saw with straightforward branch and bound, the counts derived from these early checks are used to avoid further constraint checks, putting forward checking ahead at a later stage.

When a value, v, is proposed, its own inconsistency count can be added to the current distance, and the total used in a manner similar to that proposed for arc consistency counts in the previous section: if the total is equal to or

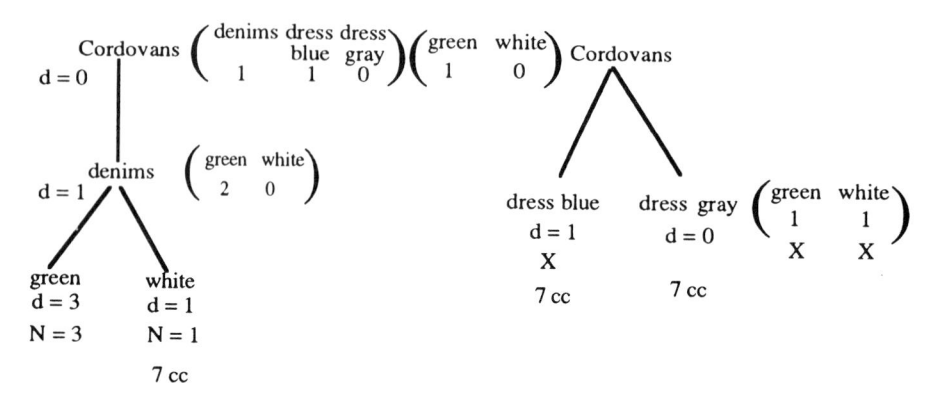

Fig. 11. Forward checking example.

greater than the bound, v fails immediately. For example, when Cordovans are tried with blue slacks, the bound is already one (set by the Cordovans, denim slacks, and white shirt combination), and the inconsistency count of blue slacks is one (set when Cordovans was chosen). This tells us that we cannot hope to choose a shirt that will permit us to do any better than our current best solution. The blue slacks fail, without any further testing.

Notice also that when gray slacks are tried with Cordovans, although they are consistent, together they eliminate all the shirt values. Cordovans raises the inconsistency count of green shirt to one, eliminating it, since the bound is one. Gray slacks raises the inconsistency count of white shirt to one, eliminating it, and leaving us with an empty domain for shirts. Reducing the domain of an uninstantiated variable to empty also, of course, signals a failure point.

Shapiro and Haralick [35] generalized the CSP look-ahead technique in their study of the "inexact matching problem". (The algorithm they call "forward checking" does more looking ahead than ours; it employs the "extended forward checking" discussed in Section 2.5.) They defined the "inexact constraint labeling problem", which involves searching for any solutions within a given error bound. The count of violated constraints that we use could be viewed as the "error". However, Shapiro and Haralick's algorithms did not seek optimal solutions and were not full branch and bound algorithms in the sense that they did not store and compare with the "best-so-far" solutions; all comparisons were with the error bound.

Different variants of forward checking can be devised, depending on the manner in which the counts for each value are used to minimize constraint checks. In contrast to Shapiro and Haralick, who stored counts in tables and did not discard values, corresponding lists can be used for domain values and associated counts, from which values are discarded if their counts are high enough to raise the distance to the bound.

In the most straightforward version, referred to as P-FC1, the values of a domain are checked against the latest value proposed, v, and the inconsistency counts associated with values inconsistent with v are incremented by one. During this revision of the domain, when a count for a value u is incremented, the incremented count is added to the distance of the search path down to v and the sum is tested against the bound. If this sum equals or exceeds the bound, it means that the search path down to v cannot be extended to a solution including u without reaching the bound. Thus u can be removed; u will not be checked again at this or at lower levels of recursion.

In the second version (P-FC2), all counts are tested in this manner against the bound during revision, not just the incremented counts. This eliminates values whose counts might now be too large, not because the count has increased, but because the bound has been lowered since the values were last considered for elimination.

In the third version (P-FC3), we take this a step further. All counts are tested before doing any constraint checking to see if counts can be incremented. Thus values may be deleted simply because the bound has been lowered, without any consistency checking to determine if their counts need to be incremented. Here, of course, any incremented counts of values that survived the first test but fail the consistency test have to be tested again during revision of the list of values.

To summarize, in P-FC1, constraint checks are done on all values and count checks on the failures; in P-FC2, constraint checks and then count checks are done on all values; in P-FC3, count checks are done on all values, constraint checks are done on viable values and then count checks are done on values that failed the consistency test. A general P-FC algorithm that does not specify the details of constraint and count checking is shown in Fig. 12.

2.3.3. Tree-structured problems

Local consistency methods have been used to support polynomial algorithms for CSPs with tree or tree-like structure [8, 15, 26]. When problems do not have such structure it may still be useful to view them as containing or being contained in such structures [6, 8, 9, 13, 15, 27]. A problem is *tree-structured* if the graph that results from viewing variables as vertices and constraints between variables as edges between vertices (the *constraint graph*) is tree-structured.

The idea of utilizing a tree which represents a subproblem is particularly attractive in the PCSP domain where the constraints that need to be removed to reduce a problem to the desired structure do not eventually have to be satisfied, but may be written off as unsatisfied constraints in the partial constraint satisfaction process. The algorithm P-T in Fig. 13 obtains an efficient solution for tree-structured maximal constraint satisfaction problems.

Tree-structured CSPs can be solved in time linear in the number of variables and quadratic in the maximum domain size, but at first blush one might

```
P-FC(Search-path, Distance, Variables, Domains, Inconsistency-counts)
    {Domains holds values for variables not yet assigned a value in Search-path
    that are consistent with the values in Search-path}
    if Variables = nil then
        Best-solution <- Search-path
        N <- Distance
        if N ≤ S then return 'finished'
        else return 'keep searching'
    else if first of Domains = nil then
        return 'keep searching'
    else if Distance + first count in Inconsistency-counts < N
        {first count in Inconsistency-counts is the number of inconsistencies
        between first value in first of Domains and values in Search-path}
        and
        while computing New-inconsistency-counts and New-domains,
        {check consistency, as needed, with first value in first of Domains;
        details determined by which version of P-FC using}
         New-domains retain at least one value in each domain
        and
        P-FC(Search-path plus first value in first of Domains,
                Distance + first count in Inconsistency-counts,
                Variables minus first variable,
                New-domains, New-inconsistency-counts) = 'finished'
            then return 'finished'
    else
        return P-FC(Search-path, Distance, Variables,
                    Domains after removing first value from first of Domains,
                    Inconsistency-counts minus count for first value
                        from first of Domains)
```

Fig. 12. Forward checking algorithm.


```
Algorithm P-T:
For each variable, L, which is a leaf node of the constraint tree:
    For each value, e, of L:
        Set Cost(e)=0
For each level in the tree starting at the level above the leaves, and working upwards:
    For each variable, V, at that level:
        For each value, v, of that variable:
            For each child, U, of that variable:
                For each value, u, of that child:
                    If v is consistent with u
                        then set Cost(v,u)=Cost(u)
                        else set Cost(v,u)=Cost(u)+1
                Link v to a u such that Cost(v,u) is minimum
                Set Cost(v) to that minimum Cost(v,u)
        Delete all v except those with minimal cost at V
Return as a minimal solution a value for the root with minimal cost,
    along with the tree of values linked to it at the other variables.
```

Fig. 13. A linear algorithm for a tree-structured maximal constraint satisfaction problem.

suppose that tree-structured maximal constraint satisfaction problems would not admit such a small bound. In fact, however, algorithm P-T does achieve this bound.

Theorem. *Algorithm P-T finds a maximal solution for a tree-structured maximal constraint satisfaction problem and has an $O(nd^2)$ complexity bound, where n is the number of variables and d the maximum number of values in a variable domain.*

Proof. As we process the tree of variables we associate costs with values. The cost represents the total number of constraints violated if we choose that value and all values we have linked to it at descendant variables. We retain only minimal cost values at each variable. We claim that the cost of a value at a variable represents in fact the minimal number of constraints that we need to violate in order to instantiate that variable and its descendants in the variable tree, while that value and its descendant values represent in fact an optimal solution for the subtree. Thus at the root variable we will have found a minimal cost instantiation, an optimal solution for the complete tree-structured problem.

The claim is trivially true at the leaves. We work our way inductively up the tree to the root. Assume that the claim is true for all the children of a variable V in the constraint tree. The algorithm only keeps values at V that minimize the additional cost vis à vis previously retained values for the children, i.e. minimize the number of constraints violated. Changing those previously retained values could not improve matters: changing a value at a child to avoid an inconsistency with the parent value means replacing the child value with one whose additional cost at the very least offsets the additional consistency. Note also that the only constraints between V and its descendants are those between V and its children. Furthermore there are no constraints between variables in different subtrees of V. Thus the cost of a value at V represents the minimal number of constraints that we need to violate in order to instantiate that variable and its descendants in the variable tree, while that value and its descendant values represents an optimal solution for the subtree rooted at V.

Working up from the leaves, the algorithm builds up optimal solutions for subtrees, all the way to the root. Essentially all $n - 1$ edges in the tree have to be processed once, with each processing requiring at most d^2 consistency checks. □

It should be emphasized that these results, indeed more powerful results, have already been obtained in a closely related context [7]. The context is a CSP with multiple solutions, where the objective is to choose a solution which maximizes the value of a criterion function. Though superficially this context appears quite distinct from the PCSP context, where there may not even be a single solution, one could presumably use the criterion function to simulate a maximal satisfaction problem.

2.4. Ordering

As usual in branch and bound it is advantageous to order the search to heuristically increase the likelihood that a good, or ideally optimal, solution will be found early. The counts produced by the arc consistency method described in Section 2.3.1 can be used to order search. This can be done either by ordering the values in each domain according to their individual counts or by ordering the variables on the basis of some statistic derived from the counts for each domain.

In the tests carried out for this paper, values are ordered by increasing counts. This allows the values most likely to produce a good solution to be tested first, so that a minimum or near-minimum distance solution should be found more quickly on average, yielding a better bound early in the search.

In the present work the statistic used for variable ordering is the mean for the counts associated with the values of each domain. (The minimum count was also considered, but, for most problems, there are too many zero counts to make this statistic sufficiently discriminating). In addition, variables are ordered by *decreasing* mean count. This is based on the premise that, once a good bound is found, checking domains with less support early in the search will increase the likelihood that the bound will be reached at higher levels of the search tree. This argument is supported by tests in which the ordering was in the opposite direction; the results were appreciably worse in most cases (and sometimes worse than the basic branch and bound), especially for sets of harder problems.

A variety of variable ordering techniques have been studied for CSPs and could be considered in the PCSP context. More sophisticated cost estimates could be associated with the variables to support additional PCSP-specific techniques. The two forms of ordering based on arc consistency counts, as well as the pruning based on arc consistency counts described in Section 2.3.1, can, of course, be combined in different ways.

2.5. Extensions

The basic techniques discussed above can be extended in a variety of directions, and other techniques considered. Obviously in this paper we can only begin a research program that requires, at the least, a recapitulation of the entire history of progress on CSPs.

One obvious line of inquiry involves combining basic techniques. We emphasize in this paper development and analysis of basic "atomic" techniques. However, we conducted some experiments with an algorithm which combines a retrospective technique—backmarking—a prospective technique—arc consistency count pruning—and an ordering technique—value ordering. We call this algorithm P-RPO.

The branch and bound context suggests looking for tighter lower bounds on the distance of the minimal distance solution that includes a given set of value choices. These can be used to obtain quicker pruning of choices that have no chance of doing better than a solution already found. The arc consistency count pruning described above does this sort of thing in a simple but efficient manner; the arc consistency counts are only computed once in a preprocessing step. The forward checking analogues utilize a kind of dynamic arc consistency count.

Shapiro and Haralick [35] suggest more elaborate lower bound computations, up to dynamically utilizing a complete arc or even path consistency [25] analogue after each value choice, for their inexact matching problems. Of course, there are tradeoffs between consistency check savings and bound computation costs. We tested an analogue, which we call *extended forward checking* for partial constraint satisfaction, of the most successful algorithm that they implemented.

Forward checking for maximal constraint satisfaction, as described above, assigns an inconsistency count to a value, v, based on the inconsistencies that would be incurred by adding v to the choices, C, which have already been made. Extended forward checking goes further by forming a lower bound estimate of the number of further inconsistencies that would accrue in the course of choosing values for each of the remaining variables. For each of these variables it finds the minimum inconsistency count assigned to the values for that variable. It then adds all of these counts to the inconsistencies incurred in choosing C and v. This sum will be a lower bound estimate on the number of constraints violated by a maximal solution that contains C and v.

Thus we could turn the P-FC algorithm into an extended forward checking algorithm, P-EFC, by changing the test:

$$Distance + \text{first count in } Inconsistency\text{-}counts < N,$$

into the test:

$$Distance + \text{first count in } Inconsistency\text{-}counts$$
$$+ \text{sum of minimum counts for each variable in } Remaining\text{-}variables < N.$$

The version of extended forward checking we tested included the forward checking refinements implemented in our P-FC3 algorithm, and is thus called P-EFC3.

Essentially we are playing a "what if" game. If we added v to the already chosen values, what would be the best we could hope for? If that is not as good as the best we have already done, we can prune v from consideration (until such time as we may change our choices, C).

3. Experiments

3.1. Overview

The algorithms described in Section 2 were tested in a series of experiments with random problems. In the first six experiments, we examined the relative efficiency of these algorithms and the relation between efficiency and problem structure. In these experiments each algorithm was run to completion, to find a maximal solution. Three preliminary studies compared the efficiency of related algorithms. The first included the retrospective algorithms, P-BJ and P-BMK, together with the basic branch and bound, P-BB. The second compared the three versions of P-FC, which differed in the number and placement of tests of distance plus counts against the bound. The third compared procedures based on the arc consistency algorithm, P-ACC. In the fourth and main experiment we tested the most promising algorithms from the first three experiments on a more extensive set of problems, in which basic problem parameters such as domain size were varied systematically. In the fifth experiment, the best algorithms were tested on problems of varying size (number of variables); this experiment also included the algorithms P-RPO and P-EFC3. In the sixth experiment we obtained data on overall efficiency, using time as a measure, with problems selected from the main experiment that presented different levels of difficulty for the algorithms.

For many problems finding a maximal solution may not be feasible because the problem is too hard to solve completely. In these cases a good submaximal solution may still be acceptable. Branch and bound techniques are useful in this situation because of their anytime feature: after an initial solution is found, the algorithm can stop at any time before completion with the best solution found so far. In Experiments 7 and 8, we examined the efficiency with which the different algorithms can find submaximal solutions with distances increasingly close to that of a maximal solution. The problems used in these experiments were larger versions of the random problems used in previous experiments and, in addition, a set of large coloring problems believed to be very hard to solve [4]. In these experiments resource bounds were established by placing a limit on the number of constraint checks that could be performed; the program terminated if this limit was reached.

3.2. Random problem generation

In generating random problems, there are four features to consider:

  (i) number of variables, n,
  (ii) number of constraints, c,

(iii) domain size, d,
(iv) number of value pairs included in a constraint, p.

In the present work, n was fixed for each set of problems. Then the values of the other three features were determined with a (constant) probability of inclusion method that is best explained by example. Consider the choice of number of constraints. For problems of ten variables with a connected constraint graph, up to 36 constraints can be added. In generating a random problem, the probability of inclusion is fixed at, say, 0.3, and each of the possible constraints is considered for inclusion using random methods to simulate this probability. With a probability of 0.3, a set of problems is obtained with an expected value for number of constraints equal to $9 + (36 * 0.3) \approx 20$. Similar procedures were used to determine d and p for each domain and constraint, respectively. The only limitation in these cases was that the value of d or p was at least one. If no element was included (zero value), the procedure was repeated beginning with the first element until a nonzero value was obtained. This method has the advantages that:

(i) each parameter value can be varied in a way that is easily characterized, i.e., by a single probability.
(ii) each element has the same probability of inclusion, which makes the sampling properties of each possible set of elements relatively easy to characterize.

For these experiments, problems without solutions were required. This limited the range of probability values that could be considered, because as d or p increases, it is more likely that problems with solutions will be produced. Values of 0.2, 0.4, and 0.6 were used to determine p, while values of 0.1, 0.2, and 0.3 were used for d, based on a maximum domain size equal to $2n$ or twice the number of variables. Values of 0.3, 0.6, and 0.9 were used to determine the number of constraints to be added to a spanning tree (which was itself derived by choosing pairs of variables at random). In the remainder of the paper, these probability values will be designated as p_c, p_d and p_p, for probability of constraint, domain, or constraint pair inclusion, respectively. (p_c is sometimes called the *density* of the problem, and p_p the (relative) *satisfiability*, while the complement of p_p is sometimes refered to as the *tightness* of a constraint.) The values chosen covered most of the range of possible values, while allowing a similar degree of variation in each case. After generation, a problem was tested for solutions. If a solution was found, the following strategy was used to obtain an insoluble problem with identical parameter values: a constraint pair that included two values in the solution was chosen at random and discarded, and another pair of values from the same domains was chosen at random as a new constraint pair; this procedure was repeated until a problem with no solutions was found.

3.3. Experimental design

Experiments 1–3. Experiments 1–3 were based on a set of ten-variable problems for which the probabilities of domain and value pair inclusion took on all the values mentioned in the last section, while the density was always 0.3. This gave nine categories of problems. Ten problems were generated for each category, for a total of 90 problems.

In Experiment 1, the algorithms tested were P-BB and two other retrospective algorithms, the backjumping and backmarking analogues, P-BJ and P-BMK. Experiment 2 compared the three variants of P-FC described in Section 2.

Experiment 3 compared several variants of P-BB that incorporated different forms of information derived from arc consistency counts, either singly or in combination. These were:

 (i) pruning based on the count for a given value,
 (ii) ordering of values in each domain by increasing count,
 (iii) ordering of variables by (decreasing) mean count of the values in their domains,
 (iv) a combination of the value and variable ordering strategies,
 (v) a combination of pruning and value ordering,
 (vi) a combination of pruning, value and variable ordering.

Experiment 4. Experiment 4 compared the most promising algorithms from each of the first three experiments. These were P-BMK, P-FC3, and two varieties of branch and bound that incorporated information from the counts obtained by P-ACC ((v) and (vi) above). P-BB was also included for reference. For this experiment the problem set was expanded to include the other two probabilities of constraint inclusion (0.6 and 0.9). It was, therefore, a fully crossed design, with each of the three probabilities of inclusion associated with each parameter, as described in Section 3.2. This gave 27 categories; ten problems were generated for each category for a total of 270 problems. (These included the 90 problems used in Experiments 1–3.)

Experiment 5. In this experiment the best retrospective and prospective algorithms from Experiment 4, P-BMK and P-FC3, along with P-BB, were compared on problems in which the number of variables, n, was varied. In addition, the extensions P-RPO and P-EFC3 were included. The number of variables ranged between 8 and 12, with ten problems for each problem size. Based on preliminary tests of feasibility for higher n, the values of 0.3, 0.2, and 0.4 were chosen for p_c, p_d, and p_p, respectively. (In Experiments 1–4, with $n = 10$, problems in this category were relatively easy to solve.)

Experiment 6. In Experiment 6, the following algorithms were compared with respect to run time: P-BB, P-BJ, P-BMK, P-FC2, and P-FC3. Problems were selected from Experiment 4 in which the order of magnitude for constraint checks was three, four, or five for branch and bound. (Similar ranges in terms of order of magnitude were obtained with the other algorithms tested.) Six problems were chosen at each level of difficulty, three for which the density, p_c, was 0.3 and three for which it was 0.9, for a total of 18 problems. These problems were also chosen so that other parameter values (probabilities of inclusion) also varied. Run times were obtained with the Lisp time function.

Experiments 7–8. In Experiment 7, problems had 12, 16, or 20 variables, with ten problems per group. The values of p_c, p_d, and p_p were the same as those in Experiment 5; in fact, the same 12-variable problems were used in both experiments. As a consequence, the distance associated with the best solution was known. For the 16-variable problems, an optimal solution was obtained using P-EFC3. This allowed a more complete evaluation of the suboptimal solutions obtained when the number of constraint checks was limited to two million. It was also used as a reference for the results with 20-variable problems, which were too large for an optimal solution to be found when the number of constraint checks was limited to five million. Five algorithms were tested with the 12-variable problems: P-BB, P-BMK, P-FC3, P-ROP, and P-EFC3, and all but P-FC3 were tested with the 16- and 20-variable problems. (Since P-FC3 was always bettered by P-EFC3, it will not be discussed further.)

In Experiment 8 a similar procedure was used with nine large, "really hard" coloring problems [4]. These were classic graph coloring problems where the objective is to color every vertex of a graph with a color, chosen from a fixed number of colors, such that no vertices joined by an edge have the same color. Vertices correspond to CSP variables, edges to CSP constraints. These problems had four colors, 130–144 variables and 620–646 constraints, giving densities of 0.05–0.06. Three algorithms were tested: P-BB, P-BMK, and P-EFC3. (P-RPO was not included since arc consistency counts are zero for all values in coloring problems of this sort.)

In all experiments except the sixth, the basic measure was the number of constraint checks, although we also recorded the number of nodes searched. In Experiment 6, the measures were execution time and time per 1000 constraint checks. Garbage collection time and basic I/O and setup time were subtracted from the total time in calculating these measures.

In these experiments, the analysis of variance (ANOVA) was used to test the statistical significance of differences due to the algorithm used and to variation in each problem parameter, as well as interactions between these factors. In these tests, one to three of the statistical factors were based on problem parameters. If more than one such factor appeared in an experiment, they were fully crossed, with each combination of factors forming a single experimental group. The algorithm used to solve the problem was a separate factor, with all problem groups "repeated" on it. (A simple fixed effects design, in which different problems are chosen from the same category for each algorithm would introduce more variation and is unnecessary, since independence of different treatments (algorithms) is not an issue in this domain.) As an example consider the design of Experiment 1. Here, the factors based on p_d and p_p are crossed to form separate categories of problems, all of which are repeated on the factor related to the three algorithms tested. Each of these factors, as well as the first and second order ($p_d \times p_p \times$ algorithm) interactions was tested for statistical significance, using the standard null hypothesis of no differences between groups related to that effect. All analyses were done with log-transformed data, to reduce differences in variance among groups. If the effect of algorithms in the ANOVA was statistically significant, algorithms were compared on their mean performance using Tukey's q test for nonorthogonal pairwise comparisons [22].

In Experiment 4, we performed several further analyses to better understand performance characteristics in relation to problem parameters. Standard deviations were obtained for each algorithm on each problem set, as well as measures of skew, or asymmetry in the distributions of performance scores. Pearson product–moment correlations between P-BB and the other algorithms were also derived, using the original scores. And, for each algorithm, multiple regression analysis with respect to the problem parameters was carried out using the log-transformed scores and a zero y-intercept.

In Experiments 7–8, statistical analysis consisted of paired comparison t tests between algorithms, beginning with 100 constraint checks and including successive powers of ten up to the highest power within the response bound. (The value of 5 million constraint checks was also tested for 20-variable problems.) For P-RPO the constraint checks required for arc consistency checking were added to the total in each case.

3.4. Results

3.4.1. Experiments 1–3: preliminary comparisons of similar algorithms

In each of the first three experiments, some of the algorithms were clearly superior to others tested on the same set of problems. In Experiment 1, P-BMK was markedly superior to both P-BB and P-BJ. In Experiment 2, P-FC3 was the most efficient in terms of constraint checks, although all three variants of P-FC were much better than P-BB. In Experiment 3, versions of P-BB that used variable and value ordering together, or pruning and value ordering, or a combination of all three strategies were generally superior to the other three variations as well as to P-BB.

These results were borne out by the statistical analysis. In all three experiments, the effect due to algorithms was statistically significant (Experiment 1,

$F[2, 243] = 12.89$, $p < 0.001$; Experiment 2, $F[2, 243] = 4.58$, $p = 0.01$; Experiment 3, $F[5, 486] = 5.85$, $p < 0.001$). In addition, the factors related to problem parameters, specifically to differences in p_d and p_p, were highly significant statistically ($F > 50$ always, $p \ll 0.001$), as was the interaction between these factors ($F > 10$ always, $p < 0.001$). With one exception in Experiment 3, none of the interactions between algorithms and the other factors was statistically significant ($F \leq 1$).

The meaning of the significant effects related to problem parameters can be understood from Fig. 14, which gives the main results for Experiment 1. As this figure shows, problems become harder as the average domain size increases, and this effect is greater with increasing tightness of constraints (decreasing p_p). This is intuitively plausible. Of greater importance is the relatively rapid change in difficulty with more extreme values, so that really difficult problems are found in only a small part of the parameter space. These results are, therefore, consistent with Dechter and Pearl's demonstration in [8] that, on average, random problems such as these are fairly easy to solve.

In Experiment 1, P-BJ was only slightly superior to P-BB, while, as stated, P-BMK was markedly superior (Fig. 14). Most importantly, P-BMK showed substantial improvement over basic branch and bound in the most difficult parts of the parameter space, i.e., the points associated with larger domain size and greater tightness of constraints. On the other hand, it appeared that for P-BMK as well as P-BJ average *relative* improvement was greatest for larger

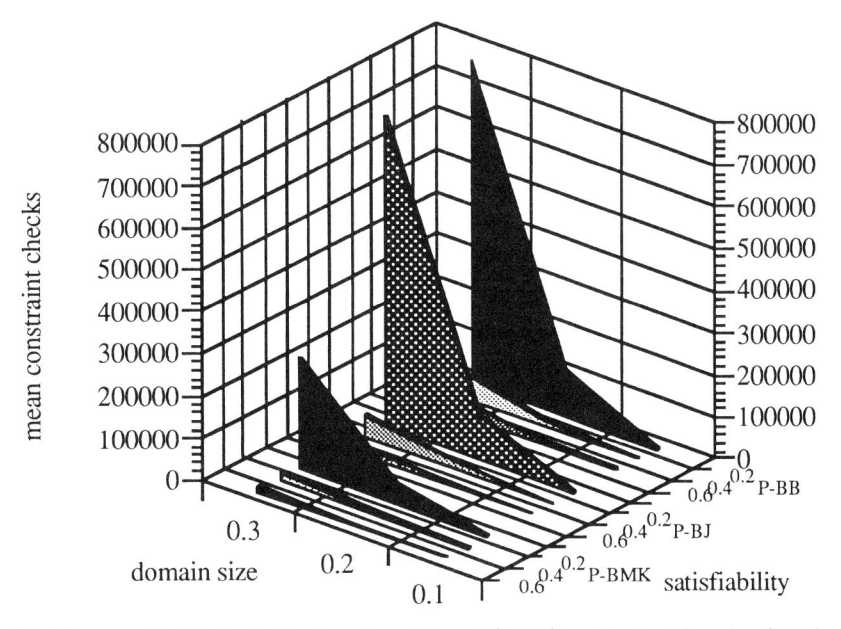

Fig. 14. Mean constraint checks for branch and bound (P-BB) and for backjumping (P-BJ) and backmarking (P-BMK) in Experiment 1, as a function of parameters for domain size (p_d) and satisfiability (p_p).

values of satisfiability and domain size, where problems were easier to solve, although this interaction was not detected by the ANOVA, probably because it was overshadowed by the corresponding changes that occurred with all three algorithms. Observed differences in performance were supported by individual comparisons of means. In this analysis, the overall difference between P-BMK and each of the other two algorithms was statistically significant ($q[2, 89] \geq 5$, $p < 0.01$ for both comparisons), while the difference between P-BJ and P-BB was not.

In Experiment 2, both methods of forward checking that employed more count checks (P-FC2 and P-FC3) were superior to the algorithm that depended more directly on constraint checks (P-FC1). However, in the individual comparisons, the differences that were statistically significant were related to P-FC3 ($q[2, 89] = 2.82$, $p < 0.05$ and $q[2, 89] = 4.20$, $p < 0.01$, for comparisons with P-FC2 and P-FC1, respectively). All versions were markedly superior to P-BB.

In Experiment 3, improvement in performance due to strategies based on arc consistency counts depended in part on domain size, which was reflected in the statistically significant interaction between algorithms and the factor based on p_d ($F[10, 486] = 2.95$, $p = 0.001$). Consider, first, the individual strategies of pruning based on counts, or ordering values, or ordering variables on the basis of counts. For $p_d = 0.1$, pruning and value ordering each reduced the number of constraint checks relative to the basic P-BB algorithm, while variable ordering resulted in increases, which were sometimes marked. For $p_d = 0.2$ or 0.3, all three strategies improved the mean performance, although the first two did so most consistently (Fig. 15). Perhaps because of this interaction, none of the comparisons of individual strategies was statistically significant, although

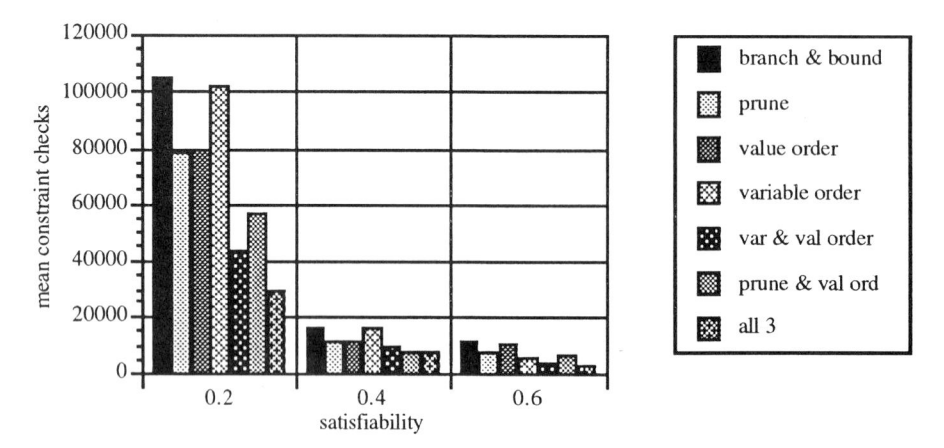

Fig. 15. Mean constraint checks required by algorithm P-BB when combined with strategies based on arc consistency counts obtained with P-ACC. Constraint checks shown as a function of constraint satisfiability, p_p; in this slice of the parameter space, $p_d = 0.2$. Results for the basic branch and bound are included for reference.

the comparison between variable ordering and pruning approached significance.

Combining strategies based on arc consistency counts resulted in greater improvement in performance (Fig. 15), and this was reflected in the individual comparisons. When pruning and value ordering were combined, performance of this algorithm was better than for either strategy alone ($q[2, 89] \geq 2.8$, $p < 0.05$ for both comparisons). Value and variable ordering combined was also better than either strategy alone, although only the latter comparison was statistically significant ($q[2, 89] = 3.43$, $p < 0.05$), in part because the superiority of the combination was only found for $p_d = 0.2$ or 0.3. Finally, the combination of all three strategies showed the best performance overall, although in comparisons with the combinations of two strategies, only the difference with the "double" ordering of variables and values was statistically significant ($q[2, 89] = 3.30$, $p < 0.05$). Again, this superiority was found only for larger domain sizes.

3.4.2. Experiment 4: comparing the best algorithms from Experiments 1–3

As indicated above, the algorithms tested in this experiment in addition to the basic branch and bound (P-BB) were P-BMK, P-FC3, and two branch and bound algorithms that used arc consistency counts: one that used pruning and value ordering and one that used all three strategies. Two algorithms based on arc consistency counts were included because the results from Experiment 3 were not altogether conclusive concerning the best algorithm in this group. Although the procedure that combined the three arc consistency count strategies was best overall, it did not perform well on problems with small domain sizes in comparison with other algorithms based on arc consistency counts, and there was considerable variability in performance even when the mean for this algorithm was better than the other means. The algorithm based on pruning and value ordering did not differ statistically from the full combination algorithm overall; moreover, unlike the combination algorithms that incorporate a variable ordering based on the counts, these strategies are less likely to result in inferior performance with respect to P-BB on individual problems.

In this experiment the factor in the ANOVA for constraint checks associated with the algorithms was highly significant statistically (Table 1; the same pattern of statistically significant results was found in the ANOVA for number of nodes checked). There was, in fact, a fairly consistent ordering over the portions of the parameter space that were tested (Fig. 16). P-BMK and P-BB incorporating arc consistency strategies generally reduced the number of consistency checks made by the basic P-BB algorithm by a factor of two to three. P-FC3 reduced this number by another factor of two. In terms of overall means the ranking of performance from worst to best was: basic branch and bound (P-BB), P-BB with the three arc consistency strategies, P-BB with

Table 1
Statistically significant effects in ANOVA for Experiment 4

Factor	df[a]	F	p
algorithm	4	43.53	0.0001
p_d	2	2070.00	0.0001
p_p	2	470.91	0.0001
p_c	2	423.81	0.0001
$p_d \times p_p$	4	81.58	0.0001
$p_d \times p_c$	4	8.56	0.0001
$p_p \times p_c$	4	21.19	0.0001
$p_d \times p_p \times p_c$	8	5.77	0.0001
alg $\times p_d$	8	4.68	0.0001
alg $\times p_c$	8	4.39	0.0001
error	1215	—	—

[a] df is degrees of freedom associated with each factor, F is the value of the test statistic, p is an upper limit on the probability of obtaining an F greater or equal to this value if there are no differences associated with this factor.

pruning based on consistency counts and value ordering, P-BMK, and P-FC3. Comparisons of mean performance following the ANOVA showed statistically significant differences between each pair of algorithms, including the two that used arc consistency counts.

The ANOVA for constraint checks also showed statistically significant effects related to each problem parameter (Table 1). In addition, all interactions between these factors were statistically significant. The effects of domain size and satisfiability and the interaction between them can be observed in Fig. 16 (and Fig. 14). For all algorithms, problem difficulty increased with increasing domain size and with diminishing satisfiability. The hardest problems were those with the largest domains and the smallest number of acceptable pairs per constraint. These effects were enhanced when the density of the constraint graph increased, which accounts for the interactions that involve this factor.

The interactions between algorithms and p_c and between algorithms and p_d were also statistically significant (Table 1). In contrast, the interaction between algorithms and p_p was not significant ($F \leq 1$); nor were any of the higher-order interactions that involved the algorithms factor. Perusal of performance means suggests that the two statistically significant interactions were due in large part to the P-ACC combination algorithm. For this algorithm, the average number of consistency checks increased more dramatically with increases in p_c or p_d than for any other algorithm. Also of interest is an apparent relation between p_p and the average difference between P-FC3 and P-BMK: for problems with higher satisfiabilities, the performance of these two algorithms was almost equal and was superior to the other algorithms; but as relative satisfiability decreased, P-FC3 became markedly superior (cf. Fig. 16). This was not

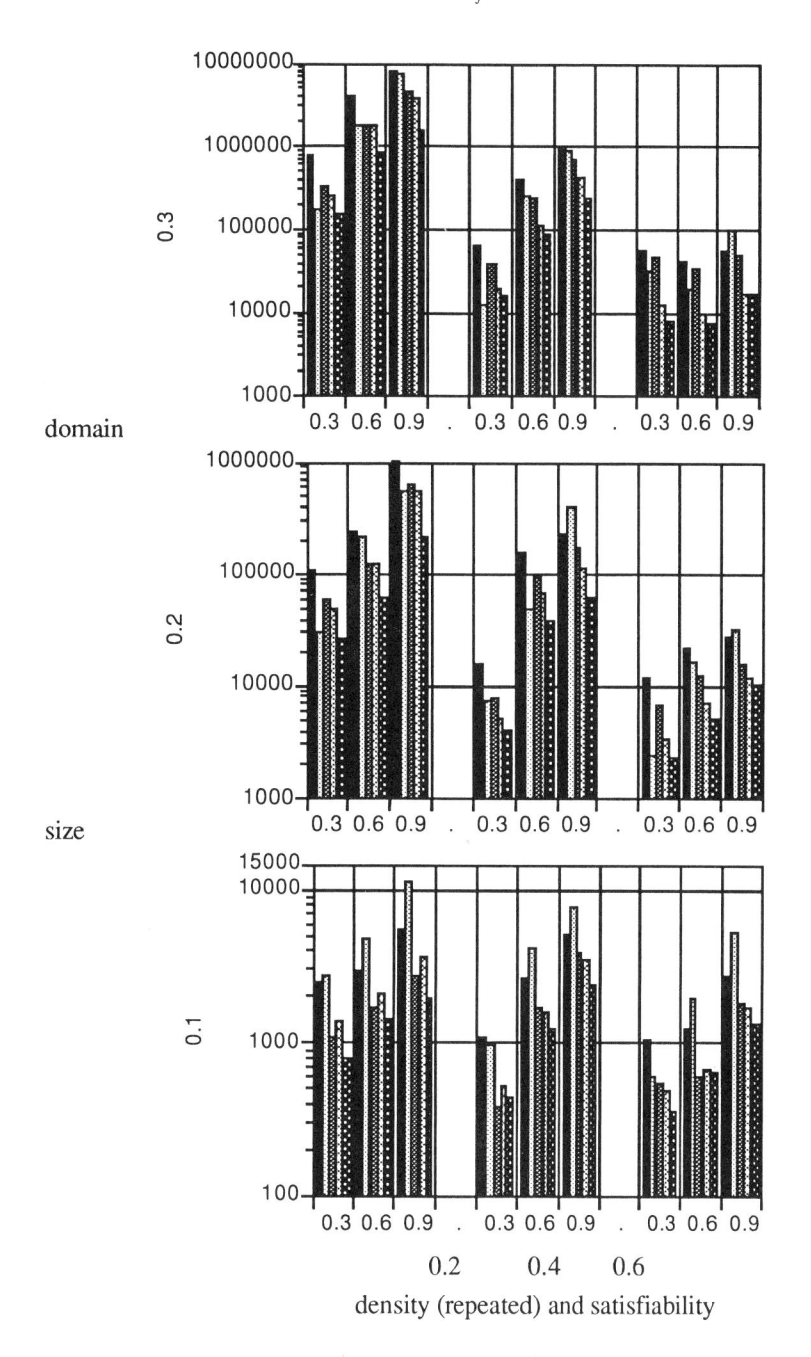

Fig. 16. Mean constraint checks per problem set for all algorithms in Experiment 4. For each combination of domain size, satisfiability, and density values, algorithms are represented in the order: branch and bound (P-BB), arc consistency counts used for value and variable ordering and pruning, arc consistency counts used for value ordering and pruning, backmarking (P-BMK), and forward checking (P-FC3).

reflected as an interaction in the ANOVA because for both algorithms amount of work increased dramatically with a decrease in p_p.

Differences in variability of performance within problem sets followed patterns similar to the differences in means. In 17 of the 27 sets of problems, the standard deviation for P-BB was greater than for any other algorithm; in the remaining problem sets the full combination P-ACC algorithm was the most variable. P-FC3 had the smallest standard deviation in performance in all but two sets. Almost all distributions showed a strong positive skew, i.e., the tail of the distribution on the right side of the median value was much longer than the tail on the left side.

Correlations between number of constraint checks performed by each algorithm were very high (≥ 0.97), with the exception of the P-ACC algorithm that incorporated the variable ordering; here the correlations were about 0.65. Since this correlation is a measure of the linear relation between two variables, it suggests that all of these algorithms have similar performance characteristics with respect to the problem parameters. Multiple regression analyses were very successful, in terms of accounting for most of the variance. The adjusted R^2 value was 97% in each case; in contrast, R^2 was about 25% when the original (untransformed) scores were used. Examination of residuals with normalized plots and other measures of influence of individual scores such as DFFITS [1] indicated that the residual values were approximately normally distributed and there were no outliers. In the multiple regression model for each algorithm, the coefficients for p_d ranged from 12.31 to 14.95 for different algorithms; for p_p the range was -0.67 to -1.00, and for p_c the range was 2.43 to 3.30. The size of these coefficients indicates the size of the effect of each parameter under the assumptions of the regression model. Clearly, domain size had the greatest influence, followed by density and then constraint satisfiability. The fundamental similarity in performance of different algorithms was also borne out.

3.4.3. Experiment 5: *effect of number of variables*

As expected, the differences in algorithm performance found in previous experiments were maintained over the range of problem sizes tested (Fig. 17). From this perspective, it appeared that P-BMK and P-FC3 have similar performance characteristics, reducing the number of constraint checks done by branch and bound by a factor of 2–3 through the range. Combining the best retrospective technique (P-BMK) with prospective and ordering techniques (pruning and value ordering based on arc consistency counts) did not materially affect this result: P-RPO reduced the effort required by P-BMK by about 1/3 throughout the range. It may be noted, however, that with few exceptions this combination outperformed P-FC3 and in a few cases (the easiest) outperformed the fastest algorithm.

The best algorithm overall was clearly P-EFC3, which computed a lower bound based on the current counts of inconsistencies. Consideration of mean

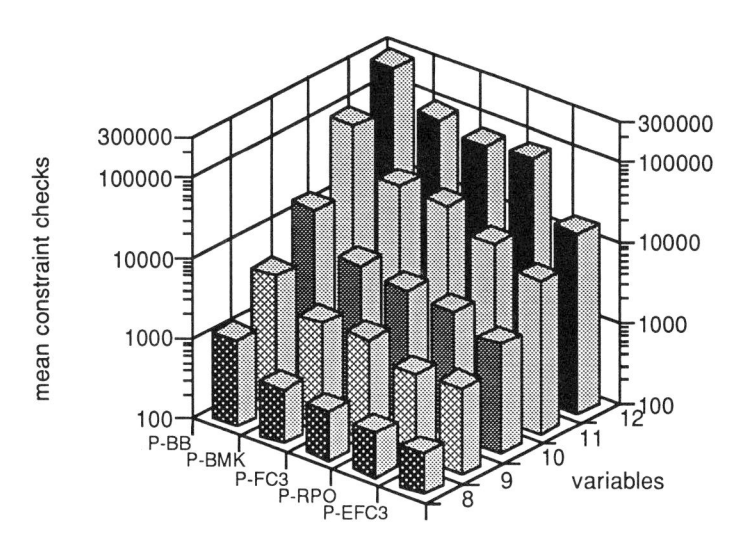

Fig. 17. Effect of number of variables on mean performance.

performance on successively greater problem sizes indicated that it, too, showed exponential growth with increasing problem size for problems with these parameters, but, as Fig. 17 shows, the rate of growth was appreciably smaller. For 12-variable problems it reduced the number of constraint checks by an order of magnitude in comparison with the other algorithms.

3.4.4. Experiment 6: evaluation of overhead using time

For total (corrected) time to solve a problem, the ranking of the algorithms resembled that for number of constraint checks. From longest to shortest time, the ranking was: P-BB, P-BJ, P-BMK, P-FC2, and P-FC3. To give an idea of the actual differences in time required, the means for the six hardest problems tested in this experiment (order of 10^5 constraint checks) are given in the same order: 382, 341, 214, 157, and 123 seconds. In the ANOVA, the effect due to algorithms was statistically significant ($F[4, 60] = 16.46$, $p < 0.001$). In the individual comparisons of means, the differences between P-BB and either P-BMK or the two forward checking algorithms were statistically significant ($p < 0.01$ in each case). The difference between P-BMK and P-FC3 was also statistically significant ($p < 0.01$), but not the difference between P-BMK and P-FC2. The difference between the two forward checking variants was also not statistically significant ($q[1, 17] = 1.58$).

For the average time per 1000 constraint checks, the ranking was considerably different. The following are mean values:

P-BB	1.61 sec
P-BJ	1.67
P-BMK	2.52

P-FC2   1.87
P-FC3   2.28

In the ANOVA the effect due to algorithms was statistically significant ($F[4, 60] = 9.25$, $p < 0.001$), as well as the effect of number of constraints ($F[1, 60] = 27.10$, $p < 0.001$), reflecting an increased efficiency for problems with denser graphs. On this measure, P-BB and P-BJ were both clearly superior to P-BMK and to P-FC3 ($p < 0.01$ for individual comparisons). P-FC2 was also superior to P-BMK ($p < 0.01$) and to P-FC3 ($p < 0.05$).

These results indicate that P-BMK and P-FC3 do incur a relatively large overhead in comparison with the other algorithms. In the case of backmarking, there is similar evidence for the CSP version [19]. But it is obvious that the decrease in number of constraint checks with these more elaborate algorithms yields a greater overall efficiency than the basic P-BB algorithm, reflected in the total time required to solve the problems.

3.4.5. Experiments 7–8: finding submaximal solutions for hard problems

The results of increasing the amount of effort applied to a problem were analyzed in two ways, by considering either, (i) the number of constraint checks required to reduce the distance by a given proportion of the total change possible (the difference between the number of constraints and the best distance), or (ii) the minimum distance found after k constraint checks. As indicated, the former measure could only be derived for 12-variable problems.

For all algorithms, after an initial drop due to the difference between the number of constraints (the initial bound) and the distance of the first solution, the relation between effort and goodness of solution approximated a simple logarithmic function (Figs. 18 and 19). Since P-EFC3 and especially P-RPO

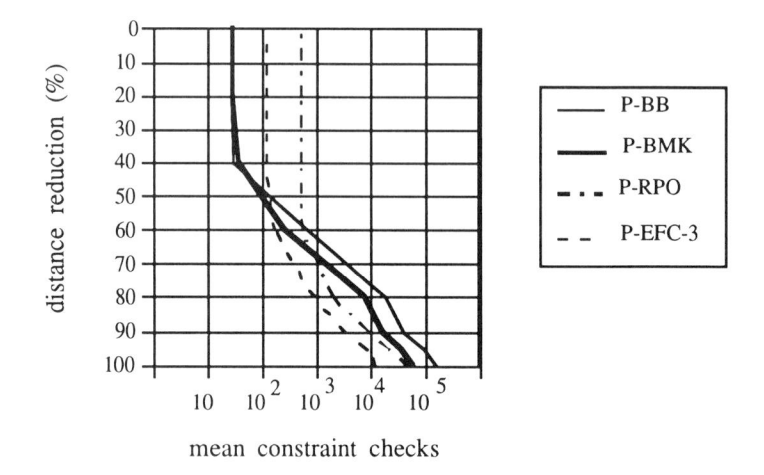

Fig. 18. Mean constraint checks required to reduce the distance as a proportion of the difference between the number of constraints and the best distance (12-variable problems).

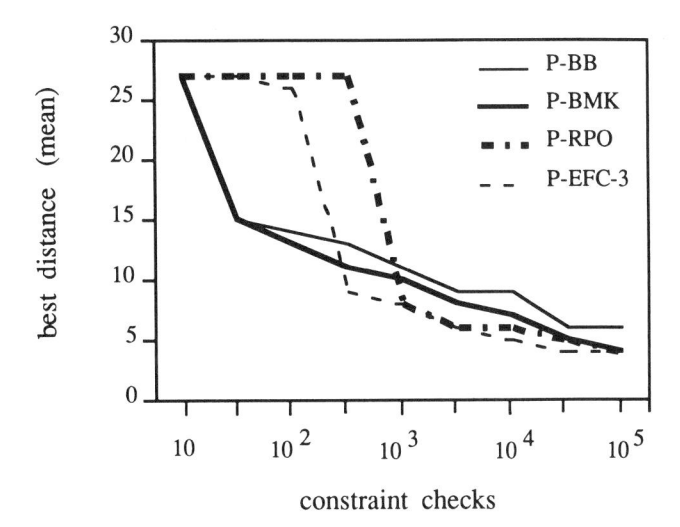

Fig. 19. Best distance found as a function of number of constraint checks for problems with 12 variables.

required more constraint checks to find an initial solution than P-BB or P-BMK, the latter algorithms were more effective initially ($p < 0.001$ for 100 constraint checks). (In the search phase per se, P-RPO actually found solutions with a given suboptimal distance faster than any other algorithm, but, in terms of constraint checks, this was overwhelmed by the cost of preprocessing.) However, for 1000 or 10,000 constraint checks, the best solutions were found by P-RPO or P-EFC3 ($p < 0.05$ for all comparisons with P-BB, for comparisons with P-BMK at 1000 constraint checks, and for the comparison between P-EFC3 and P-BMK at 10,000 constraint checks). Difference between P-RPO and P-EFC3 were never statistically significant. By 100,000 checks all algorithms except P-BB had found maximal solutions for most of the problems.

For the 20-variable problems (Fig. 20) the effects were similar, although here the superiority of P-EFC3 was more noticeable (and was statistically significant for each order of magnitude beginning with 1000 checks). In addition, the difference between P-RPO and P-BMK, while present, was never statistically significant. However, in general the trends found for smaller problems appear to hold as problem size is scaled up. (The results for 16-variable problems were also consistent with these results.)

The results for the hard coloring problems were also similar (Fig. 21). Here, the retrospective algorithm, P-BMK, achieved a better solution after a small number of constraint checks than P-EFC3, although the latter eventually surpassed it. However, the difference between P-BMK and P-EFC3 was never great, although it eventually attained statistical significance at ten million constraint checks ($p < 0.05$). In this case, the degree of local consistency in

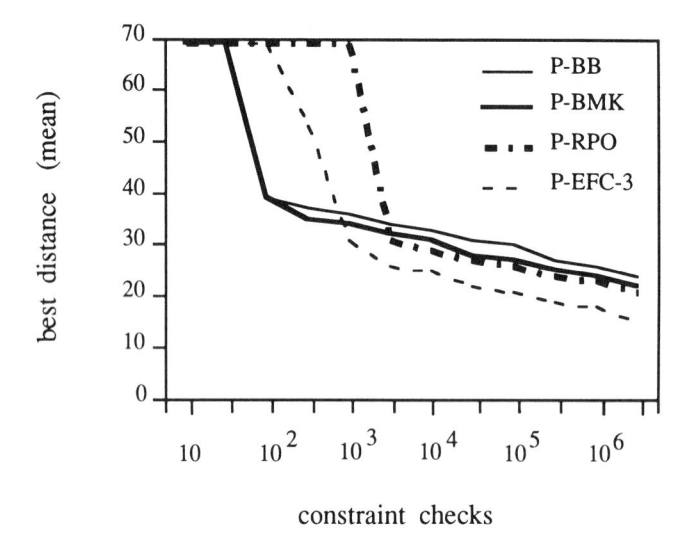

Fig. 20. Best distance found as a function of number of constraint checks for problems with 20 variables.

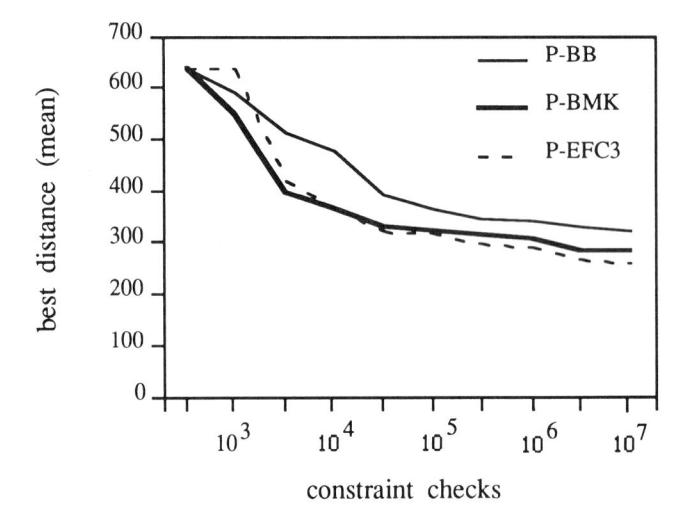

Fig. 21. Best distance found as a function of number of constraint checks for hard coloring problems.

these problems may have been responsible for the less impressive performance of P-EFC3 relative to P-BMK.

3.5. Summary of experimental results

In general, analogues of algorithms that perform well on CSPs performed well on maximal constraint satisfaction problems. Among a basic set of strategies, over the range of parameter values tested, using the measures of constraint checks and total time to obtain an optimal solution, one analogue of forward checking was generally superior. Moreover, this superiority was most evident for parts of the parameter space in which the problems were most difficult. In less extensive testing, more elaborate algorithms reduced the work required even further; here also an extension of forward checking performed better than any other algorithm. On a set of 12-variable problems, for example, the best algorithm reduced the average number of constraint checks from approximately 300,000 to approximately 20,000.

Despite the general superiority of one type of prospective strategy (forward checking), other techniques based on local consistency (arc consistency count preprocessing) or sophisticated retrospective algorithms (P-BMK) also improved on the basic branch and bound algorithm, sometimes by a factor of 4–5. In addition, for some parts of the parameter space, P-BMK was comparable in performance to P-FC3. We conclude that these techniques merit further study, especially if they can be efficiently combined with forward checking methods.

The data from Experiment 3 suggest that for sparse problems, combining arc consistency counts with a variable ordering that puts high counts at the beginning of the search sequence was efficient on average. A key factor appears to be the size of the counts in comparison to the best distance; when the distance is small, putting higher counts at the beginning is very effective in pruning the search tree. This strategy can be incorporated into the P-RPO algorithm, and preliminary data suggest that this may be an extremely effective technique for many, but not all, problems with low densities. ($p_c = 0.1$ for the problems tested.)

The main result from the anytime experiments was that solutions within ten percent of the optimum, in terms of the total distance reduction, could be obtained with a reduction in effort equal to or greater than one order of magnitude. As in earlier experiments, P-EFC3 was the best algorithm through most of the range of effort. However, P-BB and P-BMK were more efficient if the criterion of goodness was relaxed sufficiently.

These experiments also show that random problem generation can be parameterized in a straightforward manner to produce subpopulations of problems that vary statistically in their basic features: number of constraints, domain size and satisfiability. This allowed us to examine algorithm performance in terms of the space of problems defined by these parameters. Regions of this space were delineated in which the typical problem was either easy or difficult to solve, and data on the population characteristics of algorithm performance in these regions was obtained. Such data should aid the potential user in deciding which algorithms to consider, as well as indicating the costs of such decisions.

4. Partial constraint satisfaction

We focused on maximal satisfaction to facilitate the presentation and testing of the algorithms. However, there are other forms of partial satisfaction, and to a large extent the algorithms generalize in obvious ways. In this section we work toward a general model of partial satisfaction.

4.1. Metrics

Our branch and bound algorithms have sought a solution that violates a minimal number of constraints. However, the difference between a perfect solution, and a partial solution can be measured in many different and more subtle ways. As our use of the term "distance" suggests, all the branch and bound technique requires is a metric that can compare the values being considered at a given stage of search with the "best" solution found so far.

Preferences have been expressed by ordering constraints [10], by representing their importance [12], by organizing constraints into hierarchies [2], by introducing priorities [11]. Preferences can be reflected in the branch and bound metric by assigning weights to constraints. Preferences could be associated with subsets of domains and constraints, individual values or pairs of values, as opposed to entire constraints. (Wearing a striped tie and a polka dot shirt might not be as bad as wearing a bow tie with a sweatshirt.)

Constraint deviations have been combined in both local and global fashion [2]. The branch and bound metric can sum the weights of the violated constraints, use the maximum weight, compute the average, as appropriate. The initial constraints may be viewed as ideal points which we seek to approximate by some measure.

There may be some "hidden agenda" embodied in the metric. For example, we may wish to drive a problem toward a weaker version that is easily solvable, e.g. by removing constraints to yield a tree-structured problem.

4.2. Problem spaces

We have been measuring the success of a partial solution by evaluating the number, or importance, of the violated constraints. There is another criterion that we believe should be directly considered. Weakening constraints in effect creates a different problem. Alternatives for weakening constraints provide alternative problems. We may well wish to solve a problem that is close to the original in the sense of having a solution set similar to the original. Removing the one set of constraints might trivialize the problem, allowing thousands of new solutions, while removing another set might allow only a single new solution.

This consideration arises, for example, when viewing constraint knowledge base debugging as a partial constraint satisfaction problem [20]. If the knowledge base is erroneously overconstrained, a change that allows a small number of new solutions is more in keeping with Occam's Razor than one that allows many.

More formally, we can consider a space of problems with an ordering based on solution sets. A *problem space* is a partially ordered set, $(PS, \leq)$. PS is a set of constraint satisfaction problems with a partial order, $\leq$, on PS defined as follows: $P_1 \leq P_2$ iff the set of solutions to P_2 is a subset of the set of solutions to P_1. If the set of solutions to P_2 is a subset of the set of solutions to P_1, but the two sets are not equal, we will write $P_1 < P_2$ and say that P_1 is *weaker than* P_2.

One natural problem space for a partial constraint satisfaction problem with initial problem P consists of all problems Q such that $Q \leq P$. This set can be obtained by considering all the ways of weakening the constraints by allowing additional consistent combinations of values. In general, PS could contain problems, Q, which are stronger than P, $P < Q$, or problems, Q, such that neither $Q \leq P$ nor $P \leq Q$; $\geq$ is only a partial order. However, if we collect all the constraints in all the problems in PS into a single problem M, then all the problems in PS can be regarded as weakenings of M.

It may be natural to consider a space which does not include all $Q \leq P$. We may wish to specify how the problem can be weakened. Some weaker problems may make more "semantic sense". It may not be possible or desirable to violate constraints by arbitrarily allowing individual pairs of values to violate the associated constraint, as we have done until now. For example, in our dressing domain, we might decide that in a fashion emergency, or a burst of avant garde creativity, we would eschew the prohibition against mixing stripes with checks, as opposed to making an individual exception for one striped tie and one checked shirt. We may establish levels of informality in our fashion constraints corresponding to the informality of the occasion for which we are dressing.

It may make more semantic sense to have a preset hierarchy of constraints, where weakening a constraint requires moving upward in the hierarchy, as opposed to making arbitrary individual exceptions. This constraint hierarchy is reminiscent of the concept hierarchies that provide initial bias in machine learning settings, and indeed it is intriguing to think of the constraint satisfaction process as a form of concept learning, synthesizing a relationship from positive and negative information.

The specification of the problem space PS can clearly affect the efficiency of the search process. One way to specify the problem space is to specify generators, or operators, that take us from one problem P to a permitted set of problems Q_i, $Q_i \leq P$. There may be "global" restrictions on these generators, e.g. choose one constraint from column A, one from column B. As we try to move through a problem space in search of a solvable problem, it may prove desirable to take into consideration how many opportunities are opened up by altering a problem in a given way, e.g. removing one fashion restriction may be more liberating than removing another.

The process of weakening CSPs can be naturally viewed as involving four options: enlarging a variable domain (buying a new shirt), enlarging a constraint domain (deciding that an old shirt and an old tie can be worn together after all), removing a variable (deciding not to wear any tie), removing a constraint (deciding not to worry if our socks match). However, all of these can in turn be expressed in terms of the basic process of enlarging constraint domains. We can view variable domains as unary constraints. Enlarging a binary constraint until it contains all pairs of values in the specified domains for the two variables is tantamount to removing the constraint (at least until such time as the variable domains may be enlarged). Removing all the constraints on a variable in this way is tantamount to removing the variable.

4.3. Partial constraint satisfaction problems

A *partial constraint satisfaction problem* can now be specified more formally by supplying an initial constraint satisfaction problem P, a problem space, PS, containing P, a metric on that space, and necessary and sufficient solution distances, N and S. A *solution to a partial constraint satisfaction problem* can be defined as a problem P' from the problem space PS along with a solution to that problem where the metric distance of P' from P is less than N. A solution is *sufficient* if the distance is less than or equal to S. An *optimal solution* is one where the metric distance of P' from P is minimal over the problem space. The optimal solution is *dominant* if there is no optimal solution which involves a problem Q such that $P' < Q$.

The metric that evaluates our solution now compares problems rather than counting or otherwise evaluating violated constraints. Of course, one way to compare problems is to compare their constraints. Ideally, however, we might like to define the metric in terms of the partial order, defining the distance between P and P' to be the number of solutions not shared by P and P'. When $P' \leq P$, this metric, M, measures the number of solutions we have added by weakening P. This is a natural measure of how "good" our partial solution is.

Of course, computing such a metric is not likely to be easy. However, after finding a set of optimal solutions with another metric we might wish to distinguish among these by considering the different problems induced by these solutions. The problem *induced* by a partial solution S for a problem P is the problem obtained by adding to the constraints of P the inconsistent pairs of values in the partial solution S. We could compute the full solution sets for the induced problems, and look for dominant, optimal solutions using the metric M, which operates on solution sets.

We also may wish to consider how well an alternative metric does tend to reflect this natural metric M. Another natural metric is a count of the number of permitted value combinations not shared by the constraints of P and P'. To some extent, this metric does reflect the metric M based on the partial order. If P' is obtained from P by weakening the constraints then $P' \leq P$, because of the monotonic nature of constraint satisfaction problems. In other words, if for each constraint C_{ij} associated with P and constraint C'_{ij} associated with P', C_{ij} is a subset of C'_{ij}, then $P' \leq P$. In particular, the simple metric used in our maximality studies, which counts the number of violated constraints, is a metric of this form.

Viewing partial constraint satisfaction as a search through a problem space facilitates consideration of integrating branch and bound at different levels of the search process to produce different algorithms. The natural points at which to perform this integration are the failure points in a standard backtracking algorithm.

Our basic branch and bound partial constraint satisfaction algorithm integrates branch and bound at the lowest level of backtrack failure. Whenever a value c for a variable V would be rejected by normal backtracking, we can view the algorithm as determining which constraints were violated, and weakening the problem by adding precisely those constraint elements needed to permit c.

In searching through the problem space for a solvable problem, it would be desirable to avoid changing the problem in ways that do not facilitate progress. For example, if two problems are equivalent, they both do not need to be considered. A nice feature of the basic branch and bound algorithm is that for the type of partial constraint satisfaction problem for which it is designed it is able to use only the minimally different problem P required to proceed at each problem choice point.

An even simpler choice for integrating branch and bound would be to add it to backtracking upon top-level failure of backtracking, when no solution is found. A branch and bound loop can be added on the outside of the backtracking algorithm. This loop will run through the problems in the problem space, keeping track of the closest problem P' to P solved so far. Problems no closer to P than P' will be rejected immediately.

Whenever alternative problems are generated in an order which reflects their distance from the original problem, closest to furthest, generation can stop at that point when the necessary bound N is reached. If we have a top-level integration of branch and bound, this point marks the termination of the PCSP algorithm.

Branch and bound can be integrated at failure points in between these extremes. The natural compromise would occur at the points where all the values for a given variable have been exhausted in standard backtrack search. At these times options for alternative problems may be explored.

There is a tradeoff involved in the choice of how to integrate branch and bound. By integrating at a lower level we take greater advantage of backtrack pruning to avoid unnecessary effort. On the other hand by integrating at a higher level we allow greater flexibility in heuristically guiding the search through the space of alternative problems. Preliminary experiments comparing a high-level and a low-level approach to partial satisfaction in the domain of debugging constraint knowledge bases reflect this tradeoff [20].

In summary, the generalized view we have reached of partial constraint satisfaction as a search through a space of alternative problems has a number of potential advantages for further work in this area. It facilitates consideration of more global concerns than the suitability of a single solution. Specifically, it encourages us to consider whether our partial solution has been devalued by weakening the problem in a manner that permits too many solutions. It naturally incorporates practical concerns about available constraint modifications. It also facilitates generation of alternate problem solving strategies that take a more global view of effective means of modifying the problem.

5. Conclusion

Standard constraint satisfaction problem (CSP) solution techniques have analogues for solving partial constraint satisfaction problems (PCSPs), which both cope with and take advantage of the differences between CSP and PCSP. Branch and bound is the natural analogue of backtrack search. Local consistency count is an analogue of local consistency. We have found PCSP analogues of retrospective, prospective, and ordering techniques for CSPs.

Extensive experimentation over random problems with different structural parameters revealed the effectiveness of a set of PCSP techniques as a function of these parameters. A general model of PCSPs was developed involving a standard CSP together with a partially ordered space of alternative problems and a metric to measure the distances between these problems and the original CSP.

In summary, a firm algorithmic, experimental and theoretical foundation has been laid for the study of problems for which it is impractical or impossible to satisfy fully a set of constraints.

Acknowledgement

Portions of this paper were taken from [14]. We thank Peter Cheeseman and Bob Kanefsky for supplying the "really hard" coloring problems.

References

[1] D.A. Belsley, E. Kuh and R.E. Welsch, *Regression Diagnostics* (Wiley, New York, 1980).

[2] A. Borning, R. Duisberg, B. Freeman-Benson, A. Kramer and M. Woolf, Constraint hierarchies, in: *Proceedings 1987 ACM Conference on Object-Oriented Programming Systems, Languages and Applications*, Orlando, FL (1987) 48–60.

[3] A. Borning, M. Maher, A. Martindale and M. Wilson, Constraint hierarchies and logic programming, in: *Proceedings Sixth International Conference on Logic Programming*, Lisbon (1989) 149–164.

[4] P. Cheeseman, B. Kanefsky and W.M. Taylor, Where the *really* hard problems are, in: *Proceedings IJCAI-91*, Sydney, Australia (1991) 331–337.

[5] M. Cooper, *Visual Occlusion and the Interpretation of Ambiguous Pictures* (Ellis Horwood, Chichester, 1992).

[6] R. Dechter, Enhancement schemes for constraint processing: backjumping, learning and cutset decomposition, *Artif. Intell.* **41** (1990) 273–312.

[7] R. Dechter, A. Dechter and J. Pearl, Optimization in constraint networks, in: R.M. Oliver and J.Q. Smith, eds., *Influence Diagrams, Belief Nets and Decision Analysis* (Wiley, New York, 1990) 411–425.

[8] R. Dechter and J. Pearl, Network-based heuristics for constraint satisfaction problems. *Artif. Intell.* **34** (1988) 1–38.

[9] R. Dechter and J. Pearl, Tree-clustering schemes for constraint processing, *Artif. Intell.* **38** (1989) 353–366.

[10] Y. Descotte and J.C. Latombe, Making compromises among antagonistic constraints in a planner, *Artif. Intell.* **27** (1985) 183–217.

[11] R. Feldman and M. Golumbic, Optimization algorithms for student scheduling via constraint satisfiability, *Comput. J.* **33** (1990) 356–364.

[12] M. Fox, *Constraint Directed Search: A Case Study of Job-Shop Scheduling* (Morgan Kaufmann, Los Altos, CA, 1987).

[13] E. Freuder, Backtrack-free and backtrack-bounded search, in: L. Kanal and V. Kumar, eds., *Search in Artificial Intelligence* (Springer, New York, 1988) 343–369.

[14] E. Freuder, Partial constraint satisfaction, in: *Proceedings IJCAI-89*, Detroit, MI (1989) 278–283.

[15] E. Freuder, Complexity of k-tree structured constraint satisfaction problems, in: *Proceedings AAAI-90*, Boston, MA (1990) 4–9.

[16] J. Gaschnig, A general backtrack algorithm that eliminates most redundant checks, in: *Proceedings IJCAI-77*, Cambridge, MA (1977) 457.

[17] J. Gaschnig, Experimental case studies of backtrack vs. Waltz-type vs. new algorithms for satisficing assignment problems, in: *Proceedings Second National Conference of the Canadian Society for Computational Studies of Intelligence*, Toronto, Ont. (1978) 268–277.

[18] S.W. Golumb and L.D. Baumert, Backtrack programming, *J. ACM* **12** (1965) 516–524.

[19] R. Haralick and G. Elliott, Increasing tree search efficiency for constraint satisfaction problems, *Artif. Intell.* **14** (1980) 263–313.

[20] S. Huard and E. Freuder, A debugging assistant for incompletely specified constraint network knowledge bases, *Internat. J. Expert Syst. Res. Appl.* (to appear).

[21] W. Hower, Sensitive relaxation of an overspecified constraint network, in: *Proceedings Second International Symposium on Artificial Intelligence*, Monterrey, Mexico (1989).

[22] R.E. Kirk, *Experimental Design* (Brooks/Cole, Pacific Grove, CA, 2nd ed., 1982).

[23] M. Lacroix and P. Lavency, Preferences: putting more knowledge into queries, in: *Proceedings 15th International Conference on Very Large Data Bases*, Brighton (1987) 217–225.

[24] E.L. Lawler and D.E. Wood, Branch-and-bound methods: a survey. *Oper. Res.* **14** (1966) 699–719.

[25] A. Mackworth, Consistency in networks of relations, *Artif. Intell.* **8** (1977) 99–118.

[26] A. Mackworth and E. Freuder, The complexity of some polynomial network consistency algorithms for constraint satisfaction problems, *Artif. Intell.* **25** (1985) 65–74.

[27] I. Meiri, R. Dechter and J. Pearl, Tree decomposition with applications to constraint processing, in: *Proceedings AAAI-90*, Boston, MA (1990) 10–16.
[28] P. Meseguer, Constraint satisfaction problems: an overview, *AI Commun.* **2** (1) (1989) 3–17.
[29] V. Kumar, Algorithms for constraint-satisfaction problems: a survey, *AI Mag.* **13** (1) (1992) 32–44.
[30] S. Mittal and B. Falkenhainer, Dynamic constraint satisfaction problems, in: *Proceedings AAAI-90*, Boston, MA (1990) 25–32.
[31] R. Mohr and G. Masini, Good old discrete relaxation, in: *Proceedings European Conference on Artificial Intelligence*, Munich (1988) 651–656.
[32] B.A. Nadel, Constraint satisfaction algorithms, *Comput. Intell.* **5** (4) (1989) 188–224.
[33] E.M. Reingold, J. Nievergelt and N. Deo, *Combinatorial Algorithms: Theory and Practice* (Prentice-Hall, Englewood Cliffs, NJ, 1977).
[34] A. Rosenfeld, R. Hummel and S. Zucker, Scene labeling by relaxation operations, *IEEE Trans. Syst. Man, Cybern.* **6** (1976) 420–433.
[35] L. Shapiro and R. Haralick, Structural descriptions and inexact matching, *IEEE Trans. Pattern Anal. Mach. Intell.* **3** (1981) 504–519.
[36] P. Snow and E. Freuder, Improved relaxation and search methods for approximate constraint satisfaction with a maximin criterion, in: *Proceedings Eighth Biennial Conference of the Canadian Society for Computational Studies of Intelligence*, Otawa, Ont. (1990) 227–230.
[37] P. Van Hentenryck, *Constraint Satisfaction in Logic Programming* (MIT Press, Cambridge, MA, 1989).

Constraint reasoning based on interval arithmetic: the tolerance propagation approach

Eero Hyvönen
Technical Research Centre of Finland (VTT), Laboratory for Information Processing, Lehtisaarentie 2A, 00340 Helsinki, Finland

Abstract

Hyvönen, E., Constraint reasoning based on interval arithmetic: the tolerance propagation approach, Artificial Intelligence 58 (1992) 71–112.

Interval constraint satisfaction (interval labeling) systems have traditionally been based on local Waltz filtering techniques that cannot in general determine global solutions. In contrast, this paper documents a related technique, tolerance propagation (TP), that generalizes the idea of numerical exact value propagation into interval propagation. In TP, consistency techniques based on the topology of the constraint net can be combined with techniques of interval arithmetic in a new fruitful way. In particular, by TP it is possible to determine global solutions for interval constraint satisfaction problems with arbitrary accuracy and without losing all attractions of simple local computations.

1. Numerical constraint satisfaction

1.1. Exact value systems

Numerical constraint propagation systems [28, 31, 48] usually deal with exact numbers. Such *exact value systems* are used to solve problems of the following kind:

Problem formulation 1.1. Given is a set E of equations relating a set of variables. The values of the *input variables* are given by the user. The task is to determine values for the *output variables* such that E is satisfied.

Correspondence to: E. Hyvönen, Technical Research Centre of Finland (VTT), Laboratory for Information Processing, Lehtisaarentie 2A, 00340 Helsinki, Finland. E-mail: hyvonen@tik.vtt.fi.

* This work was partly supported by Academy of Finland, Technology Development Centre of Finland, Finnish Cultural Foundation, Science and Technology Agency of Japan, and Electrotechnical Laboratory, Cognitive Science Section, in Japan.

For example, the temperature conversion between degrees Celsius (C) and Fahrenheit (F),

$$F = C * 1.8 + 32, \tag{1.1}$$

can be represented by the constraint net of Fig. 1. If C (input) is known, then F (output) can be computed by combining two local computations $X = C * 1.8$ and $F = X + 32$. By applying the inverse local functions $X = F - 32$ and $C = X/1.8$, C can be computed from F, too. By such local *value propagation* any variable from a constraint net can be solved globally in terms of the others without solving the corresponding equations algebraically, which is usually difficult and in the general case impossible [52].

Exact value systems also employ iterative relaxation schemes [18, 47] in problem solving, especially the well-known Newton method [13, 28]. Here some input variables are considered as *guess variables* with user-given initial values and the task is to determine their actual values in a function at its zero point $f(\cdots) = 0$. For example, in the single variable case $f(x)$, a new value x_{n+1} for x can be estimated iteratively by

$$x_{n+1} = x_n - f(x_n)/f'(x_n) \tag{1.2}$$

until a solution x_{n+1} satisfying $0 \approx f(x_{n+1})$ is hopefully reached beginning from an initial guess value x_0.

Exact value systems have several limitations:

(1) *Dealing with inexact data*

Exact value systems accept as input only exact numbers and correspondingly produce only crisp values for output. In many applications, however, input data may be noisy, uncertain or incomplete. In such cases more inexact input values should result in more inexact output values. Exact value systems are inappropriate in such situations. For example, assume that we have two approximate interval-valued temperature measurements $C = [1, 5]$ and $F = [27, 35]$ in (1.1) and want to know under what circumstances they are coherent. This problem could be represented in terms of exact values by using inequality constraints:

$$f = c * 1.8 + 32,$$
$$1 \leq c \leq 5, \quad 27 \leq f \leq 35. \tag{1.3}$$

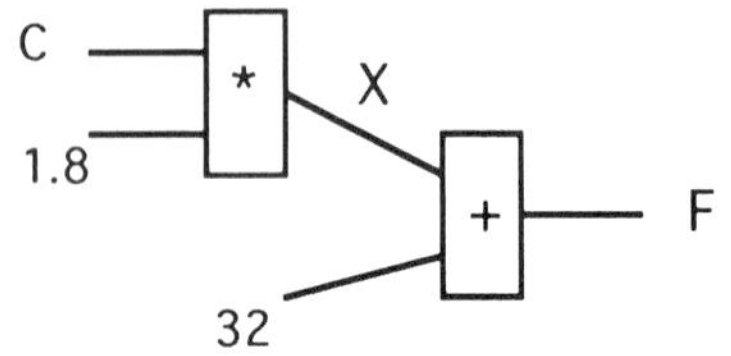

Fig. 1. A constraint net for temperature conversion.

However, the problem has infinitely many exact solutions, such as $c = 1$, $f = 33.8$. Some kind of generalization/abstraction mechanism of the solutions is needed and the generalization must be determined without enumerating solutions.

(2) *Solving underconstrained problems*

Value propagation can proceed only if there is at least one local constraint in which all but one of the related variables have values, i.e., the situation is not *locally underconstrained*. For example, equations

$$x + t = y, \quad y + t = z,$$
$$x := 1, \quad z := 11, \quad y := ?, \quad t = ? \tag{1.4}$$

constrain y to be the mean value 6 of x and z. However, $y = 6$ cannot be determined by local reasoning because the two constraints are connected to two unknown variables. This problem can be approached numerically by applying relaxation to the locally unknown variables, or algebraically by exploiting redundant views or algebraic transformations [15]. Unfortunately, numerical relaxation is computationally expensive, sensitive to initial guess values, and does not always converge towards a solution. On the other hand, algebraic transformations are applicable only to simple equations. One can also try to avoid the problem in the first place by helping the user in determining sufficient input variable sets for computing needed output values.

Even more severe problems are encountered when the problem is *globally underconstrained*, i.e., it has several or usually infinitely many solutions. Value propagation or relaxation schemes cannot deal properly with such situations. The problem has been approached in two major ways. Firstly, in constraint logic programming systems, like CLP(R) [25–27, 29–30], Prolog III [7], and CAL [1], unsolvable constraints are returned as a symbolic solution when exact numerical solutions cannot be generated. The problem here is the well-known difficulty of algebraic equation solving; typically only linear equations can be handled properly. Furthermore, it is usually computationally expensive to derive symbolic solutions and the solutions can be very complicated [52] and difficult to interpret. The second approach is interval labeling systems [8, 19–23, 38–40], the topic of this paper, where variables in solutions get interval values in underconstrained situations.

(3) *Solving overconstrained problems*

A numerical constraint satisfaction problem can also be *overconstrained*, i.e., it has no solutions. As a remedy, truth maintenance [48] has been proposed for regaining consistency. However, a fundamental difficulty here is that there are usually infinitely many possibilities for making the problem solvable again. Various strategies can be used for selecting the variables to be modified. For example, we can select randomly some variable and modify it, ask advice from the user, never modify constants, always change as few values as possible, prefer modifying variables with smaller changes, prefer modifying variables that have been modified earlier, or never change a value given by the user [15]. Unfortunately, all such strategies are *ad hoc* and cannot maintain consistency properly. Interval relaxation [23] seems to offer a new possibility for dealing with the problem.

(4) *Fixing variable types*

In value propagation, variable types (input/output) must be fixed before computation. However, it is often impossible to make the distinction. If a given variable value is modified by the propagation engine, then the variable is *simultaneously* an input and an output variable. For example, the ranges of possible values in (1.3) are $1 \leq c \leq 1.666\ldots$, $33.8 \leq f \leq 35$, i.e., ranges of both c and f must be modified and the variables are used for both input and output.

This paper argues that the above problems (1)–(4) can be approached effectively by generalizing from exact value constraint reasoning into interval constraint reasoning. Benefits of interval reasoning are obtained without losing the possibility for using exact values that can always be represented by singleton intervals $[x, x]$.

1.2. *Interval constraint satisfaction*

The idea of interval-based reasoning has been applied in several fields of AI, such as uncertain inference [37, 41, 44, 45], temporal [4], physical, and spatial reasoning [8]. Studies have been pursued mainly in connection with a particular application area. More generic approaches to interval constraint satisfaction include [6, 8, 19–23, 38–40]. The problem addressed here can be characterized roughly as the following *interval constraint satisfaction problem* (ICSP):

Problem formulation 1.2. Given is a set E of equations relating a set of variables associated with interval domains. Refine the domains as far as possible without losing possible exact solutions of E, i.e., determine for each variable the minimal *consistent* subinterval within its domain.

Problem formulation 1.1 can be obtained as a special case of 1.2 by distinguishing between input and output variables and by assigning singleton domains $[x, x]$ to the input variables and infinite domains $[-\infty, \infty]$ to the output variables. Problem formulation 1.2 differs from traditional mathematical optimization because of its symmetrical nature: the problem is to determine possible ranges of all variables of an equation set simultaneously. Furthermore, the search is for intervals rather than exact points. For example, optimization techniques, such as the Simplex algorithm, focus on determining the minimum or maximum points of a goal function. It will be argued that interval arithmetic [3, 35, 36, 43] should be applied as the basis in interval constraint reasoning. A fundamental difference between global optimization and interval arithmetic techniques is that seemingly none of the former "can be guaranteed to locate the global minimum" [12]. In contrast, "interval methods can guarantee always the location of the global extremum and, in most cases, with arbitrary accuracy" [43].

There are two major approaches to solving ICSPs:

(1) *Local Waltz filtering systems*. In this approach, constraints are decomposed into a set of primitive constraints. The Waltz filtering algorithm [50] adapted for intervals [8] or other similar local consistency filtering [38–40] is then used for screening impossible values from the variable domains.

(2) *Tolerance propagation*. In tolerance propagation (TP) [19–23] exact value propagation techniques discussed above are generalized into the interval case by replacing exact value arithmetic with interval arithmetic and by using additional global consistency techniques. The underlying idea of TP is to combine constraint satisfaction techniques with interval arithmetical techniques in a new fruitful way. (In this paper the term "tolerance" will be used as a synonym for a continuous or discontinuous interval; more generally a tolerance can be a set of any values.)

These approaches are closely related. In particular, both approaches exploit the *locality principle*: a globally hard algebraic problem is solved more easily numerically, if it is considered in terms of simple *local* constraints. Local reasoning is simple, but the problem is that one obtains only locally consistent solutions in which variables are guaranteed to be consistent only with directly related variables. A major unanswered question of the local Waltz filtering approach is how to obtain globally consistent interval solutions. The main goal of this paper is to show how to obtain such solutions by TP with arbitrary accuracy and without losing all attractions of simple local computations. In addition, a precise formulation of the notion of ICSP within a lattice-theoretic framework will be presented and general techniques are developed for determining conditions under which interval constraint satisfaction can be applied without losing completeness or soundness of reasoning. Since Waltz filtering and TP are closely related, many of the results of this paper can be applied in Waltz filtering algorithms, too.

In the following, the notions of ICSP and its solutions are first defined (Section 2). A local tolerance propagation algorithm generalizing Waltz filtering is then given (Section 3) and techniques for determining application conditions for it are presented (Section 4). In Section 5, problems of local reasoning are discussed. Local TP is then generalized into global TP for determining global solutions (Section 6). Finally, contributions of the TP approach are summarized.

2. Interval constraint satisfaction problems

2.1. Syntax

An *interval constraint satisfaction problem* (ICSP) is represented in the form:

$$E_1, \ldots, E_n,$$
$$P_1 := X_1, \quad \ldots, \quad P_m := X_m. \tag{2.1}$$

Here E_i are equations, P_j are (explicit) variables used in them, and X_j are closed real intervals $[a, b] = \{x \mid a \leq x \leq b\}$. $P := X$ assigns interval X to variable P. If some variable P is not given a value in (2.1), we assume by default $P := [-\infty, \infty]$. Two examples of ICSPs are given below:

$$\begin{aligned} &F = C * 1.8 + 32 \qquad ; \text{ Temperature conversion}, \\ &C := [1, 5], \quad F := [27, 35], \end{aligned} \tag{2.2}$$

$$\begin{aligned} &Z = X * Y \qquad ; \text{ Equation triple}, \\ &e^X + Z = -0.2, \\ &\sin(-Z) + X + Y = -0.4. \end{aligned} \tag{2.3}$$

For practical purposes, open interval bounds can be represented approximately by closed ones by using notation x^+ and x^- for a slightly larger and smaller number than x, respectively. For example: $(0, 2] \approx [0^+, 2]$. x^+ and x^- are the nearest representable numbers of x within the accuracy used in an actual implementation of an interval reasoner. This choice is coherent with interval arithmetic that is also based on closed intervals.

Nested functions $y = f(x_1, \ldots, x_n)$ in equations can be represented equivalently as (infinite) constraint relations $\{\langle x_1, \ldots, x_n, y \rangle\}$ (notation $\langle \cdots \rangle$ denotes a tuple). Hence, $E_1, \ldots, E_n$ in (2.1) can easily be decomposed into an equivalent set of simple relational constraints, the *constraint net*, by representing each different embedded function $f(x_1, \ldots, x_n)$ by a constraint with a unique (internal) *value variable* y, and by using y in the host constraint instead of $f(x_1, \ldots, x_n)$. For example, (2.3) is equivalent to

$$\{X * Y = Z, e^X = X_1, X_1 + Z = -0.2, \\ -Z = X_2, \sin(X_2) = X_3, X_3 + X = X_4, X_4 + Y = -0.4\}, \tag{2.4}$$

where X_i are value variables. Net (2.4) is represented graphically in Fig. 2.

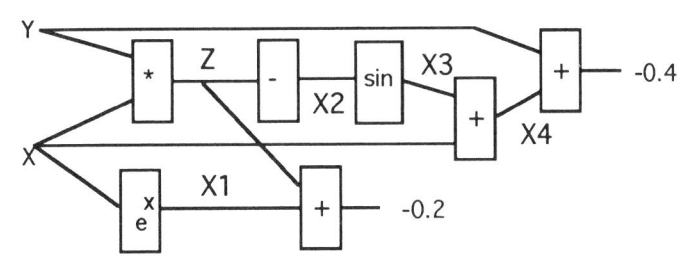

Fig. 2. Constraint net representing (2.3) and (2.4).

2.2. Semantics

The *tolerance situation* $\{P_1 := X_1, \ldots, P_m := X_m\}$ in an ICSP (2.1) refers to a set of exact value situations $\{P_1 := x_1, \ldots, P_n := x_n \mid x_j \in X_i, i = 1, \ldots, n\}$ to be called *extensions*. A constraint relation $\{\langle x_1, \ldots, x_n \rangle\}$ corresponding to a function $x_n = f(x_1, \ldots, x_{n-1})$ is *satisfied* by an extension iff $x_n = f(x_1, \ldots, x_{n-1})$ in it. An ICSP is *admissible* iff its tolerance situation has an extension satisfying all constraints (i.e., the equations have a solution within the intervals):

$$\exists \{P_1 := x_1 \in X_1, \ldots, P_m := x_m \in X_m\}:$$
All constraints of $E_1, \ldots, E_n$ are satisfied.

For example, (2.2) is admissible because $C := 1 \in [1, 5]$ and $F := 33.8 \in [27, 35]$ satisfy the equation.

A variable $P_i := X_i$ is *consistent* iff *each* interpretation $P_i := x, x \in X_i$, can be satisfied with respect to all constraints by some extension:

$$\forall x \in X_i \; \exists \{P_1 := x_1 \in X_1, \ldots, P_i := x, \ldots, P_m := x_m \in X_m\}:$$
All constraints of $E_1, \ldots, E_n$ are satisfied.

Intuitively, a tolerance should not contain "extra" values that cannot be satisfied within the given intervals. A tolerance situation is (*globally*) *consistent*, i.e., it is a (global) *tolerance solution*, iff its every variable is consistent. This definition corresponds to the notions of "global consistency" or "consistent labeling" used in constraint satisfaction and interval labeling literature. A variable is *locally* consistent iff it is consistent with respect to all directly connected constraints. Local consistency of a tolerance situation (solution) means that all variables are locally consistent. For example, (2.2) is globally and locally *in*consistent, because $C := 4 \in [1, 5]$ cannot be satisfied by any $F \in [27, 35]$.

A tolerance situation $S = \{P_1 := X_1, \ldots, P_n := X_n\}$ is more *general* than $S' = \{P_1 := X'_1, \ldots, P_n := X'_n\}$, marked as $S' \subseteq_s S$, iff $X'_i \subseteq X_i, i = 1, \ldots, n$. The generality relation $\subseteq_s$ is clearly reflexive, antisymmetric, and transitive and hence defines a partial ordering in the set of tolerance situations of an ICSP.

Intuitively, the situations form a generality hierarchy defined by $\subseteq_s$. For example, part of the $\subseteq_s$-relation corresponding to (2.2) is depicted in Fig. 3 with the more general situations appearing in the upper part of the lattice. Consistent situations (solutions) are represented in bold font and inconsistent situations in plain font. Inadmissibility is represented by italic font. Inconsistent situations may be admissible or inadmissible.

Mathematically, the resulting structure is a lattice $L = \langle S, \cup_s, \cap_s \rangle$, where $\cup_s$ is the union and $\cap_s$ is the intersection of situations S defined as:

$$\{P_i := X_i\} \cup_s \{P_i := Y_i\} = \{P_i := X_i \cup Y_i\}, \quad i = 1, \ldots, n,$$

$$\{P_i := X_i\} \cap_s \{P_i := Y_i\} = \{P_i := X_i \cap Y_i\}, \quad i = 1, \ldots, n. \quad (2.5)$$

The least upper bound of the solutions of an ICSP is called its *least general common solution* (LGCS). LGCS generalizes the exact numerical solutions S_j of the ICSP, as well as the more general tolerance solutions, by LGCS = $\cup_s \{S_j\}$.

Variable values in the LGCS cannot always be represented as continuous intervals. If $P := X_1$ in solution S_1, $P := X_2$ in solution S_2, and $X_2 \cap X_1 = \{\}$, then $P := X_1 \cup X_2$ is a discontinuous interval in LGCS = $S_1 \cup_s S_2$. For instance, the LGCS of

$$X^2 = Y, \quad Y := [4, 9]$$

is $\{X := [-3, -2] \cup [2, 3], Y := [4, 9]\}$. We will call a union set $D = X_1 \cup \cdots \cup X_n$ of mutually exclusive intervals a *division* and represent it as

$$D = [x_{1,1}, x_{1,2} | x_{2,1}, x_{2,2} | \cdots | x_{n,1}, x_{n,2}],$$

where $X_i = [x_{i,1}, x_{i,2}]$, $i = 1, \ldots, n$, and $x_{i,2} < x_{i+1,1}$, $i = 1, \ldots, n-1$. Inter-

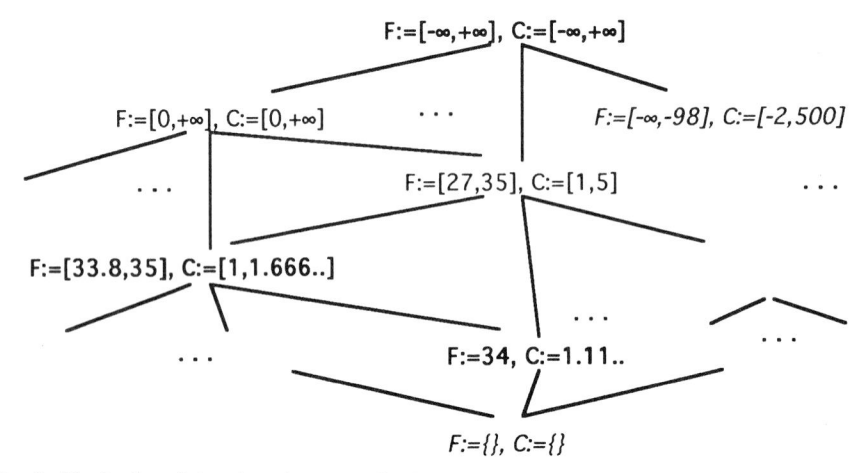

Fig. 3. The lattice of situations for constraint $F = C * 1.8 + 32$. Consistency is represented in bold and inconsistency in plain font. Italic font denotes inadmissibility.

vals X_i are called the *constituents* of division D. For simplicity, constituency will be denoted by $X_i \in D$, although division D is actually a set of real values. A singleton interval $[x, x]$ in a division is represented simply as the exact value x. For example:

$$[-\infty, 0^-] \cup [0, 0] \cup [0^+, 1] = [-\infty, 0^- \mid 0, 0 \mid 0^+, 1]$$
$$= [-\infty, 0^- \mid 0 \mid 0^+, 1].$$

Here x^+ and x^- denote a slightly larger and smaller number than x, respectively.

By generalizing the notion of interval into the notion of division, any set of solutions for an ICSP can be represented by a unique LGCS. We can always use continuous intervals as the special case, if needed. The idea of using divisions instead of intervals contrasts our approach with other interval constraint reasoning systems [8, 38] in which solutions are always interval-valued. The problem of using only intervals is that in order to keep reasoning complete, one either has to generate sets of interval solutions, which may lead to a very large number of solutions and be computationally infeasible, or allow inadmissible subintervals within solution intervals, which weakens the notion of solution and the inferential power of the reasoning system.

2.3. ICSP solutions

Problem formulation 1.2 of solving an ICSP (2.1) can now be restated precisely in terms of the situation lattice:

Problem formulation 2.1. Given is an ICSP (2.1). What is its LGCS?

For example, (2.2) states the problem of determining mutually consistent $C \subseteq [1, 5]$ and $F \subseteq [27, 35]$ intervals (divisions). An intelligent reasoner can notice inconsistencies and refine the tolerances within the lattice (Fig. 3) down to solution $\{C := [1, 1.666\ldots], F := [33.8, 35]\}$. Refining the tolerances more would remove numerical extensional solutions of the equation; the LGCS is the "tightest" solution generalizing all solutions for the ICSP.

In ordinary discrete constraint satisfaction [32, 34], exact value systems, and logic programming systems, the goal is to generate a set of exact value solutions. When the problem has infinitely many solutions and this is not possible, some kind of solution abstraction mechanism is needed. In constraint logic programming schemes, symbolic answer constraints are used as abstract solutions. Even if the idea of returning abstract answer constraints is often useful, it suffers from a fundamental problem: it sacrifices the simple and clear logic programming notion of solution as a consistent value assignment. It is often much harder for the user (or for another program) to interpret solutions containing complicated answer constraint expressions that may be represented in some internal "canonical" form. In contrast, solution abstraction in interval constraint satisfaction is uniformly based on numerical values, not on algebraic formulas. In many applications like in financial spreadsheets [23] this approach is more useful. Of course, logic programming can be extended to deal with interval solutions, as has been done in [38–40].

The idea of reasoning and representing abstract solutions in terms of set-valued variables can be applied to discrete variables and truth values as well. The general idea of tolerance constraint reasoning in multivalued and predicate logic with different quantifier constraints has been developed in [21, 24]. A related approach of extending the notion of interval solution further is presented in [51].

3. Local tolerance propagation

In this section, the notion of an interval function is first introduced. A local interval propagation algorithm is then presented.

3.1. Basic interval functions

Interval arithmetic (IA) [3, 35, 36, 43] deals with closed *intervals* $X = [a, b] = \{x \mid a \leq x \leq b\}$. Value $(a + b)/2$ is called the *centre* and value $b - a$ is called the *width* of interval X. IA generalizes ordinary exact value arithmetic; any real number x can be represented as a singleton interval $[x, x]$.

IA also generalizes real functions $f(x_1, \ldots, x_n)$ into the corresponding interval functions $F(X_1, \ldots, X_n)$:

$$F(X_1, \ldots, X_n) = \{f(x_1, \ldots, x_n) \mid x_i \in X_i, i = 1, \ldots, n\}.$$

Capital letters are used for interval concepts. Intuitively, $F(X_1, \ldots, X_n)$ simply evaluates the range of f-values when $x_1, \ldots, x_n$ *independently* get values within the corresponding intervals. For example, rational interval functions can be defined as:

$$\begin{aligned}
A + B &= \{a + b \mid a \in A, b \in B\}, \\
A - B &= \{a - b \mid a \in A, b \in B\}, \\
A * B &= \{a * b \mid a \in A, b \in B\}, \\
A / B &= \{a/b \mid a \in A, b \in B\}, \quad \text{if } 0 \notin B.
\end{aligned} \quad (3.1)$$

Here the same function symbols are used for both rational and interval functions; the distinction can be made by the arguments. Interval generalizations for the other basic functions like X^n, $\exp(X)$, $\sin(X)$ etc. can be defined easily as well.

For computational purposes, definitions relating the limits of argument intervals to the limits of the resultant interval can be derived. For example, for (3.1) we get:

$$[a, b] + [c, d] = [a + c, b + d],$$
$$[a, b] - [c, d] = [a - d, b - c],$$
$$[a, b] * [c, d] = [\min(ac, ad, bc, bd), \max(ac, ad, bc, bd)],$$
$$[a, b] / [c, d] = [a, b] * [1/d, 1/c], \quad \text{if } 0 \notin [c, d].$$
(3.2)

In interval arithmetic, an interval function F is called an *extension* of its *real restriction* f if $F(X_1, \ldots, X_n) = f(x_1, \ldots, x_n)$ for all real arguments. For complicated nested functions f, it is often difficult or impossible to define accurate interval extensions like (3.2) but we usually have to do with extensional forms

$$F(X_1, \ldots, X_n) \supseteq \{f(x_1, \ldots, x_n) \mid x_i \in X_i, i = 1, \ldots, n\}$$

that may evaluate larger intervals than the actual range of f-values. We return to extensional forms of complicated functions later.

3.2. Local interval propagation

Any exact function $x_n = f(x_1, \ldots, x_{n-1})$ can be defined equivalently by the relation constraint $\text{REL}(f) = \{\langle x_1, \ldots, x_n \rangle \mid x_n = f(x_1, \ldots, x_{n-1})\}$. In local interval propagation, local consistency conditions of the f-constraint are defined in terms of symmetrical *solution functions*:

$$F_i(X_1, \ldots, X_{i-1}, X_{i+1}, \ldots, X_n)$$
$$= \{x_i \mid \langle x_1, \ldots, x_i, \ldots, x_n \rangle \in \text{REL}(f), x_j \in X_j, j = 1, \ldots, n\}.$$
(3.3)

$F_i(X_1, \ldots, X_n)$ evaluates the interval of possible values for the ith variable as the other variables vary independently within their tolerances. Because this is exactly what interval functions in IA do, solution functions can be derived algebraically from the constraint expressions. With simple functional constraints, like basic algebraic functions, this is easy. For instance, the solution functions of the addition constraint $X + Y = Z$ are $X = Z - Y$, $Y = Z - X$, and $Z = X + Y$.

If the solution functions of a constraint F are $Y_1 = F_1(X_1, \ldots, X_n), \ldots, Y_n = F_n(X_1, \ldots, X_n)$, then, by definition of consistency, the variables are locally consistent with respect to F iff:

$$Y_1 \subseteq F_1(X_1, \ldots, X_n), \quad \ldots, \quad Y_n \subseteq F_n(X_1, \ldots, X_n). \tag{3.4}$$

The condition for local consistency in an ICSP is obtained by demanding (3.4) with respect to every constraint: a situation is locally consistent iff all solution functions of the ICSP evaluate larger intervals ($\subseteq$) than their value variables. Procedure 3.1 can be used to determine the local LGCS. The procedure gets as input the solution functions of an ICSP and an initial tolerance value assignment for its variables. During computation impossible values are removed cautiously by the intersection operation in step (3.2) until $Y \subseteq F(X_1, \ldots, X_n)$ holds for every function.

Procedure 3.1. *Local tolerance propagation.*
(1) *Agenda* := the solution functions of the constraints in the ICSP (in some order).
(2) *S* := tolerance value assignment for the variables in the ICSP.
(3) For each $X := F(\cdots)$ in *Agenda* until *Agenda* = { } do
   (3.1) $X' := F(\cdots)$
      ; Evaluate the next solution function in *Agenda*.
   (3.2) If X' = the value of X in S,
      then remove from *Agenda* all solution functions originating
         from the same constraint as $F(\cdots)$ (because they must be
         satisfied) and return to step (3),
      else $Int := X' \cap$ the value of X in S.
   (3.3) If $Int = \{\}$, then return $\{\}$.
      ; Inadmissible, no solutions.
   (3.4) If $X \subseteq X'$,
      then remove $X := F(\cdots)$ from *Agenda*,
      else set $X := Int$ in S,
         Agenda := *Agenda* $\cup$
            {Solution functions with X as argument} –
            $\{X := F(\cdots)\}$.
(4) Return to step (3).

For example, consider the earlier temperature conversion problem in Fig. 1:

$$C * 1.8 = X, \quad X + 32 = F,$$
$$C := [1, 5], \quad X := [-\infty, +\infty], \quad F := [27, 35].$$

The solution functions corresponding to the constraints are:

Constraint	Solution functions
$C * 1.8 = X$	$X = C * 1.8, \quad C = X/1.8$
$X + 32 = F$	$F = X + 32, \quad X = F - 32$

These interval functions are defined in (3.2). The initial agenda of the solution functions of this network is, for example (any ordering of the functions is possible):

$$X = C * 1.8, \qquad X = F - 32, \qquad C = X/1.8, \qquad F = X + 32.$$

If one assumes that new solution functions in Procedure 3.1 are added to the end of the agenda, the procedure assigns new values to variables and updates the agenda as shown in Table 1. Hence, the final values for the variables are:

$$C := [1, 1.666\ldots], \qquad X := [1.8, 3], \qquad F := [33.8, 35].$$

3.2.1. Comparison with Waltz filtering

Both local TP and Waltz filtering [8, 50] can be used to obtain similar locally consistent solutions. The main difference between the approaches is that in TP the solution functions of the constraints are used in the agenda while in Waltz filtering constraints themselves are used. The TP approach is argued to have the following benefits: Firstly, consistency conditions can be defined in terms of interval solution functions. (This is simple for primitive algebraic functions; problems related to nested functions will be discussed later.) Secondly, control of propagation is more flexible; the order of function evaluations can be redefined after each step. Thirdly, the TP procedure is essentially a forward chaining rule system whose rules are solution functions. This suggests that rule compilation techniques and techniques for generating explanations used in exact value systems [48] can be applied in TP, too. Fourthly and most importantly, it will be later seen that local TP can be generalized into global TP for determining globally consistent solutions in a way not possible in the local Waltz filtering approach.

A problem with TP as well as with Waltz filtering in infinite domains is that it easily goes into an infinite loop even with quite simple ICSPs. For example, in solving the proposition

$$Y = 2 * X, \qquad X = Y,$$
$$X := [0, \infty], \qquad Y := [0, \infty],$$

the values of X and Y are bisected over and over again and the situation converges only asymptotically towards the solution $\{X := 0, Y := 0\}$. Asymptotically converging propositions like this set a challenge for developing

Table 1

Next function	New value	New agenda
		$X = C * 1.8, \quad X = F - 32,$
		$C = X/1.8, \quad F = X + 32$
$X = C * 1.8$	$[1, 5] * 1.8 \cap [-\infty, +\infty] = [1.8, 9]$	$X = F - 32, \quad C = X/1.8, \quad F = X + 32$
$X = F - 32$	$([27, 35] - 32) \cap [1.8, 9] = [1.8, 3]$	$C = X/1.8, \quad F = X + 32$
$C = X/1.8$	$([1.8, 3]/1.8) \cap [1, 5] = [1, 1.666\ldots]$	$F = X + 32, \quad X = C * 1.8$
$F = X + 32$	$([1.8, 3] + 32) \cap [27, 35] = [33.8, 35]$	$X = C * 1.8, \quad X = F - 32$
$X = C * 1.8$	$[1.8, 3] \subseteq [1, 1.666\ldots] * 1.8$	$X = F - 32$
$X = F - 32$	$[1.8, 3] \subseteq [33.8, 35] - 32$	$\{\}$

techniques by which ICSPs can be represented in a computationally more efficient form and for developing strategies for agenda management in Procedure 3.1 or in Waltz filtering. In practice, this problem can be solved by defining a precision level after which two intervals are considered equal and propagation is terminated. In any case, the precision of the computing machinery sets one such precision level. Problems of rounding errors can be handled in interval arithmetic nicely: by rounding lower limits downwards and upper limits upwards solutions are never lost. Such safety is not possible in exact value systems.

3.2.2. Tractability of interval propagation

Local consistency techniques for discrete CSPs can be implemented efficiently. For example, arc consistency can be obtained in linear time with respect to the number of (binary) constraints [33]. In the interval case, however, it is easy to formulate computationally time-consuming ICSPs that converge only asymptotically towards the solution(s). This makes it difficult to estimate the time complexity of interval reasoning schemes. The complexity also heavily depends on the accuracy desired. In terms of theoretical time complexity, interval reasoning schemes behave badly. Fortunately, empirical evaluations have shown that "in practice [various interval labeling systems] run quickly and effectively on problems of realistic size (hundreds of nodes and constraints)" [8].

3.2.3. Application example

Let us apply local TP to a design problem. The task is to allocate the working time of n researchers consistently in m projects. For example, assume that three researchers a, b, and c with working capacities A, B, and C hours should be allocated to three projects p_1, p_2, and p_3 that require resources for P_1, P_2, and P_3 hours, respectively. Let variable XY denote the working time that a researcher with capacity X spends in a project requiring resources Y. For example, AP_1 is the time allocation of researcher a in project p_1. The algebraic constraints for the problem are (cf. Fig. 4):

$$
\begin{aligned}
& A + B + C = P_1 + P_2 + P_3 = \text{TOTAL} \quad &&; \text{Total working hours,} \\
& AP_1 + BP_1 + CP_1 = P_1 \quad &&; \text{Project resources,} \\
& AP_2 + BP_2 + CP_2 = P_2, \\
& AP_3 + BP_3 + CP_3 = P_3, \\
& AP_1 + AP_2 + AP_3 = A \quad &&; \text{Researcher capacities,} \\
& BP_1 + BP_2 + BP_3 = B, \\
& CP_1 + CP_2 + CP_3 = C.
\end{aligned}
\quad (3.5)
$$

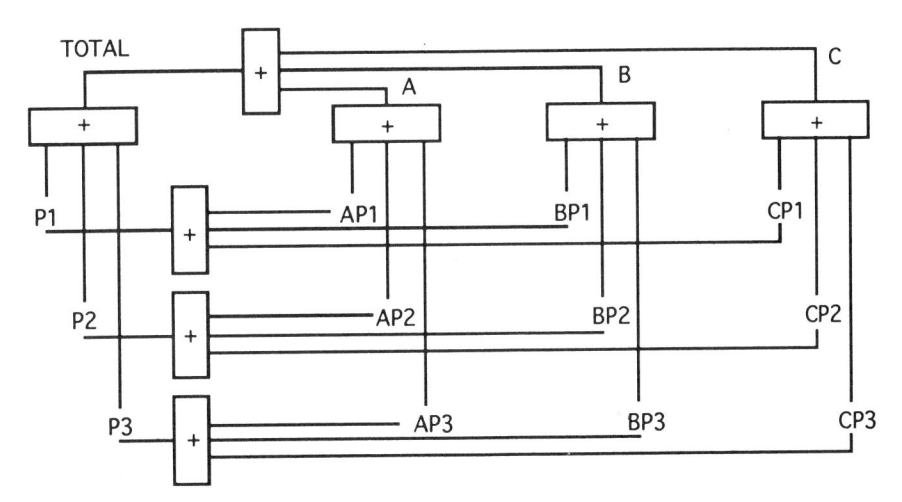

Fig. 4. Constraint net for (3.5).

The problem can be represented as a spreadsheet table where AP_i, BP_i, and CP_i, $i = 1, 2, 3$, are used as input variables and A, B, C, P_1, P_2, and P_3 are the output variables to be computed. However, by current spreadsheet or exact value propagation systems arithmetic computations cannot be performed unless the problem is perfectly constrained. Here this is not possible: in the beginning of problem solving, most researcher allocations are more or less unknown and are to be settled simultaneously. Uncertain variable values cannot be represented by exact numbers at all. It is also quite hard to see what are the input variable combinations from which a set of desired output parameters could be computed. A change in any variable value may affect any other variable values. It is quite difficult for the user to keep track of all possible interactions.

By using exact value techniques we end up in a tedious iteration where input variable values are guessed, output values computed, and results evaluated with respect to the problem constraints until a satisfiable variable assignment emerges. Relaxation schemes (that are used to automate this kind of iteration) are difficult to apply in situations like this where the number of values to be guessed is large. Furthermore, only one solution can be found, the solution is always exact, and it cannot reflect inexactness of input data.

TP-based problem solving [23] solves these problems. The user can initially set the intervals for the variables as wide or as strict as he wants. In inconsistent interval allocations suggested by the user, the system can refine the intervals further by determining the least general common solution for the problem. Problem solving proceeds not by iteration but in a top-down fashion: the problem is stepwise refined by the user and by the system until a satisfactory exact solution is found. For example, the initial intervals may be:

$$\{AP_i := BP_i := CP_i := A := B := C := [0, 160],$$
$$P_i := \text{TOTAL} := [0, 480]\},$$
$$i = 1, 2, 3.$$

If the user sets $P_2 := [160, 480]$, local TP can infer refinements $P_1 := [0, 320]$, $P_3 := [0, 320]$, and $\text{TOTAL} := [160, 480]$. If we acknowledge this and constrain the problem further by saying that A should not work in project P_1 less than 120 hours, i.e., $AP_1 := [120, 160]$, then local TP can infer seven necessary modifications:

$$P_1 := [120, 320], \qquad P_3 := [160, 360], \qquad P_3 := [0, 200],$$
$$AP_2 := [0, 40], \qquad AP_3 := [0, 40], \qquad A := [120, 160],$$
$$\text{TOTAL} := [280, 480].$$

Here only one limit of one parameter was changed in a quite simple constraint net. In the general case, both lower and higher limits of several variables can be modified simultaneously, and more complicated constraints than simple additions may be present.

Local TP refines monotonically inconsistent but admissible ICSPs. The TP approach has been extended also for dealing with inadmissible ICSPs in [23]. Here tolerances provide the means for determining minimal interval *enlargements* for the inadmissible variables based on the information present in the ICSP. This kind of "nonmonotonic" inference step is needed in order to help the user of an interval-based spreadsheet program in reformulating ICSP situations intelligently.

4. Application conditions

4.1. The problem

In both local TP and Waltz filtering, variable intervals must be computed with respect to the related variables in one way or another. However, such computations cannot always be performed straightforwardly. Preconditions for the intervals of the ICSP must be set for two major reasons:

(1) *Definability of constraints*. Certain values for the variables must be excluded by the definition of the constraints. For example, in the constraint $X/Y = Z$ all situations with $0 \in Y$ are implicitly disallowed. In general, Y may be an expression of arbitrary complexity.

(2) *Applicability of interval functions*. Needed interval functions cannot always be defined or applied easily:

(2.1) *Definability*. A solution function may not be defined for all argument values. For example, in the constraint $X * Y = Z$, the solution function $X = Z/Y$ cannot be computed if $0 \in Y$. However, in this case, value $Y := 0$ is not excluded by the definition of the constraint as with the $X/Y = Z$ constraint above: constraint $X * Y = Z$ can be satisfied for any X if $Y := 0$ and $Z := 0$.

(2.2) *Discontinuous (multiple) values.* A solution function may not evaluate to a single continuous interval. For example, in the constraint $X^2 = Y$, the solution function for X should evaluate two values $X := [1, 2]$ and $X := [-2, -1]$ if $Y := [1, 4]$.

(2.3) *Monotonicity.* For simple interval functions, like the rational functions (3.2), values are obtained easily by considering the lower and upper bounds of the argument intervals because the functions behave monotonically. However, with more complicated functions this is not the case, and more complicated interval analysis is needed.

In the following, two general techniques for solving these *application condition problems* (1)–(2) will be presented. Both techniques are based on the idea of decomposing an ICSP exhaustively into a set of well-behaved subsituations without "losing" solutions or introducing new ones. We first show how to do this.

4.2. Situation decomposition

A set of divisions D_i for the variables P_i, $i = 1, \ldots, n$, of an ICSP defines its *decomposition* into a set S of subsituations, i.e., into an *interval space*:

$$S = \{\{P_1 := X'_1, \ldots, P_n := X'_n\} \mid X'_i \in D_i, i = 1, \ldots, n\}.$$

For example, the interval space corresponding to divisions $X \in [-\infty, 0^- \mid 0, 1]$ and $Y \in [-1, 1^- \mid 1, \infty]$ is:

$$\{\{X := [-\infty, 0^-], Y := [-1, 1^-]\}, \{X := [-\infty, 0^-], Y := [1, \infty]\},$$
$$\{X := [0, 1], Y := [-1, 1^-]\}, \{X := [0, 1], Y := [1, \infty]\}\}.$$

We are interested in decompositions S satisfying two properties:

(1) *Completeness.* Each exact value solution within the intervals of the original situation is a solution of one situation in space S, i.e., the decomposition does not "lose" or duplicate solutions.

(2) *Soundness.* Each exact value solution of the situations in S is a solution of the original situation, i.e., the decomposition does not introduce new exact solutions.

The application condition problem can be solved by decomposing the original situation of the ICSP in a complete and sound way into an *actual application space*, in which interval reasoning can be performed. This space is determined as follows:

Step 1. For each constraint type (e.g., $X*Y = Z$, $X/Y = Z$, etc.), a *local definition* (*interval*) *space* is determined in which the constraint is defined. We will assume that variable divisions are finite.

Step 2. Each local definition space (Step 1) is decomposed further into the *local application space* in order to make it possible to define the solution functions conveniently.

Step 3. For a particular constraint net, local application spaces (Step 2) are combined into a *global application space*, in which interval propagation is possible.

Step 4. The actual application space for a particular ICSP is constructed by intersecting the global application space (Step 3) with the intervals of the ICSP.

Steps 1–3 can be performed *a priori* for a particular constraint net of an ICSP; only Step 4 has to be taken dynamically with respect to a particular situation. In the following, Steps 1–4 are explained in more detail.

4.2.1. Local definition space

Each primitive algebraic function constraint ($X/Y = Z$, $\log_X Y = Z$, etc.) defines a local definition space within which the constraint is defined and which contains all possible exact value solutions of the constraint. For example, the local definition space of constraint $\log_X(Y) = Z$ has two situations,

$$\{\{X \in [0^+, 1^- \mid 1^+, \infty], Y := [0^+, \infty], Z := [-\infty, \infty]\}\},$$

because the base X of the logarithm function cannot be negative or equal to 1 and the argument Y must be positive. The local definition space of constraint $Y = X^Z$ would be different.

4.2.2. Local application space

In order to guarantee that solution functions can be defined and computed easily, we often have to decompose the local definition space further into the *local application space*. In the following, two useful criteria for this task are presented:

Definability criterion. First of all, a solution function $X_1 = F(X_2, \ldots, X_n)$ must be *defined* for all argument values $x_2 \in X_2, \ldots, x_n \in X_n$ and must evaluate a continuous unique interval within X_1 (otherwise F would not be a function). For example, the definition space of the multiplication constraint $X*Y = Z$ is a singleton:

$$\{(X := [-\infty, \infty], Y := [-\infty, \infty], Z := [-\infty, \infty]\}\}. \tag{4.1}$$

However, the solution function $Y = Z/X$ in $X * Y = Z$ cannot be computed if $0 \in X$ although $X := 0$ is possible in the definition space. An analogous situation holds for function $X = Z/Y$. Decomposing (4.1) further solves the problem: exceptional cases with $0 \in X$ and $0 \in Y$ can be considered separately by using the following local application space of nine situations:

$$\{\{X \in [-\infty, 0^-\,|\,0\,|\,0^+, \infty], Y \in [-\infty, 0^-\,|\,0\,|\,0^+, \infty], Z \in [-\infty, \infty]\}\}. \tag{4.2}$$

Now situations with $0 \in X$ or $0 \in Y$ occur only when $X := 0$ or $Y := 0$, and the solution functions for X and Y in these cases can be defined based on the constraints $0 * Y = Z$ and $X * 0 = Z$, respectively:

X: if $Y = 0$ then X else Z/Y,

Y: if $X = 0$ then Y else Z/X,

Z: $X * Y$.

Intuitively, in the local application space exceptional cases are separated into distinct subspaces for which solution functions can be defined separately by the different branches of the conditional function definitions.

Monotonicity criterion. In evaluating an interval (solution) function, the minimum and maximum points of the corresponding exact function must be determined. This can be done conveniently by decomposing the definition space into subsituations in which the solution functions can be defined in terms of the bounds of the argument intervals in the same way as in (3.2). A sufficient condition for this is monotonicity: we say that an interval function $P_1 = F(P_2, \ldots, P_n)$ is *monotonic* in a situation $\{P_1 := X_1, \ldots, P_n := X_n\}$ iff the corresponding exact function f is monotonic with respect to each argument P_i within interval X_i, $i = 2, \ldots, n$. This means that if we increase any argument within its interval, the value of the function always either increases or decreases independently of the values of the other arguments (within their intervals). For example, $Z = X/Y$ is monotonic when $X \subseteq [0, \infty]$ and $Y \subseteq [0^+, \infty]$, because $z = x/y$ increases with respect to increasing x, $y \in [0^+, \infty]$, and decreases with respect to increasing y, $x \in [0, \infty]$. Monotonicity conditions can be determined by considering the partial derivatives $df(x_1, \ldots, x_n)/dx_i$, $i = 1, \ldots, n$, of the function: function $Y = F(X_1, \ldots, X_n)$ is monotonic if the partial derivatives do not change sign within the given intervals $x_i \in X_i$, $i = 1, \ldots, n$.

A monotonic function necessarily has its minimum and maximum values at the boundaries of the given intervals. Hence, the value of a monotonic solution function $Y = F(X_1, \ldots, X_n)$ corresponding to an exact value function $y = f(x_1, \ldots, x_n)$ can be computed easily by

$$Y = [\min(\{f(\underline{x}_1, \ldots, \underline{x}_n) \mid \underline{x}_i = \min(X_i) \text{ or } \underline{x}_i = \max(X_i),$$
$$i = 1, \ldots, n\}),$$
$$\max(\{f(\underline{x}_1, \ldots, \underline{x}_n) \mid \underline{x}_i = \min(X_i) \text{ or } \underline{x}_i = \max(X_i),$$
$$i = 1, \ldots, n\})]$$

where $\min(\{v_1, \ldots, v_n\})$ and $\max(\{v_1, \ldots, v_n\})$ mean the minimum and maximum of values v_i, $i = 1, \ldots, n$, respectively, and $\min(X)$ and $\max(X)$ are the minimum and maximum of interval X.

Monotonicity guarantees that solution function bounds can be computed from argument bounds. However, a function may have its absolute maximum and minimum values at argument interval bounds but be nonmonotonic. In such cases, monotonicity is an unnecessarily strong criterion and the application space will consist of unnecessarily many situations. In principle, this is not a problem since no solutions are erroneously lost or introduced as long as the decomposition is sound and complete. However, unnecessarily large decompositions result in unnecessary computations.

For example, constraint $X^a = Y$, $a \in \{2, 4, \ldots\}$, has definition space $\{\{X := [-\infty, +\infty], Y := [0, +\infty]\}\}$ and exact value solution functions:

$$x = f_x(y) = \pm y^{1/a}, \qquad y = f_y(x) = x^a.$$

The interval function for X is defined, i.e., evaluates a unique interval, if positive and negative X-values are considered separately: $X \in [-\infty, 0^- \mid 0, \infty]$. With this condition, the partial derivatives,

$$\mathrm{d}f_x(y)/\mathrm{d}y = \pm(1/a)y^{1/a-1}, \qquad \mathrm{d}f_y(x)/\mathrm{d}x = ax^{a-1},$$

do not change sign. The local application space is hence:

$$\{\{X \in [-\infty, 0^- \mid 0, \infty], Y := [0, \infty]\}\}. \tag{4.3}$$

For $X := [x_1, x_2]$ and $Y := [y_1, y_2]$ we get solution functions:

X: if $X \subseteq [0, \infty]$ then $[y_1^{1/a}, y_2^{1/a}]$ else $[-y_2^{1/a}, -y_1^{1/a}]$,

Y: $[\min(x_1^a, x_2^a), \max(x_1^a, x_2^a)]$.

These definitions solve the problem of multiple interval values. For example, if $X := [-\infty, \infty]$, $Y := [1, 4]$, and $a = 2$, the problem can be considered with respect to values $X := [-\infty, 0^-]$ and $X := [0, \infty]$ separately and the two results with $X := [-2, -1]$ and $X := [1, 2]$ are found, one in each subsituation.

In the above, the monotonicity condition suggests that positive and negative X-values should be considered separately. This is actually an unnecessarily strict condition in situations where Y is of form $Y := [0, y_2]$ because then X-values could be represented by a continuous interval. For example, if $Y := [0, 4]$ and $a = 2$, then $X := [-2, 2]$. By using (4.3) we would get two solutions $X := [-2, 0^-]$ and $X := [0, 2]$. The more general solution $X := [-2, 2]$ could be obtained by generalizing the two solutions by the $\cup_s$-operation in the situation lattice. However, it would be more efficient not to consider X in parts but define the solution function directly in such a way that the special case $Y := [0, y_2]$ is evaluated properly.

More complicated situations occur if exponent "a" above is allowed to have interval values, i.e., it is a variable. Let the resulting constraint $X^Y = Z$ have definition space:

$$\{\{X := [0, \infty], Y := [-\infty, \infty], Z := [0, \infty]\}\} .$$

Exact solution functions are:

$$x = f_x = z^{1/y}, \qquad y = f_y = \log_x(z), \qquad z = f_z = x^y .$$

Definability conditions for these functions give us the following divisions:

$$X \in [0 \,|\, 0^+, 1^- \,|\, 1 \,|\, 1^+, \infty] \quad ; \text{Due to } y = \log_x(z) ,$$
$$Y \in [-\infty, 0^- \,|\, 0 \,|\, 0^+, \infty] \quad ; \text{Due to } x = z^{1/y} ,$$
$$Z \in [0 \,|\, 0^+, \infty] \qquad\qquad ; \text{Due to } y = \log_x(z) .$$

The partial derivatives of the solution functions are:

$$df_x/dz = z^{(1/y - 1)}/y , \qquad df_x/dy = (z^{1/y})(\ln(z))(-y^{-2}) ,$$
$$df_y/dz = 1/(z \ln(x)) , \qquad df_y/dx = -\ln(z)/(x \ln(x)^2) ,$$
$$df_z/dy = x^y \ln(x) , \qquad df_z/dx = y x^{y-1} .$$

From the derivatives df_x/dy and df_y/dx we get one additional division point, $Z = 1$, due to the monotonicity criterion. By using the refined division $Z \in [0 \,|\, 0^+, 1^- \,|\, 1, \infty]$, the following solution functions are obtained:

$X = [x_1, x_2]$: if $Y = 0$ then (if $Z = 0$ then 0 else X),
     elseif $Z = 0$ then 0,
     else $[\min(\{z_i^{1/y_i}\}), \max(\{z_i^{1/y_i}\})]$, $i = 1, 2$;

$Y = [y_1, y_2]$: if $Z = 0$ then (if $X = 0$ then Y else $\{\}$)
     elseif $X = 1$ then Y,
     else $[\min(\{\log_{x_i}(z_i)\}), \max(\{\log_{x_i}(z_i)\})]$, $i = 1, 2$;

$Z = [z_1, z_2]$: if $X = 0$ then 0
     else $[\min(\{x_i^{y_i}\}), \max(\{x_i^{y_i}\})]$, $i = 1, 2$.

For example, no value (denoted by $\{\}$) for Y can satisfy the $X^Y = Z$ constraint if $Z = 0$ and $X \neq 0$.

To sum up, the local solution functions and the local application space are determined by splitting the local definition space of a constraint further in such a way that the solution functions in each subsituation can be defined conveniently. The definability and monotonicity criteria give us a recipe for selecting the splitting points: the solution functions should be defined and monotonic in each subsituation.

4.2.3. Global application space

A variable X can be used in a constraint net in k constraints, $k \geq 1$, that constrain X-values with local application divisions $D_1, \ldots, D_k$. We say that the *global application division* for X is:

$$D = \{X_1 \cap \cdots \cap X_k \mid X_i \in D_i, i = 1, \ldots, k\}.$$

This division intuitively states ranges in which all constraints in the net are defined with respect to X and solution functions in which X is used as argument can be applied. No exact values for X in possible solutions are excluded or introduced (within the accuracy used). This means that applicability of interval propagation in a net of variables $P_1, \ldots, P_n$ with respect to all constraints and all solution functions can be guaranteed in a complete and sound fashion in the *global application space* S defined as:

$$S = \{\{P_1 := X_1, \ldots, P_n := X_n\} \mid$$
$$X_i \in D_i, D_i \text{ is the global application division of } P_i,$$
$$i = 1, \ldots, n\}.$$

For example, consider the constraint net:

$$X^2 + PX = Q \equiv \{X^2 = Y_1, P*X = Y_2, Y_1 + Y_2 = Q\}. \tag{4.4}$$

The local application spaces for constraints $P*X = Y_2$ and $X^2 = Y_1$ are given in (4.2) and (4.3), respectively; the application space for addition constraint $X + Y = Z$ is $\{\{X := [-\infty, \infty], Y := [-\infty, \infty], Z := [-\infty, \infty]\}\}$. The global application space of (4.4) is hence:

$$S = \{\{X \in [-\infty, 0^-\,|\,0, \infty] \cap [-\infty, 0^-\,|\,0\,|\,0^+, +\infty] = [-\infty, 0^-\,|\,0\,|\,0^+, +\infty],$$
$$Y_1 := [0, \infty] \cap [-\infty, \infty] = [0, \infty],$$
$$P \in [-\infty, 0^-\,|\,0\,|\,0^+, +\infty],$$
$$Y_2 := [-\infty, \infty] \cap [-\infty, \infty] = [-\infty, \infty],$$
$$Q := [-\infty, \infty]\}\}. \tag{4.5}$$

Notation $X \in D$ means here that X can be any constituent interval within division D; (4.5) represents a set of nine interval situations.

4.2.4. Actual application space

Assume an ICSP with interval assignment $S = \{P_1 := X_1, \ldots, P_n := X_n\}$ and global application space $G = \{\{P_1 := Y_1 \in D_1, \ldots, P_n := Y_n \in D_n\}\}$. In order to solve the ICSP we have to consider S with respect to each subsituation in G, i.e., in situations:

$$S' = \{\{P_1 := X_1 \cap Y_1, \ldots, P_n := X_n \cap Y_n\} \mid$$
$$\{P_1 := Y_1, \ldots, P_n := Y_n\} \in G\}$$
$$= \{\{P_1 \in X_1 \cap D_1, \ldots, P_n \in X_n \cap D_n\}\}. \tag{4.6}$$

S' is called the *actual application space*. The actual application space contains every possible exact solution of the ICSP in exactly one of its subsituations.

For example, the problem of solving equation $X^2 - 2X = 3$ corresponds to an ICSP with net (4.4) and initial situation:

$$\{X := [-\infty, \infty], P := -2, Q := 3, Y_1 := [-\infty, \infty], Y_2 := [-\infty, \infty]\} . \tag{4.7}$$

The actual application space is obtained by intersecting it and (4.5) by (4.6):

$$\{\{X \in [-\infty, 0^-\,|\,0\,|\,0^+, +\infty], Y_1 \in [0, \infty], \\ P := -2, Y_2 := [-\infty, \infty], Q := 3\}\} . \tag{4.8}$$

4.3. Search in application space

An ICSP can be solved after determining its actual application space S. Each subsituation of S may contain solutions. Procedure 4.1 below can be used for searching the solution(s) of an ICSP exhaustively in a given actual application space. The idea here is to instantiate the variables in some order to the constituent intervals of the divisions that define the actual application space. After each instantiation, all solution functions applicable and not yet satisfied with respect to already instantiated variables are applied. By this way dead ends are detected as soon as possible and common computations in different subsituations can be shared. One good heuristic for the instantiation ordering is to instantiate nodes with small divisions, tight intervals, and high connectivity first. In this way dead ends are likely to be found earlier and more common computations can be shared.

Procedure 4.1. *Solve ICSP.*
  (1) *Solutions* := { }.
  (2) *Divs* := divisions defining the actual application space of the ICSP in some order.
  (3) If some $D \in Divs$ is empty, then return { }.
      ; Trivially inadmissible.
  (4) Instantiate divisions (*Divs* := *Divs*, *Vars* := { }, S := { }).
      ; Defined by Procedure 4.2 below.
  (5) Return $\bigcup_s$ *Solutions* (or *Solutions*, if a set of interval solutions is desired).

Procedure 4.2. *Instantiate divisions* (*Divs*, *Vars*, S).
  (1) If *Divs* = { }, then *Solutions* := {S} ∪ *Solutions*, return.
      ; All variables instantiated and a solution found.
  (2) D := next variable division in *Divs*.
  (3) *Var* := the variable of D.

(4) *Vars* := {*Var*} ∪ *Vars*.
   ; Instantiated variables.
(5) *Fns* := $\{X_1 = F(X_2, \ldots, X_n) \mid X_i \in \textit{Vars}, i = 1, \ldots, n\}$.
   ; Applicable solution functions of the ICSP with instantiated variables.
(6) *NewFns* := $\{X_1 = F(X_2, \ldots, X_n) \in \textit{Fns} \mid \textit{Var} \in \{X_1, \ldots, X_n\}\}$.
   ; These solution functions are applicable due to *Var*.
(7) For each *Int* ∈ *D* do:
   ; Search over division constituents.
   (7.1) *S'* := *S* ∪ {*Var* := *Int*}.
      ; Instantiate *Var* in the current situation *S*.
   (7.2) *S'* := apply local TP (Procedure 3.1) with *Agenda* := *NewFns* and initial situation *S'*, but consider only applicable functions *F* ∈ *Fns* during propagation.
   (7.3) If *S'* ≠ { },
      then instantiate divisions (*Vars* := *Vars*, *S* := *S'*, *Divs* := *Divs* − *D*), ; Recursion
      else continue with next *Int* in step (7).
         ; Inadmissible dead end

For example, in solving (4.4),

$$X^2 + PX = Q \equiv \{X^2 = Y_1, P * X = Y_2, Y_1 + Y_2 = Q\},$$

in the actual application space (4.8),

$$\{\{X \in [-\infty, 0^- \mid 0 \mid 0^+, +\infty], Y_1 \in [0, \infty],$$
$$P := -2, Y_2 := [-\infty, \infty], Q := 3\}\},$$

we can use ordering P, Q, Y_1, Y_2, X. After instantiating $P := -2$, $Q := 3$, $Y_1 := [0, \infty]$, and $Y_2 := [-\infty, \infty]$, the solution functions of constraint $Y_1 + Y_2 = Q$ can be applied by Procedure 3.1 (step (7.2)). The resulting situation is then considered by instantiating X with the constituents of $[-\infty, 0^- \mid 0 \mid 0^+, \infty]$ and by additional solution functions (*NewFns*) that have X as an argument (functions originating from $X^2 = Y_1$ and $P * X = Y_2$). As a result, we actually find by local TP the two roots $X := -1$ and $X := 3$ as fixed points corresponding to instantiations $X := [-\infty, 0^-]$ and $X := [0^+, \infty]$, respectively ($X := 0$ is found inadmissible).

4.4. Division propagation

Although Procedure 4.1 worked well in this example, its application in the general case often has problems. The size of the application space grows exponentially with respect to the number of variables with nonsingleton divisions. This is computationally costly because computations along different search paths may be partly redundant (solution functions have to be evaluated in overlapping situations). Furthermore, we may end up generating overwhelmingly (although not infinitely) many solutions although we were originally interested in deriving a unique interval (or division) solution. In practice, Procedure 4.1 can be applied only to small problems.

As a solution to these problems, I propose generalization from interval propagation into *division propagation*. In this scheme one can propagate values immediately in the application space with all variables instantiated to divisions, and a unique division-valued solution is obtained. Although computing with divisions is slightly more complicated than with intervals, division propagation, as described below, is more feasible in situations with large application spaces (i.e., spaces consisting of several interval subsituations).

It may seem that in division propagation all one has to do is to generalize the definitions of interval (solution) functions into division-valued functions. However, it turns out that application of such functions in many cases splits a division into an ever larger set of intervals, and propagation becomes computationally extremely inefficient. For example, assume $X := [-\infty, 0^- \mid 0^+, \infty]$. If one of its solution functions evaluates interval $[-\infty, 1^- \mid 1 \mid 1^+, 10]$, then we get a new splitted value $X := [-\infty, 0^- \mid 0^+, 1^- \mid 1 \mid 1^+, 10]$. In asymptotically converging problems, the number of intervals in a division can grow quite large. For instance, this happens to X in $X^2 + PX = Q$ (4.4) with situation (4.8). The phenomenon of growing divisions in division propagation will be called the *splitting problem*. In the following, we first show how to define division-valued solution functions and after that how the *splitting problem* can be solved.

4.4.1. Division arithmetic

Let us denote the interval and division functions corresponding to an exact value function f by f_i and f_d, respectively (e.g., $+_i$ means interval addition). The division function $f_d(D_1, \ldots, D_n)$ corresponding to an interval function $f_i(I_1, \ldots, I_n)$ can be defined as follows:

$$f_d(D_1, \ldots, D_n) = \bigcup \{f_i(I_1, \ldots, I_n) \mid I_1 \in D_1, \ldots, I_n \in D_n\}.$$
(4.9)

Intuitively, the interval function is applied with every combination of the constituent intervals of the arguments, which guarantees that the resulting intervals contain exactly all the possible values of the exact function f. The union operation creates the division corresponding to the possibly partly overlapping intervals. For instance, by generalizing interval multiplication $*_i$ defined in (3.2) into division multiplication $*_d$, the following evaluation example is obtained:

$$[-2, -1 \mid 3, 4] *_d [2, 3 \mid 4, 5]$$
$$= ([-2, -1] *_i [2, 3]) \cup ([-2, -1] *_i [4, 5])$$
$$\cup ([3, 4] *_i [2, 3]) \cup ([3, 4] *_i [4, 5])$$

$$= [-6, -2] \cup [-10, -4] \cup [6, 12] \cup [12, 20]$$
$$= [-10, -2 \mid 6, 20] \ .$$

The number of constituents in the resultant division in (4.9) varies between 1 and $k_1 * k_2 * \cdots * k_n$, where k_i is the number of intervals in division D_i, $i = 1, \ldots, n$. In the above example, the maximum number $2 * 2 = 4$ was reduced to 2 because two pairs of intervals were overlapping and could be combined by the union operation.

When generalizing from interval propagation into division propagation no additional assumptions with respect to the application conditions are needed because (4.9) reduces the evaluation of a division function into interval computations. The actual application space can hence be used for division propagation, too.

4.4.2. Solving the splitting problem

As a solution to the splitting problem, application of the following *do-not-split* principle is proposed: During division propagation in Procedure 3.1, the intersection operation in step (3.2) is replaced by the nonsplitting division intersection operation $\cap_n$

$$D' \cap_n D = \bigcup \{[\min(X_i \cap_n D'), \max(X_i \cap_n D')] \mid X_i \in D\} \ ,$$

where D' is a new division value evaluated by a solution function and D is the old division value in situation S. Intuitively, the constituents of a division may be constrained only from both ends but not split further. In contrast to Procedures 4.1 and 4.2, Procedure 3.1 with the do-not-split principle does not consider the subspaces of an ICSP separately but determines the division solution directly.

The do-not-split principle makes division propagation computationally feasible. However, the price to be paid is that, in the general case, we have to alter our interpretation of the intervals in a solution. It cannot be guaranteed any more that *every* value in the division intervals is consistent (locally or globally), i.e., is extendable into a full exact (local or global) solution. However, we can be sure that at least the lower and upper bounds of the division constituents can be extended into full exact (local or global) solutions and that all other solutions must reside with the divisions. For example, in ICSP

$$X + Y = Z$$
$$X := [1, 2 \mid 8, 9], \quad Y := 0, \quad Z := [-\infty, \infty]$$

we get

$$Z = X +_d Y = ([1, 2] + [0, 0]) \cup ([8, 9] + [0, 0]) = [1, 2 \mid 8, 9]$$

(interval addition is defined in (3.2)). However, by applying the do-not-split principle we get

$$Z := [1, 2 | 8, 9] \cap_n [-\infty, \infty] = [1, 9]$$

although values $2 < Z < 8$ are not consistent. By using division propagation with the do-not-split principle one cannot filter values within a constituent interval of a division if the boundary values are consistent. Division propagation is inferentially weaker than pure interval propagation combined with the search procedure (Procedure 4.1 and 4.2). However, division propagation never loses solutions or introduces new ones. For example, if we apply local nonsplitting division propagation to (4.4) with actual application space divisions (4.8), we cannot find the actual roots $X := -1$ and $X := 3$ that were obtained earlier by Procedures 4.1 and 4.2. Instead, we get the division solution $X := [-1.5 \ldots, 0^- | 0 | 0^+, 3.0 \ldots]$.

The main benefit of division propagation is the possibility of dealing with large application spaces in which the search scheme 4.1–4.2 becomes computationally infeasible. After determining rougher bounds of possible values by division propagation more precise solutions can be solved more easily by considering the different constituent intervals separately. If only continuous divisions are used, division propagation is equivalent to interval propagation; if the intervals are singletons for "known" (input) variables and large intervals for "unknown" (output) variables, division propagation means conventional exact value propagation.

5. Global consistency

5.1. Local versus global consistency

Global consistency always implies local consistency; any global solution G is a specialization of the local LGCS L, $G \subseteq_s L$. Local TP never loses global solutions or introduces new ones. However, local tolerance reasoning suffers from two major drawbacks:

(1) Finding the "tightest" solution

By local consistency techniques one can always determine safe outer bounds for the solution but not necessarily the "tightest" of them. Consider the ICSP version of (1.4) below constraining Y to be the average of X and Z (cf. Fig. 5):

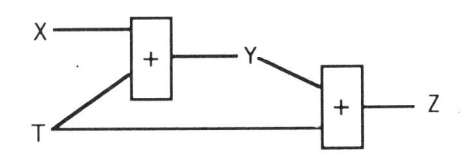

Fig. 5. The constraint net of (5.1).

$$X + T = Y, \qquad Y + T = Z,$$
$$X := 1, \qquad T := [0, \infty], \qquad Y := [0, \infty], \qquad Z := 11. \tag{5.1}$$

By local TP we get the local solution:

$$\{X := 1, T := [0, 10], Y := [1, 11], Z := 11\}. \tag{5.2}$$

This solution is not globally consistent because T and Y are not globally consistent. If, for example, $T = 9$ we get $Y = X + T = 10$ from the first constraint but the second constraint cannot be satisfied because $Y + T = 19 \not\subseteq Z = [11, 11]$. The global LGCS of (5.1) is, of course, the ordinary solution of the equation pair, i.e.,

$$\{X := 1, T := 5, Y := 6, Z := 11\}. \tag{5.3}$$

(2) *Detection of global inconsistency*

If an ICSP does not have a global solution it still may have a local solution. For example, the local LGCS of polynomial

$$X^4 + 2X^3 + 3X^2 + 4X + 5 = 0 \tag{5.4}$$

composed of $X^n = Y$, $X * Y = Z$, and $X + Y = Z$ constraints is

$$X := [-2.34\ldots, -0.1\ldots] \tag{5.5}$$

although (5.4) has no roots. What the local LGCS only tells is that *if* the problem has global solutions they *must* be within the local LGCS tolerances. This means that if local propagation fails, then the problem has no exact value or other global solutions for sure. However, from the existence of a local solution, existence of a global solution cannot be deduced: global consistency implies local consistency but not vice versa.

There are, however, ICSP categories in which local consistency implies, i.e., is equivalent to global consistency. For such problems local TP is sufficient for finding global solutions. In particular, this is the case with ICSPs whose constraint net is acyclic. Theorem 5.1 below follows directly from research on discrete CSPs where a globally consistent tree-structured CSP enables backtrack-free generation of exact solutions [10, 11, 14]:

Theorem 5.1. *An acyclic constraint net is globally consistent iff it is locally consistent.*

Proof. Intuitively, by selecting a value for a variable the locally related variable values can be selected in a satisfiable way in a locally consistent situation if the variables are not related to themselves, i.e., the net is acyclic. This means that the variables are globally consistent, i.e., local consistency implies global consistency. On the other hand, global consistency trivially implies local consistency. □

For example, the problems with (5.1) and (5.4) were due to cyclicity.

In some cases, loops can be removed by rewriting parts of the equations in equivalent acyclic form. For example, (5.1) can be rewritten in acyclic form $Y = (X + Z)/2$ by eliminating T. By applying local TP to this network global solutions are always obtained.

Theorem 5.2 below states an important special case in which any cyclic ICSP can be solved globally by local TP (here a "cutset" is, intuitively, a minimal set of nodes that "cuts" every cycle in a net):

Theorem 5.2. *If the variables of any cutset of a constraint net S are singleton-valued, then S is globally consistent iff it is locally consistent.*

Proof. Intuitively, assigning the variables of a cutset to singletons transforms the variables into exact constants. This breaks the loops and makes the network acyclic in which local and global consistency conditions are equivalent (Theorem 5.1). □

Unfortunately, ICSPs cannot usually be represented in acyclic form or have an exact value cutset. For such cases stronger global consistency techniques are needed. In the following, two such techniques, dynamic splitting and global TP, are developed.

5.2. Dynamic splitting

Theorems 5.1 and 5.2 suggest that one should focus on constraining cutset variables in global constraint satisfaction. (This strategy has been found useful also in generating exact value solutions for discrete CSPs [9].) The *dynamic splitting* procedure (Procedure 5.3 below) employs this idea. Here the easily available local solution S is first determined. After this, S is decomposed into subsituations with respect to a cutset variable. Local solutions within the subsituations are then determined, results decomposed again, and so on until globally consistent solutions hopefully emerge. A suitable cutset (or several ones) for an ICSP can be determined in a separate compilation phase before applying the procedure in different situations. The procedure assumes in step (4) that global solutions can be identified or that some other criterion for terminating splitting is available (for example, the number of recursive splittings may be bounded). A partial criterion for identifying global solutions is given by Theorem 5.2.

Procedure 5.3. *Dynamic splitting* (ICSP).
 (1) $S :=$ local LGCS obtained by Procedure 3.1.
 (2) If $S = \{\}$, then return "ICSP is inadmissible".

(3) If ICSP is acyclic, then return S as the global solution.
(4) If S is globally consistent (e.g., the variables of some cutset have singleton values) or if some other termination criterion is satisfied, then return S as the solution.
(5) Select a cutset variable $P := X$ in S by some criterion (e.g., select the variable with the largest width).
(6) Split X exhaustively into intervals $\{X_1, \ldots, X_n\}$ by some criterion (e.g., bisect X).
(7) Create decomposition $\{S_1, \ldots, S_n\}$ corresponding to $P := X_1, \ldots, P := X_n$.
(8) Apply dynamic splitting to each $S_1, \ldots, S_n$.
(9) Return generalization $\bigcup_s \{S'_i\}$, where S'_i are the solutions obtained in step (8). Optionally, set $\{S'_i\}$ can be returned if we are interested in obtaining solution sets.

Dynamic splitting works because with more constrained variable values, global solutions can be determined by local criteria more accurately. For example, consider the problem of finding the positive roots of:

$$X^3 - 9X + 4 = 0. \tag{5.6}$$

From initial value $X := [0, +\infty]$ local TP finds the local LGCS $X := [0.45, \ldots, 2.74 \ldots]$ (step (1)). In step (5), cutset variable X can be split. If we bisect X into $X := [0.45 \ldots, 1.6^-]$ and $X := [1.6, 2.74 \ldots]$ and solve the corresponding ICSPs (step (8)), global solutions $X := 0.45 \ldots$ and $X := 2.74 \ldots$ are found without further splitting.

Dynamic splitting offers an approach to solving the problem of incompleteness of numerical exact value relaxation techniques. With these techniques, as with Newton's iterative method, one cannot always find all solutions or determine whether there exists a solution. By TP, it is possible to consider infinite problem spaces without losing solutions. If local TP fails, we can be sure that there is no solution to be found within the intervals. For example, the fourth-order polynomial (5.4) is found inadmissible by bisecting the local solution (5.5) once. By this way, one can actually numerically *prove* that (5.4) has no roots. Tolerance propagation could also be applied in exact value relaxation schemes for determining plausible ranges of initial values for the guess variables.

The dynamic splitting scheme has, however, two major drawbacks:

(1) *Termination condition*. The procedure presumes that globally consistent variables and situations can be identified (step (4)). In the general case this is difficult and the use of some *ac hoc* termination condition is needed. Theorem 5.2 states only an unnecessarily strict condition for global consistency. More general criteria are needed in globally under-

constrained situations in which cutset variables may have nonsingleton tolerance values and still be globally consistent. Otherwise useless, possibly infinite, splitting may result when it is attempted to determine more and more precise solutions with respect to the cutset variables.
(2) *Efficiency*. Even if globally consistent solutions could be identified and their number were finite (or some other good termination condition is available), splitting may generate a large number of locally consistent intermediate solutions that can be identified as globally inadmissible only after several further splits, which is computationally inefficient.

The global TP scheme of the next section is an approach to solving these problems.

6. Global tolerance propagation

6.1. The idea

Assume a constraint net S with variables $P_1, \ldots, P_n$. Function $P_i = F(P_1, \ldots, P_{i-1}, P_{i+1}, \ldots, P_n)$, $2 \leq i \leq n$, is called the *global solution function* with respect to S if it evaluates the actual values of P_i as the argument variables $P_1, \ldots, P_{i-1}, P_{i+1}, \ldots, P_n$ vary independently within their tolerances. Hence, P_i is globally consistent in S iff $P_i \subseteq F(P_1, \ldots, P_{i-1}, P_{i+1}, \ldots, P_n)$. Obviously, by using global solution functions instead of the local ones during local TP, global solutions with respect to S could be determined. Intuitively, S is abstracted into a single global constraint. This, however, is usually infeasible: Firstly, solving global solution functions algebraically is usually difficult or impossible. Secondly, in this way an ICSP would always have to be solved globally even if it were possible to solve it more economically by local considerations in some part of the network. Thirdly, application conditions for the global solution functions become complicated. In general, we would like to solve an ICSP in simple local parts when this is possible and use more complicated global techniques only when necessary.

One of the key ideas of this section is the observation that it suffices to determine global solution functions only with respect to some critical variables and only with respect to some subnets of the original constraint net. In this way global solutions can be determined without sacrificing all benefits of simple local reasoning. In the following it is shown which solution functions actually need to be applied during TP in order to guarantee global consistency. The technique of applying both local and other solution functions defined over larger contexts of the ICSP in the local TP Procedure 3.1 will be called *global TP*.

Theorem 5.1 shows that local consistency is not equivalent to global consistency because of the loops. A loop is a set of variables connected circularly to each other by a chain of mutually different constraints to be called the corresponding *looping constraints*. For example, the net of Fig. 5 has one loop $\{T, Y\}$ with two looping constraints. If all loop variables were globally consistent in a locally consistent situation, then the situation would also be globally consistent. It hence suffices to determine global solution functions only with respect to loop variables. Furthermore, it suffices to determine the functions only with respect to the looping constraints corresponding to the loops going through the variables, because local consistency with respect to the remaining acyclic constraints is achieved by local TP. Moreover, we do not have to consider loops that are subsets of other loops; it suffices to deal with the set of largest loops LS containing all other loops. We call such a selection of loops *loop cover*. More precisely, the agenda of solution functions in Procedure 3.1 needed for global consistency in global TP is obtained by Procedure 6.1 below.

Procedure 6.1. *Agenda for global TP.*
(1) Find the loop variables $P_1, \ldots, P_n$ of the constraint net and their loop cover LS. Let the sets of the (largest) loops going through $P_1, \ldots, P_n$ be $LS_1 \subseteq LS, \ldots, LS_n \subseteq LS$, respectively.
(2) Determine the set G_i of global solution functions for each variable P_i, $i = 1, \ldots, n$, corresponding to the loops $L \in LS_i$ (this will be explained in the text below). The solution functions for each P_i, $i = 1, \ldots, n$, in the agenda are: $G_i \cup \{$Local solution functions for P_i excluding such local functions that originate from the looping constraints corresponding to loops LS_i (i.e., loops that go through P_i)$\}$.
(3) For the non-loop variables $P_{j \neq i}$ add ordinary local solution functions into the agenda.

Determination of global solution functions

The global solution function of a variable P with respect to a loop (step (2)) can be determined in two steps:

Step A. Construct a single algebraic equation equivalent to the looping constraints of the loop by eliminating the other loop variables.

Step B. Solve P from the equation obtained in (1) algebraically, i.e., derive the global solution function.

Step B above may turn out to be difficult or impossible to perform due to limitations of algebra or the algebraic problem solver used. Furthermore, interval algebraic rules must be taken into account. We first present an example in which these problems are not severe and discuss the general case afterwards.

ICSP (5.1) (Fig. 5) has loop $\{Y, T\}$. The equations (Step A) for solving Y and T are obtained by eliminating T and Y, respectively:

$$X + (Z - Y) = Y,$$
$$X + T = Z - T.$$

The global solution functions for Y and T are solved easily in Step B:

$$Y = (X + Z)/2,$$
$$T = (Z - X)/2. \tag{6.1}$$

The agenda for global TP is obtained by Procedure 6.1 as follows.

Step 1. Loop variables are $\{Y, T\}$ and the loops going through them are $LS = \{\{Y, T\}\}$.

Step 2. The corresponding global solution functions are (6.1). Local solution functions $Y = X + T$, $Y = Z - T$, $T = Y - X$, and $T = Z - Y$ are not needed any more because they are due to the looping constraints.

Step 3. For the other variables X and Z local solution functions $X = Y - T$ and $Z = Y + T$ are used. The agenda for global TP is hence:

$$Y = (X + Z)/2, \qquad T = (Z - X)/2,$$
$$X = Y - T, \qquad Z = Y + T. \tag{6.2}$$

By this agenda one can always find the global solution. For example, (5.3) is found from the local solution (5.2).

Notice that the length of the agenda in global TP is smaller than in local propagation because for loop parameters the local functions corresponding to a loop are replaced by a single global function. However, the global solution functions are more complicated functional expressions.

In this example, global solution functions could be derived and applied easily. However, in the general case two major problems are encountered:

(1) *Algebraic limitations*. Global solution functions cannot usually be solved by algebraic means at all. This is a problem common to all algebraic reasoning systems. However, in our approach the difficulty of manipulating a network algebraically is reduced because it suffices to derive the global solution functions only with respect to the looping constraint sets corresponding to loops. Such sets are usually, although not always, smaller than the whole constraint net. Furthermore, it is possible to derive and apply only some global functions during TP depending on the limitations of the algebraic problem solver available. This would typically result in better than local but worse than global solutions. Notice also that even in cyclic ICSPs local TP sometimes finds the global solution. For example, solution $\{X := -1.25\ldots, Y := 0.38\ldots, Z := -0.48\ldots\}$ is obtained from the highly cyclic ICSP (2.3) (Fig. 2) by local TP alone.

(2) *Interval arithmetic evaluations*. In addition to algebraic equation solving

problems, numerical evaluation of interval arithmetic functions brings along some interval-specific problems.

In the following, these problems (1) and (2) are discussed in more detail and additional techniques for solving them are presented based on interval arithmetic.

6.2. Interval analysis

A key problem in global TP is how to evaluate the range of values of nested global interval solution functions $F(X_1, \ldots, X_n)$. The main difficulty here is that interval arithmetic (IA) differs from exact value arithmetic with respect to some basic algebraic laws. For example, the distributive law $I*(J+K) = I*J + I*K$ does not hold in IA but only the *subdistributivity law*:

$$I(J+K) \subseteq IJ + IK. \tag{6.3}$$

For instance:

$$[1,2]*([-1,1]+[1,2]) = [0,6]$$
$$\subseteq [1,2]*[-1,1] + [1,2]*[1,2] = [-1,6].$$

As a result, different interval extensions F of an exact value function f may evaluate different interval values with the same arguments even if F and f were equivalent in the exact value sense. If extension F evaluates the actual range of values, it is called *optimal*. Basic interval functions like (3.2) are, of course, optimal but problems arise when they are combined into more complicated nested forms, as in (6.3).

Various forms for representing and evaluating interval functions F have been developed [43]. The simplest of these is the *natural extension* that is obtained by simply replacing real variables by interval variables in the real restriction f. The natural extension is not necessarily optimal. However, it can be shown to be *inclusion monotonic*. This means, that [35, 36] if $F(X_1, \ldots, X_n)$ is a finite natural extension based on the interval variables $X_1, \ldots, X_n$ and optimal basic IA operations, then

$$X_1' \subseteq X_1, \quad X_2' \subseteq X_2, \quad \ldots, \quad X_n' \subseteq X_n$$
$$\text{implies } F(X_1', \ldots, X_n') \subseteq F(X_1, \ldots, X_n)$$

for every set of intervals $X_1, \ldots, X_n$ for which the IA operations in F are defined. Intuitively, the natural extension is guaranteed to evaluate a superset ($\subseteq$) of the actual values; by constraining argument intervals, the extension gets more constrained values, too. However, unless equality $F(X_1', \ldots, X_n') = F(X_1, \ldots, X_n)$ holds, F is not optimal. Natural extensions of global solution functions derived by using ordinary algebraic rules can therefore be applied during global TP without losing completeness or soundness of reasoning. In this way, tighter intervals are more often obtained than by pure local TP, but global consistency cannot be guaranteed unless optimal functions are used.

There is an important class of interval functions that are known to be optimal [36]:

Theorem 6.2. *If an interval function expression* $Y = F(X_1, \ldots, X_n)$ *do not have multiple instances of variables (or if the variables with multiple instances have exact values, which makes the variables constants), then F is optimal if the basic operations are defined and optimal.*

For example, the solution functions (6.2) in the earlier example do not have multiple variable instances, are optimal, and hence find the global interval solution. Theorem 6.2 has a topological interpretation: interval functions without multiple instances of variables correspond to acyclic constraint nets.

Unfortunately it is usually not possible to derive (optimal) global solution functions without multiple variable instances. In such cases the net does not necessarily (although it may) converge towards the global solution. Even worse, it is usually not even possible to derive global functions in the first place due to limitations of algebra, unless one deals only with simple algebraic equations like linear ones. However, it is always possible to determine (by eliminating the other loop variables) at least a recursive global function of form

$$X = F(\ldots, X, \ldots), \qquad (6.4)$$

where the value variable X possibly occurs one or more times in the functional expression of F. In order to determine the actual global range of X-values, deeper interval analysis is needed.

In IA, both numerical and algebraic approaches have been developed for evaluating optimal or at least more precise values for interval functions than can be obtained by the straightforward evaluation of the natural extension. These techniques can be applied to recursive functions of type (6.4), too, and are reviewed below.

6.2.1. Numerical approaches

There is a theoretically simple, always applicable way of computing the actual range of values of interval functions numerically. Assume an interval function $F(X_1, \ldots, X_k, X_{k+1}, \ldots, X_n)$, where $X_1, \ldots, X_k$ occur more than once and $X_{k+1}, \ldots, X_n$ occur only once in F. Let us divide each $X_i = [a, b]$, $i = 1, \ldots, k$, into m subintervals D_i:

$$D_i = \{[a, x_1], [x_1, x_2], \ldots, [x_{m-1}, b]\} \, .$$

Then $F(X_1, \ldots, X_k, X_{k+1}, \ldots, X_n)$ can be computed by:

$$F(X_1, \ldots, X_k, X_{k+1}, \ldots, X_n)$$
$$= \bigcup \{F(Y_1, \ldots, Y_k, X_{k+1}, \ldots, X_n) \mid Y_i \in D_i, \quad i = 1, \ldots, k\}. \tag{6.5}$$

Skelboe [46] shows that by considering $X_1, \ldots, X_k$ in smaller and smaller parts, i.e., by increasing m, arbitrarily close approximations for the actual F-value can be obtained. This technique theoretically solves the problem of computing global solution function values. However, straightforward application of (6.5) means that F should be evaluated m^k times, which is computationally expensive. A simple algorithm for reducing function evaluations in (6.5) is presented in [46], refined in [36] (here only $O(\log_2(m^k))$ function evaluations are needed), and developed further in [5]. The technique can be extended for recursive functions of form (6.4) by iterating with converging X-values until a fixed point (with some precision) is reached.

The problem with the numerical methods above, too, is inefficiency especially if F-values converge slowly, i.e., F is far from optimal. In the following, we discuss how more optimal and more quickly converging forms of $F(X_1, \ldots, X_n)$ than the natural extension can be derived.

6.2.2. *Algebraic approaches*

A central research problem in IA is: "What is the most optimal and quickly converging extension for representing an interval function?" [43]. In the general case, this question remains unanswered but several useful ways for representing interval extensions have been developed. Some of the best known forms are briefly described below:

(1) *Algebraic modifications*. The natural extension can be modified by IA laws. For example, based on the subdistributivity law (6.3) it is always useful to apply the form $I * (J + K)$ instead of $I * J + I * K$. For polynomials $y = \sum a_i x^i$, say $y = ax^3 + bx^2 + cx + d$, the corresponding extension in the Horner scheme $y = d + x(c + x(b + ax))$ usually evaluates tighter intervals (with less work, too) than the natural extension.

(2) *Mean value and Taylor forms*. Based on the mean value theorem, the extension can be represented in the mean value form [35] F_m. For a single-variable function $F(X)$ this form is $F_m(X) = f(c) + F'(X)(X - c)$ where c is the centre of X (or more generally $c \in X$). The mean value form of an n-argument function $F(X_1, \ldots, X_n)$ is defined concisely by the matrix equation

$$F_m(\mathbf{X}) = f(\mathbf{c}) + F'_i(\mathbf{X})(X_i - c_i), \quad i = 1, \ldots, n,$$

where $\mathbf{X}$ denotes vector $\langle X_1, \ldots, X_n \rangle$ and $F'_i(\mathbf{X})$ is the vector of partial derivatives of F with respect to X_i. The mean value form has been shown to be inclusion-monotonic and can be derived easily for ordinary rational and irrational expressions. Often, but not always, F_m evaluates intervals of less width than the natural extension. The mean value form is used as the basis for the iterative interval Newton method [16] that can be used in evaluating interval function ranges with arbitrary precision. The mean value form $F_m(X)$ is the order $k = 1$ case of the more general Taylor form [43] $T_k(X)$ based on the function's Taylor expansion

$$T_k(X) = f(c) + \sum_{\lambda = 1, \ldots, k-1} \frac{f^{(\lambda)}(c)}{\lambda!}(X-c)^\lambda + \frac{F^{(k)}(X)}{k!}(X-c)^k,$$

where $f^{(n)}(x)$ denotes the nth derivative of function $f(x)$. The multivariable case is analogous.

(3) *Centred forms.* The classical centred form [35] for function $F(X_1, \ldots, X_n)$ is defined by

$$F_c(X_1, \ldots, X_n) = f(c_1, \ldots, c_n) + G(X_1 - c_1, \ldots, X_n - c_n),$$

where c_i is the centre of X_i. The idea of centred forms is to shift the origin by c_i so that argument intervals fall around 0. This minimizes absolute values of interval limits, and interval functions are likely to evaluate intervals of less width. In [42, 43], general canonical representations of G for rational functions F are derived. Centred forms usually give better results than natural extensions but are not necessarily optimal or inclusion-monotonic. For example, a centred form of $f(x) = x(x-1)$ is

$$F_c(X) = c - (1 - 2c)(X - c) - (X - c)^2 \,;$$

it evaluates $[0, 0.25]$ for $X = [0, 1]$ but a larger interval $[0, 0.2925]$ for the stricter value $X = [0, 0.9]$.

Different extensions may evaluate radically different values [2]. For instance, values of the above-mentioned extensional forms of the polynomial

$$y = x^4 - 10x^3 + 35x^2 - 50x + 24 \tag{6.6}$$

with $X := [0, 4]$ are:

Extension	Value
Natural extension (6.6)	$[-816, 840]$
Horner scheme	$[-256, 384]$
Mean value form	$[-116, 116]$
Centred form	$[-24, 36]$
Actual value	$[-1, 24]$

Here none of the extensions evaluates the actual range, i.e., is optimal. The extensions are arranged in the order of increasing precision with respect to the example. Empirically, this ordering seems to hold often at least with polynomials [2] but in the general case the order may be different with different functions. Furthermore, some forms may be better with large argument intervals, some with stricter ones.

For the time being, there is no universal method for determining the most optimal extension; it may be useful to evaluate the function by different extensions and use the intersection of the results as the best approximation. The best way for determining the actual value of an interval function is to combine numerical and algebraic techniques discussed above, i.e., derive efficient extensional forms and apply the Skelboe method (or its modifications) to them. One suggested heuristic is to use the second-order Taylor form, because it is simple, can be derived easily for rational and irrational functions, and has a quadratic convergence ratio [43]. Evaluating complicated interval functions by numerical techniques is often computationally expensive. It is therefore advisable in global TP to place such functions at the end of the agenda.

The above extensional forms cannot only be applied in evaluating interval functions in one direction but also as alternative ways of representing the ICSP in the first place. In this way, it is often possible to obtain more optimal solutions with less computation by local or global propagation.

6.2.3. Application conditions

Interval arithmetical techniques discussed above assume that the real restriction of the interval function is bounded and defined within the argument intervals. In our earlier example (6.2) such assumptions held but in the general case application conditions for global TP must be formulated. In local TP, such conditions could be determined easily for basic algebraic functions due to their algebraic simplicity. Determination of the conditions for nested function expressions is slightly more complicated. For example, function

$$X = A/(B - C*D) \tag{6.7}$$

can be applied only if $0 \notin (B - C*D)$.

The application condition problem in global TP can be solved by evaluating each basic function $F(X_1, \ldots, X_n)$ in a nested expression by

$$F(D_1 \cap X_1, \ldots, D_n \cap X_n),$$

where D_i, $i = 1, \ldots, n$, is the local application space division of argument X_i, and functions are evaluated by using division arithmetic (Section 4). For example, (6.7) consists of three nested basic functions:

$$\{X = A/X_1, X_1 = B - X_2, X_2 = C*D\}. \tag{6.8}$$

Evaluation in situation $\{A := 1, B := [1, 2], C := [-1, 3], D := [-2, 0 | 0^+, 2]\}$ proceeds as follows:

$$X_2 = C * D = [-6, 6], \qquad \text{No conditions: } D_C = D_D = [-\infty, \infty],$$

$$X_1 = B - X_2 = [-5, 8], \qquad \text{No conditions: } D_B = D_{X_2} = [-\infty, \infty],$$

$$X = A/(X_1 \cap [-\infty, 0^- | 0^+, \infty]) \quad D_A = [-\infty, \infty],$$
$$= [-\infty, -1/5 | 1/8, \infty]. \qquad D_{X_1} = [-\infty, 0^- | 0^+, \infty],$$

After evaluating a nested basic function, the union operation of division arithmetic (4.9) should not be applied: more optimal results are obtained by applying it only once after evaluating the outermost function.

Also the following *solution function localization* technique could be used in function evaluation. The nested global solution function $Y = F(\cdots)$ can be represented as a constraint net S. If S is acyclic, i.e., $Y = F(\cdots)$ does not have multiple variable occurrences, then if we add the solution functions of S into the agenda and apply local TP, P will eventually have the actual interval value $F(\cdots)$. However, it suffices to add into the agenda only such local solution functions of $Y = F(\cdots)$ that correspond to its explicit nested functions. If $Y = F(\cdots)$ has multiple variable occurrences, then the problem of determining the actual Y-values can be represented recursively as an ICSP with net $Y = F(\cdots)$. In this way the problem of solving a larger ICSP globally can be reduced to a smaller ICSP if $Y = F(\cdots)$ has less constraints than the original ICSP.

In summary, current numerical IA techniques make it possible to evaluate the actual range of an interval function with arbitrary precision. This means that by evaluating the global solutions of an ICSP by such techniques, global solutions of an ICSP can be determined with arbitrary precision. How efficiently this can be done depends on the extensional forms used in representing the ICSP and its global solution functions (and the numerical evaluation algorithm used). More research is needed on computationally optimal algebraic representation of ICSPs.

7. Conclusions

Interval constraint satisfaction makes it possible to

- represent inexact and general problems in terms of intervals (divisions),
- perform computations at a more abstract level by interval functions,
- reason numerically in underconstrained situations and with inconsistent data, and
- represent inexact and generalized solutions.

The tolerance propagation approach of this paper generalizes numerical exact value propagation into interval propagation. The main semantic difference between exact value and TP approach is: In TP, the situations constitute a lattice (hierarchy) defined by the partial generality relation between them. Tolerance constraint satisfaction means determination of the least upper bound of the exact value and other tolerance solutions of the problem, i.e., their generalization. By propagating tolerances instead of exact values several of the problems of exact value systems (Section 1) can be solved: solutions of both locally and globally underconstrained problems can be determined and represented, and the type (input/output) of each variable is determined dynamically.

It is argued that the TP approach has benefits with respect to other interval schemes [8, 38–40] based on local Waltz filtering. In particular, it is shown that techniques for determining global interval solutions of arbitrary precision can be developed naturally within the global TP framework without losing all advantages of local computations. Other major contributions of this paper include mathematical formalization of the ICSP by the division lattice apparatus, development of generic application conditions for interval constraint reasoning, and further generalization of interval propagation into division propagation.

A fundamental computational question of the TP approach is how optimal the solutions need to be in a particular application, because computational demands for global solutions can be much higher than for local solutions. It is important from this practical viewpoint that in the TP approach one can trade computational costs for solution quality (optimality) and vice versa by changing solution functions used in the agenda. However, more theoretical and empirical work is needed on this trade-off in practical systems. Since global solutions are the ultimate goal of the user, methods for deriving quickly converging topological forms of constraint nets, optimal extensions for global functions, efficient numerical evaluation of interval functions, and control of global TP remain major research topics in the TP approach.

References

[1] A. Aiba, Y. Sakai, H. Sato, D. Hawley and R. Hasegawa, Constraint logic programming language CAL, in: *Proceedings International Conference on Fifth Generation Computer Systems*, Tokyo (1988) 263–276.
[2] J. Alander, On interval arithmetic range approximation methods of polynomials and rational functions, *Comput. Graph.* **9** (4) (1985) 365–372.
[3] G. Alefeld and J. Herzberger, *Introduction to Interval Computations* (Addison-Wesley, Reading, MA, 1983).
[4] J. Allen, Maintaining knowledge about temporal intervals, *Commun. ACM* **26** (1983) 832–843.
[5] N. Asaithambi, S. Zuhe and R. Moore, On computing the range of values, *Computing* **28** (1982) 225–237.
[6] J.C. Cleary, Logical arithmetic, *Future Comput. Syst.* **2** (2) (1987) 125–149.
[7] A. Colmerauer, Opening the Prolog III universe, *Byte* (August 1987) 177–182.
[8] E. Davis, Constraint propagation with interval labels, *Artif. Intell.* **32** (1987) 281–331.

[9] R. Dechter and J. Pearl, The cycle-cutset method for improving search performance in AI applications, in: *Proceedings 3rd IEEE Conference on AI Applications*, Orlando, FL (1987) 224–230.
[10] R. Dechter and J. Pearl, Network-based heuristics for constraint-satisfaction problems, *Artif. Intell.* **34** (1988) 1–38.
[11] R. Dechter and J. Pearl, Tree clustering for constraint networks, *Artif. Intell.* **38** (1989) 353–366.
[12] L. Dixon and G. Szezö, Towards a global optimization technique, in: L. Dixon and G. Szezö, eds., *Towards Global Optimization* (North-Holland, Amsterdam, 1974) 29-54.
[13] A.L. Elias, Knowledge engineering of the aircraft design process, in: J.S. Kowalik, ed., *Knowledge Based Problem Solving* (Prentice-Hall, Englewood Cliffs, NJ, 1986) 213 256.
[14] E.C. Freuder, A sufficient condition for backtrack-free search, *J. ACM* **29** (1) (1982) 24–32.
[15] J. Gosling, *Algebraic constraints*, Ph.D. Thesis, Carnegie-Mellon University, Department of Computer Science, Pittsburgh, PA (1983).
[16] E. Hansen, An overview of global optimization using interval analysis, in: R. Moore, ed., *Reliability in Computing* (Academic Press, New York, 1988) 289–307.
[17] N. Heintze, S. Michaylov and P. Stuckey, CLP(R) and some electrical engineering problems, Tech. Rept. 84, Monash University, Department of Computer Science, Clayton, Victoria, Australia (1987).
[18] G.H. Hostetter, M.S. Santina and P. D'Carpio-Montalvo, *Analytical, Numerical, and Computational Methods for Science and Engineering* (Prentice-Hall, Englewood Cliffs, NJ, 1991).
[19] E. Hyvönen, Constraint reasoning based on interval arithmetic, in: *Proceedings IJCAI-89*, Detroit, MI (1989) 1193–1198.
[20] E. Hyvönen, Application conditions for interval constraint propagation, in: *Proceedings 11th International Conference on Expert Systems and Their Applications*, Vol. 1, Avignon, France (1991) 269–282.
[21] E. Hyvönen, Constraint reasoning with incomplete knowledge: the tolerance propagation approach, Doctoral Dissertation, Technical Research Centre of Finland, VTT Publications 72, Espoo,, Finland (1991).
[22] E. Hyvönen, Global consistency in interval constraint satisfaction, in: B. Mayoh, ed., *Proceedings 3rd Scandinavian Conference on Artificial Intelligence* (IOS Press, Amsterdam, 1991) 241–251.
[23] E. Hyvönen, Interval constraint spreadsheets for financial planning, in: *Proceedings First International Conference on Artificial Intelligence Applications on Wall Street* (IEEE Press, New York, 1991).
[24] E. Hyvönen, Solution abstraction in logical problem solving, in: *Working notes of the AAAI-92 Workshop on Approximation and Abstraction of Computational Theories*, San Jose, CA (1992).
[25] J. Jaffar and J.-L. Lassez, Constraint logic programming, in: *Proceedings Fourteenth Conference on Principles of Programming Languages (POPL-87)*, Munich, Germany (1987) 111–119.
[26] J. Jaffar and J.-L. Lassez, Constraint logic programming, Tech. Rept., Monash University, Department of Computer Science, Clayton, Victoria, Australia (1986).
[27] J. Jaffar and S. Michaylov, Methodology and implementation of a CLP system, in: *Proceedings Fourth International Conference on Logic Programming*, Melbourne, Victoria, Australia (1987).
[28] M. Konopasek and S. Jayaraman, *The TK!Solver Book* (McGraw-Hill, Berkeley, CA, 1984).
[29] C. Lassez, Constraint logic programming, *Byte* (August 1987) 171–176.
[30] C. Lassez, K. McAloon and R. Yap, Constraint logic programming and option trading, *IEEE Expert* **2** (3) (1987) 42–50.
[31] W. Leler, *Constraint Programming Languages: Their Specification and Generation* (Addison-Wesley, Reading, MA, 1988).
[32] A.K. Mackworth, Constraint satisfaction, in: S.C. Shapiro, ed., *Encyclopedia of Artificial Intelligence*, Vol. 1 (Wiley, New York, 1987) 205–211.
[33] A.K. Mackworth and E.C. Freuder, The complexity of some polynomial network consistency algorithms for constraint satisfaction problems, *Artif. Intell.* **25** (1985) 65–74.

[34] P. Meseguer, Constraint satisfaction problems: an overview, *AI Commun.* **2** (1) (1989) 3–17.
[35] R.E. Moore, *Interval Arithmetic* (Prentice-Hall, Englewood Cliffs, NJ, 1966).
[36] R.E. Moore, *Methods and Applications of Interval Analysis*, SIAM Studies in Applied Mathematics (SIAM, Philadelphia, PA, 1979).
[37] N.J. Nilsson, Probabilistic logic, *Artif. Intell.* **28** (1986) 71–87.
[38] W. Older, Interval arithmetic specification, Working Paper, Bell-Northern Research, Computing Research Laboratory, Ottawa, Ont. (1989).
[39] W. Older and A. Vellino, Extending Prolog with constraint arithmetic on real intervals, in: *Proceedings Canadian Conference on Electrical and Computer Engineering* (1990).
[40] W. Older and A. Vellino, Constraint arithmetic on real intervals, in: F. Benhamou and A. Colmerauer, eds., *Constraint Logic Programming*, *Collected Papers* (MIT Press, Cambridge, MA, to appear).
[41] J.R. Quinlan, Inferno: a cautious approach to uncertain inference, *Comput. J.* **26** (3) (1983) 255–269.
[42] H. Ratscheck, Centred forms, *SIAM J. Numer. Anal.* **17** (3) (1980) 333–337.
[43] H. Ratscheck and J. Rokne, *Computer Methods for the Range of Functions* (Ellis Horwood, Chichester, UK, 1984).
[44] G. Shafer, *A Mathematical Theory of Evidence* (Princeton University Press, Princeton, NJ, 1976).
[45] G. Shafer and J. Pearl, eds., *Uncertain Reasoning* (Morgan Kaufmann, Los Altos, CA, 1990).
[46] S. Skelboe, Computation of rational interval functions, *BIT* **14** (1) (1974) 87–95.
[47] P.A. Stark, *Introduction to Numerical Methods* (Collier-Macmillan, Toronto, Ont., 1970).
[48] G.L. Steele, The definition and implementation of a computer programming language based on constraints, Ph.D. Thesis, MIT, Department of Electrical Engineering and Computer Science, Cambridge, MA (1980).
[49] P. Van Hentenryck, *Constraint Satisfaction in Logic Programming* (MIT Press, Cambridge, MA, 1989).
[50] D. Waltz, Understanding line drawings of scenes with shadows, in: P.H. Winston, ed., *The Psychology of Computer Vision* (McGraw-Hill, New York, 1975) 19–91.
[51] A. Ward, T. Lozano-Pérez and W. Seering, Extending the constraint propagation of intervals, in: *Proceedings IJCAI-89*, Detroit, MI (1989) 1453–1458.
[52] S. Wolfram, *Mathematica: A System for Doing Mathematics by Computer* (Addison-Wesley, Reading, MA, 1988).

ARTINT 951

Constraint satisfaction using constraint logic programming

Pascal Van Hentenryck

Brown University, Box 1910, Providence, RI 02912, USA

Helmut Simonis and Mehmet Dincbas

Cosytec, Parc Club Orsay-University, 4, rue Jean-Rostand, 91893 Orsay Cedex, France

Abstract

Van Hentenryck, P., H. Simonis and M. Dincbas, Constraint satisfaction using constraint logic programming, Artificial Intelligence 58 (1992) 113–159.

Constraint logic programming (CLP) is a new class of declarative programming languages whose primitive operations are based on constraints (e.g. constraint solving and constraint entailment). CLP languages naturally combine constraint propagation with nondeterministic choices. As a consequence, they are particularly appropriate for solving a variety of combinatorial search problems, using the global search paradigm, with short development time and efficiency comparable to procedural tools based on the same approach. In this paper, we describe how the CLP language cc(FD), a successor of CHIP using consistency techniques over finite domains, can be used to solve two practical applications: test-pattern generation and car sequencing. For both applications, we present the cc(FD) program, describe how constraint solving is performed, report experimental results, and compare the approach with existing tools.

1. Introduction

The purpose of our research is to support, within constraint programming languages, computational paradigms underlying combinatorial search problems. It is motivated by the hope of reducing significantly the develop-

Correspondence to: P. Van Hentenryck, Brown University, Department of Computer Science, 115 Waterman St., 4th floor, Providence, RI 02906, USA. E-mail: pvh@cs.brown.edu.

0004-3702/92/$05.00 © 1992 — Elsevier Science Publishers B.V. All rights reserved

ment time of these applications while preserving most of the efficiency of procedural languages.

Combinatorial problems are ubiquitous in computer science. They appear in areas as diverse as operations research (e.g. scheduling), hardware design (e.g. circuit verification), biology (e.g. DNA sequencing), finance (e.g. option trading), and software design (e.g. simulation and testing of protocols), to name a few. Many of these problems are of high complexity (NP-complete or worse), which means that there is no efficient algorithm for solving them. Much research, however, has been spent on designing algorithms to tackle these problems and one of the interesting outcomes has been the development of constraint solving algorithms for various classes of problems.

Constraint programming has a long tradition in artificial intelligence. It can be traced back to the use of constraints in Sutherland's SKETCHPAD [67], the CONSTRAINT programming language of Sussman and Steele [66] and the work of Borning on ThingLab [2] among others. Mackworth also advocated, as early as 1977, the use of consistency techniques (a paradigm emerging from artificial intelligence to solve combinatorial search problems) in declarative languages as an alternative to chronological backtracking [42]. Constraint processing itself has also been present in many systems related to constraint solving such as REF-ARF [23], Alice [40], (assumption-based) truth maintenance systems (e.g. [15,21]), and various scheduling and planning systems (e.g. [24]).

The starting point of our research was, however, slightly different. We began by recognizing that logic programming is an appropriate language for stating combinatorial search problems: its relational form makes it easy to state constraints while its (don't-know) nondeterminism removes the need for programming a search procedure. Unfortunately, traditional logic programming languages can also be very inefficient when presented with a natural formulation of combinatorial search problems, largely because of their passive use of constraints to test potential values instead of pruning the search space in an active manner [27]. As a consequence, traditional logic programming languages (e.g. Prolog) often lead to "generate and test" or "standard backtracking" approaches that exhibit the pathological behavior known as thrashing [42].

Early (CLP) languages such as CHIP [20], CLP($\mathcal{R}$) [37], Prolog II [13], and Prolog III [12] attempted to preserve the advantages of logic programming while removing their limitations. The fundamental idea behind these languages, to use constraint solving instead of unification as the kernel operation of the language, was elegantly captured in the CLP scheme [36]. The CLP scheme defines a family of programming languages based on constraint solving and sharing the same semantic properties. It can be instantiated to produce a specific language by defining a constraint system (i.e. defining a set of primitive constraints and providing a constraint solver for the constraints). Thus CHIP contains constraint systems over finite domains [72], Booleans [6], and rational numbers [30,74], Prolog III is endowed with constraint systems over Booleans, rational numbers, and lists, while CLP($\mathcal{R}$) solves constraints over real numbers. The CLP scheme was further generalized into the cc framework of concurrent constraint programming [54–56] to accommodate additional constraint operations (e.g. constraint entailment [43]) and new ways of combining them (e.g. implication or blocking ask [54] and cardinality [73]). More precisely, the cc framework accommodates all operations on constraints that can be defined as closure operators. The generalization significantly extends the scope of CLP languages by enabling issues such as concurrency, control, and extensibility to be addressed at the language level.

CLP languages[1] support, in a declarative way, the solving of combinatorial search problems using the global search paradigm. The global search paradigm amounts to recursively dividing a problem into subproblems until the subproblems are simple enough to be solved in a straightforward way, and includes, as special cases, implicit enumeration, branch and bound, and constraint satisfaction. It is best contrasted with the local search paradigm, which proceeds by modifying an initial configuration locally until a solution is obtained. These approaches are orthogonal and complementary. The global search paradigm has been used successfully to solve a large variety of combinatorial search problems with reasonable efficiency (e.g. scheduling [7], graph coloring [39], Hamiltonian circuits [9], and microcode labeling [19]) and provides, at the same time, the basis for exact methods as well as approximate solutions (giving rise to the so-called "anytime algorithms" [14]).

The purpose of this paper is to illustrate how CLP languages can be used to solve two practical combinatorial search problems: test-pattern generation and car sequencing. Test-pattern generation is a standard problem in hardware design and many algorithms have been proposed for the task. We show how to use constraint logic programming to design a simple algorithm whose behavior is similar in spirit to some of the best algorithms for the task and whose efficiency is competitive with specialized implementations of these algorithms. The second problem, car sequencing, was motivated by its presentation as a challenge for AI tools [48,49]. We propose a solution to this problem that can be described concisely in constraint logic programming and whose efficiency enables to solve large instances.

The CLP language used in the above problems is cc(FD), an instance of the cc framework over finite domains that is best seen as a successor to the

---

[1] In the following, we use the term *CLP languages* generically to denote both CLP and cc languages.

finite-domain part of CHIP. Both languages support the use of consistency techniques and local propagation in conjunction with don't-know nondeterminism approximated by backtracking. In addition, they support depth-first branch and bound for combinatorial optimization problems. The novel aspects of cc(FD) include the definition of new general-purpose combinators (such as cardinality, implication, constructive disjunction, and indexical constraints) and the availability of constraint entailment and constraint generalization as primitive operations on constraints. cc(FD) generalizes in an elegant way (and thus makes unnecessary) several features and constraints of CHIP that were difficult to justify theoretically. As a consequence, it provides additional operational expressiveness, flexibility, and efficiency and lets us tackle problems such as disjunctions of constraints and the definition of primitive constraints. Preliminary solutions of the two problems described here were first expressed in CHIP (see [60] and [18]). The presentation proposed in this paper subsumes them, both in the algorithmic methods, which are more advanced, and in the statement, which is simpler, more natural, and based on a solid theoretical foundation.

The rest of the paper is organized as follows. Section 2 presents a tutorial overview of cc(FD). Since the focus here is on applications, this overview is limited to those aspects of direct relevance to the two problems considered. Important combinators such as constructive disjunctions and indexical constraints are omitted here but can be found in [75]. Sections 3 and 4 present respectively the test generation and car sequencing problems. For each application, we describe in detail how the problem can be stated and how constraint solving is performed and we also report a number of experimental results and comparisons. Section 5 contains our conclusions.

2. Overview of cc(FD)

Here we give an informal overview of the relevant parts of cc(FD). A more formal presentation, following the style of operational semantics in [54], is given in the appendix.

Our overview proceeds in several steps. Section 2.1 sketches the syntax of the language and Section 2.2 introduces the CLP scheme. Sections 2.3, 2.4, and 2.5 discuss constraint entailment, the implication combinator, and the cardinality combinator, and Section 2.6 discusses the details of constraint solving in cc(FD). Note that the presentation separates the generic aspects of the language from the details of its constraint solver. This indicates that the combinators are general-purpose.

2.1. Syntax

Figure 1 shows an outline of the syntax of a cc(FD) program. A cc(FD)

```
Program    ::=   Clauses
Clauses    ::=   Head :- Body | Clauses Clauses
Head       ::=   Atom
Goal       ::=   Atom
Body       ::=   true | Goal | c | Body ,
                 Body | c → Body | #(l,u,[c_1,...,c_n])
```

Fig. 1. An outline of the syntax.

```
p(X,Y,X) :-
  X ∈ {0,...,10}, Y ∈ {0,...,10}, Z ∈ {0,...,10},
  X ⩾ Z + 3,
  Y ⩽ Z,
  q(X,Y,Z).
q(X,Y,Z) :-
  r(X,Y).
q(X,Y,Z) :-
  Z ⩾ Y + 2.
r(X,Y) :-
  X ⩽ Y + 2.
```

Fig. 2. A simple program.

is a set of clauses in which each clause has a head and a body. A head is an atom, i.e. an expression of the form $p(t_1,...,t_n)$ where $t_1,...,t_n$ are terms. A term is a variable (e.g. X) or a function symbol of arity n applied to n terms (e.g. f(X,g(Y))). A body is either true (the empty body), a goal (procedure call), a constraint (constraint solving), an implication, or a cardinality combinator. In this paper, variables are denoted by uppercase letters, constraints by the letter c, conjunctions of constraints by the letter σ, terms by letters t and s, atoms by letters H and B, goals by the letter G, and integers by the letters l, u, and v, all possibly subscripted or superscripted. We also use $\mathcal{C}$ to denote a constraint system and D, possibly subscripted, to denote a finite domain. To illustrate the operational semantics of (part of) cc(FD), we use the simple program depicted in Fig. 2.

2.2. The CLP scheme

At least from a conceptual standpoint, the operational semantics of the CLP scheme is a simple generalization of the semantics of logic programming. It can be described as a goal-directed derivation procedure from the initial goal using the program clauses. A *computation state* is best described by

(1) a *goal part*: the conjunction of goals to be solved;
(2) a *constraint store*: the set of constraints accumulated so far.

Initially the constraint store is empty and the goal part is the initial goal. In the following, we denote the computation state by pairs $\langle G \square \sigma \rangle$, where G is the goal part and σ is the constraint store. We use ε to denote an empty goal part or constraint store. An example computation state is

$$\langle q(X,Y,Z) \square X,Y,Z \in \{0,\ldots,10\} \ \& \ X \geq Z + 3 \ \& \ Y \leq Z \rangle.$$

A *computation step* (i.e. the transition from one computation state to another) can be of two types depending upon the selection of an atom or a constraint in the goal part. In the first case, a computation step amounts to

(1) selecting an atom in the goal part;
(2) finding a clause that can be used to resolve the atom; this clause must have the same predicate symbol as the atom, and the equality constraints between the goal and head arguments must be consistent with the constraint store;
(3) defining the new computation state as the old one where the selected atom has been replaced by the body of the clause and the equality constraints have been added to the constraint store.

In the second case, a computation step amounts to

(1) selecting a constraint in the goal part that can be satisfied with the constraint store;
(2) defining the new computation state as the old one where the selected constraint has been removed from the goal part and added to the constraint store.

For instance, given a computation state

$$\langle q(X,Y,Z) \square X,Y,Z \in \{0,\ldots,10\} \ \& \ X \geq Z + 3 \ \& \ Y \leq Z \rangle$$

a computation step can be performed using the second clause of q (see Fig. 2) to obtain a new computation state

$$\langle Z \geq Y + 2 \square X,Y,Z \in \{0,\ldots,10\} \ \& \ X \geq Z + 3 \ \& \ Y \leq Z \rangle.$$

Another computation step leads to the configuration

$$\langle \varepsilon \square X,Y,Z \in \{0,\ldots,10\} \ \& \ X \geq Z + 3 \ \& \ Y \leq Z \ \& \ Z \geq Y + 2 \rangle,$$

since the resulting constraint store is satisfiable. Note that, strictly speaking, equations should have appeared between the variables in the above example; they were omitted for clarity, since the variables have the same names in the program.

As should be clear, the basic operation of the language amounts to deciding the satisfiability of a conjunction of constraints. Note also that each computation state has a satisfiable constraint store. This property is exploited inside CLP languages to avoid solving the satisfiability problem from scratch at each step. Instead, CLP languages keep a reduced (e.g. solved) form of the constraints and transform the existing solution into a solution including the new constraints. Hence the constraint solver is made incremental. For instance, the last constraint store may be represented as

$$\langle \varepsilon \square\ X \in \{5,\ldots,10\}\ \&\ Y \in \{0,\ldots,5\}\ \&\ Z \in \{2,\ldots,7\}\ \&\ X \geq Z + 3\ \&\ Y \leq Z\ \&\ Z \geq Y + 2 \rangle.$$

A computation state is *terminal* if

- the goal part is empty;
- no clause can be applied to the selected atom to produce a new computation state or the selected constraint cannot be satisfied with the constraint store.

A *computation* is simply a sequence of computation steps that either ends in a terminal computation state or diverges. A finite computation is *successful* if the final computation state has an empty goal, and *fails* otherwise.

To illustrate computations in a CLP language, consider our simple program again. The program has only one successful computation, namely

$$\langle \mathtt{p(X,Y,Z)}\ \square\ \varepsilon \rangle$$
$$\downarrow \text{ (selecting the first constraint)}$$
$$\ldots$$
$$\downarrow \text{ (selecting the last constraint)}$$
$$\langle \mathtt{q(X,Y,Z)}\ \square\ X,Y,Z \in \{0,\ldots,10\}\ \&\ X \geq Z + 3\ \&\ Y \leq Z \rangle$$
$$\downarrow \text{ (using the second clause of q)}$$
$$\langle Z \geq Y + 2\ \square\ X,Y,Z \in \{0,\ldots,10\}\ \&\ X \geq Z + 3\ \&\ Y \leq Z \rangle$$
$$\downarrow \text{ (selecting the constraint)}$$
$$\langle \varepsilon\ \square\ X,Y,Z \in \{0,\ldots,10\}\ \&\ X \geq Z + 3\ \&\ Y \leq Z\ \&\ Z \geq Y + 2 \rangle$$

The program has also one failed computation:

⟨p(X,Y,Z) □ ε⟩

　↓ (selecting the first constraint)

...

　↓ (selecting the last constraint)

⟨q(X,Y,Z) □ X,Y,Z ∈ {0,...,10} & X ⩾ Z + 3 & Y ⩽ Z⟩

　↓ (using the first clause of q)

⟨r(X,Y,Z) □ X,Y,Z ∈ {0,...,10} & X ⩾ Z + 3 & Y ⩽ Z⟩

　↓ (using the clause of r)

⟨X ⩽ Y + 2 □ X,Y,Z ∈ {0,...,10} & X ⩾ Z + 3 & Y ⩽ Z⟩.

The last computation state is terminal since the conjunction of constraints

$$X \geqslant Z + 3 \ \& \ Y \leqslant Z \ \& \ X \leqslant Y + 2$$

is not satisfiable.

Note that the results of the computation are the constraint stores of the successful computations. Also, nothing has been said so far on the strategy used to explore the space of computations. Most CLP languages use a computation model similar to Prolog: atoms are selected from left to right in the clauses, clauses are tried in textual order, and the search space is explored in a depth-first manner with chronological backtracking in case of failures.[2] For instance, on the simple program, a CLP language typically uses the first clause for p, then the first clause for q, and finally encounters a failure when trying to solve r. Execution then backtracks to the second clause of q, giving the successful computation.

2.3. Constraint entailment

As mentioned previously, the cc framework considers other operations on constraints beyond constraint solving as well as additional ways of combining them. An important operation on constraints is *constraint entailment*, which amounts to finding out if a single constraint is implied by a conjunction of constraints, i.e.

$$\mathcal{C} \models (\forall)(\sigma \rightarrow c).$$

Constraint entailment was introduced in the context of concurrent logic programming (e.g. [58]) by Maher [43] to endow these languages with a logical semantics. It can be viewed as well as a generalization of languages allowing coroutining and delay mechanisms (e.g. [10,13,17,28,47]), and is

---

[2] We see below that the additional combinators of cc(FD) permit more sophisticated search procedures.

one of the cornerstones of the cc framework, where it is used to synchronize concurrently executing agents. It was also used in CHIP (see [20,31]) inside the if_then_else construct and was instrumental in simulating hybrid circuits. Its interest for CLP languages lies in the opportunity it gives to reason about the constraints and to use the information gained in pruning. As we will see, it can be used to express non-primitive constraints following general principles from artificial intelligence and operations research.

Both implication and cardinality, the two cc(FD) combinators used in our applications, make use of constraint entailment. The implication combinator was introduced in [54] in the context of concurrent logic programming, while the cardinality combinator was proposed explicitly for CLP languages in [73].

2.4. The implication combinator

Motivation

Local propagation is one of the key ideas behind constraint programming languages such as CONSTRAINTS [66] and ThingLab [2]. Local propagation (or value propagation) amounts to deducing values for some variables from those of other variables. For instance, an "and-gate" in a digital circuit may be defined by rules of the form

"If one input is 0 then the output is 0",
"If the output is 1 then the inputs are both 1".

To implement a program achieving this form of propagation, it is necessary to introduce a form of data-driven computation in which goals are suspended when not enough information is available and reactivated when new information allows them to be reconsidered. The purpose of the implication combinator for CLP languages is to achieve this form of behavior, to generalize it to any constraint system, and to combine it with nondeterministic choice.

Description

As mentioned previously, the implication combinator has the form $c \rightarrow A$ where c is a constraint and A is a body. Its declarative semantics is simply given by logical implication.

The main originality of the implication combinator lies in its operational semantics. The implication $c \rightarrow A$ ensures that A is executed only when (and as soon as) c is entailed by the constraint store. In other words, if c is entailed by the constraint store, $c \rightarrow A$ reduces to A. If $\neg c$ is entailed by the constraint store, $c \rightarrow A$ reduces to *true*. Otherwise, the computation blocks, waiting for more information.

Consider again the description of an and-gate using local propagation techniques:

```
and(X,Y,Z) :-
  X = 0 → Z = 0,
  Y = 0 → Z = 0,
  Z = 1 → (X = 1 , Y = 1),
  X = 1 → Y = Z,
  Y = 1 → X = Z,
  X = Y → X = Z.
```

The first rule says that, as soon as the constraint store entails X = 0, the constraint Z = 0 must be added to the constraint store. Note that the last three rules actually do more than local value propagation; they also propagate symbolic equalities and one of them is conditional to a symbolic equality. Now the goal ⟨and(X,Y,Z) □ X = 0⟩ produces a constraint store X = 0 & Z = 0, since the goal ⟨X = 0 → Z = 0 □ X = 0⟩ reduces to ⟨Z = 0 □ X = 0⟩ and hence to the constraint store X = 0 & Z = 0. However the goal ⟨and(X,Y,Z) □ ε⟩ does not modify the constraint store, since none of the constraints in the implication constructs are entailed by the constraint store.

As mentioned previously, a goal that is blocked can be resumed when new information become available in the constraint store. Assume for instance the computation state

⟨X = 0 → Z = 0 , T = 0 → X = 0 □ T = 0⟩.

The first goal X = 0 → Z = 0 blocks since X = 0 is not entailed by the constraint store. But the second goal can be executed, leading eventually to the computation state

⟨X = 0 → Z = 0 □ X = 0 & T = 0⟩.

Now X = 0 is entailed by the constraint store and hence the first implication can be executed. The final constraint store will be X = 0 & T = 0 & Z = 0.

Now consider building a full-adder using logical gates:

```
fa(X,Y,Cin,S,C) :-
  and(X,Y,C1),
  xor(X,Y,S1),
  and(Cin,S1,C2),
  xor(Cin,S1,S),
  or(C1,C2,C).
```

In the above circuit, X and Y are two input bits, Cin is the carry-in, S is the result bit, and C is the carry-out. If we use the implication combinator to define all logical gates, the query fa(X,Y,1,S,0) produces the constraint store

```
X = 0 & Y = 0 & S = 1.
```

The reason is the following. Since the result of the or-gate is 0, its two inputs C1 and C2 must be 0. Since the second and-gate has output C2 equal to 0 and input Cin equal to 1, it follows that S1 must be 0, which implies that X and Y must be equal because of the first xor-gate. Since X and Y appear both as inputs in the same and-gate, they must be equal to its output C1, which is 0.

The implication combinator thus introduces a notion of coroutining between goals in the language, and the execution of goals can be interleaved in complex ways. Note that the goals synchronize by "asking" if some constraints are entailed by the constraint store and that a suspended goal can be resumed by a modification of the constraint store by other goals. Moreover, the implication combinator is not restricted to simple constraints, as illustrated above, but allows arbitrary constraints of the language.

2.5. The cardinality combinator

Motivation

The cardinality combinator is a declarative and relational operator, intended for the handling of general forms of disjunctions which often occur in practical applications. It can be used to enforce arc-consistency on any arbitrary finite-domain constraints (within the complexity bound of the optimal algorithm of [44]) but, as should be clear from the presentation, it is not limited to finite-domain constraints. The cardinality has been used in numerous applications including scheduling, assignment, Hamiltonian circuit, and warehouse location problems. It will be important in the car sequencing application.

Before entering into the description of the combinator, let us give an example to motivate the reader. Consider, for instance, a scheduling problem and assume that we face a disjunctive constraint between two tasks, i.e. the execution of the two tasks cannot overlap. Assume that S1 and S2 represent the starting dates of the tasks and D1 and D2 their durations, the constraint can be expressed as

```
disjunctive(S1,D1,S2,D2) :-
  S1 + D1 ⩽ S2.
disjunctive(S1,D1,S2,D2) :-
  S2 + D2 ⩽ S1.
```

Unfortunately the above constraint is nondeterministic and introduces choice points during the execution. The first alternative, i.e. the second task is scheduled after the first task, will be selected and its constraint will be added to the constraint store. Subsequent execution may lead to a failure and require this choice to be reconsidered. The second alternative, i.e. the first task is scheduled after the second task, will then be considered. In general, it is better to postpone choices as long as possible. The above constraint can be used in two ways to achieve pruning: (1) if the maximal start date of S2 is smaller than the minimal start date of S1 added to D1, then the second task cannot be scheduled after the first task and (2) if the maximal start date of S1 is smaller than the minimal start date of S2 added to D2, then the first task cannot be scheduled after the second task. The cardinality combinator enables us to express this pruning in a natural way.

Description

As mentioned previously, the cardinality combinator has the form

$$\#(l, u, [c_1, \ldots, c_n])$$

where l and u are integers and $c_1, \ldots, c_n$ are constraints.

The declarative semantics is given as follows. $\#(l, u, [c_1, \ldots, c_n])$ is true iff the number of constraints c_i ($1 \leq i \leq n$) satisfiable is not less than l and not more than u. It is false otherwise.

Note that this combinator is quite expressive. A conjunction $c_1 \wedge \cdots \wedge c_n$ can be expressed as $\#(n, *, [c_1, \cdots, c_n])$ where $*$ is a don't-care value, a disjunction $c_1 \vee \cdots \vee c_n$ as $\#(1, *, [c_1, \ldots, c_n])$, and a negation $\neg c$ as $\#(*, 0, [c])$. Other connectives such as equivalence $\Leftrightarrow$ can now be obtained easily. In the applications, we feel free to use the logical operators instead of the cardinality combinator when convenient.

Using the cardinality combinator, the disjunctive constraint can be implemented as follows:

```
disjunction(S1,D1,S2,D2) :-
    #(1,*,[S1 + D1 ≤ S2, S2 + D2 ≤ S1]).
```

Once again, the main interest of the cardinality combinator lies in its operational semantics. The combinator implements a principle well known in operations research and artificial intelligence: "infer simple constraints from difficult ones". The intuitive idea is to make sure that the cardinality combinator can be satisfied in some way. Moreover, if there is only one way to satisfy it, then the constraints necessary to satisfy it are introduced in the constraint store. Constraint entailment is used to check if there is a way to satisfy the constraint. In the disjunctive example, the system makes sure that either the first task can be scheduled before the second one or the second task can be scheduled before the first one (or both). If the constraint store makes it impossible to schedule the first task before the second, then a constraint forcing the second task to be scheduled first is added to the constraint store.

Consider a simple example:

```
⟨#(1,2,[X=4, Y=10]) & X>6 □ ε⟩
        ↓
⟨#(1,2,[X=4, Y=10]) □ X>6⟩
        ↓
⟨#(1,2,[Y=10]) □ X>6⟩
        ↓
X>6 & Y=10
```

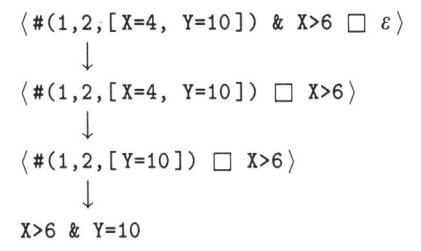

This example contains a cardinality combinator requiring that X = 4 or Y = 10 be true. Initially neither these two constraints nor their negations are entailed by the constraint store, so the execution of the cardinality combinator blocks. The second goal X > 6 is selected, which implies that X ≠ 4 is entailed by the constraint store. There is now only one way to satisfy the cardinality combinator, i.e. adding the constraint Y = 10 to the constraint store.

The cardinality combinator can be used to enforce arc-consistency on any binary constraint in time $O(ed^2)$, where e is the number of constraints and d is the size of the largest domain. Given a constraint $c(X, Y)$ with $X \in D_x$ and $Y \in D_y$, it is sufficient to generate for each value $v \in D_x$ a constraint of the form

$$X = v \Leftrightarrow Y \in D$$

where $D = \{w \in D_y \mid c(v, w)\}$ and vice versa for Y. The equivalence can be rewritten easily into two cardinality formulas. The optimal bounds of Mohr and Henderson [44] can be obtained by using counters to implement cardinality and entailment.

2.6. Constraint system

Here we give an informal presentation of the constraint part of cc(FD).

Syntax

Definition 2.1. An arithmetic term is defined inductively as follows:
(1) A variable is an arithmetic term.
(2) A natural number is an arithmetic term.
(3) $t_1 + t_2$, $t_1 * t_2$, and $t_1 - t_2$ are arithmetic terms if t_1 and t_2 are arithmetic terms.

The primitive constraints of the language are as follows:

Definition 2.2. A primitive constraint in cc(FD) can be of two forms:
(1) $x \; \delta_1 \; \{v_1, \ldots, v_n\}$;
(2) $t_1 \; \delta_2 \; t_2$,

where x is a variable, $v_1, \ldots, v_n$ are natural numbers, $\delta_1 \in \{\in, \notin\}$, t_1 and t_2 are arithmetic terms, and $\delta_2 \in \{>, \geq, =, \neq, \leq, <\}$. Constraints of the first type are called domain and non-membership constraints respectively, while constraints of the second type are called arithmetic constraints.

Note that in cc(FD) each variable appearing in an arithmetic constraint must also occur in a domain constraint.

Constraint solving

There are various ways of implementing a constraint solver for the above constraints. Since the problem is decidable (because all variables must appear in a domain constraint), a decision procedure is possible for consistency and entailment. However, a complete constraint solver would necessarily require exponential time (unless P = NP). The approach taken in cc(FD) (and in CHIP as well) is to use consistency techniques instead and amounts to replacing constraint solving by arc-consistency and constraint entailment by arc-entailment.

Definition 2.3. A constraint $c(x_1, \ldots, x_n)$ is *arc-consistent* with respect to $D_1, \ldots, D_n$ if, for each variable x_i and value $v_i \in D_i$, there exist values $v_1, \ldots, v_{i-1}, v_{i+1}, \ldots, v_n$ in $D_1, \ldots, D_{i-1}, D_{i+1}, \ldots, D_n$ such that $c(v_1, \ldots, v_n)$ holds.

A set of constraints is arc-consistent with respect to a set of domains for its variables iff all constraints are arc-consistent with respect to the domains.

Definition 2.4. A constraint $c(x_1, \ldots, x_n)$ is *arc-entailed* by $D_1, \ldots, D_n$ iff, for all values $v_1, \ldots, v_n$ in $D_1, \ldots, D_n$, $c(x_1, \ldots, x_n)$ holds.

The operational semantics of the parts of cc(FD) presented in this paper can be understood informally as an instance of the generic scheme presented earlier in which consistency is replaced by the weaker notion of arc-consistency and entailment by the weaker notion of arc-entailment. Enforcing arc-consistency does not in general produce a decision procedure (see [16] however for subclasses having that property). In conjunction with nondeterminism, it produces the kind of languages advocated in [42]. Arc-consistency algorithms have been intensively studied [42,44,45,77] but with the primitive constraints considered in cc(FD), more efficient algorithms can be exhibited. For instance, with binary constraints, arc-consistency can be enforced in $O(ed)$ where e is the number of constraints and d is the size of the largest domain [16].

A formal semantics of cc(FD) in terms of the cc framework requires decision algorithms for constraint solving and entailment. The key idea is to divide the primitive constraints into two classes: (1) basic constraints (those allowing an efficient decision procedure) and (2) non-basic constraints defined in terms of the combinators.[3] The main benefit of investigating the formal semantics has been the identification of a number of new combinators (e.g. constructive disjunction and indexical constraints) that support, at the language level, pruning principles previously hidden in the implementation.

3. Test-pattern generation

The first application we consider is in the field of digital circuit design: automatic test-pattern generation (ATPG). Problems from circuit design are useful in evaluating general problem solving techniques, since many special-purpose methods have been developed in this area and different approaches can be compared, using widely available benchmarks. CLP in general, and CHIP in particular, have been applied to a number of problems from digital circuit design, including formal verification [65], diagnosis [63], synthesis [64] as well as simulation of hybrid circuits [31]. The use of CLP for test generation has been discussed before [59,60,62]. The method described here is based on [61]. We show that cc(FD) allows a simple and declarative formulation of test generation as a constraint satisfaction problem. Moreover, by using the implication operator to define demons, it is possible to design an efficient test generation algorithm that requires only a fraction of the development effort necessary with conventional approaches.

3.1. Problem statement

VLSI chips are produced by complex processes in which errors can arise, hence only a certain percentage of chips will be error free. This *yield* varies with different circuit types and processes, but can be as low as a few percent for a new fabrication process. The manufacturer, on the other hand, wants to sell chips with a low *defect level*, i.e. a low percentage of faulty chips passing quality control. *Test generation* is the process of defining the tests to apply to a circuit in order to detects faults. Williams [78] has presented a model expressing the defect level as a function of yield and *fault coverage*, the percentage of all faults detected by testing. This model makes clear the necessity of finding a very high percentage of all faults in order to obtain a low defect level for a process with a low yield.

---

[3]These constraints need not be considered primitive constraints in the language, since they can be defined at the language level.

3.1.1. Fault models

Since many different physical failures can occur in a circuit, the only way to test for all possible faults is to test all circuit behaviors over time, which is clearly impractical. The principal idea of *structural testing* is to use knowledge about the structure of a circuit and the underlying technology to limit the number of cases we have to consider. There have been many attempts to describe what types of faults can occur in different technologies [1]. One of the earliest and still widely used fault models is the "stuck-at" model. This assumes that all faults lead to the situation where some signal in a circuit is permanently set to "1" or "0". The signal is then said to be "stuck-at 1" (sa1) or "stuck-at 0" (sa0). This fault model covers many, though not all, device faults inside a VLSI circuit. It has been shown that a test set that detects all single stuck-at faults also covers many other faults (with the exception of time-sensitive faults). Most test generation systems restrict themselves to the detection of single stuck-at faults at the logical gate level. We will use this model and, in the rest of the section, *fault coverage* should be understood as the percentage of all detected single stuck-at errors.

Note also that testing for stuck-at faults in a circuit does not require generating tests for each fault, as some faults are *covered* by other faults [51]. For instance, testing the output of an and-gate for sa0 automatically tests the gate inputs for sa0. We can easily generate this more interesting *collapsed fault set* in a preprocessing step.

3.1.2. Test generation and fault simulation

The ATPG problem is conceptually split into two subproblems: *test generation* and *fault simulation*. *Test generation* entails finding a test that detects a certain fault for some component inside the circuit; *fault simulation* detects which faults are covered by a particular pattern. Often the two parts are intertwined and the whole process terminates when either a preset fault coverage is obtained or a time limit is exceeded. The presentation here is restricted to the test generation phase, which typically consists of three steps [3]:

- *Setup*: To test a fault at the output of a certain gate, it is necessary to ensure different behavior for the good and faulty circuits for this signal. This can be achieved by *controlling the gate*, i.e. by applying certain signals to the inputs of the gate. For instance, testing an and-gate for a stuck-at-zero fault requires us to set both inputs of the gate to 1.
- *Propagation*: It is clearly not enough to create an internal difference between the behavior of the good and the faulty circuit. This difference must be *observable* at some output of the circuit. The propagation step creates a *sensitized path* from the gate under test to some circuit output. In general, one or several symbolic values are introduced and

the propagation step amounts to propagating these symbolic values towards the primary outputs. The symbolic values represent the value or the negation of the value at the gate under test and indicate where the result of the test can be observed.
- *Justification*: The last step assigns values to all signals in the circuit in order to satisfy the conditions enforced by the setup and propagation steps. Generating a test basically amounts to finding an assignment of values for each of the primary inputs, that satisfies the constraints imposed by the setup and propagation steps on the signals throughout the circuit.

How these steps are implemented makes the difference between the various test generation algorithms.

3.2. Problem solution

In this section, we present the test generation program in cc(FD). We proceed in several steps. Section 3.2.1 discusses how circuits can be represented in logic programming. Section 3.2.2 shows how ATPG can be seen as a constraint satisfaction problem. Section 3.2.3 shows how to implement the basic elements as demons using the implication operator. Section 3.2.4 presents the basic test generation program, and Section 3.2.5 shows how heuristics can improve the algorithm efficiency.

3.2.1. Circuit description

Logic programming can be considered as a simple but powerful hardware description language. It supports in a natural way top-down development and mixing of various hierarchical levels of circuit description. In logic programming, a circuit can be specified by means of *clauses* that describe components and modules and the interactions between them. A general description of a full-adder can be given as follows:

```
fa(M,N,X,Y,Z,S,C) :-
  and(M,[1|N],X,Y,C1),
  xor(M,[2|N],X,Y,S1),
  fanout(M,[3|N],S1,S11,S12),
  and(M,[4|N],Z,S11,C2),
  xor(M,[5|N],Z,S12,S),
  or(M,[6|N],C1,C2,C).
```

For simulation, the definition of the basic elements and, xor, and or can be given by a set of ground clauses (the truth table definition). For instance, an and-gate can be expressed as

```
and(simul,N,0,0,0).
```

```
and(simul,N,0,1,0).
and(simul,N,1,0,0).
and(simul,N,1,1,1).
```

Here the first argument contains the operation mode (for instance, "test" for test generation, "simul" for circuit simulation or "time" for delay time computation) to distinguish between several user-defined operation modes. The second argument assigns a unique identifier to each part (module or basic component) of the circuit. Thus a hierarchical naming convention can be easily implemented. The other arguments are the inputs and outputs of the components. Note that no distinction is necessary between inputs and outputs. Multiple internal connections between components are represented by *fanout points*, since they are of special interest in test generation. In previous examples (see Section 2.5), connections were represented by shared logical variables.

The full-adder can now be used in other circuit descriptions and parameterized libraries of modules can be generated using hierarchical descriptions. This kind of hierarchical description of circuits follows the style of logic programming in top-down development: one can replace the description of a lower-level component without affecting the higher-level circuit definition. The same circuit description can be used in various applications including simulation, formal verification and fault diagnosis (see [62]). Similar ways of describing hardware in logic programming are reported in [11,22,32,33,68].

3.2.2. ATPG as a constraint satisfaction problem

Our strategy is based on treating the test generation problem as a consistent labeling problem. We use six symbolic values, 0, 1, d, dnot, e, and enot. The values *d* and *e* represent the value at the gate under test while *dnot* and *enot* represent their negations. The basic difference between *d*, *dnot*, and *e*, *enot* is in the way these values are propagated. *d* is assigned to the gate under test and the goal of test generation is to propagate *d* or *dnot* to a primary output so that the gate can be observed. Once a test has been found, it is sufficient to run the circuit with the test and to observe the value of the gate at a suitable primary output. The values *e* and *enot* are introduced because of fanout points: without the values *e* and *enot*, a fanout point would need to propagate a *d* or *dnot* value to all outputs. Since the values *d* and *dnot* impose severe constraints on the gates in order to propagate them towards the primary outputs, the algorithm may be unable to find a test in some cases. With the values *e* and *enot*, a fanout point propagates a *d* (or a *dnot*) on one output and an *e* (or an *enot*) on the other outputs. Since it devotes no effort to propagating *e* and *enot*, the algorithm avoids the

and	0	1	d	$\bar{d}$	e	$\bar{e}$
0	0	0	--	--	0	0
1	0	1	d	$\bar{d}$	e	$\bar{e}$
d	--	d	--	--	d	--
$\bar{d}$	--	$\bar{d}$	--	--	--	$\bar{d}$
e	0	e	d	--	e	0
$\bar{e}$	0	$\bar{e}$	--	$\bar{d}$	0	$\bar{e}$

Fig. 3. Definition of an and-gate in six-value logic.

xor	0	1	d	$\bar{d}$	e	$\bar{e}$
0	0	1	d	$\bar{d}$	e	$\bar{e}$
1	1	0	$\bar{d}$	d	$\bar{e}$	e
d	d	$\bar{d}$	--	--	--	--
$\bar{d}$	$\bar{d}$	d	--	--	--	--
e	e	$\bar{e}$	--	--	0	1
$\bar{e}$	$\bar{e}$	e	--	--	1	0

Fig. 4. Definition of an xor-gate in six-value logic.

not	0	1	d	$\bar{d}$	e	$\bar{e}$
	1	0	$\bar{d}$	d	$\bar{e}$	e

Fig. 5. Definition of a not-gate in six-value logic.

above-mentioned drawback. The resulting algorithm is complete (it finds a test if one exists), which is not the case for the algorithm using a five-value logic.

Figures 3–5 give the definitions of some gates (*dnot* and *enot* are represented by $\bar{d}$ and $\bar{e}$). These definitions are intended to propagate the values *d* and *dnot* towards the primary outputs and hence some input combinations are prohibited. Consider for example the and-gate. If an input is a value *d*, then the other input must be either 1 or *e* in order to propagate *d* to the output. The handling of the value *dnot* is similar. Note also that the values *e* and *enot* are not necessarily propagated to the output of the gate; this illustrates the main difference between the values *e*, *enot* and the values *d*, *dnot*. The xor-gate is also interesting to analyze. As soon as an input is *d* or *dnot*, the other input must be 0 or 1 respectively. Note that a value *d* can thus be propagated as a *dnot* on the output. The not-gate is straightforward.

The possible values for a fanout point are given by the predicate definition in Fig. 6. Note especially how the value *d* is propagated: only one of the outputs is assigned to *d*, the other being given the value *e*. There are of course two possible ways of propagating *d* depending upon the output chosen.

Test generation is then performed by the following method. Variables

```
% fanout(Mode,Label,Stem,Branch1,Branch2)
fanout(M,N,0,0,0).
fanout(M,N,1,1,1).
fanout(M,N,d,d,e).
fanout(M,N,d,e,d).
fanout(M,N,dnot,dnot,enot).
fanout(M,N,dnot,enot,dnot).
fanout(M,N,e,e,e).
fanout(M,N,enot,enot,enot).
```

Fig. 6. Definition of a fanout in the six-value logic.

throughout the circuit are required to take one of the six signal values. In addition, the primary inputs can only take values 0 or 1. One primary output will have a *d* or *dnot* value and some others can have *e* or *enot* values. The circuit gates impose local constraints between their inputs and outputs (defined by the truth tables above). The gate under test will have a *d* as output and suitable inputs to control the gate. The key advantage of this description is that all constraints can be expressed just as local constraints. The existence of a *d*-path from the *gate under test* to a primary output is guaranteed by the constraints. This is the main difference from the classical ATPG algorithms [26,29,53], which use a five-value logic and rely on a global control strategy to create the *d*-path and choose between alternatives. Note also that the solution is not described algorithmically by changes to be applied to an empty assignment, but rather as a constraint satisfaction problem.

3.2.3. Gates as demons

A simple definition of the gates as truth tables would lead to an extremely inefficient program. For a better approach, we exploit two features of cc(FD): domain constraints and the implication operator. Each line in the circuit is associated with a variable constrained to take one of the six possible values. In addition, the primary inputs are constrained to be 0 or 1. The implication operator is then used to define a demon for each type of gate. The demons make sure that the gates propagate values as soon as possible and reduce the search space whenever possible by removing values from the variables. The demon definition is a generalization of that presented in the description of the implication operator. For instance, the demon for an and-gate is depicted in Fig. 7.

Note that the implications use both equations and non-membership and domain constraints to reduce the search space by removing variable values. Also, each implication solves the constraint, i.e. if an implication has been

```
and_demon(X,Y,Z):-
  X = 0 → (Z = 0, Y ∉ {d,dnot}),
  Y = 0 → (Z = 0, X ∉ {d,dnot}),
  Z = 1 → (X = 1, Y = 1),
  X = 1 → Y = Z,
  Y = 1 → X = Z,
  X = Y → (X = Z, X ∉ {d,dnot}),
  X = d → (Y ∈ {1,e}, Z = d),
  Y = d → (Y ∈ {1,e}, Z = d),
  X = dnot → (Y ∈ {1,enot}, Z = dnot),
  Y = dnot → (Y ∈ {1,enot}, Z = dnot),
  X = e → Y = enot → Z = 0,
  X = enot → Y = e → Z = 0.
```

Fig. 7. Implementation of an and-gate in the six-value logic.

```
and(test(Gate1,Fault),Gate,X,Y,d) :-    % this is the g.u.t.
  Gate1 = Gate,                          % to test the fault
  inverse(Fault,Setup),                  % setup opposite value
  and(X,Y,Setup).                        % use the 0-1 demon
and(test(Gate1,Fault),Gate,X,Y,Z):-
  Gate1 ≠ Gate,                          % it is not the g.u.t.
  Z ∈ {0,1,d,dnot,e,enot},               % domain constraint
  and_demon(X,Y,Z).                      % use the six-valued demon
```

Fig. 8. The and-gate definition for ATPG.

applied, then *all* remaining values for its variables are valid. Finally, note that we do not enforce an assignment of the gate inputs in the case where the output takes the value 0. The constraint blocks until an assignment is made to an input either by propagation or by a labeling routine.

3.2.4. *The basic ATGP program*

We can now present the basic program.

Each type of gate is associated with a new procedure. Figure 8 illustrates the approach for an and-gate. Besides the inputs and output, the procedure receives two arguments: a term test(Gate,Fault), which is the same for all gates, and a unique identifier for the gate. The term test(Gate,Fault) indicates which gate Gate is under test for a given fault Fault; for example, test([2],1) is used for testing a sa1 fault at gate 2.

The procedure for each type of gate is defined by two clauses. The first clause handles the case of the gate under test (g.u.t.), recognized by the

```
% test(+,+,+,-):  generate test for output of Gate at Fault sa0 or sa1
%                 the third arg is a list of inputvars of the circuit
test(Gate,Fault,Inputlist,Output):-
  domain_constraints(Inputlist,0,1),
  circuit(test(Gate,Fault),[],Inputlist,Output),
  labeling(Inputlist).

% labeling(+):  assign 0 or 1 to all inputs of the circuit
labeling([]).
labeling([X|T]):-
  member(X,[0,1]),
  labeling(T).
```

Fig. 9. ATPG program.

equality Gate1 = Gate, where Gate1 is the unique identifier of the gate under test and Gate is the gate currently considered. The clause simply assigns the value d to the output. In addition, the clause controls the gate by stating a constraint on the inputs to produce the desired output. The desired output is obtained from the type of fault by the procedure inverse and the constraint is enforced using the 0-1 definition of the and-gate as described in Section 2.4. For example, an sa0 fault for the and-gate would produce 1 as the desired output (i.e. Setup is 1) and the 0-1 and-gate is called with X, Y, and Setup as arguments. In this case, the 0-1 definition assigns X and Y to 1. The second clause handles the general case, i.e. when the gate under consideration is not the gate under test. The clause simply enforces a domain constraint for the output and calls the six-value definition.

The complete program for test generation is shown in Fig. 9. It uses a circuit description and the predicate definitions above. The first argument of test is the label of the gate to test, the second argument is the fault type to test, and the third argument must be instantiated to the list of variables for the primary inputs of the circuits (this list is assigned 0-1 values by the labeling routine). The predicate domain_constraints generates suitable domain constraints for the primary inputs to guarantee that they are given a 0-1 value. The second goal enforces the constraints associated with each gate relating its inputs to outputs. The last goal simply assigns values to the primary inputs. As usual in constraint programming, the generation phase is interleaved with the constraint propagation part at run time, although they are separated in the problem statement.

The algorithm described so far is complete, i.e. it finds a test pattern if one exists and fails otherwise. We now explore several ways of improving its efficiency.

3.2.5. Heuristics

The basic procedure described so far requires making many possible choices. To obtain an efficient system, it is necessary to develop heuristics that avoid making the *wrong* choices. In this section we describe some of the heuristics used in our test generation program. We show that this information can easily be added into the program.

Controllability and observability

When propagating a d-value from the fault to a primary output, no choices are needed as long as there is a unique path. When a d-value reaches a fanout stem however, the d-path can continue along any of the stems and we have to decide which one to follow. Several measures have been proposed to estimate the difficulty of finding a path from some point inside the circuit to an output [4]. This value, called an *observability* measure, can be precomputed in a preprocessing step. For each fanout point, we obtain an ordering for the fanout stems, and try to propagate the d-value along the path with highest observability first.

A similar measure estimates how difficult it is to set a point inside the circuit to a particular value, 0 or 1. This *controllability* is used to decide which values to assign to controlling inputs of xor-gates in the d-path. If it is easy to set a point to 0, we use this value; if not, we set it to 1.

Both controllability and observability are heuristic values. Since they are obtained by simple computations, for example ignoring reconvergent fanout, they give only hints on which values to test first, and do not eliminate the need for backtracking completely.

Labeling

The choice of an appropriate labeling routine is crucial for many constraint satisfaction problems but turns out not to be as important for test generation. We use a routine that assigns the variables in the order given, but chooses randomly between 0 and 1 for the first assignment. For most of the example circuits tested below, the labeling is done without any deep backtracking.

Limiting backtracking

Some faults in circuits can be untestable; they are *redundant*. The program may not be able to detect this in reasonable time. Tests for other faults can be very difficult to obtain. To avoid spending too long trying to find a test, we have to limit the search performed on any one fault. This can be done in two ways: one is to limit the number of backtrack steps performed in the search, the other is to limit the execution time spent on each case. Both methods are rather simple to add to the program.

Fig. 10. Test generation example.

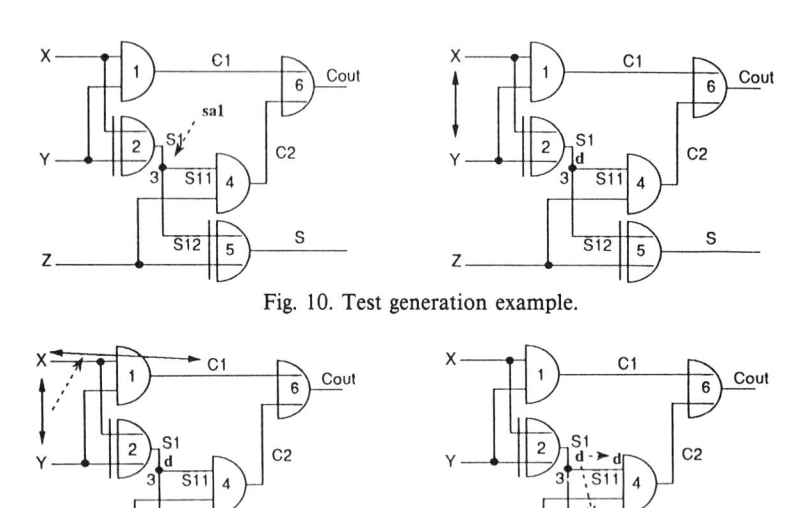

Fig. 11. Test generation example (continued).

3.3. Example

We use the full-adder circuit described above to illustrate the behavior of the program. We explain the steps required to generate a test for an sa1 fault at the output of xor-gate 2 (see Fig. 10).

The query to execute is

```
?- test([2],1,[X,Y,Z],[S,Cout]).
```

The program enforces all constraints imposed by the circuit. To control gate 2, S1 is assigned the value d. In addition, since the test is an sa1 fault, the variable Setup is assigned to 0. The xor-demon for the gate is then executed with the output equal to 0. This assignment entails, by definition of the xor-gate, the equality of both inputs of gate 2 (see Fig. 10 where the equality is shown as a double arrow), which is the weakest constraint necessary to make sure that the output is 0. All other gates use the six-value definitions; their purpose is to propagate the value d (or dnot) towards the primary outputs. Let us review how this is done.

The equality between X and Y enables one of the implications of the and-gate to be reduced (shown in the picture as a dotted arrow), leading to the equality of X with C1 and the removal of d and dnot from C1 (see Fig. 11). Then the rule for fanout point 3 is executed, creating the constraints S11 = d and S12 = e (see Fig. 11). This triggers another implication for and-gate 4, binding Z to 1 and C2 to d, which in turn triggers an implication for gate 5, binding S to enot (see Fig. 12). The rule for gate 6 now binds Cout to d and C1 to 0 and, by unification, X to 0 and Y to 0 (see Fig. 12).

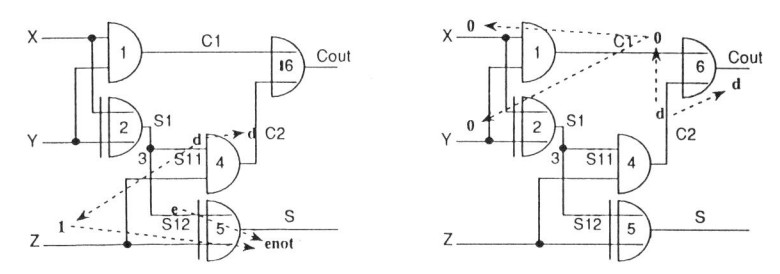

Fig. 12. Test generation example (continued).

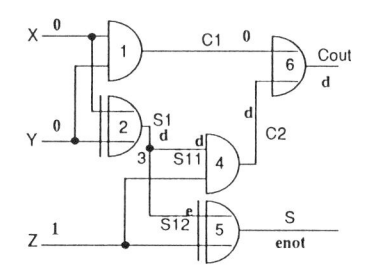

Fig. 13. Test generation example (continued).

The final solution is then

```
X = Y = C1 = 0,    S1 = d,
S11 = d,           S12 = e,
C2 = d,            Cout = d,
Z = 1,             S = enot
```

(as shown in Fig. 13). The test pattern generated for the sa1 fault at the output of gate 2 is [0,0,1].

This example is unusual in that all constraints are ultimately solved, i.e. all variables are instantiated to values. No generation of values for the primary inputs is thus necessary. For more complex examples however, this will not be the case: some constraints will block and wait until variables are instantiated by the labeling procedure in the test predicate.

3.4. Computation results

An evaluation of a test generation method must include experiments with large, realistic circuits. We use the ISCAS benchmark set [35] to test our method. The results show that a constraint-based ATPG system, while currently not as fast as specialized programs, finds test sets even in large circuits in a reasonable time with a high fault coverage.

The benchmark set was defined in 1985 to compare different test generation systems [35]. The results on a Sun 3/260 are given in Table 1, which shows the name of the circuit, the number of gates, the size of the collapsed fault set, and the number of primary inputs and outputs. For each circuit,

Table 1
Benchmark results.

Name	Gates	Faults	In	Out	Red	Ab	%	#	Time
432	160	524	36	7	1	3	99.24	68	34.0
499	202	758	41	32	8	0	98.94	62	32.6
880	383	942	60	26	0	0	100	74	68.3
1355	546	1574	41	32	8	2	99.36	92	126.7
1908	880	1879	33	25	5	5	99.47	124	245.2
2670	1193	2747	233	140	97	41	94.98	105	433.2
3540	1669	3428	50	22	127	25	95.57	175	703.9
5315	2307	5350	178	123	59	22	98.49	141	819.3
6288	2406	7744	32	32	34	0	99.56	37	265.5
7552	3512	7550	207	108	88	122	97.22	281	2223.6

we show the number of redundant faults detected (Red), the number of aborted faults (Ab), for which the procedure did not find a test or could not detect redundancy, the fault coverage (%), and the number of test patterns (#) generated. Execution times are shown for test generation only (Time).

The program obtains quite high fault coverage for all test examples. The first test patterns detect many new faults and then the number decreases slowly. The same behavior can be observed for the other systems. This shows a *tradeoff* between fault coverage and execution time. By investing more time, a slightly better fault coverage can be obtained.

The average time needed to find one test pattern for each of the example circuits grows nearly linearly with the size of the circuit. This is to be expected since, with our program, the whole circuit must be simulated to find a test pattern.

Table 2 shows the results of several special-purpose systems. It is very hard to compare two different test generation algorithms in a fair way. Fault coverage can be compared relatively easily since most systems use the same fault set. Execution times vary widely. Systems are implemented

Table 2
Benchmark comparison.

Name	Socrates %	Socrates sec	FAN %	D-Alg %	AIDSTG %	AIDSTG sec
432	99.24	5.3	94.7	97.4	99.05	70
499	98.94	24.9	93.5	68.5	99.29	101
880	100	5.7	100	100	100	107
1355	99.49	34.3	93.5	58.2	99.64	301
1908	99.52	63.1	94.6	95.0	99.59	533
2670	95.49	61.1	93.2	95.3	96.25	809
3540	95.95	89.0	92.0	94.4	95.90	1398
5315	98.88	45.4	98.2	98.5	99.21	934
6288	99.56	32.8	98.5	99.1	99.48	892
7552	98.25	243.5	93.7	96.3	98.26	2121

on different machines in different languages. For some systems, only total time is given, for others only test generation time. However, we can observe two main points. First, the fault coverage of our approach is quite good, in some cases exceeding some of the specialized programs. This means that the model and the propagation mechanisms used are quite powerful, finding a test pattern even in difficult cases. Second the experimental results indicate that the performance of the program is within a constant factor of the best specialized algorithms. This is encouraging given the effort spent in the development of these hand-crafted programs, the specialized nature of the problem, and the room left for optimization in constraint languages. It shows that a general and flexible programming language like cc(FD), especially designed for short development time and rapid prototyping, enables us to design a small declarative program whose efficiency is within a constant factor of the best special-purpose algorithms.

4. The car sequencing problem

The second application we consider is the so-called car sequencing problem. This was motivated by an article published in *AI Expert* [48] which posed the problem as a challenge for AI technology. We describe a solution using cc(FD).

4.1. Problem statement

Cars in production are placed on an assembly line that moves through various production units responsible for installing such options as air-conditioning, radios, etc. The assembly line can be viewed as composed of slots, and each car must be allocated to a single slot. However, the cars cannot be allocated arbitrarily: the production units have limited capacity

9V		10V(M)	ATWIG	Brglez	FAN	
%	sec	%	%	%	%	sec
99.1	8.1	98.9	95.9	99.24	93.7	3.6
98.9	18.1	98.9	88.0	98.94	99.4	16.2
100	26.3	100	99.2	100	100	1.3
99.5	72.6	98.7	86.7	97.27	99.5	13.5
99.6	143.2	99.4	81.9	99.52	99.5	13.5
95.4	517	93.7	81.1	95.34	95.7	49.4
96.1	452	94.7	90.0	95.71	96.0	42.9
98.9	844	98.6	96.4	98.82	98.9	19.7
99.6	1039	69.9	99	99.56	99.5	31.7
98.1	1446	96.6	92.2	98.19	98.2	118.6

Table 3
A car sequencing example.

Classes	1	2	3	4	5	6	Capacity
Option 1	y	–	–	–	y	y	1/2
Option 2	–	–	y	y	–	y	2/3
Option 3	y	–	–	–	y	–	1/3
Option 4	y	y	–	y	–	–	2/5
Option 5	–	–	y	–	–	–	1/5
Cars	1	1	2	2	2	2	

Table 4
Car sequencing: a solution.

	S_1	S_2	S_3	S_4	S_5	S_6	S_7	S_8	S_9	S_{10}
Class 1	+	–	–	–	–	–	–	–	–	–
Class 2	–	+	–	–	–	–	–	–	–	–
Class 3	–	–	–	+	–	–	–	–	+	–
Class 4	–	–	–	–	–	+	+	–	–	–
Class 5	–	–	–	–	+	–	–	+	–	–
Class 6	–	–	+	–	–	–	–	–	–	+

and they need time to set up the options on the cars as the assembly line is moving in front of the unit. These *capacity constraints* are formalized using constraints of the form *r outof s*, which indicate that the unit is able to produce at most *r* cars with the option out of each sequence of *s* cars. The car sequencing problem amounts to finding an assignment of cars to the slots that satisfies the capacity constraints.

We illustrate the problem on a simple example. In the example and the algorithm below, cars requiring the same set of options are clustered into classes, since they cannot be distinguished for any useful purpose in the algorithm. Table 3 presents a problem with five options, six classes, and ten cars. Here "y" means that a particular option is required by the class, "–" means that it is not required. The capacity constraint *r/s* should be read as *r outof s*. For example, two cars of class 6 need to be produced. They require options 1 and 2. The capacity unit for option 1 has a constraint "1 outof 2", indicating that no two consecutive cars can require the option since the unit cannot set up the option on the two consecutive cars while the line is moving.

The search space in this problem is made up by the possible values for the slots of the assembly line. Tables 4 and 5 depict a solution to the simple example, where "–" denotes an inconsistent value and "+" an assigned value; the assembly line itself is best described by the options selected for each slot.

Table 5
Car sequencing: the assembly line in a solution.

	S_1	S_2	S_3	S_4	S_5	S_6	S_7	S_8	S_9	S_{10}
Option 1	+	−	+	−	+	−	−	+	−	+
Option 2	−	−	+	+	−	+	+	−	+	+
Option 3	+	−	−	−	+	−	−	+	−	−
Option 4	+	+	−	−	−	+	+	−	−	−
Option 5	−	−	−	+	−	−	−	−	+	−

4.2. Problem solution

As is typical of finite-domain programs, the program contains two parts: a constraint part that generates the problem constraints and a choice part that assigns values to some of the problem variables. In this section we describe the variables used in modeling the problem, the constraints expressed in terms of these variables as well as short programs describing how these constraints may be generated, and the way choices are performed. We then describe the basic program and show how to improve its efficiency.

Conventions. We assume that we are given n classes of cars. Each class i contains n_i cars ($n_i \geq 0$) such that the total numbers of cars is $ns = \sum_{i=1}^{n} n_i$. We also assume m different options. For each class i and option j, we have a Boolean o_{ij} which is true if class i requires option j and false otherwise. For convenience, we represent *true* by 1 and *false* by 0.

4.2.1. Problem variables

The first step towards the solution is to identify the problem variables in terms of which the constraints are stated. To each slot i ($1 \leq i \leq ns$), we associate a variable S_i denoting the class of cars assigned to the slot. These variables, called the *slot variables*, represent the main output of the program.

Each slot i is also associated with m variables, one for each option denoted $O_i^1, O_i^2, \ldots, O_i^m$. O_i^j ($1 \leq i \leq ns$ and $1 \leq j \leq m$) is equal to 1 if the class S_i (the class assigned to slot i) requires option j and 0 otherwise. These variables are called the *option variables*. There are $O(ns)$ slot variables and $O(ns \times m)$ option variables. In the above example, there are 10 slot variables ($S_1, \ldots, S_{10}$) and 50 option variables $O_1^1, \ldots, O_1^5, \ldots, O_{10}^1, \ldots, O_{10}^5$.

4.2.2. Domain constraints

We now turn to the problem constraints. The first constraints are the domain constraints for the slot and option variables. Each slot variable S_i has a constraint $S_i \in \{1, \ldots, n\}$ and each option variable O_i^j has a constraint $O_i^j \in \{0, 1\}$. In other words, each slot variable can be assigned a class of cars while each slot variable is assigned a Boolean value. A simple recursive program can be used to generate these constraints:

```
state_domains([],Low,High).
state_domains([F|T],Low,High) :-
    F ∈ Low..High,
    state_domains(T,Low,High).
```

The goal state_domains(L,0,1) imposes a Boolean domain to all variables in the list L.

The domain constraints generated for the example in Table 3 are as follows:

$$S_1 \in \{1,\ldots,6\}, \ldots, S_{10} \in \{1,\ldots,6\},$$
$$O_1^1 \in \{0,1\}, \ldots, O_1^5 \in \{0,1\}, \ldots, O_{10}^1 \in \{0,1\}, \ldots, O_{10}^5 \in \{0,1\}.$$

4.2.3. Capacity constraints

The capacity constraints are stated in terms of the slot variables. If the capacity constraint for option j ($1 \leq j \leq m$) is of the form r *outof* s, constraints must be generated of the form

$$O_i^j + \cdots + O_{i+s-1}^j \leq r, \quad 1 \leq i \leq ns - s + 1.$$

For instance, option 1 (1 outof 2) generates the constraints

$$O_1^1 + O_2^1 \leq 1,$$
$$\ldots$$
$$O_9^1 + O_{10}^1 \leq 1,$$

while option 2 (2 outof 3) generates the constraints

$$O_1^2 + O_2^2 + O_3^2 \leq 2,$$
$$O_2^2 + O_3^2 + O_4^2 \leq 2,$$
$$\ldots$$
$$O_8^2 + O_9^2 + O_{10}^2 \leq 2.$$

A program can be written to generate all constraints of the form "r outof s". Specialized to a constraint of the type "1 outof 2", it looks like

```
atmost1outof2([]).
atmost1outof2([O]).
atmost1outof2([O1,O2|Os]) :-
    O1 + O2 ≤ 1,
    atmost1outof2([O2|Os]).
```

The above program generates linear inequalities for the variables. Overall there are $O(ns \times m)$ capacity constraints.

4.2.4. Demand constraints

It is also necessary to make sure that the cars requested are produced. For each class i $(1 \leq i \leq n)$, a constraint

$$exactly(n_i, [S_1, \ldots, S_{ns}], i)$$

has to be generated, where $S_1, \ldots, S_{ns}$ are the slot variables and n_i is the number of cars in class i. The constraint exactly(N,L,M) holds iff there are exactly N variables in the list L whose values are equal to M.

In fact, since there are *ns* slot variables and each of them will be assigned to a class (and thus a car), it is only necessary to make sure that the assignment produces no more cars from a class than are actually necessary. Hence the above constraints reduce to atmost constraints,

$$atmost(n_i, [S_1, \ldots, S_{ns}], i).$$

A constraint atmost(N,L,M) holds iff there are at most N variables in the list L whose values are equal to M.

To express the atmost constraint, we make use of the cardinality combinator. The idea is that a constraint

$$atmost(n_i, [S_1, \ldots, S_{ns}], i)$$

corresponds to the cardinality formula

$$\#(*, n_i, [S_1 = i, \ldots, S_{ns} = i]).$$

In other words, the cardinality formula makes sure that at most n_i constraints in $[S_1 = i, \ldots, S_{ns} = i]$ hold, and hence that at most n_i slots are assigned a car from class i. There are n demand constraints. The following constraints are generated for our example:

```
#(*,1,[S₁ = 1,...,S₁₀ = 1]),
...
#(*,2,[S₁ = 6,...,S₁₀ = 6]).
```

These cardinality formulas can be generated in a simple way by the following program which, given a list L and two integers N and M, makes sure that at most N elements of the list L are assigned to M.

```
atmost(N,L,M) :-
  collect_equalities(L,M,Eqs),
  #(*,N,Eqs).

collect_equalities([],M,[]).
collect_equalities([F|T],M,[F = M | Eqs]) :-
  collect_equalities(T,M,Eqs).
```

The first goal in the atmost predicate collects equalities between the value M and the elements of the list L, while the cardinality combinator makes sure that at most N of them are true.

4.2.5. Link constraints

Although all constraints seem to have been enforced at this point, an important step is still missing. The option variables and slot variables have been left completely unconnected so that a slot variable can be assigned a value without influencing its corresponding option variables and vice versa. To ensure correctness and to perform effective pruning, it is necessary to link the slot and option variables. The link is achieved by generating constraints of the form element(I,L,V) which hold iff element I of the list L is equal to V. Each option j will be connected with slot i by the constraint

$$element(S_i, [o_{1j}, \ldots, o_{nj}], O_i^j),$$

where $o_{1j}, \ldots, o_{nj}$ are the 0–1 values specifying which classes require option j. In the example, the connection between the slots and options is enforced by the constraints

```
element(S₁,[1,0,0,0,1,1],O₁¹),
...
element(S₁,[0,0,1,0,0,0],O₁⁵),
...
element(S₁₀,[1,0,0,0,1,1],O₁₀¹),
...
element(S₁₀,[0,0,1,0,0,0],O₁₀⁵).
```

There are $O(ns \times m)$ relation constraints.

How should a constraint element(I,L,V) be defined? Obviously, it is desirable that, as soon as I is given a value, V is assigned its corresponding value (for instance, in the above first constraint, if S_1 is assigned to 3, O_1^1 must be assigned to 0). On the other hand, much more pruning can be achieved. In particular, as soon as S_1 is restricted to the values 1, 4, and 5, O_1^1 must be given the value 1. In the same way, as soon as O_1^1 is assigned the value 1, S_1 is restricted to take values in $\{1,4,5\}$. In other words, we would like element(I,L,V) to be *arc consistent*.

To enforce arc-consistency on element(I,L,V), it is sufficient to generate cardinality constraints of the form

$$V = e \Leftrightarrow I \in \{i_1, \ldots, i_p\}$$

where e is a value in L and $i_1, \ldots, i_p$ are all the positions in list L whose value is e. In general, a constraint must be generated for each value in L, although this is not necessary in the car sequencing application (since only

Boolean values are used). For instance, the first element constraint of our example generates the constraint

$$O_1^1 = 1 \Leftrightarrow S_1 \in \{1,5,6\}.$$

A simple program can be written to generate the above constraints. The equivalence $\Leftrightarrow$ should be understood as an abbreviation for a cardinality formula and illustrates the fact that the cardinality operator can be used to enforce arc-consistency of any constraint (preserving the complexity bounds of the optimal algorithm of [44]).

4.2.6. Basic program

We now present the basic program, which amounts to stating the constraints and generating values for the slots variables.

```
sequencing(Line,InstanceData) ←
  state_constraints(Line,InstanceData),
  generate_values(Line).

state_constraints(Line,
                  [NbSlots,NbOptions,NbClasses,
                   OptionInfo,CarInfo]):-
  generate_slots(Line,NbSlots),
  generate_option_variables(Options,NbSlots,NbOptions),
  state_domain_constraints(Line,1,NbClasses),
  state_domain_constraints(Options,0,1),
  state_demand_constraints(Line,CarInfo),
  state_capacity_constraints(Options,OptionInfo),
  state_link_constraints(Line,Options,OptionInfo).
```

The arguments of the predicate are the list of slots variables and the data characterizing the instance. The generation of constraints creates as many variables as there are slots in the assembly line, creates the option variables, and states all the above-mentioned constraints. Generating the constraints can be done by simple recursive programs (as has been shown in the above presentation) and poses no particular difficulty. Assigning a value to the slot variables produces a solution satisfying the constraints. The generation of values simply assigns to each of the slot variables a value between 1 and n, that is, a class of cars.

4.2.7. Improving efficiency

The above program provides us with a reasonably efficient solution to the car sequencing problem. It is possible, however, to speed up the program significantly by exploiting properties of the solutions and making choices wisely.

Redundant (surrogate) constraints

A traditional technique in operations research amounts to generating *surrogate constraints*: constraints which are not strictly necessary to guarantee correctness of the application but perform pruning by exploiting properties that must be satisfied by the solutions. In other words, the constraints are redundant semantically but not operationally.

The car sequencing problem has a surrogate constraint worth exploiting. Assume that option j has a capacity constraint r outof s. We know that the last s slots contain only r cars, so the other slots must contain all the remaining cars having that option. If p cars require option j, we can generate a constraint

$$O_1^j + \cdots + O_{ns-s}^j \geq p - r.$$

More generally, the last $k \times s$ ($k = 1, 2, \ldots, ns/s$) slots can contain only $k \times r$ cars and hence the constraints

$$O_1^j + \cdots + O_{ns-k \times s}^j \geq p - k \times r$$

can be generated.

In our example, for instance, option 1 is requested by five cars and has capacity "1 outof 2". Since only one car can be scheduled in the last two slots, four cars must be sequenced in the first eight slots. Pursuing the reasoning, we can generate the following constraints:

$$O_1^1 + \cdots + O_8^1 \geq 4,$$
$$O_1^1 + \cdots + O_6^1 \geq 3,$$
$$O_1^1 + \cdots + O_4^1 \geq 2.$$

The effect of these constraints is to prune the search space early and to escape deep backtracking and thrashing by recognizing and avoiding failures as soon as possible. It is not difficult to write a recursive program generating the above constraints.

First-fail principle

Following [34], we make use of the first-fail principle in the choice process: that is we try to choose the most constrained variable to be instantiated next. In the car sequencing, this is done by choosing the variable with the smallest domain (i.e. the one that can be given the smallest number of values) and, in case of equality, the more demanding one in terms of the options.

Table 6
Car sequencing: search space after one choice.

	S_1	S_2	S_3	S_4	S_5	S_6	S_7	S_8	S_9	S_{10}
Class 1	+	−	−	−	−	−	−	−	−	−
Class 2	−									
Class 3	−									
Class 4	−									
Class 5	−	−	−							
Class 6	−	−								

Table 7
Car sequencing: the assembly line after one choice.

	S_1	S_2	S_3	S_4	S_5	S_6	S_7	S_8	S_9	S_{10}
Option 1	+	−								
Option 2	−									
Option 3	+	−	−							
Option 4	+									
Option 5										

4.3. Example

The above program first states the constraints and then makes choices. After the first choice (i.e. $S_1 = 1$), the search space and the assembly line are depicted in Tables 6 and 7. Now, giving to S_2 its first possible value, i.e. 2, leads directly to the solution presented at the beginning of the example. Indeed, this choice immediately removes the value 2 for all other slot variables and prevents variables S_3, S_4, and S_5 from taking the value 4 because of option 4. This intermediate state is depicted in Tables 8 and 9.

But the surrogate constraints for option 2 require that S_3 and S_4 be assigned a class including option 2, since six cars with option 2 must be produced. The effect of these assignments is to fix all option variables concerning option 2 and to remove possible values from the slot variables. The search space and assembly line at that stage are depicted in Tables 10 and 11.

At this point, the demand constraints for class 5 come into play. Two cars of class 5 must be produced; since only two places are left for them, they

Table 8
Car sequencing: search space after two choices (part I).

	S_1	S_2	S_3	S_4	S_5	S_6	S_7	S_8	S_9	S_{10}
Class 1	+	−	−	−	−	−	−	−	−	−
Class 2	−	+	−	−	−	−	−	−	−	−
Class 3	−	−								
Class 4	−	−	−	−						
Class 5	−	−	−							
Class 6	−	−								

Table 9
Car sequencing: the assembly line after two choices (part I).

	S_1	S_2	S_3	S_4	S_5	S_6	S_7	S_8	S_9	S_{10}
Option 1	+	−								
Option 2	−	−								
Option 3	+	−	−							
Option 4	+	+	−	−	−					
Option 5		−								

Table 10
Car sequencing: search space after two choices (part II).

	S_1	S_2	S_3	S_4	S_5	S_6	S_7	S_8	S_9	S_{10}
Class 1	+	−	−	−	−	−	−	−	−	−
Class 2	−	+	−	−	−	−	−	−	−	−
Class 3	−	−								
Class 4	−	−	−	−	−					
Class 5	−	−	−	−			−	−		
Class 6	−	−								

are assigned immediately. This leads to the search space and assembly line depicted in Tables 12 and 13. The final step amounts to using the surrogate constraints for option 1. These constraints fix all options concerning option 1 and lead to the solution depicted earlier in this paper. Note that here a solution was found in two choices without any backtracking.

Table 11
Car sequencing: the assembly line after two choices (part II).

	S_1	S_2	S_3	S_4	S_5	S_6	S_7	S_8	S_9	S_{10}
Option 1	+	−								
Option 2	−	−	+	+	−	+	+	−	+	+
Option 3	+	−	−							
Option 4	+	+	−	−	−					
Option 5		−								

Table 12
Car sequencing: search space after two choices (part III).

	S_1	S_2	S_3	S_4	S_5	S_6	S_7	S_8	S_9	S_{10}
Class 1	+	−	−	−	−	−	−	−	−	−
Class 2	−	+	−	−	−	−	−	−	−	−
Class 3	−	−			−		−			
Class 4	−	−	−	−			−			
Class 5	−	−	−		+	−	−	+	−	−
Class 6	−	−			−		−			

Table 13
Car sequencing: the assembly line after two choices (part III).

	S_1	S_2	S_3	S_4	S_5	S_6	S_7	S_8	S_9	S_{10}
Option 1	+	−		−	+	−	−	+		
Option 2	−	−	+	+	−	+	+	−	+	+
Option 3	+	−	−	+			+			
Option 4	+	+	−	−	−			−		
Option 5		−			−			−		

4.4. Computation results

A large number of experiments have been run to evaluate the efficiency of the algorithm on various problem instances. Remember that, since the problem is NP-complete, it is always possible to construct an instance that will require exponential time (whatever the proposed program).

The basic assumption in our experiments was that the assembly line supported five different options with the following capacity constraints: 1 outof 2, 2 outof 3, 1 outof 3, 2 outof 5, and 1 outof 5. Given this assumption, several parameters were still left free: the number of cars ns, the particular requirements for the cars, and the utilization of each production unit. In our experiments, ns varied from 5 to 200 and random data were generated for the utilization percentage and the options required by the cars. This random generation guarantees an overall percentage of utilization of the resources. Typically, we would ask for 70% or 80% but experiments have shown that it is possible to make this percentage even higher. For each experiment, large data samples (around 100) were generated.

When $ns < 50$, the program finds a solution in a few seconds, generally with very little if any backtracking. When $ns = 50$, the scheduling time is around 15 seconds on a Sun 3/160. Once again, little backtracking was needed to reach a solution.

When $ns = 100$, the average scheduling time is less than a minute with

Table 14
100 cars sequencing with about 70% of option utilization.

ns	n	%-1	%-2	%-3	%-4	%-5	CPU time
100	24	72	72	72	67	70	52 sec.
100	24	74	75	100	90	60	58 sec.
100	21	84	68	75	60	75	56 sec.

Table 15
100 cars sequencing with about 80% of option utilization.

ns	n	%-1	%-2	%-3	%-4	%-5	CPU time
100	25	88	84	72	77	75	62 sec.
100	22	78	80	84	90	70	58 sec.
100	21	80	81	75	72	75	59 sec.

Table 16
100 cars sequencing with about 70% of option utilization.

ns	n	%-1	%-2	%-3	%-4	%-5	CPU time
200	29	86	77	89	85	85	336 sec.
200	29	89	82	83	83	95	340 sec.
200	31	84	81	95	82	100	345 sec.

a utilization percentage around 70%. Table 14 reports some typical results. The first column *ns* is the number of cars, the second column *n* indicates the number of different classes, the next five columns indicate the utilization percentage of each option and the last column shows the CPU time required to generate the constraints and find a schedule. Increasing the utilization percentage to 80% increases the CPU time by only a few seconds. Typical results are shown in Table 15.

When $ns = 200$, the average scheduling time is around 5 minutes for an overall utilization percentage of 70% and thus scheduling time does not change when we increase the percentage to 80%. Table 16 reports some typical results.

Note that the potential search space to explore in the last example is 200^{31}. The program must generate 200 slots variables, 1000 option variables, more than 1000 cardinality constraints, and about 3000 numerical constraints. Only the slot variables, however, need to be instantiated to give a solution however, whereas an integer programming solution would require more than 7000 variables, of which 6000 would need to be instantiated to find a solution.

In the experiments, the execution time was found to increase quadratically in the average. No instance was found that could not be solved (even when $ns = 400$) although such instance could be constructed since the problem is NP-complete.

5. Conclusion

We have shown how to solve two practical combinatorial search problems using cc(FD), a successor to CHIP using consistency techniques on finite domains. The test generation problem is a well-known problem in digital circuit design and we have presented an original and complete algorithm for the task based on constraint satisfaction. The car sequencing problem was posed as a challenge for AI technology and a constraint-based solution has also been presented.

Both problems can be expressed concisely and declaratively in cc(FD) and require a small fraction of the development necessary to obtain "equivalent" procedural programs. The resulting programs can be easily extended, modified, and specialized due to the declarative nature of the language. In addition, the resulting algorithms can solve large instances of the problems in reasonable time and are competitive with procedural programs to a constant factor.

Current and future research is devoted to (1) design aspects in order to capture more abstractions useful in combinatorial search problems and (2) to implementation issues (to reduce the constant factor with respect to procedural languages).

Appendix A. Formalization of the semantics of cc(FD)

Here we formalize, following [54], the operational semantics of cc(FD) using a structural operational semantics [50]. Those interested in a broader and more rigorous handling of the semantics can refer to [36] and [55,56]; [36] contains a complete description of the CLP scheme while [55,56] respectively describe the operational and denotational semantics (in terms of information systems and closure operators) of the cc framework.

A.1. The CLP scheme

The operational semantics makes use of a transition system.

Definition A.1. A *transition system* is a triple $\langle \Gamma, T, \longmapsto \rangle$ where Γ is a set of configurations, $T \subseteq \Gamma$ is the set of terminal configurations and $\longmapsto \subseteq \Gamma \times \Gamma$ is the transition relation satisfying

$$\forall \gamma \in T, \quad \forall \gamma' \in \Gamma, \quad \gamma \not\longmapsto \gamma'.$$

The configurations of the transition system are the computation states $\langle G \ \square \ \sigma \rangle$. When the goal part is empty, we represent the configuration by the constraint part only; when the constraint part is empty, we represent the configuration by the goal part only. Terminal configurations are simply successful computation states (i.e. constraint stores) or the terminal `block` to denote blocking.

A transition $\gamma \longmapsto \gamma'$ can be read as "configuration γ nondeterministically reduces to γ'". The transition rules in this paper are presented using the format

$$\frac{\langle \text{condition 1} \rangle \\ \ldots \\ \langle \text{condition } n \rangle}{\gamma \longmapsto \gamma'}$$

expressing the fact that a transition from γ to γ' can take place if the conditions are fulfilled. We are now ready to present the various transition rules.

Goal Reduction. A goal can be reduced to the body of a clause if the constraint store is consistent with the equality constraints.

$$\frac{\begin{array}{l} p(s_1,\ldots,s_n) :- B_1,\ldots,B_m \ \in P \\ \mathcal{C} \models (\exists)\,(\sigma \wedge t_1 = s_1 \wedge \cdots \wedge t_n = s_n) \end{array}}{\begin{array}{l} \langle\, p(t_1,\ldots,t_n)\ \square\ \sigma\,\rangle \\ \quad \longmapsto \langle\, B_1,\ldots,B_m\ \square\ \sigma \wedge t_1 = s_1\ \&\ \cdots\ \&\ t_n = s_n\,\rangle \end{array}}$$

In the above transition rule, $p(t_1,\ldots,t_n)$ is the atom selected, P denotes the program, $(\exists)\,(\psi)$ represents the existential closure of ψ, and the program clause has been renamed properly to avoid sharing any variable with the goal.[4] The rule expresses formally the first kind of computation step described in the informal presentation. If there exists a clause in the program with the same predicate name as the selected atom (condition 1) and if the equality constraints are consistent with the constraint store (condition 2), then a computation step is possible. The new computation state is obtained from the old one by replacing the selected atom by the clause body and adding the equality constraints to the constraint store.

Constraint Solving. A constraint can be removed from the goal part iff it is consistent with the constraint store.

$$\frac{\mathcal{C} \models (\exists)\,(\sigma \wedge c)}{\langle c\ \square\ \sigma\,\rangle \longmapsto \sigma\ \&\ c}$$

This rules captures what was informally described by the second type of computation step.

Conjunction. If any of the goals in a conjunction can make a transition, the whole conjunction can make a transition as well and the constraint store is updated accordingly. This is the traditional interleaving rule.

$$\frac{\langle\, G_1\ \square\ \sigma\,\rangle \longmapsto \langle\, G_1'\ \square\ \sigma'\,\rangle}{\begin{array}{l}\langle\, G_1, G_2\ \square\ \sigma\,\rangle \longmapsto \langle\, G_1', G_2\ \square\ \sigma'\,\rangle \\ \langle\, G_2, G_1\ \square\ \sigma\,\rangle \longmapsto \langle\, G_2, G_1'\ \square\ \sigma'\,\rangle\end{array}}$$

---

[4] In recent work [56], Saraswat et al. give an operational semantics precluding the need for renaming.

$$\frac{\langle G_1 \ \Box \ \sigma \rangle \longmapsto \sigma'}{\langle G_1, G_2 \ \Box \ \sigma \rangle \longmapsto \langle G_2 \ \Box \ \sigma' \rangle}$$

$$\langle G_2, G_1 \ \Box \ \sigma \rangle \longmapsto \langle G_2 \ \Box \ \sigma' \rangle$$

These are the only rules necessary for the CLP scheme.

A.2. The implication combinator

We now describe precisely the semantics of the implication combinator.

Implication. An implication $c \to A$ never fails. If c is entailed by the constraint store, it reduces to the body A. If $\neg c$ is entailed by the constraint store, the implication terminates successfully. Otherwise, the implication blocks.

$$\frac{\mathcal{C} \models (\forall)(\sigma \to c)}{\langle c \to A \ \Box \ \sigma \rangle \longmapsto \langle A, \sigma \rangle}$$

$$\frac{\mathcal{C} \models (\forall)(\sigma \to \neg c)}{\langle c \to A \ \Box \ \sigma \rangle \longmapsto \sigma}$$

$$\frac{\mathcal{C} \models \neg(\forall)(\sigma \to c)}{\mathcal{C} \models \neg(\forall)(\sigma \to \neg c)}$$
$$\langle c \to A \ \Box \ \sigma \rangle \longmapsto block$$

A.3. The cardinality combinator

The precise behavior of the combinator can be described by the following transition rules taken from [73].

Trivial Satisfaction. If $l \leq 0$ and u is greater than or equal to the number of constraints $c_1, \ldots, c_n$, then $\#(l, u, [c_1, \ldots, c_n])$ is trivially satisfied:

$$\frac{l \leq 0 \ \land \ n \leq u}{\langle \#(l, u, [c_1, \ldots, c_n]) \ \Box \ \sigma \rangle \longmapsto \sigma}$$

Positive Satisfaction. A formula $\#(n, u, [c_1, \ldots, c_n])$ with $n \leqslant u$ can be satisfied only if the conjunction $c_1 \wedge \cdots \wedge c_n$ is consistent with the constraint store:

$$\frac{\begin{array}{l} l \leqslant u \wedge l = n \\ \mathcal{C} \models (\exists)(\sigma \wedge c_1 \wedge \ldots \wedge c_n) \end{array}}{\langle \#(l, u, [c_1, \ldots, c_n]) \,\square\, \sigma \rangle \longmapsto \sigma \,\&\, c_1 \,\&\, \ldots \,\&\, c_n}$$

Negative Satisfaction. A formula $\#(l, 0, [c_1, \ldots, c_n])$ with $l \leqslant 0$ can be satisfied only if the conjunction $\neg c_1 \wedge \cdots \wedge \neg c_n$ is consistent with the constraint store:

$$\frac{\begin{array}{l} l \leqslant u \wedge u = 0 \\ \mathcal{C} \models (\exists)(\sigma \wedge \neg c_1 \wedge \ldots \wedge \neg c_n) \end{array}}{\langle \#(l, u, [c_1, \ldots, c_n]) \,\square\, \sigma \rangle \longmapsto \sigma \,\&\, \neg c_1 \,\&\, \cdots \,\&\, \neg c_n}$$

The above three rules make up the basic cases for the cardinality combinator. Two of them allow the inference of primitive constraints, and hence prune the search space with the help of the transition rules for conjunction.

Positive Reduction. When a constraint c_i is entailed by the constraint store, the cardinality formula can be simplified by dropping the constraint and decrementing the bounds.

$$\frac{\begin{array}{l} \mathcal{C} \models (\forall)(\sigma \rightarrow c_i) \\ 0 < l < n \wedge l \leqslant u \;\vee\; 0 < u < n \wedge l \leqslant 0 \end{array}}{\begin{array}{l} \langle \#(l, u, [c_1, \ldots, c_i, \ldots, c_n]) \,\square\, \sigma \rangle \\ \longmapsto \langle \#(l-1, u-1, [c_1, \ldots, c_{i-1}, c_{i+1}, \ldots, c_n]) \,\square\, \sigma \rangle \end{array}}$$

The condition on l and u forces the rule to be mutually exclusive with the three satisfaction rules.

Negative Reduction. When the negation of a constraint c_i is entailed by the constraint store (i.e. c_i inconsistent with σ), the cardinality formula can be simplified by dropping the constraint:

$$\frac{\begin{array}{l} \mathcal{C} \models (\forall)(\sigma \rightarrow \neg c_i) \\ 0 < l < n \wedge l \leqslant u \;\vee\; 0 < u < n \wedge l \leqslant 0 \end{array}}{\begin{array}{l} \langle \#(l, u, [c_1, \ldots, c_i, \ldots, c_n]) \,\square\, \sigma \rangle \\ \longmapsto \langle \#(l, u, [c_1, \ldots, c_{i-1}, c_{i+1}, \ldots, c_n]) \,\square\, \sigma \rangle \end{array}}$$

The above two rules achieve progress towards the satisfaction rules by reducing the number of constraints and (possibly) the bounds. But the computation with the cardinality combinator may now block as none of the constraints can be decided upon (for entailment) with respect to the constraint store.

Blocking. The cardinality combinator blocks if there is no constraint c_i such that either c_i or its negation $\neg c_i$ is entailed by the constraint store and none of the satisfaction rules apply:

$$\frac{\begin{array}{l} C \not\models (\forall)(\sigma \to c_j) \quad \text{for all } 1 \leq j \leq n \\ C \not\models (\forall)(\sigma \to \neg c_j) \quad \text{for all } 1 \leq j \leq n \\ 0 < l < n \wedge l \leq u \ \vee \ 0 < u < n \wedge l \leq 0 \end{array}}{\langle \#(l, u, [c_1, \ldots, c_n]) \ \square \ \sigma \rangle \longmapsto block}$$

We now reconsider our simple example and indicate the transition rules used in the derivation.

```
⟨#(1,2,[X=4, Y=10]) & X>6 □ ε⟩
      ↓ (conjunction)
⟨#(1,2,[X=4, Y=10]) □ X>6⟩
      ↓ (negative reduction)
⟨#(1,2,[Y=10]) □ X>6⟩
      ↓ (positive satisfaction)
X>6 & Y=10
```

A.4. Operational semantics

The actual operational semantics of the language can be defined in terms of its success, divergence, and failure sets. We use the notation $P \vdash$ to denote the fact that the transition occurs in the context of program P. We denote by $\stackrel{*}{\longmapsto}$ the transitive closure of $\longmapsto$ and say that a configuration γ diverges in program P if there exists an infinite sequence of transitions

$$P \vdash \gamma \longmapsto \gamma_1 \longmapsto \cdots \longmapsto \gamma_i \longmapsto \cdots.$$

The operational semantics is now given in terms of three sets: the success, divergence, and blocking sets:

$$\begin{aligned} SS[P] &= \{G \mid P \vdash G \stackrel{*}{\longmapsto} \sigma\}, \\ DS[P] &= \{G \mid G \text{ diverges in } P\}, \\ BS[P] &= \{G \mid P \vdash G \stackrel{*}{\longmapsto} block\}. \end{aligned}$$

The failure set can now be defined in terms of the above three sets:

$$FS[P] = \{G \mid G \notin SS[P] \cup DS[P] \cup BS[P]\}.$$

Another semantic definition can be given to capture the results of the computation:

$$RES[P, G] = \{\sigma \mid P \vdash G \stackrel{*}{\longmapsto} \sigma\}$$

In order to achieve the above semantics, the CLP language should be embedded with a complete constraint solver; this means that, given a constraint σ, the constraint solver should return *true* if $\mathcal{C} \models (\exists)(\sigma)$ and *false* otherwise.

Acknowledgement

The initial solutions of the applications were proposed while the authors were at ECRC (Munich). Conversations with Yves Deville and Vijay Saraswat significantly improved our presentation. We also thank the three reviewers for their careful comments and suggestions. In particular, the comments (and humor) of the second reviewer (who will recognize herself or himself easily) are (greatly) appreciated. Trina Avery helped correcting our English. This research was supported in part by the National Science Foundation under grant number CCR-9108032 and by the Office of Naval Research and the Defense Advanced Research Projects Agency under Contract N00014-91-J-4052.

References

[1] J.A. Abraham, Fault modeling in VLSI, in: T.W. Williams, ed., *VLSI Testing*, Advances in CAD for VLSI **5** (North-Holland, Amsterdam, 1986) 1–27, Chapter 1.

[2] A. Borning, The programming language aspects of ThingLab, a constraint-oriented simulation laboratory, *ACM Trans. Programm. Lang. Syst.* **3** (4) (1981) 353–387.

[3] P.S. Bottorff, Test generation and fault simulation, in: T.W. Williams, ed., *VLSI Testing*, Advances in CAD for VLSI **5** (North-Holland, Amsterdam, 1986) 29–64, Chapter 2.

[4] F. Brglez, P. Pownall and R. Hum, Applications of testability analysis: from ATPG to critical delay path tracing, in: *Proceedings IEEE International Test Conference* (1984).

[5] F. Brglez, P. Pownall and R. Hum, Accelerated ATPG and fault grading via testability analysis, in: *Proceedings IEEE International Symposium on Circuits and Systems*, Kyoto, Japan (1985) 695–698.

[6] W. Buttner and H. Simonis, Embedding Boolean expressions into logic programming, *J. Symbol. Comput.* **4** (1987) 191–205.

[7] J. Carlier and E. Pinson, Une methode arborescente pour optimiser la durée d'un JOB-SHOP, Tech. Rept. ISSN 0294-2755, I.M.A. (1986).

[8] W.T. Cheng, The back algorithm for sequential test-generation, in: *Proceedings IEEE International Conference on Computer Design: VLSI in Computers and Processors (ICCD88)*, Rye Brook, NY (1988).

[9] N. Christofides, *Graph Theory: An Algorithmic Approach* (Academic Press, New York, 1975).

[10] K.L. Clark and F. McCabe, The control facilities of IC-PROLOG, in: D. Michie, ed., *Expert Systems in the Microelectronic Age* (Edinburgh University Press, Edinburgh, 1979) 122–149.

[11] W.F. Clocksin, Logic programming and digital circuit analysis, *J. Logic Programm.* **4** (1) (1987) 59-82.
[12] A. Colmerauer, An introduction to Prolog III, *Commun. ACM* **28** (4) (1990) 412-418.
[13] A. Colmerauer, H. Kanoui and M. Van Caneghem, Prolog, bases théoriques et developpements actuels, *T.S.I. (Techniques et Sciences Informatiques)* **2** (4) (1983) 271-311.
[14] T. Dean and M. Boddy, An analysis of time-dependent planning, in: *Proceedings AAAI-88*, St. Paul, MN (1988) 49-54.
[15] J. de Kleer, An assumption-based TMS, *Artif. Intell.* **28** (1986) 127-162.
[16] Y. Deville and P. Van Hentenryck, An efficient arc consistency algorithm for a class of CSP problems, in: *Proceedings IJCAI-91*, Sidney, Australia (1991).
[17] M. Dincbas and J.-P. Lepape, Metacontrol of logic programs in METALOG, in: *Proceedings International Conference on Fifth Generation Computer Systems (FGCS'84)*, Tokyo, Japan (1984) 361-370.
[18] M. Dincbas, H. Simonis and P. Van Hentenryck, Solving the car sequencing problem in constraint logic programming, in: *Proceedings European Conference on Artificial Intelligence (ECAI-88)*, Munich, Germany (1988).
[19] M. Dincbas, H. Simonis and P. Van Hentenryck, Solving large combinatorial problems in logic programming, *J. Logic Programm.* **8** (1-2) (1990) 75-93.
[20] M. Dincbas, P. Van Hentenryck, H. Simonis, A. Aggoun, T. Graf and F. Berthier, The constraint logic programming language CHIP, in: *Proceedings International Conference on Fifth Generation Computer Systems*, Tokyo, Japan (1988).
[21] J. Doyle, A truth maintenance system, *Artif. Intell.* **12** (1979) 231-272.
[22] K. Eshghi, Application of meta-level programming to fault finding in logic circuits, in: *Logic Programming and Its Applications* (Ablex, Norwood, NJ, 1985) 208-219.
[23] R.E. Fikes. A heuristic program for solving problems stated as non-deterministic procedures, Ph.D. Thesis, Computer Science Department, Carnegie-Mellon University, Pittsburgh, PA (1968).
[24] M.S. Fox, Constraint-directed search: a case study of job-shop scheduling, Tech. Rept. CMU-CS-83-161, Carnegie-Mellon University, Pittsburgh, PA (1983).
[25] H. Fujiwara, FAN: a fanout oriented test pattern generation algorithm, in: *Proceedings. IEEE International Symposium on Circuits and Systems*, Kyoto, Japan (1985) 671-674.
[26] H. Fujiwara and T. Shimono, On the acceleration of test generation algorithms, *IEEE Trans. Comput.* **32** (1983) 1137-1144.
[27] H. Gallaire, Logic programming: further developments, in: *Proceedings IEEE Symposium on Logic Programming*, Boston, MA (1985) 88-99 (Invited Paper).
[28] H. Gallaire and C. Lasserre, Metalevel control for logic programs, in: *Logic Programming* (Academic Press, New York, 1982) 173-185.
[29] P. Goel, An implicit enumeration algorithm to generate tests for combinational logic circuits, *IEEE Trans. Comput.* **30** (1981) 215-222.
[30] T. Graf, Extending constraint handling in logic programming to rational arithmetic, Internal Report, ECRC, Munich, Germany (1987).
[31] T. Graf, P. Van Hentenryck, C. Pradelles and L. Zimmer, Simulation of hybrid circuits in constraint logic programming, *Comput. Math. Appl.* **20** (9-10) (1990) 45-56; Preliminary version in: *Proceedings IJCAI-89*, Detroit, MI (1989).
[32] E. Gullichsen, Heuristic circuit simulation using PROLOG, *Integr. VLSI J.* **3** (1985) 283-318.
[33] R. Gupta, Test-pattern generation for VLSI circuits in a Prolog environment, in: *Proceedings Third International Conference on Logic Programming*, London (1986) 528-535.
[34] R.M. Haralick and G.L. Elliot, Increasing tree search efficiency for constraint satisfaction problems, *Artif. Intell.* **14** (1980) 263-313.
[35] ISCAS, Special Session on ATPG, in: *Proceedings IEEE International Symposium on Circuits and Systems*, Kyoto, Japan (1985) 663-698.
[36] J. Jaffar and J.-L. Lassez, Constraint logic programming, in: *Proceedings 14th ACM Symposium on Principles of Programming Languages (POPL-87)*, Munich, Germany

(1987).

[37] J. Jaffar and S. Michaylov, Methodology and implementation of a CLP system, in: *Proceedings Fourth International Conference on Logic Programming*, Melbourne, Australia (1987).

[38] M. Kawai, K. Oozeki, M. Takahashi, M. Ono, Y. Ishizaka and T. Masui, Automatic test pattern generator for large combinational circuits, in: *Proceedings IEEE International Symposium on Circuits and Systems*, Kyoto, Japan (1985) 663–666.

[39] M. Kubale and D. Jackowski, A generalized implicit enumeration algorithm for graph coloring, *Commun. ACM* **28** (4) (1985) 412–418.

[40] J.-L. Lauriere, A language and a program for stating and solving combinatorial problems, *Artif. Intell.* **10** (1) (1978) 29–127.

[41] A. Lioy, Adaptive backtrace and dynamic partitioning enhance ATPG, in: *Proceedings IEEE International Conference on Computer Design: VLSI in Computers and Processors (ICCD88)*, Rye Brook, NY (1988).

[42] A.K. Mackworth, Consistency in networks of relations, *Artif. Intell.* **8** (1) (1977) 99–118.

[43] M.J. Maher, Logic semantics for a class of committed-choice programs, in: *Proceedings Fourth International Conference on Logic Programming*, Melbourne, Australia (1987) 858–876.

[44] R. Mohr and T.C. Henderson, Arc and path consistency revisited, *Artif. Intell.* **28** (1986) 225–233.

[45] U. Montanari, Networks of constraints: fundamental properties and applications to picture processing, *Inf. Sci.* **7** (2) (1974) 95–132.

[46] M. Muarkami and H. Kikuchihara, Test generation for LSI circuits using extended nine-valued method, in: *Proceedings IEEE International Symposium on Circuits and Systems*, Kyoto, Japan (1985) 675–678.

[47] L. Naish, Negation and control in Prolog, Ph.D. Thesis, University of Melbourne, Australia (1985).

[48] B.D. Parrello, CAR WARS: the (almost) birth of an expert system, *AI Expert* **3** (1) (1988) 60–64.

[49] B.D. Parrello, W.C. Kabat and L. Wos, Job-shop scheduling using automated reasoning: a case study of the car-sequencing problem, *J. Autom. Reasoning* **2** (1) (1986) 1–42.

[50] G.D. Plotkin, A structural approach to operational semantics, Tech. Rept. DAIMI FN-19, CS Department, University of Aarhus, Denmark (1981).

[51] D.K. Pradhan, *Fault Tolerant Computing* (Prentice Hall, Englewood Cliffs, NJ, 1986).

[52] B.C. Rosales and P. Goel, Results from application of a commercial ATG system to large-scale combinatorial circuits, in: *Proceedings IEEE International Symposium on Circuits and Systems*, Kyoto, Japan (1985) 667–670.

[53] J. Roth, Diagnosis of automata failure: a calculus and a method, *IBM J. Res. Dev.* **10** (1966) 278–291.

[54] V.A. Saraswat, Concurrent constraint programming languages, Ph.D. Thesis, Carnegie-Mellon University, Pittsburgh, PA (1989).

[55] V.A. Saraswat and M. Rinard, Concurrent constraint programming, in: *Proceedings 17th ACM Symposium on Principles of Programming Languages*, San Francisco, CA (1990).

[56] V.A. Saraswat, M. Rinard and P. Panangaden, Semantic foundations of concurrent constraint programming, in: *Proceedings 19th ACM Symposium on Principles of Programming Languages*, Orlando, FL (1991).

[57] M. Schulz, E. Trischler and T. Sarfert, Socrates: a highly efficient automatic test pattern generation system, in: *Proceedings International Test Conference*, Washington, DC (1987).

[58] E. Shapiro, The family of concurrent logic programming languages, *Comput. Surv.* **21** (3) (1990) 413–510.

[59] H. Simonis, Test generation using logic programming, Tech. Rept. TR-LP-34, ECRC, Munich, Germany (1988).

[60] H. Simonis, Test generation using the constraint logic programming language CHIP, in: *Proceedings 6th International Conference on Logic Programming*, Lisbon, Portugal (1989).

[61] H. Simonis, ATPG revisited, Tech. Rept. TR-LP-56, ECRC, Munich, Germany (1990).
[62] H. Simonis and M. Dincbas, Using an extended Prolog for digital circuit design, in: *Proceedings IEEE International Workshop on AI Applications to CAD Systems for Electronics*, Munich, Germany (1987) 165-188.
[63] H. Simonis and M. Dincbas, Using logic programming for fault diagnosis in digital circuits, in: *Proceedings German Workshop on Artificial Intelligence (GWAI-87)*, Geseke, Germany (1987) 139-148.
[64] H. Simonis and T. Graf, Technology mapping in CHIP, Tech. Rept. TR-LP-44, ECRC, Munich, Germany (1990).
[65] H. Simonis, H.N. Nguyen and M. Dincbas, Verification of digital circuits using CHIP, in: G.J. Milne, ed., *Proceedings IFIP WG 10.2 International Working Conference on the Fusion of Hardware Design and Verification*, Glasgow, Scotland (1988).
[66] G.J. Sussman and G.L. Steele Jr, CONSTRAINTS—a language for expressing almost-hierarchical descriptions, *Artif. Intell.* **14** (1) (1980) 1-39.
[67] I.E. Sutherland, SKETCHPAD: A man-machine graphical communication system, MIT Lincoln Labs, Cambridge, MA (1963).
[68] D. Svanaes and E.J. Aas, Test generation through logic programming, *Integr. VLSI J.* **2** (1984) 49-67.
[69] Y. Takamatsu and K. Kinoshita, An efficient test generation method by 10-V algorithm, in: *Proceedings IEEE International Symposium on Circuits and Systems*, Kyoto, Japan (1985) 679-682.
[70] Y. Tohma and K. Goto, Test generation for large-scale combinational circuits by using Prolog, in: *Proceedings 6th International Conference on Logic Programming*, Lisbon, Portugal (1987).
[71] E. Trischler and M. Schulz, Applications of testability analysis to ATG: methods and experimental results, in: *Proceedings IEEE International Symposium on Circuits and Systems*, Kyoto, Japan (1985) 691-694.
[72] P. Van Hentenryck, *Constraint Satisfaction in Logic Programming*, Logic Programming Series (MIT Press, Cambridge, MA, 1989).
[73] P. Van Hentenryck and Y. Deville, The cardinality operator: a new logical connective and its application to constraint logic programming, in: *Proceedings Eighth International Conference on Logic Programming (ICLP-91)*, Paris, France (1991).
[74] P. Van Hentenryck and T. Graf, Standard forms for rational linear arithmetics in constraint logic programming, in: *Proceedings International Symposium on Artificial Intelligence and Mathematics*, Fort Lauderdale, FL (1990).
[75] P Van Hentenryck, V. Saraswat and Y. Deville, Constraint Logic Programming over Finite Domains: the Design, Implementation, and Applications of cc(FD), Tech. Rept., Brown University, Providence, RI (1992).
[76] P. Varma and Y. Tohma, Protean, a knowledge based test generator, in: *Proceedings IEEE 1987 Custom Integrated Circuits Conference*, Portland, OR (1987).
[77] D. Waltz, Generating semantic descriptions from drawings of scenes with shadows, Tech. Rept. AI271, MIT, Cambridge, MA (1972).
[78] T.W. Williams, VLSI Testing, Advances in CAD for VLSI **5** (North-Holland, Amsterdam, Netherlands, 1986).

Minimizing conflicts: a heuristic repair method for constraint satisfaction and scheduling problems

Steven Minton
Sterling Federal Systems, NASA Ames Research Center, AI Research Branch, Mail Stop: 269-2, Moffett Field, CA 94035, USA

Mark D. Johnston
Space Telescope Science Institute, 3700 San Martin Drive, Baltimore, MD 21218, USA

Andrew B. Philips
Sterling Federal Systems, NASA Ames Research Center, AI Research Branch, Mail Stop: 269-2, Moffett Field, CA 94035, USA

Philip Laird
NASA Ames Research Center, AI Research Branch, Mail Stop: 269-2, Moffett Field, CA 94035, USA

Abstract

Minton, S., M.D. Johnston, A.B. Philips and P. Laird, Minimizing conflicts: a heuristic repair method for constraint satisfaction and scheduling problems, Artificial Intelligence 58 (1992) 161–205.

The paper describes a simple heuristic approach to solving large-scale constraint satisfaction and scheduling problems. In this approach one starts with an inconsistent assignment for a set of variables and searches through the space of possible repairs. The search can be guided by a value-ordering heuristic, the *min-conflicts heuristic*, that attempts to minimize the number of constraint violations after each step. The heuristic can be used with a variety of different search strategies.

We demonstrate empirically that on the n-queens problem, a technique based on this approach performs orders of magnitude better than traditional backtracking techniques. We also describe a scheduling application where the approach has been used successfully. A theoretical analysis is presented both to explain why this method works well on certain types of problems and to predict when it is likely to be most effective.

Correspondence to: S. Minton, Sterling Federal Systems, NASA Ames Research Center, AI Research Branch, Mail Stop: 269-2, Moffett Field, CA 94035, USA.

1. Introduction

One of the most promising general approaches for solving combinatorial search problems is to generate an initial, suboptimal solution and then to apply local *repair* heuristics [19, 28, 30, 32, 36, 38, 44]. Techniques based on this approach have met with empirical success on many combinatorial problems, including the traveling salesman and graph partitioning problems [20]. Such techniques also have a long tradition in AI, most notably in problem-solving systems that operate by debugging initial solutions [37, 40]. In this paper, we describe how this idea can be extended to constraint satisfaction problems (CSPs) in a natural manner.

Most of the previous work on CSP algorithms has assumed a "constructive" bracktracking approach in which a partial assignment to the variables is incrementally extended. In contrast, our method creates a complete, but inconsistent assignment and then repairs constraint violations until a consistent assignment is achieved. The method is guided by a simple ordering heuristic for repairing constraint violations: identify a variable that is currently in conflict and select a new value that minimizes the number of outstanding constraint violations.

We present empirical evidence showing that on some standard problems our approach is considerably more efficient than traditional constructive backtracking methods. For example, on the n-queens problem, our method quickly finds solutions to the one million queens problem [30]. We argue that the reason that repair-based methods can outperform constructive methods is because a complete assignment can be more informative in guiding search than a partial assignment. However, the utility of the extra information is domain dependent. To help clarify the nature of this potential advantage, we present a theoretical analysis that describes how various problem characteristics may affect the performance of the method. This analysis shows, for example, how the "distance" between the current assignment and solution (in terms of the minimum number of repairs that are required) affects the expected utility of the heuristic.

The work described in this paper was inspired by a surprisingly effective neural network developed by Adorf and Johnston [2, 22] for scheduling astronomical observations on the Hubble Space Telescope. Our heuristic CSP method was distilled from an analysis of the network. In the process of carrying out the analysis, we discovered that the effectiveness of the network has little to do with its connectionist implementation. Furthermore, the ideas employed in the network can be implemented very efficiently within a symbolic CSP framework. The symbolic implementation is extremely simple. It also has the advantage that several different search strategies can be employed, although we have found that hill-climbing methods are particularly well-suited for the applications that we have investigated.

We begin the paper with a brief review of Adorf and Johnston's neural network, and then describe our symbolic method for heuristic repair. Following this, we describe empirical results with the *n*-queens problem, graph-colorability problems and the Hubble Space Telescope scheduling application. Finally, we consider a theoretical model identifying general problem characteristics that influence the performance of the method.

2. Previous work: the GDS network

By almost any measure, the Hubble Space Telescope scheduling problem is a complex task [21, 34, 43]. Between ten thousand and thirty thousand astronomical observations per year must be scheduled, subject to a great variety of constraints including power restrictions, observation priorities, time-dependent orbital characteristics, movement of astronomical bodies, stray light sources, etc. Because the telescope is an extremely valuable resource with a limited lifetime, efficient scheduling is a critical concern. An initial scheduling system, developed using traditional programming methods, highlighted the difficulty of the problem; it was estimated that it would take over three weeks for the system to schedule one week of observations. As described in Section 4.2, this problem was remedied by the development of a successful constraint-based system to augment the initial system. At the heart of the constraint-based system is a neural network developed by Adorf and Johnston, the guarded discrete stochastic (GDS) network, which searches for a schedule [2, 22].

From a computational point of view the network is interesting because Adorf and Johnston found that it performs well on a variety of tasks, in addition to the space telescope scheduling problem. For example, the network performs significantly better on the *n*-queens problem than methods that were previously developed. The *n*-queens problem requires placing n queens on an $n \times n$ chessboard so that no two queens share a row, column or diagonal. The network has been used to solve problems of up to 1024 queens, whereas most heuristic backtracking methods encounter difficulties with problems one-tenth that size [39].

The GDS network is a modified Hopfield network [18]. In a standard Hopfield network, all connections between neurons are symmetric. In the GDS network, the main network is coupled asymmetrically to an auxiliary network of *guard neurons* which restrict the configurations that the network can assume. This modification enables the network to rapidly find a solution for many problems, even when the network is simulated on a serial machine. Unfortunately, convergence to a stable configuration is no longer guaranteed. Thus the network can fall into a local minimum involving a group of unstable states among which it will oscillate. In practice, however, if the network fails to converge after some number of neuron state transitions, it can simply be stopped and started over.

To illustrate the network architecture and updating scheme, let us consider how the network is used to solve binary constraint satisfaction problems. A problem consists of n variables, $X_1, \ldots, X_n$, with domains $D_1, \ldots, D_n$, and a set of binary constraints. Each constraint $C_\alpha(X_j, X_k)$ is a subset of $D_j \times D_k$ specifying incompatible values for a pair of variables. The goal is to find an assignment for each of the variables which satisfies the constraints. (In this paper we only consider the task of finding a single solution, rather than that of finding all solutions.) To solve a CSP using the network, each variable is represented by a separate set of neurons, one neuron for each of the variable's possible values. Each neuron is either "on" or "off" and in a solution state, every variable will have exactly one of its corresponding neurons "on", representing the value of that variable. Constraints are represented by inhibitory (i.e., negatively weighted) connections between the neurons. To insure that every variable is assigned a value, there is a guard neuron for each set of neurons representing a variable; if no neuron in the set is on, the guard neuron will provide an excitatory input that is large enough to turn one on. (Because of the way the connection weights are set up, it is unlikely that the guard neuron will turn on more than one neuron.) The network is updated on each cycle by randomly picking a set of neurons that represents a variable, and flipping the state of the neuron in that set whose input is *most inconsistent* with its current output (if any). When all neurons' states are consistent with their input, a solution is achieved.

To solve the n-queens problem, for example, each of the $n \times n$ board positions is represented by a neuron whose output is either one or zero depending on whether a queen is currently placed in that position or not. (Note that this is a local representation rather than a distributed representation of the board.) If two board positions are inconsistent, then an inhibiting connection exists between the corresponding two neurons. For example, all the neurons in a column will inhibit each other, representing the constraint that two queens cannot be in the same column. For each row, there is a guard neuron connected to each of the neurons in that row which gives the neurons in the row a large excitatory input, enough so that at least one neuron in the row will turn on. The guard neurons thus enforce the constraint that one queen in each row must be on. As described above, the network is updated on each cycle by randomly picking a row and flipping the state of the neuron in that row whose input is most inconsistent with its current output. A solution is realized when the output of every neuron is consistent with its input.

3. Why does the GDS network perform so well?

Our analysis of the GDS network was motivated by the following question: "Why does the network perform so much better than traditional backtracking methods on certain tasks"? In particular, we were intrigued by the results on the n-queens problem, since this problem has received considerable attention from previous researchers. For n-queens, Adorf and Johnston found empirically that the network requires a linear number of transitions to converge. Since each transition requires linear time, the expected (empirical) time for the network to find a solution is $O(n^2)$. To check this behavior, Johnston and Adorf ran experiments with n as high as 1024, at which point memory limitations became a problem.[1]

3.1. Nonsystematic search hypothesis

Initially, we hypothesized that the network's advantage came from the nonsystematic nature of its search, as compared to the systematic organization inherent in depth-first backtracking. There are two potential problems associated with systematic depth-first search. First, the search space may be organized in such a way that poorer choices are explored first at each branch point. For instance, in the n-queens problem, depth-first search tends to find a solution more quickly when the first queen is placed in the center of the first row rather than in the corner; apparently this occurs because there are more solutions with the queen in the center than with the queen in the corner [39]. Nevertheless, most naive algorithms tend to start in the corner simply because humans find it more natural to program that way. However, this fact by itself does not explain why nonsystematic search would work so well for n-queens. A backtracking program that randomly orders rows (and columns within rows) performs much better than the naive method, but still performs poorly relative to the GDS network.

The second potential problem with depth-first search is more significant and more subtle. As illustrated by Fig. 1, a depth-first search can be a disadvantage when solutions are not evenly distributed throughout the search space. In the tree at the left of the figure, the solutions are clustered together. In the tree on the right, the solutions are more evenly distributed. Thus, the average distance between solutions is greater in the left tree. In a depth-first search, the average time to find the first solution increases with the average distance between solutions. Consequently depth-first search performs relatively poorly in a tree where the solutions are clustered, such as that on the left [13, 29]. In comparison, a search strategy which examines the leaves of the tree in random order is unaffected by solution clustering.

We investigated whether this phenomenon explained the relatively poor performance of depth-first search on n-queens by experimenting with a ran-

---

[1] The network, which is programmed in LISP, requires approximately 11 minutes to solve the 1024 queens problem on a TI Explorer II. For larger problems, memory becomes a limiting factor because the network requires approximately $O(n^2)$ space. (Although the number of connections is actually $O(n^3)$, some connections are computed dynamically rather than stored.)

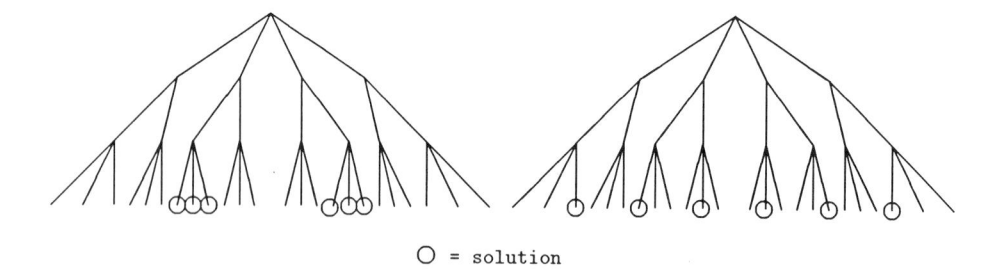

Fig. 1. Solutions clustered vs. solutions evenly distributed.

domized search algorithm, called a Las Vegas algorithm [5]. The algorithm begins by selecting a path from the root to a leaf. To select a path, the algorithm starts at the root node and chooses one of its children with equal probability. This process continues recursively until a leaf is encountered. If the leaf is a solution the algorithm terminates, if not, it starts over again at the root and selects a path. The same path may be examined more than once, since no memory is maintained between successive trials.

The Las Vegas algorithm does, in fact, perform better than simple depth-first search on n-queens. In fact, this result was already known [5]. However, the performance of the Las Vegas algorithm is still not nearly as good as that of the GDS network, and so we concluded that the systematicity hypothesis alone cannot explain the network's behavior.

3.2. Informedness hypothesis

Our second hypothesis was that the network's search process uses information about the current assignment that is not available to a constructive backtracking program. We now believe this hypothesis is correct, in that it explains why the network works so well. In particular, the key to the network's performance appears to be that state transitions are made so as to reduce the number of outstanding inconsistencies in the network; specifically, each state transition involves flipping the neuron whose output is most inconsistent with its current input. From a constraint satisfaction perspective, it is as if the network reassigns a value for a variable by choosing the value that violates the fewest constraints. This idea is captured by the following heuristic:

> **Min-Conflicts heuristic:**
> *Given*: A set of variables, a set of binary constraints, and an assignment specifying a value for each variable. Two variables *conflict* if their values violate a constraint.

Procedure: Select a variable that is in conflict, and assign it a value that minimizes the number of conflicts.[2] (Break ties randomly.)

We have found that the network's behavior can be approximated by a symbolic system that uses the min-conflicts heuristic for hill climbing. The hill-climbing system starts with an initial assignment generated in a preprocessing phase. At each choice point, the heuristic chooses a variable that is currently in conflict and reassigns its value, until a solution is found. The system thus searches the space of possible assignments, favoring assignments with fewer total conflicts. Of course, the hill-climbing system can become "stuck" in a local maximum, in the same way that the network may become "stuck" in a local minimum. In the next section we present empirical evidence to support our claim that the min-conflicts approach can account for the network's effectiveness.

There are two aspects of the min-conflicts hill-climbing method that distinguish it from standard CSP algorithms. First, instead of incrementally constructing a consistent partial assignment, the min-conflicts method *repairs* a complete but inconsistent assignment by reducing inconsistencies. Thus, it uses information about the current assignment to guide its search that is not available to a standard backtracking algorithm. Second, the use of a hill-climbing strategy rather than a backtracking strategy produces a different style of search.

Extracting the method from the network enables us to tease apart and experiment with its different components. In particular, the idea of repairing an inconsistent assignment can be used with a variety of different search strategies in addition to hill climbing. For example, we can backtrack through the space of possible repairs, rather than using a hill-climbing strategy, as follows. Given an initial assignment generated in a preprocessing phase, we can employ the min-conflicts heuristic to order the choice of variables and values to consider, as described in Fig. 2. Initially, the variables are all on a list of VARS-LEFT, and as they are repaired, they are pushed onto a list of VARS-DONE. The algorithm attempts to find a sequence of repairs, such that no variable is repaired more than once. If there is no way to repair a variable in VARS-LEFT without violating a previously repaired variable (a variable in VARS-DONE), the algorithm backtracks.

Notice that this algorithm is simply a standard backtracking algorithm

---

[2] In general, the heuristic attempts to minimize the number of other variables that will need to be repaired. For binary CSPs, this corresponds to minimizing the number of conflicting variables. For general CSPs, where a single constraint may involve several variables, the exact method of counting the number of variables that will need to be repaired depends on the particular constraint. The space telescope scheduling problem is a general CSP, whereas the other tasks described in this paper are binary CSPs.

```
Procedure INFORMED-BACKTRACK (VARS-LEFT VARS-DONE)
  If all variables are consistent, then solution found, STOP.
  Let VAR = a variable in VARS-LEFT that is in conflict.
  Remove VAR from VARS-LEFT.
  Push VAR onto VARS-DONE.
  Let VALUES = list of possible values for VAR ordered in ascending order
               according to number of conflicts with variables in VARS-
               LEFT.
  For each VALUE in VALUES, until solution found:
    If VALUE does not conflict with any variable that is in VARS-DONE,
    then Assign VALUE to VAR.
      Call INFORMED-BACKTRACK(VARS-LEFT VARS-DONE)
    end if
  end for
end procedure

Begin program
  Let VARS-LEFT = list of all variables, each assigned an initial value.
  Let VARS-DONE = nil
  Call INFORMED-BACKTRACK(VARS-LEFT VARS-DONE)
End program
```

Fig. 2. Informed backtracking using the min-conflicts heuristic.

augmented with the min-conflicts heuristic to order its choice of which variable and value to attend to. This illustrates an important point. The backtracking repair algorithm incrementally extends a consistent partial assignment (i.e., VARS-DONE), as does a constructive backtracking program, but in addition, uses information from the initial assignment (i.e., VARS-LEFT) to bias its search. Thus, it is a type of *informed backtracking*. We still characterize it as repair-based method since its search is guided by a complete, inconsistent assignment.

4. Experimental results

In this section we evaluate the performance of the min-conflicts heuristic on some standard tasks. These experiments identify problems on which min-conflicts performs well, as well as problems on which it performs poorly. The experiments also show the extent to which the min-conflicts approach approximates the behavior of the GDS network.

Our experiments focus on the two search strategies described in the previous section, the hill-climbing repair strategy and the backtracking repair strategy.

These strategies provide a starting point for our analysis, although many more sophisticated search strategies exist. In general, these two strategies have the following advantages and disadvantages:

(1) *Hill climbing.* This strategy most closely replicates the behavior of the GDS network. The disadvantage is that a hill-climbing program can get caught in local maxima, in which case it will not terminate.
(2) *Informed backtracking.* As described earlier, this strategy is a standard backtracking strategy augmented with the min-conflicts heuristic for ordering the assignment of variables and values; this can be viewed as backtracking in the space of possible repairs. The advantage of this strategy is that it is complete—if there is a solution, it will eventually be found; if not, failure will be reported. Unfortunately, this is of limited significance for large-scale problems because terminating in a failure can take a very long time.

4.1. The n-queens problem

The n-queens problem, originally posed in the 19th century, has become a standard benchmark for testing CSP algorithms. In a sense, the problem of finding a single solution has been solved, since there are a number of analytic methods which yield a solution in linear time [1]. For example, there are certain well-known patterns that can be instantiated to produce a solution. Nevertheless, the problem has been perceived as relatively "hard" for heuristic search methods. Several studies of the n-queens problem [15, 25, 39] have compared heuristic backtracking methods such as search rearrangement backtracking (e.g., most-constrained first), forward checking, dependency-directed backtracking, etc. To the best of our knowledge, the GDS network was the first search method which could consistently solve problems involving hundreds of queens in several minutes.

On the n-queens problem, Adorf and Johnston [2] reported that the probability of the GDS network converging increases with the size of the problem. For large problems, e.g., $n > 100$ (where n is the number of queens), they observed that the network almost always converges. Moreover, the median number of transitions required for convergence is only about $1.16n$. Since it takes $O(n)$ time to execute a transition (i.e., picking a neuron and updating its connections), the expected time to solve a problem is (empirically) $O(n^2)$.

To compare the network with our min-conflicts approach, we constructed a hill-climbing program that operates as follows. A preprocessing phase creates an initial assignment using a greedy algorithm that iterates through the rows, placing each queen on the column where it conflicts with the fewest previously placed queens (breaking ties randomly). In the subsequent repair phase the program keeps repairing the assignment until a solution is found. To make a repair, the program selects a queen that is in conflict and moves it to the column (within the same row) where it conflicts with the fewest other queens (breaking ties randomly). A repair can be accomplished in $O(n)$ time by maintaining a list of the queens currently in conflict and an array of counters indicating the number of queens in each column and diagonal.

Interestingly, in our initial experiments we found that the hill-climbing program performs significantly *better* than the network. For $n \geq 100$ the program has never failed to find a solution. Moreover, the required number of repairs appears to remain *constant* as n increases. For comparison, recall that the required number of repairs for the network increases linearly with n. After further analysis, we found that this discrepancy can be accounted for by the network's and the hill-climbing program's different initialization processes. In particular, whereas the network starts with no queens assigned in the initial state, the hill-climbing program's preprocessing phase invariably produces an initial assignment that is "close" to a solution. As shown in Table 1, the number of conflicting queens in the initial assignment grows extremely slowly, from a mean of 3.1 for $n = 10$ to a mean of 12.8 for $n = 10^6$. We found that if we start the network in an initial state produced by our preprocessing algorithm, the network and the hill-climbing program perform comparably. (We note, however, that the network requires $O(n^2)$ space, as compared to the $O(n)$ space required by the hill-climbing program, which prevented us from running very large problems on the network.) On the other hand, if we start the hill-climbing program with a random initial assignment, the required number of repairs tends to grow linearly. This is not surprising, since the number of conflicts in a random finitialization also tends to grow linearly.

Table 2 compares the efficiency of our hill-climbing program and several backtracking programs. Each program was run one hundred times for n increasing from ten to one million. Each entry in the table shows the mean number of queens moved, where each move is either a backtrack or a repair, depending on the program. A bound of $n \times 100$ queen movements was employed so that the experiments could be conducted in a reasonable amount of time; if the program did not find a solution after moving $n \times 100$ queens, it was terminated and credited with $n \times 100$ queen movements. For the cases

Table 1
Number of conflicts after initialization.

n	Conflicts after initialization
$n = 10^1$	3.11
$n = 10^2$	7.35
$n = 10^3$	9.75
$n = 10^4$	10.96
$n = 10^5$	12.02
$n = 10^6$	12.80

Table 2
Number of backtracks/repairs for n-queens algorithms.

	Constructive		Repair-based	
n	Standard backtrack	Most constrained backtrack	Min-conflicts hill climbing	Min-conflicts backtrack
$n = 10^1$	53.8	17.4	57.0	46.8
$n = 10^2$	4473 (70%)	687 (96%)	55.6	25.0
$n = 10^3$	88650 (13%)	22150 (81%)	48.8	30.7
$n = 10^4$	*	*	48.5	27.5
$n = 10^5$	*	*	52.8	27.8
$n = 10^6$	*	*	48.3	26.4

* = exceeded computational resources.

when this occurred, the corresponding table entry indicates in parentheses the percentage of times the program completed successfully. The first column shows the results for a standard constructive backtracking program. For $n \geq 1000$, the program was ineffective. The second column in the table shows the results for informed backtracking using the "most-constrained first" heuristic. This program is a constructive backtracking program that selects the row that is most constrained when choosing the next row on which to place a queen. In an empirical study of the n-queens problem, Stone and Stone [39] found that this was by far the most powerful heuristic for the n-queens problem out of several described earlier by Bitner and Reingold [4]. The program exhibited highly variable behavior. At $n = 1000$, the program found a solution on only 81% of the runs, but three-quarters of these successful runs required fewer than 100 backtracks. Unfortunately, for $n > 1000$, one hundred runs of the program required considerably more than 12 hours on a SPARCstation1, both because the mean number of backtracks grows rapidly and because the "most-constrained first" heuristic takes $O(n)$ time to select the next row after each backtrack. Thus we were prevented from generating sufficient data for $n > 1000$. The next column in the table shows the results for hill climbing using the min-conflicts heuristic. As discussed above, this algorithm performed extremely well, requiring only about 50 repairs irrespective of problem size. The final column shows the results for an informed backtracking program that uses the min-conflicts heuristic, backtracking within the space of possible repairs as described in the previous section. We augmented this program with a pruning heuristic that would prune a path when the number of constraint violations began to increase significantly. However, this proved unnecessary for large n. For $n \geq 100$, this program never backtracked (i.e., no queen had to be repaired more than once). This last program performs better than the hill-climbing program (although there is little room for improvement) primarily because the hill-climbing program may move the same queen repeatedly, which degrades its performance.

A disadvantage of the min-conflicts heuristic is that the time to accomplish a repair grows with the size of the problem. For n-queens, as noted above, each repair requires $O(n)$ time in the worst case. Of course, most heuristic methods require time to determine the best alternative at a choice point. For example, the "most-constrained" heuristic also requires $O(n)$ time at each choice point. However, with min-conflicts the tradeoff is clearly cost effective, at least for n-queens. Since the number of repairs remains approximately constant as n grows, the program's runtime is approximately linear. This is illustrated by Fig. 3, which shows the average runtime for the hill-climbing program. In terms of realtime performance, this program solves the million queens problem in less than four minutes on a SPARCstation1.

The cost of making a repair can be optimized for large problems, in which case the average solution time for the million-queens problem is reduced to less than a minute and a half. The program maintains a list of queens that are in conflict, as well as three arrays of counters indicating the number of queens in each column, row and diagonal. Rather than scanning a row for the position with the fewest conflicts, the optimized program maintains a list of empty columns (which tends to be quite small); it first checks for a zero-conflict position by looking for an empty column with no conflicts along the diagonals. If there is no zero-conflict position, the program repeatedly looks for a position with one conflict by randomly selecting a position and checking the number of conflicts in that position. Since there tend to be many positions with one conflict, this technique tends to succeed after just a few tries, so the total number of positions examined is generally very low.

One obvious conclusion from these results is that n-queens is actually a very easy problem given the right method. Interesting, two other heuristic methods that can quickly solve n-queens problems have also recently been invented. (These two other methods and our method were all developed and published

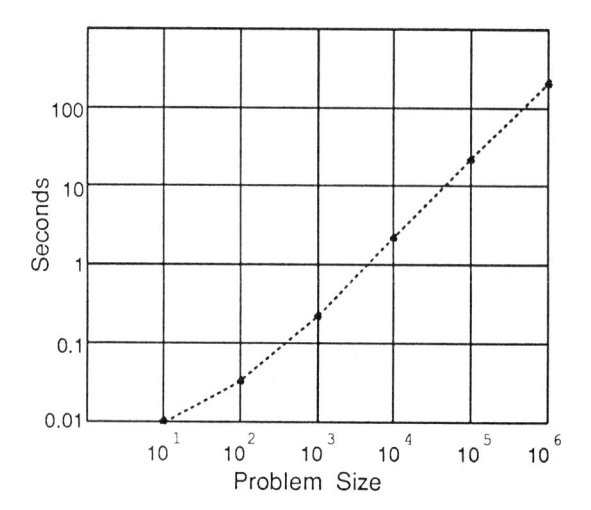

Fig. 3. Mean solution time for hill-climbing program on n-queens problem.

independently.) While both methods are specific to *n*-queens, one method is a repair-based method that is similar to ours in spirit [38], whereas the other employs a constructive backtracking approach [23]. This latter method uses a combination of variable and value-ordering heuristics which take advantage of the particular structure inherent in *n*-queens. This shows that one *can* solve *n*-queens problems quickly with a traditional, constructive backtracking method. Nevertheless, given the comparative simplicity of our method, it would seem that *n*-queens is more naturally solved using a repair-based approach.

4.2. Scheduling applications

Whereas the *n*-queens problem is only of theoretical interest, scheduling algorithms have many practical applications. A scheduling problem involves placing a set of tasks on a time line, subject to temporal constraints, resource constraints, preferences, etc. The Hubble Space Telescope scheduling problem can be considered a constrained optimization problem [10, 12] where we must maximize both the number and the importance of the constraints that are satisfied. As noted earlier, the initial scheduling system developed for this application had difficulty producing schedules efficiently. The constraint-based system, SPIKE, that was developed to augment (and partially replace) the initial system has performed quite well using a relatively simple approach.

In part, the HST scheduling problem was made more tractable by dividing it into two parts, a long-term scheduling problem and a short-term scheduling problem. Currently SPIKE handles only the long-term problem. The long-term problem involves assigning approximately one year's worth of exposures to a set of "bins" or time segments of several days length. (The short-term problem involves deriving a detailed series of commands for the telescope and is addressed using different techniques [34].) The input to SPIKE is a set of detailed specifications for exposure that are to be scheduled on the telescope. The constraints relevant to the long-term problem are primarily temporal constraints. As outlined in [21], some exposures are designed as calibrations or target acquisitions for others, and so must proceed them. Some must be executed at specific times, or at specific phases in the case of periodic phenomena. Some observations must be made at regular intervals, or grouped within a specified time span. The constraints vary in their importance; they range from "hard" constraints that cannot be violated under any circumstances, to "soft" constraints that represent good operating practices and scheduling goals.

SPIKE operates by taking the exposure specifications prepared by astronomers and compiling them into a set of tasks to be scheduled and a set of constraints on those tasks. Among other things, the compilation process takes the transitive closure of temporal constraints and explicitly represents each inferred constraint. For example, if task A must be before task B, and task B must be before task C, then the system will explicitly represent the fact that task A must be before task C as well. This explicit representation enables the scheduler to obtain a more accurate assessment of the number of conflicts in a given schedule.

In searching for a schedule, the GDS network follows the constraint satisfaction approach outlined in Section 2. In effect, if a task is currently in conflict then it is removed from the schedule, and if a task is currently unscheduled then the network schedules it for the time segment that has the fewest constraint violations. However, the network uses only the hard constraints in determining the time segment with the fewest violations. Soft constraints are consulted when there are two or more "least conflicted" places to move a task.

The min-conflicts hill-climbing method has been shown to be as effective as the GDS network on representative data sets used for testing SPIKE, and it was recently incorporated into the SPIKE system. One advantage in using the min-conflicts method, as compared to the GDS network, is that much of the overhead of using the network can be eliminated (particularly the space overhead). Moreover, because the min-conflicts heuristic is so simple, the min-conflicts module was quickly coded in C and is extremely efficient. (The min-conflicts scheduler runs about an order of magnitude faster than the network, although some of the improvement is due to factors such as programming language differences, making a precise comparison difficult.) While this may be regarded as just an implementation issue, we believe that the clear and simple formulation of the method was a significant enabling factor. In addition, the simplicity of the method makes it easy to experiment with various modifications to the heuristic and the search strategy. This has significant practical importance, since SPIKE is currently being used on other types of telescope scheduling problems where a certain amount of modification and tuning is required.

In general, scheduling appears to be an excellent application area for repair-based methods. Supporting evidence comes from recent work on other real-world scheduling applications by Zweben [44], Biefeld and Cooper [3] and Kurtzmann [27]. Each of these projects use iterative improvement methods which can be characterized as repair-based. There are several reasons why repair-based methods are well-suited to scheduling applications. First, as Zweben et al. [45] have pointed out, unexpected events may require schedule revision, in which case dynamic rescheduling is an important issue. Repair-based methods can be used for rescheduling in a natural manner. Second, most scheduling applications involve optimization, at least to some degree, and repair-based methods are also naturally extended to deal with such issues. For example, in scheduling the Hubble Space Telescope, the goal is to maximize the amount of observing time and the priority of the chosen observations. The telescope is expected to remain highly over-subscribed, in that many more proposals will be submitted than can be accommodated by any schedule. On such problems, repair-based methods offer an alternative to traditional branch-and-bound techniques. Finally, as Biefeld and Cooper [3] have pointed out, there are real-world scheduling problems where humans find repair-based methods very natural. For example, human schedulers at JPL employ repair-based methods when constructing mission schedules for robotic spacecraft. For such problems, it may be relatively easy for people using a repair-based system to understand the system's solution and how it was arrived at.

4.3. Graph coloring

In addition to n-queens problem and HST scheduling, Adorf and Johnston also tested the GDS network on graph 3-colorability problems. A graph 3-colorability problem consists of an undirected graph with n vertices. Each vertex must be assigned one of three colors subject to the constraint that no neighboring vertex is assigned the same color. Graph 3-colorability is a well-studied NP-complete problem that is used to model certain types of scheduling and resource allocation problems, such as examination scheduling and register allocation.

Adorf and Johnston found that the performance of the network depended greatly on the connectivity of the graph. On densely-connected graphs the network converged rapidly to a solution, while on sparsely-connected graphs the network performed much more poorly. We have repeated Adorf and Johnston's experiments using the min-conflicts approach, and found similar results. We have also found that there is a simple, well-known backtracking algorithm for coloring graphs that performs much better than either the network or any of our min-conflicts algorithms on sparsely-connected graphs. This provides a useful case for comparative analysis.

We used the same procedure for generating test problems as Adorf and Johnston. Solvable problems with n nodes and m arcs are generated as follows:

(1) Create three groups of nodes, each with $n/3$ nodes.
(2) Randomly create m arcs between nodes in different groups.
(3) Accept the graph if it has no unconnected components.

Johnston and Adorf experimented with two classes of problem instances; one set with $m = 2n$ (i.e., average vertex degree of 4) and another with $m = n(n-1)/4$. We will refer to the former as the sparsely-connected graphs, and the latter as the densely-connected graphs.

Figure 4 compares the results published by Adorf and Johnston with our results. In Adorf and Johnston's experiments, graphs were tested in the range from $n = 30$ to $n = 180$. For each of the two types of graphs, three different instances of each size were generated, and the network was run 3000 times per graph. Our experiments with the min-conflicts hill-climbing algorithm employed the same experimental design.

Because the network is started with all nodes "uncolored", we employed a similar approach with the hill-climbing program so that the comparison would be fair. Thus, in the initialization phase, each vertex is labeled as "uncolored". An uncolored node is defined to conflict with each of its neighbors, regardless of their color.

The results demonstrate that the hill-climbing algorithm behaves similarly to the GDS network on both types of problems. This supports our hypothesis that the hill-climbing algorithm captures the essential characteristics of the network. As shown in Fig. 4(a), the densely-connected graphs are easy to solve. Both methods tend to converge rather quickly on average. Specifically, the mean number of transitions required for convergence appears to grow linearly with n. The sparsely-connected graphs are much harder. In these experiments, the network was given a bound of $9n$ transitions, after which the run was terminated. (The bound was chosen arbitrarily, but means in principle that each of the $3n$ neurons in the main network can transition three times.) The hill-climbing algorithm was therefore given a bound of $9n$ repairs. As illustrated in Fig. 4(b), for both methods, the probability of success appears to decline exponentially with n.[3] Adorf and Johnston observed that as the number of nodes increases, it is highly likely that the network will become caught in a local minimum in which a small number of neurons transition repeatedly. That is, the network becomes trapped, vacillating between several states. The hill-climbing algorithm behaves in a similar manner.

To determine whether the min-conflicts approach would be practical for graph-coloring applications, we compared our min-conflicts hill-climbing algorithm to a simple constructive backtracking algorithm that is known to perform well on graph-coloring problems. The algorithm, originally proposed by Brelaz [6, 41], can be described as the repeated application of the following rule for choosing a node to color:

> Find the uncolored node that has the fewest consistent colorings with its neighbors. If there is more than one, then choose one that has the maximum degree in the uncolored subgraph. Break ties randomly.

---

[3] The use of an identical bound for both programs may give the hill-climbing algorithm a slight advantage. The GDS network requires separate transitions to deassign a variable and to assign a new value. In the hill-climbing program a single repair, in effect, simulates two transitions by the network (unless an initial "uncolored" value is being repaired). Additional experimentation has revealed that this advantage is relatively small, however. In fact, Fig. 4(b) shows that on the sparse graphs, the hill-climbing program performed a bit worse than the network for small n, although the significance of this is unclear due to the relatively large statistical variation in the difficulty of the smaller problems. Unfortunately, the network is no longer running, so additional experiments cannot be run.

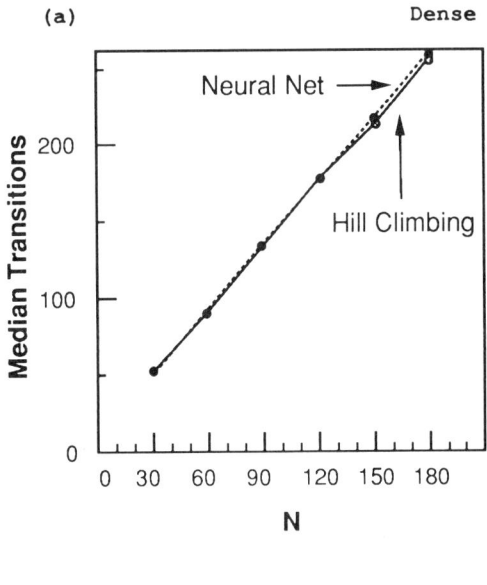

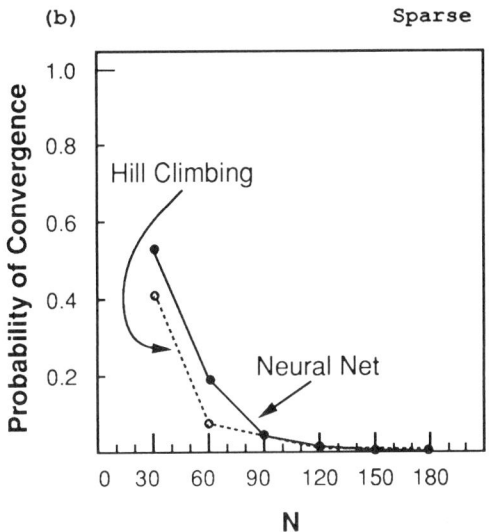

Fig. 4. Comparing the GDS network to min-conflicts hill climbing on dense and sparse graph-coloring problems.

Essentially, this is a variable order rule consisting of two criteria. The first criterion is a preference for the "most-constrained" variable. The tie-breaking criterion is a preference for the "most-constraining" variable. Thus, this rule is composed of two generic variable-ordering heuristics. No value-ordering heuristic is required.

The rule can be incorporated in a standard backtracking algorithm in the obvious manner. Turner [41] has shown that this algorithm will optimally color "almost all" random *k*-colorable graphs without backtracking. This result actually says more about the distribution of random *k*-colorable graphs than about the effectiveness of the algorithm, but nonetheless, the Brelaz algorithm outperforms other algorithms we have tried.

For a fair comparison between the Brelaz algorithm and our min-conflicts algorithm, a good initialization method for the min-conflicts algorithm is presumably required. We can use the Brelaz rule itself to arrive at an initialization for our min-conflicts algorithm. Specifically, the initialization process makes one pass through the vertices of the graph, using the Brelaz variable ordering rule to pick the next vertex to color. If no color consistent with the node's neighbors is available, a color is chosen that minimizes the number of conflicts. This process results in initial colorings with many fewer conflicts than random colorings. Table 3 shows the percentage of times that the initialization routine, by itself, finds a solution, for graphs of size n. Each entry in the table is based on 100 runs of the initialization routine for eight problems of size n to the sparsely-connected and densely-connected graphs described computed problems.

Since the initialization process consistently finds solutions for the densely-connected graphs (eliminating the need for a repair phase), we restricted our experiments to the hard sparsely-connected graphs. Figure 5 compares the performance of the Brelaz algorithm with min-conflicts hill climbing. For completeness, the figure also shows a third algorithm, an informed backtracking problem that uses min-conflicts to search through the space of repairs. For each method, we tested eight randomly generated problems of size n, for 100 runs per problem. The graph shows the probability of finding a solution within $9n$ repairs/backtracks. (The results do not include trials where no repairs were required, or where Brelaz found the solution without backtracking. This is fair since the two repair-based methods use the Brelaz rule for initialization.)

The conclusion from this experiment is that the Brelaz backtracking algorithm obviously outperforms both of the min-conflicts methods. Of the two latter methods, informed backtracking performs slightly better. In addition, comparing the performance of hill climbing with and without the Brelaz

Table 3
Probability that initialization alone will solve the problem.

n	Sparse graphs	Dense graphs
30	63.19%	100.00%
60	50.13%	100.00%
90	40.37%	100.00%
120	32.75%	100.00%
150	32.87%	100.00%
180	23.75%	100.00%

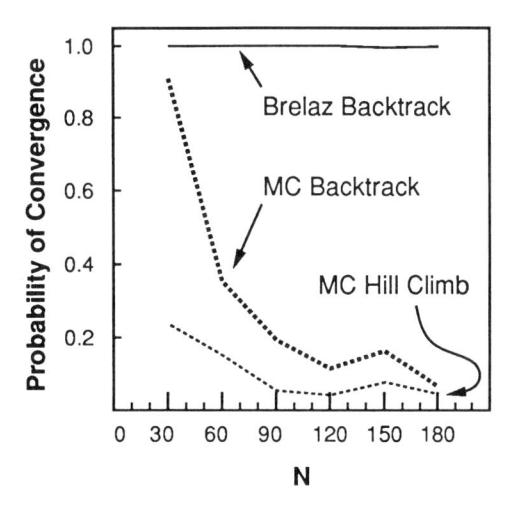

Fig. 5. Comparing Brelaz backtracking with two min-conflicts methods.

initialization method (Fig. 5 and Fig. 4) shows that the initialization method improves performance, but not dramatically.[4]

The experiments also demonstrate clearly that sparse graphs are much harder to color than dense graphs, for both the Brelaz method as well as for the min-conflicts methods. Intuitively, the reason that dense graphs are easy to color is that they are so overconstrained that a mistake is both unlikely and easily corrected. For min-conflicts, a mistake is easily corrected because the choice of color at a vertex is greatly influenced by the colors of all of its neighbors. For the Brelaz backtracking method, a mistake is easily corrected since the subsequent choices will be pruned quickly due to the overconstrained nature of the problem. In a study motivated in part by these experiments, Cheeseman et al. [7] have shown that as the average connectivity of a (connected) graph increases, a "phase transition" occurs, and it is at this point that most of the hard graph colorability problems are found. In other words, sine a constraint satisfaction problem is easy if it is either underconstrained or overconstrained, hard problems can be expected to lie within the boundary between underconstrained and overconstrained problems. Our sparsely-connected graphs lie within this boundary area.

Figure 6 illustrates how the difficulty of sparsely-connected connected graphs manifests itself for min-conflicts. The group of nodes on the left of the graph represents one consistent coloring, and the group on the right represents a different consistent coloring. But the two colorings are inconsistent with each other. This situation frequently arises as a result of the initialization process. On the surface, the assignment would appear to be a good one, since there are

---

[4] Interestingly, the Brelaz initialization method actually degrades performance of the smallest graphs (where $n = 30$). This is an anomaly which we cannot as yet explain.

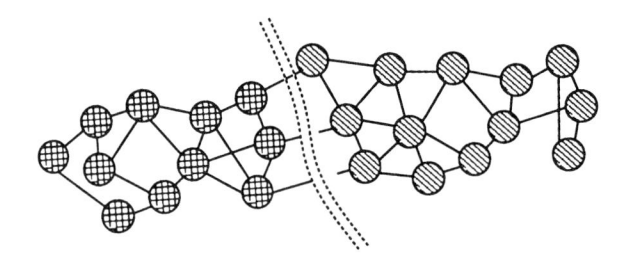

Fig. 6. An unlucky initialization.

at most three pairs of nodes in conflict. However, to achieve a solution, the boundary between the consistent colorings must be "pushed" completely to the left or right during the repair phase. Unfortunately, in this situation, there is not enough information locally available to direct min-conflicts. We have observed, in animations of the hill-climbing program, that the boundary tends to vacillate back and forth with little overall progress being made.

The excellent performance of the Brelaz algorithm led us to experiment with backtracking repair algorithms that are a hybrid of Brelaz and min-conflicts. The best hybrid algorithm we found first employs the Brelaz initialization routine described above. Then a modified version of the Brelaz variable selection rule is used:

> Of the nodes that have not yet been repaired, find the node that has the fewest consistent colorings with its already-repaired neighbors. If there is more than one, then choose one that is in conflict with a previously repaired node. If there is still more than one candidate, choose the one with the maximum degree in the unrepaired subgraph.

The hybrid algorithm uses this rule for variable ordering and min-conflicts heuristic for value ordering. Interestingly, once the initial assignment is made, this algorithm has a higher probability of finding a solution without backtracking than Brelaz. On the other hand, when the algorithm does backtrack, it tends to require more backtracking on average than Brelaz, probably because it does not make as effective use of the "most constraining" criteria for variable selection. Unfortunately, the total time required by the hybrid algorithm tends to increase faster than the total time required by Brelaz, and thus the hybrid method appears to be primarily of academic interest.

4.4. Summary of experimental results

For each of the three tasks we have examined in detail, n-queens, HST scheduling and graph 3-colorability, we have found that the GDS network's behavior can be approximated by the min-conflicts hill-climbing algorithm. To this extent, we have a theory that explains the network's behavior. Obviously, there are certain practical advantages to having "extracted" this method from the network. First, the method is very simple, and so can be programmed extremely efficiently, especially if done in a task-specific manner. Second, the heuristic we have identified, that is, choosing the repair which minimizes the number of conflicts, is very general. It can be used in combination with different search strategies and task-specific heuristics, an important factor for most practical applications.

For example, the min-conflicts heuristic can be used in combination with a variety of variable ordering heuristics. In the previous section, for instance, we described a hybrid program in which the Brelaz variable ordering heuristic is adapted for use with min-conflicts value-ordering heuristic. We have also experimented with a hill-climbing program that uses "max-conflicts" as a variable ordering heuristic in conjunction with the min-conflicts value ordering heuristic. On graph-coloring problems, the resulting program tends to outperform min-conflicts alone, although performance is still not as good as the Brelaz algorithm.

Insofar as the power of our approach is concerned, our experimental results are encouraging. We have identified two tasks, n-queens and HST scheduling, which appear more amenable to our repair-based approach than the traditional constructive approach that incrementally extends a consistent partial assignment. This is not to say that a repair-based approach will do better than *any* constructive approach on these tasks, but merely that our simple, repair-based approach has done relatively well in comparison to the obvious constructive strategies we tried. We also note that repair-based methods have a special advantage for scheduling tasks, since they can be used for overconstrained problems and for rescheduling problems in a natural manner. Thus it seems likely that there are other applications for which our approach will prove useful.

5. Analysis

The previous section showed that, compared to constructive approaches, our repair-based approach is extremely effective on some tasks, such as placing queens on a chessboard, and less effective on other tasks, such as coloring sparsely-connected graphs. We claimed that the min-conflicts heuristic takes advantage of information in the complete assignment to guide its search; this information is not available to a constructive backtracking algorithm that incrementally extends a partial assignment. Thus the advantage of the min-conflicts heuristic over constructive approaches depends on how "useful" this information is. In this section we formalize this intuition. Specifically, we investigate how the use of a complete assignment informs the choice of which value to pick. The analysis reveals how the effectiveness of the min-conflicts heuristic is influenced by various characteristics of a task domain. The analysis is independent of any particular search strategy, such as hill climbing or backtracking.

5.1. Modeling the min-conflicts heuristic

Consider a constraint satisfaction problem with n variables, where each variable has k possible values. We restrict our consideration to a simplified model where every variable is subject to exactly c binary constraints, and we assume that there is only a single solution to the problem, that is, exactly one satisfying assignment. We address the following question: What is the probability that the min-conflicts heuristic will make a mistake when it assigns a value to a variable that is in conflict? We define a mistake as choosing an incorrect value that will have to be changed before the solution is found. We note that for our informed backtracking program a mistake of this sort may prove quite costly, since an entire subtree must be explored before another value can be assigned.

For any assignment of values to the variables, there is a set of d variables whose values must be changed to convert the assignment into the solution. We can regard d as a measure of distance to the solution. The key to our analysis is the following observation. Given a variable V to be repaired, only one of its k possible values will be correct[5] and the other $k-1$ values will be incorrect (i.e., mistakes). Whereas the correct value may conflict with at most d other variables in the assignment, an incorrect value may conflict with as many as c other variables. Thus, as d shrinks, the min-conflicts heuristic should be less likely to make a mistake when it repairs V. In fact, if each of the $k-1$ incorrect values has more than d conflicts, then the min-conflicts heuristic cannot make a mistake—it will select the correct value when it repairs this variable, since the correct value will have fewer conflicts than any incorrect value.

We can use this idea to bound the probability that the min-conflicts heuristic will make a mistake when repairing variable V. Let V' be a variable related to V by a constraint. We assume that an incorrect value for V conflicts with an arbitrary value for V' with probability p, independent of the variables V and V'. Consider an arbitrary incorrect value for V. Let N_b be the total number of conflicts between this incorrect value and the assigned values for the other variables. Given the above assumptions, the expected value of N_b is pc, because there are exactly c variables that share a constraint with V, and the probability of a conflict is p. As mentioned above, the min-conflicts heuristic

---

[5] Although a variable is in conflict, its assigned value may actually be the correct value. This can happen when the variable with which it conflicts has an incorrect value. In this paper we have defined the min-conflicts heuristic so that it can choose *any* possible value for the variable, including the variable's current value.

will not make a mistake if the number of conflicts N_b for each incorrect value is greater than d. We can, therefore, bound the probability of making a mistake by bounding the probability that N_b is less than or equal to d.

To bound N_b, we use Hoeffding's inequality, which states that the sum N of n independent, identically distributed random variables is less than the expected value $\bar{N}$ by more than sn only with probability at most e^{-2s^2n}, for any $s \geq 0$. In our model, N_b is the sum of c potential conflicts, each of which is either 1 or 0, depending on whether there is a conflict. The expected value of N_b is pc. Thus:

$$\Pr(N_b \leq pc - sc) \leq e^{-2s^2c}.$$

Since we are interested in the behavior of the min-conflicts heuristic as d shrinks, let us suppose that d is less than pc. Then, with $s = (pc - d)/c$, we obtain:

$$\Pr(N_b \leq d) \leq e^{-2(pc-d)^2/c}.$$

To account for the fact that a mistake can occur if *any* of the $k - 1$ incorrect values has d or fewer conflicts, we bound the probability of making a mistake on any of them by multiplying by $k - 1$:

$$\Pr(\textit{mistake}) \leq (k - 1)\, e^{-2(pc-d)^2/c}.$$

Note that as c (the number of constraints per variable) becomes large, the probability of a mistake approaches zero if all other parameters remain fixed. This analysis thus offers an explanation as to why 3-coloring densely-connected graphs is relatively easy. We also see that as d becomes small, a mistake is also less likely, explaining our empirical observation that a "good" initial assignment can be important. (Of course, an assignment with few conflicts does not necessarily imply small d, as was illustrated by the 3-colorability problem in Fig. 6.) In a recent paper, Musick and Russell [35] present an analysis which supports this result. They model heuristic repair algorithms as Markov processes, and show that under this model the choice of initial state can have a significant impact on the expected solution time.

Finally, we note that the probability of a mistake also depends on p, the probability that an incorrect value conflicts with another variable's value, and k, the number of values per variable. The probability of a mistake shrinks as p increases or k decreases.

5.2. A statistical model for CSP repair

The simple model presented in the previous section shows, in a qualitative way, how various problem characteristics influence the effectiveness of the min-conflicts heuristic. While the analysis is helpful for understanding how the min-conflicts heuristic works, it is not quantitatively useful, since only very gross characteristics of the problem are considered. In this section we augment the model with statistical assumptions about the task domain, assumptions that enable us to analyze the heuristic's behavior quantitatively on particular problems. Specifically, we discard the assumptions that there is a uniform probability of a conflict between an erroneous value for a variable and an arbitrary value for any related variable and instead assume that conflicts between variables can be characterized by independent probability distribution functions determined by the problem. We retain the assumption that there is a unique solution. While these assumptions are seldom met in practice on any particular CSP, the augmented model turns out to be a surprisingly accurate predictor of the performance of several heuristics, including min-conflicts, on some interesting classes of problems.

We continue to assume a binary CSP with n variables and k possible values per variable; for a given assignment, the distance d is the number of variables that must be corrected to obtain a solution. As a measure of heuristic performance, we use the probability that, after a particular repair step, *the distance d is decreased*. This only occurs when the heuristic selects a variable that is assigned an incorrect (non-solution) value and changes it to the unique correct (solution) value. This probability is given by

$$P_{d \to d-1} = P_{\bar{s}} P_{c|\bar{s}},$$

where $P_{\bar{s}}$ is the probability that the variable selection heuristic chooses a variable currently assigned an incorrect (non-solution) value, and $P_{c|\bar{s}}$ is the probability that the value selection heuristic chooses the correct value given that the selected variable has an incorrect value currently assigned. (Subscripts s and $\bar{s}$ indicate variables assigned solution and non-solution values, respectively. For a given variable, the subscripts c and $\bar{c}$ refer to correct and incorrect values, respectively.)

Similarly, the probability of *increasing* the distance from the solution is

$$P_{d \to d+1} = P_s(1 - P_{c|s}),$$

where $P_s = 1 - P_{\bar{s}}$ is the probability that the variable selection heuristic will choose a variable currently assigned a correct value, and $P_{c|s}$ is the probability that the value selection heuristic will choose the correct value given that the chosen variable already has the correct value assigned. The third possibility, that d will remain unchanged, has probability

$$P_{d \to d} = 1 - P_{d \to d-1} - P_{d \to d+1}.$$

The ratio $P_{d \to d-1}/P_{d \to d+1}$ is of particular interest, since as long as it is greater than 1 a heuristic is more likely to move *towards* the solution than *away* from it.

5.3. Conflict probability distributions

An expression for the performance measures $P_{d \to d, d \pm 1}$ can be derived for variable and value selection heuristics given the probability distributions for conflicts. Four such distributions are required:

For variables currently assigned the correct value:

$$\theta_{cs}(v) = \begin{bmatrix} \text{Probability that the correct value has } v \text{ conflicts,} \\ 0 \leq v \leq d \end{bmatrix},$$

$$\theta_{\bar{c}s}(v) = \begin{bmatrix} \text{Probability that an incorrect value has } v \text{ conflicts,} \\ 0 \leq v \leq n-1 \end{bmatrix}.$$

For variables currently assigned an incorrect value:

$$\theta_{c\bar{s}}(v) = \begin{bmatrix} \text{Probability that the correct value has } v \text{ conflicts,} \\ 0 \leq v \leq d-1 \end{bmatrix},$$

$$\theta_{\bar{c}\bar{s}}(v) = \begin{bmatrix} \text{Probability that an incorrect value has } v \text{ conflicts,} \\ 0 \leq v \leq n-1 \end{bmatrix}.$$

For the cumulative distributions we use the following notation:

$$\theta_{\bar{c}\bar{s}}(>v) = \sum_{w>v} \theta_{\bar{c}\bar{s}}(w).$$

In the remainder of this section we discuss the derivation of these conflict probability distributions θ for two classes of CSPs: those with random independent constraints, and those with more structured constraints. For the readers convenience, Table 4 summarizes the notation we employ.

5.3.1. Random CSPs

Random CSPs can be characterized by two probabilities as follows:

- $p_{c \Rightarrow \bar{c}} \equiv p_{\bar{c} \Rightarrow c}$ is the probability that a *correct* value for variable V conflicts with an *incorrect* value for variable V', and
- $p_{\bar{c} \Rightarrow \bar{c}}$ is the probability that an *incorrect* value for variable V conflicts with an *incorrect* value for variable V',

Note that, by definition, $p_{c \Rightarrow c} = 0$ (there can be no conflicts between correct values).

Consider a state in which there are d variables assigned incorrect values. If a variable is assigned the correct value, then it can conflict with at most the d variables assigned incorrect values. Assuming that *the probability of each conflict is independent*, the total number of conflicts follows a binomial distribution:

$$B(x, p, N) = \binom{N}{x} p^x (1-p)^{N-x}$$

Table 4
Summary of notation.

n	Number of variables
k	Values per variable
c	Binary constraints per variable
d	Distance to solution (number of variables with incorrect values)
$P_{d \to d-1}$	Probability that after a repair step d decreases
$P_{d \to d+1}$	Probability that after a repair step d increases
$P_{d \to d}$	Probability that after a repair step d is unchanged
$P_{\bar{s}}$	Probability that the variable chosen is currently assigned a non-solution (i.e., incorrect) value
$P_{c\mid\bar{s}}$	Probability of choosing a correct value, given that a non-solution value is currently assigned
$\theta_{\bar{c}s}(v)$	For a variable currently assigned a solution value, probability that an incorrect value has v conflicts
$p_{c \Rightarrow \bar{c}}$	Probability that a correct value for variable V conflicts with an incorrect value for variable V'

In general, subscripts s and $\bar{s}$ indicate variables assigned solution and non-solution values, respectively. For a given variable, the subscripts c and $\bar{c}$ refer to correct and incorrect values, respectively.

where x is the number of "successes", p is the probability of success in a single "trial", and N is the number of trials. Thus

$$\theta_{cs}(v) = B(v, p_{\bar{c} \Rightarrow c}, d) .$$

Incorrect values can conflict with the d incorrectly assigned variables, each with probability $p_{\bar{c} \Rightarrow \bar{c}}$, and with the other $n - d - 1$ correctly assigned variables, each with probability $p_{c \Rightarrow \bar{c}}$. The distribution is:

$$\theta_{\bar{c}s}(v) = \sum_{k=0}^{v} B(k, p_{\bar{c} \Rightarrow \bar{c}}, d) B(v - k, p_{c \Rightarrow \bar{c}}, n - d - 1) .$$

This is the distribution for the sum of two binomially-distributed variables with different values for N and p. In the case where $p_{\bar{c} \Rightarrow \bar{c}} = p_{c \Rightarrow \bar{c}} = p_c$, this reduces to $\theta_{\bar{c}s}(v) = B(v, p_c, n - 1)$.

For variables currently assigned incorrect values, the correct value can conflict with at most the $d - 1$ other variables assigned incorrect values, each with probability $p_{c \Rightarrow \bar{c}}$:

$$\theta_{c\bar{s}}(v) = B(v, p_{c \Rightarrow \bar{c}}, d - 1) .$$

Incorrect values can conflict with the other $d - 1$ incorrect variables, each with probability $p_{\bar{c} \Rightarrow \bar{c}}$, and with the $n - d$ correct variables, each with probability $p_{c \Rightarrow \bar{c}}$. The distribution function is:

$$\theta_{\bar{c}s}(v) = \sum_{k=0}^{v} B(k, p_{\bar{c} \Rightarrow \bar{c}}, d-1) B(v-k, p_{c \Rightarrow \bar{c}}, n-d).$$

In the case where $p_{\bar{c} \Rightarrow \bar{c}}$ and $p_{c \Rightarrow \bar{c}} = p_c$, this reduces to $\theta_{\bar{c}s}(v) = B(v, p_c, n-1) = \theta_{\bar{c}s}(v)$.

To calculate $p_{\bar{c} \Rightarrow \bar{c}}$ and $p_{c \Rightarrow \bar{c}}$, suppose that each variable constrains on average c other variables, and, if there is a constraint between any two variables V and V', then each value for V conflicts with an average k' values for V'. Then the probability that V constrains V' is $c/(n-1)$, and the probability that the correct value for V conflicts with an incorrect value for V' is $k'/(k-1)$, where k is the domain size. Thus we have

$$p_{c \Rightarrow \bar{c}} = \frac{c}{n-1} \frac{k'}{k-1}.$$

A similar argument for incorrect values yields

$$p_{\bar{c} \Rightarrow \bar{c}} = \frac{c}{n-1} \frac{k'}{k-1} \frac{k-2}{k-1} = \frac{k-2}{k-1} p_{c \Rightarrow \bar{c}}.$$

Values for $p_{c \Rightarrow \bar{c}}$ and $p_{\bar{c} \Rightarrow \bar{c}}$ are given in Table 5 for some illustrative problem types, including sparse and dense graph 3-colorability problems. For comparison, the table also shows the corresponding values for the random problem described by Dechter and Pearl [8].

Table 5
Probabilities of conflicts between solution and non-solution values $p_{c \Rightarrow \bar{c}}$, and between non-solution and non-solution values $p_{\bar{c} \Rightarrow \bar{c}}$, for some CSPs that can be treated as "random". For graph 3-colorability problems the mean vertex degree (VD) of the problem graph is indicated. The Dechter–Pearl problem, shown for comparison, has probability p_1 of a constraint between variables, and p_2 that a constraint permits any specific pair of values. c is the mean number of variables constrained by any variable, k' is the mean number of values prohibited by a constraint between two variables and k is the domain size.

Problem	c	k'	k	$p_{c \Rightarrow \bar{c}}$	$p_{\bar{c} \Rightarrow \bar{c}}$
Sparse graph 3-colorability VD = 4	4	1	3	$\dfrac{2}{n-1}$	$\dfrac{1}{n-1}$
Dense graph 3-colorability VD = $2n/3$	$\dfrac{2}{3} \cdot n$	1	3	$\dfrac{1}{3} \cdot \dfrac{n}{n-1}$	$\dfrac{1}{6} \cdot \dfrac{n}{n-1}$
Dechter–Pearl general case	$p_1 n$	$(1-p_2)k$	k	$\dfrac{p_1(1-p_2)kn}{(k-1)(n-1)}$	$\dfrac{p_1(1-p_2)k(k-2)n}{(k-1)^2(n-1)}$
Dechter–Pearl $k=5$ $p_1 = 0.5$, $p_2 = 0.6$	$\dfrac{1}{2} \cdot n$	2	5	$\dfrac{1}{4} \cdot \dfrac{n}{n-1}$	$\dfrac{3}{16} \cdot \dfrac{n}{n-1}$

5.3.2. Highly-structured CSPs

The conflict distribution functions for random CSPs derived above predict significant variance in conflict counts in the solution state. For example, when $d = 0$ the distribution $\theta_{\bar{c}s}(v)$ reduces to $B(v, p_{c \Rightarrow \bar{c}}, n-1)$ which has mean $(n-1)p_{c \Rightarrow \bar{c}}$ and variance $(n-1)p_{c \Rightarrow \bar{c}}(1 - p_{c \Rightarrow \bar{c}})$. For some CSPs, the variance in the solution state is demonstrably much less than this, and can be essentially zero for problems with sufficiently strong regularities. For example, treating n-queens as random would predict that many incorrect values would have zero conflicts for large n, but in fact, in the solution state, each incorrect value has at least one conflict. This structure can be incorporated into the calculation of θ, as illustrated in Appendix A for a simplified n-queens model which assumes that exactly three other queens conflict with each incorrect value.

5.4. Value selection heuristics

In this section we derive expressions for the probability of choosing a correct value ($P_{c|s}$ and $P_{c|\bar{s}}$) based on the conflict probability distributions defined in Section 5.3. It is important to note that the derived probabilities depend only on the existence of the θ distributions, and not on their specific form.

5.4.1. Min-conflicts value selection

The min-conflicts value selection heuristic can be stated as:

> Choose a value which has the *minimum* number of conflicts with the assigned values for the other variables. If there is more than one such value, select one at random.

Note that with this rule there need be no change in the assignment.

$P_{c|s}$: variable with correct value assigned

Conflicts on the correct value must be due to one or more of the d variables which have incorrect assignments. Suppose there are $v > 0$ conflicts on the correct value (if there are $v = 0$ conflicts, the variable would not have been selected for repair). We seek the probability of leaving the assigned value unchanged, which is the right decision in this case. If any of the $k-1$ incorrect values has less than v conflicts, then the min-conflicts heuristic will choose one of these values. The correct value will be chosen only if all $k-1$ incorrect values have at least v conflicts. Of the $k-1$ incorrect values, let m be the number which have exactly v conflicts, while the remaining $k-1-m$ have $>v$ conflicts. The probability of such a configuration is:

$$\theta_{\bar{c}s}(v)^m \theta_{\bar{c}s}(>v)^{k-1-m}$$

while the total number of such configurations is $\binom{k-1}{m}$. Since, in this configuration, there are m values other than the correct value with an equal number v of conflicts, the probability of choosing the correct value is $1/(m + 1)$. Thus the total probability of choosing the correct value, given that it has v conflicts, is:

$$P^{\text{sol}}(v) = \sum_{m=0}^{k-1} \binom{k-1}{m} \theta_{\bar{cs}}(v)^m \theta_{\bar{cs}}(>v)^{k-1-m} \frac{1}{m+1}.$$

The probability of v conflicts on the correct value, given that it has >0 conflicts, is $\theta_{cs}(v)/[1 - \theta_{cs}(0)]$. Combining these yields the total probability that the heuristic will leave the assignment unchanged:

$$P_{c|s} = \sum_{v=1}^{d} \frac{\theta_{cs}(v)}{1 - \theta_{cs}(0)} P^{\text{sol}}(v).$$

$P_{c|\bar{s}}$: *variable with incorrect value assigned*

Suppose the number of conflicts on the correct value is v, and that there are w conflicts on the current (incorrect) assigned value. Let $P^{\text{sol}}(v, w)$ denote the probability of choosing the correct value in this situation. There are three cases:

(1) $v > w$. The correct value will not be chosen since the current value has fewer conflicts, so $P^{\text{sol}}(v, w)|_{v>w} = 0$.

(2) $v = w$. In this case we have to consider the other $k - 2$ incorrect values. Summing over configurations where m have exactly v conflicts, and the remaining $k - 2 - m$ have $>v$ conflicts, yields:

$$P^{\text{sol}}(v, w)|_{v=w} \equiv R^{v=w}(v) = \sum_{m=0}^{k-2} \binom{k-2}{m} \theta_{\bar{cs}}(v)^m \theta_{\bar{cs}}(>v)^{k-2-m} \frac{1}{m+2}.$$

(3) $v < w$. Similar to case (2) except that in this case the heuristic will certainly not leave the assignment unchanged, so the probability of choosing the correct value increases from $1/(m + 2)$ to $1/(m + 1)$:

$$P^{\text{sol}}(v, w)|_{v<w} \equiv R^{v<w}(v) = \sum_{m=0}^{k-2} \binom{k-2}{m} \theta_{\bar{cs}}(v)^m \theta_{\bar{cs}}(>v)^{k-2-m} \frac{1}{m+1}.$$

The total probability of choosing the correct value is

$$P_{c|\bar{s}} = \sum_{w=1}^{n-1} \sum_{v=0}^{d-1} \theta_{cs}(v) \frac{\theta_{\bar{cs}}(w)}{1 - \theta_{\bar{cs}}(0)} P^{\text{sol}}(v, w),$$

using the fact that the probability of v conflicts on an incorrect value, given that the value has >0 conflicts, is $\theta_{\bar{cs}}(v)/[1 - \theta_{\bar{cs}}(0)]$.

5.4.2. Random-conflicts value selection

The min-conflicts heuristic examines the *number* of conflicts on each value to determine which to assign. A less-informed heuristic could simply check *whether or not* there are any conflicts on values. This approach is captured by the "random-conflicts" rule:

> If one or more values has *no* conflicts, select one of these values (at random). If *all* values have conflicts, select one at random.

The assignment is not required to change (although it must change if at least one value has zero conflicts).

The derivation of $P_{c|s}$ and $P_{c|\bar{s}}$ follows the same argument as above, with the results:

$$P_{c|s} = \theta_{cs}(>0)^{k-1} \frac{1}{k}$$

and

$$P_{c|\bar{s}} = \theta_{c\bar{s}}(0) P^{\text{sol}}(v, w)\big|_{v=0} + [1 - \theta_{c\bar{s}}(0)] P^{\text{sol}}(v, w)\big|_{v>0},$$

where

$$P^{\text{sol}}(v, w)\big|_{v=0} = \sum_{m=0}^{k-2} \binom{k-2}{m} \theta_{c\bar{s}}(0)^m \theta_{c\bar{s}}(>0)^{k-2-m} \frac{1}{m+1},$$

$$P^{\text{sol}}(v, w)\big|_{v>0} = \theta_{c\bar{s}}(>0)^{k-2} \frac{1}{k}.$$

$P^{\text{sol}}(v, w)$ is the probability of choosing the correct value for a variable with v conflicts on the correct value and $w > 0$ conflicts on an incorrect value.

5.4.3. Random value selection

This is the "least-possible-informed" value selection rule:

> Select and value at random, regardless of conflicts.

With this rule, the probability of choosing the correct value is independent of the variable's currently assigned value:

$$P_{c|s} = P_{c|\bar{s}} = 1/k.$$

5.5. Variable selection

In this section we develop expressions for the probability of selecting a variable to be repaired (P_s or $P_{\bar{s}}$) based on the following simple rule:

> Select for repair a variable at random from the set of all variables that are currently in conflict.

Consider first a variable that is assigned an incorrect value. The probability that there are one or more conflicts on its assigned value is $1 - \theta_{c\bar{s}}(0)$. Since there are a total of d such variables, the expected number with conflicts is

$$N_{\bar{s},\text{conf}} = d[1 - \theta_{c\bar{s}}(0)].$$

Now consider a variable that is assigned a correct value. The probability that there are one or more conflicts on its assigned value is $1 - \theta_{cs}(0)$. Since there are a total of $n - d$ such variables, the expected number with conflicts is

$$N_{s,\text{conf}} = (n - d)[1 - \theta_{cs}(0)].$$

Thus, for a variable with conflicts that is picked at random, the probability that is currently assigned a correct value is:

$$P_s = \frac{N_{s,\text{conf}}}{N_{\bar{s},\text{conf}} + N_{s,\text{conf}}},$$

while the probability that is currently assigned an incorrect value is:

$$P_{\bar{s}} = 1 - P_s = \frac{N_{\bar{s},\text{conf}}}{N_{\bar{s},\text{conf}} + N_{s,\text{conf}}}.$$

5.6. Evaluation of the statistical model

We have numerically evaluated the expressions above for $P_{d \to d, d \pm 1}$, $P_{c|\bar{s}}$, $P_{c|s}$, etc. on two random CSP problem types, and on the simplified n-queens model, in order to compare the predicted performance of the three value selection heuristics discussed above. For the random CSPs we have also generated sample problems and computed the probabilities empirically for comparison with the model. These results are described in this section.

5.6.1. Random CSPs

We have taken two graph 3-colorability problems for comparison of the heuristics:

- *H3C*. "Hard" 3-colorability, random sparsely-connected graph, mean vertex degree = 4. In the solution state the expected number of conflicts on incorrect values is 2, approximately independent of problem size n.
- *E3C*. "Easy" 3-colorability, random densely-connected graph, mean vertex degree = $2n/3$. In the solution state the expected number of conflicts on incorrect values is $n/3$, i.e. increasing linearly with problem size

The relevant conflict probabilities for these two problems are given in Table 5. Probabilities were calculated for both problem types for $n = 90$. Value selection heuristics are labelled as follows in Figs. 8–10: MC min-conflicts (Section 5.4.1); RC random-conflicts (Section 5.4.2); and R random (Section 5.4.3).

Variable selection

Figure 7 shows $P_{\bar{s}}$ vs. d/n, the probability that a variable currently assigned an incorrect value will be chosen for repair. The probability is lower for the densely-connected E3C problem, since even a small number of incorrectly assigned variables can introduce a large number of conflicts.

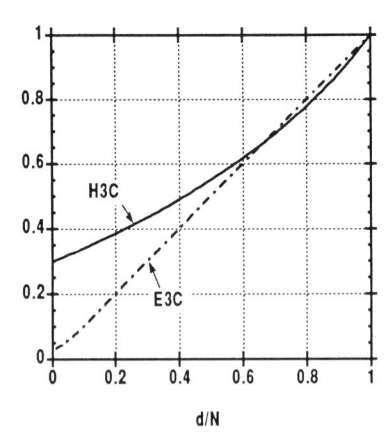

Fig. 7. Probability of selecting a variable that is assigned an incorrect value for H3C and E3C random problems.

Value selection

Figure 8 compares value selection for the two problems. Here it is desirable that both $P_{c|s}$ (Figs. 8(a), (b)) and $P_{c|\bar{s}}$ (Figs. 8(c), (d)) be as large as possible. Random value selection (labelled R in the figures) has uniform probability $\frac{1}{3}$ making the correct choice in both problems. For H3C variables with correct values assigned (Fig. 8(a)), RC does worse than random, and MC does better only for small d/n. In contrast, for variables that have incorrect values (Fig. 8(c)), the probability is fairly high for both MC and RC that the correct value will be selected, with MC showing slightly better performance. For E3C (Figs. 8(b), (d)), MC has probability near unity of choosing the correct value, whether or not the current value is correct. RC does no better than random except for variables currently assigned incorrect values and $d/n < 0.2$ (Fig. 8(d)).

Combined variable and value selection

Figure 9 shows the probabilities of moving towards ($P_{d \to d-1}$, Figs. 9(a), (b)) or away from ($P_{d \to d+1}$, Figs. 9(c), (d)) the solution for the variable selection method combined with each of the three value selection methods. For H3C (Figs. 9(a), (c)), all three value selection methods have higher probability of *worsening* the state than of improving it. MC shows the best performance, with the largest values for $P_{d \to d-1}$ and the smallest for $P_{d \to d+1}$ in the range $d/n < \frac{2}{3}$. For E3C (Figs. 9(b), (d)), both RC and R tend to worsen the state, while MC has a much higher probability of improving it.

The ratio $P_{d \to d-1}/P_{d \to d+1}$ provides a useful comparison of combined variable and value selection performance: it is greater than unity when a heuristic is

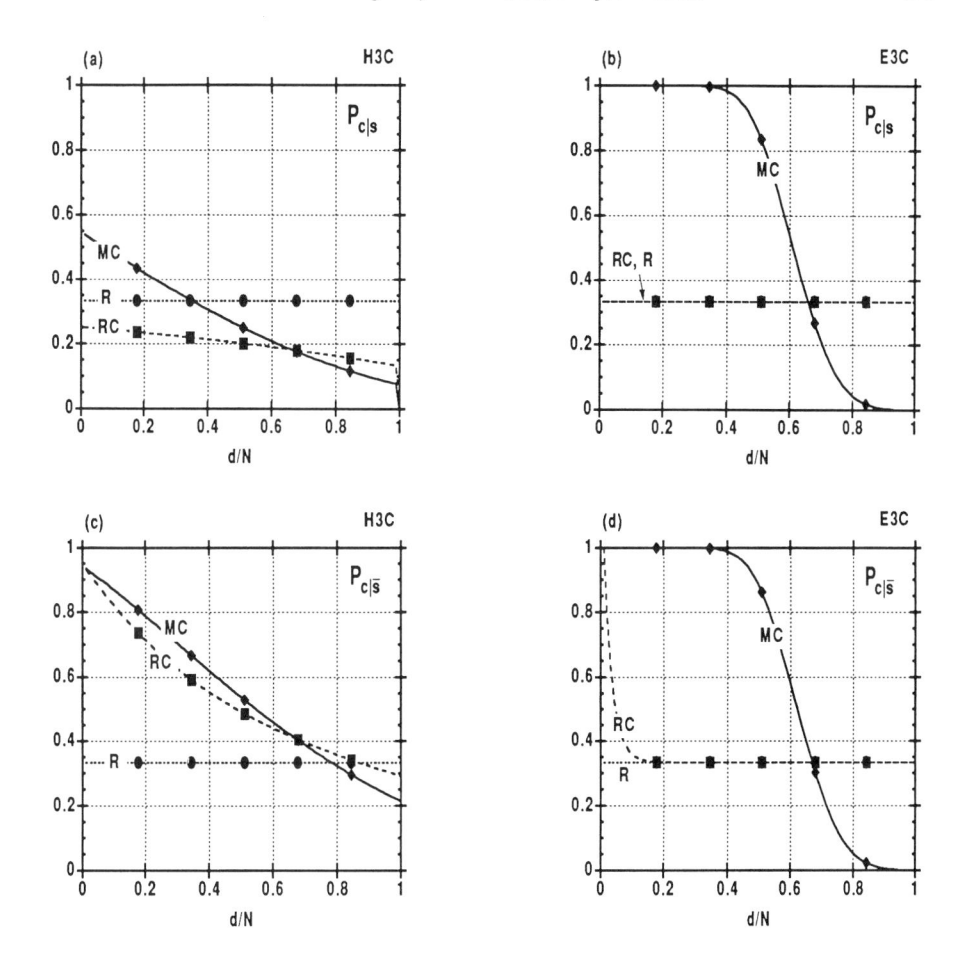

Fig. 8. Probability of choosing correct values for variables currently assigned correct or incorrect values.

more likely to improve the state than to worsen it. Figure 10 plots this ratio on a logarithmic scale vs. d/n for each of the three value selection methods. For H3C (Fig. 10(a)), MC is best (for $d \ll n$), followed by RC and R, but in all cases the ratio is <1. For E3C (Fig. 10(b)) the results are very different: MC shows a much higher chance of improving the state, while both RC and R worsen it. RC is significantly better than R only for very small d/n.

Comparison with empirical results

To see how well the model captures features of the heuristics when applied to actual problems, we have generated random problem instances with known solutions,[6] then assigned incorrect values to some of the variables and calcu-

---

[6] The random problem instances were not guaranteed to have unique solutions; simple relabelling of colors will yield several.

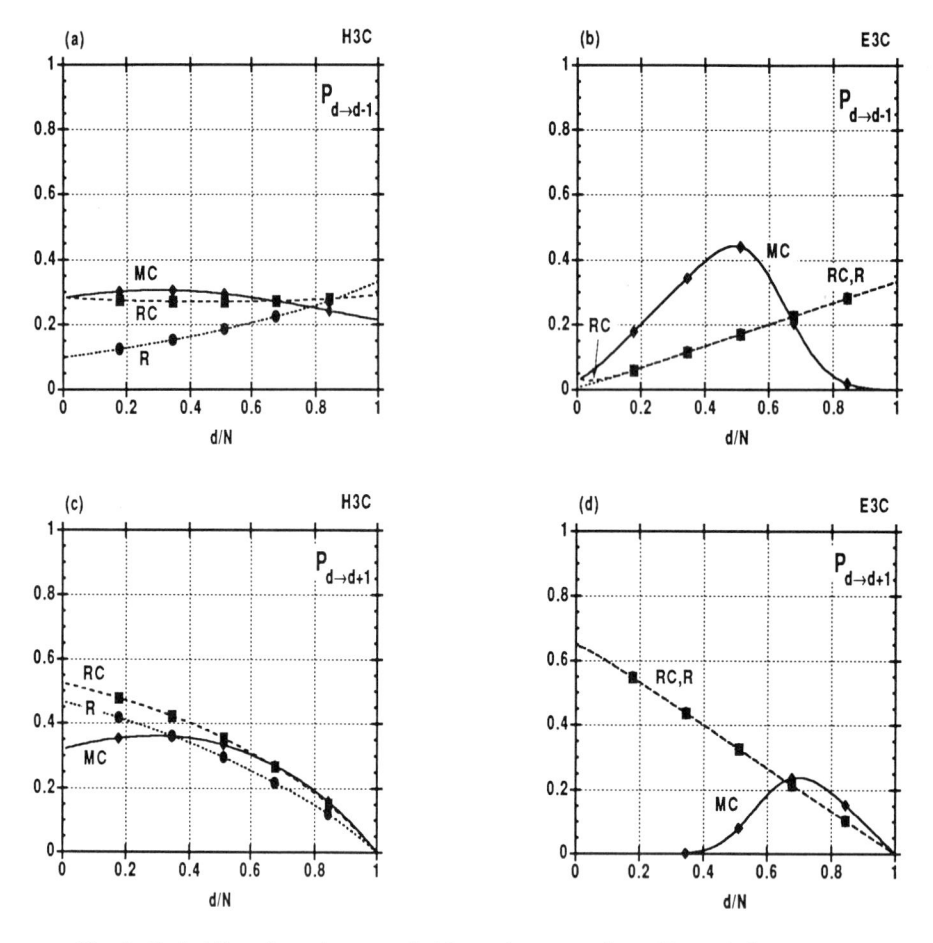

Fig. 9. Probability of moving towards ($P_{d \to d-1}$) or away from ($P_{d \to d+1}$) the solution.

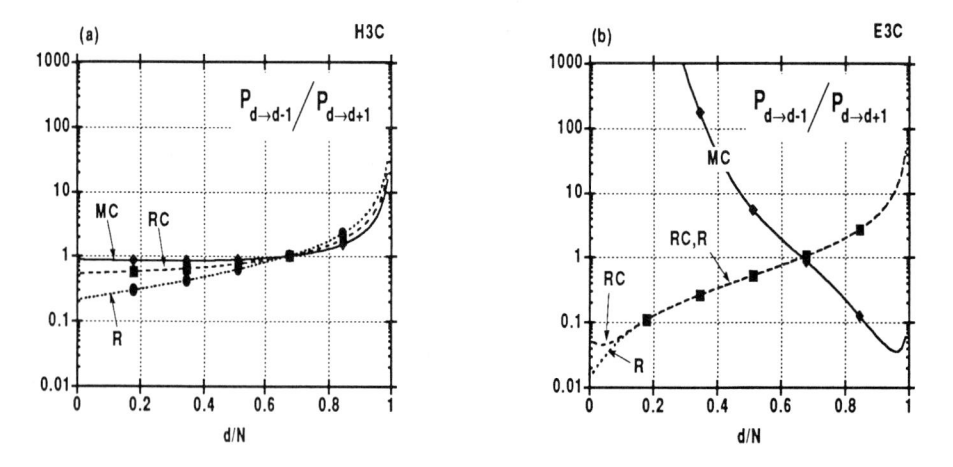

Fig. 10. $P_{d \to d-1}/P_{d \to d+1}$ for the three value selection heuristics.

lated empirically the same probabilities that are predicted by the statistical model. Fig. 11 shows the comparison for MC value selection: the empirical data points, indicated by the + and × symbols, show the results of averaging 200 states for each value of d. The agreement with the model probability calculations is excellent.

5.6.2. n-queens

We have evaluated the simplified n-queens model of Section 5.3.2 and Appendix A for min-conflicts value selection. Figure 12 shows the quantities $P_{d \rightarrow d-1}$, $P_{d \rightarrow d+1}$, and the ratio $P_{d \rightarrow d-1}/P_{d \rightarrow d+1}$ for small d for $n = 64, 96, 128$, and 256. As n increases, the relative probability of moving towards the solution increases as well. While this is in accordance with the experimental results, the

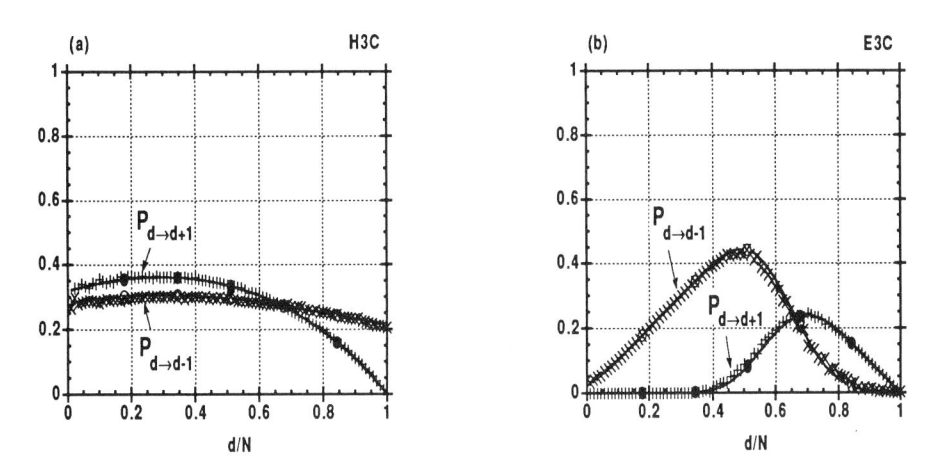

Fig. 11. Comparison of predicted results with empirical results for min-conflicts value selection.

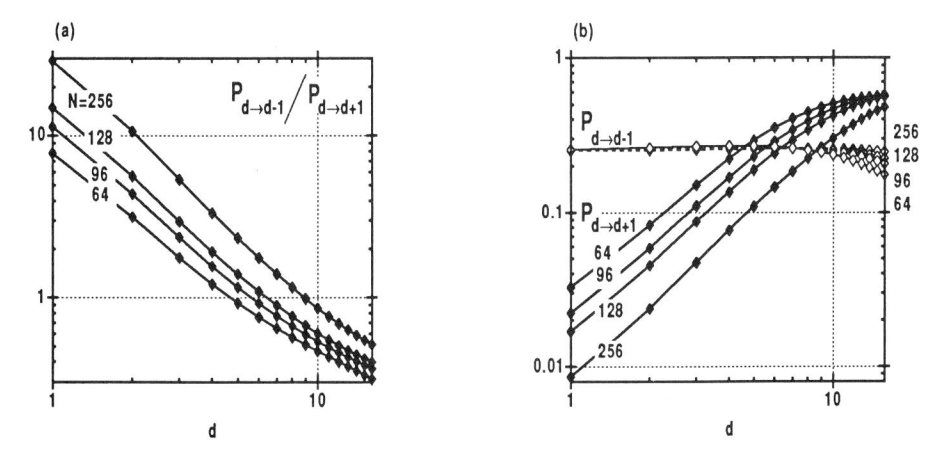

Fig. 12. Performance probabilities for the n-queens model.

model does not permit more quantitative comparison due to the simplifying assumption that the mean conflicts on incorrect values is 3 (instead of the actual ~2.5). The situation for *n*-queens is further complicated by the fact that solutions appear to be relatively numerous, violating the model assumption that there is a unique solution.

5.7. Limiting behavior for random CSPs

There are two interesting limiting cases of the model for random CSPs, corresponding to limiting forms of the conflict probability distribution functions θ (see Section 5.3.1). These limits are discussed in this section.

5.7.1. Poisson limit

In the case $n \to \infty$, $p_{\bar{c} \Rightarrow \bar{c}} \to p_{c \Rightarrow \bar{c}} = p_c$, and $np_c \to$ constant, the conflict distribution functions approach the Poisson distribution: $\theta_{cs}(v) \approx \theta_{c\bar{s}}(v) \approx P_{\text{poisson}}(v, dp_c)$, and $\theta_{\bar{c}s}(v) \approx \theta_{\bar{c}\bar{s}}(v) \approx P_{\text{poisson}}(v, np_c)$, where $P_{\text{poisson}}(v, \mu) = e^{-\mu} \mu^v / v!$. If we let $d = fn$, i.e. f is the fraction of variables assigned incorrect values, we can write the distributions for $\theta_{cs}(v)$ and $\theta_{c\bar{s}}(v)$ as:

$$\theta_{cs}(v) \approx \theta_{c\bar{s}}(v) \approx \frac{(e^{-\mu})^f (f\mu)^v}{v!},$$

here $\mu = np_c$. The result is independent of n, and thus we have the important conclusion that *the performance of value selection heuristics depends only on d/n in the Poisson limit $p_c \propto 1/n$ for small np_c.* This is also true of the variable selection method used in the model (which depends only on $\theta_{\bar{c}s}(0)$ and $\theta_{cs}(0)$). Figure 13(a) illustrates this dependence on d/n for the H3C problem for $n = 30$, 60, and 90: the differences are already nearly indistinguishable.

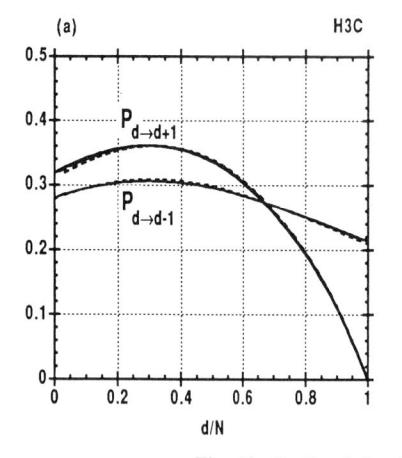

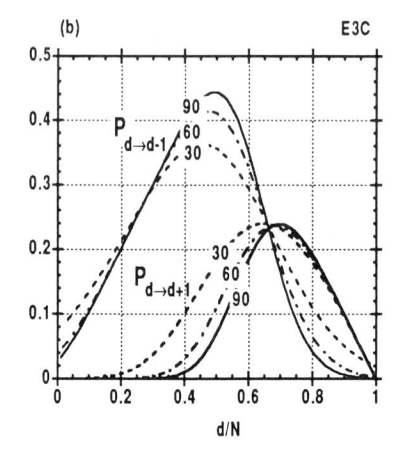

Fig. 13. Scaling behavior with *n* for variable selection method.

5.7.2. Gaussian limit

At the other extreme, consider the case when the mean number of conflicts *increases* with n, e.g. when $p_{c \Rightarrow \bar{c}}$ is approximately constant, and $np_{c \Rightarrow \bar{c}}$, the expected number of conflicts for an incorrect value for a variable when in the solution state, increases linearly with n. In this case, for sufficiently large n, the distributions can be approximated by Gaussian distributions with mean $np_{c \Rightarrow \bar{c}}$ and variance $\sigma^2 = np_{c \Rightarrow \bar{c}}(1 - p_{c \Rightarrow \bar{c}})$. We can derive the dominant behavior of min-conflicts value selection in the limit $n \gg d \gg 1$ by approximating the sums in the expressions for $P_{c|\bar{s}}$ and $P_{c|s}$ by integrals over the Gaussian distribution. Only values near the peak of the Gaussian make significant contributions, and in the limit $P_{c|\bar{s}} \approx P_{c|s} \approx 1$. The probability of choosing a variable with an incorrect value becomes $P_{\bar{s}} \approx d/n$ since $N_{\bar{s},\text{conf}} \approx d$ and $N_{s,\text{conf}} \approx n - d$. From this it follows that $P_{d \to d-1} \approx d/n$ and $P_{d \to d+1} \approx 0$. This linear dependence of $P_{d \to d-1}$ on d for large n is evident in Fig. 13(b), which shows $P_{d \to d-1}$ and $P_{d \to d+1}$ for $n = 30, 60$, and 90 for MC value selection.

5.7.3. Global performance of min-conflicts hill-climbing repair

The simple limiting forms above permit some general statements to be made about the behavior of hill-climbing repair methods based on min-conflicts value selection. Hill-climbing repair can be modelled as a random (Markovian) walk described by the probabilities $P_{d \to d, d \pm 1}$ of moving towards or away from an "absorbing barrier" at $d = 0$.

In the Gaussian limit where $P_{d \to d+1} \approx 0$, $P_{d \to d-1} \approx d/n$ (cf. Fig. 9(b)), the expected number of hill-climbing steps to transition from d to $d - 1$ is $1/P_{d \to d-1} = n/d$. From an initial distance d_0, the expected number of steps t to reach $d = 0$ is thus

$$t_{d_0 \to 0} = \sum_{i=1}^{d_0} \frac{n}{i} \approx n \left[\gamma + \ln d_0 + O\left(\frac{1}{d_0^2}\right) \right]$$

where $\gamma = 0.577\ldots$ is Euler's constant. Thus *the expected number of steps to reach the solution is linear in the problem size n and depends only logarithmically on how far away the initial guess is from the solution.*

In the Poisson limit where $P_{d \to d+1} > P_{d \to d-1}$ but both are nearly constant (cf. Fig. 9(a)), the distance from the solution after t steps can be written as $d(t) = d_0 + \sum_{i=1}^{t} \xi_i$ where ξ_i is a random variable representing the change in d with each step. The probability distribution for ξ has mean $\mu = P_{d \to d+1} - P_{d \to d-1}$ and variance $\sigma^2 = P_{d \to d+1} + P_{d \to d-1} - (P_{d \to d+1} - P_{d \to d-1})^2$. After a sufficiently large number of steps, the distribution for $d(t)$ is approximately Gaussian with mean $\mu_d = d_0 + t\mu$ and variance $\sigma_d^2 = t\sigma^2$. The mean μ_d represents a drift of the expected value of $d(t)$ *away* from the solution $d = 0$. The probability of reaching the solution after t steps is approximately given by the tail of the Gaussian distribution for $d \leq 0$, which approaches

$$\frac{\sigma}{\mu\sqrt{2\pi t}} \exp\left(-\frac{\mu^2 t}{2\sigma^2}\right)$$

for large t. The important point is the predicted *exponential decline in the probability of reaching the solution as the number of hill-climbing steps increases*. This result provides an explanation for the observed behavior of the GDS network and of min-conflicts hill climbing on sparse 3-colorable graphs as described above in Section 4.3: when the number of steps is limited to $t \propto n$, there is an exponential decline with problem size n of the probability of finding the solution.

5.8. Summary and caveats

The statistical model of CSP repair described here is a surprisingly good predictor of "conflict-informed" value selection performance for random CSPs. The model has both theoretical and practical benefits. It permits average-case comparisons of different variable and value selection heuristics, from which can be drawn general conclusions about their relative effectiveness. For particular problem types, limiting behavior for large n can be derived, including general statements as to whether heuristics will show better or worse performance as problem size increases. For random CSPs discussed in detail above, these conclusions include:

- min-conflicts is the most effective value selection method among those considered;
- min-conflicts performs relatively better as n increases, particularly when $p_{c\Rightarrow\bar{c}}$ increases with n or remains constant;
- if the Gaussian limit applies, then hill climbing with min-conflicts is an effective repair strategy, showing only weak dependence on the initial guess and $O(n)$ dependence on problem size n;
- if the Poisson limit applies, then the probability of reaching the solution declines exponentially with the number of hill-climbing steps.

Application of the model to other problem types is the subject of future research.

There are, however, several factors that limit the applicability of the model. The most important are that conflicts are assumed to be independent, and that a single solution state is assumed. The presence of multiple solutions may not be a serious limitation so long as the model is applied in the vicinity of a solution, and that solutions are not so dense as to render this meaningless. Conflict independence is more significant, since highly structured problems which occur in practice may violate this assumption. Nevertheless, to the extent that the statistical properties of classes of problems can be established, it may still be possible to use the model to perform average-case analysis of heuristics.

Two other limitations are worth noting, since we have analyzed the min-conflicts heuristic independent of the initialization process and search strategy. First, the model permits no conclusions about the assignment being repaired, yet the construction of a good initial guess (i.e. an assignment such that d is small) is a key problem for repair methods. Second, since the model ignores all fine structure in the problem, the possibility of pathological configurations is not considered. This can manifest itself in hill-climbing techniques as "cycles", where the same variables are repaired again and again, but no progress is made towards the solution. To model the performance of the min-conflicts heuristic in conjunction with a particular search strategy, such as hill-climbing a more detailed analysis is required. For example, in a recent paper, Morris [33] examines the structure of the n-queens problem, and shows analytically that, for min-conflicts hill-climbing, almost all local minima are solutions.

6. Discussion

The heuristic hill-climbing method described in this paper can be characterized as a *local search* method [20], in that each repair minimizes the number of conflicts for an individual variable. Local search methods have been applied to a variety of important problems, often with impressive results. For example, the Kernighan–Lin method, perhaps the most successful algorithm for solving graph-partitioning problems, repeatedly improves a partitioning by swapping the two vertices that yield the greatest cost differential. The much-publicized simulated annealing method can also be characterized as a form of local search [19]. However, it is well known that the effectiveness of local search methods depends greatly on the particular task.

In fact, it is easy to imagine problems on which the min-conflicts heuristic will fail. The heuristic is poorly suited to problems with a few highly critical constraints and a large number of less important constraints. For example, consider the problem of constructing a four-year course schedule for a university student. We may have an initial schedule which satisfies almost all of the constraints, except that a course scheduled for the first year is not actually offered that year. If this course is a prerequisite for subsequent courses, then many significant changes to the schedule may be required before it is fixed. In general, if repairing a constraint violation requires completely revising the current assignment, then the min-conflicts heuristic will offer little guidance. This intuition is partially captured by the analysis presented in the previous section, which shows that the effectiveness of the heuristic is inversely related to the distance to a solution.

The problems investigated in this paper, especially the HST and n-queens problem, tend to be relatively uniform in that critical constraints rarely occur.

In part, this is due to the way the problems are represented. For example, in the HST problem, as described earlier, the transitive closure of temporal constraints is explicitly represented. For example, if task A must precede task B, then all tasks that precede A must also precede B, and all such constraints are explicitly represented. This improves performance because the min-conflicts heuristic is less likely to violate a set of constraints than a single constraint. In some cases, we expect that more sophisticated techniques will be necessary to identify critical constraints [11]. To this end, we are currently evaluating explanation-based learning techniques [9] as a method for identifying critical constraints.

The algorithms described in this paper also have an important relation to previous work in AI. In particular, there is a long history of AI programs that use repair or debugging strategies to solve problems, primarily in the areas of planning and design [37, 40]. This approach has recently had a renaissance with the emergence of case-based [14, 26] and analogical [17, 24, 42] problem solving. To solve a problem, a case-based system will retrieve the solution from a previous, similar problem and repair the old solution so that it solves the new problem.

The fact that the min-conflicts approach performs well on n-queens, a well-studied, "standard" constraint-satisfaction problem, suggests that AI repair-based approaches may be more generally useful than previously thought. Additional evidence also comes from a very recent study by Selman, Levesque and Mitchell [36], in which they showed that a repair-based algorithm (very similar to the hill-climbing algorithms investigated here) performs well on hard satisfiability problems. However, as we have pointed out, in some cases it can be more time-consuming to repair a solution than to construct a new one from scratch. It may be that our analysis of min-conflicts for CSP problems can be extended to repair methods for other tasks, such as case-based planning methods. We conjecture that for each of the factors affecting the performance of min-conflicts, such as the expected "distance" from the initial assignment to the solution and the degree that each variable is constrained, there are analogous factors for other tasks.

There are many possible extensions to the work reported here, but three are particularly worth mentioning. First, we expect that there are other applications for which the min-conflicts approach will prove useful. Conjunctive matching, for example, is an area where preliminary results appear promising. This is particularly true for matching problems that require only that a good partial-match be computed. Second, we expect that there are interesting ways in which the min-conflicts heuristic could be combined with other heuristics. For example, as mentioned earlier, when a "most-conflicted" variable ordering strategy is used together with min-conflicts, the resulting program outperforms min-conflicts alone on graph 3-colorability problems. Finally, there is the possibility of employing the min-conflicts heuristics with other search techniques. In this paper, we only considered two very basic methods, hill climbing and backtracking. However, more sophisticated techniques such as best-first search are obvious candidates for investigation, since the number of conflicts in an assignment can serve as a heuristic evaluation function. Another possibility is Tabu search [16], a hill-climbing technique that maintains a list of forbidden moves in order to avoid cycles. Morris [31, 32] has also proposed a hill-climbing method which can break out of local maxima by systematically altering the cost function. The work by Morris and much of the work on Tabu search bears a close relation to our approach.

7. Conclusions

In this paper we have analyzed a very successful neural network algorithm and shown that a simple heuristic search method behaves similarly. Specifically, we carried out extensive experiments in three task domains in which the min-conflicts hill-climbing algorithm and the GDS network exhibited similar performance. Based on our experience with both programs, we conclude that the min-conflicts heuristic captures the critical aspects of the GDS network. In this sense, we have explained why the network is so effective.

We have also demonstrated that the min-conflicts heuristic can be employed in conjunction with other types of symbolic search methods besides hill-climbing. In particular, we showed that it can be used as a value-ordering heuristic by an informed backtracking algorithm. This is an important consideration, since we expect that in many applications the choice of search strategy may be critical to producing satisfactory solutions.

By isolating the min-conflicts heuristic from the search strategy, we distinguished the idea of a repair-based CSP method from the particular strategy employed to search within the space of repairs. This enabled us to carry out a strategy-independent analysis of the heuristic. The analysis identified several factors that effected the utility of the min-conflicts heuristic, such as the expected distance between the initial assignment and the solution. We believe that this analysis may be relevant to repair-based problem solving methods in general.

There are also several practical implications of this work. First, the scheduling system for the Hubble Space Telescope, SPIKE, now employs our symbolic method, rather than the network, reducing the overhead necessary to arrive at a schedule. Perhaps even more importantly, it is easy to experiment with variations of the symbolic method, which should facilitate transferring SPIKE to other scheduling applications, Finally, by demonstrating that repair-based methods are applicable to standard constraint satisfaction problems, such as N-queens, we have provided a new tool for solving CSP problems.

8. Acknowledgement

The authors wish to thank Hans-Martin Adorf, Don Rosenthal, Richard Franier, Peter Cheeseman and Monte Zweben for their assistance and advice. We also thank Ron Rusick and our anonymous reviewers for their comments. The Space Telescope Science Institute is operated by the Association of Universities for Research in Astronomy for NASA.

Appendix A. *n*-queens conflict probability distributions

In this appendix we derive conflict distribution functions for the simplified *n*-queens model discussed in Section 5.3.2, which assumes that in the solution state exactly three queens conflict with non-solution queen placements.

Consider first a non-solution value $Q_R^{\text{non-sol}}$ for a queen in row R. In the solution state there are three other queens which constrain $Q_R^{\text{non-sol}}$: denote this set by q. Let the number of queens other than R which have non-solution assignments be i. If R has a solution assignment, then $i = d$; and if R has a non-solution assignment, then $i = d - 1$. The probability of a conflict on $Q_R^{\text{non-sol}}$ due to a queen in q is:

$$p_1^q = \begin{bmatrix} \text{Probability conflict} \\ \text{on } Q_R^{\text{non-sol}} \text{ from} \\ \text{queen in } q \end{bmatrix} = \begin{bmatrix} \text{Probability queen} \\ \text{in } q \text{ has non-solution} \\ \text{value} \end{bmatrix} \times \begin{bmatrix} \text{Probability non-} \\ \text{solution value} \\ \text{conflicts with } Q_R^{\text{non-sol}} \end{bmatrix}$$
$$+ \begin{bmatrix} \text{Probability queen} \\ \text{in } q \text{ has} \\ \text{solution value} \end{bmatrix} \times \begin{bmatrix} \text{Probability solution} \\ \text{value conflicts} \\ \text{with } Q_R^{\text{non-sol}} \end{bmatrix}.$$

Now the probability that a queen in q has a non-solution value is $i/(n-1)$, and the probability that a non-solution value for a queen in q conflicts with $Q_R^{\text{non-sol}}$ is $2/(n-1)$ (i.e. two other placements would be either on the same row or diagonal as $Q_R^{\text{non-sol}}$). The probability that a solution value for a queen in q conflicts with $Q_R^{\text{non-sol}}$ is one by definition. Thus:

$$p_1^q = \frac{i}{n-1} \frac{2}{n-1} + \left(1 - \frac{i}{n-1}\right) = 1 - \frac{i(n-3)}{(n-1)^2}.$$

A similar argument leads to the probability of conflict with the $n - 4$ queens *not* in q:

$$p_1^{\bar{q}} = \frac{3i}{(n-1)^2}.$$

The probability of v conflicts on $Q_R^{\text{non-sol}}$ is the sum of two binomially-distributed variables

$$P(v \text{ conflicts on } Q_R^{\text{non-sol}}) = \sum_{x=0}^{v} B(x, p_1^q, 3) B(v - x, p_1^{\bar{q}}, n - 4),$$

assuming that the conflicts are independent. When there are no erroneous assignments, this distribution has a mean value of 3 and variance of zero, capturing the assumption that, in the solution state, each non-solution value has exactly three conflicts.

For a solution value Q_R^{sol} for a queen in row R, conflicts can arise only from non-solution assignments of the $n - 1$ other queens. Assuming independence, the distribution of conflicts is

$$P(v \text{ conflicts on } Q_R^{\text{sol}}) = B(v, p_2, n - 1),$$

where $p_2 = 3i(n - 1)^2$.

References

[1] B. Abramson and M. Yung, Divide and conquer under global constraints: a solution to the n-queens problem, *J. Parallel Distrib. Comput.* **61** (1989) 649–662.

[2] H.M. Adorf and M.D. Johnston, A discrete stochastic neural network algorithm for constraint satisfaction problems, in: *Proceedings International Joint Conference on Neural Networks*, San Diego, CA (1990).

[3] E. Biefeld and L. Cooper, Bottleneck identification using process chronologies, in: *Proceedings IJCAI-91*, Sydney, Australia (1991).

[4] J. Bitner and E.M. Reingold, Backtrack programming techniques, *Commun. ACM* **18** (1975) 651–655.

[5] G. Brassard and P. Bratley, *Algorithmics—Theory and Practice* (Prentice Hall, Englewood Cliffs, NJ, 1988).

[6] D. Brelaz, New methods to color the vertices of a graph, *Commun. ACM* **22** (1979) 251–256.

[7] P. Cheeseman, B. Kanefsky and W.M. Taylor, Where the *really* hard problems are, in: *Proceedings IJCAI-91*, Sydney, Australia (1991).

[8] R. Dechter and J. Pearl, Network-based heuristics for constraint-satisfaction problems, *Artif. Intell.* **34** (1988) 1–38.

[9] M. Eskey and M. Zweben, Learning search control for constraint-based scheduling, in: *Proceedings AAAI-90*, Boston, MA (1990).

[10] M.S. Fox, *Constraint-Directed Search: A Case Study of Job-Shop Scheduling* (Morgan Kaufmann, San Mateo, CA, 1987).

[11] M.S. Fox, N. Sadeh and C. Baykan, Constrained heuristic search, in: *Proceedings IJCAI-89*, Detroit, MI (1989).

[12] E.C. Freuder, Partial constraint satisfaction, in: *Proceedings IJCAI-89*, Detroit, MI (1989); also: *Artif. Intell.* **58** (1992) 21–70 (this volume).

[13] M.L. Ginsberg and W.D. Harvey, Iterative broadening, in: *Proceedings AAAI-90*, Boston, MA (1990).

[14] K.J. Hammond, Case-based planning: an integrated theory of planning, learning and memory, Ph.D. Thesis, Yale University, Department of Computer Science, New Haven, CT (1986).

[15] R.M. Haralick and G.L. Elliot, Increasing tree search efficiency for constraint satisfaction problems, *Artif. Intell.* **14** (1980) 263–313.

[16] A. Hertz and D. de Werra, Using tabu search techniques for graph coloring, *Computing* **39** (1987) 345–351.

[17] A.K. Hickman and M.C. Lovett, Partial match and search control via internal analogy, in:

[18] J.J. Hopfield, Neural networks and physical systems with emergent collective computational abilities, *Proc. Nat. Acad. Sci.* **79** (1982).
[19] D.S. Johnson, C.R. Aragon, L.A. McGeoch and C. Schevon, Optimization by simulated annealing: an experimental evaluation, Part II, *J. Oper. Res.* **39** (3) (1991) 378–406.
[20] D.S. Johnson, C.H. Papadimitrou and M. Yannakakis, How easy is local search?, *J. Comput. Syst. Sci.* **37** (1988) 79–100.
[21] M.D. Johnston, Automated telescope scheduling, in: *Proceedings Symposium on Coordination of Observational Projects* (Cambridge University Press, Cambridge, UK, 1987).
[22] M.D. Johnston and H.M. Adorf, Learning in stochastic neural networks for constraint satisfaction problems, in: *Proceedings NASA Conference on Space Telerobotics*, Pasadena, CA (1989).
[23] L.V. Kale, An almost perfect heuristic for the n nonattacking queens problem, *Inf. Process. Lett.* **34** (1990) 173–178.
[24] S. Kambhampati, Supporting flexible plan reuse, in: S. Minton, ed., *Machine Learning Methods for Planning and Scheduling* (Morgan Kaufmann, San Mateo, CA, 1992).
[25] N. Keng and D.Y.Y. Yun, A planning/scheduling methodology for the constrained resource problem, in: *Proceedings IJCAI-89*, Detroit, MI (1989).
[26] J.L. Kolodner, R.L. Simpson Jr and K. Sycara-Cyranski, A process model of case-based reasoning in problem solving, in: *Proceedings IJCAI-85*, Los Angeles, CA (1985).
[27] C.R. Kurtzman, Time and resource constrained scheduling, with applications to space station planning, Ph.D. Thesis, Department of Aeronautics and Astronautics, MIT, Cambridge, MA (1988).
[28] C.R. Kurtzman and D.L. Aiken, The Mfive space station crew activity scheduler and stowage logistics clerk, in: *Proceedings AIAA Computers in Aerospace VII Conference*, Monterey, CA (1989).
[29] P. Langley, Systematic and nonsystematic search strategies, in: *Proceedings AAAI-92*, San Jose, CA (1992).
[30] S. Minton, M. Johnston, A.B. Philips and P. Laird, Solving large scale constraint sastisfaction and scheduling problems using a heuristic repair method, in: *Proceedings AAAI-90*, Boston, MA (1990).
[31] P. Morris, Solutions without exhaustive search: an iterative descent method for binary constraint satisfaction problems, in: *Proceedings AAAI-90 Workshop on Constraint-Directed Reasoning*, Boston, MA (1990).
[32] P. Morris, An iterative improvement algorithm with guaranteed convergence, Tech. Rept. TR-M-91-1, Intellicorp Technical Note (1991).
[33] P. Morris, On the density of solutions in equilibrium points for the queens problem, in: *Proceedings AAAI-92*, San Jose, CA (1992).
[34] N. Muscettola, S.F. Smith, G. Amiri and D. Pathak, Generating space telescope observation schedules, Tech. Rept. CMU-RI-TR-89-28, Carnegie Mellon University, Robotics Institute, Pittsburgh, PA (1989).
[35] R. Musick and S. Russell, How long will it take?, in: *Proceedings AAAI-92*, San Jose, CA (1992).
[36] B. Selman, H.J. Levesque and D. Mitchell, A new method for solving hard satisfiability problems, in: *Proceedings AAAI-92*, San Jose, CA (1992).
[37] R.G. Simmons, A theory of debugging plans and interpretations, in: *Proceedings AAAI-88*, St. Paul, MN (1988).
[38] R. Sosic and J. Gu, A polynomial time algorithm for the n-queens problem, SIGART **1** (3) (1990).
[39] H.S. Stone and J.M. Stone, Efficient search techniques—an empirical study of the n-queens problem, *IBM J. Res. Dev.* **31** (1987) 464–474.
[40] G.J. Sussman, *A Computer Model of Skill Acquisition* (American Elsevier, New York, 1975).
[41] J.S. Turner, Almost all k-colorable graphs are easy to color, *J. Algorithms* **9** (1988) 63–82.
[42] M.M. Veloso and J.G. Carbonell, Towards scaling up machine learning: a case study with

derivation analogy in prodigy, in: S. Minton, ed., *Machine Learning Methods for Planning and Scheduling* (Morgan Kaufmann, San Mateo, CA, 1992).
[43] M. Waldrop, Will the Hubble space telescope compute?, *Science* **243** (1989) 1437–1439.
[44] M. Zweben, A framework for iterative improvement search algorithms suited for constraint satisfaction problems, Tech. Rept. RIA-90-05-03-1, NASA Ames Research Center, AI Research Branch (1990).
[45] M. Zweben, M. Deale and R. Gargan, Anytime rescheduling, in: *Proceedings Workshop on Innovative Approaches to Planning, Scheduling and Control* (Morgan Kaufmann, San Mateo, CA, 1990).

Arc consistency: parallelism and domain dependence

Paul R. Cooper
Institute for the Learning Sciences, Northwestern University, 1890 Maple Avenue, Evanston, IL 60201, USA

Michael J. Swain
Artificial Intelligence Laboratory, Department of Computer Science, University of Chicago, 1100 E 58th St., Chicago, IL 60637, USA

Abstract

Cooper, P.R. and M.J. Swain, Arc consistency: parallelism and domain independence, Artificial Intelligence 58 (1992) 207–235.

This paper discusses how better arc consistency algorithms for constraint satisfaction can be developed by exploiting parallelism and domain-specific problem characteristics. A massively parallel algorithm for arc consistency is given, expressed as a digital circuit. For a constraint satisfaction problem with n variables and a labels, this algorithm has a worst-case time complexity of $O(na)$, significantly better than that of the optimal uniprocessor algorithm. An algorithm of intermediate parallelism suitable for implementation on a SIMD machine is also given. Analyses and implementation experiments are shown for both algorithms.

A method for exploiting characteristics of a problem domain to achieve arc consistency algorithms with better time and space complexity is also discussed. A general technique for expressing domain knowledge and using it to develop optimized arc consistency algorithms is described. The domain-specific optimizations can be applied analogously to any of the arc consistency algorithms along the sequential/parallel spectrum.

1. Introduction

Many artificial intelligence problems can be formulated as constraint satisfaction problems, from planning [34] and plan recognition through

---

Correspondence to: P.R. Cooper, Institute for the Learning Sciences, Northwestern University, 1890 Maple Avenue, Evanston, IL 60201, USA. E-mail: cooper@ils.nwu.edu.

0004-3702/92/$ 05.00 © 1992 — Elsevier Science Publishers B.V. All rights reserved

low and high level vision [7,38]. Efficiently solving constraint satisfaction problems is thus important to AI. Since the first step in the solution of any constraint satisfaction problem is the elimination of locally inconsistent solutions, much work has gone into the development of arc consistency algorithms [13,16,24,30,38]. Recently, the optimal uniprocessor algorithm for arc consistency was shown [29]. Further improving the performance of arc consistency algorithms requires exploiting parallelism, or exploiting domain dependence, or both. In this paper, we develop both strategies, further closing the book on arc consistency.

We give two parallel algorithms for arc consistency with differing degrees of parallelism. These algorithms illustrate a time/space tradeoff spectrum for arc consistency algorithms. Furthermore, we show how to exploit domain dependence to develop arc consistency algorithms with improved performance anywhere along such a spectrum.

Taking the extreme in a strategy of trading processing units (or space) for time, we first show an algorithm whose run-time performance would be virtually instantaneous. The algorithm is expressed as a massively parallel digital circuit that requires only a small constant number of time steps for many problem instances. Even in the unlikely worst case, its time complexity is only $O(na)$, for a problem with n variables and a values or labels per variable. This compares favorably to the optimal uniprocessor algorithm, with time complexity $O(n^2a^2)$ [29]. We also show an algorithm that corresponds to an intermediate choice of spatial parallelism. This second algorithm is more suited to implementation on a highly parallel SIMD machine such as the Connection Machine. The first part of the paper concludes with a discussion on the limits of parallelism for arc consistency algorithms.

In the second part of the paper, we show a general method for exploiting domain dependence to further improve the performance of arc consistency algorithms. In this approach, completely general-purpose constraint satisfaction schemes are not used. Instead, the algorithms are optimized to perform in a specific domain by exploiting regularities in the classes of problem instances. An example of this strategy is the work of Mackworth et al. [27], who show how hierarchic domains can be exploited to yield a more efficient constraint satisfaction process. For massively parallel algorithms, performance improvement reduces the amount of space (or number of processing elements) required. We show how this process works in general, by providing a way in which domain-specific regularities may be expressed, and by providing an algorithm that takes a domain description and generates an optimized arc consistency circuit for it. Significant reductions in space requirements can be achieved in this way, and these optimizations can be translated to time speedups for less parallel algorithms.

2. General-purpose arc consistency algorithms

2.1. Constraint satisfaction: problem definition

We first review the constraint satisfaction problem as classically formulated [13,21,24,29]. Formally, a constraint satisfaction problem (CSP) is defined as follows: Given a set of n variables each with an associated domain and a set of constraining relations each involving a subset of the variables, find an n-tuple that is an instantiation of the n variables satisfying the relations. We consider only those CSPs in which the domains are discrete, finite sets and the relations are unary and binary.

The CSP problem, as formulated above, is NP-complete. Thus, unless $P = NP$ a general solution will take, in the worst case, exponential time. Many algorithms, such as backtracking search, have been used in the solution of CSPs. Network consistency methods have been developed as a way to improve the efficiency of these search algorithms. They work by the elimination of locally inconsistent partial solutions, in a preprocessing or filtering phase. Arc consistency algorithms detect and eliminate inconsistencies involving two variables, and are not guaranteed to find a unique solution to a CSP.

A typical arc consistency problem consists of a set of variables, a set of possible labels or values for the variables, a unary predicate, and a binary predicate with an associated constraint graph. For each i of the n variables, the unary predicate $P_i(x)$ defines the list of allowable labels x taken from the domain of the variables. For each pair of variables (i, j) in the constraint graph, the binary predicate $Q_{ij}(x, y)$ defines the list of allowable label pairs (x, y). To compute the n-tuples which satisfy the overall problem requires that the local constraints are propagated among the variables and arcs until no inconsistencies remain.

2.1.1. Consistency methods and problem classes

Low-order network consistency algorithms are not guaranteed to find a unique solution to a CSP, and subsequent processing may still be required. A k-consistency algorithm removes all inconsistencies involving all subsets of size k of the n variables [13]. In particular, node and arc consistency algorithms detect and eliminate inconsistencies involving $k = 1$ and 2 variables, respectively. Reviews of network consistency algorithms and their use in the solution of constraint satisfaction problems can be found in Mackworth [25] and Henderson [19].

There thus exists a range of increasingly powerful and costly network consistency methods, as well as a variety of sophisticated heuristic methods for solving the CSPs that remain after network consistency methods have been applied. A range of constraint satisfaction problems of differing degrees of difficulty also arise. It is useful to match the solution technique to the problem type.

Node and arc consistency are computationally cheapest. In problem domains with rich local representations, arc consistency alone frequently yields adequate solutions [1,5]. Even for those problems where arc consistency does not yield unique solutions, the initial arc consistency phase is often useful and can involve a substantial amount of computation. Improving the performance of arc consistency algorithms is thus relevant for most constraint satisfaction problems.

Problem classes may exist where arc consistency algorithms are of little or no utility, since the initial problem may already involve an arc-consistent network. In some such cases, it may be useful to apply path consistency [25] or higher-order network consistency algorithms. Such algorithms are computationally more costly. The optimal sequential path consistency algorithm takes $O(n^3 a^3)$ [17] and the fastest parallel algorithm using a polynomial number of processors is $O(n^2 a^2)$ [35]. As Dechter shows [8], arc consistency and path consistency together are sufficient to allow backtrack-free depth-first solution of the class of CSPs with constraint graphs of a particular form, called *regular width-2*, that can be recognized in linear time.

Finally, CSPs exist for which network consistency methods alone are not appropriate, since eventually the cost of enforcing local consistency meets or exceeds the cost of backtracking to find a solution [9]. A variety of approaches to the solution of these problems have been explored, as well as various kinds of restricted classes of CSPs and the appropriate algorithms for each. For more complex problems, Dechter has developed effective heuristic techniques to speed up backtracking. One, called the *cycle cutset method*, instantiates enough variables so that the remaining constraint graph is a tree. Another, *backjumping*, minimizes thrashing by backtracking to the source of the failure guided by the constraint graph. A third, *learning*, records constraints generated by the search when dead ends are encountered.

2.2. Uniprocessor solution

In this section, we illustrate the computation of variable and arc consistency with a discussion of algorithms for a uniprocessor. The most efficient algorithm for achieving arc consistency on a uniprocessor is AC-4 [29]. Predecessors to AC-4 include the original Waltz filtering application [38] and AC-3 [24,26]. As Mohr and Henderson show [29], AC-4 is the optimal algorithm for the uniprocessor case.

Achieving node consistency is easy. One simply eliminates all labels x at a variable i which do not conform to the unary predicate $P_i(x)$. This can be done with a single pass over the variables. One can make an analogous pass over the arcs, and eliminate labels which do not take part in consistent label pairs on that arc (i.e. do not conform to $Q_{ij}(x,y)$). However, this does not guarantee that the network is arc-consistent. This is because eliminating a label from a variable may make neighboring variables inconsistent. Therefore, the process of checking for arc consistency must be iterated until no more eliminations occur, and the network is arc-consistent. This is the "relaxation" phase of the computation, when the constraints are propagated from variable to variable.

The simplest idea for achieving arc consistency sequentially is to iterate a process which checks each arc for consistency, until no further changes occur. This process does much unnecessary work. As stated above, elimination of a label from a variable can only affect the consistency of labels at neighboring variables. Therefore, only neighboring variables need be checked, not every variable (or arc) in the network. The algorithm AC-3 exploits this fact. AC-4 exploits an additional observation. A label x at some variable i is arc-consistent if it has some minimum of support at each of its neighboring variables. The label x only becomes inconsistent when the last of its support at a neighbor (e.g., the last consistent label) is eliminated. AC-4 makes this notion explicit with the use of counters which measure support for a label. Relevant counters are decremented when a label is eliminated, and search is in this way minimized. This strategy yields an optimal algorithm for a uniprocessor, with time complexity $O(ea^2)$, where e is the number of edges in the constraint graph (e is at most $O(n^2)$). The space complexity of AC-4 is also $O(ea^2)$ (although it is possible to reduce the space complexity to $O(ea)$).

The notion that a label has lost sufficient support from its neighbors and is now inconsistent can be stated independent of a sequential or parallel control strategy for its implementation. This notion was expressed by Hummel and Zucker [21] as the *label discarding rule*: discard a label x at a variable i if there exists a neighbor j of i such that *every* label y currently assigned to j is incompatible with x at i, that is, $\neg Q_{ij}(x,y)$ for all y in the domain of j. In the next section, we will give an algorithm which applies the label discarding rule in a parallel fashion.

We are not the first to study parallel algorithms for arc consistency. Rosenfeld [32] described a parallel algorithm for a class of machines called web automata. Henderson and Samal [33] designed shared memory parallel algorithms for arc consistency. We reduce the "processors" to their simplest form, latches and gates, and show how a single chip can compute arc consistency in a highly parallel manner.

2.3. Massively parallel solution

2.3.1. Algorithm

In this section, we describe a fast parallel algorithm for computing arc consistency. The algorithm is specified as a massively parallel digital circuit we call the Arc Consistency (AC) Chip. The design is derived from an earlier purely connectionist algorithm [5], and is based upon the use of the unit/value principle [2,12]. In massively parallel or connectionist designs using the unit/value principle, very simple processing elements are assigned to every single value which may take part in the computation. Only simple messages are passed between the processing elements or units, and it is the pattern of connections between the units that encodes the information necessary to solve the problem. In the case of the AC Chip, the processing elements are logic gates (**and**, **or**, and **not** gates) and memory elements, and the messages are digital signals. The result is a digital circuit potentially amenable to implementation in VLSI.

In essence, the AC Chip consists of two arrays of JK flip-flops and suitable amounts of combinational circuitry. The most important part of the design is the representation for the two constraint predicates $P_i(x)$ and $Q_{ij}(x,y)$. Adopting the unit/value principle, we assign one memory element to represent every possible value of $P_i(x)$ and $Q_{ij}(x,y)$. (As will be seen, JK flip-flops are used as the memory elements because of their convenient reset characteristics.) To allow the hardware to compute any arc consistency problem, the two arrays must be able to represent any given $P_i(x)$ and $Q_{ij}(x,y)$ of sizes bounded by n and a.

The first (node) array will be designated the *labeling array*. It consists of na flip-flops we call $u(i,x)$. The array of flip-flops serves two purposes. First, it represents all possible solutions to the problem, and eventually, after the constraint satisfaction is completed, the set of solutions which are arc-consistent. That is, the array explicitly represents the variables of the CSP and all possible labels for each variable. The second purpose of the labeling (or node) array is to represent and apply the unary constraint predicate $P_i(x)$. This is accomplished by initializing each flip-flop $u(i,x)$ of the labeling array to the value of the corresponding element of the unary constraint predicate $P_i(x)$. That is, if x is a valid label at variable i, then the flip-flop $u(i,x)$ is initialized to **on**. Thus initially at least, the flip-flops which are **on** all correspond to labelings of a variable which are valid considering only the local (unary) constraint at that variable. Note that all flip-flops are initialized. The final answer to the computation (which labels are arc-consistent at each variable) will be contained in this array at the end of the computation.

The second (arc) array consists of $a^2 n(n-1)$ flip-flops we designate $v(i,j,x,y)$ which are initialized to conform to the arc constraint predicate $Q_{ij}(x,y)$, if i is adjacent to j in the constraint graph, and to 1 (no constraint) otherwise. Note that the arc array is static; it does not change throughout the computation.

The basic structure of the two arrays of flip-flops is shown in Fig. 1. It remains only to develop combinational circuitry that causes the flip-flop

Labeling Array   **Arc Array**

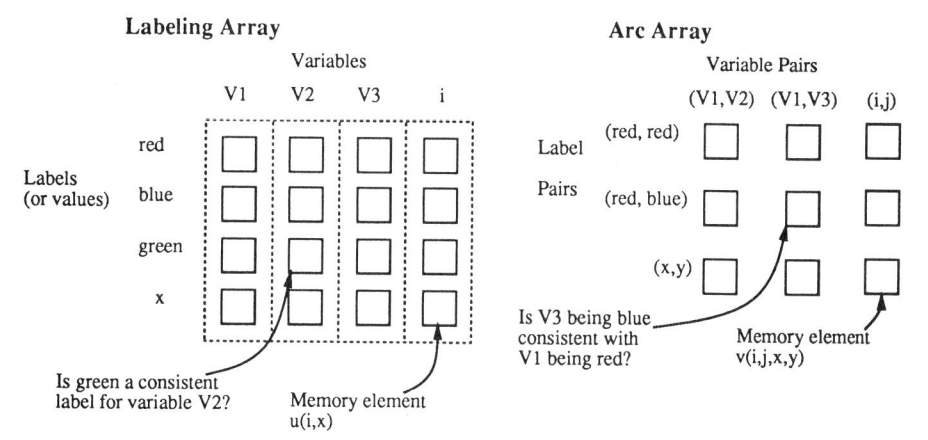

Fig. 1. Unary and binary constraint table.

representing the label x at variable i to be reset to zero if it becomes inconsistent. In other words, we want circuitry which implements the label discarding rule at each variable. Arc consistency is then achieved when a limiting label set is obtained.

To implement the arc consistency label discarding rule, the combinational circuitry is designed so that the K (reset) input of the JK flip-flop $u(i,x)$ receives the value:

$$reset(u(i,x)) = \neg \bigwedge_{j=1, j \neq i}^{n} \bigvee_{y=1}^{a} (u(j,y) \wedge v(i,j,x,y)).$$

The J input of each JK flip-flop is tied to 0. A partial circuit diagram for this equation is given in Fig. 2. This figure shows the reset circuitry for one flip-flop in the labeling array $u(i,x)$. In the figure, the entire labeling array is present, but only the part of the arc table $v(i,j,x,y)$ useful for this variable is drawn. An analogous circuit for each element of the labeling array completes the whole circuit.

To interpret the equation and circuit, consider first the inner term $u(j,y) \wedge v(i,j,x,y)$ for a particular case of $u(i,x)$. The fact that $v(i,j,x,y)$ is true tells us that there is an arc between i and j, and (x,y) is a consistent label pair for this arc. We already know that $u(i,x)$ is true; **and**ing with $u(j,y)$ checks that the other end of the arc has a valid label. Point A on the circuit diagram in Fig. 2 shows where this term is computed. (In Fig. 7, a particular **and** gate of this type is referred to as $A(i,j,x,y)$.)

At this point, as far as variable i is concerned, x is a label consistent with variable neighbor j's label y. The $\bigvee_{y=1}^{a}$ simply ensures that at least *one* label y on neighboring variable j is consistent. This function has been computed after the **or** gate at point B in Fig. 2. (In Fig. 7 these **or** gates are designated $B(j)$.)

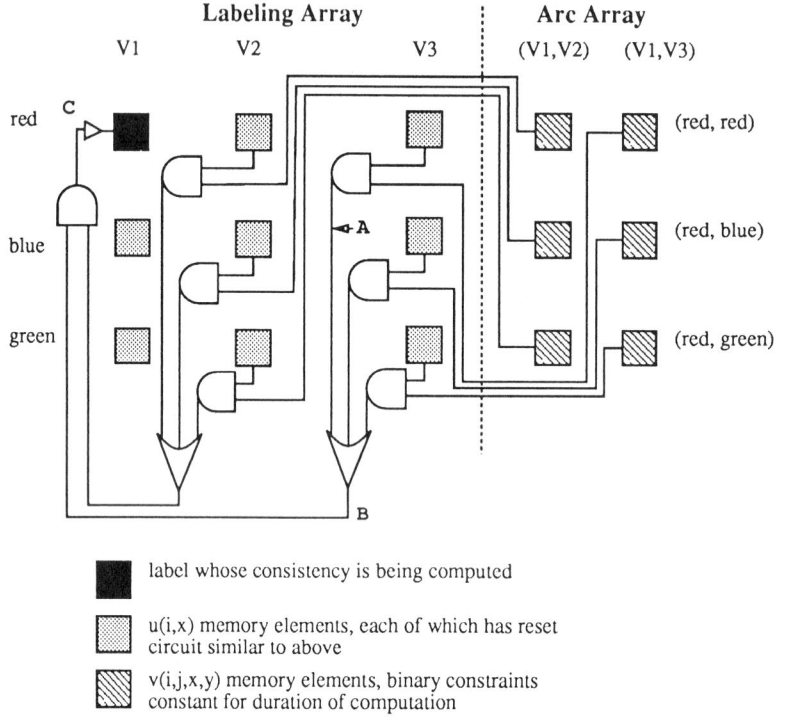

Fig. 2. Partial circuit diagram for the AC Chip.

- ■ label whose consistency is being computed
- ▨ u(i,x) memory elements, each of which has reset circuit similar to above
- ▩ v(i,j,x,y) memory elements, binary constraints constant for duration of computation

Label x on variable i is thus consistent with its neighbor j. But what about variable i's other neighbors? The $\bigwedge_{j=1, j \neq i}^{n}$ ensures that there is arc consistency among *all* variable i's neighbor's. The **and** gate at C in Fig. 2 ensures this.

If the signal is **on** at point C, that means that label x is consistent for variable i—therefore, the flip-flop need not be reset. Thus the **not** gate is required.

To reverse the analysis, if some variable j does not have a consistent labeling, then at point B, the signal will be **off**. The **and** will fail, so the signal at C will also be 0, and then the **not** gate will cause flip-flop $u(i,x)$ to be reset.

2.3.2. Analysis

Correctness. To begin with, recall that we are interested in discarding labels, an operation which corresponds to resetting **on** flip-flops to 0. Furthermore, since the J input of each JK flip-flop in the variable array is tied to 0, the flip-flops can only ever be reset to 0, never set. Once they are **off** they must stay off, so the whole process is clearly monotonic. Therefore, all we need to show for correctness is to show that the network correctly applies the label discarding rule. If the network discards labels when they should be discarded, and does not discard them when they should be kept, then it implements the label discarding rule correctly.

The label discarding rule can be formally expressed as follows:

$$\exists j (j \neq i) \forall y [u(j,y) \wedge v(i,j,x,y) = 0].$$

But this expression is equivalent to

$$\bigwedge_{j=1, j \neq i}^{n} \bigvee_{y=1}^{a} (u(j,y) \wedge v(i,j,x,y)) = 0$$

or

$$\neg \bigwedge_{j=1, j \neq i}^{n} \bigvee_{y=1}^{a} (u(j,y) \wedge v(i,j,x,y)) = 1,$$

which is just the condition under which (i,x) is reset. Therefore, the network correctly discards labels when it should. The converse follows from negating the above equations.

Complexity. The circuit requires na JK flip-flops for the labeling array, and $a^2 n(n-1)$ flip-flops for the arc array. From Fig. 2 we see that there is an **and** gate for every flip-flop in the arc array, so $a^2 n(n-1)$ two-input **and** gates are required for this purpose. For each of the na flip-flops in the labeling array $n-1$ **or** gates are required, each taking a inputs—a total of $an(n-1)$ **or** gates. Finally, there are na **and** and **not** gates (**nand** gates), each taking $n-1$ inputs. There are also $O(a^2 n^2)$ wires.

The worst-case time complexity of the network occurs when only one JK flip-flop is free to reset at a time. So if propagation through the **and** and **or** gates is considered instantaneous, the worst-case time complexity is na. If a logarithmic time cost is assigned to the large fan-in **and** and **or** gates the worst-case time complexity is $O(a \log(a) n \log(n))$.

2.3.3. Application

The AC Chip algorithm could be used in any arc consistency application. As might be expected, the highly parallel implementation runs very fast. Although worst-case running time is linear in the number of variables and labels, it is more reasonable to expect that the network runs in a small constant number of time steps. For example, the crossword puzzle example developed by Mackworth [25] takes about 342 sequential time steps for solution with AC-4, the optimal uniprocessor algorithm, while the AC Chip would take only two time steps to solve the same problem. The Tinkertoy graph matching problem described later (see Table 1) is a more substantial problem, requiring 35588 time steps for solution by AC-4. Even on this larger problem, the AC Chip would require only 8 time steps to obtain an arc-consistent solution. Clearly, the time performance of the parallel network could be expected to be much better than that of the best sequential implementations.

For sufficiently small problems it would be straightforward to construct our Arc Consistency Chip. In general, however, two problems arise from the $O(a^2n^2)$ resources required to represent an arbitrary system of binary constraints. First, a potential I/O bottleneck exists. If the node and arc arrays must be initialized serially, loading them takes more time ($O(a^2n^2)$ steps) than executing the algorithm, and the run-time complexity becomes similar to that expected from standard uniprocessor implementations of arc consistency. A direct way to overcome this I/O bottleneck is to supply parallel input to the AC Chip. Alternatively, the design can be specialized to address a particular class of problems. In this case, regularities in the problem instances can be exploited so the binary constraint can be specified with less than $O(a^2n^2)$ information. A special-purpose circuit could then be built to efficiently supply the required constraint values to the remaining circuitry, whose job it is to propagate and apply the constraints. This possibility is explored in the second part of the paper.

Physical realization can also be a problem if $O(a^2n^2)$ space is required. It is easy to see that the limits of current VLSI technology are reached for problems with relatively small numbers of variables and values. Specialization for domains also provides a solution to this problem.

Constructing special-purpose hardware is effective in environments where classes of problem instances are well-understood and repeat frequently, and where extremely fast performance is required. (For example, a robot vision system designed for industrial application might meet these criteria.) An alternative to using special-purpose hardware is to implement a parallel algorithm on a general-purpose parallel computer. This possibility is explored in the next section.

2.4. SIMD solution

Here we present a parallel algorithm for constraint satisfaction that requires na processors and $O(na \log(na))$ time. The algorithm is Single Instruction, Multiple Data (or SIMD), and requires only local memory and modest communication requirements. Experiments have shown that a constraint satisfaction problem of size $na = 32K$ will run in 16 seconds on the Connection Machine multiprocessor.[1]

---

[1] Connection Machine is a registered trademark of Thinking Machines Corporation.

2.4.1. Algorithm

The algorithm, called ACP, is given in Figure 3. It, like the AC Chip and AC-4 algorithms from which it was derived, relies on the notion of support. In ACP, there is a processor for every member of the labeling array. Each such member of the labeling array will be referred to as a candidate label, and corresponds to one possible label at one variable. At each processor there is a set of counters which denote the support given by each other variable to the candidate label.

ACP has four phases:

(1) Initialize the processor array according to the values of $P_i(x)$.
(2) Accumulate support.
(3) Iteratively remove inconsistent candidate labels.
(4) Read answer back from the machine.

One candidate label is removed at a time. It broadcasts its identity to all the other processors which, in parallel, check to see if that candidate label supported them. If it did, the appropriate counter is decremented. If a counter becomes zero, the *dying* flag is set, indicating that the processor has become eligible to broadcast its identity as an inconsistent pair.

Unlike Mohr and Henderson's AC-4, there are no support lists, simply because they are unnecessary. The List data structure of AC-4 is also not present in ACP; it simply corresponds to the set of processors for which the variable *dying* is **true**.

In the algorithm ACP, it is assumed there is a processor for every element of the array *candidate_label*. We use the operator **one of** to arbitrarily select and return one of the values of a variable which exists in each of the processors. **If** and **while** statements are executed only in the processors for which the associated expression is true. This notation is similar to the programming language C* [31].

2.4.2. Analysis

Complexity. Since there are na candidate labels and one inconsistent candidate label is removed per iteration, the **while** loop commencing at line 27 will be executed at most na times. If the individual Connection Machine operations are considered to take $O(1)$ the complexity of the algorithm is $O(na)$. In fact, there is a logarithmic component of complexity associated with the broadcast network, but this is fixed for a given machine. Including this complexity term gives a total complexity of $O(an \log(an))$.

Correctness. The proof of correctness for AC-4 given by Mohr and Henderson [29] works for ACP as well. We repeat the proof here for ease of reference.

```
1.      procedure acp(P,Q,result)
2.      begin
3.          j, y, ia, xa, jd, yd: integer;
4.          candidate_label: poly array[1..n,1..a] of
5.              record
6.                  counter: array[1..n] of integer;
7.                  alive, dying: boolean;
8.                  i,x: integer;
9.              end;
10.
11.         (* Initialize data structures *)
12.         for each (ia,xa) do
13.             candidate_label[ia,xa].alive := P(ia,xa);
14.
15.         for each candidate_label in parallel do
16.             begin
17.                 dying := false;
18.                 (* Accumulate support *)
19.                 if alive do
20.                     for j := 1 to n do
21.                         begin
22.                             for y in P_j do
23.                                 if Q_{ix}(j,y) then counter[j] := counter[j] + 1;
24.                             if counter[j] = 0 then dying := true;
25.                         end
26.                 (* Remove inconsistent variable-label pairs *)
27.                 while dying do
28.                     begin
29.                         (jd,yd) := one of (i,x);
30.                         if Q_{ix}(jd,yd) then
31.                             begin
32.                                 counter[jd] := counter[jd] - 1;
33.                                 if counter[jd] = 0 then
34.                                     if alive then dying := true;
35.                             end
36.                         candidate_label[jd,yd].alive := false;
37.                     end
38.                 (* Find out which processors are still alive *)
39.                 result := false;
40.                 while alive do
41.                     begin
42.                         (ia,xa) := one of (i,x);
43.                         result[ia,xa] := true;
44.                     end
45.             end
46.     end acp
```

Fig. 3. The algorithm ACP.

Step 1. By induction, each label deleted from A_i is not admissible for any arc consistency solution: The label is removed if one of its counters goes to zero, so it has no more corresponding labels at one edge; by induction all the previously removed labels could not belong to any solution, so this one cannot belong to any solution.

Step 2. The result is arc-consistent: for all (i, j), for all labels b for i, we have Counter$[(i, j), b] > 0$ so b has a corresponding label variable j; therefore, ACP builds an arc-consistent solution.

Step 3. From Steps 1 and 2 we conclude that the algorithm builds the largest arc-consistent solution.

2.4.3. Application experiment: Connection Machine implementation

The Connection Machine 2 is ideal for implementing ACP. The machine used for the implementation was configured with 32K processors (1K = 1024), each with 64K bits of memory. The algorithm was implemented in C*.

The problem that the algorithm was tested on was similar to the example used in [33]. For $i, j = 1, \ldots, n$ and $x, y = 1, \ldots, a$ we have $P(i, x) =$ true and

$$Q(i, x, j, y) = \neg([i - j]_n = 1 \wedge x > y).$$

We assumed the constraint graph to be complete, although for this problem a sparser constraint graph could have been used. We did this to compare the sequential and parallel algorithms on a problem for which the parallel algorithm was well-suited. Problems with truly complete constraint graphs tend to be more complex than the one we used.

The experimental results are shown in Fig. 4. The graph is a log–log plot, the slope of which gives the degree of the polynomial expression of complexity. The slope for the Connection Machine results is 0.992, with a coefficient of correlation $r = 0.999$, showing an almost perfect fit to a straight line of slope 1, indicating a complexity of $\Theta(na)$ with na processors.

After 32K processors the Connection Machine we used in these experiments ran out of real processors. One might expect the complexity to grow quadratically after this point, but the slope of the line from $na = 32$K to $na = 64$K is only 1.3. The explanation for the low growth in complexity lies in the overhead in decoding an instruction from the host. Because a processor simulating more than one virtual processor only needs to decode the instruction once for all virtual processors, it can simulate k processors in less than k times the time to simulate one processor. As k grows, the instruction decoding time becomes less important, but from $k=1$ to $k=2$ the effect is significant.

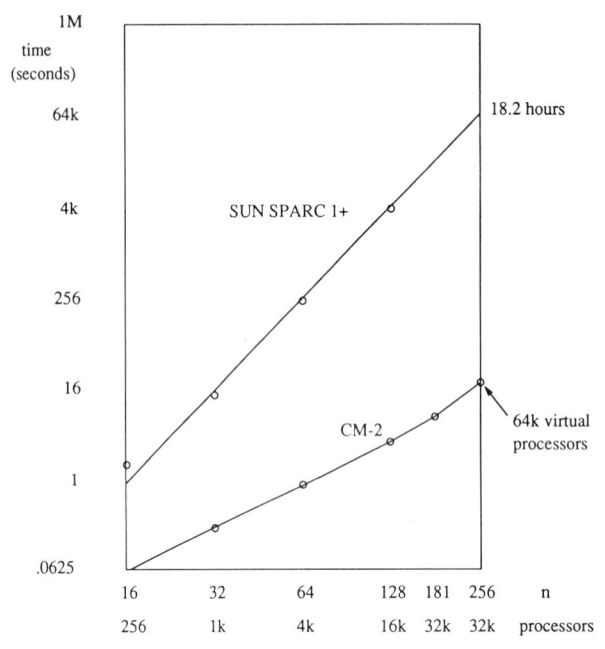

Fig. 4. Parallel versus sequential arc consistency.

As expected, the slope of the log–log plot of the sequential run-times is 2, indicating a complexity of $O(a^2 n^2)$. The largest problem tried on the Connection Machine, $na = 64K$, took 16.5 seconds whereas the estimated time on a Sparc 1+ would be 18.2 hours.

2.5. Relating the algorithms

The AC-4 uniprocessor algorithm for arc consistency, the AC Chip massively parallel solution, and the ACP SIMD solution are all closely related. The algorithm is most explicitly expressed in the AC Chip solution—each element of the solution is a visible element of the chip. The less parallel versions of the solution all group some elements of the AC Chip solution at a processor or in a variable.

Consider the ACP algorithm of the previous section, compared to the AC Chip specification. In ACP, a processor is assigned to every element of the AC Chip labeling array. The functionality of the tree of gates in Fig. 2 for the AC Chip solution is replaced by equivalent code at each variable in the labeling array. In effect, the **or** gate in each row of Fig. 2 is replaced by a counter maintained on each processor. When an element of the labeling array goes off, it broadcasts a message. Upon receipt of a message that an element has gone off, each still-active element of the labeling array decrements the appropriate support counter. If some counter at a processor goes to zero, that element of the labeling array has become inconsistent.

AC-4 can also be seen as a uniprocessor simulation of the functionality of the AC Chip representation. It uses support counters for each **or** gate of Fig. 2 in a manner analogous to ACP. If a support counter falls to zero, that candidate label is marked inconsistent by adding it to a list of inconsistent candidate labels. The list is required because AC-4 must deal sequentially with events, and must deal with the consequences of each candidate label becoming inconsistent one at a time. When a particular inconsistent label at a variable is being processed, the neighbors of the variable must also be visited in sequence, decrementing the appropriate counters if necessary.

2.6. Limits to parallelism

2.6.1. Intrinsic sequentiality

So far, we have seen parallel schemes for arc consistency that achieve faster worst-case and expected-case running times than more sequential algorithms. A natural question arises: "How fast can arc consistency be accomplished?" It has long been recognized (e.g., [20]) that there is an intrinsically parallel aspect to relaxation type computations. Consistency can be computed locally and in parallel, as we have seen. But there is also an intrinsically serial aspect to these computations, because a globally consistent answer cannot be found without constraint propagation and constraints may only propagate one arc per time step.

This latter suggestion of inherent sequentiality is borne out by the analysis of Kasif [22] who showed that constraint satisfaction by arc consistency is log-space complete for P. (P is the class of problems that require polynomial time for their solution, given a polynomial number of processors.) This suggests that finding an algorithm for arc consistency with significantly sublinear time complexity is unlikely [36]. A class of problems with faster solutions is NC. (NC is the class of problems solvable in logarithmic parallel time with polynomially many processors.) Kasif's result shows that unless NC = P, a result thought as unlikely as P = NP [28], a logarithmic time polynomial-processor algorithm for arc consistency does not exist. This also suggests that a linear lower bound for arc consistency will be extremely difficult to prove—it would be equivalent to proving that NC ≠ P.

Problems in NC are typically those thought of as having a fast parallel solution, and those in P are typically regarded as being in some way intrinsically sequential. But it is important to remember that these results analyze only worst-case performance. Consider arc consistency. As discussed in the worst-case analysis of the AC Chip in Section 2.3.2, it is possible that only one variable/label possibility is eliminated in every time step.

It is easy to imagine a case where this is true—all that is required is a linear chain of constraint dependencies. Although expected-case analysis is problematic as usual, it is obvious enough that many real problems do not consist solely of long chains of dependent constraints. In these cases, near constant time performance by the AC Chip algorithm would be expected.

In short, although the possible existence of algorithms with time complexities slightly below linear cannot be discounted, it is likely that the AC Chip algorithm has the fastest possible worst-case time complexity for arc consistency. Certainly, the AC Chip algorithm can be expected to operate much faster than linear on many problems.

2.6.2. Sublinear time algorithms

If the limitation of polynomially-many processors is abandoned, significantly faster algorithms for arc consistency than the AC Chip can be constructed [36]. These algorithms are interesting primarily from a theoretical point of view. They prove that linear-time algorithms are not the fastest possible, and offer insights into how arc consistency algorithms might be designed to be faster.

It is possible to construct an algorithm for node and arc consistency that takes $O(\log(na))$ time on a PRAM with $O(n^2 a^2 2^{na})$ processors. Such an algorithm works by finding (in parallel) the maximum cardinality consistent set of variable–label pairs, which is equivalent to the result of applying variable and arc consistency [36].

2.6.3. Parallelism for general constraint satisfaction

The design strategies adopted for the development of parallel algorithms for arc consistency can be extended for algorithms that enforce k-consistency. Since space is being traded off for time in such strategies, and since NP-complete problems are solvable with k-consistency for arbitrarily large k, combinatorially large space resources would ultimately be required.

The middle ground offers some possibilities. For increasing cost, other low-order constraints may be used. Third-order constraints have been represented and exploited in parallel, for example, at the cost of cubic space requirements [4]. In addition, a small number of specific higher-order constraints useful in solving a particular problem can be represented and exploited in parallel, if they can be identified or learned.

Other interesting alternatives are also being explored. Güsgen [15], for example, has proposed augmenting an AC Chip style architecture with a Gödel encoding scheme that would allow the global solution, in parallel, of general constraint satisfaction problems limited to binary constraints. It remains to develop a strategy for the parallel solution of more difficult CSPs in the general case.

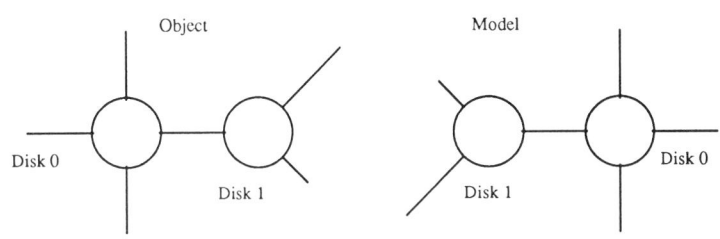

Fig. 5. Tinkertoy objects.

3. Domain-specific constraint satisfaction

If the space of input problem instances is in some way restricted, the potential for specialized and more efficient solution algorithms exists. A problem domain is just such a restricted set of problem instances. Domains can be thought of as classes of problem instances with invariant properties. We now describe a general-purpose method for developing efficient arc consistency algorithms for any domain.

Invariants arise during the problem formulation process, which is described first. A general scheme for exploiting any invariant properties of a problem class requires a representation language for expressing the invariants. Finally, a procedure is described that automatically generates an efficient arc consistency algorithm for the domain, given the description of the invariants for that domain. We develop these ideas in the context of the AC Chip algorithm described earlier, and show how the algorithmic optimizations can be transferred to uniprocessor algorithms.

An alternative strategy for developing efficient domain-specific arc consistency algorithms has been described [10]. In that work a parameterized arc consistency algorithm for a uniprocessor is used, with procedures developed and instantiated to suit specific invariant properties on a case-by-case basis.

3.1. Example problem formulation

A particular problem or class of problems is formulated as a constraint satisfaction problem by defining the elements of the general constraint satisfaction problem (CSP) in terms of the specific application being investigated. That is, a set of variables and a set of labels must be defined in terms of the problem at hand. Likewise, the unary and binary predicates P and Q must be defined in terms relevant to the application problem.

In this part of the paper, we use as an example problem the task of matching descriptions of objects comprised of link-and-junction structure, such as the Tinkertoy objects in Fig. 5. This problem, which arises in the recognition of objects from images [5] or structure matching in analogy [11], is nontrivial and similar to graph isomorphism. The problem formulation process establishes a mapping between elements of the application problem,

Tinkertoy matching, and the CSP framework. If one of the objects to be matched is called the object, and the other the model, one formulation maps object parts to CSP variables, and model parts to CSP labels [5]. A unique label for every CSP variable then corresponds to the partwise matching of object and model parts.

It is convenient to discretize the points where links can attach to junctions; these will be called *slots*, and the links will be *rods*. Junction geometry can then be represented implicitly, by treating both slots and rods as parts. With this problem formulation, we can establish basic predicates applying to the variables and labels in the problem. The predicates $rod(i)$ and $slot(j)$ designate the type of variable, and predicates $length(i)$ and $filled(j)$ specify the basic geometric unknown for each type of variable. Additionally, we use $connected(i, j)$ to specify whether a rod and slot are connected, $offset(i, j)$ to specify the number of slots between two slots i and j in the clockwise sense, and $sd(i, j)$ to specify whether two slots belong to the same disk. Finally, with the following terms defined for conciseness,

$$rr(i, j) = rod(i) \land rod(j),$$

$$sr(i, j) = slot(i) \land rod(j) \lor rod(i) \land slot(j),$$

we have the language necessary to specify the unary and binary constraint predicates.

The unary and binary constraint predicates are defined as:

$$P(i, x) = (rod(i) \land rod(x)) \land (length(i) = length(x)) \lor$$
$$(slot(i) \land slot(x)) \land (filled(i) = filled(x)),$$

$$Q(i, x, j, y) = \begin{cases} \mathbf{t} & \text{if } i = j \text{ and } x = y, \\ \mathbf{f} & \text{if } i = j \text{ or } x = y \text{ but not both,} \\ sd(i, j) \land sd(x, y) \land offset(i, j) \\ \quad = offset(x, y) \lor sr(i, j) \land sr(x, y) \\ \quad \land connected(i, j) \\ \quad = connected(x, y) \lor rr(i, j) \land rr(x, y), \\ & \text{otherwise.} \end{cases}$$

A solution to the CSP framed in this way constitutes a correspondence between a Tinkertoy object and model. But these definitions provide no restrictions on the problem instances that can arise, so the resulting CSP still requires a solution algorithm of complete generality. Sequential simulations of the AC Chip algorithm have been used to solve small instances of this problem [6]. For realistic structure matching problems, the number of variables and labels is about 100, and the AC Chip algorithm becomes infeasible, requiring over 100 million gates.

3.2. Domain description

In this section a meta-language is described that can express invariant properties of a problem domain. Consider for example the Tinkertoy matching problem as framed above. For all problem instances, it is never the case that a rod can match a slot. To exploit such characteristics in general requires a domain description language.

The purpose of the domain description is to represent invariant properties that hold over different problem instances. In constraint satisfaction problems, the variables and labels are the entities that can have properties. In a problem instance, the variable i might represent a rod part, and thus have the property $rod(i)$. If the variable i is used to represent a rod part for all problem instances, $rod(i)$ is a property invariant for all problem instances. Note that the mapping between Tinkertoy parts and the variables of the CSP must maintain the invariant property across problem instances. It is straightforward to arrange that a certain subset of variables represents rods and a different subset of variables represents slots for all problem instances.

Once an invariant is established in this way, it can be conveniently described with a three-valued meta-term. A meta-term C' is defined in terms of an object term describing $C(i)$ as follows. By defining a domain as a (possibly infinite) set δ of problem instances designated α,

$$C'(i) = \begin{cases} t, & \text{if } C(i) = \mathbf{t} \text{ for all } \alpha \text{ in } \delta, \\ f, & \text{if } C(i) = \mathbf{f} \text{ for all } \alpha \text{ in } \delta, \\ u, & \text{otherwise (if } C(i) = \mathbf{t} \text{ for some } \alpha \text{ in } \delta \text{ and} \\ & C(i) = \mathbf{f} \text{ for some } \alpha \text{ in } \delta). \end{cases}$$

Invariants in a domain are, of course, represented by those meta-terms that evaluate to **t** or **f**. For example, $rod'(i)$ would be **t** if $rod(i)$ was true for all problem instances in the domain. Many properties will not be invariant, and their meta-description will evaluate to **u**.

Once the meta-terms describing the invariants are defined, it is a simple matter to define meta-predicates P' and Q'. These are exactly the same as the unary and binary constraint predicates P and Q, with meta-terms used in place of the object terms of P and Q. The meta-predicates are evaluated with Kleene's three-valued logic [37], as in Fig. 6.

Consider for example:

A	¬ A
t	f
f	t
u	u

A ∧ B

		B		
	∧	t	f	u
	t	t	f	u
A	f	f	f	f
	u	u	f	u

A ∨ B

		B		
	∨	t	f	u
	t	t	t	t
A	f	t	f	u
	u	t	u	u

Fig. 6. Truth tables for Kleene's three-valued logic.

$$P'(i,x) = (rod'(i) \land rod'(x)) \land (length(i) = length(x))' \lor \\ (slot'(i) \land slot'(x)) \land (filled(i) = filled(x))'.$$

Domain invariants can be exploited when the meta-predicates P' or Q' evaluate as invariant on some arguments. As a concrete example, consider the meta-unary-predicate $P'(i,x)$ for some $\bar{i}$ where $rod(\bar{i})$ is always true $(rod'(\bar{i}) = t)$, and for some $\bar{x}$ where $slot(\bar{x})$ is always true. Because a rod does not correctly correspond to a slot, the predicate $P'(\bar{i}, \bar{x})$ will evaluate to **f** *for all problem instances*. This fact is known in advance of runtime, and can be exploited in developing the algorithms to solve the CSP in this domain. We demonstrate this optimization in the next section.

3.3. Circuit optimization

If the meta-predicates P' or Q' are **t** or **f** for some arguments, this translates to flip-flops which are always **on** or **off** in the AC Chip arc consistency algorithm. Systematically modifying the circuit to exploit the ramifications of these constants constitutes the domain-dependent optimization of the algorithm. For example, if for some i and x $P'(i,x)$ is **f**, the entire circuit of Fig. 2 is not required for the $u(i,x)$ element. The algorithm that performs these simplifications in general is given in Fig. 7, and is called *Circ_Min*.

Circ_Min consists of five phases: *P_elimination*, *Q_elimination*, *Replace_By_Hierarchical_Gates*, *Merge_With_Same_Inputs*, and *Flatten_Hierarchies*.

P_elimination deletes any flip-flops $u(i,x)$ that represent impossible candidate labels along with the trees of gates that feed into them. *Q_elimination* removes **and** gates that are not necessary and replaces each one by a wire when $Q' =$ **true**. These two optimizations are often the most important.

The purpose of the remaining three procedures is to factor out common subterms in the circuit and eliminate the redundant circuitry that computes them. The procedure *Replace_By_Hierarchical_Gates* (Fig. 8) replaces a single gate by a hierarchy of gates in the pattern set by the template *or_hier* (for **or** gates) or *and_hier* (for **and** gates). These hierarchies are supplied by the user, and represent additional description of the domain. The hierarchy must correspond to natural groupings of the labels for hierarchical gate

procedure Circ_Min
    inputs: domain meta-predicates P' and Q'
                     variable tree node_hier
                     label tree label_hier
    modifies: circuit, as in Figure 2
begin
  (* P elimination *)
  forall (i, x) *in* P' **do**
    if $P'(i, x) = $ **f** **then**
      Recursive_Delete(flip-flop $u(i, x)$)

  (* Q elimination *)
  forall (i, j, x, y) *in* Q' **do**
    if $P'(j, y) = $ **f** **or** $Q'(i, j, x, y) = $ **f** **then**
      Recursive_Delete(and gate $A(i, j, x, y)$)
    else if $Q'(i, j, x, y) = $ **t** **then**
      begin
        wire output of flip-flop $u(j, y)$ to or gate $B(j)$
        Recursive_Delete(and gate $A(i, j, x, y)$)
      end

  Replace_By_Hierarchical_Gates(circ, label_hier, node_hier);
  Merge_With_Same_Inputs(circ);
  Flatten_Hierarchies(circ);
end

Fig. 7. Procedure *Circ_Min*.

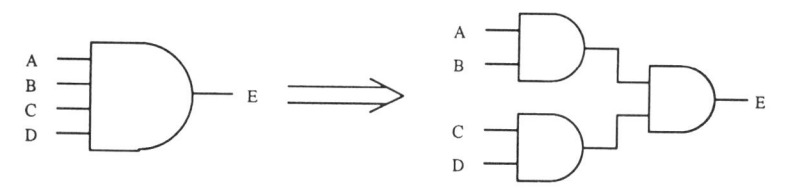

Fig. 8. Procedure *Replace_By_Hierarchical_Gates*.

replacement to enable more wires to be eliminated in the merge phase. The procedure *Merge_With_Same_Inputs* (Fig. 9) replaces redundant gates by one gate (thus also eliminating redundant input wires), and wires the output appropriately to the multiple places it is used. Finally, the procedure *Flatten_Hierarchy* (Fig. 10) replaces hierarchies of gates of the same type with functionally equivalent multiple-input gates. *Flatten_Hierarchy* thus inverts the function of *Replace_By_Hierarchical_Gates* where it is still possible after common subterms have been eliminated. It is reasonable to apply this function only to minimize the number of gates and wires. If other complexity measures (wire length or wire crossings) are important, the functionality of

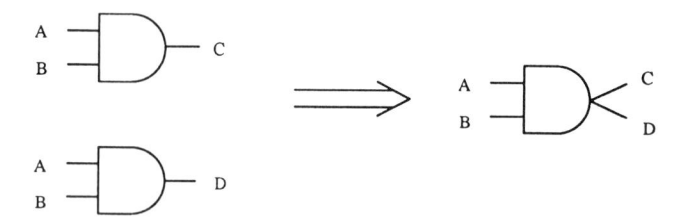

Fig. 9. Procedure *Merge_With_Same_Inputs*.

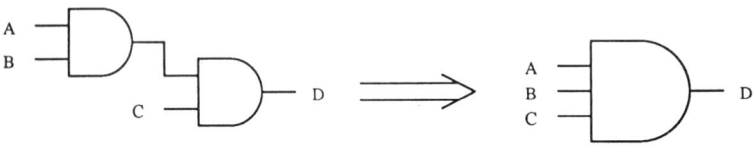

Fig. 10. Procedure *Flatten_Hierarchy*.

Flatten_Hierarchy might be undesirable.

The procedure *Recursive_Delete* deletes the gate that is its argument, and recursively deletes any gates which become redundant by its deletion because they have no inputs or no outputs.

3.4. Analysis and performance

The correctness of the algorithm can be determined by noting that each transformation transforms one or more gates into an equivalent set of gates. Therefore, the function of the AC circuit is preserved throughout the algorithm.

A straightforward analysis shows that the algorithm takes $O(a^2n^2)$ time and space. Since the circuit reduction algorithm is run offline, the exact value of its complexity is not important. However, it should be noted that the algorithm does not need combinatorial resources; in fact it needs time and space linear in the original size of the AC circuit.

Circ_Min may reduce the complexity of an AC circuit by orders of magnitude. For instance, for Tinkertoy domain problems with a number of disks d, number of rods r, and number of slots per disk s, the number of gates is reduced from almost $2(r+ds)^4$ to about $2r^2d^2s^2$. For the Tinkertoy domain with a maximum of five rods and three disks, each with eight slots, this is a twenty-fold decrease (see Table 1 and Fig. 11). The order of magnitude of decrease is given for an arbitrary Tinkertoy domain in Table 2.

As an example, Fig. 12 gives part of the reduced circuit for a Tinkertoy matching problem with at most three rods and three disks, with two slots per disk. The figure gives the input circuit to a single target candidate labeling—the match of slot 1 on disk 1 of the object, to slot 2 of disk 3 of the model. This candidate labeling is shaded in Fig. 12.

In the figure, the square and rectangular boxes represent the array of

Table 1
Optimizations for Tinkertoy domain with five rods and three disks with eight slots.

Optimization	Gates saved (thousands)	Gates remaining (thousands)	Wires saved (thousands)	Wires remaining (thousands)
Original AC circuit	—	1390	—	2085
P flip-flop elimination	678	712	1026	1059
Q flip-flop elimination	637	75	803	256
or gate merging	9	66	147	109
Hierarchical gates		66	9	100

Table 2
Efficiency of optimizations for Tinkertoy domain.

Optimization	Gates saved	Gates remaining
Original AC circuit	—	$(ds+r)^4$
P flip-flop elimination	$d^3s^3r + d^2s^2r^2 + dsr^3$	$d^4s^4 + r^4$
Q flip-flop elimination	$d^4s^4 + r^4$	$d^3s^3 + d^2s^2r^2 + r^3$
or gate merging	$d^3s^3 + r^3$	$d^2s^2r^2$
Hierarchical gates	—	—

Optimization	Wires saved	Wires remaining
Original AC circuit	—	$(ds+r)^4$
P flip-flop elimination	$d^3s^3r + d^2s^2r^2 + dsr^3$	$d^4s^4 + r^4$
Q flip-flop elimination	$d^4s^4 + r^4$	$d^4s^4 + r^4$
or gate merging	$d^3s^3 + r^3$	$d^3s^3 + d^2s^2r^2 + r^3$
Hierarchical gates	$d^3s^3 + r^3$	$d^2s^2r^2 + d^3 + r^3$

flip-flops $u(i,x)$ (holding $P(i,x)$) and the array of flip-flops $v(i,j,x,y)$ (holding $Q(i,j,x,y)$) respectively. All four types of optimizations have been made to this circuit. *P_elimination* has eliminated $u(i,x)$ flip-flops (and their associated circuitry) from the upper left-hand corner and lower right-hand corners of the $u(i,x)$ array. *Q_elimination* has eliminated the $v(i,j,x,y)$ flip-flops associated with all of the slot–slot matches. Slot–slot matches can be divided into two groups—those compatible with the target candidate labeling ($Q' = t$) and those incompatible with the target candidate labeling ($Q' = f$). Those that are compatible have an output wire and can affect the consistency of the candidate labeling. The **or** gates receiving input from slot–slot matches have been broken up into a two-level hierarchy, with slots from the same disk grouped together at the lower level.

We do not claim to be able to generate the optimal (most reduced) circuit for any problem. First, subtle optimizations not discovered by *Circ_Min* might be feasible. Since, in general, circuit optimization is a difficult problem

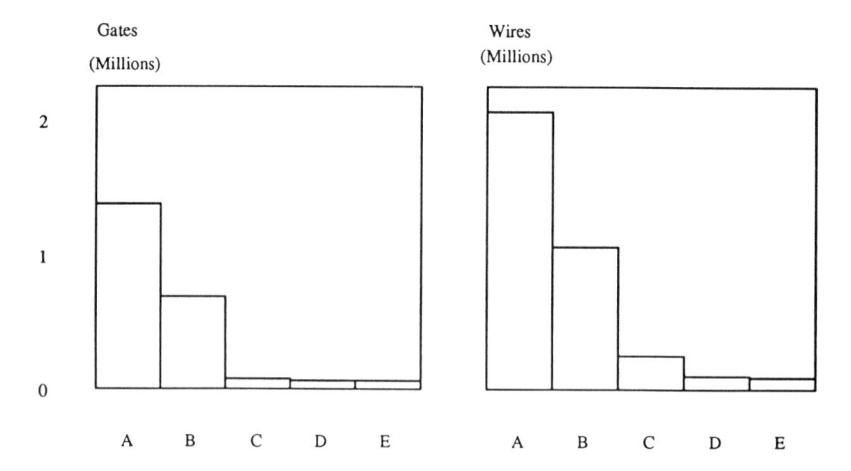

Fig. 11. Gates (left) and wires (right) in AC circuit after each optimization, for the Tinkertoy domain with five rods and three disks with eight slots. A: original, B: *P* flip-flop elimination, C: *Q* flip-flop elimination, D: **or** gate merging, E: hierarchical gates.

and must be approached heuristically [3], we do not expect there to be a tractable algorithm that finds the optimal circuit.

Second, domain knowledge not expressed in the meta-predicates might be exploitable. For example, the meta-language described above is intended to describe invariant semantic properties of application problems. In contrast, Deville and Van Hentenryck [10] describe syntactic properties of the variables' domains and show on a case-by-case basis how they may be used to generate efficient arc consistency algorithms. The AC Chip circuit could be optimized for each case analogously, and still allow further general-purpose optimizations. More interestingly, the meta-language and optimization procedure could be extended to handle such syntactic invariants in general. For example, to address "functional constraints" (where at most one constraint exists between any two labels, independent of which variables are being constrained) would require the ability to specify term equality and remove redundant circuit elements.

3.5. *Mapping the optimizations to AC-4*

As discussed in Section 2.5, there is a close relationship between the arc consistency algorithms at various levels of parallelism. The AC Chip to AC-4 mapping can be used to take the optimizations described above for the AC Chip and apply them to the AC-4 algorithm.

Since AC-4 only iterates over the candidate labels for which $P(i, x)$ is **true** and not all (i, x) it already incorporates an optimization similar to *P_flip_flop elimination*. Because the optimizations of AC-4 overlap the optimizations achieved by circuit minimization, we do not see as great reductions in the example Tinkertoy match done above. In a typical Tinkertoy experiment,

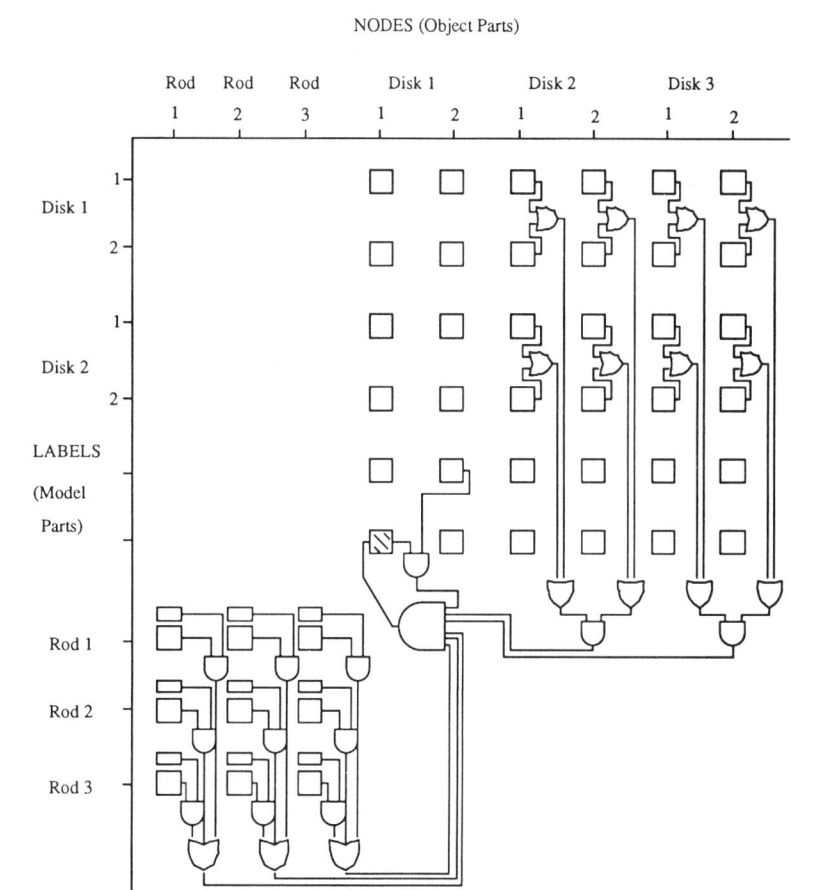

Fig. 12. Reduced circuit for slot–slot Tinkertoy match.

AC-4 took 195,000 steps. The optimized algorithm *AC4_Min* took 45,000 steps, about one-fifth as many.

The processor and time reductions the optimizations achieve for the AC Chip, ACP and AC-4 (in one experiment) are shown in Fig. 14. Processor reductions for the AC Chip are translated into time reductions for AC-4.

4. Conclusions

The utility of constraint satisfaction methods in the solution of many AI problems suggests that efficient implementations might be widely useful. For arc consistency, a uniprocessor algorithm optimal in time complexity is now known, so further improvements must come through parallelization or specialization for specific problems. In this paper, we have explored both possibilities.

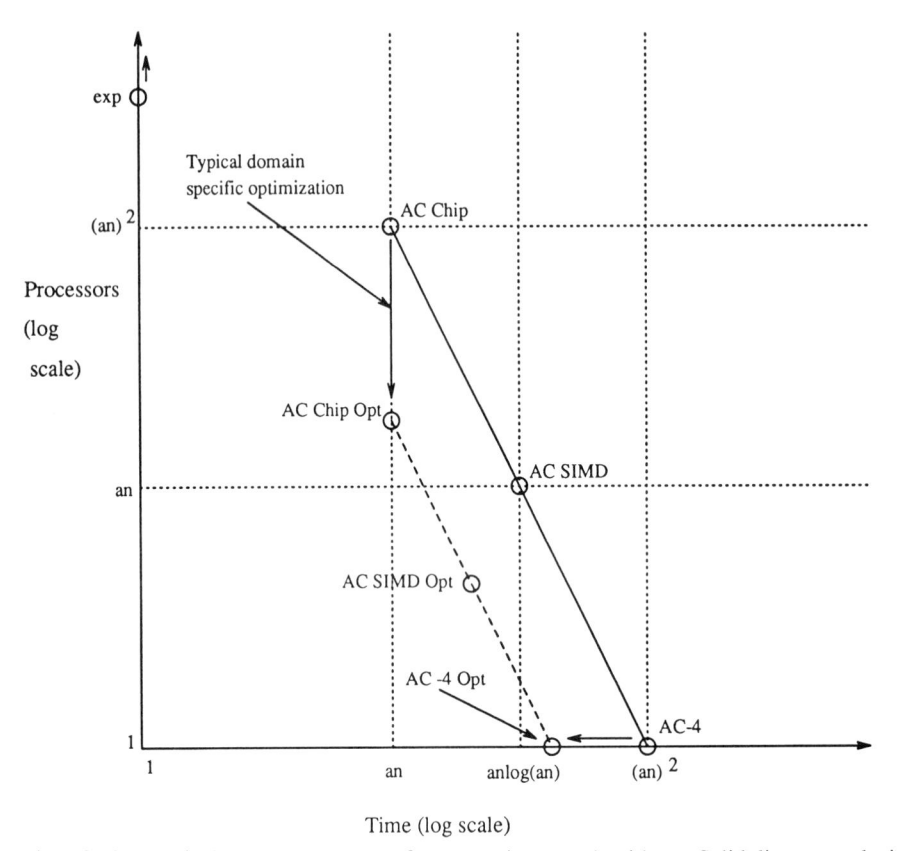

Fig. 13. Sequential/parallel spectrum of arc consistency algorithms. Solid line: complexity spectrum for general-purpose algorithms. Dashed line: complexity spectrum for domain-specific algorithms.

We have shown the AC Chip, a massively parallel algorithm for the arc consistency problem. As might be expected, the highly parallel implementation runs very fast. Although worst-case running time is linear in the number of variables and labels, it is more reasonable to expect that the network runs in a small constant number of time steps. A slightly less parallel version of the algorithm has also been specified and tested on the Connection Machine.

We have also shown how to exploit domain-specific meta-constraints to optimize arc consistency algorithms for a particular domain. For highly parallel spatially intensive algorithms such as the AC Chip, this specialization amounts to reducing the space requirements (or number of processing elements) for the algorithm. But the close relationship between all the algorithms allows us to port the optimizations from one form of the algorithms to another, such as the AC-4 uniprocessor algorithm.

Consider Figs. 13 and 14. These figures show a spectrum of algorithms for the arc consistency problem, from sequential to parallel. In this paper

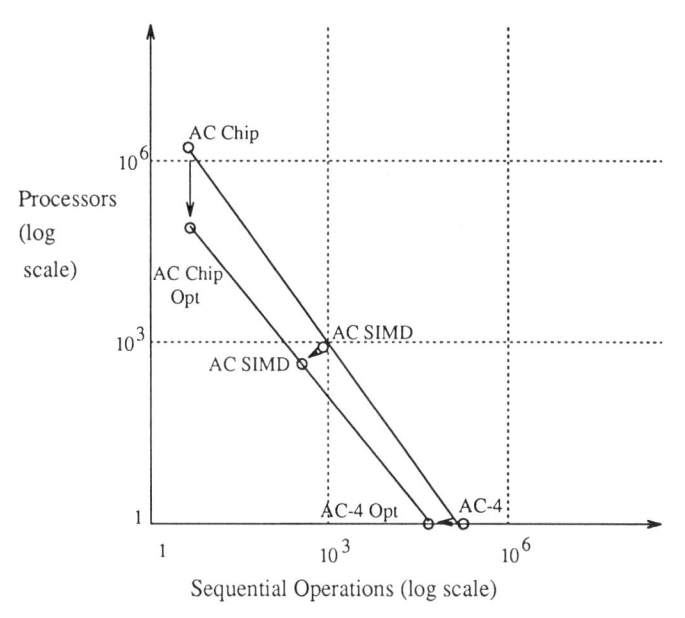

Fig. 14. Optimizations to arc consistency algorithms on one experiment (Tinker Toy circuit with rods = 5, disks = 3, and slots/disk = 8).

we have added to the spectrum of algorithms. The solid line (line A) in Fig. 13 represents the space–time trade-offs for completely general-purpose algorithms. The AC Chip algorithm we have specified in this paper provides a definition for the parallel end of the spectrum of general-purpose arc consistency algorithms. The parallelism in this algorithm reflects the unit/value design principle. A less extreme choice of parallelism leads to the SIMD algorithm implemented on the Connection Machine. This algorithm is found somewhere between the sequential and parallel extremes.

Equally important, we have shown how to define a second sequential/parallel trade-off line with better performance. The height of line A in the figure is intended to represent the optimal achievable algorithm (e.g., AC-4, which takes $O(n^2 a^2)$ time and is known to be optimal) for a given space–time trade-off. But by exploiting domain-specific problem characteristics, better performance of arc consistency algorithms can be achieved right across the spectrum of sequential-to-parallel algorithms, as diagrammed by line B.

While Fig. 13 represents the spectrum of algorithms with their worst-case complexity, Fig. 14 represents the performance of the algorithms on a real experiment, and thus could be considered more representative.

With an understanding of the complete spectrum of possible algorithms for the arc consistency problem comes the freedom to choose appropriately. If optimum time performance is required for completely general problems, the AC Chip can be constructed. If an IBM PC is to be used to perform arc consistency in some repetitive vision task in a well understood domain, the time-optimized version of AC-4 can be selected.

Acknowledgement

This work was supported in part by NSF grant #IRI-9110482 and by Andersen Consulting, through its support for The Institute for the Learning Sciences, and by ONR grant #N00014-91-J-1185. Parts of this work were done at the University of Rochester, supported by a Canadian NSERC post-graduate scholarship, by the Air Force Systems Command, Rome Air Development Center, Griffis Air Force Base, New York 13441-15700 and the Air Force Office of Scientific Research, Bolling AFB, DC 20332 under Contract No. F30602-85-C-0008. The latter contract supported the Northeast Artificial Intelligence Consortium (NAIC).

References

[1] J.F. Allen, H.A. Kautz, R. Pelavin and J. Tenenberg, *Formal Models of Plan Reasoning*, (Morgan Kaufmann, San Mateo, CA, 1990).
[2] H.B. Barlow, Single units and sensation: A neuron doctrine for perceptual psychology? *Perception* **1** (1972) 371–394.
[3] R.K. Brayton, G.D. Hachtel, C.T. McMullen and A.L Sangiovanni-Vincentelli, *Logic Minimization Algorithms for VLSI Synthesis* (Kluwer Academic Publishers, Boston, MA, 1984).
[4] P.R. Cooper, Parallel structure recognition with uncertainty: Coupled segmentation and matching, Tech. Rept. 5, Institute for the Learning Sciences, Northwestern University, Evanston, IL (1990).
[5] P.R. Cooper, Structure recognition by connectionist relaxation: formal analysis, *Comput. Intell.* **8** (1) (1992).
[6] P.R. Cooper and M.J. Swain, Parallelism and domain dependence in constraint satisfaction, Tech. Rept. TR 255, Department of Computer Science, University of Rochester, Rochester, NY (1988).
[7] L.S. Davis and A. Rosenfeld, Cooperating processes for low-level vision: a survey, *Artif. Intell.* **17** (1981) 245–263.
[8] R. Dechter and J. Pearl, Network-based heuristics for constraint-satisfaction problems, *Artif. Intell.* **34** (1988) 1–38.
[9] J. de Kleer, A comparison of ATMS and CSP techniques, in: *Proceedings IJCAI-89*, Detroit, MI (1989) 290–296.
[10] Y. Deville and P. Van Hentenryck, An efficient arc consistency algorithm for a class of CSP problems, in: *Proceedings IJCAI-91*, Sydney, Australia (1991) 325–330.
[11] B. Falkenhainer, K.D. Forbus and D. Gentner, The structure-mapping engine: algorithm and examples, *Artif. Intell.* **41** (1990) 1–63.
[12] J.A. Feldman and D.H. Ballard, Connectionist models and their properties, *Cogn. Sci.* **6** (1982) 205–254.
[13] E.C. Freuder, Synthesizing constraint expressions, *Commun. ACM* **21** (1978) 958–966.
[14] J. Gu, W. Wang, and T.C. Henderson, A parallel architecture for discrete relaxation algorithm, *IEEE Trans. Pattern Anal. Mach. Intell.* **9** (1987) 816–831.

[15] H.-W. Güsgen, A connectionist approach to symbolic constraint satisfaction, Tech. Rept. 90-018, International Computer Science Institute (1990).

[16] H.-W. Güsgen and J. Hertzberg, Some fundamental properties of local constraint propagation, *Artif. Intell.* **36** (1988) 237-247.

[17] C.-C. Han and C.-H. Lee, Comments on Mohr and Henderson's path consistency algorithm, *Artif. Intell.* **36** (1988) 125-130.

[18] R.M. Haralick and L.G. Shapiro, The consistent labeling problem: Part 1, *IEEE Trans. Pattern Anal. Mach. Intell.* **1** (1979) 173-184.

[19] T.C. Henderson, *Discrete Relaxation Techniques*, (Oxford University Press, Oxford, 1990).

[20] G.E. Hinton, Relaxation and its role in vision, Ph.D. Thesis, University of Edinburgh (1977).

[21] R.A. Hummel and S.W. Zucker, On the foundations of relaxation labeling processes, *IEEE Trans. Pattern Anal. Mach. Intell.* **5** (1983) 267-287.

[22] S. Kasif, On the parallel complexity of discrete relaxation in constraint satisfaction networks, *Artif. Intell.* **45** (1990) 275-286.

[23] E. Leung and X. Li, Matrix formulation and parallel algorithms for relaxation object labeling, in: *Proceedings: Vision Interface 88*, Edmonton, Alta. (1988) 146-151.

[24] A.K. Mackworth, Consistency in networks of relations, *Artif. Intell.* **8** (1977) 99-118.

[25] A.K. Mackworth, Constraint satisfaction, in: S.C. Shapiro, ed., *Encyclopedia of Artificial Intelligence* (Wiley, New York, 1987) 205-211.

[26] A.K. Mackworth and E.C. Freuder, The complexity of some polynomial network consistency algorithms for constraint satisfaction problems, *Artif. Intell.* **25** (1985) 65-74.

[27] A.K. Mackworth, J.A. Mulder, and W.S. Havens, Hierarchical arc consistency: exploiting structured domains in constraint satisfaction problems, *Comput. Intell.* **1** (1985) 118-126.

[28] P. McKenzie and S.A. Cook, The parallel complexity of abelian permutation group problems, *SIAM J. Comput.* **16** (1987) 880-909.

[29] R. Mohr and T.C. Henderson, Arc and path consistency revisited, *Artif. Intell.* **28** (1986) 225-233.

[30] U. Montanari, Networks of constraints: Fundamental properties and applications to picture processing, *Inf. Sci.* **7** (1974) 95-132.

[31] J. Rose and G. Steele, C*: an extended C language for data parallel programming, Tech. Rept. PL87-5, Thinking Machines Corporation (1987).

[32] A. Rosenfeld, Networks of automata: some applications, *IEEE Trans. Syst. Man Cybern.* **5** (1975) 380-383.

[33] A. Samal and T.C. Henderson, Parallel consistent labeling algorithms, *Int. J. Parallel Program.* **16** (1987) 341-364.

[34] M. Stefik, Planning with constraints, *Artif. Intell.* **16** (1981) 111-139.

[35] S.Y. Susswein, T.C. Henderson, J.L. Zachary, C. Hansend, P. Hinker and G.C. Marsden, Parallel path consistency, Tech. Rept. UUCS-91-010, Department of Computer Science, University of Utah, Salt Lake City, UT (1991).

[36] M.J. Swain, Comments on Samal and Henderson: "Parallel consistent labeling algorithms", *Int. J. Parallel Program.* **17** (1988) 523-528.

[37] R. Turner, *Logics for Artificial Intelligence* (Ellis Horwood, Chichester, England, 1984).

[38] D. Waltz, Understanding line drawings of scenes with shadows, in: P.H. Winston, ed., *The Psychology of Computer Vision*, (McGraw-Hill, New York, 1975) 19-91.

Structure identification in relational data *

Rina Dechter
Information and Computer Science, University of California, Irvine, CA 92717, USA

Judea Pearl
Cognitive Systems Laboratory, Computer Science Department, University of California, Los Angeles, CA 90024, USA

Abstract

Dechter, R. and J. Pearl, Structure identification in relational data, Artificial Intelligence 58 (1992) 237–270.

This paper presents several investigations into the prospects for identifying meaningful structures in empirical data, namely, structures permitting effective organization of the data to meet requirements of future queries. We propose a general framework whereby the notion of identifiability is given a precise formal definition similar to that of learnability. Using this framework, we then explore if a tractable procedure exists for deciding whether a given relation is decomposable into a constraint network or a CNF theory with desirable topology and, if the answer is positive, identifying the desired decomposition. Finally, we address the problem of expressing a given relation as a Horn theory and, if this is impossible, finding the best k-Horn approximation to the given relation. We show that both problems can be solved in time polynomial in the length of the data.

1. Introduction

Discovering meaningful structures in empirical data has long been regarded as the hallmark of scientific activity. Yet, despite the mystical aura surrounding such discoveries, we often find that computational considerations of efficiency and economy play a major role in determining what

---

Correspondence to: R. Dechter, Information and Computer Science, University of California, Irvine, CA 92717, USA. E-mail: dechter@ics.uci.edu.
*This work was supported in part by the Air Force Office of Scientific Research grant AFOSR 900136, NSF grant IRI-9157636, GE Corporate R&D and Micro grant 91-125.

structures are considered meaningful by scientists. In this paper we address the task of finding a computationally attractive description of the data, a description that both is economical in storage and permits future queries to be answered in a tractable way.

Invariably, the existence of such a desirable description rests on whether the dependencies among the data items are decomposable into local, more basic dependencies, possessing some desirable features. A classic example would be finding a finite state machine (with the least number of states) that accounts for observed dependencies among successive symbols in a very long string. In more elaborate settings, the dependencies can form a graph (as in the analysis of Markov fields [24]) or a hypergraph (as in relational databases [19]), and the task is to find the topology of these structures. Structure identification includes tasks such as finding effective representations for probability distributions [7,16,30], devising economical decompositions of database schemas, synthesizing simple Boolean expressions for truth tables [6], and casting logical theories that render subsequent processing tractable.

Despite the generality of the task, very few formal results have been established, and those that exist were confined primarily to probabilistic analysis of statistical data [7,18,24,25]. In this paper we focus on relational (nonstatistical) data and deterministic descriptions of the data. Given a relation ρ in the form of an explicit listing of the tuples of ρ, we ask whether we can find a more desirable description of ρ, say a constraint network possessing desirable topological features or a logical theory possessing desirable syntactic features (e.g., Horn theories). In both cases the desirable features would be those that facilitate efficient query processing routines.

We view this task as an exercise in automatic *identification*, because our main concerns are to recognize cases for which desirable descriptions exist and to identify the parameters of at least one such description. Thus, we explore the existence of a tractable identification procedure that takes data as input, returns a structure, and works in time polynomial in the size of the input and output. Given that the data were generated from a model that has a desirable structure, our procedure should identify either the underlying structure when it is unique, or an equivalent structure when it is not unique. Conversely, if the data does not lend itself to effective organization, we wish our procedure to acknowledge this fact, so as to save further exploration. Sometimes an additional requirement is imposed on the procedure, namely, to identify a "best" approximated theory, when an exact desirable theory does not exist. We call this latter requirement "strong identifiability".

Our analysis bears a close relation to that of Selman and Kautz [27], where theory formation is treated as a task of "knowledge compilation". The main difference between the two approaches is that Selman and Kautz begin with a preformed *theory* in the form of a (reasonably sized) set of clauses, while we start with the bare *observations*, namely, a (reasonably sized) set of tuples that represent the models of the desired theory. This enables us to easily project the tuples onto subsets of variables and to solve subtasks that would be intractable had we started with a causal theory. Another difference is that we require definite determination of whether the theory approximates or describes the data.

This paper is organized as follows: Section 2 introduces a general framework of the identification task. We define weak and strong notions of identifiability and, using familiar examples, compare them to Valiant's [30] notion of learnability. Section 3 investigates the identifiability of structure-based tractable classes of constraint networks and propositional theories. We show that stars and trees are identifiable, while chains and k-trees are not. Section 4 focuses on identifying theories whose tractability stems from syntactic rather than structural features. In particular, we show that relations describable by Horn theories can readily be recognized (Theorem 4.9), and that corresponding Horn theories can be found in time polynomial in the length of the data (Theorem 4.10). Additionally, we show that a best approximation in k-Horn theory (in which every clause contains at most k literals) can be identified in $O(|\rho|n^{k+1})$ time, where n is the number of variables (Corollary 4.11).

2. Preliminaries and basic definitions

2.1. Theories: networks and formulas

We denote propositional symbols, also called *variables*, by uppercase letters $P, Q, R, X, Y, Z, \ldots$, propositional literals (i.e., $P, \neg P$) by lowercase letters $p, q, r, x, y, z, \ldots$, and disjunctions of literals, or *clauses*, by $\alpha, \beta, \ldots$. The complement operator $\sim$ over literals is defined as usual: If $p = \neg Q$, then $\sim p = Q$; if $p = Q$ then $\sim p = \neg Q$. A *formula* in conjunctive normal form (CNF) is a set of clauses $\varphi = \{\alpha_1, \ldots, \alpha_t\}$, implying their conjunction. The *models* of a formula φ, $M(\varphi)$, is the set of all satisfying truth assignments to all of the formula's symbols. A clause α is *entailed* by φ, written $\varphi \models \alpha$, iff α is true in all models of φ. A clause α is a *prime implicate* of φ iff $\varphi \models \alpha$ and $\not\exists \beta \subseteq \alpha$ such that $\varphi \models \beta$. A Horn formula is a CNF formula whose clauses all have at most one positive literal. A k-CNF formula is one in which clauses are all of length k or less, and a k-Horn formula is defined accordingly.

To characterize the structure of a formula φ we define its *scheme* as the set of variable sets on which clauses are defined. Formally:

Definition 2.1 (*Scheme*). Let $\varphi = \{\alpha_1, \ldots, \alpha_r\}$, and let $base(\alpha)$ be the set of all propositional symbols on which clause α is defined, then

$$scheme(\varphi) = \{base(\alpha_j) \mid 1 \leqslant j \leqslant r\}. \tag{1}$$

Example 2.2. Consider the formula

$$\varphi = \{(\neg P \vee Q \vee R), (P \vee S), (\neg P \vee \neg S), (\neg P \vee R)\}. \tag{2}$$

In this case,

$$scheme(\varphi) = \{\{P, Q, R\}, \{P, S\}, \{P, R\}\}. \tag{3}$$

We next define the notions of *constraint networks* and *relations*, which parallel the notions of formulas and their satisfying models, for multivalued variables. A *relation* associates a set of multivalued variables with a set of tuples specifying their allowed combinations of values. A *constraint network* is a set of such relations, each defined on a subset of the variables. Taken together, this set represents conjunction of constraints, namely, it restricts value assignments to comply with each and every constituent relation. The theory of relations has been studied extensively in the database literature [19].

Definition 2.3 (*Relation and network*). Given a set of multivalued variables $X = \{X_1, \ldots, X_n\}$, each associated with a domain of discrete values $D_1, \ldots, D_n$, respectively, a *relation* (or, alternatively, a *constraint*) $\rho = \rho(X_1, \ldots, X_n)$ is any subset

$$\rho \subseteq D_1 \times D_2 \times \cdots \times D_n. \tag{4}$$

A *constraint network* N over X is a set $\rho_1, \ldots, \rho_t$ of such relations. Each relation ρ_i is defined on a subset of variables $S_i \subseteq X$. The set of subsets $S = \{S_1, .., S_t\}$ is called the *scheme* of N (also denoted $scheme(N)$). The *dimension* of scheme S, denoted $dim(S)$, is defined as the cardinality of the largest component in S. The network N represents a unique relation $rel(N)$ defined over X, which stands for all consistent assignments (or all solutions), namely,

$$rel(N) = \{x = (x_1, \ldots, x_n) \mid \forall S_i \in S, \Pi_{S_i}(x) \in \rho_i\}, \tag{5}$$

where $\Pi_{S_i}(x)$ is the projection of x onto S_i. The *projection* of a relation ρ onto a subset of variables R, denoted $\Pi_R(\rho)$, is the set of tuples defined on the variables in R that can be extended to a tuple in ρ. If $rel(N) = \rho$ we say that N *describes* or *represents* ρ.

Clearly, any CNF formula can be viewed as a special kind of constraint network, where the domains are bivalued and where each clause specifies a constraint on its propositional symbols. We say that a bivalued relation $\rho = \rho(x_1, \ldots, x_n)$ is *described* (or *represented*) by a formula $\varphi = \varphi(x_1, \ldots, x_n)$ iff $M(\varphi) = \rho$. We will use the term *theory* to denote either a network or a formula and, correspondingly, will use $M(T)$ and $rel(T)$ interchangeably.

Example 2.4. The relation

$$\rho(P, Q, R, S) = \{(1010), \\ (1110), \\ (0101), \\ (0011), \\ (0111), \\ (0001)\}$$

can be described by the network

$$N = \{(\rho(P, Q, R) = \{(101), (111), (010), (001), (011), (000)\}), \\ (\rho(P, S) = \{(01), (10)\}), \\ (\rho(P, R) = \{(00), (01), (11)\})\},$$

since the consistent assignments of N coincide with ρ. Being bivalued, ρ can also be described by the formula

$$\varphi = \{(\neg P \vee Q \vee R), (P \vee S), (\neg P \vee \neg S), (\neg P \vee R)\}, \tag{6}$$

since $M(\varphi) = \rho$.

When considering ways of approximating a relation ρ by a theory T, we will examine primarily upper bound approximations, namely, theories T such that $\rho \subseteq M(T)$.

Definition 2.5 (*Tightest approximation*). A theory $T \in C$ is said to be a *tightest approximation* of ρ relative to a class C of theories if $\rho \subseteq M(T)$ and there is no $T' \in C$ such that $\rho \subseteq M(T') \subset M(T)$.

2.2. Identifiability

We are now ready to give a formal definition of identifiability: A property that is intrinsic to any class of theories and that governs our ability to decide whether a given relation ρ has a description within the class. As the preliminary example, we will use the class of k-CNF formulas. We will show that, while this class is identifiable for $k = 2$, it may not be identifiable for any $k > 2$. In other words, there may not be any tractable way of deciding whether an arbitrary relation ρ has a description as a k-CNF formula for $k > 2$. The class of 2-CNF theories will turn out to be *strongly* identifiable, namely, not only can we decide the existence of a 2-CNF description, and produce such a description if it exists, but we can also produce a tightest 2-CNF formula (as well as a k-CNF, $k > 2$) if a precise description does not exist (hence the term "strong").

Not surprisingly, the decisions above would depend on our prior knowledge about the observed relation ρ. For example, if we were given assurance that ρ has a description in k-CNF, it would be easy to produce such a description. Thus, it is necessary to define the notion of identifiability relative to a background class C' of theories from which ρ is chosen. We will adopt the convention that, unless stated otherwise, C' is presumed to be the class of all theories, namely, ρ is an arbitrary relation. We will denote by $|\rho|$ the number of tuples in ρ.

Definition 2.6 (*Identifiability*). A class of theories C is said to be *identifiable* relative to a background class C' if there is an algorithm A, polynomial in the size of its input and output, such that:
  (1) *Recognition*: For every relation ρ that is describable by some theory T in C', A determines whether ρ has a description in C.
  (2) *Description*: If the answer to (1) is positive, algorithm A finds one theory $T \in C$ that describes ρ (i.e., $\rho = M(T)$).
  (3) *Tightness*: C is said to be *strongly* identifiable if, in addition to (1) and (2) above, A always finds a theory T_0 in C that is a tightest approximation of ρ.

By convention, a class in which the problems associated with the recognition or description tasks are NP-hard will be defined as nonidentifiable. Note that in conditions (2) and (3) the complexity of A is measured relative to the size of ρ as well as to the size of the theories that describe ρ. In the analysis of structure-based constraint networks and CNFs (Section 3), the description length will usually be insignificant, so $|\rho|$ will be the dominant factor in the complexity of A. In Section 4, however, where we analyze Horn approximations, the two factors will play equal roles. Practically speaking, taking the size of ρ as the basis for measuring complexity amounts to focusing the identification task on highly constrained data, where the number of distinct observations grows polynomially with the number of variables.

Coming back to our k-CNF example, we consider again the question of whether the class C_k of all relations expressible by k-CNF theories is identifiable relative to $C' = C_n$, the class of all CNFs. As we will show in Section 3, although algorithms for condition (3) (and hence condition (2)), namely, of constructing a tightest k-CNF approximation, do exist for any ρ, we do not have an effective way of fulfilling condition (1), namely, of testing whether this approximation represents the relation ρ exactly or a superset thereof. (Even generating a single model of a tightest k-CNF theory may be NP-hard for $k > 2$.) We will thus conclude that C_k is not identifiable.[1] On the other hand, C_k is strongly identifiable relative to itself, since recognition is trivially satisfied and any tightest approximation must be exact.

2.3. Identifiability versus learnability

There is a strong resemblance between the notion of identifiability and of learnability [30]. If we associate theories with concepts (or functions) and the models of a theory with the learning examples, we see that in both cases we are seeking a polynomial algorithm that will take in a polynomial number of examples and will produce a concept (or a function) which is consistent with those examples, from some family of concepts C. Moreover, for a family C to be learnable from positive examples (with one-sided errors), we know that it must be closed under intersection and that the algorithm must produce the tightest concept in C consistent with the observations [23]. This is identical to condition (3) (strong identifiability).

The main difference between the problems described in this paper and those addressed by learning models is that in learnability we are given the concept class C and our task is to identify an individual member of C that is (either surely or probably) responsible for the observed instances. By contrast, in structure identification we are not given the concept class C. Rather, one of our primary objectives is to decide whether a fully observed concept ρ, taken from some broad class C' (e.g., all relations), is also a member of a narrower class C of concepts, one that possesses desirable syntactical features (e.g., a 2-CNF, a constraint tree, or a Horn theory). Thus, the task is not to infer the extension of a concept from a subset of its examples (the entire extension is assumed to be directly observed), but to decide whether the concept admits a given syntactical description.

It turns out that deciding whether the tightest approximation exactly describes a given concept, even when the concept is of small size, might be computationally expensive—a problem not normally addressed in the learning literature.

The differences between learnability and identifiability can be well demonstrated using our previous example of the class C_k of k-CNF theories. We have argued earlier that while C_k may not be identifiable relative to the class C' of all relations, it is nevertheless strongly identifiable relative to

---

[1]The nonexistence of a tractable procedure for testing exact match with ρ is subject to Conjecture 3.10 (see Section 3.1).

$C' = C_k$. By comparison the class C_k is known to be polynomially learnable [30] since, given a collection of instances I of $M(\varphi)$, one can find in polynomial time the tightest k-CNF expression that contains I (see Section 3). The fact that C_k is not identifiable is not too disturbing in learning tasks, because there we assume that the examples must be drawn from some k-CNF theory φ, so in the long run the tightest k-CNF approximation to the data will coincide with φ. However, nonidentifiability can be very disturbing if the examples are taken from a theory outside C_k. In this case, the tightest k-CNF theory consistent with the examples might lead to substantial (one-sided) errors.

In general, if we set $C' = C$, then, if C is learnable from positive and negative examples, it must also be identifiable, because identification is an easier task under this condition. Assuming that ρ contains *all* instances of a concept amounts to observing both positive and negative examples and, compared to PAC-learning, we are effectively provided with an answer to every membership query without having to wait for examples to be generated by a random process. Likewise, if C is one-sided learnable, it must be strongly identifiable, because condition (1) is satisfied automatically, and the one-sided learnability requirement of zero error on negative examples is equivalent to condition (3). There are, of course, concept classes that are identifiable but not one-sided learnable under the condition $C' = C$ (a trivial example of which is the class of relations ρ having size $|\rho| = k$), again because, in identification, negative examples are implicit through their absence from the data.

3. Topology-based identification

A given relation ρ can be represented by many networks or formulas (if ρ is bivalued), each having a different scheme. All such representations will be called *equivalent* (denoted by $\approx$). In this section we will focus on networks and CNF formulas parameterized by their corresponding schemes. We will first analyze the identifiability of several classes of constraint networks and then show, using a simple translation, that most results are extensible to the scheme-based identifiability of CNF formulas.

3.1. Identifying constraint networks

We will first make some observations that generalize Montanari's [21] notion of *minimal networks* (originally defined on binary networks) to constraint networks having arbitrary schemes. Some of these observations were also made in [22], albeit under a different notation.

We denote by N_S the class of all constraint networks having a common scheme S, assuming all networks are defined on n variables with the same set of domain values.

Definition 3.1 (*Projection network*). Given a relation ρ and a scheme $S = \{S_1,\ldots,S_r\}$, the projection of ρ on S, $\Pi_S(\rho)$, is defined as the network obtained by projecting ρ onto each component of S:

$$\Pi_S(\rho) = \{\Pi_{S_i}(\rho) |\ \forall S_i \in S\}. \tag{7}$$

Clearly, generating $\Pi_S(\rho)$ from ρ is polynomial:

Lemma 3.2. *The network $\Pi_S(\rho)$ can be constructed in* $\mathrm{O}(|\rho||S|)$ *steps.*

Theorem 3.3 (Montanari and Rossi [22]). *The network $\Pi_S(\rho)$ is a tightest approximation of ρ relative to the class N_S.*

As in [21,22], we next observe that among all networks $R \in N_S$ that are equivalent to $\Pi_S(\rho)$, $\Pi_S(\rho)$ has a unique syntactic property called *minimality* with respect to the partial order $\subseteq$ defined as follows:

Definition 3.4 (*Network ordering*).

$$R \subseteq Q \quad \text{iff} \quad \forall S_i \in S, R_{S_i} \subseteq Q_{S_i}, \tag{8}$$

where R_{S_i} is the relation associated with S_i in network R.

Similarly, we define the *intersection of networks* R and Q in N_S as the network created by the intersection of the corresponding constraints.

Definition 3.5 (*Network intersection*). Let $R, Q \in N_S$. The intersection $\cap$ of R and Q is given by:

$$R \cap Q = \{R_{S_i} \cap Q_{S_i} |\ \forall S_i \in S\}. \tag{9}$$

Note that $R \in N_S$ and $Q \in N_S$ implies that $R \cap Q \in N_S$.

The next theorem states the existence of a unique (with respect to $\subseteq$) *minimal* network M_S of ρ having scheme S.

Theorem 3.6 (Montanari and Rossi [22]). . *Let $R, Q \in N_S$ and let $\rho = rel(R)$, then*
  (1) $R \approx Q \implies R \cap Q \approx R$,
  (2) *there exists a unique minimal (with respect to $\subseteq$) network M_S representing ρ, and it is given by $M_S = \Pi_S(\rho)$.*

Proof. The first part is clear and implies the existence of a unique minimal network M_S, which equals the intersection of all equivalent networks. We will show that $M_S = \Pi_S(\rho)$. Clearly, $M_S \approx \Pi_S(\rho)$. By definition, $M_S \subseteq \Pi_S(\rho)$. However, if we eliminate even a single tuple from any constraint in $\Pi_S(\rho)$, the resulting network will not allow a legal tuple of ρ, contradicting the fact that M_S describes ρ. Consequently, $M_S = \Pi_S(\rho)$. □

Corollary 3.7. *Among all tightest approximations to ρ from N_S, $\Pi_S(\rho)$ is the minimal one.*

We are now ready to discuss identifiability relative to specific schemes. The negative result that follows hinges on Conjecture 3.10 and Lemma 3.8.

Lemma 3.8 (Ullman[29]). *Given a relation ρ and an arbitrary scheme S, deciding whether $rel(\Pi_S(\rho)) = \rho$ is NP-hard.*

Theorem 3.9. *Given an arbitrary scheme S, the class N_S is not identifiable relative to all networks N, but is strongly identifiable relative to N_S.*

Proof. We will show a polynomial reduction from the decision problem of whether $rel(\Pi_S(\rho)) = \rho)$ (which is NP-complete) to the problem of deciding the identifiability of N_S (for any S). Given a relation ρ and a scheme S, if we can identify in polynomial time whether ρ is representable by scheme S, then, due to condition (1), we can also determine whether $rel(\Pi_S(\rho)) = \rho)$: If ρ is identifiable, $rel(\Pi_S(\rho)) = \rho$; if not, $rel(\Pi_S(\rho)) \supset \rho$. Since the projection formula can be computed in time proportional to $|\rho||S|$, the reduction is polynomial. Consequently, based on Lemma 3.8, unless P = NP, the identifiability of N_S relative to all networks is NP-hard. When the background is N_S, the exactness decision is trivially satisfied (the projection $\Pi_S(\rho)$ is guaranteed then to represent ρ) and hence N_S is strongly identifiable. □

Let S_k be the set of all subsets of size k or less of $X = \{X_1, \ldots, X_n\}$. Although we believe that the NP-completeness result of Lemma 3.8 extends to these special schemes, we are unable to prove it as yet. For convenience we will use the shorthand $N_k = N_{S_k}$.

Conjecture 3.10. *Given a relation ρ and an integer k, deciding whether $rel(\Pi_{S_k}(\rho)) = \rho$ is NP-hard.*

Corollary 3.11. *The class N_k is not identifiable relative to N.*

Example 3.12. The class N_2 of all binary multivalued constraint networks is not identifiable (unless the number of values is 2). This class is characterized by a scheme consisting of all variable pairs (i.e., the complete graph) for which, subject to Conjecture 3.10, we cannot establish whether $rel(\Pi_{S_2}(\rho)) = \rho$ in polynomial time.

When the scheme S has topological properties that permit solution in polynomial time, N_S is identifiable. We say that a scheme S is tractable when there exists a polynomial algorithm for deciding the consistency of every constraint network in the class N_S. For instance, any tree or acyclic hypergraph [10] is a tractable scheme.

Theorem 3.13. *Let S be a tractable scheme. Then the class of networks N_S is strongly identifiable.*

Proof. The projection $\Pi_S(\rho)$ provides a tightest N_S approximation to ρ and can be computed in polynomial time. The tractability of S assures that the equality $|rel(\Pi_S(\rho))| = |\rho|$ can also be tested in polynomial time. It was recently shown [11] that for every theory T satisfiable in time t, deciding whether $|M(T)| > c$ takes time $O(ct)$. Now, since S is tractable, it is satisfiable in polynomial time; therefore, deciding $rel(\Pi_S(\rho)) \supset \rho$ can be accomplished in polynomial time. □

3.2. Identifying CNF formulas

In this section we shift our attention to bivalued relations and to the task of identifying tractable classes of CNF formulas. We will show that there is great similarity between the identifiability of scheme-based constraint networks and that of scheme-based CNF having the same scheme. This will become clear through a simple translation from bivalued relations into CNFs. As in the multivalued case, we will first extend the auxiliary notions of *projection network* and *minimal network* to *projection formula* and *maximal formula*.

Definition 3.14 (*Canonical representation*).
(1) Let ρ be a bivalued relation over $X = X_1, \ldots, X_n$. We define

$$canonical(\rho) = \{(\sim x_1 \vee \sim x_2 \vee \cdots \vee \sim x_n) | (x_1, x_2, \ldots, x_n) \notin \rho\}. \qquad (10)$$

(2) Given a constraint network $N = \{\rho_1, \ldots, \rho_t\}$, we define $canonical(N)$ as the formula generated by collecting the canonical formulas of every

constituent relation in N. Namely,

$$canonical(N) = \bigcup \{canonical(\rho_i) | \rho_i \in N\}. \tag{11}$$

The equivalence of the relational and propositional representations of this translation, as stated in the following lemma, is quite immediate:

Lemma 3.15. *The models of the canonical formula of network N coincide with the solutions of N. Namely, $M(canonical(N)) = rel(N)$.*

We now extend the notion of projection network to projection formula.

Definition 3.16 (*Projection formula*). Given a relation ρ and a scheme S, the *projection formula* of ρ with respect to S, denoted $\Gamma_S(\rho)$, is given by

$$\Gamma_S(\rho) = canonical(\Pi_S(\rho)). \tag{12}$$

Example 3.17. Let

$$\rho(P, Q, R) = \{(100), (010), (001)\}$$

and

$$S = \{\{P, Q\}\{P, R\}\{Q, R\}\}.$$

Then,

$$\Pi_S(\rho) = \{(\rho(P, Q) = \{(10), (01), (00)\}),$$
$$(\rho(P, R) = \{(10), (01), (00)\}),$$
$$(\rho(Q, R) = \{(10), (01), (00)\})\},$$

and

$$\Gamma_S(\rho) = \{(\neg P \vee \neg Q), (\neg P \vee \neg R), (\neg R \vee \neg Q)\}.$$

Generating $\Gamma_S(\rho)$ from $\Pi_S(\rho)$ may be exponential in the size of the largest component in S, as it requires enumerating all tuples defined on each component. Consequently, for schemes of bounded dimension, this construction is polynomial.

Lemma 3.18. *Let $dim(S) \leq k$. The complexity of generating $\Gamma_S(\rho)$ is $O(|\rho||S| + |S|2^k)$.*

Let C_S be the class of CNF formulas having scheme S. Parallel to Theorem 3.3, we have:

Theorem 3.19. *The formula $\Gamma_S(\rho)$ is a tightest approximation of ρ relative to C_S.*

Proof. Follows immediately from the facts that $\Pi_S(\rho)$ is a tightest approximation to ρ and $M(\Gamma_S(\rho)) = rel(\Pi_S(\rho))$. □

Parallel to the notion of minimal networks in multivalued relations, we will now show that among all formulas φ in C_S that are equivalent to $\Gamma_S(\rho)$, $\Gamma_S(\rho)$ is *maximal* with respect to the partial order $\subseteq$ defined by set inclusion (of clauses). Clearly the class C_S is closed under union. The next lemma (parallel to Theorem 3.6) proves that among all equivalent formulas in C_S, $\Gamma_S(\rho)$ is the unique maximal formula.

Lemma 3.20. *Let $\varphi, \tau \in C_S$ and let $\rho = M(\varphi)$. Then*
  (1) $\varphi \approx \tau \implies \varphi \cup \tau \approx \varphi$,
  (2) *there exists a unique maximal (with respect to $\subseteq$) formula μ_S representing ρ, and it is given by $\mu_S = \Gamma_S(\rho)$.*

Proof. The first part is immediate, since the union of formulas stands for their conjunction. The second part is similar to the proof of Theorem 3.6. □

When the scheme S has components containing each other, the corresponding clauses may subsume each other and thus present redundancy. We clearly prefer to consider formulas in *reduced* form, without subsumption.

Definition 3.21 (*Reduced formula*). A formula φ is *reduced* if none of its clauses contain another clause. The formula obtained after eliminating clause subsumption from φ is denoted $reduced(\varphi)$.

Lemma 3.22. *Reduced($\Gamma_S(\rho)$) contains all (but not only) the prime implicates of $\Gamma_S(\rho)$ that are restricted to the subsets in S.*

Proof. Being maximal, $\Gamma_S(\rho)$ must contain all prime implicates restricted to S. □

We now state a scheme-based correspondence between scheme-based identification of constraint networks and CNFs.

Theorem 3.23. *If N_S is identifiable relative to all constraint networks and if scheme S has a bounded dimension, then the class C_S is also identifiable relative to all CNFs.*

Proof. Given a bivalued relation ρ and a scheme S, since N_S is identifiable we can decide in polynomial time whether the projection network $\Pi_S(\rho)$ represents ρ. moreover, since $dim(S)$ is bounded the translation from $\Pi_S(\rho)$ to $\Gamma_S(\rho)$ is polynomial. Hence, the conclusion follows because $\Pi_S(\rho)$ describes ρ iff $\Gamma_S(\rho)$ describes ρ. □

The following theorem shows that the converse is not true. Although N_2 is not identifiable, C_2 is, because the satisfiability of 2-CNF is tractable. Consequently, testing of whether $|\Gamma_{S_2}(\rho)| > |\rho|$ can be done in polynomial time [11].

Theorem 3.24. *The class of 2-CNFs is strongly identifiable relative to all CNFs.*

The negative results ahead are based on an extended version of Lemma 3.8 and on the bivalued version of Conjecture 3.10.

Lemma 3.25 (Parallel to Lemma 3.8). *Given a bivalued relation ρ and an arbitrary scheme S, deciding whether $M(\Gamma_S(\rho)) = \rho$ is NP-complete.*

Proof. The proof follows from a simple polynomial translation of any multivalued relation to a bivalued relation and from Lemma 3.8. □

Theorem 3.26 (Parallel to Theorem 3.9). *Given a parameterized scheme class SC_n of bounded dimension, the class C_{SC_n} is not identifiable relative to the class of all CNFs, but is strongly identifiable relative to itself.*

Proof. The proof of the first part is identical to that of Theorem 3.9. The reason that C_{SC_n} is identifiable relative to itself is that the translation from $\Pi_{SC_n}(\rho)$ to $\Gamma_{SC_n}(\rho)$ is polynomial for bounded schemes. □

Conjecture 3.27 (Parallel to Conjecture 3.10). *Given a bivalued relation ρ and an integer k, deciding whether $M(\Gamma_{S_k}(\rho)) = \rho$ is NP-hard.*

Consequently,

Corollary 3.28. *The class of k-CNF is not identifiable relative to all CNFs.*

3.3. Identifying constraint trees

We saw in the previous section that the class N_2 of binary constraint networks is not identifiable, while the class C_S of constraint networks with some specific scheme S is identifiable if S is tractable. We now study a unique class of tractable schemes, those structured as constraint trees, which is identifiable not only when we present one specific scheme (i.e., a particular tree), but also when we have no knowledge of the underlying scheme except that it is a tree.

Let N_T be the class of all constraint networks that have a tree-structured scheme. The following theorem [9] shows that N_T is identifiable.

Theorem 3.29. *Given an arbitrary relation ρ, let $n(x_i)$ be the number of n-tuples in ρ for which $X_i = x_i$, and let $n(x_i, x_j)$ be the number of n-tuples in ρ for which $X_i = x_i$ and $X_j = x_j$. Define the arc-weights $m(X_i, X_j)$ as*

$$m(X_i, X_j) = \frac{1}{|\rho|} \sum_{(x_i,x_j) \in \Pi_{X_i X_j}(\rho)} n(x_i, x_j) \log \frac{n(x_i, x_j)}{n(x_i) n(x_j)}. \tag{13}$$

If ρ has a constraint-tree representation, then any maximum-weight spanning tree (MWST) formed with the arc-weights defined above constitutes a scheme of such a representation.

Example 3.30. Consider the relation ρ over the binary variables A, B, C, D and E given in Fig. 1. The first step in the algorithm computes the quantities $n(X_i = x_i)$ and $\{n(X_i = x_i, X_j = x_j)\}$ for all variables and their values, obtaining

$$n(A = 0) = 8, \quad (B = 1) = 6, \quad n(B = 0) = 2,$$
$$n(B = 0, C = 1) = 2, \quad n(B = 1, C = 1) = 3, \quad \text{etc.}$$

Next, for each pair of variables (X_i, X_j), we compute the weights $m(X_i, X_j)$, according to equation (13).

$$m(A, B) = m(A, C) = m(A, D) = m(A, E) = -16.63,$$
$$m(B, C) = -13.97, \quad m(B, D) = -15.95, \quad m(B, E) = -16.55,$$
$$m(C, D) = -16.55, \quad m(C, E) = -17.13, \quad m(D, E) = -15.50.$$

Finally, using the MWST algorithm on these weighted arcs, the tree shown in Fig. 2 is produced. The relations associated with the arcs of the tree are the projections of ρ on pairs of connected variables. For instance, the relation associated with variables D and B is given in Fig. 2(a). The tree generated in this example, together with its associated database (see Fig. 2), represents the original relation, in the sense that it provides a lossless decomposition.

A	B	C	D	E
0	0	1	1	1
0	0	1	1	0
0	1	1	1	1
0	1	1	1	0
0	1	1	0	1
0	1	0	1	1
0	1	0	1	0
0	1	0	0	1

Fig. 1. The input relation ρ for Example 3.30.

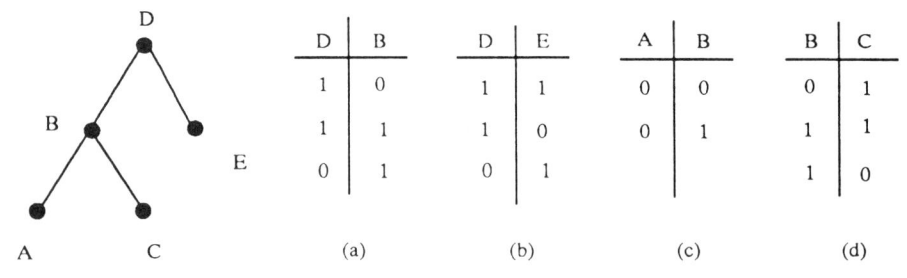

Fig. 2. The tree decomposition of ρ.

In other words, the set of all solutions to this network coincide with relation ρ and they can be recovered efficiently.

Corollary 3.31. N_T is identifiable in time $O((|\rho| + \log n)n^2)$.

Proof. The MWST can be constructed in $O((|\rho| + \log n)n^2)$ steps. To verify that the generated tree t represents the input relation ρ, we project ρ onto the arcs of t, compute (in linear time) the number of n-tuples represented by the resulting constraint tree, and compare it to the size of ρ. If the two numbers are equal, the constraint tree represents ρ precisely. Otherwise, we know that no tree representation exists for ρ. □

An alternative method of identifying and constructing tree representations, avoiding the numerical precision required for computing equation (13), is described in [20]. We first project ρ onto all triplets of variables, then examine each triplet for possible redundancy, namely, whether the constraint on one of the pairs is implied by the other two. Next we assign integer weights to the edges (X_i, X_j) in such a way that any redundant edge should always receive a lower weight than that of a nonredundant edge in the same triangle. Finally, we construct an MWST according to the integer weights thus assigned. It can be shown that the resulting tree has all the properties of the tree constructed by the weights of equation (13).

Although the class of constraint trees is identifiable, it is still open to question whether this class is strongly identifiable; we were not able to prove (or disprove) that the MWST method returns a tightest tree containing ρ when the input relation ρ does not have a tree representation. In all examples examined so far, the returned tree was a tightest one.

Note that although the class of constraint trees is identifiable, it is not learnable with one-sided error, because it is not closed under intersection—the intersection of two trees may form a graph with cycles. Hence, there is no unique tightest tree that contains every subset of positive examples, and this implies that N_T is not learnable with one-sided error.

3.4. Chains, stars, and k-trees

The previous analysis might leave the impression that any class of networks is identifiable as long as the scheme of each network in the class is tractable. To see that this may not be so, consider the class N_c of constraint chains. Being a special kind of a tree, each individual member of N_c is clearly tractable. Yet deciding whether an arbitrary relation ρ can be described by some chain seems an insurmountable task. We do not know of any method of solving this decision problem, save for exhaustive enumeration of all $n!$ chains or all spanning trees that tie for the minimal weight. The difficulty is that since chains are not matroids we do not have a greedy algorithm similar to the MWST for identifying the correct ordering of the variables.

Another class of trees that are not matroids are stars, namely, trees in which one node is adjacent to all the others. This class is (strongly) identifiable, however, primarily due to its low cardinality; there are exactly n stars on n variables. To identify a star, we simply test whether any of the n possible stars represents the input relation ρ. This test, as usual, involves projecting ρ on the edges of the tested star, then counting (in linear time) the number of solutions of the resulting constraint network and testing whether it is equal to $|\rho|$.

An important class of networks is k-trees (or chordal graphs), a powerful generalization of trees (where $k = 1$) investigated in [3,4], and, more recently, [13]. k-Trees can be viewed as trees of clusters, where each cluster consists of a clique of variables with cardinality not exceeding k. Like trees, they are tractably satisfiable. However, not being matroids, k-trees are probably not identifiable. We know of no method (save for exhaustive enumeration) of testing whether an arbitrary relation is representable as a

k-tree for any $k > 1$. In [9] we provide a heuristic algorithm for identifying k-trees which is a generalization of the one for 2-trees.

4. Identifying Horn theories

In this section we shift our attention to bivalued relations and to the task of identifying tractable classes of CNF formulas, such as Horn theories.

In general, determining whether a given query formula follows from a given CNF formula is intractable [8]. However, when the latter contains only Horn clauses, the problem can be solved in linear time [14]. The tractability of Horn theories stems not from the topology of the interactions among their clauses, but rather from a syntactic restriction imposed on each individual clause. This restriction is, in general, less constraining than those imposed by topological considerations; experience with logic programming and databases suggests that humans find it natural to communicate knowledge in terms of Horn expressions. Additionally, the tractability of Horn theories covers a wide range of queries, including, for example, membership, equivalence, disjointness, and entailment. In contrast, the data compression techniques used in classification learning, such as decision trees [26], are effective only for certain membership queries.[2] Thus, it would be useful to determine whether a given set of observations (the data ρ) can be described as a Horn theory.

We shall show that Horn theories are polynomially identifiable; the recognition test of whether ρ has a Horn description can be decided in time proportional to $|\rho|^2 \log |\rho|$, while the time needed to find such a description is proportional to $|\rho|^2 n^2$. However, there are several impediments to using Horn theories as effective approximations to relational data. Selman and Kautz [27], have shown that finding a tightest Horn approximation to a given CNF formula is NP-hard and that any tightest approximation might sometimes require exponentially many clauses (in the size of the source theory). All indications are that similar problems would surface in using Horn expressions to approximate empirical data. First, we have no guarantee that the length of the best approximation would not be exponential in the input $|\rho|$ and, second, we still have no polynomial method of finding the best approximation, even if we take the length of the minimal output theory as the basis for analysis.

In such cases it might be futile to use Horn approximations instead of the observations themselves. A more practical question to ask, then, is whether

---

[2]For example, decision trees are efficient for determining class membership from a set of properties but do not permit us to effectively infer properties from class membership (and other properties) or to decide whether two decision trees are equivalent or disjoint.

a given relation can be approximated by a Horn theory of a reasonable size. To that end, we analyze the identifiability of k-Horn formulas, namely, Horn formulas in which every clause contains at most k literals. We show that this class of formulas is strongly identifiable.

4.1. Preliminaries

We will assume that all Horn clauses are represented as implications $v_1 \wedge v_2 \wedge \cdots \wedge v_l \longrightarrow z$, where $v_1, v_2, \ldots, v_l$ are positive literals and z may be either a positive literal or 0 (0 stands for "false" and 1 for "true").

Definition 4.1. Let $x = (x_1, x_2, \ldots, x_n)$ be a tuple where $x_i \in \{1, 0\}$. Then $true(x)$ is the set of variables assigned 1 by x and $false(x)$ is the set of variables assigned the value 0 by x.

Definition 4.2 (*Intersection and closure*). Let x and y be two tuples. Then $x \cap y$ is defined to be the tuple z such that $true(z) = true(x) \cap true(y)$. A set of tuples X is said to be *closed under intersection* if $x \cap y \in X$ whenever $x \in X$ and $y \in X$. A set X^* is said to be the *intersection closure* of X if it is the smallest set containing X that is closed under intersection.

We shall show that a relation ρ has a precise Horn representation iff it is closed under intersection, namely, $\rho = \rho^*$. The proof is based on the notion of *extreme tuples*[3], and on Lemma 4.4 below.

Definition 4.3 (*Extreme tuples*). Given a set X of tuples, $x \in X$ is said to be *extreme* (relative to X) if it is not in the intersection closure of $\{X - x\}$. A tuple that is not extreme is called *interior*, and the set of extreme tuples will be called the *basis* of X, denoted $B(X)$.

Remarks. It is easy to show that every set X has a unique basis $B(X)$ and, moreover, that $B(X)$ is the minimal set having the same closure as X, namely, $[B(X)]^* = X^*$. $B(X)$ is also the maximal subset of X that is the basis of itself, that is, $B(X)$ is the maximal $Y \subseteq X$ satisfying $B(Y) = Y$. Finally, the basis of any set X can be found in time quadratic in $|X|$; we simply check for every $x \in X$ whether it is extreme (relative to X) by intersecting all tuples $y \in X$ such that $true(y) \supset true(x)$ and then testing whether the intersection differs from x.

---

[3]This notion, and its connection to Horn approximation (Corollary 4) was brought to our attention by H. Kautz. Lemma 4.5 which makes this connection possible, appears to be a general folklore among many researchers, although we could not trace its precise origin. An explicit proof for the propositional case is presented below; alternative treatment is given in [28].

Lemma 4.4. *Given a set X of tuples and another tuple t such that t is not in the intersection closure of X, there exists a Horn theory H that contains X and excludes t.*

Proof. Construct H as follows: Start with the set of all Horn clauses and remove every clause that conflicts with any tuple $x \in X$. We will show that among the remaining clauses, there must be at least one clause c' that excludes t. Consider the set of variables $T(t)$ such that:

$$T(t) = \bigcap_{x : true(x) \supset true(t)} true(x),$$

and assume $T(t)$ is nonempty. Since t is not in the intersection closure of X, $true(t)$ is a proper subset of $T(t)$, and we can choose an element z from $\{T(t) - true(t)\}$ and form the clause $c' : \bigwedge_i v_i \longrightarrow z$ where $v_i \in true(t)$. This clause will not be removed during the construction of H, because it is not violated by any $x \in X$. For c' to be violated by a tuple x, $true(t)$ must be a subset of $true(x)$ and z must be in $false(x)$, but c' was chosen such that each set $true(x)$ that contains $true(t)$ also contains z. Thus, since t violates c' and H contains c', t will not be a model of H. The argument remains valid in case $T(t)$ is empty, because in that case we have $z = 0$, thus, c' will eliminate t but nothing else. □

Lemma 4.5. *Let ρ be a set of tuples. Then ρ is the set of models of some Horn theory H if and only if it is closed under intersection.*

Proof. Let ρ be closed under intersection, and let H be the tightest Horn theory containing ρ. Suppose H has a model t that is not in ρ. Since ρ is closed under intersection, t cannot be in the intersection closure of ρ and, according to Lemma 4.4, it is possible to form a Horn theory, H_1, that contains ρ and excludes t. The Horn theory $H \cap H_1$ is clearly a tighter approximation of ρ, contrary to our assumption. This establishes the "if" part of the lemma. The "only if" part follows from showing that any clause that satisfies x and y also satisfies $x \cap y$ (see [31] and [2, Lemma 3]). □

Corollary 4.6. [4] *Let $h(\rho)$ stands for any tightest Horn approximation of an arbitrary relation ρ, and let $B(\rho)$ stand for the basis of ρ. Then*

$$h[B(\rho)] \approx h(\rho) \approx h(\rho^*).$$

---

[4] Independently proved in [28].

Proof. For any ρ, we have $h(\rho) \approx h(\rho^*)$, because Lemma 4.5 dictates $M[h(\rho^*)] = \rho^*$, and so, if $M[h(\rho)]$ were a proper subset of $M[h(\rho^*)] = \rho^*$, it would constitute a set closed under intersection containing ρ that is properly contained in ρ^*, thus violating the status of ρ^* as the closure of ρ (see Definition 4.2). Therefore, substituting $B(\rho)$ for ρ, we also have $h[B(\rho)] \approx h[B(\rho)^*]$. Moreover, since $[B(\rho)]^* = \rho^*$, we get $h[B(\rho)] \approx h(\rho^*) \approx h(\rho)$, which proves the corollary. □

Corollary 4.7. *Let X be a set of extreme tuples. Then, for every subset Y of X, there exists a Horn theory H that contains $X - Y$ and excludes Y. Conversely, if such a theory can be found for every subset Y of X, then X must be a set of extreme tuples.*

Proof. Let $Y = \{y_1, y_2, \ldots\}$. From Lemma 4.4, there exists a set of Horn theories $\{H_1, H_2, \ldots\}$ such that H_i contains $\{X - y_i\}$ and excludes y_i. Clearly, the union of clauses in $\{H_1, H_2, \ldots\}$ is a Horn theory that satisfies the condition of the corollary. The converse follows from the fact that if some member of X is given by the intersection of several other elements of X then every Horn theory that contains the latter must also contain the former. □

Corollary 4.8. *The VC-dimension of (the class of) Horn theories is $O[\exp(n/2)]$.*

Proof. The VC-dimension is defined as the maximum number of points that can be "shattered" by Horn theories, in the sense of Corollary 4.7 [5]. Accordingly, this number is equal to the maximum number of n-tuples such that none is in the intersection closure of the rest, namely,

$$\binom{n}{n/2} = O[\exp(n/2)]. \qquad \square$$

The VC-dimension plays an important role in the framework of PAC-learning, where it is used to assess the number of random samples needed before the error associated with learning an incorrect theory can be bounded [5]. Roughly speaking, Corollary 4.8 states that approximately as many samples as the square root of the 2^n possible tuples are needed before one can be fairly confident that the Horn theory learned does not deviate substantially from the one generating the data. Since the VC-dimension grows exponentially in n, we conclude that Horn theories are not polynomially learnable (in the PAC sense) from random examples [5]. This negative result has no significant impact on identification tasks, where we assume that all models of the learned theory are available explicitly. It does mean, however, that every Horn theory H can be completely characterized by at most $\exp(n/2)$

of its models. Conversely, at most $\exp(n/2)$ tuples would ever be needed to characterize ρ if we are determined to approximate ρ by a Horn theory.

4.2. Recognition, description, and approximation

This subsection analyzes the three conditions required for the identifiability of Horn theories. We first show that Horn theories are identifiable by analyzing the recognition and description conditions. We later address difficulties in finding tightest Horn approximations—the condition needed for strong identifiability.

Theorem 4.9. *Deciding whether an arbitrary set ρ of tuples can be represented by a Horn theory can be done in $O(|\rho|^2 \log|\rho|)$ time.*

Proof. According to Lemma 4.5, it is enough to test whether ρ is closed under intersection. This can be done by simply checking whether the intersection of any two elements in ρ is in ρ [17]. This method requires $O(|\rho|^2 \log|\rho|)$ steps (the number of pairs times the time to check whether the intersection of the pair is in ρ), thus proving the theorem. □

Theorem 4.9 establishes the recognition part of the identification task. We remark that of all the classes considered in this paper, the class of Horn theories is unique in that we can decide the existence of a description in the class without actually producing one. Consequently, the time required for reaching this decision is independent of the length of the final theory (if such exists).

To fully establish the identifiability of Horn theories, there remains to show that whenever ρ is describable by a Horn theory, it is possible to find one such theory in polynomial time. This task is facilitated by a learning algorithm called HORN, recently devised by Angluin, Frazer, and Pitt [2].[5] The learning algorithm of Angluin et al. assumes that an oracle possesses a target Horn theory H^* having m clauses, and tries to find a Horn theory equivalent to H^* by asking the oracle two types of queries: *equivalence* and *membership*. An equivalence query asks whether some conjectured Horn theory H is equivalent to H^*, and its answer is either a confirmation or a counterexample (i.e. an assignment that satisfies H^* but not H, or vice versa). When there are no counterexamples, the learning algorithm has clearly succeeded in identifying a correct theory. Membership queries allow the algorithm to ascertain whether a given tuple satisfies the target theory

---

[5] This algorithm and the possibility of simulating it on relational data was brought to our attention by an anonymous reviewer. These results were independently recognized by Kautz, Kearns, and Selman [17]. A direct and more efficient algorithm is described in the appendix.

H^*; they are answered "yes" or "no" by the oracle. Angluin et al. have shown that HORN finds a theory equivalent to H^* in polynomial time, making $O(mn)$ equivalence queries and $O(m^2n)$ membership queries. Moreover, every theory H that HORN presents as a conjecture (including, of course, the final output theory) has at most $m(n + 1)$ clauses.

To find a Horn description of a given relation ρ, we simply simulate HORN by addressing its queries to the data ρ rather than to the oracle's theory H^*. A membership query is answered by simply checking whether the tuple presented is in ρ. Equivalence queries can be answered as follows: Given a conjectured Horn theory H, we first check that every tuple of ρ satisfies H. If not, we return the unsatisfying tuple as a counterexample. Otherwise, $M(H)$ contains ρ, and we then determine whether $M(H) = \rho$ by the polynomial enumeration method of [11].

Thus, since we can correctly answer the two basic queries of HORN, the simulation algorithm must output an exact Horn representation of ρ if one exists. Moreover, since every membership query takes $O(n \log |\rho|)$ time, and every equivalence theory takes $O(|\rho||H|)$ time, we conclude that a Horn description of ρ can be found in

$$O(mn|\rho||H| + m^2n^2 \log |\rho|) = O(m^2n^2(|\rho| + \log |\rho|))$$
$$= O(m^2n^2|\rho|)$$

time, where m is the minimum number of clauses in any Horn theory describing ρ.

This essentially establishes the identifiability of Horn theories as prescribed in Definition 2.6, according to which a description must be found in time polynomial in both the input ($|\rho|$) and the shortest possible output ($m(n + 1)$). However, we can establish an even stronger result by showing that m is polynomial in $|\rho|$, namely, the size of the shortest output theory cannot be substantially larger than the input. Indeed, it is possible to show (see appendix) that every Horn theory with K models can be expressed by a Horn formula that employs at most Kn^2 clauses. Translated to our setting, this means that m cannot exceed $|\rho|n^2$ and hence that the simulation algorithm will find a Horn description for ρ of length $O(|\rho|n^3)$ clauses. Moreover, while the time it takes the HORN algorithm to find this description is $O(|\rho|^3n^6)$, a simpler algorithm can be found (see appendix), which works directly on ρ, finds a description of length $O(|\rho|n^2)$ clauses, and runs in only $O(|\rho|^2n^2)$ steps.

We summarize this analysis by stating:

Theorem 4.10. *If a relation ρ has a Horn description, then one such description, having at most $|\rho|n^2$ clauses, can be found in $O(|\rho|^2n^2)$ time.*

Combining Theorems 4.9 and 4.10 we now have:

Corollary 4.11. *Horn theories are identifiable in input-polynomial time.*

We remark that the tight connection between the number of models and the number of clauses renders Horn theories a useful tool in data compression. Short relations are guaranteed to have short theories, whereas the converse does not hold; some extremely long relations may have short Horn descriptions. For example, the theory containing a single clause, say $a \longrightarrow b$, has exponentially many models. Recent study reveals that such a tight connection does not exist between the length of a Horn theory and the number of extreme models it may have [17]. In other words, the number of extreme models of some Horn theory with m clauses is exponential in m and, conversely, the length of the shortest Horn theory having K extreme models may be exponential in K and n. This implies that the tightest Horn approximation of some long relations may be much shorter than the relation, even if the input data consists of only extreme models. Conversely, it raises the interesting possibility that the basis of ρ, which can be computed in $O(|\rho|^2)$ steps, could serve as a more economical description of ρ than any Horn approximation of ρ.

This brings us to the complexity of finding tightest Horn approximations to relations ρ that do not have precise Horn descriptions. In principle, we can find such approximations by simulating the HORN algorithm again, this time referring all its queries to the closure ρ^* of ρ, which we can keep implicit. We know from Corollary 4 that $B(\rho)$ contains all the information about ρ^*, and that ρ^* has a Horn representation that is the tightest Horn approximation of ρ. This simulation would have a difficulty answering equivalence queries, however. Whereas previously we were able to answer equivalence queries in time polynomial in $|\rho|$, the size of ρ^* may be exponential in ρ, and we do not have a way of testing whether $M(H) \subseteq \rho^*$ except by enumerating $M(H)$ and ρ^*. Thus, the strong identifiability of Horn theory remains an open problem.

We can still assert a weaker result:

Corollary 4.12. *Horn theories are strongly identifiable for every dataset whose intersection closure is of a polynomial size.*

Corollary 4.12 might seem weak in view of the fact that there is no simple method of estimating the size of ρ^*, short of actually enumerating ρ^*. However, if the size of ρ^* is substantially larger than that of ρ, we know that any Horn approximation is bound to be very poor. It is only when $|\rho^* - \rho|$ is a fraction of $|\rho|$ that Horn theories can offer a reasonable approximation to ρ, and it is precisely in those cases that we can find a tightest Horn approximation in a reasonable time. This suggests a strategy of focusing the development of Horn approximations on those cases only that can benefit from such approximations. Given a relation ρ and a tolerance level τ, we begin to generate the closure of ρ and test whether its size exceeds $(1+\tau)|\rho|$. If it does, we know that no acceptable Horn approximation is feasible. If $|\rho^*| < (1+\tau)|\rho|$, we proceed to find a tightest Horn approximation using either the HORN simulation or the envelope-based algorithm described in the appendix.

4.3. Identifying k-Horn formulas

We now restrict our attention to the identifiability of k-Horn formulas.

As before, S_k denotes the set of all subsets of X of size k or less. A tightest k-Horn approximation can be generated by first constructing the tightest CNF approximation over the scheme S_k and then eliminating all non-Horn clauses from that approximation. In other words: given a relation ρ on n variables and a constant k, we generate the formula $\Gamma_{S_k}(\rho)$ and throw away all non-Horn clauses. We claim that the resulting Horn theory is the tightest k-Horn approximation of ρ (which may have, of course, many equivalent syntactic representations). Since, as we will show, this is also the longest form of the tightest approximation, we then generate an equivalent reduced version by eliminating subsumptions. To test if the resulting Horn theory represents ρ exactly, we enumerate its models. Note, however, that while there are 2^k clauses over a set of k symbols, there are only $k+1$ Horn clauses over the same set. Thus, it makes more sense to go in the opposite direction: first enumerate all possible Horn formulas over scheme S_k, then eliminate those clauses that conflict with any tuple of ρ. It can be shown that these two methods yield the same expression. Given a CNF formula φ, we denote by $Horn(\varphi)$ the formula resulting from eliminating all non-Horn clauses from φ. Given a relation ρ, let $\Omega_k(\rho)$ be the set of all possible Horn formulas over scheme S_k that are consistent with all tuples of ρ.

Theorem 4.13. *Let ρ be an n-ary bivalued relation, k a constant, $\pi = \Gamma_{S_k}(\rho)$, and $\eta = Horn(\pi)$. Let H_k be the family of k-Horn formulas, then*
  (1) *η is a tightest k-Horn approximation of π,*
  (2) *η is maximal with respect to H_k,*
  (3) *if $M(\eta) \supset \rho$, no k-Horn formula describes ρ,*
  (4) *reduced(η) equals the set of all k-Horn prime implicates of η,*
  (5) *$\eta = \Omega_k(\rho)$.*

Proof. (1) and (2) follow from the fact that π already contains all k-Horn clauses consistent with ρ. (3) follows immediately from the tightness of η. Since the scheme S_k contains all subsets of size k or less, it follows

Algorithm Horn-generation(ρ, k)

Input: A relation ρ on n variables and an integer k.
Output: A k-Horn formula describing ρ or a k-Horn tightest approximation of ρ.

(1) Enumerate Ω_k, the set of all Horns over S_k.
(2) Eliminate any Horn clause that violates ρ, resulting in $\Omega_k(\rho)$.
(3) $\eta \Leftarrow reduced(\Omega_k(\rho))$ (by eliminating subsumptions).
(4) Enumerate the models of η, $\{m_1, m_2, \ldots\}$, using the method in [11], and, if for some $i \leq |\rho|$, $m_i \notin \rho$, or if $M(\eta)$ contains more than $|\rho|$ elements, then return: "η is a tightest k-Horn approximation"; else, return "η describes ρ".

Fig. 3. Algorithm Horn-generation.

from Lemma 3.22 that $reduced(\eta)$ contains all and only the k-Horn prime implicates of η, thus proving (4). Finally, (5) follows from (2) and from the observation that by definition, $\Omega_k(\rho)$ is the tightest maximal k-Horn of ρ. □

Theorem 4.13 implies that algorithm *Horn-generation* in Fig. 3 which outputs the formula $reduced(\Omega_k(\rho))$, is guaranteed to return the tightest k-Horn approximation of ρ relative to H_k. The algorithm also returns a statement as to whether the formula found is an exact representation of ρ.

To summarize:

Corollary 4.14. *Algorithm Horn-generation provides a tightest k-Horn approximation of an arbitrary relation ρ. Moreover, this approximation equals the k-Horn prime implicates of ρ.*

Example 4.15. Consider again the relation

$$\rho(PQR) = \{(100), (010), (001)\}$$

and let $k = 2$. For this example, it is easier to first list the tightest k-CNF approximation and then eliminate non-Horn clauses. We have

$$\begin{aligned}\Pi_{S_2}(\rho) = \{&(\rho(P,Q) = \{(10), (01), (00)\}), \\ &(\rho(P,R) = \{(10), (01), (00)\}), \\ &(\rho(Q,R) = \{(10), (01), (00)\})\},\end{aligned}$$

and $P = \{0, 1\}$, $Q = \{0, 1\}$, $R = \{0, 1\}$. When applying the canonical transformation to each of these relations, we get the (already reduced) formula

$$\Gamma_{S_2}(\rho) = \{(\neg P \vee \neg Q), (\neg P \vee \neg R), (\neg R \vee \neg Q)\}.$$

Since this is a Horn formula, we need not throw any clauses away. Computing the number of models of this theory yields four models (there is an additional (0,0,0) tuple), so we conclude that the formula is a tightest 2-Horn approximation of ρ and that ρ is not 2-Horn identifiable. If we generate the 3-Horn approximation for ρ, we get the same formula (because, in this case, the 2-Horn approximation already contains all its Horn prime implicates). Going through algorithm *Horn-generation*, step (2) yields:

$$\Omega_k(\rho) = \{(\neg P \vee \neg Q \vee R), (P \vee \neg Q \vee \neg R), (\neg P \vee Q \vee \neg R),$$
$$(\neg P \vee \neg Q \vee \neg R), (\neg P \vee \neg Q), (\neg P \vee \neg R), \neg R \vee \neg Q)\}.$$

The result of further eliminating subsumptions yields the same formula:

$$reduced(\Omega_k(\rho))) = \{(\neg P \vee \neg Q), (\neg P \vee \neg R), (\neg R \vee \neg Q)\}. \quad (14)$$

Example 4.15 suggests an *anytime* variation of the algorithm described in Fig. 3. Instead of applying the algorithm to all subsets of size k, we first apply the algorithm to subsets of size 2, then add the result of processing subsets of size 3, and so on, until we get a satisfying approximation. The algorithm is given in Fig. 4. Let us denote by $S_{(k)}$ all subsets of size exactly k and by $\Omega_{(k)}$ the set of all Horn clauses of length k that are consistent with ρ.

Note that the algorithm always retains the unreduced formula generated in the previous iteration.

We next assess the complexity of our approximation and the size of its resulting Horn theory.

Theorem 4.16 (Complexity).
(1) *The length (number of clauses) of $reduced(\Omega_k(\rho))$ is $O(kn^{k+1})$.*
(2) *The complexity of Horn-generation(ρ, k) is $O(|\rho|kn^{k+1})$.*

Proof. Since worst-case analysis is unable to distinguish between a maximal formula and its reduced form, we assume that the algorithm generates the former.

(1) Since there are $i + 1$ distinct Horn clauses on a subset of size i and since there are n^{k+1} subsets in scheme S_k, the overall number of Horn clauses is $O(kn^{k+1})$.

Algorithm Anytime-Horn-generation(ρ, k)

Input: A relation ρ and a constant k.
Output: A Horn formula describing ρ or a k-Horn tightest approximation to ρ.

(1) $\pi \Longleftarrow \Omega_{(1)}(\rho)$
(2) For $i = 2$, while $i \leq k$, do
  - $\pi \Longleftarrow \pi \cup \Omega_{(i)}(\rho)$
  - $\eta \Longleftarrow reduced(\pi)$
  - if $|M(\eta)|$ equals $|\rho|$, then return "η describes ρ".
(3) endwhile.
(4) Return η and a statement "η is a tightest k-Horn approximation of ρ".

Fig. 4. Algorithm Anytime-Horn-generation.

(2) Generating all possible Horn clauses over S_k not in conflict with ρ takes $O(|\rho|kn^{k+1})$. Eliminating subsumption may take additional $O((2n)^k)$, resulting in an overall time complexity of $O((|\rho| + kn + 2^k)n^k)$. Finally, computing the number of models of a Horn theory is linear in the theory size and the number of models [11]. Therefore, testing whether this number exceeds $|\rho|$ takes $O(kn^{k+1}|\rho|))$ steps. □

Corollary 4.17. *The class of k-Horn theories is strongly identifiable in $O(|\rho|n^{k+1})$ time.*

Interestingly, algorithm Horn-generation can easily be converted into an on-line version, which is useful for stream processing. Assume the tuples of ρ are not available all at once, but are obtained sequentially as a stream of observations, normally containing many repetitions. In this case it might be advantageous to store a parsimonious theory of past data, rather than the data itself, and to update the theory incrementally whenever an observation arrives that contradicts the theory. If storage space permits, the update can be made particularly easy if in addition to the reduced approximation η we also keep the maximal tightest Horn approximation π. Then, whenever a new tuple arrives, all clauses in π that conflict with it are eliminated, and the resulting theory can now be reduced to form a new η so as to facilitate query answering. When the size of π is much larger than that of η, it might be advantageous to store only η and compute the maximal π on the fly, update π to conform with the new tuple and reduce it back to more economical form. The time it takes for this operation is $O(n^k)$ per update.

5. Conclusions

This paper summarizes several investigations into the prospects for identifying meaningful structures in empirical data. The central aim is to identify a computationally attractive description, in cases where the observed data possess such a description and a best approximate description otherwise. The feasibility of performing this task in reasonable time has been given a formal definition through the notion of identifiability, which is normally weaker (if $C' = C$) than that of learnability.

In exploring the decomposition of data into a given scheme of smaller relations, it was shown that, whereas a best approximation can always be found, it is only in cases where the scheme is tractable that we can (tractably) decide whether the resulting approximation constitutes an exact representation of the data. It is worth noting that the difficulty associated with this decision can be mitigated by allowing approximation through sampling. It is a known result by Angluin [1] that polynomial-time algorithms for exact identification of concepts using equivalence and membership queries can be transformed into polynomial-time PAC learning algorithms using membership queries only. In our case, the difficulty associated with confirming the exactness of the tightest theory amounts to that of answering an equivalence query, and hence, it can be transformed to answering a sequence of (randomly sampled) membership queries, yielding an approximately correct confirmation of the exactness of the output theory.[6]

The decomposition of data into a structure taken from a *class* of schemes turned out to be a harder task, one that is intractable even in cases where each individual member of the class is tractable. The class of tree structured schemes is an exception. Here it was shown that an effective procedure exists for determining whether a given relation is decomposable into a tree of binary relations and, if the answer is positive, identifying the topology of such a tree. The procedure runs in time proportional to the size of the relation, but whether it provides a tightest tree-structured approximation in cases where the answer is negative is still an open question.

Focusing on bivalued data, we then explored the identification of descriptions whose tractability stems from syntactic rather than structural features. In particular, we showed that Horn theories can be identified in input-polynomial time, that is, one can decide whether the input data possesses an exact Horn description and find such a description (whenever

---

[6] For further detail see [17].

possible) in time polynomial with the length of the input. The strong identifiability of Horn theories, that is, the problem of finding a tightest Horn approximation, remains open. Since there are small sets of models with exponentially long tightest Horn approximations [17], the best one can hope for is an output-polynomial algorithm for generating such approximations. So far, only sampling algorithms are known for this task, namely, algorithms which guarantee that the output theory is "probably almost tightest", thus rendering Horn theories "strongly PAC-identifiable". Whether there is an output-polynomial algorithm that returns the tightest Horn approximation is still an open question.

By contrast, k-Horn theories were shown to be strongly identifiable in polynomial time, when k is bounded. Both anytime and on-line algorithms where discussed for identifying these theories.

An important issue not dealt with in this paper is assessment of the goodness of the approximations provided by Horn theories. Another issue is the feasibility of constructing both an upper bound and a lower bound approximations of ρ, in the manner discussed in [27] and also in [9]. Finally, we should mention that the methods presented in this paper will also handle partial observations, namely, observations of truncated tuples of ρ.

Appendix A. Proof of Theorem 4.10

In this appendix we prove the two assertions stated in Theorem 4.10, Section 4.2:[7]

(1) Every Horn formula with K models has an equivalent Horn formula that employs at most Kn^2 clauses.
(2) Given a relation ρ, closed under intersection, it is possible to find a Horn description of ρ in time $O(|\rho|^2 n^2)$.

Let x and y be two arbitrary tuples. We say that x is an ancestor of y (equivalently, y is a descendant of x) if $true(x) \supset true(y)$; we say that x is a parent of y (equivalently, y is a child of x) if x is an ancestor of y and $|true(x)| = |true(y)| + 1$. Let ρ be a set of tuples closed under intersection, we say that x is a least ancestor of y (relative to ρ) if x is in ρ and y has no other ancestor z in ρ such that $true(z) \subset true(x)$. Note that if y is not in ρ, then it either has a unique least ancestor (since the intersection of any two ancestors in ρ yields another ancestor in ρ), or it has no ancestor in ρ, in which case we say that the least ancestor of y is $\emptyset$.

---

[7]We are indebted to Dana Angluin for outlining the method used in this proof.

Define the *envelope* $E(\rho)$ of ρ as the set of tuples *not* in ρ that either have a child in ρ or have no child at all (the latter corresponds to the tuple containing all zeros). Clearly, there are at most $n|\rho|$ elements in $E(\rho)$. Also, every tuple that is not in $E(\rho)$ must either be in ρ or have a descendant in $E(\rho)$.

Let e be an element in $E(\rho)$ and let e' be the (unique) least ancestor of e in ρ (possibly $\emptyset$). Attach to every pair (e, e') a Horn theory $H(e, e')$ containing one clause, $c_i = antecedent \to v_i$ for every variable v_i in $true(e') - true(e)$, where *antecedent* stands for the conjunction of all positive literals of $true(e)$.[8] If $true(e) = \{\emptyset\}$, then $c_i = v_i$ and if $e' = \emptyset$, then $v_i = 0$. Note that $H(e, e')$ excludes those and only those tuples that are ancestors of e and not of e'.

Lemma A.1. *Let ρ be a relation closed under intersection and let $H(\rho)$ be the Horn formula formed by collecting the clauses from all the subtheories $H(e, e')$, where e ranges over all elements of $E(\rho)$. Then $H(\rho)$ constitutes a precise description of ρ, and contains at most $|\rho|n^2$ clauses.*

Proof. It is easy to show that every tuple in ρ is a model of $H(\rho)$. For if a tuple x in ρ conflicts with any $H(e, e')$ then x must be an ancestor of e and not of e', and then the intersection $x \cap e'$ which is in ρ would also be an ancestor of e with a smaller number of ones than e'. Hence e' cannot be the least ancestor of e in ρ.

To prove that every model of $H(\rho)$ is in ρ we show that the opposite alternative leads to a contradiction. Suppose there is a model y of $H(\rho)$ that is not in ρ. Since $H(\rho)$ excludes all tuples in $E(\rho)$, it is clear that y cannot be in $E(\rho)$. Since y itself is not in ρ or in $E(\rho)$, there must be at least one descendant of y that is in $E(\rho)$; let z be a maximal such descendant (i.e., there is no $x \in E(\rho)$ that is an ancestor of z and a descendant of y. Being in $E(\rho)$, z must contribute a set of clauses $H(z, z')$ to H, where z' is the least ancestor of z in ρ and $H(z, z')$ excludes all ancestors of z unless they are also ancestors of z'. Thus, if y is a model of H, it must be that y is also an ancestor of z'. Now consider any descending path P from y to z (i.e., every pair of successive elements along P consists of a parent followed by its child). Since y is not in $E(\rho)$ and z' is in ρ, P must contain an element $z'' \in E(\rho)$ such that z'' is an ancestor of z' and a descendant of y. But this contradicts our assumption that z is the maximal descendant of y in $E(\rho)$. □

---

[8] For example, for variables a, b, c, d, and $e = (1, 0, 1, 0)$, $e' = (1, 1, 1, 1)$, we have $true(e) = \{a, c\}$, $true(e') = \{a, b, c, d\}$, and $H(e, e') = \{a \wedge c \to b, a \wedge c \to d\}$.

Theorem A.2. *Every Horn formula with K models has an equivalent Horn formula that employs at most Kn^2 clauses.*

Proof. The proof follows immediately from Lemma A.1. If ρ stands for the models of a Horn formula H', then ρ must be closed under intersection and contain precisely K models. From Lemma A.1, an equivalent Horn formula H can be constructed from the elements of $E(\rho)$ that describes ρ precisely and employs at most $n|E(\rho)|$ clauses. Since, each of the K elements in ρ can contribute at most n elements to $E(\rho)$, we conclude that the number of clauses in H is at most Kn^2. □

We will now prove the second claim by analyzing the complexity of constructing H.

Theorem A.3. *Given a relation ρ, closed under intersection, it is possible to find a Horn description of ρ in time $O(|\rho|^2 n^2)$.*

Proof. Assume $|\rho| = K$. The construction of H consists of three parts:

(a) identifying the elements of the envelope $E(\rho)$,
(b) identifying the pair (e, e') for every element in $E(\rho)$, and
(c) constructing the formulas $H(e, e')$ for every pair found in (b).

Part (a) can be done in $O(nK \log K)$ time, simply testing which of the n parents of each member of ρ is not in ρ.

Part (b) requires the identification of the least ancestor $e' \in \rho$ for each member $e \in E(\rho)$. Clearly, there are at most nK elements e in $E(\rho)$, and identifying e' requires at most $2nK$ steps (i.e., taking each element of ρ and testing whether it is an ancestor of e, then taking its intersection with that of previously found ancestors of e). This takes a total of at most $2n^2K^2$ operations.

Part (c) requires at most n operations for each of the (e, e') pairs, of which there are at most nK. This gives a total of $n^2 K$ operations.

The dominant effort is clearly part (b), yielding a total of $O(K^2 n^2)$ steps, thus confirming the theorem. □

We remark that while the envelope-based algorithm described in the proof of Theorem A.3 yields a theory of size $O(|\rho|n^2)$ and the HORN simulation algorithm produces a theory of size $O(|\rho|n^3)$, the latter has the advantage of always producing theories that lie within a factor $(n+1)$ of the shortest possible theory representing ρ. Thus, in cases where a long ρ is suspected of having a short Horn description, it is worth running HORN instead of the envelope-based algorithm. Alternatively, it is possible in such cases to run the HORN algorithm directly on the theory H found by the envelope-based algorithm, so as to reduce its length. Given any Horn theory H, if we use H to answer the queries of HORN, then HORN is guaranteed to yield a theory equivalent to H, whose length is within a factor $n + 1$ of $H_{\min}$, the shortest Horn equivalent of H. This simplification procedure runs in time proportional to $n|H|^2|H_{\min}|$.

Acknowledgement

We are indebted to many colleagues for most generous assistance. We deeply appreciate the insightful comments of three anonymous referees, who were responsible for many improvements and for illustrating how we could use the HORN algorithm. Conversations with Henry Kautz, Michael Kearns, and Bart Selman have pushed us toward many of the results in Sections 4.1 and 4.2, and the ideas of Dana Angluin were responsible for the claims and proof of Theorem 4.10. Jeff Ullman has been most helpful in generating a proof of Lemma 3.8, and Itay Meiri and Amir Weinstein contributed several ideas in the early stages of this paper.

References

[1] D. Angluin, Queries and concept learning, *Mach. Learn.* **2** (1988) 319-342.
[2] D. Angluin, M. Frazier and L. Pitt, Learning conjunctions of Horn clauses, in: *Proceedings 31st Annual Symposium on Foundations of Computer Science, Vol. I* (IEEE Computer Society Press, St. Louis, MO, 1990).
[3] S. Arnborg, Efficient algorithms for combinatorial graphs with bounded decomposability—a survey, *BIT* **25** (1985) 2-23.
[4] C. Beeri, R. Fagin, D. Maier and M. Yannakakis, On the desirability of acyclic database schemes, *J. ACM* **30** (1983) 479-513.
[5] A. Blumer, A. Ehrenfeucht, D. Haussler and M. K. Warmuth, Learnability and the Vapnik-Chervonenkis dimension, *J. ACM* **36** (1989) 929-965.
[6] R.K. Brayton, G.D. Hachtel and A.L. Sangiovanni-Vincentelli, Multilevel logic synthesis, *Proc. IEEE* **78** (2) (1990).
[7] C.K. Chow and C. N. Liu, Approximating discrete probability distributions with dependence trees, *IEEE Trans. Inf. Theor.* **14** (1968) 462-467.
[8] S.A. Cook, The complexity of theorem-proving procedures, in: *Proceedings 3rd Annual ACM Symposium on the Theory of Computing*, New York (1971) 151-158.
[9] R. Dechter, Decomposing a relation into a tree of binary relations, *J. Comput. Syst. Sci.* **41** (1990) 2-24 (Special Issue on the Theory of Relational Databases).
[10] R. Dechter, Constraint networks, in: *Encyclopedia of Artificial Intelligence* (Wiley, New York, 2nd ed., 1992) 276-285.
[11] R. Dechter and A. Itai, The complexity of finding all solutions, UCI Rept., University of California, Irvine, CA (1991).
[12] R. Dechter and J. Pearl, Network-based heuristics for constraint-satisfaction problems, *Artif. Intell.* **34** (1) (1987) 1-38.
[13] R. Dechter and J. Pearl, Tree clustering for constraint networks, *Artif. Intell.* **38** (3) (1989) 353-366.
[14] W.F. Dowling and J.H. Gallier, Linear time algorithms for testing the satisfiability of propositional Horn formula, *J. Logic Program.* **3** (1984) 267-284.

[15] E.C. Freuder, Complexity of k-structured constraint satisfaction problems, in: *Proceedings AAAI-90*, Boston, MA (1990) 4–9.
[16] C. Glymour, R. Scheines, P. Spirtes and K. Kelly, *Discovering Causal Structure* (Academic Press, Orlando, FL 1987).
[17] H.A. Kautz, M. Kearns and B. Selman, *Horn Approximations of Empirical Data*, AT&T Bell Laboratories (1992).
[18] P.F. Lazarsfeld, Latent structure analysis, in: S.A. Stouffer, L. Guttman, E.A. Suchman, P.F. Lazarsfeld, S.A. Star and J.A. Claussen, eds., *Measurement and Prediction* (Wiley, New York, 1966).
[19] D. Maier, *The Theory of Relational Databases* (Computer Science Press, Rockville, MD, 1983).
[20] I. Meiri, R. Dechter and J. Pearl, Tree decomposition with applications to constraint processing, in: *Proceedings AAAI-90*, Boston, MA (1990) 10–16.
[21] U. Montanari, Networks of constraints, fundamental properties and applications to picture processing, *Inf. Sci.* **7** (1974) 95–132.
[22] U. Montanari and F. Rossi, Fundamental properties of networks of constraints: a new formulation, in: L. Kanal and V. Kumar, eds., *Search in Artificial Intelligence* (Springer, New York, 1988) 426–449.
[23] B.K. Natarajan, On learning Boolean functions, in: *Proceedings 19th Annual ACM Symposium on Theory of Computation*, New York (1987) 296–304.
[24] J. Pearl, *Probabilistic Reasoning in Intelligent Systems: Networks of Plausible Inference* (Morgan Kaufmann, San Mateo, CA, 1988).
[25] J. Pearl and T. Verma, A theory of inferred causation, in: J.A. Allen, R. Fikes and E. Sandewall, eds., *Principles of Knowledge Representation and Reasoning: Proceedings Second International Conference* (Morgan Kaufmann, San Mateo, CA, 1991) 441–452.
[26] J.R. Quinlan, Induction of decision trees, *Mach. Learn.* **1** (1986) 81–106.
[27] B. Selman and H.A. Kautz, Knowledge compilation using Horn approximation, in: *Proceedings AAAI-91*, Anaheim, CA (1991).
[28] B. Selman and H.A. Kautz, Tractability through theory approximation, AI Tech. Rept., AT&T Bell Laboratories, Murray Hill, NJ (1992).
[29] J. Ullman, Personal communication (1991).
[30] L.G. Valiant, A theory of the learnable, *Commun. ACM* **27** (11) (1984) 1134–1142.
[31] M.A. van Emden and R.A. Kowalski, The semantics of the predicate logic as a programming language, *J. ACM* **23** (1976) 733–742.

Learning to improve constraint-based scheduling

Monte Zweben
NASA Ames Research Center, M.S. 269-2, Moffett Field, CA 94035, USA

Eugene Davis
Recom Technologies, NASA Ames Research Center, M.S. 269-2, Moffett Field, CA 94035, USA

Brian Daun
Recom Technologies, NASA Ames Research Center, M.S. 269-2, Moffett Field, CA 94035, USA

Ellen Drascher
Sterling Software, NASA Ames Research Center, M.S. 269-2, Moffett Field, CA 94035, USA

Michael Deale
Lockheed Space Operations Company, 1100 Lockheed Way, Mail Stop LSO-459, Titusville, FL 32780, USA

Megan Eskey
NASA Ames Research Center, M.S. 269-2, Moffett Field, CA 94035, USA

Abstract

Zweben, M., E. Davis, B. Daun, E. Drascher, M. Deale and M. Eskey, Learning to improve constraint-based scheduling, Artificial Intelligence 58 (1992) 271–296.

This paper describes an application of an analytical learning technique, plausible explanation-based learning (PEBL), that dynamically acquires search control knowledge for a constraint-based scheduling system. In general, the computational efficiency of a scheduling system suffers due to resource contention among activities. Our system

Correspondence to: Monte Zweben, NASA Ames Research Center, M.S. 269-2, Moffett Field, CA 94035, USA. E-mail: zweben@shepard.arc.nasa.gov.

Elsevier Science Publishers B.V.

learns the general conditions under which *chronic* contention occurs and uses search control to avoid repeating mistakes. Because it is impossible to prove that a chronic contention will occur with only one example, traditional EBL techniques are insufficient. We extend classical EBL by adding an empirical component that creates search control rules only when the system gains enough confidence in the plausible explanations. This extension to EBL was driven by our observations about the behavior of our scheduling system when applied to the real-world problem of scheduling tasks for NASA Space Shuttle payload and ground processing.

1. Introduction

This paper describes a methodology for learning search control knowledge for a constraint-based scheduling system. The general approach is to detect those characteristics that contribute to inefficiencies in search, and to use the learned knowledge to avoid poor performance in future problems. We demonstrate the impact of learning by applying the technique to two search methods:

(1) depth-first backtracking through the space of partial schedules and,
(2) iterative repair through the space of complete schedules.

For backtracking search, our system learns *variable ordering* control knowledge. Variable ordering control knowledge guides the selection of which variable to instantiate. Value ordering knowledge guides the selection of a value for the variable. For the iterative repair method the system learns to select between a less-informed (but fast) repair heuristic and a more-informed (but computationally expensive) repair heuristic.

Our learning method, *plausible explanation-based learning* (*PEBL*), extends previous work in explanation-based learning (EBL) by incorporating an empirical component that is used to confirm plausible explanations. Initially, PEBL uses a domain theory to conjecture, rather than to prove, why a particular search process was inefficient, and confirms these conjectures if they apply to multiple scenarios. Then the aspects of the search problem that contributed to the poor search performance are extracted, generalized, and used as control knowledge for similar problems. We confirm the utility of our learning technique by empirically testing the method on a suite of typical scheduling problems. These test cases are various scheduling problems based on NASA Space Shuttle scheduling scenarios. We test the system both with and without the learned control knowledge. Our experiments indicate that the learned knowledge improves the efficiency of the system for both iterative repair and backtracking search.

We begin the paper by specifying scheduling as a constraint satisfaction problem and then present the general learning framework. We then describe each search method and the application of PEBL to that method. Finally we present related work, conclusions, and future plans.

2. Scheduling: problem specification

The scheduling problem accepts tasks, resource pools, and constraints as input. Each task has a given duration and a set of resource requests; each resource request designates a resource type (e.g., technician) and quantity. Resource requests are filled by drawing the necessary quantity from a resource pool. Resource pools are specified by type and initial capacity. There may be several pools for a given resource type. Constraints represent the restrictions made on value assignments for the tasks and resource pools.

Each task has associated with it the following variables:

- *start(T)*: the start time of the task,
- *end(T)*: the end time of the task,
- *duration(T)*: the duration of the task,
- *resource-type(T, i)*: the type of the ith resource pool needed for task T,
- *resource-qty(T, i)*: the quantity of the ith resource pool needed for task T,
- *resource-pool(T, i)*: the resource pool assigned to the ith resource request for task T.

The variables of a resource pool are:

- *type(r)*: the type of the pool,
- *capacity(r)*: the maximum amount available of the given pool,
- *availability(r)*: the availability of the pool over time.

The following are constraints for scheduling:

- $t_1 \prec t_2$: time variable t_1 must be less than t_2,
- $t_1 \preceq t_2$: time variable t_1 must be less than or equal to t_2,
- $AVL(t_1, t_2, qty, rp)$: during the interval designated by $[t_1, t_2]$ there must be at least qty allocatable in the resource availability variable rp,
- *isa(type, pool)*: the resource assigned to *pool* must be of the class defined by *type*,
- $t_1 + t_1 = t_3$: the sum of the first two time points must be equal to the third time point.

Scheduling is the process of assigning times and resource pools to a set of tasks subject to temporal and resource capacity constraints.

Temporal constraints relate the start and end points of tasks. Milestone constraints are a specialization of temporal constraints such that the start or end time of a task is constrained to a time constant. Temporal constraints enforce predecessor/successor relationships as well as more complex temporal relations [1,39], and milestone constraints enforce due dates.

When tasks overlap in time, they are likely to contend for available resources. Resource capacity constraints are used to ensure that no resource pool is overallocated. For example, an activity for testing an engine of the Space Shuttle could overlap with an inspection of the forward reaction control thrusters. In this case, both tasks compete for technicians of the same skill level. If each requires 10 of the 15 technicians available during that time, then the capacity constraints on the activities would be violated. The scheduling system monitors the availability of a resource pool and makes it a function of the previous assignments made to tasks. The system creates a *resource-available* constraint for every resource request.

The scheduling system's goal is to produce an assignment of start times, end times, and resource pools for each of the tasks, such that all constraints are satisfied.

3. Plausible explanation-based learning

In order to avoid combinatorial explosion, the control of search is essential for domain-independent problem solvers. Search control can be captured opportunistically through heuristic evaluations to indicate the best course of action [37], or it can be learned from experience and transferred to new problems [25,29]. Explanation-based learning (EBL) [8,29,32] is a technique that depends on a strong domain theory to draw generalizations. Explanation-based generalization (EBG) [32] is a specific EBL algorithm that starts with a high-level target concept and a training example. Using a set of axioms (the domain theory), EBG generates an explanation that serves as a proof that the training example satisfies the target concept. The weakest preconditions of the explanation are determined, and a learned description is produced. This description must be *operational* or useful for the performance task [23]. Since the description is a generalization of the training example, it might apply in future situations similar to the training example.

Our extension to EBG allows the system to empirically address an aspect of the *utility problem* originally discussed in [28]. The utility problem states that learned knowledge may not necessarily be useful to a problem solver, and in some cases may actually degrade system performance. PEBL is a technique that enables the learning system to draw conclusions from a distribution of examples rather than from a single exemplar. The empirical component is essential for learning a target concept such as a *chronic* resource bottleneck, where the idea of chronic cannot be confirmed without multiple examples of search failure. In many cases, a bottleneck may be unique to a particular example and not relevant to other problems. PEBL enables a system to generalize a target concept over a distribution of examples. Other work combining EBL with an empirical component [5,6,19,33] uses multiple examples to further generalize explanations. In contrast, PEBL does not use multiple examples to make inductive leaps but rather to confirm conjectured explanations. A decision function, $D_{useful-explan}$, indicates when a conjectured explanation is no longer simply a conjecture, but is instead a good candidate for a new search control rule. $D_{useful-explan}$ is based on the probability that the explanation is correct, the deleterious matching costs of the learned knowledge, and the impact learning has on solution quality. It is important to note that if learning degrades the quality of a solution, then the solution is unacceptable regardless of the speed of the problem solver. Previous work on the *utility problem* primarily focused on the matching cost of learned knowledge (e.g., [30]) and did not consider solution quality or explanation confidence. The PEBL algorithm is described in Fig. 1.

Consider an example of a PEBL domain theory in a robot planning system. Suppose a robot's domain theory describes its potential mechanical failures and the manifestation of these faults in its plan execution. If one axiom of the domain theory is: "whenever the robot's goal is to be one step in front of its current location, and it attempted to go forward one step but found itself one step northeast of its current location, then it is plausible that a wheel is frozen in a skewed position". A direct application of standard EBG would conclude that the wheel is skewed and would change the robot's strategy whenever attempting to go forward. Since mechanical devices occasionally exhibit temporary mechanical failures, this scenario could be anomalous. A PEBL application to the same scenario would delay learning such a control rule until the confidence in the explanation was sufficient, and would therefore be less prone to learning information that could degrade the robot's performance.

The semantics of a domain theory can be viewed as *plausible implications* modeled as conditional probabilities (with strong independence assumptions) [34]. The $D_{useful-explan}$ can be described as:

$$D_{useful-explan} : P_{explan} \times C_{match} \times C_{quality} \longrightarrow \{0, 1\}.$$

P_{explan} is the probability that the explanation is correct, C_{match} is the expected cost to match the search control rule [30], and $C_{quality}$ is a measure of the expected degradation in the quality of the solution.

We now present two search methods used by our scheduling system and describe how PEBL can be used to improve each method.

Given:
(1) A domain theory
(2) A target concept
(3) An example instance
(4) A library of previously generated explanations

(1) Try to instantiate one of the previously generated explanations for the given example instance.
(2) If no explanation applies to the example instance, then use EBL to explain the instance: using the domain theory, prove that the example instance entails the target concept, and generalize the explanation. Go to 5.
(3) If an explanation applies to the example instance, augment the confidence in the explanation.
(4) If the stored explanation has reached its confidence level (based on some decision function, $D_{useful-explan}$), then extract an operational concept from the explanation and form a search control rule.
(5) Continue problem solving.

Fig. 1. The PEBL procedure.

4. Backtracking: searching the space of partial schedules

For simple constraint satisfaction problems, backtracking search may be sufficient to find valid solutions efficiently. Here the search mechanism systematically extends a valid but incomplete schedule until all variables have legal assignments.

Our system performs backtracking search by selecting a task from the subset of tasks currently available for scheduling[1] and assigning values to all of its variables. Variable and value ordering knowledge guide the selection process. Once a variable's value is chosen, all attached constraints are tested with forward checking [17], which dynamically enforces arc-consistency [12,27]. That is, the value is immediately rejected if there does not exist a consistent value for every variable constrained by the current variable. For example, if a start time has been assigned to a task such that no resource can be assigned consistently to a resource variable, then the system will reject the current start time and will assign a new time to the variable. Forward checking will also filter any values from the domains of related variables inconsistent with the constraints. This significantly reduces the search spaces

---

[1] Tasks are considered "available" if they are on the frontier of unscheduled tasks in a topological sort.

required for the assignment of variables.

If the constraints are satisfied for the variable assignment, the system will repeat the value selection process with a new unassigned variable from the same task. When all of the variables of a task are successfully instantiated, a new task is selected. If all values for all variables of a task are exhausted, the scheduler "backtracks" to the previously assigned task and selects new values for its variables. This process continues until all variables have legal assignments, indicating that a valid schedule has been found.

4.1. Domain: Space Shuttle payload processing

The backtracking search mechanism has been applied to the NASA problem of *Space Shuttle payload processing*. Payload processing includes the receiving, testing, inspecting, and installing of payloads into the shuttle cargo bay [4,15]. Payloads that fly on the shuttle rest on modular containers called carriers. Each carrier requires a distinct set of tasks to prepare and process the payloads for a mission. These tasks form a hierarchy and every task in the hierarchy has temporal constraints and resource requirements. A Space Shuttle mission is defined as a set of payload/carrier pairs and a launch date. The launch date is a milestone for the *fly-mission* task associated with each mission.

For backtracking search in scheduling, there are four domain-dependent control strategies that can be declaratively stated as rules:

(1) task ordering,
(2) value ordering,
(3) constraint ordering, and
(4) variable ordering.

Task ordering (for our experiments) depends on a topological sorting of tasks with respect to temporal constraints. The system schedules backwards from *fly-mission* starting with its immediate prerequisites. Then it schedules forward from *fly-mission* starting with its immediate postrequisites. Value ordering depends on the direction of scheduling. When scheduling forward, the earliest possible times are chosen for the two time variables. When scheduling backward the latest possible times are assigned. The selection of which resource and what value to choose is arbitrary. Constraint ordering is used to enable more efficient forward checking.

Variable ordering in scheduling has been a topic of extensive research [35,37]. Consider scheduling from a *temporal perspective* where start and end time variables are instantiated before resource variables. When scheduling backwards in the temporal perspective, the end time is instantiated first, then the start time, and finally the resources. Thus, the system will find the latest time when all resources can be assigned. Forward scheduling assigns the start time first, then the end time, and finally the resources. Both strategies provide a bias to minimize the *work-in-process* time of the schedule by condensing the schedule as tightly as possible with respect to time. While this strategy creates compact schedules, it can be computationally expensive if resource constraint violations cause significant backtracking. A resource bottleneck situation occurs when a great deal of the resource has been used by other tasks, thus making it difficult to find a time interval that satisfies the resource capacity constraints.

An alternative variable ordering is to assign resources first. Then, by forward checking, the first available times for the assigned resource are the next values chosen for the start and end times. Although scheduling from the *resource perspective* can significantly increase the efficiency of the system, the resulting schedules are unacceptably long. This is because the next available time is assigned, regardless of how far it is from its closest temporally related task. In contrast, the temporal perspective attempts to systematically place tasks as closely together as possible.

A composite strategy is to opportunistically determine whether any resources are bottlenecks and only then use the resource perspective. This type of analysis is similar to the dynamic search strategies in OPIS [37]. CORTES also performs opportunistic bottleneck detection for task ordering [35]. Our system avoids the overhead of in-line bottleneck detection by learning criteria that predict resource bottlenecks. The next section presents this learning component.

5. Learning variable ordering

In this section, we describe an example of learning variable ordering. We also present the empirical results of applying PEBL to scheduling in the payload processing domain using backtracking search.

5.1. An example in the payload processing domain

In the payload processing domain, the target concepts to be learned are the plausibly chronic resource bottlenecks. The domain theory contains information describing the conditions under which contention might occur, such as proximity of multi-mission launch dates, types of carriers, types of tasks, and types of resources. The training example is an instance of a task whose resource requirements were not met. In Appendix A we illustrate the generalization problem for a plausibly chronic resource bottleneck between tasks in two different missions. The domain theory is used to create a specialized instance of the target concept (with each of the variables instantiated). Then a goal regression algorithm generalizes the description

```
If
    TASK-TYPE(task1, SPACELAB-EXPERIMENT-INTEGRATION) ∧
        RESOURCE-TYPE(res, AUTOMATIC-TEST-EQUIPMENT) ∧
        IN-MISSION(task1, miss1) ∧
        LAUNCH(miss1, time1) ∧
        ISA(miss2, MISSION) ∧
        LAUNCH(miss2, time2) ∧
        MINUS(time1, time2, diff) ∧
        ABS-VAL(diff, abs-val) ∧
        LESS-THAN(abs-val, SIX-MONTHS) ∧
        USES-CARRIER(miss1, carr1) ∧
        CARRIER-TYPE(carr1, BIOLOGICAL) ∧
        USES-CARRIER(miss2, carr2) ∧
        CARRIER-TYPE(carr2, BIOLOGICAL) ∧
Then
    SCHEDULING-PERSPECTIVE(task1, RESOURCE-BASED)
```

Fig. 2. An example search control rule.

by regressing the target concept's preconditions back through the results of the inference process, and finds the weakest preconditions under which the explanation holds.

For example, consider a task *spacelab-systems-experiment-test* that is a subtask of *spacelab-experiment-integration*. *Spacelab-systems-experiment-test* is part of a biological mission that uses a long-module-2 carrier. Among its resource requirements is a request for automatic test equipment. If there is no automatic test equipment available at the first time consistent with its temporal constraints, learning would be initiated. All previously generated explanations are tested to see if their preconditions apply to this particular example. If no explanation holds, a new one is generated that describes the current situation. In this example, by using the domain theory, the system would determine that the bottleneck is a result of contention with a set of previously scheduled tasks in some other biological mission that use all of the automatic test equipment. Both missions have launch dates within six months of each other.

If a previously generated explanation held, its confidence would be augmented. If the confidence in the explanation, as determined by the decision function, $D_{useful-explan}$, was sufficient, a new search control rule would be generated. This and other rules would be used to guide search in future scheduling runs. If, in this example, the confidence was high, the search control rule shown in Fig. 2 would be created.

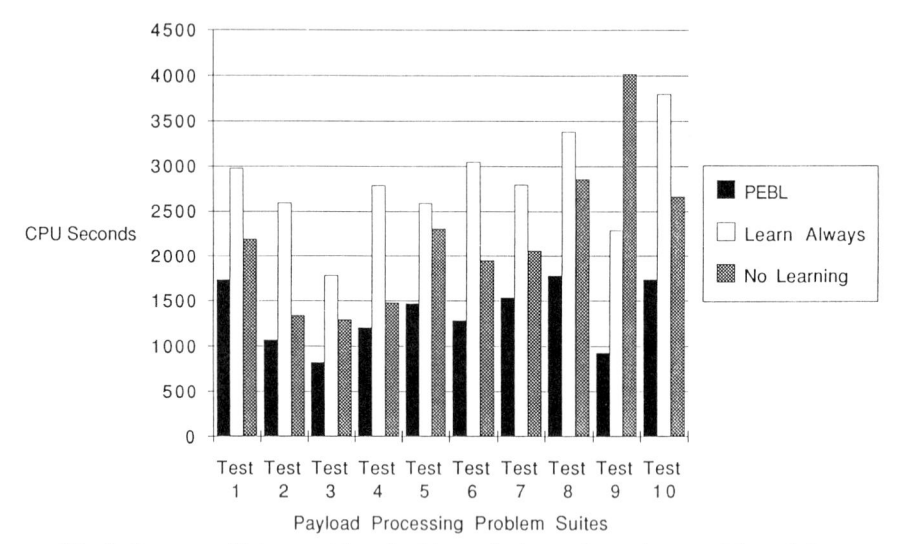

Fig. 3. Program efficiency with and without the learned search control knowledge.

5.2. Evaluating the method

In this section we describe the empirical analysis of the PEBL method as applied to backtracking search.

5.2.1. Empirical results

To evaluate the success of our approach, we randomly generated sixteen sets of missions with varying proximity of launch dates and various carrier types. For the training phase, we used six sets of missions (with ~300 examples of resource contention). The decision function, $D_{useful-explan}$, was a simple threshold value. We analyzed the characteristics of the search space of scheduling this training set of missions to determine a likely range of threshold values. In this problem, a rule was created from an explanation if it was applicable to four examples in a sample of one hundred. After training, we compared the respective speeds and work-in-process (WIP) times for the schedules generated with and without the learned search control rules created by PEBL, and for the schedules generated with rules created by using a zero threshold on ten different sets of missions. Using a threshold of zero is analogous to using standard EBL, where each explanation would be used to create a search control rule. This falsely implies that every resource bottleneck is chronic; we refer to this as the "Learn Always" method. The results of the efficiency gain of synthesizing schedules using the learned knowledge are shown in Fig. 3. The results of the increased WIP times for the schedules generated with search control rules are shown in Fig. 4.

The number of tasks in each set of missions varied from 362 in Test 3 to 652 in Test 8. From 296 examples, PEBL created 19 search control rules.

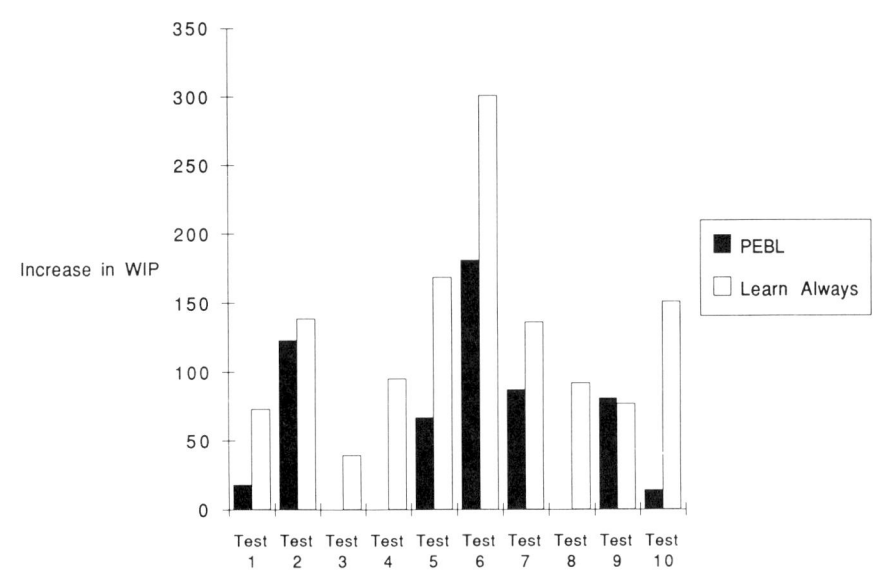

Fig. 4. WIP time with and without the learned search control knowledge.

The number of times that the search control rules applied in each set of missions varied from 70 times in Test 3 to 138 times in Test 7 and Test 10. The rules were tested before scheduling each task. When using the Learn Always technique, 78 search control rules were created. The number of times the rules applied ranged from 117 times in Test 3 to 233 times in Test 10.

5.2.2. Discussion of the results

In our experiments, the empirical component of PEBL proved essential. With too many rules, scheduling with the learned knowledge was slower than scheduling without the learned knowledge. The cost of testing the rules resulted in decreased system efficiency, and over-applying the non-optimizing search strategy created poor schedules.

The results of our empirical analysis indicate that we must address the utility problem in terms of solution quality. The speed-up of the system is significant, ranging from ~19% to ~77% when the search control knowledge is applied. Test 9 shows the most significant efficiency improvement (77%) because of the configuration of carriers and launch dates (three biological carriers with launch dates within six months, thus, high contention for human resources). The overall average speed-up is 34%. However, the increase in WIP time varies from one set of missions to another. In some instances, the degradation in the quality of the synthesized schedules is noticeable; in others, the total WIP time is maintained. In this and other real-world domains, however, the ability to rapidly generate viable schedules is essential, and in some cases, worth marginal increases in WIP time.

When scheduling from the resource perspective, we select resources randomly and then choose times based on the resources' availability. Some processing to select the "best" resource (which has the maximum availability or a sufficient quantity available closest to the desired time) may improve schedules because the choice of resource determines start and end times. This is similar to the look-ahead schemes of [37], and would incur additional costs to the efficiency of the system.

Additionally, we believe that scheduling tasks from individual missions to minimize WIP time does not necessarily create schedules in which total WIP time is minimized. That is, there may be cases when sparse resource utilization in one mission allows tasks in a second mission to interleave with those in the first mission; this would reduce total WIP time across both missions.

6. Iterative repair: searching the space of complete schedules

For more complex scheduling problems, and particularly for problems that require extensive rescheduling, backtracking search may prove unacceptably inefficient. In this case, an iterative repair search mechanism may be preferable. *Iterative repair* is a general search method that has been applied to complex scheduling and constraint satisfaction problems with good results (e.g., [3,21,26,31,42]). Iterative repair methods construct an initial, possibly-flawed schedule and then iteratively modify it until no constraints remain violated. The primary difference between iterative repair methods and more traditional constraint-based approaches is that iterative repair modifies a complete, imperfect schedule, instead of incrementally constructing a conflict-free[2] schedule.

In reviewing previous research on repair-based scheduling we have found that one of the essential differences among such systems is how informed the repair process is. As illustrated by Fig. 5, an informed repair system (i.e., a point near the right of the x-axis) will generally require fewer, more computationally expensive iterations to find a solution. In contrast, a less-informed system may require more iterations to reach a solution, but each iteration can be accomplished with less computational cost. Ideally an equilibrium point exists where neither adding repair knowledge nor removing it yields a system that produces conflict-free solutions more quickly.

Here we present a learning method for dynamically selecting between a less-informed repair heuristic and a more-informed, but computationally expensive, heuristic. The system begins with the inexpensive repair strategy and then uses PEBL to learn when the less-informed heuristic leads the

---

[2] In this paper we refer to a constraint violation as a *conflict*.

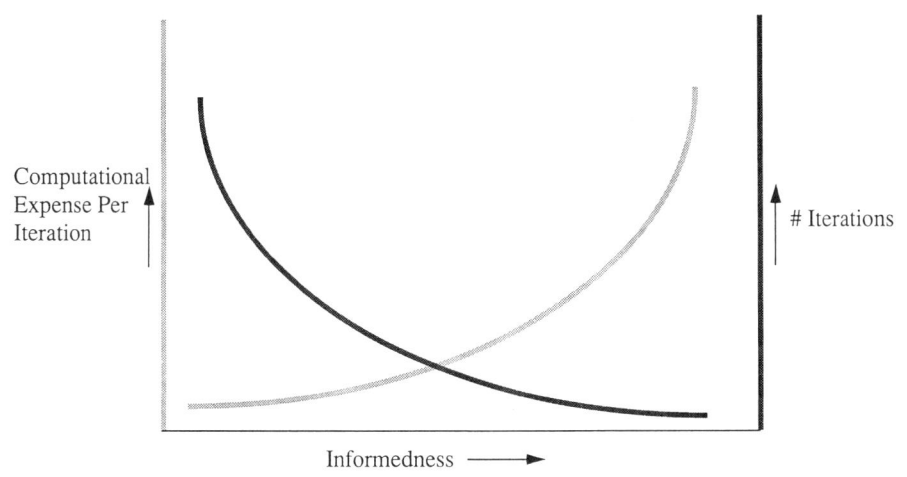

Fig. 5. Informedness versus computational cost of repairs.

search awry. When similar situations arise after learning, the system adopts the more-informed strategy.

6.1. Problem specification

We used the *Space Shuttle ground processing* problem as a test domain for our experiments in iterative repair. Ground processing encompasses all activities necessary to prepare a shuttle for launch. This includes a multitude of inspection, repair, and refurbishment tasks, which must be completed by a designated deadline. Each task demands some amount of resources such as technicians, engineers and quality inspectors. Tasks are also temporally related to each other.

The Columbia and Endeavour flow management teams that coordinate ground processing use our scheduling system operationally. We expect our system to evolve into the primary scheduling and rescheduling tool used by all four orbiter teams.

6.1.1. Preemptive scheduling

In some scheduling problems (including Space Shuttle ground processing), preemption is a complicating factor. In preemptive scheduling, each task is associated with a calendar of legal work periods that determine when the task must be preempted and restarted. For example, suppose a task has a duration of 16 hours and a calendar indicating that only the first shift of each non-weekend day is legal. Given that the first shift of the day extends from 8:00 am to 4:00 pm, if the task is started on Monday at 8:00 am, then it will be suspended at the end of the shift (at 4:00 pm). It would restart on Tuesday at 8:00 am and would complete the same day at 4:00 pm. If the task were started on Friday, however, it would not complete until the following Monday at 4:00 pm.

Preemption effectively splits a task into a set of suspended and restarted subtasks. Resource constraints are annotated as to whether they should be enforced only during each individual subtask (and not during the suspended periods between subtasks) or during the entire time spanning from the first subtask until the last. Labor is not typically required during the suspended periods, and is therefore an example of the former constraint type. In contrast, heavy machinery is difficult to relocate and may remain allocated during the suspended periods.

Preemptive scheduling requires substantial computational overhead because, for each assignment, preemption times must be computed and appropriate constraint manipulation must be performed.

6.1.2. Components of a shuttle mission

For each shuttle mission, a set of *generic* tasks (called the generic flow) must be performed in preparation for every launch. In addition to the generic tasks, other groups of tasks (called *options*) are appended. An option is a set of temporally related tasks, each having individual resource requirements. Options may be added for a variety of reasons; for example, certain maintenance operations are only required after every fifth flight.

A mission is composed of the tasks and constraints from the generic flow and the necessary options. Options are attached as a postrequisite to one generic task and as a prerequisite to another and are thus anchored into the generic flow.

PEBL attempts to transfer learned information from a training set of missions to a different set of missions that share similar options.

6.2. Constraint-based iterative repair

PEBL was applied to the constraint-based iterative repair system described in [41,42]. This system begins with an assignment of all variables and improves the assignments until the cost function reaches zero. For the experiments reported here, the cost function is simply the number of conflicts in the schedule. Each repair constitutes re-assigning one or more variables with different values. To simplify our discussion below, we will often refer to repairing a conflict by "moving a task", which is a prototypical repair for scheduling problems.

An initial schedule is determined by the *critical path method* (CPM) [18]. This algorithm schedules all tasks as early as possible by considering only temporal constraints. It is an $O(n)$ algorithm that results in a schedule with only resource violations.

In the system, repairs are associated with constraints. This allows knowledge engineers to encode local repair heuristics likely to satisfy the constraint without requiring them to anticipate how repairs interact with other constraints. Of course, local repairs do occasionally yield globally undesirable states.

In our experiments, the system repairs up to ten constraint violations per iteration. Repairing a violation involves moving a set of tasks to different times: at least one task participating in the constraint violation is moved, along with any other tasks whose temporal constraints would be violated by the move. In other words, all temporal constraints are preserved after the repair. We use the Waltz constraint propagation algorithm over time intervals [7,40] to carry this out (this affecting a form of arc-consistency). The algorithm recursively enforces temporal constraints until there are no outstanding temporal violations. This scheme can be computationally expensive, since moving tasks involves checking resource constraints, calculating preemption intervals, etc.

At the end of each iteration, the system re-evaluates the cost function to determine whether the new schedule resulting from the repairs is better than the current one. If the new schedule is an improvement, it becomes the current schedule for the next iteration. If it is not an improvement, with some probability (see below) it is either accepted anyway, or it is rejected and the previous solution is restored.

The system will sometimes accept a new solution that is worse than the current solution in order to escape local minima. This stochastic technique is referred to as simulated annealing [24]. The probability distribution function for accepting an inferior solution s' from solution s is:

$$Escape(s, s', T) = e^{-|Cost(s) - Cost(s')|/T},$$

where T is a "temperature" parameter that is gradually reduced during the search process. Note that s' is less likely to be accepted from s for higher values of $|Cost(s) - Cost(s')|$ and/or lower values of T.

To summarize, the repair algorithm begins with a complete but flawed schedule and isolates the violated constraints. Tasks are moved according to the repairs embodied in the violated constraints. A new schedule is accepted if the new cost is lower than the previous cost, or if a random number exceeds the value of the escape function; otherwise it is rejected and new repairs are attempted on the previous schedule. The process repeats until the cost of the solution is acceptable to the user, or until the user terminates the repair cycle. The system may also terminate itself if a prespecified number of iterations have been attempted or if a prespecified CPU time bound has been reached.

6.2.1. The dimensions of repair knowledge

In [43], the authors outline five different dimensions of repair-based techniques that affect the tradeoff between informedness and computational complexity. This paper is concerned with two of these dimensions: the depth of repairs and the evaluation criteria used to select repairs.

The *depth* of a repair strategy is the degree of look-ahead employed when choosing a repair. A strategy with depth 0 only considers the current state (current schedule). A strategy with depth 1 evaluates a potential repair by considering the state resulting after the repair. For example, the *min-conflicts* method [31] is a depth 1 method since it selects the repair that most reduces the total number of conflicts. Similarly, a strategy with depth 2 would evaluate a repair by considering the repairs required *after* the current repair was executed. Some systems employ variable depth look-ahead: moving one task may require additional moves if the system automatically preserves temporal constraints.

The evaluation criteria measure the quality of a repair. After a set of candidate repairs has been generated, each is evaluated and one selected. Examples of evaluation criteria are the number of conflicts in a resulting schedule or the amount of perturbation from a previous state. Ideally, a good evaluation criterion should accurately measure both the quality of the resulting schedule with respect to the applicable criteria, and the likelihood of reaching a conflict-free state from the resulting schedule.

6.2.2. Two heuristic repair methods

In this section we present two repair strategies for resource capacity constraints that differ in depth of look-ahead and evaluation criteria. One repair strategy uses no look-ahead (depth 0) and evaluates the quality of the repair with a simple function over specific task attributes. The other strategy employs a form of min-conflicts that uses a variable depth look-ahead.

A depth-0 repair strategy

To repair a violated resource capacity constraint, an offending task is selected and reassigned to a new time. The heuristic used to select a candidate considers the following information:

- *Fitness*: Move the task whose resource requirement most closely matches the amount of overallocation. A task using a significantly smaller amount is not likely to have a large enough impact on the current violation being repaired. A task using a far greater amount is more likely to be in violation wherever it is moved.
- *Temporal dependents*: Move the task with the fewest number of temporal dependents. A task with many dependents, if moved, is likely to cause temporal constraint violations.

For each of the tasks contributing to the violation, the system considers only the *next earlier* and *next later* available times for a move, rather than exploring many or all possible times. The system scores each candidate move by using a linear combination of the *fitness* and *temporal dependents* heuristic values. The repair then chooses the move stochastically with respect to the scores calculated. After the repair is performed, the Waltz algorithm moves other tasks in order to preserve temporal constraints.

In summary, this repair strategy only considers two possible moves for a task participating in a violation: one earlier and one later. The evaluation criterion used to select a repair is based upon two computationally inexpensive heuristic criteria: degree of fitness and number of temporal dependents.

A variable-depth repair strategy

As before, for each of the tasks contributing to a violation, the system considers moving the task to the next earlier and next later available time. However, this method selects the repair that minimizes the constraint violations in the resulting state. This method uses a variable depth look-ahead because it counts conflicts *after* the Waltz algorithm moves an arbitrary number of tasks. The main advantage of this strategy is that it can identify interactions (i.e., new constraint violations) that would occur after a candidate repair. However, this technique is more computationally expensive than the depth-0 strategy because each candidate move must be performed, the resulting state evaluated, and original state restored in order to evaluate the next move.

6.3. Learning to select repair strategies

Here we describe a general method for learning to select between repair strategies. We define *goodness* as a quality metric which, for these experiments, is simply the number of conflicts resulting after a repair. For example, a repair which results in fewer conflicts would have a high goodness rating. The first step of the training process is to gather goodness statistics for each task moved within a repair. During this first phase, the system uses the depth-0 heuristic over a training set of missions, resulting in a table of goodness statistics. Figure 6(a) depicts a typical statistics table for a training suite.

After ample statistics are gathered, the system enters a second phase which employs PEBL. The PEBL domain theory is used to conjecture that our variable depth strategy should be used when the goodness statistics contradict the advice offered by the depth 0 strategy. More specifically, if the highest candidate tasks proposed by the depth 0 strategy are not suggested by the statistical data as one of the top candidates to move, then

Goodness statistics					PEBL-conjectures				
Tasks	\multicolumn{4}{c|}{Options}	Tasks	\multicolumn{4}{c}{Options}
	G	O_1	O_2	O_3		G	O_1	O_2	O_3
G_1	1	1	1	3	G_1	0	0	0	0
G_2	2	1	2	1	G_2	0	0	0	0
⋮	⋮	⋮	⋮	⋮	⋮	⋮	⋮	⋮	⋮
O_{11}	2	1	1	1	O_{11}	0	0	0	0
O_{12}	2	1	2	1	O_{12}	0	0	0	0
⋮	⋮	⋮	⋮	⋮	⋮	⋮	⋮	⋮	⋮
O_{21}	3	6	7	10	O_{21}	0.4	0.5	0.8	0.9
O_{22}	2	5	9	12	O_{22}	0.3	0.6	0.9	0.9
⋮	⋮	⋮	⋮	⋮	⋮	⋮	⋮	⋮	⋮
O_{31}	4	9	12	15	O_{31}	0.5	0.6	0.9	0.7
O_{32}	3	8	13	16	O_{32}	0.5	0.6	0.7	0.7
⋮	⋮	⋮	⋮	⋮	⋮	⋮	⋮	⋮	⋮

Fig. 6. (a) *Goodness statistics*: each cell O_{ij}, O_k is the expected violations that will result from moving task j of option i when option O_k is part of the mission. (b) *PEBL-conjectures*: each cell O_{ij}, O_k is the probability that moving task j of option i will contradict the goodness statistics when option O_k is part of the mission.

it is likely that the depth 0 criteria has over-abstracted the problem details, and may create unnecessary constraint violations. PEBL then conjectures that since this local strategy has been myopic, a contradiction exists that can only be resolved with more global information. When training is terminated, the system is capable of selecting repair strategies according to this evidence.

To foster transfer between problems, the goodness statistics and PEBL conjectures are organized into tables that relate tasks to the generic flow and options as shown in Fig. 6(b). New problems can exploit learned knowledge when they contain options that appeared in the training set.

After learning, when selecting a task to move for a repair, the system uses the PEBL conjectures to decide whether it should believe its less-informed heuristic or use the look-ahead strategy. To make this decision, the system averages the relevant PEBL conjectures for the task selected by the depth-0 strategy. If this result exceeds a threshold, then look-ahead is performed. In our experiments, the threshold is set at 0.5.

For example, suppose some mission is composed of options O_1 and O_3, and task O_{31} is selected by the depth-0 repair. Since the PEBL conjectures of $(O_{31}, G) = 0.5$, $(O_{31}, O_1) = 0.6$, $(O_{31}, O_3) = 0.7$ average to 0.6, and since this exceeds the 0.5 threshold, our system will employ the look-ahead strategy.

To summarize, learning proceeds with a statistics gathering phase followed by a PEBL stage. The statistics quantify the goodness of the depth-0 strategy. Then the PEBL phase is used to conjecture contradictions between the depth-0 strategy and the statistics. This technique can be used with any two repair heuristics and a variety of goodness metrics.

6.4. Evaluating the method

To evaluate the success of our approach, we generated a set of scheduling problems by specifying range limits for various problem parameters as input to the system. An individual scheduling problem consists of a generic flow, a set of option flows, and a set of resource pools. A "suite" of scheduling problems can be considered a single scheduling domain. That is, for each suite, the generic flow, the set of resource pools and the set of options are fixed. A generic flow is comprised of 100 to 150 tasks. For each suite, there is a set of 8 possible options, each consisting of 10 to 50 tasks. There are 6 resource pools for each suite, with capacities ranging from 7 to 10 units.

We generated three major testing problem sets: (D)ifficult, (F)ew options, and (L)oose. In problem sets (D) and (L), each option has a 50% chance of being included in a particular problem, so that each problem on average consists of 4 of the 8 options. In problem set (F) there was only a 20% chance that each option would be included in a problem. Thus problem set (F) was easier than (D) because fewer options cause less interaction. All missions have an overall due date that all tasks must precede. Both the (D) and (F) problem sets have earlier due dates for each mission while the (L) problem set has later due dates. In short, problem set (D) includes many options in a tight time bound; problem set (F) is easier than (D) because there are fewer options; problem set (L) is easier than (D) because its time bound is less restrictive.

For the training phase, we randomly selected 10 (out of the 256 possible) scheduling problems to learn the characteristics of the likely task/option interactions. After training, we compared the respective speed of convergence to an acceptable solution (i.e., no constraint violations or reaching a prespecified time bound) for the variable depth look-ahead approach, the depth-0 approach, and the approach suggested by PEBL on new problems from the same problem suite (see Fig. 7). Testing consisted of more than 1600 runs for the three problem sets.

6.4.1. Discussion of the results

The (D)ifficult problem set consisted of numerous tasks with multiple resource requests and tight milestone constraints. In this problem set, the system tended to favor look-ahead and performed only 4% better than the look-ahead strategy. However, the system did appear to learn about interactions because it performed 51% better than the depth-0 strategy.

The (F)ew options set had fewer interacting tasks in each problem and were therefore considerably easier than the (D) set. Here learning performed

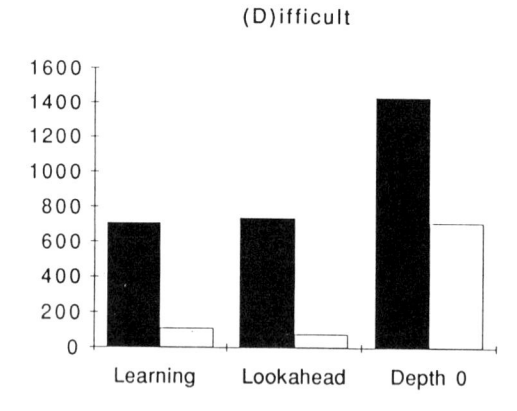

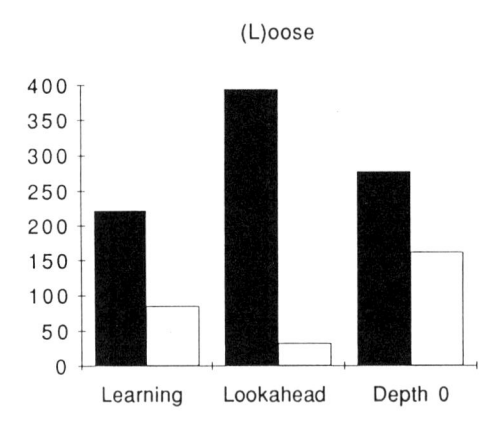

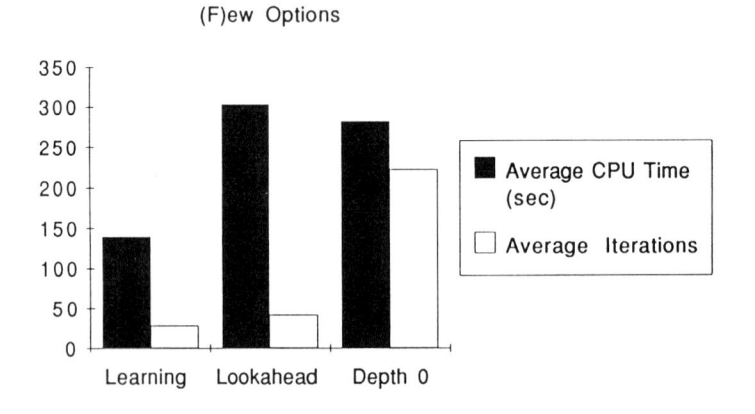

Fig. 7. Average CPU time and iterations.

54% better than look-ahead and again 51% better than the depth-0 strategy.

In the (L)oose problem set, the depth-0 strategy performed much better than the look-ahead strategy. Here learning performed 44% better than look-ahead and 20% better than the depth-0 strategy.

The computational expense of look-ahead was clearly worthwhile for problem set (D), but in (F) and (L) using look-ahead was overkill. The learning method outperformed the other strategies because it only invests in look-ahead when its experience suggests that the depth-0 strategy would make the wrong decision.

7. Related work

The PEBL approach extends previous work in EBL [8,29,32] by applying it to a real-world problem and by adding an empirical component to confirm plausible explanations. PEBL is similar to other empirical learning techniques [5,6,11,19,33]. However, our empirical component is not used to make inductive leaps. Rather, the target concept itself cannot be proved without a distribution of examples. Another empirical approach is that of [2]. In their system, explanations are created which describe how a plan can be "tuned". If multiple conflicting explanations are created, either a compromise is attempted, or a new plan is constructed.

In the PEBL framework, the decision to create a rule is determined by the expected cost to solution quality, the conditional probabilities associated with plausible implications, and the expected match cost of applying a rule. Prior work in learning search control rules calculates the utility of a rule as the function of the frequency of application, the match cost and the efficiency gain. This is similar to learning macro-operators [20]; a macro-operator is deemed useful if its expanded length does not exceed some threshold, and if it appears in a successful solution path. Since our system does not create rules from every plausible explanation, we avoid having to reject useless or incorrect knowledge.

Since the initial publication of our work [9], Gratch and DeJong [13] have successfully applied a nearly identical technique to the two domains in [29] and the domain in [10]. In their implementation, rules are proposed to have *conditional utility*. This value is empirically approximated by conjecturing candidate rules, applying the rules to a distribution of problems, and extracting savings and match cost statistics. If conditional utility has been accurately estimated, those rules with positive conditional utility will increase the efficacy of the search strategy.

Our idea of taking statistics on the frequency of interactions between option tasks was inspired by the calibration techniques of Hansson and Mayer [16], who built a heuristic error model from problem solving instances. In their work on decision-theoretic control of scheduling systems, they maintain a multi-dimensional histogram, where each dimension is a heuristic value or an outcome attribute. They use the data to determine what heuristics (e.g., variable and value ordering knowledge) are likely to lead to good solutions.

The repair-based scheduling methods considered here are related to the repair-based methods that have been previously used in AI planning systems such as the "fixes" used in the Hacker planning system [38] and, more recently, the repair strategies used in the GORDIUS [36] generate–test–debug system, in the PRIAR plan modification system [22], and the CHEF cased-based planner [14].

Another system that uses explanations and multiple examples is presented by Bennett and DeJong [2]. In their system, explanations are created which describe how a plan can be "tuned". If multiple conflicting explanations are created, either a compromise between conflicting explanations is attempted, or a new plan is constructed.

Finally, we extend previous work in scheduling using multiple perspectives [37] by applying machine learning techniques to minimize the changes in the search strategy to the most critical points in the search space based on experience.

8. Conclusions and future work

The overall conclusion of our work is that PEBL is an effective method for learning search control for both backtracking and iterative repair search. However, the empirical results indicate clear avenues of improvement. In general, the approach requires some hand-tuning and human analysis. Various enhancements to the system could make this process more transparent. In the case of backtracking search, a metric of solution quality during the learning phase would help guide the decision of whether or not to create a new search control rule. For the iterative repair search strategy, a cost analysis should be incorporated into the domain theory to provide a better indication of when the use of look-ahead is beneficial. The domain theory currently reasons about the predicted accuracy of the repair heuristic. Information about the computational expense of a more informed repair heuristic should be incorporated into the domain theory to determine the optimal balance between the two metrics. In future work, we plan to augment PEBL with utility information and perform more comprehensive testing on problems of variable complexity.

Another problem indicated by our empirical analysis is that the iterative repair method is prone to cycle as it approaches a final solution. Often, the system rapidly converges to few constraint violations, but is unable to jump out of the local minimum. In these cases the system terminates when it reached a time threshold, but the final solutions are non-optimal. One idea is to use PEBL to isolate these local minima situations. If this proves to be a successful approach, it has potential to apply to related problems and domains.

Finally, we intend to apply our learning technique to the deployed version of our system at Kennedy Space Center. We believe that in domains where scheduling problems are largely repetitive with occasional discrepancies (such as in the Space Shuttle processing domain), the PEBL technique will capture the likely interactions and has the potential to significantly improve scheduling.

Appendix A. The plausibility-chronic-resource-bottleneck-across-two-missions generalization problem

Given:
- *Target concept*: Class of instances of a chronic resource bottleneck across two missions where:
  PLAUSIBLY-CHRONIC-RESOURCE-BOTTLENECK
   -ACROSS-TWO-MISSIONS(*task1,res*)
  ⇔
  IN-MISSION(*task1,miss1*)
  ∧ CONFLICTING-TASKS(*task1,res,task-list*)
  ∧ ISA(*miss2*,MISSION)
  ∧ NOT-EQUAL(*miss1,miss2*)
  ∧ NEARBY(*miss1,miss2*)
  ∧ CONFLICT-IN-MISSION(*task-list,miss2,task2*)
  ∧ USES-CARRIER(*miss1,carr1*)
  ∧ USES-CARRIER(*miss2,carr2*)
  ∧ CARRIER-TYPE(*carr1,carr-type1*)
  ∧ CARRIER-TYPE(*carr2,carr-type2*)
  ∧ RESOURCE-TYPE(*res,res-type*)
  ∧ TASK-TYPE(*task1,task-type1*)
  ∧ TASK-TYPE(*task2,task-type2*).

- *Training example*:
  RESOURCE-BOTTLENECK(*spacelab-systems-experiment-test1,*
   automatic-test-equipment1)
  ISA(*spacelab-systems-experiment-test1,*
   SPACELAB-SYSTEMS-EXPERIMENT-TEST)
  IN-MISSION(*spacelab-systems-experiment-test1,sts-62*)
  ISA(*sts-62*,MISSION)

USES-CARRIER(*sts-62,lm2-1*)
ISA(*lm2-1*,LONG-MODULE-2)
• • •

- *Domain theory*:
  USERS(*res,task-list*)
  ∧ EQ(*parallel-tasks*,{*task* ∈ *task-list* | INTERSECTS(*task,task1*)})
  → CONFLICTING-TASKS(*task1,res,parallel-tasks*)

  START-TIME(*task1,st1*) ∧ END-TIME(*task1,et1*)
  ∧ START-TIME(*task2,st2*) ∧ END-TIME(*task2,et2*)
  ∧ (LEQ(*st1,et2*) ∧ LEQ(*et2,et1*))
  ∨ LEQ(*st1,st2*) ∧ LEQ(*st2,et1*))
  → INTERSECTS(*task1,task2*)

  ISA(*m1*,MISSION) ∧ ISA(*m2*,MISSION) ∧ NOT-EQUAL(*m1,m2*)
  ∧ LAUNCH(*m1,time1*) ∧ LAUNCH(*m2,time2*)
  ∧ MINUS(*time1,time2,diff*) ∧ ABSOLUTE-VALUE(*diff,abs-val*)
  ∧ LESS-THAN(*abs-val*,SIX-MONTHS)
  → NEARBY(*m1,m2*)

  CONFLICTING-TASKS(*conf-task,res,task-list*)
  ∧ ∃ *task* ∈ *task-list* IN-MISSION(*task,miss*)
  → CONFLICT-IN-MISSION(*task-list,miss,task*)

  ISA(*task*,SPACELAB-SYSTEMS-EXPERIMENT-TEST)
  → TASK-TYPE(*task*,SPACELAB-EXPERIMENT-INTEGRATION)

  ISA(*task*,PAD-OPERATIONS) → TASK-TYPE(*task*,LEVEL-1)
  •

  EQ(*res*,AUTOMATIC-TEST-EQUIPMENT1)
  → RESOURCE-TYPE(*res*,AUTOMATIC-TEST-EQUIPMENT)
  EQ(*res*,EAST-CRANE) → RESOURCE-TYPE(*res*, CRANE)
  •

  ISA(*c*,MPRESS) → CARRIER-TYPE(*c*,MISSION-PECULIAR)
  ISA(*c*,LONG-MODULE-1) ∨ ISA(*c*,LONG-MODULE-2)
  ∨ ISA(*c*,PALLET-IGLOO)
  → CARRIER-TYPE(*c*,BIOLOGICAL)
  • • •

- *Operationality criterion*: The concept definition must be expressed in terms of the predicates used to describe the examples (e.g., IN-MISSION(*task,miss*), USES-CARRIER(*miss,carr*)) or other selected, easily evaluated predicates from the domain theory (e.g., MINUS,LAUNCH,TASK-TYPE).

Determine:

A generalization of the training example that is a sufficient concept definition for the target concept and that satisfies the operationality criterion.

Acknowledgement

We thank Steve Minton for many valuable discussions and the use of Prodigy's rule system, John Bresina for his ideas about plausibility and John, Steve, Peter Friedland and Holly Pease for carefully reviewing this paper.

References

[1] J.F. Allen, Towards a general theory of action and time, *Artif. Intell.* 23 (1984) 123–154.
[2] S. Bennett and G. DeJong, Comparing stochastic planning to the acquisition of increasingly permissive plans for complex, uncertain domains, in: *Proceedings Eighth International Workshop on Machine Learning* (1991).
[3] E. Biefeld and L. Cooper, Bottleneck identification using process chronologies, in: *Proceedings IJCAI-91*, Sydney, Australia (1991).
[4] R.H. Brown, Knowledge-based scheduling and resource allocation in the CAMPS architecture, in: *Proceedings IEEE International Conference on Expert Systems and the Leading Edge in Planning and Control* (Benjamin/Cummings, Menlo Park, CA, 1987).
[5] W. Cohen, Concept learning using explanation based generalization as an abstraction mechanism, Ph.D. Thesis, Rutgers University, New Brunswick, NJ (1990).
[6] A. Danyluk, Finding new rules for incomplete theories, in: *Proceedings Sixth International Workshop on Machine Learning*, Ithaca, NY (1989).
[7] E. Davis, Constraint propagation with interval labels, *Artif. Intell.* 32 (3) (1987) 281–331.
[8] G.F. DeJong and M.R. Mooney, Explanation-based generalization: an alternative view, *Mach. Learn.* 1 (1986) 145–176.
[9] M. Eskey and M. Zweben, Learning search control for a constraint-based scheduling system, in: *Proceedings AAAI-90*, Boston, MA (1990).
[10] O. Etzioni, Why Prodigy/EBL works, in: *Proceedings AAAI-90*, Boston, MA (1990).
[11] N. Flann and T.G. Dietterich, A study of explanation-based methods for inductive learning, *Mach. Learn.* 4 (1989).
[12] E.C. Freuder, A sufficient condition for backtrack-free search, *J. ACM* 29 (1) (1982) 24–32.
[13] J. Gratch and G.F. DeJong, A hybrid approach to guaranteed effective control strategies, in: *Proceedings Eighth International Workshop on Machine Learning* (1991).
[14] K.J. Hammond, CHEF: a model of case-based planning, in: *Proceedings AAAI-86*, Philadelphia, PA (1986).
[15] G.B. Hankins, J.W. Jordan, J.L. Katz, A.M. Mulvehill, J.N. Dumoulin and J. Ragusa, EMPRESS: expert mission planning and re-planning scheduling system, in: *Expert Systems in Government Symposium* (1985).
[16] O. Hansson and A. Mayer, Decision-theoretic control of artificial intelligence scheduling systems, Tech. Rept. Heuristicrats Research Inc., Berkeley, CA (1991).
[17] R.M. Haralick and G.L. Elliot, Increasing tree efficiency for constraint satisfaction problems, *Artif. Intell.* 14 (1980) 263–313.

[18] F.S. Hillier and G.J. Lieberman, *Introduction to Operations Research* (Holden-Day, San Francisco, CA, 1980).
[19] H. Hirsh, Combining empirical and analytical learning with version spaces, in: *Proceedings Sixth International Workshop on Machine Learning*, Ithaca, NY (1989).
[20] G. Iba, A heuristic approach to the discovery of macro-operators, *Mach. Learn.* **3** (4) (1989) 285–318.
[21] D. Johnson, C. Aragon, L. McGeoch and C. Schevon, Optimization by simulated annealing: an experimental evaluation, Part II, *J. Oper. Res.* **39** (3) (1990) 378–406.
[22] S. Kambhampati, A theory of plan modification, in: *Proceedings AAAI-90*, Boston, MA (1990).
[23] R.M. Keller, Defining operationality for explanation-based learning, in: *Proceedings AAAI-87*, Seattle, WA (1987).
[24] S. Kirkpatrick, C.D. Gelatt and M.P. Vecchi, Optimization by simulated annealing, *Science* **220** (4598) (1983).
[25] J.E. Laird, P.S. Rosenbloom and A. Newell, *Universal Subgoaling and Chunking* (Kluwer Academic Publishers, Hingham, MA, 1986).
[26] S. Lin and B. Kernighan, An effective heuristic for the travelling salesman problem, *Oper. Res.* **21** (1973) 498–515.
[27] A.K. Mackworth, Consistency in networks of relations, *Artif. Intell.* **8** (1) (1977) 99–118.
[28] S. Minton, J.G. Carbonell, O. Etzioni, C.A. Knoblock and D.R. Kuokka, Acquiring effective search control rules: explanation-based learning in the Prodigy system, in: *Proceedings Fourth International Workshop on Machine Learning*, Irvine, CA (1987).
[29] S. Minton, Learning effective search control knowledge: an explanation-based approach, Ph.D. Thesis, Carnegie Mellon University, Pittsburgh, PA (1988).
[30] S. Minton, Quantitative results concerning the utility of explanation-based learning, in: *Proceedings AAAI-88*, St. Paul, MN (1988).
[31] S. Minton, A. Phillips, M. Johnston, and P.E. Laird, Solving large scale CSP and scheduling problems with a heuristic repair method in: *Proceedings AAAI-90*, Boston, MA (1990).
[32] T.M. Mitchell, R.M. Keller and S.T. Kedar-Cabelli, Explanation-based learning: a unifying view, *Mach. Learn.* **1** (1986) 47–80.
[33] M. Pazzani, M. Dyer and M. Flowers, The role of prior causal theories in generalization, in: *Proceedings AAAI-86*, Philadelphia, PA (1986).
[34] J. Pearl, *Probabilistic Reasoning in Intelligent Systems: Networks of Plausible Inference* (Morgan Kaufmann, San Mateo, CA, 1988).
[35] N. Sadeh and M.S. Fox, Preference propagation in temporal/capacity constraint graphs, Tech. Rept., The Robotics Institute, Carnegie Mellon University, Pittsburgh, PA (1989).
[36] R. Simmons, Combining associational and causal reasoning to solve interpretation and planning problems, Tech. Rept., MIT Artificial Intelligence Laboratory, Cambridge, MA (1988).
[37] S. Smith and P. Ow, The use of multiple problem decompositions in time constrained planning tasks, in: *Proceedings IJCAI-85*, Los Angeles, CA (1985).
[38] G.J. Sussman, A computational model of skill acquisition, Ph.D. Thesis, AI Laboratory, MIT, Cambridge, MA (1973).
[39] M. Vilain and H.A. Kautz, Constraint propagation algorithms for temporal reasoning, in: *Proceedings AAAI-86*, Philadelphia, PA (1986).
[40] D. Waltz, Understanding line drawings of scenes with shadows, in: P. Winston, ed., *The Psychology of Computer Vision* (McGraw-Hill, New York, 1975).
[41] M. Zweben, E. Davis, B. Daun and M. Deale, Iterative repair for scheduling and rescheduling, *IEEE Syst. Man Cybern.* (1992), to appear.
[42] M. Zweben, M. Deale and R. Gargan, Anytime rescheduling, in: *Proceedings DARPA Workshop on Innovative Approaches to Planning and Scheduling* (1990).
[43] M. Zweben and S. Minton, Repair-based scheduling: informedness versus computational cost, Tech. Rept., NASA Ames Research Center, Moffett Field, CA (1991).

ARTINT 956

Reasoning about qualitative temporal information *

Peter van Beek

Department of Computing Science, University of Alberta, Edmonton, Alberta, Canada T6G 2H1

Abstract

Van Beek, P., Reasoning about qualitative temporal information, Artificial Intelligence 58 (1992) 297–326.

Representing and reasoning about incomplete and indefinite qualitative temporal information is an essential part of many artificial intelligence tasks. An interval-based framework and a point-based framework have been proposed for representing such temporal information. In this paper, we address two fundamental reasoning tasks that arise in applications of these frameworks: Given possibly indefinite and incomplete knowledge of the relationships between some intervals or points, (i) find a scenario that is consistent with the information provided, and (ii) find the feasible relations between all pairs of intervals or points.

For the point-based framework and a restricted version of the interval-based framework, we give computationally efficient procedures for finding a consistent scenario and for finding the feasible relations. Our algorithms are marked improvements over the previously known algorithms. In particular, we develop an $O(n^2)$-time algorithm for finding one consistent scenario that is an $O(n)$ improvement over the previously known algorithm, where n is the number of intervals or points, and we develop an algorithm for finding all the feasible relations that is of far more practical use than the previously known algorithm. For the unrestricted version of the interval-based framework, finding a consistent scenario and finding the feasible relations have been shown to be NP-complete. We show how the results for the point algebra aid in the design of a backtracking algorithm for finding one consistent scenario that is shown to be useful in practice for planning problems.

Keywords. Temporal reasoning, interval algebra, point algebra, constraint satisfaction.

Correspondence to: P. van Beek, Department of Computing Science, University of Alberta, Edmonton, Alberta, Canada T6G 2H1. Telephone: (403) 492-7741 (Office). Fax: (403) 492-1071. E-mail: vanbeek@cs.ualberta.ca.

*A preliminary version of this paper appeared in: *Proceedings AAAI-90*, Boston, MA (AAAI Press/MIT Press, Cambridge, MA, 1990) 728–734.

1. Introduction

Representing and reasoning about incomplete and indefinite qualitative temporal information is an essential part of many artificial intelligence tasks. Allen [2] has proposed an interval algebra framework and Vilain and Kautz [41] have proposed a point algebra framework for representing such qualitative information. The frameworks are influential and have been applied in such diverse areas as natural language processing [3], planning [4], plan recognition [20], and diagnosis [18]. In this paper, we address two fundamental temporal reasoning tasks that arise in these application areas: Given possibly indefinite and incomplete knowledge of the relations between some intervals or points,

- find a scenario that is consistent with the information provided, and
- find the feasible relations between all pairs of intervals or points.

The frameworks have in common that the representations of temporal information can be viewed as binary constraint networks and that constraint satisfaction techniques can be used to reason about the information.

For point algebra networks and a restricted class of interval algebra networks, we present new, more efficient, algorithms for both of the reasoning tasks. In particular, for finding one consistent scenario, we develop an $O(n^2)$-time algorithm that is an $O(n)$ improvement over the previously known algorithm [22], where n is the number of points. For finding the feasible relations, we develop an $O(\max(mn^2, n^3))$-time algorithm for finding all pairs of feasible relations, where n is the number of points and m is the number of pairs of points that are asserted to be not equal. The new algorithm is of far more practical use than the previously known algorithm [40].

For general interval algebra networks, finding a consistent scenario and finding the feasible relations has been shown to be NP-complete and thus almost assuredly intractable in the worst case [41,42]. For finding a consistent scenario, we show how the results for the point algebra aid in the design of a backtracking algorithm. The algorithm is shown experimentally to be useful in practice for planning problems and problems with similar characteristics. For finding the feasible relations, the intractability of finding solutions for the general problem has led us elsewhere to explore algorithms that find approximate solutions [40].

The rest of the paper proceeds as follows. We begin by reviewing each of the frameworks and illustrating each with examples from natural language, showing how the temporal information is represented and giving examples of the reasoning tasks. We then formalize the reasoning tasks as binary constraint satisfaction problems. We then develop our algorithms for solving the two reasoning tasks, first for point algebra networks and a restricted class of interval algebra networks and, second for general interval algebra networks.

2. Representing temporal information

In this section, we review Allen's framework [2] for representing relations between intervals and Vilain and Kautz's framework [41] for representing relations between points, and illustrate the kinds of temporal information that can be represented within each framework. We then formalize the reasoning tasks using networks of binary constraints [27].

2.1. Allen's framework

There are thirteen *basic* relations that can hold between two intervals (see Fig. 1, [2,6]). In order to represent indefinite information, the relation between two intervals is allowed to be a disjunction of the basic relations. Sets are used to list the disjunctions. For example, the relation {m,o,s} between events A and B represents the disjunction,

(A meets B) ∨ (A overlaps B) ∨ (A starts B).

Let I be the set of all basic relations,

$I = \{b, bi, m, mi, o, oi, s, si, d, di, f, fi, eq\}$.

Allen allows the relation between two events to be any subset of I.

We use a graphical notation where vertices represent events and directed edges are labeled with sets of basic relations. As a graphical convention, we never show the edges (i,i), and if we show the edge (i,j), we do not show the edge (j,i). Any edge for which we have no explicit knowledge of the relation is labeled with I; by convention such edges are also not shown. We call networks with labels that are arbitrary subsets of I, interval algebra or IA networks.

Example 2.1. As an example of representing temporal information using IA networks and of the reasoning tasks of finding a consistent scenario and of finding the feasible relations, consider the description of events shown in Fig. 2(a). Not all of the temporal relations between events are explicitly or unambiguously given in the description. The first sentence tells us only that the interval of time over which Fred read the paper intersects with the interval of time over which Fred ate breakfast. We represent this as "paper {o, oi, s, si, d, di, f, fi, eq} breakfast". The second sentence fixes the relationship between some of the end points of the intervals over which Fred read his paper and over which Fred drank his coffee but it remains

Relation	Symbol	Inverse	Meaning
x before y	b	bi	x before y (disjoint, x first)
x meets y	m	mi	x meets y (x ends where y begins)
x overlaps y	o	oi	x overlaps y
x starts y	s	si	x and y start together, x shorter
x during y	d	di	x during y
x finishes y	f	fi	x finishes y
x equal y	eq	eq	x equal y

Fig. 1. Basic relations between intervals.

indefinite about others. We represent this as "paper {o, s, d} coffee".[1] But we also know that drinking coffee is a part of breakfast and so occurs during breakfast. We represent this as "coffee {d} breakfast". Finally, the information in the third sentence is represented as "walk {bi} breakfast". The resulting network is shown in Fig. 2(a), where we have drawn a directed edge from "breakfast" to "walk" and so have labeled the edge with the inverse of the "bi" (after) relation.

One scenario consistent with the description of events is shown in Fig. 2(c). Another possible consistent scenario is one where Fred starts to read his paper before he starts his breakfast. The feasible relations between all pairs of intervals are shown in Fig. 2(b). Determining the feasible relations can be viewed as determining the deductive consequences of our temporal knowledge. We are able to derive, for example, that Fred went for a walk after reading his paper and drinking his coffee and that Fred finished his paper before he finished his breakfast.

2.2. Vilain and Kautz's framework

There are three *basic* relations that can hold between two points: $<$, $=$, and $>$. In order to represent indefinite information, the relation between two points is allowed to be a disjunction of the basic relations. Sets are used to list the disjunctions. For example, the relation $\{<, =\}$ between points A

---

[1] Another possibility is the relation {b, m, o, s, d}, since the scenario where reading the paper occurred entirely before drinking the coffee is not explicitly ruled out by the sentence.

and B represents the disjunction, $(A < B) \vee (A = B)$. Let ? be the set of all basic relations, $\{<, =, >\}$. The set of possible relations between two points is $\{\emptyset, <, \leqslant, =, >, \geqslant, \neq, ?\}$, where $\leqslant$, for example, is an abbreviation of $\{<, =\}$. We call networks with labels that are subsets of ?, point algebra or PA networks.

Example 2.2. As an example of representing temporal information using PA networks, consider the description of events shown in Fig. 3(a). As discussed in Example 2.1, this sentence fixes the relationship between some of the end points of the intervals of time over which Fred read his paper and over which Fred drank his coffee but it remains indefinite about others. We represent this by the network shown in Fig. 3(a), where paper⁻ and paper⁺ represent the start and end points of the event. One scenario consistent with the temporal information is shown in Fig. 3(b). If a directed edge from paper⁻ to coffee⁺ labeled < was added to the network shown in Fig. 3(a), the resulting network would show the feasible relations between all pairs of points.

2.3. Translations between representations

Vilain and Kautz [41] show that a restricted class of IA networks, denoted here as SA networks, can be translated without loss of information into PA networks. In IA networks, the relation between two intervals can be any subset of I, the set of all thirteen basic relations. In SA networks, the allowed relations between two intervals are only those subsets of I that can be translated, using the relations $\{<, \leqslant, =, >, \geqslant, \neq, ?\}$, into conjunctions of relations between the end points of the intervals. For example, the IA network in Fig. 2(a) is also an SA network. As a specific example, the part of the interval network "paper {o, s, d} coffee" can be expressed as the conjunction of point relations,

$$(paper^- < paper^+) \wedge (coffee^- < coffee^+) \wedge$$
$$(paper^+ > coffee^-) \wedge (paper^+ < coffee^+),$$

and the equivalent representation as a PA network is shown in Fig. 3(a), where paper⁻ and paper⁺ represent the start and end points of the interval denoted paper, respectively. (See [40] for an enumeration of the allowed relations for SA networks and the translation into PA relations; also enumerated by Güther [17] and Ladkin and Maddux [23], where the relations are called the "pointisable" relations.)

The allowed relations for SA networks is a small but important and useful subset of the 2^{13} relations allowed for IA networks, as many applications of IA networks in the literature actually only use SA networks. For example,

(a) Example:

Fred was reading the paper while eating his breakfast. He put the paper down and drank the last of his coffee. After breakfast he went for a walk.

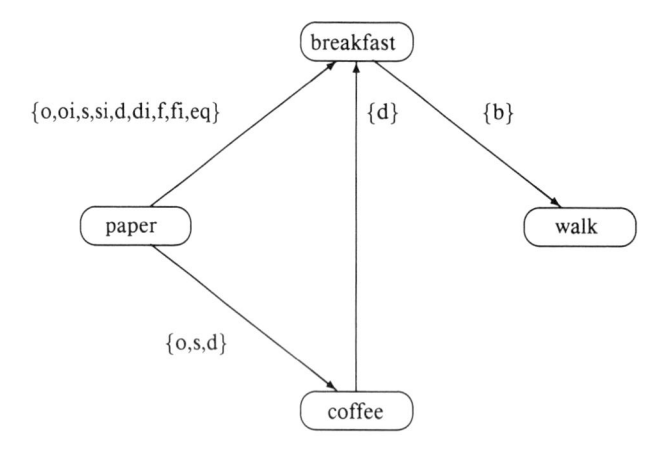

(b) Feasible relations:

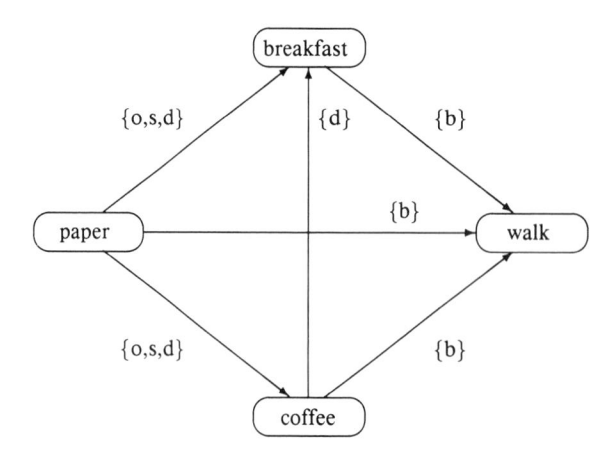

(c) Consistent scenario:

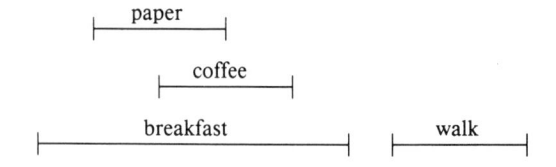

Fig. 2. Representing qualitative relations between intervals.

(a) Example:
Fred put the paper down and drank the last of his coffee.

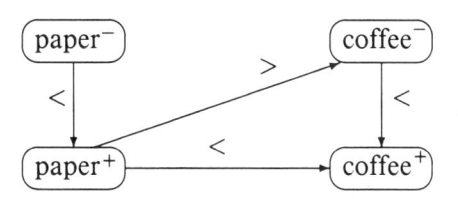

(b) Consistent scenario:

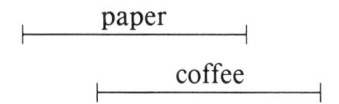

Fig. 3. Representing qualitative relations between points.

Almeida [5] and Song [35], in independent work on computer understanding of English narratives, both adopt Allen's framework but choose to use only relations that are allowed for SA networks. Hamlet and Hunter [18] adopt Allen's framework for representing temporal information in medical expert systems but, with the exception of the disjointedness relation {b, bi, m, mi}, choose to use only relations that are allowed for SA networks (in their example, later temporal information is used to strengthen the disjointedness relation to {b, m} which is allowed). Nökel [29] uses SA networks in a diagnostic setting. With the exception of Nökel [29], it does not appear that the authors intentionally restricted their representation language or were aware of the computational advantages; rather, the relations used were simply the right ones for the task at hand.

As alluded to above, what *cannot* be expressed in SA networks that can be expressed in IA networks is "disjointedness" of intervals. For example, we cannot say that "A {b, bi} B", i.e., that A is either before or after B, since this interval relation cannot be expressed as simply a conjunction of point relations between the end points of the two intervals. It requires the disjunction,

$$((A^- < B^-) \wedge (A^- < B^+) \wedge (A^+ < B^-) \wedge (A^+ < B^+)) \vee$$
$$((A^- > B^-) \wedge (A^- > B^+) \wedge (A^+ > B^-) \wedge (A^+ > B^+)).$$

The nearest approximation using only conjunction is

$$(A^- \neq B^-) \wedge (A^- \neq B^+) \wedge (A^+ \neq B^-) \wedge (A^+ \neq B^+),$$

and so, the nearest approximation to "A {b, bi} B" in SA networks is "A {b, bi, o, oi, d, di} B". But as can be seen, this allows, for example, A to overlap B, which we did not intend.

2.4. Formalization of the reasoning tasks

We formalize our reasoning tasks using networks of binary constraints [27]. The reasoning tasks are then special cases of a general class of problems known as constraint satisfaction problems. Our development borrows from that found by Dechter et al. [12] and Ladkin and Maddux [22,23]. This approach allows us to use some previously known algorithms and eases the development of new algorithms.

A *network of binary constraints* [27] is defined as a set X of n variables $\{x_1, x_2, ..., x_n\}$, a domain D_i of possible values for each variable, and binary constraints between variables. A *binary constraint*, C_{ij}, between variables x_i and x_j, is a subset of the Cartesian product of their domains that specifies the allowed pairs of values for x_i and x_j (i.e., $C_{ij} \subseteq D_i \times D_j$). For the networks of interest here, we require that $(x_j, x_i) \in C_{ji} \Leftrightarrow (x_i, x_j) \in C_{ij}$. An *instantiation* of the variables in X is an n-tuple $(X_1, X_2, ..., X_n)$, representing an assignment of $X_i \in D_i$ to x_i. A *consistent instantiation* of a network is an instantiation of the variables such that the constraints between variables are satisfied. A network is *inconsistent* if no consistent instantiation exists.

An *IA network* is a network of binary constraints where the variables represent time intervals, the domains of the variables are the set of ordered pairs of rational numbers $\{(s, e) \mid s < e\}$, with s and e representing the start and end points of the interval, respectively, and the binary constraints between variables are represented implicitly by sets of the basic interval relations.[2] For example, let $C_{ij} = \{m,o\}$ be the relation between variables x_i and x_j in some IA network. The set of allowed pairs of values for variables x_i and x_j is given by,

$$\{((s_i, e_i), (s_j, e_j)) \mid (s_i, e_i) \text{ meets } (s_j, e_j) \vee \\ (s_i, e_i) \text{ overlaps } (s_j, e_j)\}.$$

A *PA network* is a network of binary constraints where the variables represent time points, the domains of the variables are the set of ratio-

---

[2]Our interests are in temporal reasoning and hence we speak of *time* intervals. However, IA networks and the results presented in this paper have other applications. Two examples are DNA sequencing and optimal arrangement of records on secondary storage (see [16, pp. 182–184]). As well, it should be noted that, by adopting the rationals as the underlying representation of time, we are committing ourselves to a particular view of time, namely, that time is dense, linear, and unbounded. This is appropriate in many temporal reasoning applications. In other applications, however, we may want discrete, branching, or bounded time.

nal numbers, and the binary constraints between variables are represented implicitly by sets of the basic point relations.[3]

The reasoning tasks that we want to solve are finding a consistent scenario and finding the feasible relations. A network S is a *consistent scenario* of a network C if and only if

(a) $S_{ij} \subseteq C_{ij}$,
(b) $|S_{ij}| = 1$, for all i, j, and
(c) there exists a consistent instantiation of S.

The basic relations are disjoint. Hence, if an instantiation of variables x_i and x_j satisfies C_{ij}, then one and only one of the basic relations in C_{ij} is satisfied. Thus, given a consistent instantiation of a PA or IA network, the basic relations between variables satisfied by that consistent instantiation define a consistent scenario. As an example, one possible consistent instantiation of the network in Fig. 2(a) that would give the consistent scenario in Fig. 2(c) is,

paper ← (1, 3),

breakfast ← (0, 5),

walk ← (6, 7),

coffee ← (2, 4).

While there are either zero or an infinite number of different consistent instantiations of a PA or IA network, there are only a finite number of different consistent scenarios.

A basic relation $B \in C_{ij}$ is *feasible* with respect to a network if and only if there exists a consistent instantiation of the network where B is satisfied. Given an IA network or a PA network, C, the *set of feasible relations* between two variables x_i and x_j in the network is the set consisting of *all and only* the $B \in C_{ij}$ that are feasible. The *minimal* network representation, M, of a network, C, is the network for which M_{ij} is the set of feasible relations between variables x_i and x_j in C for every $i, j = 1, \ldots, n$. As an example, the network in Fig. 2(b) is the minimal network of the network in Fig. 2(a).

---

[3]With the exclusion of the $\neq$ relation, a PA network is simply a system of linear inequalities where each inequality is in two variables and each variable has unit coefficient. This is discussed further in Section 3.1. Along similar lines, Dean and McDermott [8] and Dechter et al. [12] propose difference constraints, and Malik and Binford [26] propose linear inequalities to represent and reason about temporal information.

3. Point algebra networks and a subclass of interval algebra networks

In this section we examine the computational problems of finding consistent scenarios and finding the feasible relations of PA networks and SA networks.

3.1. Finding a consistent scenario

3.1.1. Related work

One method of finding a consistent scenario of a PA network is to first find a consistent instantiation of the network. The basic relations between variables satisfied by the consistent instantiation then give a consistent scenario.

Topological sort (see Knuth [21]) can be used to find a consistent instantiation if the temporal information is a strict partial order; i.e., if the allowed relations are restricted to $\{<, >, ?\}$. Topological sort is $O(n^2)$.

If the allowed relations are restricted to $\{<, \leqslant, =, >, \geqslant, ?\}$, i.e., we do not allow disequality, PA networks can be viewed as a set of linear equalities and inequalities. The equalities and inequalities are of the form: $x_i - x_j < 0$, $x_i - x_j \leqslant 0$, and $x_i - x_j = 0$. A solution to the set of linear inequalities is precisely a consistent instantiation of the network. Solving a set of linear inequalities—or recognizing that no solution exists—is easily done using algorithms for solving linear programs (see Chvátal [7]). Thus, the simplex algorithm or Karmarkar's algorithm can be used to find a solution. However, more efficient algorithms are known if the linear program is of a particular form that arises in what is known as the shortest-path problem.

The shortest-path problem is to find the shortest path in a labeled graph from a vertex s to a vertex t. This can be made into a linear program as follows (see Papadimitriou and Steiglitz [31]). Let l_{ij} be the label on the directed edge (i, j) and let x_i denote the length of the shortest path from s to i. The shortest path from s to itself is 0. We want to minimize x_t, the length of the shortest path from s to t. Since the shortest path from s to j might pass through i, we must have $x_j \leqslant x_i + l_{ij}$, i.e., $x_j - x_i \leqslant l_{ij}$. The result is a linear program of the form,

$$\min x_t,$$
$$x_i - x_j \leqslant l_{ij}, \quad i, j = 1, \ldots, n,$$
$$x_i \text{ unconstrained},$$
$$x_s = 0.$$

If all the l_{ij} are non-negative then we can use Dijkstra's algorithm [13] to find a solution to this linear program. Dijkstra's algorithm is $O(n^2)$. If some of the l_{ij} are negative then we can use the Floyd–Warshall algorithm [1] to find a solution. The Floyd–Warshall algorithm is $O(n^3)$.

It remains to show how much of our problem can be translated into a shortest-path problem. The translation is as follows,

$$x_i = x_j \quad \rightarrow \quad x_i - x_j \leqslant 0, \quad x_j - x_i \leqslant 0,$$
$$x_i \leqslant x_j \quad \rightarrow \quad x_i - x_j \leqslant 0, \quad x_j - x_i \leqslant +\infty,$$
$$x_i < x_j \quad \rightarrow \quad x_i - x_j \leqslant -\varepsilon, \quad x_j - x_i \leqslant +\infty,$$

where the left column shows the relation between variables in a PA network and the right columns shows the translation into constraints for the shortest-path linear program. Note the use of a small negative value, $-\varepsilon$, for turning a strict inequality into a weak inequality (see [7, p. 451] for how to choose a value for ε such that solutions are preserved and no new solutions are introduced). In summary, if the allowed relations are restricted to $\{\leqslant, =, \geqslant, ?\}$, then Dijkstra's algorithm can be used to find a consistent instantiation in $O(n^2)$ time. If the allowed relations are restricted to $\{<, \leqslant, =, >, \geqslant, ?\}$, then the Floyd–Warshall algorithm can be used to find a consistent instantiation in $O(n^3)$ time.

Finally, Ladkin and Maddux [22] give an algorithm for finding one consistent scenario for PA networks that takes $O(n^3)$ time with n points. If no consistent scenario exists, the algorithm reports the inconsistency. Their algorithm relies on first applying the path consistency algorithm [24,27] before finding a consistent scenario.

3.1.2. An improved algorithm

We develop an algorithm for finding one consistent scenario that takes $O(n^2)$ time for PA networks with n points. Our starting point is an observation by Ladkin and Maddux [22, p. 34] that topological sort alone will not work as the labels may be any one of the eight different relations, $\{\emptyset, <, \leqslant, =, >, \geqslant, \neq, ?\}$, and thus may have less information about the relation between two points than is required. For topological sort we need all edges labeled with $<$, $>$, or ?. The "problem" labels are then $\{=, \emptyset, \leqslant, \geqslant, \neq\}$. The intuition behind the algorithm is that we somehow remove or rule out each of these possibilities and, once we have, we can then apply topological sort to give a consistent scenario. The algorithm is summarized in Fig. 6 and a proof of correctness is given in Appendix A. The input to the algorithm is a PA network represented as an adjacency matrix C where element C_{ij} is the label on edge (i, j).

The $=$ relation. To remove the $=$ relation from the network, we identify all pairs of points that are necessarily equal and condense them into one vertex. When saying that two points are necessarily equal, we mean that in every consistent scenario the relation between the two vertices is the $=$ relation. More formally, we want to partition the vertices into equivalence classes S_i, $1 \leqslant i \leqslant m$, such that vertices v and w are in the same equivalence class if

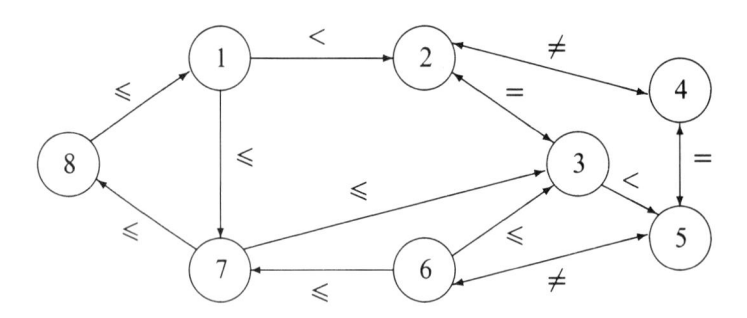

Fig. 4. Example PA network.

and only if they are necessarily equal. It turns out that the vertices v and w are necessarily equal precisely when there is a cycle of the form,

$$v \leqslant \cdots \leqslant w \leqslant \cdots \leqslant v,$$

where one or more of the $\leqslant$ can be $=$ (see Appendix A for a proof). This is the same as saying v and w are in the same equivalence class if and only if there is a path from v to w and a path from w to v using only the edges labeled with $\leqslant$ or $=$. This is a well-known problem in graph theory. Determining the equivalence classes is the same as identifying the strongly connected components (SCCs) of the graph and an efficient $O(n^2)$ algorithm is known (Tarjan [36]).

We condense the graph by collapsing each strongly connected component into a single vertex. Let $\{S_1, S_2, \ldots, S_m\}$ be the SCCs we have found. The S_i partition the vertices in the graph in that each vertex is in one and only one of the S_i. We construct the condensed graph and its matrix representation, $\hat{C}$, as follows. Each S_i is a vertex in the graph. The labels on the edges between all pairs of vertices is given by,

$$\hat{C}_{S_i S_j} \leftarrow \bigcap_{\substack{v \in S_i \\ w \in S_j}} C_{vw}, \quad i, j = 1, \ldots, m.$$

Example 3.1. The network shown in Fig. 4 is used to illustrate the discussion. As usual, all edges (i, i) and all edges labeled ? are omitted. The four strongly connected components, S_1, S_2, S_3, and S_4, of the network are as shown in Fig. 5(a). The condensed graph of the network of Fig. 4 is shown in Fig. 5(b). To illustrate, condensing the strongly connected component S_1 gives,

$$\hat{C}_{S_1 S_1} \leftarrow C_{17} \cap C_{18} \cap C_{71} \cap C_{78} \cap C_{81} \cap C_{87}$$

(a) Strongly connected components:

$S_1 = \{1, 7, 8\}$, $S_3 = \{4, 5\}$,
$S_2 = \{2, 3\}$, $S_4 = \{6\}$.

(b) Condensed PA network:

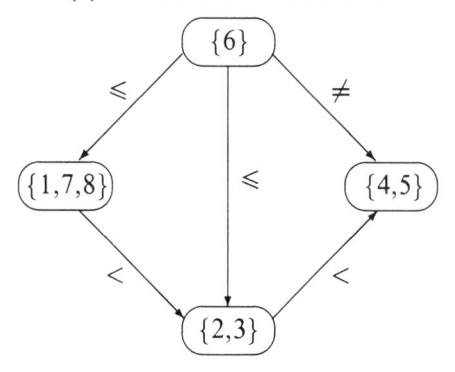

```
           {6}
          / | \
         ≤  |  ≠
        /   ≤   \
   {1,7,8}  |   {4,5}
        \   |   /
         <  |  <
          \ | /
          {2,3}
```

Fig. 5. Condensing the strongly connected components.

$$\leftarrow \{<, =\} \cap \{>, =\} \cap \{>, =\} \cap \{<, =\} \cap \{<, =\} \cap \{>, =\}$$
$$\leftarrow \{=\},$$

where we have omitted the self-loops C_{ii} (these loops are always labeled with $\{=\}$ and so do not affect the result). As a further illustration, the labels on the edges between S_2 and S_3 are given by,

$$\hat{C}_{S_2 S_3} \leftarrow C_{24} \cap C_{25} \cap C_{34} \cap C_{35}$$
$$\leftarrow \{<, >\} \cap \{<, =, >\} \cap \{<, =, >\} \cap \{<\}$$
$$\leftarrow \{<\}.$$

The ∅ relation. To rule out the ∅ relation we must determine if the network is inconsistent. It turns out that the network is inconsistent precisely when there is a cycle of the form,

$$v = \cdots = w \neq v,$$

or of the form,

$$v \leq \cdots \leq w \leq \cdots \leq v \neq w,$$

where some or all of the $\leq$ can be $=$, or of the form,

$$v < \cdots < w < \cdots < v,$$

CSPAN(C)

1. Identify the strongly connected components (SCCs) of C using only edges labeled with $\{<\}$, $\{<,=\}$, and $\{=\}$. Let $S_1,\ldots,S_m$ be the SCCs found.
2. **for** $i,j \leftarrow 1,\ldots,m$
3.   **do** $\hat{C}_{S_iS_j} \leftarrow \{<,=,>\}$
4.   **for each** $v \in S_i$, $w \in S_j$
5.   **do** $\hat{C}_{S_iS_j} \leftarrow \hat{C}_{S_iS_j} \cap C_{vw}$
6.   **if** $\hat{C}_{S_iS_j} = \emptyset$
7.   **then return**("Inconsistent network")
8. Replace any remaining $\{<,=\}$ labels in $\hat{C}$ with $\{<\}$.
9. Perform a topological sort using only the edges in $\hat{C}$ labeled with $\{<\}$.

Fig. 6. Consistent scenario algorithm for PA networks.

where all but one of the $<$ can be $\leq$ or $=$ (see Appendix A for a proof). The first two cases are already detected when we identify all pairs of points that are necessarily equal and condense them into one vertex. That is, the inconsistencies are detected when the strongly connected components are condensed. But we can identify the third case simply by also looking at edges labeled with $<$ when identifying the strongly connected components. As before, the inconsistencies are then detected when the strongly connected components are condensed.

Example 3.2. Suppose the label on the edge $(1, 7)$ in the graph shown in Fig. 4 was $<$ instead of the $\leq$ shown. Condensing the strongly connected component S_1 would give,

$$\hat{C}_{S_1S_1} \leftarrow C_{17} \cap C_{18} \cap C_{71} \cap C_{78} \cap C_{81} \cap C_{87}$$
$$\leftarrow \{<\} \cap \{>,=\} \cap \{>\} \cap \{<,=\} \cap \{<,=\} \cap \{>,=\}$$
$$\leftarrow \emptyset,$$

where again we have omitted the self-loops C_{ii}.

The $\leq$ and $\geq$ relations. To remove the $\leq$ relation from the network, we simply change all $\leq$ labels to $<$. This is valid because, assuming that the $\emptyset$ and $=$ relations have been removed, we know that a consistent scenario exists and that no remaining edge is forced to have $=$ as its label in all consistent scenarios. So, for any particular edge labeled with $\leq$ there exists a consistent scenario with $<$ as the singleton label. But, changing a $\leq$ to a

< can only force other labels to become <; it cannot force labels to become =. (Using the terminology of the algorithm in Fig. 6, no new strongly connected components are introduced by this step; hence no new labels are forced to be equal and no new inconsistencies are introduced.) So, after all the changes, a consistent scenario still exists.

The ≠ relation. We can now perform topological sort to find one consistent scenario. It can be shown that, because of the previous steps of the algorithm, the ≠ relations are now handled correctly (and implicitly) by topological sort. The output of topological sort is an assignment of numbers to the vertices that is consistent with the information provided.

Example 3.3. Consider the network shown in Fig. 5(b). Depending on the particular implementation of topological sort, one possible result is that vertex {6} is assigned the number 0, vertex {1, 7, 8} is assigned 1, vertex {2, 3} is assigned 2, and vertex {4, 5} is assigned 3. The consistent scenario of the original network (Fig. 4) is easily recovered from this information.

Theorem 3.4. *Procedure CSPAN correctly finds a consistent scenario of a PA network in $O(n^2)$ time, where n is the number of points.*

Proof. See Appendix A for a detailed proof of correctness. For the time bound, finding the strongly connected components is $O(n^2)$ [36], condensing the graph looks at each edge only once, and topological sort is $O(n^2)$ [21]. □

We can find a consistent scenario of an SA network by first translating it into a PA network and using algorithm CSPAN to find a consistent instantiation. The consistent instantiation of the PA network also gives a consistent instantiation of the original SA network and hence also defines a consistent scenario of the original SA network. Each of the steps of (i) recognizing that an IA network is the special case of an SA network, (ii) translating it into a PA network, and (iii) finding a consistent scenario, can be done in $O(n^2)$ time.

Example 3.5. Consider the (small) SA subnetwork shown in Fig. 2(a) consisting of "paper {o, s, d} coffee" and its translation into a PA network shown in Fig. 3(a). One consistent instantiation of the corresponding PA network is the assignments, paper$^-$ ← 1, coffee$^-$ ← 2, paper$^+$ ← 3, and coffee$^+$ ← 4. The corresponding consistent instantiation of the original SA network is simply, paper ← (1, 3) and coffee ← (2, 4), and the consistent scenario is given by, "paper {o} coffee".

To summarize, if our temporal networks are PA networks or SA networks we can find a consistent scenario quickly using algorithm CSPAN.

3.2. Finding the feasible relations

3.2.1. Related work

Allen [2] shows that a path consistency algorithm [24,27] can be used to find an approximation to the sets of all feasible relations (see Fig. 8; the path consistency procedure shown there is due to Mackworth [24] but is slightly simplified because of properties of the algebras). Path consistency algorithms, as their name suggests, ensure that a network is path-consistent. A network is *path-consistent* [24] if and only if, for every triple (i,k,j) of vertices,

$$\forall x_i \forall x_j [(x_i, x_j) \in C_{ij} \Rightarrow$$
$$\exists x_k (x_k \in D_k \wedge (x_i, x_k) \in C_{ik} \wedge (x_k, x_j) \in C_{kj})].$$

In words, for every instantiation of x_i and x_j that satisfies the direct relation, C_{ij}, there exists an instantiation of x_k such that C_{ik} and C_{kj} are also satisfied. To use the path consistency algorithm, we need the operators composition and intersection of relations (see [2,41] for discussions of how the operations are implemented in this context).

Previous work has identified classes of relations for which the path consistency algorithm will find the minimal network. Montanari [27] shows that the path consistency algorithm finds the minimal network for a restricted class of binary constraint relations. However, the relations of interest here do not all fall into this class. Valdés-Pérez [37] shows that the path consistency algorithm finds the minimal network for IA networks which use only the basic interval relations. In [38,40], we show that the path consistency algorithm finds the sets of feasible relations for the subclass of PA networks that do not contain the $\neq$ relation, and for a corresponding subclass of SA networks. But we also give examples there that show that, earlier claims to the contrary, the path consistency algorithm is not sufficient for finding the minimal network for general PA networks nor for general SA networks and we develop an $O(n^4)$ consistency algorithm that is sufficient, where n is the number of intervals or points.

3.2.2. An improved algorithm.

Here we give an $O(\max(mn^2, n^3))$-time algorithm for finding all feasible relations, where n is the number of points and m is the number of pairs of points that are asserted to be not equal. The algorithm is of far more practical use than our previous algorithm (that algorithm is still of importance as an approximation algorithm for instances of the problem from the full interval algebra; see [38,40] for the details).

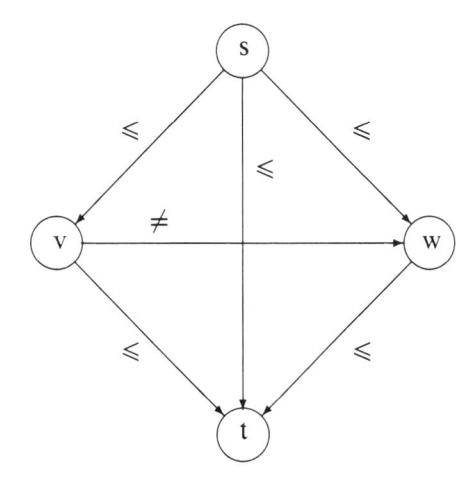

Fig. 7. "Forbidden" subgraph.

Our strategy for developing an algorithm for PA networks is to first identify why path consistency is sufficient if we exclude ≠ from the language and is not sufficient if we include ≠. Figure 7 gives the smallest counter-example showing that the path consistency algorithm does not correctly determine the minimal network representation of all PA networks. The network is path-consistent. But it is easy to see that not every basic relation in the label between s and t is feasible. In particular, asserting $s = t$ forces v and w to also be equal to s and t. But this is inconsistent with $v \neq w$. Hence, the = relation is not feasible as it is not capable of being part of a consistent scenario. The label between s and t should be <.

This is one counter-example of four vertices. But are there other counter-examples for $n \geq 4$? The following theorem answers this question and is the basis of an algorithm for finding all feasible relations for PA networks.

Theorem 3.6 (van Beek and Cohen [40]). *Any path-consistent PA network which is not the minimal network, has a subgraph of four vertices isomorphic to the network in Fig. 7.*

The counter-example then is unique, up to isomorphism, if the network is path-consistent. This leads to the following algorithm. We solve an instance of the feasible relations problem by first applying the path consistency algorithm and then systematically searching for "forbidden" subgraphs and appropriately changing the labels. The algorithm is shown in Fig. 8. The input to the algorithm is a PA network represented as an adjacency matrix C where element C_{ij} is the label on edge (i, j). The algorithm also makes use of adjacency lists. For example, $\text{adj}_\leq (v)$ is the list of all vertices, w, for which there is an edge from v to w that is labeled with "≤".

FEASIBLE(C)

1. PATH-CONSISTENCY(C)
2. FIND-SUBGRAPHS(C)

PATH-CONSISTENCY(C)

1. $Q \leftarrow \bigcup_{1 \leq i < j \leq n}$ RELATED-PATHS(i, j)
2. **while** (Q is not empty)
3.   **do** select and delete a path (i, k, j) from Q
4. $t \leftarrow C_{ij} \cap C_{ik} \cdot C_{kj}$
5.   **if** ($t \neq C_{ij}$)
6.   **then** $C_{ij} \leftarrow t$
7. $C_{ji} \leftarrow$ INVERSE(t)
8. $Q \leftarrow Q \cup$ RELATED-PATHS(i, j)

RELATED-PATHS(i, j)

1. **return** $\{(i, j, k), (k, i, j) \mid 1 \leq k \leq n, k \neq i, k \neq j\}$

FIND-SUBGRAPHS(C)

1. **for** each edge (v, w) such that $w \in \text{adj}_{\neq}(v)$
2.   **do** $S \leftarrow (\text{adj}_{\geq}(v) \cap \text{adj}_{\geq}(w))$
3. $T \leftarrow (\text{adj}_{\leq}(v) \cap \text{adj}_{\leq}(w))$
4.   **for** each $s \in S, t \in T$
5.   **do** $C_{st} \leftarrow$ "<"
6. $C_{ts} \leftarrow$ ">"

Fig. 8. Feasible relations algorithm for PA networks.

Changing the label on some edge (s, t) from "$\leq$" to "<" may further constrain labels on other edges. The question immediately arises of whether we need to again apply the path consistency algorithm following our search for "forbidden" subgraphs to propagate the newly changed labels? Fortunately, the answer is no. Given a new label on an edge (s, t), if we were to apply the path consistency algorithm, the set of triples of vertices that would be examined is given by

$$\{(s, t, k), (k, s, t) \mid 1 \leq k \leq n, k \neq s, k \neq t\}$$

(see RELATED-PATHS in Fig. 8). Thus there are two cases. For both, we can show that any changes that a second application of the path consistency algorithm would make will already have been made by procedure FIND-SUBGRAPHS.

Case 1: (s,t,k). Changing the label on the edge (s,t) from "$\leq$" to "$<$" would cause the path consistency algorithm to change the label on the edge (s,k) only in two cases:

- $s \leq t$, $t \leq k$, and $s \leq k$,
- $s \leq t$, $t = k$, and $s \leq k$.

In both, the label on (s,k) will become "$<$". For (s,t) to change we must have the situation depicted in Fig. 7, for some v and w. But $v \leq t$ and $w \leq t$ together with $t \leq k$ (or $t = k$) imply that $v \leq k$ and $w \leq k$ (we can assume the relations were propagated because we applied the path consistency algorithm before the procedure for finding "forbidden" subgraphs). Hence, (s,k) also belongs to a "forbidden" subgraph and the label on that edge will have been found and updated.

Case 2: (k,s,t). Similar argument as Case 1.

Theorem 3.7. *Procedure* FEASIBLE *correctly finds the feasible relations between all pairs of points when applied to PA networks and requires* $O(\max(mn^2, n^3))$ *time, where m is the number of edges labeled with "$\neq$" and n is the number of points.*

Proof. Let P, M, and S be the propositions that "the network is path-consistent", "the network is not the minimal network", and "the network contains a "forbidden" subgraph", respectively. By Theorem 3.6 we have, $P \wedge \neg M \Rightarrow S$. Taking the contrapositive gives, $\neg S \Rightarrow \neg P \vee M$. But the algorithm removes all "forbidden" subgraphs, so $\neg S$ is true, and, by the case analysis above, the network remains path-consistent, so $\neg P$ is false. Hence, the network is the minimal network. For the time bound, the path consistency procedure is $O(n^3)$, where n is the number of points [25]. The FIND-SUBGRAPHS procedure can be seen to be $O(mn^2)$, where m is the number of edges labeled with "$\neq$". Hence the overall algorithm is $O(\max(mn^2, n^3))$. □

We can find all pairs of feasible relations of an SA network by first translating it into a PA network, applying algorithm FEASIBLE to the PA network, and translating the result back into an SA network. For many applications of SA networks in the literature, the translation into a PA network results in a network with few or no $\neq$ relations between points. Thus, a desirable feature of procedure FIND-SUBGRAPHS is that its cost is proportional to the number of edges labeled "$\neq$".

To summarize, if our temporal networks are PA networks or SA networks we can find all pairs of feasible relations quickly using algorithm FEASIBLE.

4. Interval algebra networks

In this section we examine the computational problems of finding consistent scenarios and finding the feasible relations of IA networks.

4.1. Finding a consistent scenario

4.1.1. Related work

Vilain and Kautz [41,42] show that finding a consistent scenario is NP-complete for IA networks. Thus the worst cases of the algorithms that we devise will be exponential and the best we can hope for is that the algorithms are still useful in practice. We discuss below to what extent this is achieved.

In the previous section we found a consistent scenario by first finding a consistent instantiation. An alternative method is as follows. Recall that a network S is a *consistent scenario* of a network C if and only if

(a) $S_{ij} \subseteq C_{ij}$,
(b) $|S_{ij}| = 1$, for all i, j, and
(c) there exists a consistent instantiation of S.

To find a consistent scenario we simply search through the different possible S's that satisfy conditions (a) and (b)—it is a simple matter to enumerate them—until we find one that also satisfies condition (c). Allen [2] was the first to propose using backtracking search to search through the potential S's. In this formulation of the problem the variables represent the relations between intervals, the domains of the variables are the set of basic interval relations, and the ternary constraints preclude certain combinations of relationships between three intervals. Note, however, that if the problem size is n in the original formulation, it is now n^2 in this alternative formulation.

There has been much work on improving the performance of backtracking that could be (or has been) adapted to this problem. This work can be classified according to the following four general considerations when designing a backtracking algorithm for a particular application [10]:

(1) What kind of preprocessing to do (e.g. [11,19]). For finding a consistent scenario, Reinefeld and Ladkin [33] give the results of extensive computational experiments characterizing how effective path consistency is in pruning as a preprocessing step before backtracking search.
(2) Which variable to instantiate next (e.g. [30,32]).
(3) Which instantiation to give the variable (e.g. [19,28]). For general constraint networks, Haralick and Elliott [19] propose a technique called forward checking where it is determined and recorded how the instantiation of the current variable restricts the possible instantiations of future variables. This technique can be viewed as a hybrid of tree search and consistency algorithms (see [30]). For finding

a consistent scenario, Reinefeld and Ladkin [33] give an algorithm that interleaves path consistency and backtracking search in the style of forward checking.

(4) How to handle backtracking (e.g. [9,15]). In chronological backtracking, when a dead end occurs in the search, the algorithm backs up to the last variable instantiated. For general constraint networks, Gaschnig [15] proposes backjumping as an improvement where the idea is to try and back up further to the source of the problem. For finding a consistent scenario, Valdés-Pérez [37] gives a backtracking algorithm in the style of backjumping.

4.1.2. Improving the algorithms

Here we show how the results for SA networks can be used to improve the performance of backtracking algorithms for finding a consistent scenario. We then design a backtracking algorithm modeled on that of Reinefeld and Ladkin [33] and present the results of experiments comparing the performance of the two algorithms on random problems drawn from two different distributions. Based on the experimental evidence, we postulate that the algorithm is useful in practice, in particular for planning problems and problems with similar characteristics.

Our proposal for improving the backtracking algorithms is the following. Rather than search directly for a consistent scenario of an IA network, as in previous work, we first search for something more general: a consistent SA subnetwork of the IA network. That is, we use backtrack search to find a subnetwork S of a network C such that,

(a) $S_{ij} \subseteq C_{ij}$,
(b) S_{ij} is an allowed relation for SA networks, for all i, j, and
(c) there exists a consistent instantiation of S.

In previous work, the search is through the alternative singleton labelings of an edge, i.e., $|S_{ij}| = 1$. The key idea in our proposal is that we decompose the labels into the largest possible sets of basic relations that are allowed for SA networks and search through these decompositions. This can considerably reduce the size of the search space. An example will clarify this. Suppose the label on an edge is {b, bi, m, o, oi, si}. There are six possible ways to label the edge with a singleton label: {b}, {bi}, {m}, {o}, {oi}, {si}, but only two possible ways to label the edge if we decompose the labels into the largest possible sets of basic relations that are allowed for SA networks: {b, m, o} and {bi, oi, si}.

Example 4.1. Consider the network shown in Fig. 9. For illustration purposes only, suppose that we perform naive backtrack search (chronological backtracking and no forward checking) to find a consistent scenario and

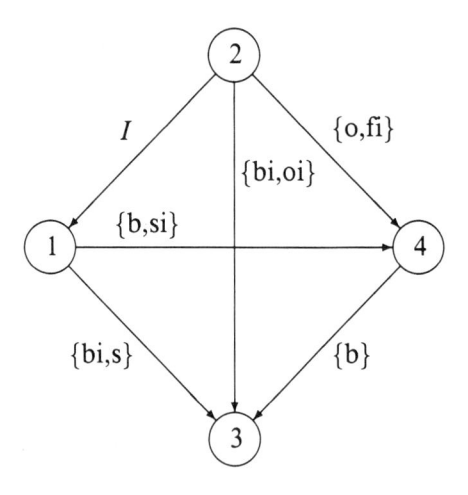

Fig. 9. Example IA network. $I = \{b, bi, m, mi, o, oi, s, si, d, di, f, fi, eq\}$.

that the search looks at the edges in the order (1,2), (1,3), (2,3), (1,4), (2,4), and (3,4). Figure 10 shows a record of the search for both methods. Moving to the right and downward in the figure means a partial solution is being extended, moving to the left and downward means the search is backtracking. In this example, when searching through alternative singleton labelings, much search is done before it is discovered that no consistent scenario exists with edge (1,2) labeled with {eq}, but when decomposing the labels into the largest possible sets of basic relations that are allowed for SA networks and searching through the decompositions, no backtracking is necessary (in general, the search is, of course, not always backtrack-free).

To test whether an instantiation of a variable is consistent with instantiations of past variables and with possible instantiations of future variables, we can either (i) translate the SA network into an equivalent PA network and use the $O(n^2)$ decision portion of procedure CSPAN (Steps 1–7 of Fig. 6), or (ii) use a path consistency algorithm. Finally, the result of the backtracking algorithm is a consistent SA subnetwork of the IA network (or a report that the IA network is inconsistent). After backtracking completes, the resulting SA network is translated into a PA network and then passed to algorithm CSPAN to find a consistent scenario of this network and, hence, a consistent scenario of the original IA network. A schema of the algorithm is shown in Fig. 11.

4.1.3. Experiments

We tested our ideas experimentally. For the purposes of the experiments we must make procedure CSIAN concrete by specifying a backtracking

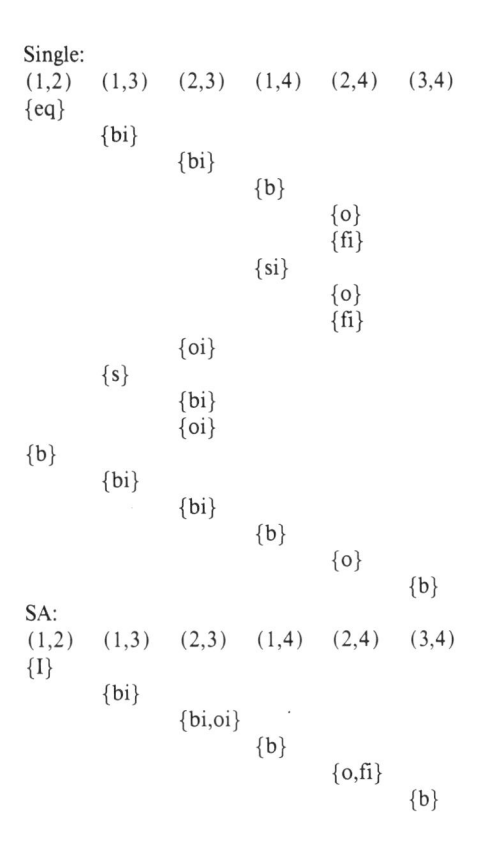

Single:
(1,2)	(1,3)	(2,3)	(1,4)	(2,4)	(3,4)
{eq}					
	{bi}				
		{bi}			
			{b}		
				{o}	
				{fi}	
		{si}			
				{o}	
				{fi}	
		{oi}			
	{s}				
		{bi}			
		{oi}			
{b}					
	{bi}				
		{bi}			
			{b}		
				{o}	
					{b}

SA:
(1,2)	(1,3)	(2,3)	(1,4)	(2,4)	(3,4)
{I}					
	{bi}				
		{bi,oi}			
			{b}		
				{o,fi}	
					{b}

Fig. 10. Record of backtrack search using naive backtracking.

procedure. We chose to model our algorithm after that of Reinefeld and Ladkin [33] as the results of their experimentation suggests that it is very successful at finding consistent scenarios quickly. Following Reinefeld and Ladkin our algorithm has the following characteristics: path consistency preprocessing, randomly chosen static order of instantiation of the variables, chronological backtracking, and forward checking or pruning using path consistency.

We randomly generated IA networks of size n as follows. We first generated

---

CSIAN(C)

1. Find a consistent SA subnetwork, S, of the IA network, C, using backtrack search.
2. Translate SA network, S, into PA network, P.
3. CSPAN(P)

Fig. 11. Schema of a consistent scenario algorithm for IA networks.

an "instantiation" by randomly generating values for the end points of n intervals. This was turned into a consistent scenario by determining the basic relations which were satisfied by the instantiation. Finally, we then added indefiniteness to the relations between intervals by adding basic relations.

All experiments were performed on a Sun 4/25 with 8 megabytes of memory. We implemented two versions of the algorithm that were identical except that one searched through the decompositions of the labels into the largest possible allowed relations for SA networks and the other searched through the decompositions of the labels into singleton labelings. The results are divided according to how the indefiniteness was randomly generated. Table 1 shows the results for random instances from a distribution designed to approximate planning applications (as estimated from a block-stacking in [4]; in planning, as formulated by Allen and Koomen [4], finding a consistent scenario corresponds to finding an ordering of the actions that will accomplish a goal). In this distribution, approximately 75% of the edges are labeled with I—meaning there is no constraint between the intervals, and the remaining edges have between 0 and 3 basic relations added as indefiniteness. For the results in Table 2, all subsets of I are equally likely to be added as indefiniteness to an edge. The timings do not include preprocessing time, as this was common to both methods, or the additional time for steps 2 and 3 of CSIAN. However, this additional cost is small (for example, for $n = 100$, it takes about 0.15 seconds). For these two distributions, the experiments suggest that decomposing into "larger" relations improves the performance of backtracking search, sometimes by a factor of almost 3. The experiments also provide additional evidence for

Table 1
Solving random instances of consistent IA networks from a distribution designed to model instances that arise in planning; 1000 tests for each n.

	SA		Single	
n	pc. calls	time (sec.)	pc. calls	time (sec.)
10	6.4	0.01	8.8	0.01
20	16.6	0.06	20.1	0.08
30	23.7	0.17	31.3	0.24
40	28.5	0.34	42.1	0.50
50	30.8	0.54	52.6	0.88
60	31.7	0.78	62.5	1.42
70	31.6	1.06	71.9	2.11
80	30.8	1.32	80.3	2.99
90	29.4	1.60	88.1	4.05
100	28.1	1.89	95.9	5.36

Table 2
Solving random instances of consistent IA networks from a distribution where all labels are added with equal likelihood; 1000 tests for each n.

n	SA pc. calls	SA time (sec.)	Single pc. calls	Single time (sec.)
10	13.3	0.02	9.9	0.02
20	30.3	0.21	96.2	0.45
30	84.8	0.88[a]	129.1	1.32[b]
40	67.9	0.85	41.6	0.49
50	27.5	0.49	52.9	0.82
60	22.9	0.57	50.6	0.96
70	20.5	0.70	54.9	1.38
80	17.8	0.82	57.7	1.87
90	15.3	0.93	59.9	2.44
100	13.8	1.07	61.5	3.08

[a] 1 test omitted as the 10^5 limit on the number of path consistency calls was exceeded.

[b] 4 tests omitted as the 10^5 limit on the number of path consistency calls was exceeded.

the efficacy of Reinefeld and Ladkin's algorithm.

To summarize, if our representation language is IA networks, we can use algorithm CSIAN, which is exponential in the worst case, to find a consistent scenario. One bright spot is that the algorithm seems to work well in practice for problems that arise in planning. The algorithm should work similarly well on any problem with the characteristics of a planning problem. The characteristics are: We do not have direct knowledge of the relations between most intervals and few of the relations are disallowed relations for SA networks. We remark that it is a simple matter to have a procedure that determines whether an IA network is also the special case of an SA network and then, depending on the outcome, calls either CSPAN or CSIAN to find a consistent scenario. This has the twofold advantage that the choice of algorithm can be hidden from the user and that no commitment need be made at the outset by the user to restrict the representation language (the more expensive CSIAN algorithm can simply be used as needed).

4.2. Finding the feasible relations

Vilain and Kautz [41,42] show that finding the feasible relations is NP-complete for IA networks. Freuder [14] and Seidel [34] give algorithms that find *all* consistent instantiations of a general constraint network. Hence, their algorithms can be used for finding the feasible relations. A difficulty is that both algorithms require the domains of the variables to be finite but IA networks have infinite domains. However, we can again reformulate the feasible relations problem as a network of ternary constraints with finite domains: the variables represent the relations between intervals, the domains of the variables are the set of basic interval relations, and the ternary constraints preclude certain combinations of relationships between three intervals. Seidel's algorithm [34] is useful for sparse constraint networks but here the networks are dense, there being a ternary constraint for every combination of three variables. For the problems of interest here, both algorithms appear to be practical only for small instances of the problem.

A backtracking algorithm similar to the one given in the previous section can be designed for finding all the feasible relations. Again, instead of searching through the alternative singleton labelings of the edges, we decompose the labels into the largest possible sets of basic relations allowed for SA networks and search through the decompositions. In the previous section when finding a consistent scenario we stopped the backtracking algorithm after one consistent SA network was found. To determine the feasible relations we must find all such consistent SA networks. For each such consistent SA network we find the feasible relations using the algorithm of Fig. 8. The feasible relations for the IA network are then just the union of all such solutions. Initial experience, however, suggests this method is practical only for small instances of the problem, or for instances where only a few of the relations between intervals fall outside of the allowed relations for SA networks. We conclude that in most cases a better approach is to, if possible, accept approximate solutions to the problem [2,40].

5. Conclusions

Allen [2] and Vilain and Kautz [41] give frameworks for representing and reasoning about qualitative temporal information. We looked at two reasoning tasks that arise in applications of these frameworks: Given possibly indefinite and incomplete knowledge of the relationships between some intervals or points, (i) find a scenario that is consistent with the information provided, and (ii) find the feasible relations between all pairs of intervals or points.

For finding one consistent scenario, we give an $O(n^2)$-time algorithm for PA and SA networks. The algorithm is an $O(n)$ improvement over the previously known algorithm. The results for the point algebra are shown to aid in the design of a backtracking algorithm for IA networks. The backtracking algorithm is shown experimentally to be useful for planning problems. For finding the feasible relations, we give an algorithm for PA and SA networks that is of more practical use than the previously known algorithm.

The algorithms are of importance as the reasoning tasks arise in such diverse applications as natural language processing, plan recognition, planning, and diagnosis and within these applications the reasoning tasks often need to be solved repeatedly. As well, in related work we show how the algorithms can be used in answering a broader range of query types, including (i) determining whether a formula involving temporal relations between events is possibly true and necessarily true; and (ii) answering aggregation questions where the set of all events that satisfy a formula are retrieved [39].

Appendix A.

In this appendix we prove Theorem 3.4 by showing statements (a) and (b) below. The rest of the algorithm is justified by the discussion in the text of Section 3.1.

(a) The vertices v and w are necessarily equal if and only if there is a cycle of the form,

$$v \leqslant \cdots \leqslant w \leqslant \cdots \leqslant v, \tag{A.1}$$

where one or more of the $\leqslant$ can be $=$.

(b) The network is inconsistent if and only if there is a cycle of the form,

$$v = \cdots = w \neq v, \tag{A.2}$$

or of the form,

$$v \leqslant \cdots \leqslant w \leqslant \cdots \leqslant v \neq w, \tag{A.3}$$

where some or all of the $\leqslant$ can be $=$, or of the form,

$$v < \cdots < w < \cdots < v, \tag{A.4}$$

where all but one of the $<$ can be $\leqslant$ or $=$.

Let M be the minimal network representation of a PA network. The idea behind the proof is that by Theorems 3.6 and 3.7, the path consistency algorithm correctly determines M_{ij} if M_{ij} is one of $\{\emptyset, <, =, >, \neq, ?\}$. That is, the path consistency algorithm correctly determines, in particular, whether a PA network is inconsistent (this was first proved in [23]) and whether two vertices are necessarily equal. Thus, we need to look at only the paths between vertices to prove statements (a) and (b).

Composition of two relations:

·	=	<	⩽	>	⩾	≠
=	=	<	⩽	>	⩾	≠
<	<	<	<	?	?	?
⩽	⩽	<	⩽	?	?	?
>	>	?	?	>	>	?
⩾	⩾	?	?	>	⩾	?
≠	≠	?	?	?	?	?

Intersection of two relations:

∩	=	<	⩽	>	⩾	≠
=	=	∅	=	∅	=	∅
<	∅	<	<	∅	∅	<
⩽	=	<	⩽	∅	=	<
>	∅	∅	∅	>	>	>
⩾	=	∅	=	>	⩾	>
≠	∅	<	<	>	>	≠

Fig. A.1. Point algebra operations (Vilain and Kautz [41]).

To make the argument precise, we first give some notation. Let $P = (v, x_1), (x_1, x_2), \ldots, (x_m, w)$ be a path (possibly containing cycles) from vertex v to vertex w in a PA network. Let the *label of a path*, denoted $l(P)$, be the composition of the labels of the edges in the path, taken in order (see Fig. A.1 for the composition table). For example, with reference to Fig. 4, let P be the path $(1, 2), (2, 3), (3, 5), (5, 4)$; the label of the path P is $< \cdot = \cdot < \cdot =$, which is simply $<$. Let $i(v, w)$ be defined as the intersection of the labels of all the paths from v to w. Montanari ([27, p. 113]; see also [24, p. 111] and [1, p. 198]) shows that the path consistency algorithm computes $i(v, w)$, for each pair of vertices (v, w). Therefore, since the path consistency algorithm correctly determines whether a PA network is inconsistent and whether two vertices are necessarily equal, it is sufficient to look at the intersection of the labels of the paths between two vertices to prove statements (a) and (b).

For vertices v and w to be necessarily equal (i.e., $i(v, w) = $ "="), there must exist paths P_i and P_j from v to w such that the intersection of the labels of these paths is the $=$ relation. The following table gives all the possibilities.

	(1)	(2)	(3)	(4)
$l(P_i)$	⩽	⩾	⩽	=
$l(P_j)$	=	=	⩾	

By examination of the composition table for the point algebra (Fig. A.1) it can be seen that these four cases arise only when there is a cycle of the form (A.1).

For the network to be inconsistent (i.e., $i(v, w) = \emptyset$), there must exist paths P_i, P_j, and P_k from v to w such that the intersection of the labels of these paths is the empty set. The following table gives all the possibilities.

	(1)	(2)	(3)	(4)	(5)	(6)	(7)
$l(P_i)$	$\leq$	$<$	$\leq$	$\geq$	$=$	$=$	$=$
$l(P_j)$	$\geq$	$>$	$>$	$<$	$<$	$>$	$\neq$
$l(P_k)$	$\neq$						

By examination of the composition table for the point algebra (Fig. A.1) it can be seen that case (1) arises only when there is a cycle of the form (A.3), cases (2)–(6) arise only when there is a cycle of the form (A.4), and case (7) arises only when there is a cycle of the form in (A.2). □

Acknowledgement

I wish to thank Robin Cohen and Peter Ladkin for many helpful comments and discussions on this work. Financial support is acknowledged from the Natural Sciences and Engineering Research Council of Canada.

References

[1] A.V. Aho, J.E. Hopcroft and J.D. Ullman, *The Design and Analysis of Computer Algorithms* (Addison-Wesley, Reading, MA, 1974).
[2] J.F. Allen, Maintaining knowledge about temporal intervals, *Commun. ACM* **26** (1983) 832–843.
[3] J.F. Allen, Towards a general theory of action and time, *Artif. Intell.* **23** (1984) 123–154.
[4] J.F. Allen and J.A. Koomen, Planning using a temporal world model, in: *Proceedings IJCAI-83*, Karlsruhe, Germany (1983) 741–747.
[5] M.J. Almeida, Reasoning about the temporal structure of narrative, Ph.D. Thesis, Tech. Rept. 87-10, Department of Computer Science, State University of New York at Buffalo (1987).
[6] B.C. Bruce, A model for temporal references and its application in a question answering program, *Artif. Intell.* **3** (1972) 1–25.
[7] V. Chvátal, *Linear Programming* (Freeman, San Francisco, CA, 1983).
[8] T.L. Dean and D.V. McDermott, Temporal data base management, *Artif. Intell.* **32** (1987) 1–55.
[9] R. Dechter, Enhancement schemes for constraint processing: backjumping, learning and cutset decomposition, *Artif. Intell.* **41** (1990) 273–312.
[10] R. Dechter, Constraint networks, in: *Encyclopedia of Artificial Intelligence* (Wiley, Chicester, UK, 2nd ed., 1992) 276–285.
[11] R. Dechter and I. Meiri, Experimental evaluation of preprocessing techniques in constraint satisfaction problems, in: *Proceedings IJCAI-89*, Detroit, MI (1989) 271–277.
[12] R. Dechter, I. Meiri and J. Pearl, Temporal constraint networks, *Artif. Intell.* **49** (1991) 61–95.
[13] E.W. Dijkstra, A note on two problems in connexion with graphs, *Numer. Math.* **1** (1959) 269–271.
[14] E.C. Freuder, Synthesizing constraint expressions, *Commun. ACM* **21** (1978) 958–966.
[15] J. Gaschnig, Experimental case studies of backtrack vs. Waltz-type vs. new algorithms for satisficing assignment problems, in: *Proceedings Second Biennial Conference of the Canadian Society for Computational Studies of Intelligence*, Toronto, Ont. (1978) 268–277.

[16] M.C. Golumbic, *Algorithmic Graph Theory and Perfect Graphs* (Academic Press, New York, 1980).
[17] S. Güther, Zur Repräsentation temporaler Beziehungen in SRL, KIT Report 69, Fachbereich Informatik, Technische Universität, Berlin, Germany (1984).
[18] I. Hamlet and J. Hunter, A representation of time for medical expert systems, in: Lecture Notes in Medical Informatics **33** (Springer, Berlin, 1987) 112–119.
[19] R.M. Haralick and G.L. Elliott, Increasing tree search efficiency for constraint satisfaction problems, *Artif. Intell.* **14** (1980) 263–313.
[20] H.A. Kautz, A formal theory of plan recognition, Ph.D. Thesis, Tech. Rept. 215, Department of Computer Science, University of Rochester, Rochester, NY (1987).
[21] D.E. Knuth, *The Art of Computer Programming, Vol. 1: Fundamental Algorithms* (Addison-Wesley, Reading, MA, 1973).
[22] P.B. Ladkin and R. Maddux, The algebra of constraint satisfaction problems and temporal reasoning, Tech. Rept., Kestrel Institute, Palo Alto, CA (1988).
[23] P.B. Ladkin and R. Maddux, On binary constraint networks, Tech. Rept., Kestrel Institute, Palo Alto, CA (1988).
[24] A.K. Mackworth, Consistency in networks of relations, *Artif. Intell.* **8** (1977) 99–118.
[25] A.K. Mackworth and E.C. Freuder, The complexity of some polynomial network consistency algorithms for constraint satisfaction problems, *Artif. Intell.* **25** (1985) 65–74.
[26] J. Malik and T.O. Binford, Reasoning in time and space, in: *Proceedings IJCAI-83* Karlsruhe, Germany (1983) 343–345.
[27] U. Montanari, Networks of constraints: fundamental properties and applications to picture processing, *Inf. Sci.* **7** (1974) 95–132.
[28] B.A. Nadel, Constraint satisfaction algorithms, *Comput. Intell.* **5** (1989) 188–224.
[29] K. Nökel, Temporal matching: recognizing dynamic situations from discrete measurements, in: *Proceedings IJCAI-89*, Detroit, MI (1989) 1255–1260.
[30] B. Nudel, Consistent-labeling problems and their algorithms: expected-complexities and theory-based heuristics, *Artif. Intell.* **21** (1983) 135–178.
[31] C.H. Papadimitriou and K. Steiglitz, *Combinatorial Optimization: Algorithms and Complexity* (Prentice-Hall, Englewood Cliffs, NJ, 1982).
[32] P.W. Purdom Jr, Search rearrangement backtracking and polynomial average time, *Artif. Intell.* **21** (1983) 117–133.
[33] A. Reinefeld and P.B. Ladkin, Fast solution of large interval constraint networks, in: *Proceedings Ninth Biennial Conference of the Canadian Society for Computational Studies of Intelligence*, Vancouver, BC (1992).
[34] R. Seidel, A new method for solving constraint satisfaction problems, in: *Proceedings IJCAI-81* Vancouver, BC (1981) 338–342.
[35] F. Song and R. Cohen, The interpretation of temporal relations in narrative, in: *Proceedings AAAI-88*, St. Paul, MN (1988) 745–750.
[36] R.E. Tarjan, Depth-first search and linear graph algorithms, *SIAM J. Comput.* **1** (1972) 745–750.
[37] R.E. Valdés-Pérez, The satisfiability of temporal constraint networks, in: *Proceedings AAAI-87*, Seattle, WA (1987) 745–750.
[38] P. van Beek, Approximation algorithms for temporal reasoning, in: *Proceedings IJCAI-89*, Detroit, MI (1989) 745–750.
[39] P. van Beek, Temporal query processing with indefinite information, *Artif. Intell. Med.*, **3** (1991) 745–750. (Special Issue on Temporal Reasoning).
[40] P. van Beek and R. Cohen, Exact and approximate reasoning about temporal relations, *Comput. Intell.* **6** (1990) 132–144,.
[41] M. Vilain and H.A. Kautz, Constraint propagation algorithms for temporal reasoning, in: *Proceedings AAAI-86*, Philadelphia, PA (1986) 132–144.
[42] M. Vilain, H.A. Kautz and P. van Beek, Constraint propagation algorithms for temporal reasoning: a revised report, in: D.S. Weld and J. de Kleer, eds., *Readings in Qualitative Reasoning about Physical Systems* (Morgan Kaufmann, San Mateo, CA, 1989) 373–381.

A geometric constraint engine

Glenn A. Kramer

Schlumberger Laboratory for Computer Science, 8311 RR 620 North, P.O. Box 200015, Austin, TX 78720-0015, USA

Abstract

Kramer, G.A., A geometric constraint engine, Artificial Intelligence 58 (1992) 327–360.

This paper describes a geometric constraint engine for finding the configurations of a collection of geometric entities that satisfy a set of geometric constraints. This task is traditionally performed by reformulating the geometry and constraints as algebraic equations which are then solved symbolically or numerically. Symbolic algebraic solution is NP-complete. Numerical solution methods are characterized by slow runtimes, numerical instabilities, and difficulty in handling redundant constraints. Many geometric constraint problems can be solved by reasoning symbolically about the geometric entities themselves using a new technique called *degrees of freedom analysis*. In this approach, a plan of measurements and actions is devised to satisfy each constraint incrementally, thus monotonically decreasing the system's remaining degrees of freedom. This plan is used to solve, in a maximally decoupled form, the equations resulting from an algebraic representation of the problem. Degrees of freedom analysis results in a polynomial-time, numerically stable algorithm for geometric constraint satisfaction. Empirical comparison with a state-of-the-art numerical solver in the domain of kinematic simulation shows degrees of freedom analysis to be more robust and substantially more efficient.

1. Introduction

Geometric reasoning plays a fundamental role in our understanding of the physical world. An important task in geometric reasoning is the geometric constraint satisfaction problem (GCSP): Given a collection of geometric entities, or *geoms*, and constraints that describe how the geoms interact with each other, find their positions, orientations, and dimensions so as to satisfy all constraints simultaneously. Solving GCSPs is central to several related domains: describing mechanical assemblies, constraint-based sketching and design, geometric modeling for computer-aided design, and kinematic analysis of robots and other mechanisms.

Correspondence to: G.A. Kramer, Schlumberger Laboratory for Computer Science, 8311 RR 620 North, P.O. Box 200015, Austin, TX 78720-0015, USA. Telephone: (512) 331-3715. E-mail: gak@slcs.slb.com.

General-purpose constraint satisfaction techniques are not well suited to the solution of constraint problems involving complicated geometry, for reasons to be explained shortly. This paper describes a novel technique, called *degrees of freedom analysis,* for solving GCSPs. It avoids a number of drawbacks associated with traditional approaches to solving GCSPs. Degrees of freedom analysis borrows from techniques originally developed for the analysis and synthesis of mechanical devices [6]. These techniques have been formalized and generalized so that they apply to a wider class of geometric constraint satisfaction problems.

Existing programs which solve GCSPs represent geoms and constraints as algebraic equations, whose real solutions yield the numerical values describing the positions, orientations, and dimensions of the geoms. Such equation sets are highly nonlinear and highly coupled, and in the general case require iterative numerical solution techniques. Iterative numerical programs are not particularly efficient, and can have problems with stability and robustness [18]. For many tasks (e.g., simulation and optimization of mechanical devices) the same equations are solved repeatedly, which makes a "hard-wired", or compiled, solution desirable.

In theory, symbolic analysis of the equations can often yield a non-iterative, closed-form solution, or can help reduce the number of redundant generalized coordinates in an iterative problem. Once found and compiled, such a closed-form solution may be executed in time nearly linearly proportional to the size of the constraint problem. However, the computational intractability of symbolic algebraic solution of the equations renders this approach impractical [11].

Degrees of freedom analysis solves GCSPs by reasoning symbolically about geometry, rather than equations, leading to more efficient algorithms. Degrees of freedom analysis uses two models of a constraint problem: a symbolic geometric model and a detailed numerical model. The geometric model is used to reason symbolically about how to assemble the geoms so as to satisfy the constraints incrementally. The "assembly plan" thus developed is then used to guide the solution of the complex nonlinear equations—derived from the numerical model—in a highly decoupled, stylized manner. This approach allows finding non-iterative, closed-form solutions to GCSPs whenever possible, and allows formulating iterative problems with a minimal number of redundant generalized coordinates when closed-form solutions do not exist.

Degrees of freedom analysis was developed for analyzing problems of rigid-body kinematics, and was tested with an implemented computer program called The Linkage Assistant (TLA) [9,10]. This paper describes extensions and alterations to degrees of freedom analysis to cover a broader range of geometric entities and constraints. A program called the Geometric Constraint

Engine (GCE) has been developed to test these extensions. All examples in this paper have been solved by GCE.

1.1. Domain

Design and analysis of physical systems often require a representation of the geometry of the system. While some problems such as finite element analysis [5] and design using deformable surfaces [4] are inherently iterative in nature, other problems can, in principle, be treated either entirely or in large part using closed-form solution techniques. In practice, many such problems are still treated iteratively, either due to the complexity of deriving a direct formulation, or due to the use of more general solution techniques that also handle the (possibly small) portions of the problem which require iteration.

Domains such as constraint-based sketching and mechanical part design fall into this latter category. They tend to rely on complex combinations of relatively simple geometric elements, such as points, lines, and circles, and a small collection of constraints such as coincidence, tangency, and parallelism. For example, profile design for mechanical devices involves defining a closed perimeter curve, usually comprised of line segments and arcs, with a set of features, such as holes and slots, in the interior. In three dimensions, collections of simple solids (e.g., spheres, cones, cylinders) are combined to yield a solid structure. While the positions of the geoms in such structures often may be computed in a closed-form, analytic manner, the sequence of transformational operations required to satisfy the constraints may be quite complex. In the past, the designer of the part had to provide the transformation sequences [19]. Degrees of freedom analysis generates such sequences of transformations automatically.

Texts in fields such as mechanical engineering or computer-aided design employ simple examples using algebraic techniques inspired by, and grounded in, the geometric nature of the problems being analyzed. Kinematic analysis of rigid-body mechanisms is an example in which geometric construction techniques are used [6]. However, real-world codes for kinematic analysis bear no resemblance to the human problem solving techniques outlined in such texts, and are quite unintuitive. Degrees of freedom analysis leads to a more understandable way of solving these problems by automatically generating the geometric constructions required for analysis.

1.2. Terminology

The objects of interest in solving GCSPs will be called *geoms*. Some examples of geoms are lines, line segments, circles, and rigid bodies. Geoms have degrees of freedom, which allow them to vary in location or size.

For example, in 3D space, a rigid body has three translational and three rotational degrees of freedom. A circle with a variable radius has three translational, two rotational, and one dimensional degree of freedom (a third rotational degree of freedom is not required because the circle is invariant under rotation about its axis).

The *configuration variables* of a geometric object are defined as the minimal number of real-valued parameters[1] required to specify the object in space unambiguously. The configuration variables parameterize an object s translational, rotational, and dimensional degrees of freedom (DOFs), with one variable required for each DOF. A *configuration* of a geom is a particular assignment of the configuration variables, yielding a unique instantiation of the geom.

Using this terminology, a GCSP is defined as follows: Given a set of geoms and constraints between them, find the configurations of the geoms such that all constraints are satisfied. The collection of entities and constraints is called the *constraint system*, or simply the *system*.

2. Degrees of freedom analysis

Degrees of freedom analysis shares much with a body of principles found in texts on the graphical analysis of mechanisms. In fact, the earliest analyses of mechanisms were entirely graphical (i.e., geometrical) in nature. As algebraic methods were developed, the graphical methods were abandoned due to the error inherent in such manual approaches. But the algebraic techniques are hardly intuitive; therefore, the graphical methods are still significant. They "maintain touch with physical reality to a much greater degree than do the algebraic methods" and "serve as useful guides in directing the course of equations" [6, p. 215]. Degrees of freedom analysis encapsulates this "intuition" in a formal method.

One way to characterize degrees of freedom analysis is as a forward chaining system performing geometric constructions to ascertain the location of the various geoms. In geometry theorem proving, forward chaining is infeasible because the space of possible inference is infinite [13]. In degrees of freedom analysis, each geometric construction (comprised of a sequence of measurements and actions) satisfies some constraint, but also reduces the number of degrees of freedom in the composite system of geoms. Eventually, all degrees of freedom are consumed by actions, and the inference process terminates. Thus, forward chaining is feasible.

---

[1] Also known as "generalized coordinates" [15].

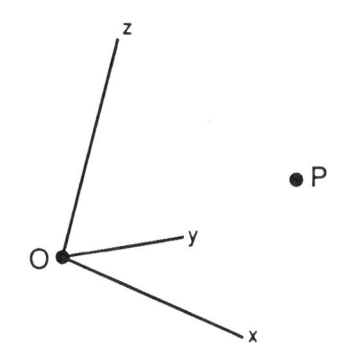

Fig. 1. A rigid body with two embedded points.

2.1. Resources, measurements, and actions

Solving GCSPs using degrees of freedom analysis relies on a representation shift from reasoning about the real-valued configuration variables to reasoning about the DOFs of the actual geometric entities. The equations that relate configuration variables to each other may be complicated, tightly coupled, and highly nonlinear; in addition, the domains of the configuration variables are continuous, yielding an infinite search space. In contrast, an object's degrees of freedom form a compact, discrete-valued description of the state of the object.

Degrees of freedom form abstract equivalence classes describing the state of a geometric entity without specifying how the constraints that lead to that state are satisfied. DOFs may be considered resources which are consumed by "physically" moving geoms to satisfy constraints. Further actions are then confined to those that do not violate any previously-satisfied constraints. Therefore, every constraint, upon being satisfied, requires that certain quantities be treated as invariant in the satisfaction of subsequent constraints, thereby restricting some number of degrees of freedom. These geometric invariants are represented explicitly.

Reasoning about DOFs is essential to decoupling the constraints. Consider the xyz coordinate frame in Fig. 1, with points O, at the origin, and P, in some arbitrary location, rigidly fixed in the coordinate frame. As a rigid body, the coordinate frame is parameterized by six configuration variables, three for the translational DOFs (x, y, z) and three for the rotational DOFs (θ, ϕ, ψ).[2] Thus, the coordinate frame is free to translate and rotate in space.

Fixing the position of either point O or P (through the satisfaction of some constraint) removes the three translational DOFs in the system; the coordinate frame may only rotate about the fixed point in order to

---

[2]In this example, the rotational DOFs are represented using Euler angles.

satisfy subsequent constraints. But consider the constraints in terms of configuration variables. Fixing the position of point O uniquely determines the three translational coordinates:

$$x = x_O,$$
$$y = y_O,$$
$$z = z_O,$$

where $[x_O, y_O, z_O]$ denotes the position of point O in the global reference frame.

In contrast, fixing the position of P (instead of O) introduces nonlinear constraint equations into the system to relate the configuration variables to the distance $\overline{OP}$:

$$(x - x_P)^2 + (y - y_P)^2 + (z - z_P)^2 = \overline{OP}^2,$$
$$\tan \theta = (y - y_P)/(x - x_P),$$
$$\tan \phi = [(y - y_P)/(z - z_P)] \csc \theta.$$

Solving constraint systems algebraically is difficult because of this type of coupling between configuration variables. The coupling is entirely an artifact of the way in which the system is modeled; for example, if the same rigid body is modeled with the coordinate frame centered at point P, then satisfying a constraint involving point O leads to coupled equations.

Using incremental movement as a constraint satisfaction scheme, the constraint that point O of the body be at a specific point in space is satisfied by measuring the vector from O to that point, and translating the body by that vector. There is no need to use the local coordinate frame representation, as long as the global position of O can be found by some means. Thus, the identical solution strategy works for point P.

Solving in DOF space is simpler because the actions can be specified independently of how the system is parameterized in terms of configuration variables. The action of translating a geom to bring a specific point (O or P) to a particular location is independent of the detailed mathematical representation of the geom. The operational semantics shields a constraint satisfaction algorithm from having to know anything about "arbitrary" internal representations.

2.2. The metaphor of incremental assembly

Degrees of freedom analysis employs the notion of *incremental assembly* as a metaphor for solving geometric constraint systems. This use of assembly should not be confused with physical interpretations of assembly as in, for example, robotics applications. In a metaphorical assembly, no physical meaning is ascribed to how the objects move from where they are to where they need to be, a factor which is quite important in a real assembly problem. In solving GCSPs, the values of the geoms' configuration variables constitute the desired answer, rather than the history of how they were calculated.

In a metaphorical assembly, geoms are treated as "ghost objects" which can pass through each other. It is therefore possible to ignore the physical constraints imposed by the boundaries of physical bodies, and instead be concerned only with purely geometric relations. The constraints between "ghost" geoms may be satisfied incrementally; no part is ever moved in a way which violates previously satisfied constraints.

In some real-world problems, like kinematic analysis or profile sketching in computer-aided design, the starting locations of the geoms and their movement toward a configuration which satisfies the constraints is of no concern. What is desired is the globally consistent locations of the geoms. In other domains, such as "real" assembly planning, the "ghost object" metaphor is clearly incorrect. However, real assembly planning can benefit from knowing the final locations of the assembled objects. Disassembling the collection of assembled objects is an easier problem than generating a physically-realizable assembly plan; the disassembly plan can then be run in reverse to create an assembly plan which takes into account the physical constraints [21].

2.3. MAPs and equation solution

A plan (a sequence of measurements and actions) for moving a set of "ghost" geoms from arbitrary configurations to ones satisfying the constraints is called a *metaphorical assembly plan,* or MAP. The generation of a MAP is a problem in symbolic geometry. The sequence of measurements and actions is determined without regard to the actual metric values of the parts.[3] The MAP describes the general form of a solution to a constraint problem. However, symbolic geometry alone is not sufficient to obtain the real values of the configuration variables describing each geom in a system.

To obtain values for configuration variables, degrees of freedom analysis requires a detailed numerical model of each geom. Relating the numerical model to the symbolic model requires a set of operators for translating, rotating, and scaling geoms, and a set of functions that can measure, relative to a global coordinate system, points and vectors embedded in any geom. These capabilities are provided by homogeneous coordinate transforms which most graphics and robotics systems use. The use of the operators allows the solution to the constraint problem to be found in a manner that is independent of the way in which the system is modeled at the detailed numerical level.

---

[3]As will be seen shortly, geometric degeneracies must be accommodated.

Table 1
Constraints used in GCE.

Constraint name	Explanation
dist:point-point(G_1, G_2, d)	Distance between point G_1 and point G_2 is d.
dist:point-line(G_{pt}, G_ℓ, d)	Distance between point G_{pt} and line G_ℓ is d.
dist:point-plane(G_{pt}, G_{pl}, d)	Distance between point G_{pt} and plane G_{pl} is d.
dist:line-circle(G_ℓ, G_c, d)	Distance between line G_ℓ and circle G_c is d. [a]
angle:vec-vec(G_1, G_2, α)	Angle between vector G_1 and vector G_2 is α.

[a] In two dimensions, $d = 0$ represents a tangency constraint.

3. Representation

3.1. Geometric entities

Geoms can be nested hierarchically in a part–whole relationship; the terms *subgeom* and *parent geom* are used to denote relative position in the hierarchy. *Aggregate* geoms are composed of combinations of *primitive* geoms—points, vectors, and dimensions. A set of measurement, or query, operators allows finding the positions and orientations of points and vectors in the global, or world, coordinate frame.

3.2. Constraints

With the exception of dimensional constraints, all constraints considered here are binary constraints—they relate two geoms. These constraints may additionally involve real parameters. Some examples of constraints used in this paper are shown in Table 1. Dimensional constraints are unary; they relate one geom to a real-valued dimension parameter.

Constraints may apply to subgeoms of a given geom. For example, to constrain two lines to be parallel, one constrains the vectors of those lines to have an angle of zero.

3.3. Invariants

In the TLA system, geometric invariants were stored as arguments to predicates indicating the translational DOFs (TDOFs) and rotational DOFs (RDOFs) of the rigid-body geoms [10]. This scheme works well for the kinematics domain, but does not always work well for other rigid-body systems or for describing geoms with dimensional DOFs.

A rigid-body geom cannot always be characterized by well-defined combinations of TDOFs and RDOFs. In some situations the degrees of freedom are coupled in ways which cannot be divided neatly into TDOFs and RDOFs.

Consider a rigid body B with two points, p_1 and p_2. Let p_1 be constrained to lie in a plane, using the **dist:point-plane** constraint. Let p_2 be constrained to lie on a line by a **dist:point-line** constraint. Then B has three degrees of freedom. But B's degrees of freedom cannot be neatly divided into TDOFs and RDOFs, as is now shown.

Let s be the tuple of TDOFs and RDOFs remaining for B after these two constraints have been applied. Now consider the case where p_1 is fixed in the plane by satisfying yet another constraint. Then the new tuple of TDOFs and RDOFs, s', is $\langle 0\text{ TDOF}, 1\text{ RDOF}\rangle$ (B may rotate about the line connecting p_1 and p_2). This would suggest that the original s was $\langle 2\text{ TDOF}, 1\text{ RDOF}\rangle$, since only translational DOFs were removed by the new constraint. But consider instead the case where the translation of p_2 along the line is fixed by a new constraint. Then $s' = \langle 0\text{ TDOF}, 2\text{ RDOF}\rangle$ (B may rotate so that p_1 remains on a circle in the plane, and it may also rotate about the line connecting p_1 and p_2). This would suggest that the original s was $\langle 1\text{ TDOF}, 2\text{ RDOF}\rangle$. Thus, depending on subsequent constraints, the degrees of freedom in s decompose into differing numbers of TDOFs and RDOFs, making it an ambiguous representation.

A more general approach to representing the degrees of freedom of a geom is to create a data structure that explicitly represents the invariants without assigning them to particular categories (e.g., TDOF or RDOF). In the expanded theory of degrees of freedom analysis, the invariants associated with each geom are stored in a structure called the *invariants record*, which contains several lists of points, vectors, or tuples. The invariants record representation has the advantage over the predicate-based representation of being easily extensible for new constraint types and for different geom types. This data structure is implemented in GCE.

The structure of the invariants record is shown in Table 2. In the table, p represents a point, v a vector, $\mathcal{L}^1$ a one-dimensional locus (e.g., circle, line, parabola), $\mathcal{L}^2$ a two-dimensional locus (e.g., sphere, hyperboloid), $\mathcal{D}$ a dimension, $v_\mathbb{R}$ a real value, and G an aggregate geom.

The "invariant points" slot of the invariants record is a list of all points embedded in the geom whose positions are invariant. The "1D-constrained points" slot is a list of $\langle$point, locus$\rangle$ tuples denoting those points embedded in the geom which are constrained to lie on one-dimensional loci (similarly for the "2D-constrained points" slot). Vectors, being two-dimensional, can be invariant, or can be constrained to one-dimensional loci (on a unit sphere). Invariant dimensions are those which have been constrained to fixed values.

The last three entries in the invariants record are placeholders for relationships that will later constrain dimensions. Their use is illustrated in Section 4.2.

Table 2
Structure of the invariants record.

Slot	Representation
Invariant points	p
1D-constrained points	$\langle p, \mathcal{L}^1 \rangle$
2D-constrained points	$\langle p, \mathcal{L}^2 \rangle$
Invariant vectors	v
1D-constrained vectors	$\langle v, \mathcal{L}^1 \rangle$
Invariant dimensions	$\langle \mathcal{D}, v_\mathbb{R} \rangle$
Fixed-distance points	$\langle p, v_\mathbb{R} \rangle$
Fixed-distance lines	$\langle G_\ell, v_\mathbb{R} \rangle$
Fixed-distance planes	$\langle G_{\text{pl}}, v_\mathbb{R} \rangle$

The cardinalities of the lists in the invariants record at any given stage of the solution process form an *invariants signature*. This signature may be used, along with the type of an as-yet-unsolved constraint, to determine the sequence of measurements and actions which will satisfy that constraint. The invariants signature is represented as a vector of integers, which when read left to right, correspond to the cardinalities of the invariants record slots as described in Table 2. For example, IR[100_10_1_000] describes a geom that has one invariant point, one invariant vector, and one invariant dimension. The underscores separate the signature into point invariants, vector invariants, dimension invariants, and fixed-distance invariants for ease of reading.

The number of DOFs remaining on a partially-constrained geom is calculated by subtracting the number of degrees of freedom restricted by the invariants (an example of this type of calculation appears in Section 4.2.3). If the number of DOFs of a geom becomes zero, the geom is said to be *grounded*, or *fixed*.

4. Action and locus analysis

The two fundamental types of reasoning carried out by degrees of freedom analysis are called *action analysis* and *locus analysis*. They are described through the use of examples. Each example will illustrate the steps used to solve the problem by following the actions of GCE, which implements degrees of freedom analysis.

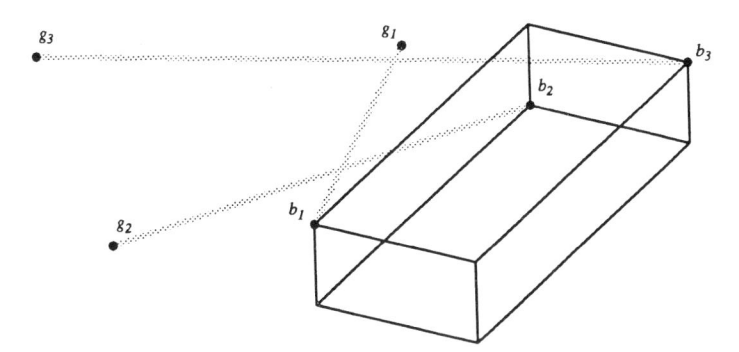

Fig. 2. Brick with three **dist:point-point** constraints.

4.1. Example 1: the brick

Consider a "brick" (a rigid-body geom) with three distinguished points[4] b_1, b_2, and b_3. Another three points, g_1, g_2, and g_3, are fixed in the global coordinate system. The problem is to find a configuration for the brick such that b_1 is coincident with g_1, b_2 with g_2, and b_3 with g_3. The constraints to be satisfied are:

dist:point-point$(g_1, b_1, 0)$,

dist:point-point$(g_2, b_2, 0)$,

dist:point-point$(g_3, b_3, 0)$.

These constraints are depicted graphically in Fig. 2. In this figure, the brick is in some arbitrary configuration, and it must be configured so that the three **dist:point-point** constraints (denoted by gray lines between the points) are all satisfied.

4.1.1. Action analysis

At each step in solving for a geom's configuration, degrees of freedom analysis searches for constraints in which one of the geoms is "fixed enough" so that the other geom can be moved to satisfied the constraint. For example, if one geom of a **dist:point-point** constraint has invariant position, it is fixed enough for the other geom to be moved to satisfy the constraint. If neither geom is fixed, then it makes sense to delay the satisfaction of the constraint, since both geoms might need to be moved subsequently. The process of finding and satisfying constraints using the above strategy is called *action analysis*.

---

[4]The shape of this "brick" is not important to degrees of freedom analysis. The important information is that this rigid-body geom contains three distinguished points.

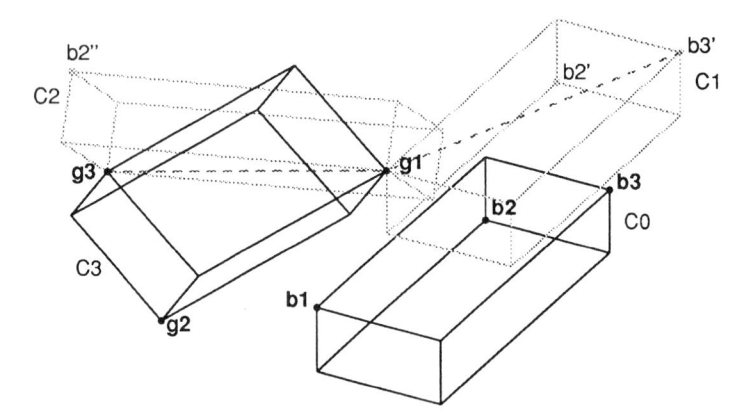

Fig. 3. Brick solution using a geometric approach.

A geom need only be "fixed enough" to allow the constraint to be satisfied; it need not be grounded. For example, if a line segment L has a fixed orientation, and one endpoint is constrained to a line parallel to the orientation of L, then L is "fixed enough" to allow a point to be moved to satisfy a **dist:point-line** constraint.[5]

The information required for action analysis is stored in a set of *plan fragment tables*, one for each type of geom. Conceptually, a plan fragment table is a dispatch table, indexed by the invariants signature of the geom and the type of constraint to be satisfied. Each plan fragment in the table specifies how to move the geom to satisfy the new constraint using only available degrees of freedom, and specifies what new invariants the geom will have after the action is performed.

4.1.2. Geometric planning

Geometric planning begins by selecting a constraint which can be satisfied, and performing the appropriate measurements and actions. While the brick is initially free to move, it does have an arbitrary configuration C_0 in the numerical model, as shown in Fig. 3. The particular values of the brick's configuration variables do not affect the symbolic model.

A trace of GCE's solution process serves to illustrate the geometric planning. GCE decides to satisfy **dist:point-point**$(g_1, b_1, 0)$ first; it could have chosen any of the constraints. To satisfy this constraint, GCE measures the vector from b_1 to g_1. It then translates the brick by that vector, leaving the brick in configuration C_1, shown in gray. If **dist:point-point**$(g_1, b_1, 0)$ is to remain satisfied when future actions alter the brick's configuration, those future

---

[5]The semantics of the **dist:point-line** constraint allows the point to be a specified distance from the infinite line which is the extension of the line segment.

actions must be restricted to rotations about g_1 (or equivalently, about b_1). GCE ensures this by marking point b_1 on the brick as being an invariant point.

GCE generates this sequence of measurements and actions by looking up the appropriate template in the plan fragment table, and binding the template's variables appropriately. Initially the brick has no invariants (i.e., its invariants signature is IR[000_00_0_000]). The plan fragment that is invoked contains the following information (descriptions in this and subsequent figures have been syntactically "cleaned up" for ease of reading):

Geom type: **rigid-body**
Constraint: **dist:point-point**(*?geom1, ?geom2, ?d*)
Invariants signature: IR[000_00_0_000]

Measurements and actions:
begin
?fixed = **fixed-geom**(*?geom1, ?geom2*);
?free = **free-geom**(*?geom1, ?geom2*);
?sphere = **make-sphere**(*?fixed, ?d*);
?dest = **projection**(*?free, ?sphere*);
?parent = **top-level-parent**(*?free*);
translate(*?parent*, **vec-diff**(**global-loc**(*?dest*),
                               global-loc(*?free*)));
end;

Bookkeeping:
if *?d* == 0
   then **add-invariant-point**(*?free, ?parent*)
   else **add-2D-constrained-point**(*?free, ?sphere, ?parent*);

Explanation:
Geom *?parent* is free to translate. A **dist:point-point** constraint must be satisfied between point *?fixed*, whose global position is known to be invariant, and point *?free* on *?parent*. Therefore *?parent* is translated by the vector from the current global position of *?free* to a point on the sphere of radius *?d* around point *?fixed* with known global position. This action removes one translational degree of freedom if *?d* is non-zero, and removes all three translational degrees of freedom if *?d* is zero.

The plan fragment specifies how to move geom of type **rigid-body**, with an invariants signature of IR[000_00_0_000], to satisfy the constraint. The fixed and free geoms—both of which are points—are determined via functions called **fixed-geom** and **free-geom**, which check the invariant statuses of

?geom1 and *?geom2*. The effect is to assign a directionality to the constraint. In this example, g_1 is the fixed geom and b_1 is the free one. Since b_1 is embedded in a rigid-body, the rigid body plan fragment table is used, and all operations (e.g., **translate**) are applied to the parent rigid body. The function **top-level-parent** follows the **parent** relation transitively until it reaches a geom which has no parent. The function **global-loc** returns the location (position for a point, orientation for a vector) of a primitive geom in the global coordinate system. The **projection** function is used to calculate the minimum alteration to the brick's current position that will satisfy the constraint. The textual explanation—with variable names replaced by their bindings—helps a user of GCE to understand the solution process.

After moving the brick, the plan fragment updates the invariants record of the brick to show that it has one invariant point, since the distance parameter of the constraint was zero. Note that the bookkeeping section of the plan fragment is responsible for noticing that a point is a degenerate case of a sphere (i.e., a sphere of radius zero). The invariants record of the brick now has a signature of IR[100_00_0_000].

GCE next chooses to satisfy **dist:point-point**$(g_3, b_3, 0)$; again, either of the remaining constraints could have been chosen. GCE measures the vector v_1 from g_1 to g_3 (where b_3 must be placed), and vector v_2 from g_1 to b_3 (shown in its new location as b_3' in Fig. 3). These two vectors are shown as dashed lines in Fig. 3. Since the desired distance between the two points is zero, the problem can be solved only if the point g_3 lies on a sphere centered at g_1, with radius $|v_2|$.

In order to move the brick, GCE requires a line about which to rotate it. The point b_1 lies on this line, and if the rotation is to move b_3 to coincide with g_3, one acceptable line direction is the normal to the plane in which v_1 and v_2 lie, i.e., $v_1 \times v_2$. The amount to rotate the brick is the angle between these vectors, measured from v_1 to v_2. Therefore, GCE rotates the brick about b_1 around vector $v_1 \times v_2$ by the angle between v_1 and v_2. This action brings the brick to configuration C_2, which satisfies **dist:point-point**$(g_3, b_3, 0)$ without violating **dist:point-point**$(g_1, b_1, 0)$. This action also removes two of the remaining rotational degrees of freedom; in order to preserve the two already-satisfied constraints, all future actions must be rotations about line segment $\overline{g_1 g_3}$.

Once again, the sequence of measurements and actions is obtained by direct lookup in the plan fragment table. The actual measurements and actions are more complicated than described above, in order to handle the general case of a non-zero distance:

> *Geom type*: **rigid-body**
> *Constraint*: **dist:point-point**(*?geom1*, *?geom2*, *d*)
> *Invariants signature*: IR[100_00_0_000]

Measurements and actions:
begin
?fixed = **fixed-geom**(*?geom1, ?geom2*);
?free = **free-geom**(*?geom1, ?geom2*);
?parent = **top-level-parent**(*?free*);
?point = **get-invariant**(*?parent*, "Invariant points", 1);
?v1 = **vec-diff**(**global-loc**(*?fixed*), **global-loc**(*?point*));
?v2 = **vec-diff**(**global-loc**(*?free*), **global-loc**(*?point*));
?sphere1 = **make-sphere**(*?fixed, ?d*);
?sphere2 = **make-sphere**(*?point*, **mag**(*?v2*));
?circle = **intersect**(*?sphere1, ?sphere2*);
if *?circle* == **null**
  begin
    if (**mag**(*?v1*) + **mag**(*?v2*) < *?d*)
      then *?error* = *?d* − (**mag**(*?v1*) + **mag**(*?v2*))
      else *?error* = **abs**(**mag**(*?v1*) − **mag**(*?v2*)) − *?d*;
    error("Dimensionally inconsistent", *?error*)
  end
?dest = **projection**(*?free, ?circle*);
?v3 = **vec-diff**(**global-loc**(*?dest*), **global-loc**(*?point*));
?cp = **cross-prod**(*?v2, ?v3*)
rotate(*?geom*, **global-loc**(*?point*), *?cp*, **vec-angle**(*?v2, ?v3, ?cp*));
end;

Bookkeeping:
if *?d* == 0
  add-invariant-point(*?free, ?parent*)
  else **add-1D-constrained-point**(*?free, ?circle, ?parent*);

Explanation:
Geom *?parent* has zero translational degrees of freedom, but may rotate about *?point*. If the points *?fixed* and *?free* have distances from *?point* which differ by no more than *?d*, the problem is solved by rotation about *?point*. Otherwise, the problem is dimensionally inconsistent. If *?d* is zero, geom *?parent* is left with one degree of freedom; otherwise it has two degrees of freedom.

A new feature of this plan fragment is the use of conditional statements to check the values of quantities. The two spheres *?sphere1* and *?sphere2* will not intersect in the following situations:

$|?v1| - |?v2| > ?d,$

$|?v2| - |?v1| > ?d,$

$|?v1| + |?v2| < ?d.$

In these situations, *?circle* will be null. An error value is calculated to indicate the severity of the problem. In all other cases, a solution is possible.[6] Since, in the brick example, *?d* is zero, another invariant point is added, and the invariants signature becomes IR[200_00_0_000].

To satisfy the final constraint, **dist:point-point**$(g_2, b_2, 0)$, GCE constructs a perpendicular from b_2 to $\overline{g_1 g_3}$, and creates a circle with radius equal to the magnitude of the perpendicular, center equal to the base of the perpendicular, and axis equal to the direction of line segment $\overline{g_1 g_3}$. If the circle is non-degenerate (i.e., has a non-zero radius), and it intersects point g_2, a solution is obtained by rotation about line segment $\overline{g_1 g_3}$. This action brings the brick to configuration C_3, which satisfies all three **dist:point-point** constraints. If the circle is degenerate (i.e., a point), no actions are taken, and no degrees of freedom are constrained. In the non-degenerate case, the action reduces the brick's remaining degrees of freedom to zero, by adding another invariant point.

4.1.3. *The canonical nature of action analysis*

Action analysis provides a simple way of decoupling the constraints pertaining to a single geom. It may be understood in the context of rewriting systems. A set of rewrite rules is *canonical* when all the normal forms of each expression are identical [3]. In such cases, the order in which the rules are applied does not matter; the result is always the same. When a set of rules is canonical, any applicable rule may be invoked, and "progress" will be made toward the solution. No ordering of the rules need be done, although it may be useful to guide the order of rule invocations to improve the efficiency of the process. Similarly, action analysis may be viewed as the process of repeatedly updating a geom's invariants record. Action analysis is canonical in the sense that, regardless of the order in which the constraints are satisfied, the invariants record of the geom at the end of the process is always the same.

Action analysis is shown to be canonical in the domain of rigid-body kinematics in [10, pp. 80–81, 247–249]. A proof has not yet been attempted in the expanded geometric domain of GCE, but it seems to be a natural extension of the existing proof.

4.2. *Example 2: constraints on a circle*

The brick problem illustrated how action analysis is used to generate a sequence of measurements and actions to satisfy a set of geometric constraints.

---

[6]If the vectors stored in registers *?v2* and *?v3* are gratuitously coincident, the cross-product vector stored in *?cp* will have a magnitude of zero. In this situation, the **rotate** operator performs no action.

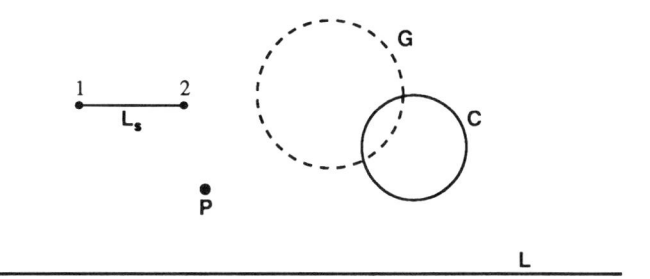

Fig. 4. Constraining a circle—initial conditions.

For each of these constraints, one geom must be invariant. This condition, however, is not always encountered in GCSPs. Often, geoms interact with each other in more complex ways that require the satisfaction of constraints between partially constrained geoms. This corresponds to the solution of nonlinear simultaneous equations in the algebraic domain.

A problem involving constraints that can only be solved by considering their interactions is shown in Fig. 4. This problem is a planar problem, i.e., all geoms are constrained to lie in a particular plane. The problem involves the following geoms:

- A circle C, of fixed position, orientation, and radius (i.e., grounded).
- An infinite line L, of fixed position and orientation (i.e., grounded).
- A grounded point P.
- A line segment L_s, of fixed length, free to translate and rotate within the same plane as C and L. The invariants of the line segment record that one endpoint is constrained to a two-dimensional locus (a plane), and the line segment's vector is constrained to a one-dimensional locus (perpendicular to the plane's normal); the invariants signature is IR[001_01_1_000].
- A circle G, free to translate in the same plane as C and L, as well as free to change radius; however, the axis of the circle is constrained to be the same as the normal to the plane: IR[001_10_0_000]. G is shown as a dashed circle in Fig. 4.

The additional constraints to be solved are:

(1) **dist:point-point**(end-1(L_s), P, 0),
(2) **dist:point-point**(end-2(L_s), center(G), 0),
(3) **dist:line-circle**(L, G, 0),
(4) **dist:circle-circle**(C, G, 0).

These constraints will be referred to by number in the following discussion. Since the constraints can be satisfied in any order, they will "arbitrarily" be attempted in the order in which they appear above.

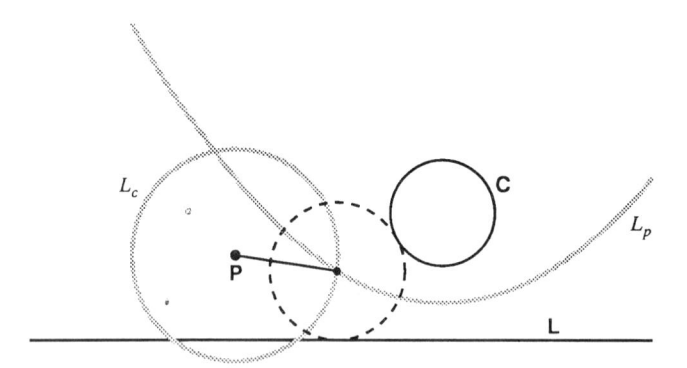

Fig. 5. Constraining a circle—solution.

4.2.1. Geometric planning: action analysis

Action analysis can be used to satisfy most of these constraints. Constraint (1) can be satisfied because point **P** is grounded. Therefore, line segment **L**$_s$ is translated to bring **end-1**(**L**$_s$) into coincidence with point **P**. Constraint (2) cannot yet be satisfied, because neither the center of circle **G** nor **end-2**(**L**$_s$) are grounded.

Constraint (3) can be satisfied by action analysis because line **L** is fixed. No restrictions can be placed on the location of the center of the **G**, nor on its radius. The invariant that is added to the invariants record is of the "fixed-distance lines" class. This invariant records the distance from the circle perimeter to the line (in this case zero). It serves to indicate that, were the radius of the circle fixed, the center would be restricted to a one-dimensional locus, or, were the center fixed, the radius would be known. This relationship restricts one degree of freedom.

Constraint (4) can be satisfied because circle **C** is fixed. The combination of constraint (4) and the fixed-distance line invariant is used to deduce that the center of **G** is in fact restricted to a one-dimensional locus; this is the parabolic locus L_p shown in Fig. 5. The center of **G**, which was previously constrained to a two-dimensional locus (the plane), is "promoted" to a one-dimensional locus.

Still, constraint (2) cannot be satisfied, since neither **center**(**G**) nor **end-2**(**L**$_s$) have become grounded through the solution of other constraints. However, there is enough information to satisfy this constraint.

4.2.2. Locus analysis

Locus analysis determines where in global space certain classes of partially constrained geoms must lie. If a subgeom is embedded in a parent geom that is not yet grounded but which has some geometric invariants, that subgeom is restricted to lie in a subregion of space. The locus of possible locations for the subgeom is a function only of the subgeom's position within its parent geom, and of the parent geom's degrees of freedom. When two partially constrained geoms are related by a constraint, the globally acceptable locations for those geoms often may be derived by intersection of their locally determined loci of possible locations. Once the global location is known, action analysis is once again used to move the relevant geoms to satisfy the constraint.

A collection of *locus tables* describes the loci of points, lines, and vectors embedded in a geom as a function of the invariants of that geom. A *locus intersection table* enables deduction of globally acceptable locations for pairs of geoms constrained by multiple loci. If the intersection yields a finite set of points, the locus intersection table also contains information about the maximum number of real roots the intersection equation may have; a *branch variable* is introduced into the solution to let a user of degrees of freedom analysis specify which branch of the solution should be used for the problem solution.

Even though an intersection may have several branches (or solutions), the solutions are topologically equivalent in that all loci resulting from the intersection are of the same dimensionality.[7] Thus, a locus intersection is a single abstract solution which can be instantiated by choosing a branch variable value. In this manner, a class of instantiable solutions are represented by a vector of branch variables associated with a metaphorical assembly plan, and a specific solution by a vector of branch variable values.

4.2.3. Geometric planning: locus analysis

At the current stage of the solution, L_s has an invariant endpoint, a vector constrained to be normal to the plan of the problem, and a fixed dimension. Thus, L_s has one degree of freedom (a line segment has six DOFs in three space; an invariant point subtracts three DOFs, a 1D-constrained vector removes one, and an invariant dimension subtracts one, leaving one remaining DOF). Therefore, any points on the line segment must have no more than one DOF. The locus tables indicate that **end-2**(L_s) is restricted to a circle locus, shown as L_c in Fig. 5.

The location of **center**(G) has already been restricted to the parabola locus L_p via the solution of constraints (3) and (4). This allows constraint (2) to be satisfied as follows:

(1) Intersect loci L_p and L_c. Since multiple intersections are possible, a branch variable is assigned to the chosen solution so that the same intersection may be chosen in a subsequent solution of the constraint system.

---

[7]For more general non-analytic or piecewise-analytic curves, such as splines, this may not be the case, thereby making locus analysis more complicated.

(2) Use action analysis to rotate L_s so that **end-2**(L_s) is coincident with the intersection point. This action grounds L_s.

(3) Use action analysis to translate circle G so **center**(G) is coincident with the intersection point. Using the information stored in the "fixed-distance lines" slot of the invariants record, set the circle's radius so the perimeter touches line L. These actions ground G.

Locus intersection, followed by another round of action analysis thus grounds the remaining geoms and completes the solution of this constraint problem.

4.3. Structure of the plan fragment tables

The plan fragments are small programs that satisfy a constraint without violating any of the invariants already pertaining to a geom. When a new geom type or constraint type expands the ontology of the system, new plan fragments must be written, and the plan fragment tables expanded. Each geom type has its own plan fragment table; thus, the plan fragment table for a circle is different from that of a line segment. Since the plan fragment table is accessed by the invariants signature of a geom, the number of entries in the plan fragment table depends on the number of possible invariants signatures for that geom.

The geom representations sometimes allow redundant descriptions of the same state. For example, a grounded line segment could be described by an invariant dimension, an invariant point, and an invariant vector (IR[001_01_1_000]). However, it could be described equally well by two invariant points (IR[002_00_0_000]). Thus, for each geometrically distinct state, a set of invariants records may describe the geom, forming an equivalence class. To minimize the number of plan fragments in each table, one member of each equivalence class is (arbitrarily) designated the "canonical" invariants record. Then, each plan fragment is written so that only canonical invariants records can result from satisfying the constraints. At present, this task is performed manually; automating this process, or at least checking it for consistency, would greatly improve the knowledge engineering process.

Many entries in the various plan fragment tables share a similar structure. For instance, moving a line segment with no invariants to satisfy a **dist:point-point** constraint uses the same measurements and actions as moving an unconstrained circle or rigid body. To re-use generic strategies, the plan fragments are written in MATHCODE, a Mathematica-based system for translating high-level code descriptions into lower-level languages [8]. A single MATHCODE routine can then be used in several different plan fragments.

Verification of the plan fragments is achieved by exhaustive unit testing which takes into account all possible geometric degeneracies. A "geometric

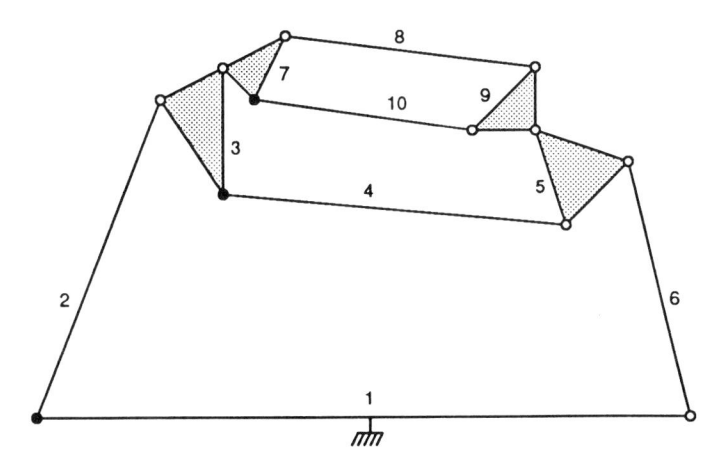

Fig. 6. A ten-bar linkage "recursively" composed of four-bar linkages.

construction checker", analogous to a theorem checker, would improve the verification process.

5. Loop and chain analysis

The previous examples were relatively simple in that all constraints could be solved with action and locus analysis being repeatedly used to "grow" the set of grounded geoms, thus allowing more constraints to be satisfied. More complex problems require solving subnetworks (e.g., loops or chains) of the constraint network in isolation, then reformulating those substructures as rigid bodies which can then be moved to solve other portions of the constraint network.

5.1. Example 3: hierarchical grouping of geoms

An example of a constraint system requiring analysis of constraint loops and chains is the ten-bar mechanical linkage shown in Fig. 6. Its structure is that of a four-bar linkage, whose coupler bar is composed of another four-bar, whose coupler is composed of yet another four-bar.

In Fig. 6, the geoms (called links in the mechanisms domain) have been labeled 1 through 10. All links are constrained to be in the plane. The joints connecting the links are modeled with **dist:point-point** constraints, all with zero distances. This system has three internal degrees of freedom, and hence requires additional constraints to fully constrain the system. The three joints in Fig. 6 which are solid black (connecting links 1 and 2, links 3 and 4, and links 7 and 10) are additionally constrained by **angle:vec-vec** constraints. In addition, link 1 is grounded (as indicated by the "foot" in the center of the link).

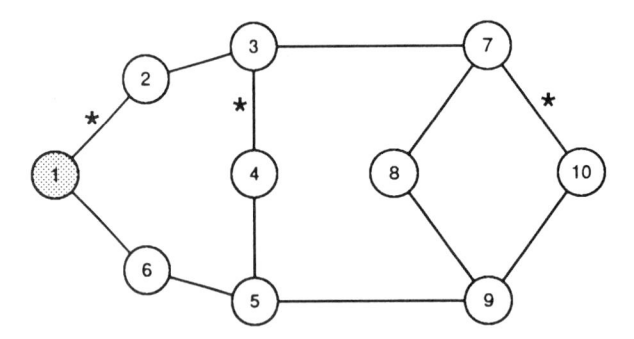

Fig. 7. Graph of the ten-bar linkage of Fig. 6.

In order to search for rigid substructures, degrees of freedom analysis employs a graph representation of the constraint system. In the constraint graph, nodes represent geoms, and arcs represent collections of one or more constraints (in subsequent discussion, the terms *geom* and *node* will be used interchangeably). Figure 7 shows the graph of the constraint system of Fig. 6 before solving. The node numbers correspond to the link numbering in Fig. 6. The grounded geom in this and subsequent graphs is shaded for easy identification.

In the absence of the constraints to be satisfied, each rigid-body geom in the system has three DOFs, since each body is constrained to the plane. The arcs in the graph of Fig. 7 which are marked with an asterisk restrict three DOFs, since they have **dist:point-point** constraints with zero distance, and angle constraints. Thus, satisfaction of the constraints on one of these arcs will cause the two geoms which they relate to be fixed rigidly with respect to each other. Acyclic collections of such geoms are called *chains*. Degrees of freedom analysis satisfies these constraints first, and reformulates each pair of geoms as a single rigid-body geom, also called a *macro-geom*. The resultant graph is shown in Fig. 8, where geoms 1 and 2 have been assembled to form geom 11, 3 and 4 have formed geom 12, and 7 and 10 have formed geom 13.

In the new graph, all remaining arcs have a single **dist:point-point** constraint that, in the plane, restricts two DOFs. No rigid chains remain, so degrees of freedom analysis next looks for rigid loops in the constraint graph. Consider what would happen if the loop of nodes 11, 12, 6, and 5 were to be satisfied using action and locus analysis. Each of the three non-grounded geoms has three DOFs, for a total of nine DOFs. The three constraints restrict only six DOFs, leaving three remaining DOFs. In other words, that loop would not be rigidly fixed. In contrast, consider loop 8-9-13-8. Were one of the geoms grounded, this loop would have zero DOFs. Finding a loop's degrees of freedom is analogous to determining the mobility of a mechanism [6], and the algorithms are quite similar.

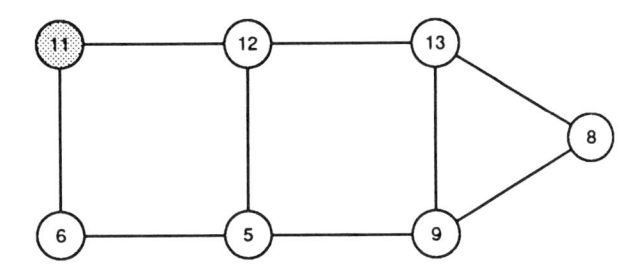

Fig. 8. Graph of Fig. 7 after replacing pairs of geoms constrained by driving inputs with macro-geoms.

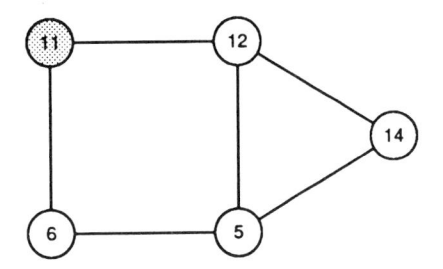

Fig. 9. Graph of Fig. 8 after assembling loop 8-9-13-8 and replacing it with the single node 14.

Degrees of freedom analysis identifies the loop with the lowest number of degrees of freedom, in this case, loop 8-9-13-8. It then temporarily grounds one of the geoms in this loop and uses action and locus analysis to solve for the constraints on the arcs connecting the three nodes. Next, it reformulates the composite geometry as a macro-geom, shown as node 14 in Fig. 9. This will in turn allow loop 12-14-5-12 to be reformulated as a macro-geom, which will enable the solution of the remaining constraints.

5.2. Position analysis

Position analysis is the term for the top-level strategy employed in degrees of freedom analysis. First, rigid chains are identified, solved, and reformulated as macro-geoms. Next, the loop with the fewest DOFs is identified, solved, and rewritten as a macro-geom. The process is repeated until the entire constraint graph is rewritten as a single node. Appendix A.3 describes the algorithm in detail.

5.2.1. Underconstrained systems and iterative solutions

Cases where no loop in the constraint system is rigid indicate one of two possible situations:

(a) the system is underconstrained, or
(b) the system has no closed-form solution.

In such cases, degrees of freedom analysis proceeds by identifying the loop with the fewest degrees of freedom, and adding as many redundant constraints to the system as are required to make the loop rigid. These redundant constraints are called *defaults*.

In case (a), the defaults serve to parameterize the remaining degrees of freedom in the system. In case (b), the constraints yield a near-minimal set of redundant generalized coordinates for use in an efficient iterative solution to the constraint system. Iterative solutions are formulated in the following manner: A set of parameter values are chosen for the defaults, and assembly of the geometry is attempted. If the geometry cannot be assembled, the **error** functions in the plan fragments accumulate an error proportional to the degree to which the assembly is incorrect. Traditional optimization schemes are then used to vary the default parameters until the error term vanishes.

Once degrees of freedom analysis has committed to solving a particular loop, it will not backtrack. Therefore, if the loop is degenerate in some way, a redundant generalized coordinate may be introduced when in fact solving a different loop first would have obviated the need for a redundant generalized coordinate. While this does not affect the quality of the answer to the GCSP, it does affect the efficiency of the solution process. The group-theoretic approach to finding degrees of freedom proposed by Hervé [7] may be useful in detecting degeneracies before loop solution, as evidenced by similar work by Popplestone et al. [17].

A complete discussion of loop and chain analysis would exceed the space limitations of this article. Extended discussion is found in [10].

5.2.2. Plan compilation issues

The TLA system was employed as a simulation "compiler" by storing the sequence of measurements and actions in a re-executable plan structure [9]. This allowed typically linear behavior, with a worst-case $O(n \log n)$, in the simulation of mechanisms, where n is the number of links. In its expanded scope, degrees of freedom analysis still utilizes a plan representation; however, rather than a linear array, a tree is used to store the plan. Each node in the plan tree has different exit points depending on the number of degrees of freedom absorbed by the constraint. Upon re-execution with different dimensions or constraint parameters, a new geometric degeneracy may arise, causing a new branch of the plan tree to be generated and stored. This allows caching solutions from various degenerate geometries. Currently, the tree-style plan representation is in prototype form.

6. Empirical and theoretical analysis

Degrees of freedom analysis provides low-order polynomial-time algorithms for the solution of GCSPs. Problems are solved in $O(cg)$ time, where c is the number of constraints, and g is the number of geoms. Details of the complexity analysis are provided in Appendix A.

6.1. Canonicality

In degrees of freedom analysis, the constraint satisfaction process is canonical. At any stage of the solution process, a number of choices may exist as to which constraint to satisfy next. Any choice may be made, with no affect on the final answer. Proving that the position analysis algorithm is canonical is done by proving that chain and loop rewriting are *confluent*, and then showing that this implies that the algorithm is canonical.

Borrowing the terminology used in [3], which applies to expression rewriting, confluence is defined in this context as the property that whenever a subgraph S in the constraint graph can be rewritten in two different ways, say to I_1 and I_2, then I_1 and I_2 can both be rewritten to some common graph S'. A proof of the canonical nature of position analysis is found in [10, pp. 140–145].

6.2. Empirical comparisons

Degrees of freedom analysis was empirically validated in the domain of kinematics with an implemented computer program called The Linkage Assistant (TLA). This program has performed kinematic simulation of complex mechanisms in a more computationally efficient manner than other existing programs. Efficiency increases of two orders of magnitude were observed on medium-sized examples involving on the order of a hundred constraints, when compared with ADAMS, a mechanism simulator using a maximally redundant generalized coordinate representation and iterative numerical solution [1].

The graph of Fig. 10 shows the timing analyses of ADAMS and TLA as a function of the number of bodies in a mechanism. The dashed line shows the time per iteration for ADAMS; it is a polynomial curve proportional to $n^{2.17}$, where n is the number of links in the mechanism. This indicates the efficiency of the sparse matrix routines employed by ADAMS. Typically, between 2 and 12 iterations are required to solve a single step of the simulation, as indicated by the gray area. In contrast, the behavior of TLA (re-using its compiled plan) is linear, and is substantially more efficient.

7. Conclusion

While symbolic solution of the algebraic equations describing geometric constraints is NP-complete in general, degrees of freedom analysis allows generating closed-form solutions, or efficient iterative solutions, to GCSPs

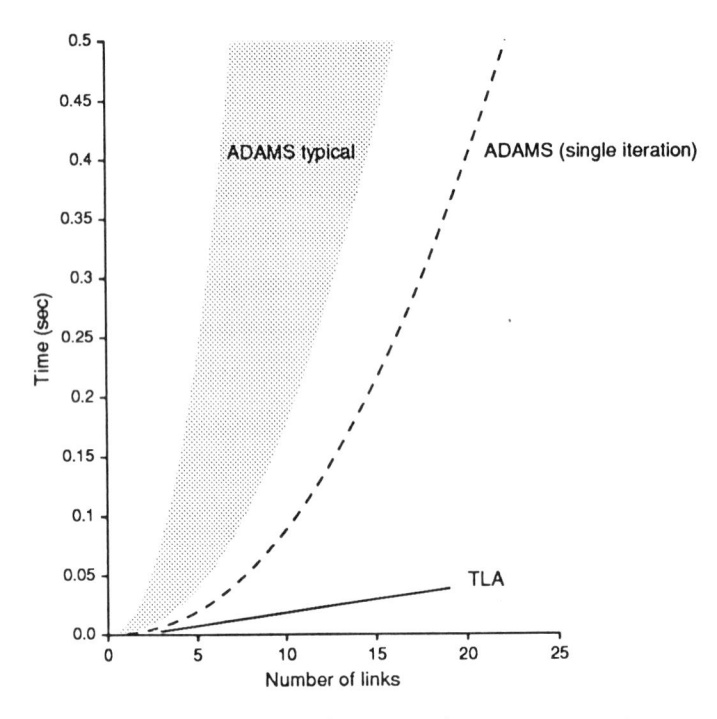

Fig. 10. Comparison of runtimes of TLA and ADAMS.

in polynomial time. This avoids the problem of computational intractability found in symbolic algebra systems. Typically, the resulting closed-form solutions may be executed in time linearly proportional to the size of the constraint system being analyzed, and are substantially more efficient than iterative numerical techniques.

The power in degrees of freedom analysis comes from the use of a metaphor of incremental assembly. This allows for maximal decoupling of the constraints. Similar operational semantics can be found in the work of Arbab and Wang [2], Pabon et al. [14], and Wilk [20]. However, in these systems, methods must be provided to solve a new constraint in the context of the object plus *all* the constraints currently satisfied. The number of constraint satisfaction methods can grow quickly with the types of objects and types of constraints—$O(c^n)$, where c is the number of constraint types, and n is the number of DOFs in an unconstrained geom. By using DOFs as equivalence classes, degrees of freedom analysis coalesces many of these states, thereby creating a more manageable search space.

The work of Arbab and Wang [2] and Pabon et al. [14] used iterative numerical techniques whenever a constraint loop was found. In contrast, locus analysis allows solving many such problems in closed form. Locus analysis can be considered a generalization of the "cycle finder" described by Popplestone in [16].

There are a number of interesting topics for further extending degrees of freedom analysis. Currently, the plan tree is recomputed whenever the topology of the constraint problem changes. This can be inefficient if constraints are only being added. However, re-use of the tree may result in the retention of previously-added redundant generalized coordinates which are no longer needed.

Experiments have begun in mixing iterative and closed-form solutions within the plan fragments themselves. For example, if a point geom is confined to a one-dimensional locus described by a sixth-degree polynomial, and must be positioned a certain distance from another point, a locally iterative solution can be used to compute the intersection of the locus and a sphere. This is more efficient than employing a general iterative solver in an "outer loop" invoking the entire assembly plan.

7.1. Relation to general constraint satisfaction

Mackworth's description of constraint graphs, and the concepts of node, arc, and path consistency, were formulated for predicates with finite, discrete-valued variable domains [12]. In GCSPs, the variables are continuous, with infinite domains. Node, arc, and path consistency are more difficult in such situations.[8]

In the context of the graph representation of general constraint systems, degrees of freedom analysis may be thought of as a layered solution to the GCSP. In the original formulation of the problem, the nodes in the constraint graph represent real values for the configuration variables of the geoms, and the arcs represent constraints. A "meta-system" may be devised in which the graph nodes represent the number of degrees of freedom of the system, and the arcs represent constraints. The meta-system maps the continuous variables into the discrete-valued DOF space.

In the meta-system, node, arc, and path consistency are used to remove degrees of freedom from the nodes (since any degrees of freedom on the nodes are incompatible with constraints on adjacent arcs). Node consistency corresponds to grounding a geom, arc consistency corresponds to solving a chain, and path consistency corresponds to solving loops. Every time a constraint is removed in the meta-system, a set of measurements and actions is posted as a side-effect. These side-effects solve the GCSP as originally formulated.

From this analogy, it is seen that there are some broad concepts that can be re-used in formulating constraint satisfaction problems for other domains. The notion of abstracting some continuous space (e.g., position,

---

[8]Interval arithmetic, while technically continuous, discretizes the domain by considering only a finite set of interval endpoints.

orientation, dimension) into a discrete space (e.g., degrees of freedom) may apply to other domains. Designing algorithms that make use of monotonic trends (such as the reduction of degrees of freedom of a geom) tend to lead to polynomial-time algorithms. Planning metaphors can help to guide search. Creative representation shifts will be required to use these principles in other domains, but if they can be found, the benefits may be substantial.

Appendix A. Algorithms

The section describes, at a high level, the algorithms for the major functional components of GCE. Algorithms for action analysis and locus analysis are not given; they are similar to those found in [10].

A.1. Solving chains

Satisfying the constraints on a rigid chain of arbitrary length proceeds recursively by satisfying the constraints between a pair of geoms, and rewriting the pair of geoms as a single macro-geom. The algorithm for identifying a pair of geoms which can be rewritten as a macro-geom, and solving the appropriate constraints is:

Algorithm SOLVE-RIGID-CHAINS. *Algorithm for recognizing and rewriting topologically rigid chains in a constraint graph as macro-geoms.*

Input: Constraint graph G.
Other variables: I for temporary storage of a geom's invariants record.

```
     procedure SOLVE-RIGID-CHAINS(G):
       begin
1        for arc a in the constraint system do
2          if a's constraints imply a rigid connection between the
               geoms (see [10])
3          then
             begin
4              g₁ ← one node connected to a
5              g₂ ← the other node connected to a
6              if grounded(g₂)
7              then swap(g₁, g₂)
```

Comment: *At this point, the following encoding has been established: If one of the geoms is grounded, it is stored in g_1.*

```
8              if not grounded(g₁)
```

```
9                  then
                   begin
10                     I ← copy-invariants-record(g₁);
11                     ground!(g₁);
                   end
12                 ACTION-ANALYSIS(constraints in a);
13                 Replace g₁, a, g₂ with macro-geom m;
14                 set-invariants-record(m, I);
              end
       end
```

Using this algorithm, all rigid chains in a constraint system can be reformulated in $O(a)$ time, where a is the number of arcs in the graph.

A.2. Solving loops

Depending on the geometric domain, there is a limit to the size of a loop which can be assembled into a rigid macro-geom. This limit is six geoms for general bodies in 3D space, and three geoms for bodies in 2D space.[9]

In the algorithm described below, loops are identified in *stages*. A stage is a list of sequences of node numbers that describe a path through the graph. Sequences in stage s each contain $s + 1$ nodes. A sequence describes a loop if the first and last numbers in that sequence are equal. To avoid identifying the same loop multiple times (e.g., 8-9-13-8 and 13-8-9-13), a canonical form is required in which the first node number in the loop is the smallest, and the second node number is less than the penultimate one:

Algorithm IDENTIFY-LOOPS. *Algorithm for identifying all loops of size l or less in a constraint graph.*

Input: G, the constraint graph
       l, the maximum number of nodes in a loop.
Other variables: Constraint graph connectivity array C,
           where $C[i]$ contains the list of nodes connected to node i.
           Stage array (stage[s] contains the sequences in stage s).
Output: The loops found.

```
       procedure IDENTIFY LOOPS(G, l):
       begin
1          C ← make-connectivity-array(G);
```

---

[9] Larger loops may be handled by degrees of freedom analysis; however, the absence of any rigid loops implies an iterative solution will be necessary. Defaults will be added to the system until one of the loops becomes rigid. In this process, rewriting the chains (formed using the defaults) as macro-geoms will reduce the loop size to the limitations specified here.

```
2       for i ∈ node numbers do
3         for j in C[i] do
4           if i < j
5             then stage[1] ← stage[1] + i, j
6       for s ← 2 until l do
7         for x_1, x_2, ..., x_s in stage[s - 1] do
8           for j in C[x_s] do
9             if x_s ≠ x_1
10              and x_1 ≤ j
11              and ∀k, 1 < k ≤ s. x_k ≠ j
12              then stage[s] ← stage[s] + x_1, x_2, ..., x_s, j
13      loops ← ∅;
14      for s ← 1 until l do
15        for x_1, x_2, ..., x_{s+1} in stage[s] do
16          if x_1 = x_{s+1} and x_2 < x_s
17            then loops ← loops + x_1, x_2, ..., x_{s+1}
18      return loops;
        end
```

Lines 9 through 11 provide the preconditions for the next node to be a valid continuation of the sequence: the first and last node numbers must not be equal (this would indicate a loop has already been found); the new node number must be greater than the first number; and, the new number must not already be a member of the sequence, unless it matches the first node number, forming a loop. Line 16 checks if a sequence is a canonical description of a loop. In the case where the number of arcs in the graph is comparable to the number of nodes (typical of many GCSPs), the complexity of this algorithm can be shown to be linear in the number of nodes [10].

The constraints in a loop are solved using the following approach: choose a ground node (if one does not exist), and then switch between action and locus analysis until constraints have been satisfied or no further inference is possible:

Algorithm SOLVE-LOOP. *Algorithm for solving the constraints pertaining to a loop.*

Input: Loop L.
Other variables: M a temporary transform matrix.
Output: RGC, a list of any redundant generalized coordinates used.

```
        procedure SOLVE-LOOP(L):
        begin
1         RGC ← ∅;
```

2   $g_1 \leftarrow$ grounded geom of L (or $\emptyset$ if no geom is grounded);
3   $g_2 \leftarrow \emptyset$;
4   **if** $g_1 = \emptyset$
5   **then** $g_2 \leftarrow$ an acceptable ground geom
        (by the kinematic inversion decision procedure—see [10])
6   **else if** g_1 is an acceptable ground geom
7   **then** $g_2 \leftarrow g_1$
8   **else** $g_2 \leftarrow$ an acceptable ground geom

Comment: *At this point, the following encoding has been established: If g_1 is null, then no geom on the original loop was grounded. Otherwise, g_1 is the original grounded geom, and g_2 is the geom being used as ground for the loop solution.*

9   **if** $g_1 \neq \emptyset$ and $g_2 \neq g_1$
10 **then** $M \leftarrow$ **transform**(g_1)
11 REPEAT: ACTION-ANALYSIS(all constraints in L);
12 LOCUS-ANALYSIS(all constraints in L)
13 **if** all constraints are satisfied
14 **then**
      begin
15   rewrite all geoms as macro-geom G;
16   **if** $g_1 \neq \emptyset$ and $g_2 \neq g_1$
17   **then** move G by **inverse**(**transform**$(g_2)) \cdot M$;
18   **return** RGC;
      end
19 **else if** any constraints were satisfied in lines 11 or 12
20 **then goto** REPEAT
21 **else**
      begin
22   add a redundant constraint restricting one DOF;
23   add corresponding generalized coordinate
            (the real argument of the redundant constraint) to RGC;
24   **goto** REPEAT;
      end
    end

A.3. Top-level algorithm

The top-level algorithm finds the positions, orientations, and dimensions of all the geoms so that all constraints are satisfied. First, any unary constraints are trivially satisfied; in GCE, these are constraints on the dimension of one geom, so the dimension is adjusted and the dimensional DOF is fixed. Then, chains and loops are solved and rewritten, until the constraint graph has been reduced to a single node.

Algorithm POSITION-ANALYSIS. *Algorithm for finding a closed-form solution to a given GCSP, if one exists. Otherwise, the algorithm finds a solution with a minimal number of redundant generalized coordinates, which can then be used by an iterative numerical solver.*

Input: G, the constraint graph,
    l, the maximum loop size.
Other variables: *loop*, a loop that is to be solved.
Output: RGC, a list of any redundant generalized coordinates used.

    procedure POSITION-ANALYSIS(G, C, l):
    begin
1   RGC $\leftarrow \emptyset$;
2   Solve all dimensional (i.e., unary) constraints;
3   REPEAT: SOLVE-RIGID-CHAINS(G);
4   **if** G is a single node
5   **then return** RGC;
6    $L \leftarrow$ IDENTIFY-LOOPS(G, l);
7   **if** $L = \emptyset$
8   **then**
      begin
9   add a redundant constraint restricting one DOF;
10   add corresponding generalized coordinate
         (the real argument of the redundant constraint) to RGC;
11   **goto** REPEAT;
      end
12   **for** $l \in L$ **do**
13   CLASSIFY-LOOP(l);
14   *loop* $\leftarrow$ PICK-LOOP(L);
15   RGC $\leftarrow$ RGC $+$ SOLVE-LOOP$(loop)$;
16   **goto** REPEAT;
    end

The PICK-LOOP algorithm is responsible for choosing the best loop to solve, given the choices available. Assuming that SOLVE-RIGID-CHAINS is linear in the number of arcs, a, the complexity of POSITION-ANALYSIS is $O(na)$, where n is the number of nodes in the constraint graph. This results from the fact that, each time the loop in lines 3 through 16 is executed, the size of the constraint graph is decreased by at least one node.

Acknowledgement

The author would like to thank Phil Agre, Harry Barrow, Phil Husbands, and Robin Popplestone for comments and discussion. Mahesh Kanumury and Walid Keirouz are principal co-implementors of GCE, and contributed greatly to the ideas in this paper. Jahir Pabon and Robert Young provided useful comments on an earlier draft of this paper.

References

[1] *ADAMS Users Manual* (Mechanism Dynamics, Inc., Ann Arbor, MI, 1987).
[2] F. Arbab and B. Wang, A constraint-based design system based on operational transformation planning, in: J.S. Gero, ed., *Proceedings 4th International Conference on Applications of Artificial Intelligence* (Spinger, Berlin, 1989).
[3] A. Bundy, *The Computer Modelling of Mathematical Reasoning* (Academic Press, London, 1983).
[4] G. Celniker and D. Gossard, Deformable curve and surface finite-elements for free-form shape design, *Comput. Graph.* **25** (4) (1991) 257-266.
[5] R.H. Gallagher, *Finite Element Analysis: Fundamentals* (Prentice-Hall, Englewood Cliffs, NJ, 1975).
[6] R.S. Hartenberg and J. Denavit, *Kinematic Synthesis of Linkages* (McGraw-Hill, New York, 1964).
[7] J.M. Hervé, Analyse structurelle des mécanismes par groupes de déplacements, *Mech. Mach. Theor.* **13** (1978) 437-450.
[8] E. Kant, F. Daube, W. MacGregor and J. Wald, Scientific programming by automated synthesis, in: M.R. Lowry and R.D. McCartney, eds., *Automating Software Development* (AAAI Press, Menlo Park, CA, 1991) 169-205.
[9] G.A. Kramer, Solving geometric constraint systems, in: *Proceedings AAAI-90*, Boston, MA (1990) 708-714.
[10] G.A. Kramer, *Solving Geometric Constraint Systems: A Case Study in Kinematics* (MIT Press, Cambridge, MA, 1992).
[11] Y. Liu and R.J. Popplestone, Symmetry constraint inference in assembly planning: automatic assembly configuration specification, in: *Proceedings AAAI-90*, Boston, MA (1990) 1038-1044.
[12] A.K. Mackworth, Consistency in networks of relations, *Artif. Intell.* **8** (1) (1977) 99-118.
[13] A. Nevins, Plane geometry theorem proving using forward chaining, Artificial Intelligence Lab Tech. Rept. No. 303, MIT, Cambridge, MA (1974).
[14] J. Pabon, R. Young and W. Keirouz, Integrating parametric geometry, features, and variational modeling for conceptual design, *Int. J. Syst. Autom. Res. Appl. (SARA)* **2** (1992) 17-37.
[15] R.P. Paul, *Robot Manipulators: Mathematics, Programming, and Control* (MIT Press, Cambridge, MA, 1981).
[16] R.J. Popplestone, A language for specifying robot assembly, Department of Artificial Intelligence Res. Rept. No. 29, University of Edinburgh, Edinburgh, Scotland (1977).
[17] R.J. Popplestone, A.P. Ambler and I.M. Bellos, An interpreter for a language for describing assemblies, *Artif. Intell.* **14** (1) (1980) 79-107.
[18] W.H. Press, B.P. Flannery, S.A. Teukolsky and W.T. Vetterling, *Numerical Recipes: The Art of Scientific Computing* (Cambridge University Press, Cambridge, England, 1986).
[19] J.R. Rossignac, Constraints in constructive solid geometry, in: *Proceedings 1986 Workshop on Interactive 3D Graphics* (1986) 93-110.

[20] M.R. Wilk, Equate: an object-oriented constraint solver, in: *Proceedings ACM Conference on Object-Oriented Programming Systems, Languages and Applications*, Phoenix, AZ (1991) 286–298.
[21] T.C. Woo and D. Dutta, Automatic disassembly and total ordering in three dimensions, *Trans. ASME, J. Eng. Indust.* **113** (2) (1991) 207–213.

A theory of conflict resolution in planning

Qiang Yang*

Department of Computer Science, University of Waterloo, Waterloo, Ontario, Canada N2L 3G1

Abstract

Yang, Q., A theory of conflict resolution in planning, Artificial Intelligence 58 (1992) 361–392.

Conflict resolution in planning is the process of constraining a plan to remove harmful interactions that threaten its correctness. It has been a major contributing factor to the complexity of classical planning systems. Traditional planning methods have dealt with the problem of conflict resolution in a local and incremental manner, by considering and resolving conflicts individually. This paper presents a theory of conflict resolution that supports a global consideration of conflicts. The theory enables one to formally represent, reason about and resolve conflicts using an extended framework of constraint satisfaction. The computational advantage of the theory stems from its ability to remove inconsistencies early in a search process, to detect dead ends with low computational overhead, to remove redundancies in a search space, and to guide the search by providing an intelligent order in which to resolve conflicts. The paper also presents empirical results showing the utilities of the theory, by investigating the characteristics of problem domains where the theory is expected to work well, and the types of planning systems for which the theory can offer a marked computational advantage.

1. Introduction

A central problem faced by classical AI planning is the composition of sets of operators, or plans, to achieve certain specified goals, given the capabilities, the environment, and the initial situation of agents. A major obstacle in the composition process is that different parts of a plan may interact in harmful ways. The harmful interactions, which are normally called *conflicts*, can often be removed by further imposing various kinds of constraints onto the plan. The

Correspondence to: Q. Yang, Department of Computer Science, University of Waterloo, Waterloo, Ontario, Canada N2L 3G1. Telephone: (519) 888-4716. E-mail: qyang@logos.waterloo.edu.

* The author is supported in part by an operating grant OGP0089686 from the Natural Sciences and Engineering Research Council of Canada, and ITRC: Information Technology Research Centre.

constraint posting process has been known as *conflict resolution*. The purpose of this paper is to develop a computational theory of conflict resolution in planning, using extended techniques of constraint satisfaction.

1.1. Background

Conflict resolution in planning is a complex computational process. A single plan may contain many different kinds of conflicts, and each conflict in turn may be resolved by several alternative sets of constraints. To make the matter even more complex, these constraints can also interact among themselves in different ways. For example, some constraints cannot be simultaneously imposed onto a plan to avoid creating inconsistency. Others may be redundant in the presence of more powerful ones. Conflict resolution is often a major contributing factor to the complexity of planning.

As an example, suppose that one wants to paint a ceiling as well as a ladder (an example used in [11]). A proposed plan may consist of two parts, one for painting the ceiling and the other for painting the ladder, such that no ordering constraint is imposed between the two parts. If the robot hand can only hold one brush at a time, then a resource conflict occurs between the part of the plan that paints the ceiling and the part of the plan that paints the ladder, because of their competition for the robot hand. Similarly, if the wet paint from painting the ladder precludes one from climbing up, then another conflict occurs because performing the former negates a precondition of the latter, which requires that the ladder be dry.

In the above example, a conflict is caused by one operator which can potentially delete a precondition of another operator. The resource conflict can be resolved by painting the ceiling either before or after painting the ladder. And the wet-paint-on-ladder conflict is resolved by painting the ceiling first. The successful resolution of both conflicts involves the recognition of the fact that one cannot paint the ceiling both before and after painting the ladder, and that the ordering constraint of painting the ceiling first, not only resolves the wet-paint-on-ladder conflict, but also resolves the resource conflict. Thus, a consistent solution to resolving both conflicts is to paint the ceiling first.

Because of its importance in planning, methods for conflict resolution were explored early on. Sussman's system HACKER [14] recognized and fixed "bugs", which were certain classes of conflicts. The bugs were fixed using a bag of hacks, which were different types of ordering constraints that could be imposed upon the operators of a plan. Sacerdoti's NOAH [11] used a partial order to represent the structure of a plan, and implemented a more elaborate set of ordering constraints that could resolve different classes of conflicts. A problem of NOAH is that given several alternative choices in the constraints, it commits to one of them, and does not have the ability to backtrack should an inconsistent situation occur later. Tate's NONLIN [15] fixed this problem and introduced a complete set of alternative ordering constraints that are capable of resolving conflicts in a completely instantiated plan. Recognizing the need to represent resources using variables in a plan, Stefik's MOLGEN [13] and Wilkins' SIPE [17] both could further impose constraints on variable bindings to resolve conflicts. Chapman's TWEAK [2] introduced an additional type of constraint on variable bindings that forces two variables to instantiate to different objects. He also provided a formal language for expressing plans that we will use as a basis for our computational theory.

1.2. Motivation

A major theme of the previous approaches to conflict reasoning is their incremental nature: conflicts are reasoned about one at a time, and in the presence of more than one conflict, no systematic theory exists that can guide the resolution process. Such incremental, local analysis has a number of drawbacks. First, in the presence of a large number of conflicts, the order in which the conflicts are resolved may have dramatic effects on efficiency. One order can lead to a reduction in the size of the search space more than others, but an arbitrarily chosen order may happen to be the worst one. For example, recall that in order to resolve the two conflicts in the painting problem, the resource conflict can be resolved by two alternative constraints, while the wet-paint-on-ladder conflict can be resolved by only one. Since each alternative choice corresponds to a branching point in the search tree, if the resource conflict is chosen first, then four states will be generated in the worst case. But if the wet-paint-on-ladder conflict is chosen first, then only two states will be generated. The difference in savings could be much larger if more conflicts were involved.

A conflict ordering heuristic can be further strengthened by recognizing "redundant" constraints, which exist because some conflict resolution constraints may be stronger than others. For example, for a set of conflicts $\mathscr{C}$, there may exist a subset $\mathscr{S}$ of $\mathscr{C}$ so that once conflicts in $\mathscr{S}$ are resolved, all other conflicts in $\mathscr{C}$ are also resolved. This *subsumption* information can further enable a planner to find a good order for resolving conflicts, since by resolving the subset first, one can avoid resolving all others. In the painting example, if a decision is made to resolve the wet-paint-on-ladder conflict by painting the ceiling first, then the resource conflict is also resolved automatically. A related issue is to use the subsumption information to guide the choices of alternative constraints for resolving each conflict.

Second, a plan in which conflicts cannot be resolved together corresponds to a dead end in a planner's search space. The ability to detect such dead ends early is vital to a planner's efficiency. In many situations, unresolvable conflicts can be detected with less cost when considered together, but may not be obvious when only a single conflict is considered at a time. Thus, a planning system based on the incremental method for conflict resolution may incur expensive computation due to the expansion of plans that eventually leads to dead ends. For example, if painting the ceiling also makes it impossible to further paint the ladder, due to the dripping paint from the ceiling, then a third conflict exists in our painting example. The only way to resolve this new conflict is to paint the ladder before the ceiling. When all three conflicts are considered together, it is apparent that there is no solution; painting the ceiling first will render the ladder unpaintable, while painting the ladder first makes it impossible to use the ladder for painting the ceiling. However, an incremental system may discover this situation after many plan-expansions.

Finally, considering conflicts in a global manner may lead to the discovery that some constraints can never participate in any final solutions. For example, by comparing the constraints for both the resource conflict and the wet-paint-on-ladder conflict, it is easy to discover that one of the ordering constraints for the resource conflict, namely that of applying paint to the ladder first, is not consistent with the only ordering constraint for the other conflict. Therefore, the constraint of applying paint to ladder first will not be part of any solution for resolving both conflicts. Noticing inconsistencies early can enable a planner to produce a smaller search tree.

A natural extension to the previous work, then, is to reason about conflicts in a global manner. This requires a formal representation of the individual conflicts and their resolution methods, an analysis of the relations among different conflicts, as well as the design of reasoning techniques that can facilitate global conflict resolution. We briefly summarize these contributions in the following section.

1.3. An overview of the paper

This paper presents a formalization of conflicts and their inter-relations, using an extended framework for solving constraint satisfaction problems (or CSPs). This formalization makes it possible to apply many existing techniques from the CSP area to aid efficient conflict resolution in planning. An additional feature of conflict resolution, which makes use of a subsumption relation, extends the existing methods for solving CSPs. The paper also explores the utilities of applying the CSP formalization to conflict resolution, by pointing out where the proposed technique is expected to be most effective. To justify the claims about improved efficiency, experiments have been conducted to show that using the CSP method for global conflict resolution can lead to dramatic improvement in planning efficiency.

To understand conflict resolution from a global viewpoint, one has to be precise about the language for expressing plans, operators, and precondition establishments. In Sections 2 and 3, we review TWEAK's plan language, and express a formal representation of conflicts using this language. Then in Section 4, we present our formulation of conflicts and conflict resolution using a CSP framework. Sections 5 to 8 explore the utilities of applying the theoretical results to planning along several dimensions and present test results. Section 9 concludes the paper.

2. Conflicts and conflict resolutions

2.1. Plan language

A formal account of conflicts and their resolutions requires a precise characterization of the language for expressing plans. We adopt the TWEAK language designed by Chapman [2], because it has been one of the most formal and influential to date. Later in the paper we point out possible extensions to other plan languages.

A plan Π consists of a set of operators, $operators(\Pi)$, and a set of precedence constraints on the operators. Each operator α is defined in terms of a set of preconditions, $Preconditions(\alpha)$, and a set of effects $Effects(\alpha)$. For simplicity, the initial state I can be represented by a special operator $Init$, where $Effects\ (Init) = I$ and $Preconditions\ (Init) = \emptyset$. The goal G can likewise be viewed as a special operator $Goal$, with $Effects\ (Goal) = \emptyset$ and $Preconditions\ (Goal) = G$. These two operators will be elements of every plan Π, such that $Init$ precedes every other operator and $Goal$ is preceded by every other operator.

Each plan is also associated with three kinds of constraints:

(1) A set of precedence constraints on operator ordering, $Ordering(\Pi)$, that enforces a *partial order* on the operators. Each ordering constraint between operators α and β is denoted by $\alpha \prec \beta$.
(2) A set of codesignation constraints $Co(\Pi)$ on variable bindings. These constraints enforce an *equivalence relation* on the variables x_i, $i = 1, 2, \ldots$, and constants C_i, $i = 1, 2, \ldots$. Each codesignation constraint between variables (or constants) x_i and x_j is denoted by $x_i \approx x_j$.
(3) A set of noncodesignation constraints, $Nonco(\Pi)$, that forces two variables to instantiate to different constants. Each noncodesignation constraint between x_i and x_j is denoted by $x_i \not\approx x_j$. The noncodesignation constraints enforce a symmetric relation on variables and constants, such that
  (a) if $x_1 \not\approx x_2$, then $x_2 \not\approx x_1$,
  (b) if $x_1 \approx x_2$, $x_3 \approx x_4$, and $x_2 \not\approx x_4$, then $x_1 \not\approx x_3$.

In addition, constraints on variable bindings can be propagated through the literals that refer to the variables. For example, let l_1 be $P(x_1, x_2, \ldots, x_n)$ and

l_2 be $Q(y_1, y_2, \ldots, y_n)$. Then $l_1 \approx l_2$ if and only if $P = Q$ and $x_i \approx y_i$, $i = 1, 2, \ldots, n$.

A partially ordered and instantiated plan can have more than one instance that satisfies the constraints. Each instance of a plan is a totally ordered set of operators, with all variables bound to constants. Each instance is called a *completion* of the plan. A constraint R *necessarily holds* in the plan if it holds in every completion of the plan.[1] A plan is *necessarily correct*, if and only if every precondition p of every operator α is true, just before α, in every completion of the plan. A plan may be incorrect because of "conflicts" among its operators, which we formalize below.

First, we define *precondition establishment* (adopted from [20]): an operator E (which stands for Establisher) is said to *establish* a precondition p_U for operator U (which stands for User), or $Est(E, U, p_U)$, if and only if

(1) $E < U$,
(2) $\exists e_E \in \textit{Effects}(E)$ such that $(e_E \approx p_U)$, and
(3) $\forall E'$ if $(E < E')$, $(E' < U)$, and $\forall e_{E'} \in \textit{Effects}(E')$, then $\neg(e_{E'} \approx p_U)$ and $\neg(e_{E'} \approx \neg p_U)$.

The last condition states that no other operators necessarily between E and U also necessarily assert or deny p_U. This ensures that operator E is the last operator that asserts the precondition p_U. For example, in a plan for going between two rooms, the operator "opening the door" can be thought of as establishing a precondition for the operator "going between the two rooms", as long as no other operators between these two either opens or closes the door. The concept of precondition establishment has been used under different names. For example, it is called "protection interval" in NONLIN, and causal link in the systematic planner by McAllester and Rosenblitt [10].

In a partially ordered and instantiated plan, an establishment relation may possibly be undone by some other operators in the same plan. Such situations are called *conflicts* in a plan. For example, in the above example of the door-opening establishment relation, if a "closing door" operator is placed between the establisher and the user, then a conflict occurs.

Formally, let E and U be operators in a plan such that $Est(E, U, p_U)$. Suppose that there is another operator C in the plan such that

(1) $\neg(C < E)$ *and* $\neg(U < C)$, that is, C can possibly be between E and U, and
(2) $\exists e_C \in \textit{Effects}(C)$ such that $\neg(e_C \not\approx \neg p_U)$, that is, possibly C denies p_U.

Then C is called a *clobberer* of the establishment relation $Est(E, U, p_U)$.

---

[1] We have chosen not to use the modal operators □ and ◇ that Chapman has defined in [2], because the meanings of necessity and possibility are already clear from the definitions of partial ordering and equivalence relations.

A clobberer in a plan can be "defeated" by imposing ordering or codesignation constraints on the plan, or by inserting a *white knight* W between the clobberer and the operator U. Intuitively, a white knight is an operator which re-establishes the clobbered precondition p_U, whenever p_U is "threatened" by the clobberer C with its effect e_C. Formally, W is a white knight for $Est(E, U, p_U)$, e_C, and C, if and only if

(1) C is a clobberer of $Est(E, U, p_U)$,
(2) $(C < W)$ and $(W < U)$, and
(3) $\exists e_W \in Effects(W)$ such that either $e_W \approx p_U$, or $(e_W \approx \neg e_C)$.

In the door-opening example, if someone reopens the door whenever it is closed, then the operator that reopens the door is a white knight.

The tuple $\langle E, U, C, p_U, e_C \rangle$ is called a *conflict* in a plan Π, if the following conditions hold:

(1) C is a clobberer of $Est(E, U, p_U)$, and
(2) there is no W in Π, such that W is a white knight for $Est(E, U, p_U)$, e_C, and C.

2.2. Conflict resolution methods

Conflicts threaten the correctness of plans. Based on the TWEAK plan language, Chapman [2] formulated a necessary and sufficient goal achievement criterion, known as the necessary modal truth criterion, or MTC, which includes "promotion", "demotion", "establishments", "separation", and "introducing white knights" as methods to make a goal true. This set of methods is sufficient for resolving a set of conflicts, in the sense that any of them can be chosen to resolve a conflict, as long as it is consistent with the existing constraints in the plan. The methods are also necessary because, as shown by Chapman, no other methods are needed.

Let $\langle E, U, C, p_U, e_C \rangle$ be a conflict in Π. Then any of the following constraints are sufficient for resolving it:

(1) promotion of clobberer: $U < C$,
(2) demotion of clobberer: $C < E$,
(3) separation: $p_U \not\approx \neg e_C$,
(4) introducing white knights: for some W, where W is either an existing operator in the plan, or a new operator, and for some $e_W \in Effects(W)$, $C < W < U$ and either (a) $e_W \approx p_U$, or (b) $e_W \approx \neg e_C$.

Suppose that a plan Π is possibly correct. That is, there is a completion of Π in which every precondition p of every operator U holds just before U. Then from the fact that the above conflict resolution methods are both necessary and sufficient, there is a set of resolution methods, one chosen for each conflict in

Π as defined above, that forces the plan Π to be also necessarily correct. This guarantee suggests the following procedure to "fix" a faulty plan: first, find out all conflicts in the plan. Then for each conflict, generate a set of conflict resolution methods. Finally, choose one method from each set and impose the selected constraints onto the plan.

Given an establishment relation $Est(E, U, p_U)$, the set of all conflicts can be found in time $O(n^2)$, where n is the total number of operators in the plan. This is because in the worst case $O(n)$ operators have to be examined for clobberers, and for each clobberer, $O(n)$ operators have to be checked to see if they are white knights. If no new operators are to be inserted in Π, then for each conflict it takes $O(n)$ time to completely generate all four types of resolution methods above, since in the worst case $O(n)$ operators have to be tested for white knights.

Let $Conf = \langle E, U, C, p_U, e_C \rangle$ be a conflict in Π, and $M(Conf)$ the set of resolution methods for resolving $Conf$, then the set of alternative methods can be represented as a disjunctive set:

$$M(Conf) = \{\{U < C\}, \{C < E\}, \{p_U \neq \neg e_C\}\} \cup WKs(Conf),$$

where $WKs(Conf)$ is the set of white knight constraints for $Conf$. In the actual implementation of this generation process, however, the total number of conflict resolution methods can be reduced by taking into account the structure of the plan. For example, if the three operators E, U, and C are ordered in a linear sequence in a plan, such that the clobberer C is located necessarily between E and U, then only the separation and white knight methods are applicable without violating the existing ordering constraints.

Consider the painting example introduced in Section 1. The plan for painting both the ceiling and the ladder consists of two unordered linear sequences of operators, as follows:

$Init <$ **getbrush**($\$cb$) $<$ **paintceiling**(Ceiling)

$<$ **returnbrush**($\$cb$) $<$ Goal,

$Init <$ **getbrush**($\$lb$) $<$ **paintladder**(Ladder)

$<$ **returnbrush**($\$lb$) $<$ Goal,

where $\$cb$ is a variable which stands for any ceiling brush and $\$lb$ is a variable that likewise refers to any ladder brush. The preconditions and effects of each operator in the plan are shown in Table 1. The conflicts in this plan are listed in Table 2.

The conflict resolution methods are:

$$M(Conf_a) = \{\{\textbf{getbrush}(\$cb) < \textbf{getbrush}(\$lb)\},$$

$$\{\textbf{returnbrush}(\$lb) < \textbf{getbrush}(\$cb)\}\},$$

Table 1
Operator definitions for the painting example.

Operator	Preconditions	Effects
getbrush	HandEmpty, Dry($b)	Have($b), ¬HandEmpty
paintceiling	Have($b), Dry(Ladder), Have(Paint)	¬Dry(Ceiling), ¬Dry($b), Painted(Ceiling)
paintladder	Have($b), Have(Paint)	¬Dry(Ladder), ¬Dry($b), Painted(Ladder)
returnbrush	Have($b)	¬Have($b), HandEmpty
Init		HandEmpty, Dry(Ladder), Dry($lb), Dry($cb), Have(Paint)
Goal	Painted(Ceiling), Painted(Ladder)	

Table 2
Conflicts in the painting example.

Conflict	Producer	User	Clobberer	Precondition	Clobbering effect
$Conf_a$	Init	**getbrush($cb)**	**getbrush($lb)**	HandEmpty	¬HandEmpty
$Conf_b$	Init	**getbrush($lb)**	**getbrush($cb)**	HandEmpty	¬HandEmpty
$Conf_c$	Init	**getbrush($cb)**	**paintladder**	Dry($cb)	¬Dry($lb)
$Conf_d$	Init	**getbrush($lb)**	**paintceiling**	Dry($lb)	¬Dry($cb)
$Conf_e$	Init	**paintceiling**	**paintladder**	Dry(Ladder)	¬Dry(Ladder)

$$M(Conf_b) = \{\{\textbf{getbrush}(\$lb) < \textbf{getbrush}(\$cb)\},$$
$$\{\textbf{returnbrush}(\$cb) < \textbf{getbrush}(\$lb)\}\},$$
$$M(Conf_c) = \{\{\textbf{getbrush}(\$cb) < \textbf{paintladder}\}, \{\$cb \neq \$lb\}\},$$
$$M(Conf_d) = \{\{\textbf{getbrush}(\$lb) < \textbf{paintceiling}\}, \{\$cb \neq \$lb\}\},$$
$$M(Conf_e) = \{\{\textbf{paintceiling} < \textbf{paintladder}\}\}.$$

3. Relations among conflict resolution methods

To find one or all of the consistent methods for resolving a set of conflicts in a plan Π, one has to take into account the various kinds of relationships among different constraints. In this section, we define and analyze two kinds of such relations, the subsumption relation and the inconsistency relation.

3.1. Inconsistency relation

Resolving conflicts involves imposing constraints onto the structure of a plan.

Some constraints cannot be imposed together, because they are *inconsistent* with each other. For example, imposing two ordering constraints $\alpha_1 < \alpha_2$ and $\alpha_2 < \alpha_1$ onto the same plan results in a cycle in operator ordering, which is disallowed in a partial order. Likewise, constraints $x_1 \approx x_2$ and $x_2 \not\approx x_3$ are inconsistent if the variables are already constrained in the plan such that $x_1 \approx x_3$.

We now formally define an inconsistency relation on constraints. For convenience, if $\mathcal{O}$ is a set of ordering constraints, then $TR(\mathcal{O})$ represents the transitive relation corresponding to $\mathcal{O}$. Also, if $\mathcal{CO}$ is a set of codesignation constraints, then $ER(\mathcal{CO})$ is the equivalence relation corresponding to $\mathcal{CO}$.

Definition 3.1. Let R_1 and R_2 be two sets of conjunctive ordering constraints. R_1 is *inconsistent with* R_2 in plan Π, or $I_\Pi(R_1, R_2)$, if and only if $\exists \alpha, \beta \in operators(\Pi)$ such that

$$(\alpha < \beta) \in TR(R_1 \cup Ordering(\Pi)),$$
$$(\beta < \alpha) \in TR(R_2 \cup Ordering(\Pi)).$$

We can similarly define an inconsistency relation among two variable binding constraints. Let R_1 and R_2 be two sets of conjunctive codesignation and noncodesignation constraints. Let $Co(R)$ be the set of all codesignation constraints in R and $Nonco(R)$ be the set of all non-codesignation constraints in R.

Definition 3.2. R_1 is *inconsistent with* R_2 in plan Π, or $I_\Pi(R_1, R_2)$, if and only if there are variables x and y such that

$$(x \approx y) \in ER(Co(R_1) \cup Co(R_2) \cup Co(\Pi)),$$
$$(x \not\approx y) \in (Nonco(R_1) \cup Nonco(R_2) \cup Nonco(\Pi)).$$

Inconsistency relations can be extended to sets of conjunctive constraints containing ordering, codesignation, and noncodesignation ones, in terms of the inconsistency relation of their respective parts. For example, let $R_1 = \{\alpha_1 < \alpha_2, x \not\approx y\}$ and $R_2 = \{\alpha_3 < \alpha_4, x \approx y\}$. Then $I_\Pi(R_1, R_2)$ holds. Two constraints R_1 and R_2 are *consistent*, if they are not inconsistent with each other.

3.2. Subsumption relation

Imposing one set of constraints R_1 may also make another set R_2 of constraints redundant. For example, let $R_1 = \{\alpha_2 < \alpha_3\}$ and $R_2 = \{\alpha_1 < \alpha_3\}$. If $(\alpha_1 < \alpha_2) \in Ordering(\Pi)$, then clearly imposing R_1 makes it unnecessary to further impose R_2.

In general, R_1 subsumes R_2 if imposing R_1 will guarantee that R_2 is also imposed. Thus, R_2 is considered to be weaker than R_1. Formally,

Definition 3.3. Let R_1 and R_2 be two sets of conjunctive ordering constraints. R_1 *subsumes* R_2 in plan Π, or $S_\Pi(R_1, R_2)$, if and only if

$$R_2 \subseteq TR(R_1 \cup Ordering(\Pi)) .$$

Let R_1 and R_2 be two sets of codesignation and noncodesignation constraints.

Definition 3.4. R_1 *subsumes* R_2 in plan Π, or $S_\Pi(R_1, R_2)$, if and only if
 (1) $Co(R_2) \subseteq ER(Co(R_1) \cup Co(\Pi))$,
 (2) $\forall r = (x \not\approx y) \in Nonco(R_2)$, $\exists r_1 = (x \approx x')$, $r_2 = (y \approx y')$, and $r_3 = (x' \not\approx y')$, where $r_1, r_2 \in ER(Co(R_1) \cup Co(\Pi))$ and $r_3 \in (Nonco(R_1) \cup Nonco(\Pi))$.

The last condition says that every noncodesignation constraint of R_2 can be inferred from the noncodesignation constraints of R_1 and Π. As an example, let $R_1 = \{(x \approx y)\}$ and $R_2 = \{(y \not\approx z)\}$. If $(x \not\approx z) \in Nonco(\Pi)$, then $S_\Pi(R_1, R_2)$.

Similar to inconsistency relations, subsumption relations can also be extended to include sets of both ordering and codesignation constraints. For example, let $R_1 = \{\alpha_2 < \alpha_3, x_1 \approx x_2\}$ and $R_2 = \{\alpha_1 < \alpha_3, x_1 \approx x_3\}$. If constraints $\alpha_1 < \alpha_2$ and $x_2 \approx x_3$ already hold in plan Π, then $S_\Pi(R_1, R_2)$ holds.

Given a plan Π, one can establish the subsumption and inconsistency relations between any pair of constraints R_1 and R_2, by computing the transitive and equivalence closures of the ordering and codesignation constraints, respectively, in R_1, R_2, and Π. Both computations take time $O(n^3)$ for n operators in Π.

For convenience, the subscript Π of both I_Π and S_Π relations is dropped in situations where it is clear about the plan under consideration.

Because the subsumption relation S is defined via subset relations, it can be easily verified that S is transitive. That is,

Lemma 3.5. *If $S(R_1, R_2)$ and $S(R_2, R_3)$, then $S(R_1, R_3)$.*

In addition, it is also easy to see that the following property holds:

Lemma 3.6. *If $S(R_1, R_2)$, $S(R_3, R_4)$, and $I(R_2, R_4)$, then $I(R_1, R_3)$.*

This lemma states that if two constraints are inconsistent, then stronger versions of the two constraints are also inconsistent. By letting R_3 and R_4 both be R', it holds as a corallary that if $S(R_1, R_2)$ and $I(R_2, R')$, then $I(R_1, R')$.

Subsumption and inconsistency relations have so far been defined between pairs of constraints. Extensions to higher-order relations can be naturally made in a similar way. For example, two sets of precedence constraints R_1 and R_2 subsume R_3 in Π if and only if $R_3 \subseteq TR(\{R_1, R_2\} \cup Ordering(\Pi))$.

3.3. Minimal solutions

Above we have defined a set of constraints R to be consistent with respect to a plan Π, as the condition that imposing R onto Π will not create any cycle in the operator ordering of Π, and will not produce any contradictory codesignation and noncodesignation constraints. If $\mathscr{C}$ is the set of all conflicts in plan Π, and if a consistent set of constraints Sol resolves all conflicts in Π, then Sol is called a *solution* to $\mathscr{C}$. Clearly, if two sets of constraints R_1 and R_2 are inconsistent, then they cannot both be part of a solution.

It is possible to find a certain amount of redundancy in a solution. For example, if $\alpha_1 < \alpha_2$ and $x \neq y$ both resolve the same conflict $Conf$, then the set of conjunctive constraints $\{(\alpha_1 < \alpha_2), (x \neq y)\}$ also resolves $Conf$. However, the latter is unnecessarily strong, because either conjunct is able to resolve the conflict without the other. Thus, it is possible to reduce a solution Sol to another solution that is in some sense minimal. A *minimal solution Sol'* for $\mathscr{C}$ is a solution for $\mathscr{C}$ such that no proper subset of Sol' also resolves all conflicts in $\mathscr{C}$.

As the previous example illustrates, a solution may have several alternative sets of minimal solutions. If Sol' is a minimal solution and if $Sol' \subset Sol$, then the constraints in set difference $Sol - Sol'$ are considered redundant with respect to Sol'. As a consequence, if R_1 and R_2 are two disjoint subsets of a solution Sol and if $S(R_1, R_2)$ is true, then removing R_2 from Sol doesn't affect the minimal solution corresponding to Sol. This observation is the basis of a constraint propagation rule presented in the next section.

As we have pointed out in Section 1, if all conflicts in a plan are known, then using a *global analysis* for conflict resolution is more advantageous than considering the conflicts one at a time. A global analysis of conflicts should then take into account both the inconsistency relation and subsumption relation. To do this, an existing problem solving paradigm, known as constraint satisfaction, provides an ideal framework for conducting such a global analysis. In the next section, we present a formalization of conflict resolution using CSP.

4. Conflict resolution as constraint satisfaction

Constraint satisfaction problems (CSPs) provide a simple but powerful framework for solving a large variety of AI problems. The technique has been successfully applied to machine vision, belief maintenance, scheduling, as well as many design tasks. An overview of the techniques can be found in [6].

4.1. CSP representations

A CSP can be formulated abstractly as consisting of a set of variables, each variable is associated with a domain of values that can be assigned to the variable. In addition, a set of constraints exists that defines the permissible subsets of assignments to variables. The goal is to find one (or all) assignment of values to the variables such that no constraints are violated. Note that one should not confuse the variables used in the parameters of a planning operator with the variables in a CSP.

As an example, consider the map coloring problem, where the variables are regions that are to be colored. A domain for a variable is the set of alternative colors that a region can be painted with. A constraint exists between every pair of adjacent variables, which states that the pair cannot be assigned the same color. A solution to the problem is a set of colors, one for each region, that satisfies the constraints.

Conflict resolution in planning can be mapped into a CSP in the following manner. For a given plan Π, each conflict $Conf_i$ in Π corresponds to a variable. The domain of $Conf_i$ is the set of alternative conflict resolution methods that are capable of resolving the conflict. The constraints among the variables are defined via the inconsistency relations among different sets of conflict resolution methods. A solution to the CSP corresponds to selecting a set of consistent resolution methods that resolves all conflicts in Π.

An advantage of the mapping from conflict resolution problems to CSPs is that many existing strategies for solving general CSPs can be directly applied to facilitate a global analysis of conflicts. In addition, the existence of subsumption relations among the variables provides new opportunities for simplifying a CSP further than permitted by traditional CSP techniques.

The methods for solving a CSP can be roughly divided into two categories: constraint propagation and heuristically guided backtracking algorithms.

4.2. Propagating constraints among conflicts

When two or more variables are considered together, certain implicit constraints among them can be inferred from the explicitly given ones. Consider, for example, a plan containing two conflicts, $Conf_A$ and $Conf_B$, where the resolution methods have been found out to be

$$M(Conf_A) = \{\{x \approx y, b < c\}\},$$
$$M(Conf_B) = \{\{x \not\approx y\}, \{c < b\}\}.$$

Then from the inconsistency relations $I(x \approx y, x \not\approx y)$ and $I(b < c, c < b)$, it is clear that the constraint set $\{x \approx y, b < c\}$, for $Conf_A$, cannot be used as part of a solution for solving both conflicts. Therefore, it can be removed from the set of resolution methods for $Conf_A$ without affecting any solutions. Furthermore, if it is also the only method for resolving $Conf_A$, then the plan Π corresponds to a dead end; it cannot be resolved by simply imposing constraints.

The above example is an instance of a general procedure known as arc-consistency in CSP. Given a CSP, an arc-consistency algorithm checks every pair X, Y of variables to search for a situation where there is a value V_X for X that is inconsistent with every value of Y. Then V_X can be removed from the domain of X without losing solutions to the CSP. The algorithm AC-3 [9] which is based on this idea, ensures that no more values can be further removed as described above. In this case, the CSP is called arc-consistent. If a CSP has n variables, and each has a domain size no more than v, then the time complexity is $O(n^2 v^2)$. As a special case, if any variable ends up with an empty domain, then the entire CSP has no solution.

Arc-consistency can be used as a preprocessing routine before a backtracking algorithm is used, or, as we'll explain later, it can also be used during backtracking. Arc-consistency computation considers pairs of conflicts, and is thus more powerful than considering individual conflicts alone. As demonstrated by the above example, an advantage of arc-consistency processing is that dead ends can be found early in many cases. In terms of search, the pruning of inconsistent choices corresponds to a reduction of the branching factor of a planner's search tree. It can also reduce a "thrashing" effect notorious for backtracking problem solving. A thrashing effect occurs when search in different parts of the search space may fail because of exactly the same reason. For example, if $Conf_i$ and $Conf_j$ are not arc-consistent, i.e., if a resolution method R_{ik} for conflict $Conf_i$ is inconsistent with every method for resolving a conflict $Conf_j$, and if $Conf_i$ is resolved first, then choosing R_{ik} for $Conf_i$ will always result in a failure, which is repeated for every selection of resolution methods for every conflict the planner chooses between $Conf_i$ and $Conf_j$. However, arc-consistency can detect and avoid such a situation with quadratic time complexity.

4.3. Redundancy removal via subsumption relation

Recall that a resolution method R_1 subsumes R_2, if R_1 can resolve any conflict that R_2 can. Therefore, with respect to a conflict $Conf_2$ that R_2 can resolve, R_1 is stronger than necessary. Subsumption relations make certain constraints in the solutions to a CSP redundant. Below, we consider two cases in which redundancy can be detected.

Consider a plan Π containing, among others, two conflicts, $Conf_1$ and $Conf_2$. Suppose that every set of constraints for $Conf_1$ subsumes some constraint for $Conf_2$. Because any solution Sol for resolving all conflicts must also resolve $Conf_1$, every choice of a resolution method from $M(Conf_1)$ must also resolve $Conf_2$. This fact holds even when a constraint chosen from $M(Conf_2)$ is removed from *Sol*. Therefore, if $Conf_2$ is removed from the CSP, the set of minimal solutions to the CSP will not be affected. The argument is summarized in the theorem below.

Theorem 4.1. *Let Π be a plan with a conflict set $\mathscr{C}$. Let $Conf_1$ and $Conf_2$ be two conflicts in $\mathscr{C}$, and let $M(Conf_1)$ and $M(Conf_2)$ be their corresponding sets of conflict resolution constraints. Suppose that*

$$\forall R_1 \in M(Conf_1), \exists R_2 \in M(Conf_2) \text{ such that } S(R_1, R_2).$$

Then $Conf_2$ can be pruned from the CSP without affecting the set of minimal solutions to $\mathscr{C}$.

In this case, $Conf_2$ is redundant. Formal proofs for this theorem and the next can be found in Appendix A.

Pruning of redundant variables from a CSP reduces the size of the CSP and therefore can lead to improved efficiency in constraint reasoning. Removal of redundancy in the above form only utilizes the subsumption information. When both inconsistency and subsumption relations are considered together, it is also possible to remove individual redundant values from a CSP.

Consider again a plan Π containing two conflicts, $Conf_1$ and $Conf_2$. Suppose that there is some constraint set R_2 in $M(Conf_2)$, such that for every method R_1 in $M(Conf_1)$, either

(1) $I(R_1, R_2)$, i.e. R_1 is inconsistent with R_2; or
(2) $\exists R_3 \in M(Conf_2)$ such that $R_2 \neq R_3$ and $S(R_1, R_3)$, that is, R_1 subsumes some other constraints in $M(Conf_2)$.

A solution *Sol* for the set of all conflicts in Π must also resolve $Conf_1$. Since R_1 satisfies the above condition, if R_1 subsumes $R_3 \in M(Conf_2)$ such that $R_3 \neq R_2$, then it is equivalent to selecting R_3 resolving $Conf_2$, instead of selecting R_2. On the other hand, if R_1 is inconsistent with R_2, then the solution cannot include both R_1 and R_2 anyway. As a result, no matter what method is chosen for $Conf_1$, R_2 will not be chosen for a minimal solution. This means that R_2 can be removed from $M(Conf_2)$ without affecting the set of minimal solutions for resolving all conflicts in Π. This conclusion is summarized in the following theorem.

Theorem 4.2. *Let Π be a plan with a conflict set $\mathscr{C}$. Let $Conf_1$ and $Conf_2$ be two conflicts in $\mathscr{C}$, and let $M(Conf_1)$ and $M(Conf_2)$ be their corresponding sets of conflict resolution constraints. Suppose that $\exists R_2 \in M(Conf_2)$ such that $\forall R_1 \in M(Conf_1)$, either*
(1) $I(R_1, R_2)$, *or*
(2) $\exists R_3 \in M(Conf_2)$ *such that* $R_2 \neq R_3$ *and* $S(R_1, R_3)$.

Then R_2 can be pruned from $M(Conf_2)$ without affecting the set of minimal solutions to $\mathscr{C}$.

Removal of redundant variables or values in a CSP is called *redundancy removal*. It can be used to augment a traditional arc-consistent algorithm in the following manner: at each time a pair of variables X, Y are examined in an arc-consistency algorithm, a check is also made to first verify where Y is redundant using Theorem 4.1. Then a second test using Theorem 4.2 can be made to test whether each value of Y is redundant due to a combined consideration of both inconsistency and subsumption relations. For a given set of constraints, the computations of both inconsistency and subsumption relations have the same time complexity. These relations are computed only once when the CSP is first initialized. Furthermore, the augmented arc-consistency algorithm takes these two relations as inputs, and considers pairs of conflicts for both of them. Therefore, the additional consideration of subsumption relations in the augmented algorithm increases the complexity of the original algorithm only by a constant factor.

Redundancy removal can also be extended in a similar manner to augment path-consistency algorithms, which examine and infer inconsistencies within groups of three variables [8]. Such an extension is straightforward, and a detailed description can be found in [18]. We will now illustrate the application of constraint propagation algorithms and then turn our attention to a consideration of possible applications of heuristically guided backtracking algorithms to global conflict resolution.

4.4. The painting example

Consider again the painting problem described in Section 1. The conflict resolution methods for this problem have been formulated in Section 2. The conflicts are listed in Table 2. The conflict resolution process is listed below.

(1) The only choice for $Conf_e$ is inconsistent with the second set of constraints for $Conf_a$. Therefore, the latter is removed from $M(Conf_a)$ by arc-consistency.

(2) After the last step, the only alternative left for $M(Conf_a)$ is

$\{\textbf{getbrush}(\$cb) < \textbf{getbrush}(\$lb)\}$,

which is inconsistent with the first choice for $Conf_b$. Thus, due to arc-consistency $M(Conf_b)$ is reduced to

$\{\{\textbf{returnbrush}(\$cb) < \textbf{getbrush}(\$lb)\}\}$.

(3) The only remaining constraint for $Conf_b$ now subsumes constraints for $Conf_a$, $Conf_c$, and $Conf_e$. Thus, from Theorem 4.1, all three conflicts become redundant in the CSP and can be removed.

(4) The remaining constraint

   {**returnbrush**(sb) < **getbrush**(lb)}

   for $Conf_b$ is inconsistent with the first constraint for $Conf_d$. Thus, the first constraint can be removed using arc-consistency
(5) Finally, the CSP contains only two conflicts, $Conf_b$ and $Conf_d$. The remaining constraints left in $M(Conf_b)$ and $M(Conf_d)$ are combined as a global solution to the CSP:

   returnbrush(cb) < **getbrush**(lb), $cb \neq lb$.

   This solution is also a minimal solution for the CSP. The resulting plan is formed by ordering all ceiling-painting operations to be before all ladder-painting operations, and making sure that the ceiling-painting brush is different from the ladder-painting brush.

4.5. Heuristically guided backtracking algorithms and their extensions

Arc-consistency algorithms may not discover all implicit constraints in a CSP, as it considers only pairs of variables. If three or more sets of constraints are inconsistent, then a problem solver may have to backtrack. For example, suppose that there are N conflicts, a resolution method for the ith one is $a_i < a_{i+1}$ for $1 \leq i < N$, and $a_N < a_1$ for $Conf_N$. Then although any pair of values for two variables may not contradict with each other, the set of all N constraints will result in a cycle in the plan. Therefore, although arc-consistency can prune many inconsistent values, in general a global constraint management algorithm, such as a backtracking algorithm, has to be used.

A backtracking algorithm instantiates the variables one at a time in a depth-first manner. It backtracks when the constraints accumulated so far signal inconsistency. With both inconsistency and subsumption relations in a CSP, a backtracking algorithm can be guided by the order of variables to be solved, and the order of value assignments to the variables.

Variable ordering corresponds directly to ordering the conflicts to be resolved in a plan. Under this mapping, one useful heuristic is to resolve a conflict with the smallest number of resolution methods first [6]. For example, if $M(Conf_1)$ has a size of two and $M(Conf_2)$ has a size of ten, then this heuristic resolves $Conf_1$ before $Conf_2$. A problem with this heuristic is that there may be many conflicts with the same number of resolution methods. Given subsumption relations among the conflicts, a tie-breaking heuristic can be further used to augment the above heuristic by preferring to resolve a conflict which resolution methods subsume a large number of others.

Given an ordering of conflicts, a value ordering heuristic could choose a resolution method that leaves choices for future variable assignments as open as possible [6], and similar to variable ordering, tie-breaking can be further achieved by preferring a value which subsumes the largest number of values belonging to the remaining variables.

After each variable assignment, a backtracking algorithm can also propagate constraints through the unassigned variables. A straightforward but powerful method, known as forward-checking [6], performs partial arc-consistency by removing from each future variable domain those values that are inconsistent with the current assignment. An extension using subsumption relations can further simplify the remaining CSP, by removing from the network any variable with a domain value subsumed by the current assignment. Specifically, let *Conf* be the current variable and *Rem* be the set of remaining conflicts yet to be resolved. If u is chosen to be the instantiation for *Conf*, then the forward-checking algorithm performs a look-ahead step:

>   **for** each $Conf_j \in Rem$ **do**
>   **if** there is a value $v \in M(Conf_j)$ such that (u, v) is inconsistent,
>   **then** delete v from $M(Conf_j)$;
>   **endif**;
>   **if** there is a value $v \in M(Conf_j)$ such that u subsumes v,
>   **then** delete $Conf_j$ from Rem;
>   **endfor**;

So far we have been concerned with the construction of reasoning tools used for resolving conflicts. We next consider how to integrate these tools with actual planning systems.

5. Planning with global conflict resolution

Classical planning systems often plan in an incremental manner, by repeatedly inserting new operators and resolving conflicts. During each iteration of a planning routine, a few existing or new operators are chosen to establish a precondition or subgoal. Then one or more conflicts are detected and resolved. This process repeats until no more conflicts exist in a plan, and when there are enough operators to establish all preconditions and goals. Some examples are Chapman's TWEAK and the systematic nonlinear planner by McAllester and Rosenblitt [10].

In a simple domain, the number of conflicts introduced and considered in each planning cycle by an incremental method may be very small in number. In blocks world domains, for example, our experience has been that the number of conflicts introduced in each cycle by TWEAK is often about two on the average. Because of the small number of conflicts, it may not appear very effective to apply the CSP conflict resolution method to incremental planning, since many of the supposed advantages of the global analysis may indeed be too small to be noticed: the order in which to resolve the conflicts may not matter much, and dead ends may not occur often enough to justify a global constraint propagation. Furthermore, the utility of our conflict resolution method based on CSP may even become a serious question; although it only takes cubic time to detect conflicts and build a CSP representation, the accumulated amount of effort over the entire search space could surpass its benefit in the long run. Therefore, a complete theory of conflict resolution should also cast a boundary indicating in what kind of domains, and with what type of planning methods, the global analysis is expected to work well.

To address the utility question, we have performed empirical tests of the algorithms. We expected from these tests that the CSP method for conflict resolution will be the most effective when a large number of conflicts could be detected in a plan. In addition, the benefit of doing the global analysis increases with the number of conflicts, relative to an incremental method.

In terms of application domains, a large number of conflicts may occur if the operators are tightly inter-related and sensitive to operator ordering and variable binding constraints. An example of such domains is where there are *nonserializable subgoals* [5], such that solutions to the individual subgoals must be properly interleaved in order to yield a correct solution. With planning techniques, our expectation leads to the following predictions. First, for planning systems that adopt a problem decomposition strategy, a global conflict analysis can be beneficial. Examples of problem-decomposition-based problem solvers are Lansky's GEMPLAN [7], which has been applied to building construction domains, Yang, Nau and Hendler's restricted interaction planner [19], which has been tested on metal cutting problems in automated manufacturing, and Simmons' GORDIUS system [12] which has been applied to geologic interpretation. Problem decomposition is the process of breaking apart a large and complex problem into several smaller, more or less self-contained parts. A solution can then be found for each individual part concurrently, by constraining problem solving activities to be focused on only that part. When the subsolutions are combined, however, the interactions among the different parts are likely to occur and need to be resolved. It is in this combination phase where the CSP-based conflict resolution method can show a marked difference. Using problem decomposition, one can generate plans for each individual subproblem from scratch. But one can also rely on problem-dependent problem solvers for providing subsolutions of decomposed parts, and use the CSP method as a problem-independent routine for combining the solution plans. For example, in a manufacturing domain there is usually a number of specialists who can provide several alternative plans and constraints for subproblems within their expertise. But when a complex part is to be produced, a domain-independent module can be used profitably for sequencing and resource control [4].

Related to problem decomposition systems, a second type of planner for which the CSP method may be useful is one that employs a task network hierarchy. A task network planning system starts with a set of subgoals and reduces each one according to a library of pre-defined networks of subplans. Each subplan may also contain more detailed subgoals that can be further reduced. The system terminates when every remaining operator in the plan can be successfully executed. Examples of such systems are SIPE, NONLIN, and DIVISER. When these systems are applied to complex domains, each task reduction may introduce many new steps that interact, which may in turn cause a large number of conflicts to occur.

Finally, the CSP method is expected to be useful in *plan revision*, where the input is a used plan that is possibly incorrect, and the output is a modified version of the plan which fits a new situation. For example, in the PRIAR system of Kambhampati and Hendler [3], a previously generated plan is first retrieved. The system then identifies those preconditions of the operators that are no longer established or conflicted in a new situation, and proposes plan modification operations for re-achieving them. The inserted new operators may render the plan possibly incorrect by creating new conflicts, and the number of such conflicts may increase with the number of faults in the original plan. In this case, our CSP method for conflict resolution can fix the remaining conflicts and arrive at a conclusion about the validity of the fix fast.

In the sections that follow, we present empirical, average-case results confirming the hypothesis that a global analysis based on CSP methods is more advantageous than an incremental method in domains where there is a large number of conflicts. We also test the prediction that with a problem decomposition strategy, the CSP-based method offers dramatic improvement in efficiency. We start by providing a detailed picture of the implementation.

6. Implementation

This section describes the implementation of two planning systems, TWEAK and WATPLAN. Both systems are coded in Allegro Common Lisp on a SUN4/Sparc Station. Care has been taken so that both planners share exactly the same unification and consistency checking routines.

6.1. TWEAK

TWEAK[2] is implemented as a cycle of two activities: establishing a precondition of an operator, and then resolving all conflicts for that establishment relation. More precisely, it can be specified as the following procedure:

(1) Select a plan state from the search frontier. Apply a correctness

---

[2] Implemented in collaboration with Steve Woods.

checking routine (the Modal Truth Criterion) to the plan to verify its necessary correctness. If the plan is correct, then exit with success.

(2) Find a precondition p of an operator A such that p is not necessarily true. Find all establishers from the operators in the plan as well by instantiating new operator schemata in a plan library. For each establisher E, construct a new establishment relation $Est(E, A, p)$ in a copy of the plan.

(3) For each successor plan, detect and resolve all conflicts with the new establishment relation. Each alternative set of constraints that resolves the conflicts gives rise to a new successor state.

(4) Extend the search frontier of TWEAK by including all resultant successors from the last step. Go to step (1).

This implementation of TWEAK is sound, in that every solution it finds is necessarily correct. With a breadth-first search control strategy, it is also complete in that it will always find a solution if one exists.

An option can also be chosen in TWEAK for performing either depth-first search or breadth-first search. Under the condition that only ordering and variable binding constraints can be imposed, both depth-first and breadth-first strategies guarantee that a correct completion of a plan can be found, if one such completion exists.

6.2. WATPLAN

The theory of conflict resolution has been implemented in a planner we call WATPLAN[3]. Its input is assumed to be a possibly incorrect plan, and it outputs a necessarily correct instance of the plan if one exists. WATPLAN consists of four modules, a conflict detection module, a preprocessing module, a variable ordering module, and a backtracking module. Each module is described briefly below.

6.2.1. Conflict detection

The first module of WATPLAN detects all conflicts with the establishment relations in the plan. It starts by trying to find an establishment relation for each operator precondition and subgoal. Then it looks for the set of all conflicts with the establishment relations in the entire plan. For each conflict, it proposes a set of resolution methods as outlined in Section 2. The conflicts, together with the conflict resolution methods, form a CSP that is the basis of the subsequent modules.

6.2.2. Preprocessing

If executed, this module will perform two tasks: using a partial arc-

---

[3] *Waterloo plan*ner.

consistency algorithm to check for dead ends and for removing inconsistencies, and using a redundancy removal algorithm for eliminating subsumed nodes or values in the CSP.

The partial arc-consistency algorithm checks for every pair X and Y of variables in the CSP whether a value of X is inconsistent with every value of Y. If so, then the value is removed from the domain of X. The difference between this algorithm and AC-3 is that it only does one pass over the network, thus, it doesn't re-check the consistency of X with other variables due to an update in X's domain. Although the partial arc-consistency enforcement does not ensure the CSP network to be completely arc-consistent, it does allow significant elimination of inconsistencies. This implementation decision is for the purpose of minimizing the complexity of preprocessing algorithms.

After performing partial arc-consistency, a redundancy elimination procedure checks every pair of variables X and Y to see if every value of X subsumes some value of Y. If so, then according to Theorem 4.1, Y can be removed from the CSP while keeping the solution set intact. This procedure also records the total number of times a value of a variable X subsumes some values of other variables. The recorded measure will be used in the next module as a variable ordering heuristic.

6.2.3. Variable ordering

The third module of WATPLAN sorts the variables of the CSP in ascending order of the cardinality of their domains. For variables of the same domain size, an option can be selected to order them in decreasing number of subsumption recordings given by the previous module. The purpose of this ordering process is for the backtracking algorithm to search a small search tree, and discover redundant nodes as soon as possible.

6.2.4. Backtracking

The last module performs depth-first search using the forward-checking algorithm augmented by subsumption pruning. The algorithm is listed in Section 4. An option has also been implemented for the algorithm to find just one solution, or the set of all solutions. Finally, the solution constraints are imposed onto the plan to produce a correct instance.

7. Fixing incorrect plans

The first experiment compares the average performance of WATPLAN and TWEAK, on a group of artificially and randomly generated plans that are possibly incorrect. Each test problem contains a user-specified number of randomly generated conflicts among a fixed number of linear sequences of operators that are unordered with each other. Each operator can have preconditions and effects. To avoid cases that favor WATPLAN over TWEAK, trivial plans in which some preconditions don't have an establisher, or plans that contain obvious unresolvable conflicts, have been rejected. Each conflict is created by randomly choosing a clobbering operator that conflicts with a randomly selected establishment relation.

The test problems are designed to simulate an important subclass of planning problems in general, which can be described as follows:

> Given an incorrect plan, impose only ordering and codesignation constraints to make it necessarily correct.

This problem is characteristic of the kinds of problems concerned by plan reuse systems such as PRIAR, the conflict resolution components of task-network-based planners such as SIPE, and the subsolution combination phase of any problem decomposition system.

The first group of data compares the average performance[4] of WATPLAN with TWEAK, with an increasing number of conflicts and increasing size of the plans. Tests were done for plans containing two, four, and six unordered linear sequences, where each sequence contains ten operators. Each operator has two preconditions, and more than two effects. For each plan size, 150 randomly generated plans are taken as inputs to WATPLAN and TWEAK with either depth-first or breadth-first search strategy. For each specific number of conflicts, ten random plans are generated and the test results are averaged.

Test results for plans with 2×10 operators are partitioned into two classes, based on whether a plan contains resolvable conflicts or not. Figure 1 shows

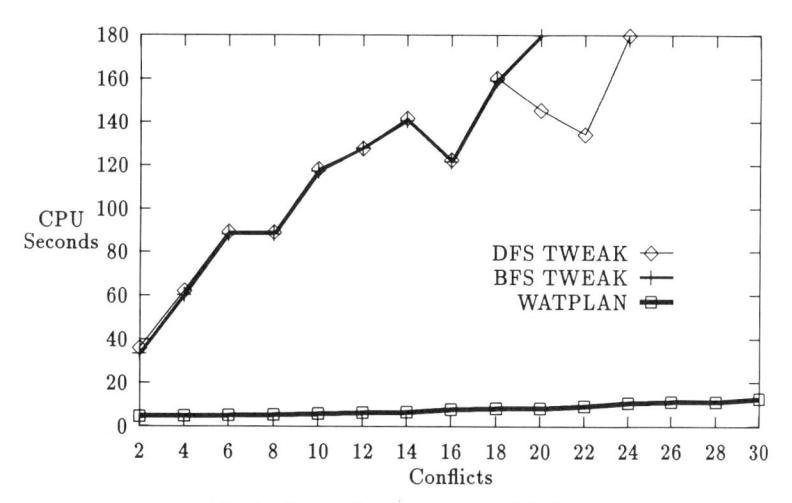

Fig. 1. Comparison over successful plans.

---

[4] In most tests, CPU seconds are used as units of measurements, as opposed to the total number of states explored, since the costs of preprocessing algorithms in WATPLAN do not show up in the number of states expanded.

the average results of the first class, where conflicts in all plans can be successfully resolved. Figure 2 shows the tests of plans with unresolvable conflicts, with the same plan size as in Fig. 1. It is clear from Fig. 1 that the average-case complexity of WATPLAN is much lower than TWEAK, and that, as the number of conflicts increases, the difference between the two also increases. For plans with unresolvable conflicts, WATPLAN displays a more stable pattern in CPU time, as compared to TWEAK. This can be attributed to the application of partial arc-consistency for global dead end detection in WATPLAN. On the other hand, TWEAK often cannot realize the dead end situation until late in the search process.

With plans containing 4×10 and 6×10 operators, TWEAK cannot finish by a limit of 180 CPU seconds. Thus, only WATPLAN is used for testing these plans. This class of tests is aimed at finding the effects of large plan size on the complexity of WATPLAN. Figure 3 shows the results, where each datum is an average of ten tests, with no distinction made between successful and unsuccessful plan revision. It is easy to observe the constant amount of increase in average time complexity of WATPLAN when the plan sizes increase. This constant factor is due to the fact that the initial setup costs—the costs of conflict detection operations—increase with plan sizes in cubic manner. But once set up, the costs for conflict resolution is a function of only the total number of conflicts in the plan.

Our second group of experiments tests the utilities of using the subsumption relation in both preprocessing and backtracking. We expect that subsumption is most useful when the conflicts are tightly coupled, in situations where a small portion of a plan contains a large number of conflicts. In such cases, it is more likely for some constraints to subsume a large number of others, making it more efficient to impose these constraints first. For example, in an extreme

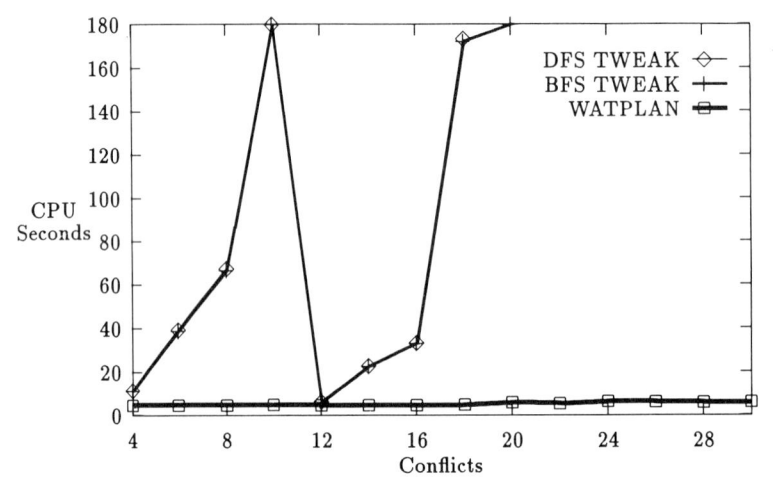

Fig. 2. Comparison over failed plans.

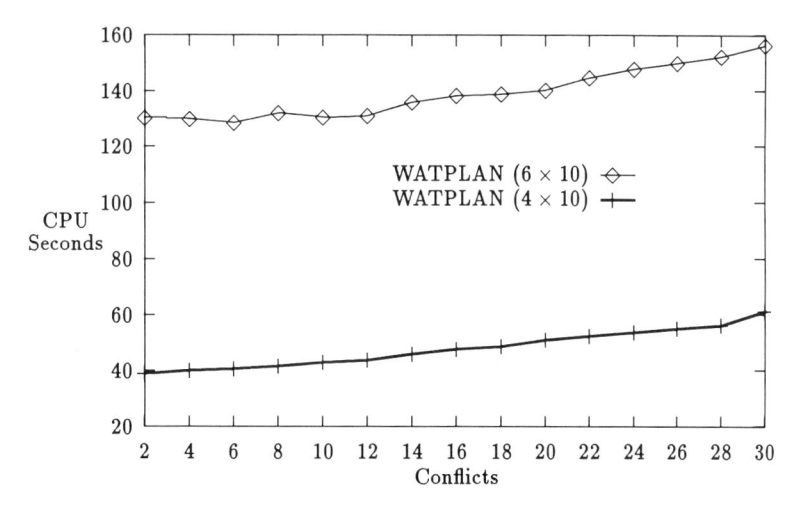

Fig. 3. Comparison over plans with large sizes.

case, there can be one clobberer in a linear branch that creates all conflicts with operators on the other branch. Figure 4 shows comparisons, in CPU seconds, of WATPLAN using and not using subsumption relations in such an extreme case (where the number of preconditions for each operator is three, the plan size is 2×10, and all the conflicts are caused by a single operator). Figure 5 further demonstrates the number of states expanded for each case of WATPLAN. The number of states expanded by WATPLAN using subsumption stays almost constant with increasing number of conflicts, because redundancy removal eliminates almost any need for search in tightly coupled plans. Therefore, our expectation about the utility of subsumption relation holds true.

However, when conflicts are only loosely coupled, using the subsumption

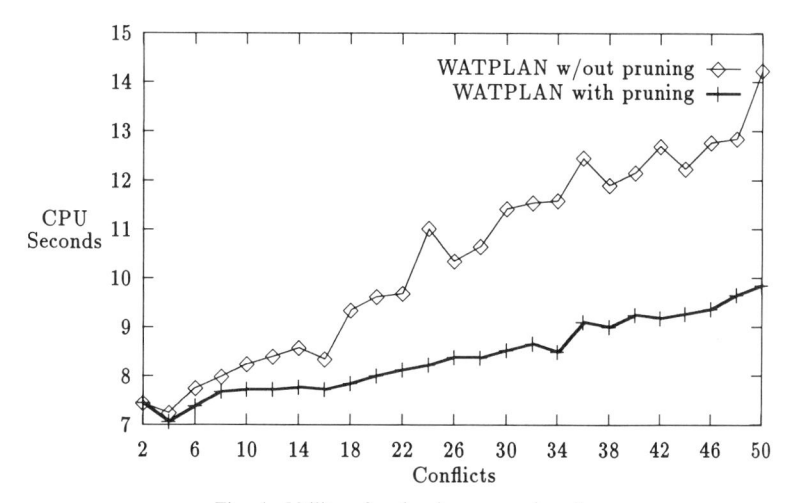

Fig. 4. Utility of redundancy pruning, I.

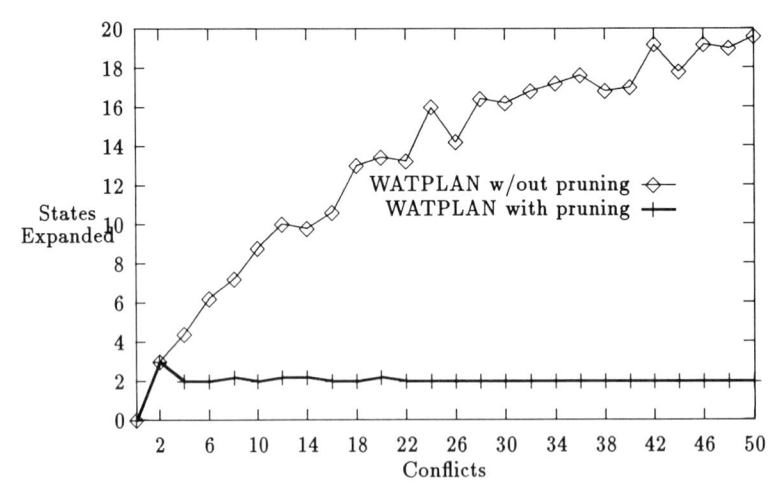

Fig. 5. Utility of redundancy pruning, II.

relation is not very different from not using it. For example, in plans containing six branches and ten operators per branch, there is no observable difference between the two instances of WATPLAN.

To sum up, the results of our experiments can be stated in the following three conclusions:

(1) A global conflict processing algorithm is more efficient than an incremental planning algorithm.
(2) With the increasing number of conflicts, the relative computational advantage of WATPLAN over TWEAK grows.
(3) Subsumption is more useful when conflicts are more tightly coupled in a small portion of a plan.

8. Problem decomposition with WATPLAN

As predicted in Section 5, a global analysis of conflicts is expected to be particularly useful for problem solvers that are based on a problem decomposition strategy. A situation in which problem decomposition can be profitably applied is where there is enough domain-dependent knowledge for generating solutions to each individual subproblem, but the conflicts among the subsolutions need to be resolved when a global solution is formed. WATPLAN is extended to interface with a set of specialists to facilitate this way of problem solving. In particular, it is assumed that an ordered set of alternative solutions has been generated by each specialist within his/her domain. WATPLAN then conducts a systematic selection of subsolutions, and applies its conflict detection, preprocessing, variable ordering, and backtracking algorithms to combine the solutions. If the resultant plan can be made correct, then one such correct plan is returned. Otherwise, it returns to the previous step to select the next set of plans for combination. The process repeats until either there is a successful combination, or there is no new combination to be considered.

To test the efficiency of this strategy, experiments have been done in the blocks world domain, where a planning problem is defined by the initial and final configurations of stacks of blocks on a table. The restrictions are that only one block can be moved at a time, and that a block cannot simultaneously support more than one block. The operators in this domain are **move**(x, y, z), for moving a block x and y to a block z, and **newtower**(x, y) for moving a block x from the top of y to Table.

One way to decompose the blocks world domain is to consider the movement of each block as the task of a specialist. Suppose that a specialist knows exactly how a block x can be moved, in the following manner: From any initial situation On(x, y) to a goal situation On(x, z), every block x is moved in precisely one of the following ways:

(1) If $y = z =$ Table, then return {(**donothing**)} as the only solution for moving block x. **donothing** denotes an empty subplan, in which all goal conditions are established by the initial situation.

(2) If $y =$ Table but $z \neq$ Table, then return {(**move**(x, Table, z))}.

(3) If $y \neq$ Table and $z =$ Table, then return {(**newtower**(x, y))}.

(4) If $y = z \neq$ Table, then return a set of two alternative solutions:

{(**donothing**), (**newtower**(x, y) < **move**(x, Table, z))} .

(5) Otherwise, return

{(**move**(x, y, z)), (**newtower**(x, y) < **move**(x, Table, z))} .

The above domain-dependent enumeration of the movement of a block completely characterizes its possible movement for any given initial and final situations. Therefore, given a blocks world problem, if there is a plan for all blocks, then a subplan exists for each individual block that can be combined to result in a correct one. In other words, WATPLAN is complete for this domain. The difficulty lies in the selection of subplans which can be combined to result in a final solution. When more than one block exists, a choice made may not only affect the successful movement of one block, but may also make the other blocks' movements either easier or harder, or even impossible in some situations. We illustrate the selection process through the following example.

The initial situation is

On(C, A), On(A, B), On(B, Table), Clear(C), Clear(Table)

and the goal is

On(A, B), On(B, C), On(C, Table).

The initial subplans, which are provided by the specialists for the blocks, are listed below.

- For block A: {(**donothing**), (**newtower**(A, B) < **move**(A, Table, B))}.
- For block B: {(**move**(B, Table, C)}.
- For block C: {(**newtower**(C, A))}.

The first choice for subplan combination includes the subplan **donothing** for block A. However, when the three subplans are combined, no operator can be found in the plan that establishes the precondition Clear(B) of **move**(B, Table, C). But the second choice for combination, listed below, can be successfully merged.

- For block A: (**newtower**(A, B) < **move**(A, Table, B)).
- For block B: **move**(B, Table, C).
- For block C: **newtower**(C, A).

In particular, when the three subplans are combined, the newly found establishment relations for precondition Clear(A) of **move**(A, Table, B) and precondition Clear(B) of **move**(B, Table, C) require the imposition of ordering constraints

newtower(C, A) < **move**(A, Table, B),

newtower(A, B) < **move**(B, Table, C).

Furthermore, the following conflicts are detected:

(1) **move**(A, Table, B) is a clobberer for the establishment relation

$Est(Init, $ **move**(B, Table, C), Clear(B)),

(2) **move**(B, Table, C) is a clobberer for

$Est(Init, $ **newtower**(C, A), Clear(C)).

A linear plan is obtained by resolving both conflicts:

newtower(C, A) < **newtower**(A, B)

< **move**(B, Table, C) < **move**(A, Table, B).

Tests have been conducted with randomly generated blocks world problems, which are simply randomly generated initial situations for a given number of blocks. For each random problem, a domain-specific routine is first applied to generate the set of alternative movements for each block. Then WATPLAN is applied for selecting subsolutions and resolving conflicts. To compare with an incremental planner, an additional run is made for each test problem using TWEAK to combine subplans and resolve conflicts. The results are shown in

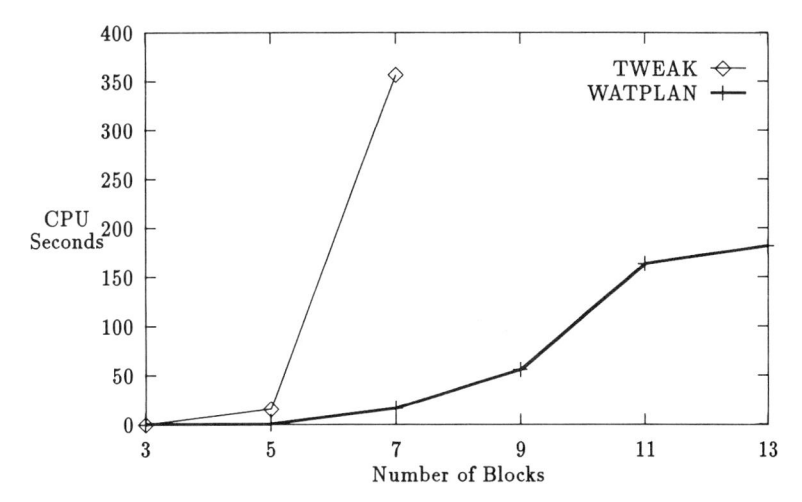

Fig. 6. Comparison in blocks world domain.

Fig. 6, where each datum is the average of ten randomly generated problems for a given number of blocks. This test again demonstrates that with WATPLAN the computational cost of the combination phase is much lower than the incremental planner, TWEAK.

9. Conclusion

We have described a theory of conflicts and conflict resolution methods in planning. Each conflict is modeled as a variable in a CSP, and the set of conflict resolution methods is modeled as the domain of a variable. Two types of relations are described. The inconsistency relation corresponds directly to its counterpart in CSPs, and the subsumption relation provides new insights into the removal of redundancy values and variables. The formalization supports a number of efficient reasoning tasks, including arc-consistency enforcement, redundancy removal, dead end detection, and the ordering of conflicts in which to conduct their resolution.

Our empirical results have also revealed that for problems where a large number of conflicts is expected to occur, the theory will work well. In addition, for planning systems that rely on problem decomposition, that are based on task networks, and that perform plan revisions for reuse, a global reasoning of conflicts based on our theory promises improved efficiency.

Our theory of conflict resolution can be considered as a framework for making inferences between time points in a temporal constraint network. In this respect, it is closely related to Allen and Koomen's work on temporal constraint propagation in planning [1]. In that work, a time interval algebra is used to express the relationship between actions, facts, and goals. When a new temporal relation is added into a plan, constraint propagation is automatically conducted, resulting in temporal relations that are more specific. This is similar to removing inconsistent or redundant relations contained in the variables in our constraint network during conflict resolution. However, as a proposal for a general plan representation language, Allen and Koomen did not focus on any specific control strategy for resolving conflicts in a plan, nor did they consider codesignation and noncodesignation constraints among the variables in a plan. One problem that faced Allen and Koomen's planning system was how to control constraint propagation when a new relation was inserted into a plan, so that only "interesting" inferences were made. Our theory on conflict resolution provides a guideline for controlling the propagation of constraints: propagations should be done only when they are useful in establishing inconsistency or subsumption relations among the conflict resolution constraints.

One advantage of our theory is its extensibility; with a more elaborate planning language, the underlying theory for global conflict resolution need not change. For example, one can extend the TWEAK language to include the time point algebra of Vilain and Kautz [16], by associating the occurrence of each action with a time point. One can also extend the TWEAK language to include Allen's interval representation of actions. With Vilain and Kautz's time point logic, the relationships between two time points include "precedes", "follows", "same", and "not-same". With the new language, one can also augment the set of conflict resolution methods by providing an additional set of constraints. For example, suppose that whenever two operators occur simultaneously, one of their combined effects will clobber an establishment relation. Then one way to resolve the conflict is to impose a "not-same" constraint onto the time points of the two operators. This augmentation only enlarges the domain of individual variables that represent conflicts in a CSP, and thus the same computational framework can be directly applied to resolve conflicts in the extended language.

Appendix A. Proofs of the theorems

Theorem 4.1. *Let Π be a plan with a conflict set $\mathscr{C}$. Let $Conf_1$ and $Conf_2$ be two conflicts in $\mathscr{C}$, and let $M(Conf_1)$ and $M(Conf_2)$ be their corresponding sets of conflict resolution constraints. Suppose that*

$$\forall R_1 \in M(Conf_1), \exists R_2 \in M(Conf_2) \text{ such that } S(R_1, R_2).$$

Then $Conf_2$ can be pruned from $\mathscr{C}$ without affecting the set of minimal solutions to $\mathscr{C}$.

Proof. Let $\mathscr{C}'$ be $\mathscr{C} - \{Conf_2\}$. We would like to show that every minimal solution to $\mathscr{C}'$ is a minimal solution to $\mathscr{C}$, and vice versa.

Let $Sol_{\mathscr{C}'}$ be a minimal solution to $\mathscr{C}'$. This implies that the constraints in $Sol_{\mathscr{C}'}$ resolve every conflict in $\mathscr{C}'$. Since $Conf_1$ is a member of $\mathscr{C}'$ and $\mathscr{C}'$ is solved by $Sol_{\mathscr{C}'}$, some constraint $R_1 \in M(Conf_1)$ must be subsumed by $Sol_{\mathscr{C}'}$. From the assumption that every constraint in $Conf_1$ subsumes some constraint in $Conf_2$, there must exist a constraint $R_2 \in M(Conf_2)$ such that R_1 subsumes R_2. Because the subsumption relation is transitive, $Sol_{\mathscr{C}'}$ subsumes R_2 also. Therefore, $Sol_{\mathscr{C}'}$ is a solution for $\mathscr{C} = \mathscr{C}' \cup \{Conf_2\}$. Furthermore, $Sol_{\mathscr{C}'}$ must also be a *minimal* solution to $\mathscr{C}$, since otherwise, a proper subset of $Sol_{\mathscr{C}'}$ could solve $\mathscr{C}$ as well as $\mathscr{C}'$, violating the assumption that $Sol_{\mathscr{C}'}$ is a minimal solution to $\mathscr{C}'$. Thus, every minimal solution to $\mathscr{C}'$ must also be a minimal solution to $\mathscr{C}$.

On the other hand, a minimal solution $Sol_{\mathscr{C}}$ to $\mathscr{C}$ is clearly a solution to $\mathscr{C}'$, since $\mathscr{C}'$ is a subset of $\mathscr{C}$. Suppose that it is *not* a minimal solution to $\mathscr{C}'$. Then a proper subset of $Sol_{\mathscr{C}}$ is a solution to $\mathscr{C}'$. This implies that, using the result from the above paragraph, the subset is also a solution to $\mathscr{C}$, violating the assumption that $Sol_{\mathscr{C}}$ is already a minimal solution to $\mathscr{C}$. Therefore, $Sol_{\mathscr{C}}$ must also be a minimal solution to $\mathscr{C}'$. □

Theorem 4.2. *Let Π be a plan with a conflict set $\mathscr{C}$. Let $Conf_1$ and $Conf_2$ be two conflicts in $\mathscr{C}$, and let $M(Conf_1)$ and $M(Conf_2)$ be their corresponding sets of conflict resolution constraints. Suppose that $\exists R_2 \in M(Conf_2)$ such that $\forall R_1 \in M(Conf_1 H)$, either*

(1) $I(R_1, R_2)$, *or*
(2) $\exists R_3 \in M(Conf_2)$ *such that* $R_2 \neq R_3$ *and* $S(R_1, R_3)$.

Then R_2 can be pruned from $M(Conf_2)$ without affecting the set of minimal solutions to $\mathscr{C}$.

Proof. Let R_2 be the constraint in $M(Conf_2)$ that satisfies the condition of Theorem 4.2, and let M'_2 be $M(Conf_2) - \{R_2\}$. We would like to show that every minimal solution to the CSP corresponding to $\mathscr{C}$ is a minimal solution to the modified CSP, obtained by removing R_2 from $M(Conf_2)$, and vice versa.

Let $Sol_{\mathscr{C}}$ be a minimal solution to $\mathscr{C}$. Since $Sol_{\mathscr{C}}$ resolves $Conf_1$, it must subsume a constraint R_1 in $M(Conf_1)$. There are two possibilities regarding R_1 and R_2:

(1) R_1 is inconsistent with R_2. Then the solution $Sol_{\mathscr{C}}$ cannot include R_2 as a member. Therefore $Sol_{\mathscr{C}}$ must subsume a member of M'_2 in order to solve $Conf_2$.
(2) R_1 is consistent with R_2. From the condition of Theorem 4.2, R_1 must also subsume some constraint R_3 in $M(Conf_2)$, where $R_3 \neq R_2$ and $R_3 \in M'_2$.

Thus, every minimal solution to $\mathscr{C}$ subsumes a constraint in M'_2. If there exists a solution to the CSP corresponding to $\mathscr{C}$, then the same solution is also a solution for the modified CSP $\mathscr{C}'$, obtained by removing R_2 from $M(Conf_2)$. On the other hand, every minimal solution to the modified CSP resolves a conflict in $\mathscr{C}$, and is clearly a solution to the original CSP as well. □

Acknowledgement

The author wishes to thank Josh Tenenberg, Peter van Beek, and Jean Patrick Tsang for many useful comments on an earlier version of the paper.

References

[1] J. Allen and J. Koomen, Planning using a temporal world model, in: *Proceedings IJCAI-83*, Karlsruhe, Germany (1983) 741–747.
[2] D. Chapman, Planning for conjunctive goals, *Artif. Intell.* **32** (1987) 333–377.
[3] S. Kambhampati, Flexible reuse and modification in hierarchical planning: a validation structure based approach, Ph.D. Thesis, University of Maryland, College Park, MD (1989).
[4] S. Kambhampati, M. Cutkosky, M. Tenenbaum and S.H. Lee, Combining specialized reasoners and general planners: a case study, in: *Proceedings AAAI-91*, Anaheim, CA (1991) 199–205.
[5] R.E. Korf, Planning as search: a quantitative approach, *Artif. Intell.* **33** (1987) 65–88.
[6] V. Kumar, Algorithms for constraint satisfaction problems: a survey, Tech. Rept. 91-28, Department of Computer Siences, University of Minnesota, Minneapolis, MN (1991).
[7] A.L. Lansky, Localized event-based reasoning for multiagent domains, *Comput. Intell.* **4** (4) (1988).
[8] A.K. Mackworth, Consistency in networks of relations, *Artif. Intell.* **8** (1977) 99–118; also in: B.L. Webber and N.J. Nilsson, eds., *Readings in Artificial Intelligene* (Morgan Kaufmann, Los Altos, CA, 1981) 69–78.
[9] A.K. Mackworth and E.C. Freuder, The complexity of some polynomial network consistency algorithms for constraint satisfaction problems, *Artif. Intell.* **25** (1985) 65–74.
[10] D.A. McAllester and D. Rosenblitt, Systematic nonlinear planning, in: *Proceedings AAAI-91*, Anaheim, CA (1991).
[11] E.D. Sacerdoti, *A Structure for Plans and Behavior* (American Elsevier, New York, 1977).
[12] R.G. Simmons, The roles of associational and causal reasoning in problem solving, *Artif. Intell.* **53** (2–3) (1992) 159–208.
[13] M. Stefik, Planning with constraints (MOLGEN: Part 1), *Artif. Intell.* **16** (2) (1981) 111–139.
[14] G.J. Sussman, A computational model of skill acquisition, MIT AI Lab Memo No. AI-TR-297, Cambridge, MA (1973).
[15] A. Tate, Generating project networks, in: *Proceedings IJCAI-77*, Cambridge, MA (1977) 888–893.
[16] M. Vilain and H.A. Kautz, Constraint propagation algorithms for temporal reasoning, in: *Proceedings AAAI-86*, Philadelphia, PA (1986) 337–382.
[17] D.E. Wilkins, *Practical Planning: Extending the Classical AI Planning Paradigm* (Morgan Kaufmann, San Mateo, CA, 1988).
[18] Q. Yang, Reasoning about conflicts in least-commitment planning, Tech. Rept. CS-90-23, Department of Computer Science, University of Waterloo, Waterloo, Ont. (1990).
[19] Q. Yang, D.S. Nau and J.V. Hendler, Merging separately generated plans in limited domains, *Comput. Intell.* **9** (1) (1993), to appear.
[20] Q. Yang and J. Tenenberg, Abtweak: abstracting a nonlinear, least commitment planner, in: *Proceedings AAAI-90*, Boston, MA (1990) 204–209.

Index

Note: Page numbers in italics indicate illustrations.

Aas, E. J., 130
Abraham, J. A., 128
Abramson, B., 169
AC-4, 217
 comparison, 220–221
 mapping optimization to, 230–231
ACP, 217, *218*
 compared, 220–221
 phases of, 217
Action analysis, 336, *337–338*
 canonical nature of, 342
 and geometric planning, 338–342, 344
Actual application space, 87–88, 92–93
 search in, 93–94
ADAMS Users Manual, 351
Adorf, Hans-Martin, 162, 169, 175–176, 202
Aggoun, A., 114, 121
Aggregate geoms, 334
Agre, Phil, 359
Aho, A. V., 306, 324
Aiba, A., 73, 79
Aiken, D. L., 162
Alander, J., 107, 108
Alefeld, G., 74, 80
Allen, J. F., 210, 274, 298, 299, 312, 316, 320, 322, 389–390
Almeida, M. J., 303
Ambler, A. P., 350
Amiri, G., 146, 163, 173
Angluin, D., 258, 265, 266n, 269
ANOVA (analysis of variance), 51–60, *56*
Anytime algorithm, 115, 263, *264*
 branch and bound and, 29, 48
 depth-first implementation and, 30
Aragon, C. R., 162, 199, 282
Arbab, F., 352
Arc array, 212, *213, 214*
Arc consistency, 38
 achieving sequentially, 211
 in CSP, 374
 in DOF, 353
 fast parallel algorithm for, 211–216
 general purpose algorithm for, 209–222
 parallelism and domain dependence, 207–235
Arc Consistency (AC) Chip, 212–216, *232, 233*
 circuit optimization, 226–228, *229, 230, 231*
 comparison, 220–221
 speed of, 222
Arc consistency counts, *57*, 63
 defined, 39

algorithm for, *40*
pruning, 39–40, 47
Arc consistency methods, and problem classes, 209–210
Arc consistent network, *12*
Arnborg, S., 253
Asaithambi, N., 79, 106
Automatic test pattern generation (ATPG), 127, *134*
 basic program of, 133–134
 as constraint satisfaction problem, 130–132
Avery, Trina, 156

Backjumping, 31–34, 210, 317
 algorithm for, *33*
 examples of, *32, 33*
Backmarking, 34–38
 algorithm for, *35*
 example of, *37*
Backto, 34–38, *37*
Backtracking
 defined, 25
 example of, *26*
 vs. hill-climbing repair strategy, 168–169
 informed, in min-conflicts, 167–*168*
 as search mechanism, 276–278, *279*
 speeding up, 210
Backtracking algorithms
 considerations for, 316–317
 heuristically guided, 377–378
Backtracking search, 316
 naive, 317, *319*
Ballard, D. H., 212
Barlow, H. B., 212
Barrow, Harry, 359
Baumert, L. D., 25
Baykan, C., 200
Beeri, C., 253
Bellos, I. M., 350
Belsey, D. A., 37, 58
Bennett, S., 291, 292
Berthier, F., 114, 121
Bibel, W., 5, 11
Biefeld, E., 174, 175, 282
Binary constraints
 in GCE, 334
 network of, 304
Binford, T. O., 305n
Bitner, J., 171
Blumer, A., 257

Boddy, M., 115
Borning, A., 22, 37, 38, 64, 114, 121
Bottorff, P. S., 128
Branch and bound technique, 25-31, 47
  algorithm for, *29*
  defined, 25
  depth-first implementation of, 30-31
  example of, *28*
  levels of, 67-68
  and resource-bound solutions, 29
Branch variable, 345
Brassard, G., 166
Bratley, P., 166
Brayton, R. K., 238
Brelaz, D., 176-180
Bresina, John, 295
Brglez, F., 135
Brown, R. H., 277
Bruce, B. C., 299
Bundy, A., 351
Buttner, W., 115

C*, 217
Canadian flag problem, 4-7
  AC resolution on, *16*
  as FCSP, *7*
Canonicality, in DOF analysis, 351
Capacity constraints, 140, 142
Carbonell, J. G., 200, 274
Cardinality combinator, 123-125
Cardinality similator, transition rules for, 153-155
Carlier, J., 115
Car sequencing, 115, 139-150, *140, 141, 147, 148, 149, 150*
  improving efficiency in, 145-147
Causal link, 366
cc(FD), 115, *117*
  formalization of semantics of, 151-156
  novel aspects of, 116
  overview of, 116-127
Celnicker, G., 319
Centred forms, 107-108
Chain analysis, 347-350
Chains, 253-254
  solving, 354-355
Chapman, D., 363, 365, 366n
Cheeseman, Peter, 68, 179, 202
CHIP, 13
Chow, C. K., 238
Christofides, N., 115
Chvátal, V., 306, 307
Circle, constraints on, 242-244, *343*
Circ_Min, 226-227
Clark, K. L., 12, 120

Clobberer, 366-367
Clocksin, W. F., 130
Closed World Assumption, 6
CLP, scheme of, 117-120
CNF formula(s)
  as constraint network, 241
  identifying, 247-251
Cohen, Robin, 298, 301, 312, 313, 322, 325
Cohen, W., 275, 291
Colmerauer, A., 73, 114, 120
Completeness, defined, 87
Computation state, 117-118
Computation step, 118
Conditional utility, 291
Configuration variables, 330
Conflict(s), 361
  and conflict resolution, 365-369
Conflict probability distributions, 185, *186*
Conflict resolution, 362
  conflicts and, 365-369
  as constraint satisfaction, 372-378
  global analysis of, 372
  methods for, 367-369
  minimal solutions to, 372
  planning with global, 378-380
  relations among methods, 369-372
Connection Machine, 232
Consistency, *78*
  constraint net for, *97*
  local vs. global, 97-98
Consistent scenario, finding a, 316-321
Constituents, 79
Constraint(s), definability of, 86
Constraint-based reasoning, introduction to, 1-2
Constraint-based scheduling, learning to improve, 271-296
Constraint checks, 26, 31, *54, 57, 60, 61*, 62
  in forward checking, 41
Constraint entailment, 120-121
Constraint graph, 43
Constraint importance, 22
Constraint logic programming, 3, 4
Constraint net, as globally consistent, 98-99
Constraint network, defined, 240
Constraint propagation, among conflicts, 373-374
Constraint reasoning, as based on interval arithmetic, 71-112
Constraint relaxation, 22
Constraint satisfaction
  conflict resolution as, 372-378
  logical framework for, 3-4
  logic of, 3-20
  partial, 21-70

and scheduling problems, 161–205
  using constraint logic programming, 113–159
Constraint satisfaction problem (CSP), 3, 364
  and CLP(D), 14
  defined, 209
  formulation of, 4
  highly structured, 188
  methods for solving, 373–374
  random, 185–*187*, 193, 196, 198
  repair, statistical model for, 183–184
Constraint store, 118
Constraint system, of cc(FD), 125–127
Constraint trees, identifying, 251
Cook, S. A., 221, 254
Cooper, L., 174, 175, 282
Cooper, M., 2, 22
Cooper, Paul R., on arc consistency, 207–235
CORTES, 278
CPU time, and iterations, 289–*290*
Critical path method (CPM), 284
CSIAN, 318–321
CSP representations, 373. *See also* Constraint satisfaction problem
CSPAN, 311–312
Cutkosky, M., 379
Cycle cutset method, 210

Danyluk, A., 275, 291
Datalog, *8*
Daube, F., 346
Daun, Brian, on constraint-based scheduling, 271–296
Davis, Eugene, 2, 14, 73, 79, 83, 84, 110
  on constraint-based scheduling, 271–296
Davis, L. S., 208
D'Carpio-Montalvo, P., 72
Deale, Michael, 2, 174
  on constraint-based scheduling, 271–296
Dean, T., 115, 305n
Dechter, A., 22, 45
Dechter, Rina, 2, 4, 11, 12, 17, 22, 43, 45, 53, 98, 99, 187, 210, 304, 305n, 316, 317
  on structure identification, 237–270
Defaults, 350
Defect level, 127
Definability, 86–87
  criterion for, 88–89
Definite clause programs (DCP), 8
Degrees of freedom (DOF), 330
  analysis of, 330–334
  as layered solution to GCSP, 353
  reasoning about, *331*
De Jong, G. F., 274, 291, 292
de Kleer, J., 14, 15, 17, 18, 114
Demand constraints, 143–144

Denavit, J., 328, 329, 330, 348
Density, 49
  and satisfiability, *57*
Deo, N., 25
Depth-first search, for GDS, 165–*166*
Depth-0 repair strategy, 286–287
Descotte, Y., 22, 64
Deville, Y., 115, 121, 126, 153, 156, 223
de Werra, D., 201
DFFITS, 58
Dietterich, T. G., 291
Dijkstra, E. W., 306
Dimension, defined, 240
Dincbas, Mehmet, 1
  on constraint satisfaction, 113–159
Discontinuous (multiple) values, 87
Distance, defined, 27, 30
DIVISER, 380
Division arithmetic, 95–96
Division propagation, 94–95
Dixon, L., 75
Domain size, and satisfiability, *53*
Dowling, W. F., 18, 254
Doyle, J., 114
Drascher, Ellen, 2
  on constraint-based scheduling, 271–296
Duisberg, R., 22, 64
Dumoulin, J. N., 277
Dutta, D., 333
Dyer, M., 275, 291
Dynamic splitting, 99–101

Ehrenfeucht, A., 257
Elias, A. L., 72
Elliot, G. L., 38, 146, 169, 276, 316
Empirical analysis, of GCE, 350–351
Enlargements, 86
Envelope, 267
  algorithm for, 268–269
Equation triple, constraint net for, *77*
Eshghi, K., 130
Eskey, Megan, 2, 200, 291
  on constraint-based scheduling, 271–296
Etzioni, O., 274, 291
Even, S., 17
Exact value systems, 71–74
Explanation-based generalization (EBG), 274
Explanation-based learning (EBL), 272
Extended forward checking, 42, 47

Fagin, R., 253
Falkenhainer, B., 23, 223
Fanout points, 130, 131, *132*
Fault coverage, defined, 127
Fault models, 128

FCS. *See* Finite constraint satisfaction
FCS decision problem (FCSDP), 5–6
FCSP, logical interpreters for, 12–13
Feasible relations, 312–315, *314*
   finding, 321–322
Feldman, J. A., 212
Feldman, R., 22, 64
Fikes, Richard E., 1, 114
Finite constraint satisfaction (FCS)
   in constraint networks, *11–12*
   as Datalog, 11
   as model finding in propositional logic, 14–18
   as theorem proving in definite theories, 10–11
   as theorem proving in propositional calculus, 9–10
Finite CSP (FCSP), 3
First-fail principle, 146
Firstmark, 36–38, *37*
Flann, N., 291
Flannery, B. P., 328
Flowers, M., 275, 291
FOPC, flag FCSP in, 7
"Forbidden" subgraph, *313–315*
Forbus, K. D., 223
Forward chaining, 330
Forward checking, 38–39, 41–43, 47, 63, 378
   and constraint checks, 41
   example of, *42*
Fox, M., 22, 64, 114, 173, 200, 277, 278
Franier, Richard, 202
Frazier, M., 258
Freeman-Benson, B., 22, 64
Freuder, Eugene C., 12, 17, 84, 98, 173, 208, 209, 210, 276, 321
   on constraint-based reasoning, 1–2
   on partial constraint satisfaction, 21–70
Friedland, Peter, 295
Fujiwara, H., 132
Full-adder, 130

Gallagher, R. H., 329
Gallaire, H., 114, 120
Gallier, J. H., 18, 254
Gargan, R., 174, 284
Gaschnig, J., 31, 34, 317
Gates
   defined, *131, 133*
   as demons, 132–133
Gaussian limit, *196*, 197
GDS network, 163–164
   constraint satisfaction approach of, 174
   vs. min-conflict hill climbing, 170, *177*, 180–181
   performance of, 164–168

Gelatt, C. D., 285
GEMPLAN, 379
Generic flow, 284
Gentner, D., 223
Geoms, 327
   configuration of, 330
   description of, 329–330
   as grounded, 336
   hierarchical grouping of, 347–349, *348*
   as links, 347
   nested, 334
   and node, 348
Geometric constraint engine (GCE), 327–360
Geometric constraint satisfaction problem (GCSP), 327–360
   constraints used in, 334
   defined, 330
Geometric planning
   and action analysis, 338–342, 344
   and locus analysis, 345, 346
Ginsberg, M. L., 165
Global application space, 92
Global conflict processing algorithm, 386
Global conflict resolution, planning with, 378–380
Global consistency, 97–101
   detection of, 98
Global search paradigm, vs. local search paradigm, 115
Global solution functions, 101
   determination of, 102–104
Global tolerance propagation, 101–109
   agenda for, 102–104
Glymour, C., 238
Goal part, 118
Goel, P., 132
Golumb, S. W., 25
Golumbis, M., 22, 64, 304n
Goodness, *288*
   defined, 287
GORDIUS, 292, 379
Gosling, J., 73, 74
Gossard, D., 329
Graf, T., 114, 115, 121, 127
Graph coloring, 175–180, *177, 178, 179*
Gratch, J., 291
Ground processing, defined, 283
Gu, J., 162, 173
Guard neurons, 163
Guess variables, 72
Gullichsen, E., 130
Gupta, R., 130
Güsgen, H.-W., 208, 222
Güther, S., 301

Hachtel, G. D., 238
HACKER, 362
Hamlet, I., 298, 303
Hammond, K. J., 200, 292
Han, C.-C., 210
Hankins, G. B., 277
Hansen, E., 107
Hansson, O., 291
Haralick, R. M., 22, 38, 40, 42, 47, 146, 169, 276, 316
Hartenberg, R. S., 328, 329, 330, 348
Harvey, W. D., 165
Hasegawa, R., 73, 79
Haussler, D., 257
Havens, W. S., 14, 208
Hawley, D., 73, 79
Henderson, T. C., 123, 125, 126, 145, 208, 209, 210, 211, 217
Hendler, J. V., 379
Hertz, A., 201
Hervé, J. M., 350
Herzberger, J., 74, 80, 208
Heuristically guided backtracking algorithms, 377–378
Hickman, A. K., 200
Hill-climbing min-conflicts, 167, 197–198
  vs. backtracking repair strategy, 168–169, 170–*171*
  run time for, *172*
Hillier, F. S, 284
Hinton, G. E., 221
Hirsh, H., 275, 291
Hopcroft, J. E., 306, 324
Hopfield, J. J., 163
HORN, 258, 268–269
Horn clauses, forms of, 8
Horn formula
  defined, 239
  with k models, 268
HornSAT algorithm, 10
Horn theories, identifying, 254–265
Hostetter, G. H., 72
Hower, W., 22
Huard, S., 68
Hubble Space Telescope
  scheduling problem of, 163, 173, 174–175
  and SPIKE, 173–174
Hum, R., 135
Hummel, R. A., 22, 209, 211
Hunter, J., 298, 303
Husbands, Phil, 359
Hybrid algorithms, 38
Hyvönen, Eero, 1
  on constraint reasoning, 71–112

Identifiability, 241–244
  defined, 241
  vs. learnability, 243–244
Identification
  automatic, 238
  topology-based, 244–254
Implication combinator, 121–123
  semantics of, 153
Inadmissibility, *78*
Inconsistency, 25, 28, *78*
Inconsistency count, 41
Inconsistency depth, 34
Inconsistency relation, 369–370
Incremental assembly, 332–333
Inexact consistent labeling problem, 22
  defined, 42
Inexact data, dealing with, 72–73
Informedness hypothesis, 166–168
Initialization routine, *178*
Input variables, 71
Interval(s)
  disjointedness of, 303–304
  qualitative relations between, *302*
  relations between two, 299–*300*
Interval algebra (IA) networks, 316–322
  consistent scenario for, *319, 320, 321*
  defined, 304
  example of, *318*
  feasible relations for, 322
  vs. SA networks, 303
Interval analysis, 104
Interval constraint satisfaction, 74–76
Interval constraint satisfaction problem (ICSP), 74–80
  semantics of, 77–79
  solutions for, 79–80
  syntax for, 76
Interval functions
  algebraic approaches to, 106–108
  applicability of, 86–87
  basic, 80–81
  computing values for, 105–106
Interval propagation, tractability of, 84
Invariants record, 335–*336*
Invariants signature, 336
ISCAS benchmark set, 137–*139, 138*
Itai, A., 17, 259
Iterative repair, 282–291
  constraint-based, 284–287
  defined, 282

Jackowski, D., 115
Jaffar, J., 14, 72, 73, 79, 82, 114, 151
Jayaraman, S., 71, 72

JK flip-flops, 212
Johnson, D. S., 162, 199, 282
Johnston, Mark D., 1, 282
  on constraint satisfaction and scheduling problems, 161–205
Jones, N. D., 17
Jordan, J. W., 277

Kabat, W. C., 115
Kale, L. V., 173
Kambhampati, S., 200, 292, 379, 380
Kanefsky, Bob, 51, 68, 179
Kanoui, H., 114, 120
Kant, E., 346
Kanumury, Mahesh, 359
Kasif, S., 14, 17, 221
Katz, J. L., 277
Kautz, Henry A., 210, 238, 254, 255n, 256n, 258n, 260, 265n, 266, 269, 274, 298, 299, 301, 312, 316, 321, 322, 390
Kearns, Michael, 258n, 260, 265n, 266, 269
Kedar-Cabelli, S. T., 274, 291
Keirouz, Walid, 352, 359
Keller, R. M., 274, 291
Kelly, K., 238
Keng, N., 169
Kernighan, B., 282
k-Horn formulas, identifying, 261–265, *262*
Kirk, R. E., 52
Kirkpatrick, S., 285
Kleene, three-valued logic of, 225–226
Knoblock, C. A., 274
Knuth, D. E., 306, 311
Kolodner, J. L., 200
Konopasek, M., 71, 72
Koomen, J. A., 298, 320, 389–390
Korf, R. E., 379
Kowalski, R. A., 13, 256
Kramer, A., 22
Kramer, Glenn, 2
  on geometric constraint engine, 327–360
k-trees, 253–254
Kubale, M., 115
Kuh, E., 37, 58
Kumar, V., 23, 372, 377, 378
Kuokka, D. R., 274
Kurtzman, C. R., 162, 174

Laaser, W. T., 17
Label discarding rule, 211
Labeling array, 212, *213, 214*
Lacroix, M., 22
Ladkin, Peter B., 298, 301, 304, 307, 316, 317, 319, 323, 325

Laird, J. E., 274
Laird, Philip E., 1, 282
  on constraint satisfaction and scheduling problems, 161–205
Langley, P., 165
Lansky, A. L., 379
Lasserre, C., 120
Lassez, C., 73
Lassez, J.-L., 14, 73, 114
Lastmark, 36–38, *37*
Las Vegas algorithm, 166
Latombe, J. C., 22, 64
Lauriere, J.-L., 114
Lavency, P. 22
Lawler, E. L., 25
Lazarsfeld, P. F., 238
Learnability, vs. identifiability, 243–244
Learned search control knowledge, *280–281*
Learning variable ordering, 278–282
Least general common solution (LGCS), 78–79
Lee, C.-H., 210
Lee, S. H., 379
Leler, W., 71
Lepape, J.-P., 120
Levesque, H. J., 162, 200
Lieberman, G. J., 284
Lien, Y. E., 17
Lin, S., 282
LINC (logical interpreter for a network of constraints), 12–13
Link constraints, 144–145
Links, *347, 348, 349*
  geoms as, 347
Liu, C. N., 238
Liu, Y., 328
Local application space, 88
Local definition space, 88
Local failure, 27
Local interval propagation, 81–82
Locality principle, 75
Local tolerance propagation, 80–86, *83*
  constraint net for, *85*
Local Waltz filtering systems, 75
Locus analysis, 336, 344–345
  as cycle finder, 352
  and geometric planning, 345–346
Locus intersection tables, 345
Locus tables, 345
Logical representation systems, *8–9*
Loop(s), 101–102
  solving, 355–357
Loop analysis, 347–350
Loop cover, 102
Looping constraints, 102

Lovett, M. C., 200
Lozano-Pérez, T., 80

McAllester, D. A., 14, 15, 378
McAloon, K., 73
McCabe, F., 120
McDermott, D. V., 305n
McGeoch, L. A., 162, 199, 282
MacGregor, W., 346
McKenzie, P., 221
Mackworth, Alan K., 38, 43, 79, 84, 114, 126, 208, 209, 210, 215, 276, 307, 312, 324, 353, 376
  on constraint-based reasoning, 1–2
  on logic of constraint satisfaction, 3–20
Maddux, R., 298, 301, 304, 307, 323
Maher, M., 22, 37, 38, 115, 120
Maier, D., 238, 253
Malik, J., 305n
Mark, 34
Martindale, A., 22, 37, 38
Masini, G., 22
Maximal constraint satsifaction, 22–23
  methods for, 24–48
  testing of, 48–63
Maximal solution, 27
Maximum-weight spanning tree (MWST), 251–253, *252*
Mayer, A., 291
Mean value, 106–107
Meiri, Itay, 43, 252, 269, 304, 305n, 316
Meseguer, P., 23, 79
Metaphorical assembly plan (MAP), and equation solution, 333–334
Metrics, 64
Michaylow, S., 72, 73, 79, 82, 114
Milestone constraints, 273–274
Min-conflicts heuristic, 166–168, 170–173, 286
  disadvantage of, 171–172
  vs. GDS network, 170, 174, *177, 179*
  hill climbing repair of, 167–172, 197–198
  and initialization, *180*
  modeling, 182–183
Minimal network, and maximal formula, 247, 249
Minton, Steven, 1, 274, 275, 282, 291, 295
  on constraint satisfaction and scheduling problems, 161–205
Mitchell, D., 162, 200
Mitchell, T. M., 274, 291
Mittal, S., 23
Modal truth criterion (MTC), 367
Mohr, R., 22, 123, 125, 126, 145, 208, 209, 217
MOLGEN, 363

Monotonicity, 87
  criterion for, 89–91
Montanari, U., 11, 12, 126, 208, 244–245, 299, 304, 307, 312, 324
Mooney, M. R., 274, 291
Moore, R., 106
Moore, R. E., 72, 74, 79, 80, 82, 104, 106
Morris, P., 162, 199, 201
Mulder, J. A., 208
Mulvehill, A. M., 277
Muscettola, N., 146, 163, 173
Musick, R., 183

Nadel, B. A., 23, 316
Naish, L., 120
Naive backtracking search, 317, *319*
Natarajan, B. K., 243
Nau, D. S., 379
Necessary bound, 28
Network, as path-consistent, 312
Nevins, A., 330
Newell, A., 274
Nguyen, H. N., 127
Nievergelt, J., 25
NOAH, 362
Node
  achieving consistency for, 210–211
  in DOF, 353
  and geom, 348
Nökel, K., 303
NONCIN, 363, 366, 380
Nonserializable subgoals, 379
Nonsystematic search hypothesis, GDS, 165–166
n-queens, *195*–196
  problem, 169–173, *171, 172*
Nudel, B., 316
Numerical constraint satisfaction, 71–76

Older, W., 73, 79, 80, 108, 110
OPIS, 278
Optimal solution, 66
Options, 284
Option variables, 141
Ordering techniques, 46
  defined, 25
Output variables, 71
Overconstrained problems, solving, 73–74
Overhead using time, 59–60
Ow, P. 274, 277, 278, 282, 292

Pabon, Jahir, 352, 359
Painting example, 362–*369*
  conflict resolution for, 376–377

Panangaden, P., 115, 151, 152n, 162, 199, 306
PA network, *308*
  consistent scenario for, *310*
  and CSPAN, 311–312
  defined, 304–305
  feasible relations algorithm for, *314*–315
Parallelism
  for general constraint satisfaction, 222
  limits to, 221–222
Parent geom, 334
Parrello, B., 115, 139
Partial constraint satisfaction, 21–70
  contexts of, 21–22
  defined, 21
Partial constraint satisfaction problems (PCSP), 66–68
  defined, 25
  solving, 25–48, 66
Pathak, D., 146, 163, 173
Path consistency, in DOF, 353
Paul, R. P., 330n
Payload processing domain, 278–279
Pazzani, M., 275, 291
P-BB procedure, 30, 50, 51, 52, *53, 54*, 55, *57*
  recursive structure of, 30, 58, 59, 60, 63
P-BJ, 50, 51, 52, 53, 54, 59, 60
P-BMK, 35, 50, 51, 52, 53, 54, 55–56, *57*, 58, 59, 60, 62, 63
p_c, 49, 50 51, 58
p_d, 49, 50, 51, 52, *53, 54*
Pearl, Judea, 2, 17, 22, 43, 45, 53, 98, 99, 187, 210, 275, 304, 305n
  on structure identification, 237–270
Pease, Holly, 295
P-EFC, 47
P-EFC3, 47, 51, 58–59, 60–61, 62, 63
Pelavin, R., 210
P-FC algorithm, 42–43, 50
P-FCC, 50, *54,* 56, 58
P-FC1, 42–43, 54
P-FC2, 43, 51, 54, 59
P-FC3, 43, 50, 51, 52, 54, 55–56, *57,* 58, 59, 60, 63
Philips, Andrew B., 1, 282
  on constraint satisfaction and scheduling problems, 161–205
Pinson, E., 115
Pitt, L., 258
Plan fragment tables, 338–342
  structure of, 346–347
Planning
  and problem decomposition, 389
  with global conflict resolution, 378–380
Plan revision, CSP in, 380

Plausible explanation–based learning (PEBL), 272, 274–*276*
  conjectures, 287–289, *288*
  and EBL, 291
Plausibility-chronic-resource-bottleneck-across-two-missions generalization problem, 293–294
Plotkin, G. D., 151
Point algebra networks, and interval algebra networks, 306–315
Points
  qualitative relations between, *303*
  relations between two, 300–301
Poisson limit, *196*
Popplestone, R. J., 328, 350, 352, 359
Position analysis, 349–350
Pownall, P. 135
Pradelles, C., 121, 127
Pradhan, D. K., 128
p_p, 49, 50, 51, 52, *53, 54,* 58
Precondition establishment, 366
Preemptive scheduling, 283–284
Preprocessing methods, consistency techniques for, 38
Press, W. H., 328
PRIAR, 380, 383
Primitive geoms, 334
Priorities, 22
Problem decomposition, planning and, 389
Problem decomposition, with WATPLAN, 386–389
Problem-decomposition-based problem solvers, 379
Problem spaces, 64–66
Projection network, and projection formula, 247–248
Prolog, 10–11
P-ROP, 51
Prospective strategies, 38–46
  defined, 25
Protection interval, 366
P-RPO, 47, 50, 52, 58, 60–61, 63
Pruning, with arc consistency counts, 39–40, 47
Purdom, P. W., Jr., 316

Quinlan, J. R., 254

Ragusa, J., 277
Random problem generation, 48–49
Ratscheck, H., 75, 80, 104, 106, 107, 108
Reasoning systems, 8–9
Redundancy
  removal of via subsumption relation, 374–376
  utility of, in WATPLAN, *385, 386*

Regular width-2, 210
Reinfeld, A., 316, 317, 319
Reingold, E. M., 25, 171
Reiter, R., 6, 11, 14, 17, 18
Relation, defined, 240
Rinard, M., 115, 151, 152n
Repair knowledge, dimensions of, 286
Repair process, informed, 282–283
Repair strategies, 286–288
    learning to select, 287–288
Representations, translations between, 301–304, 302, 303
Resource-available constraint, 274
Resource-bounded satisfaction, 23
Retrospective techniques, 25–38
    defined, 25
Robot clothing problem, 23–42, 23, 42
Rod variables, 224, 225
Rokne, J., 75, 80, 104, 106, 107, 108
Rose, J., 217
Rosenblitt, D., 378
Rosenbloom, P. S., 274
Rosenfeld, A., 22, 208, 211
Rosenthal, Don, 202
Rossi, F., 12, 244, 245
Rossignac, J. R., 329
Rotational DOFs (RDOFs), 334–336
Roth, J., 132
Rusick, Ron, 202
Russell, S., 183

Sacerdota, E. D., 362
Sadeh, N., 200, 277, 278
Sakai, Y., 73, 79
Samal, A., 211
SA networks, 301
    consistent scenario for, 302, 311
    and CSPAN, 311–312
    feasible relations algorithm for, 315, 322
Sangiovanni-Vincentelli, A. L., 238
Santina, M. S., 72
Saraswat, V. A., 115, 116, 121, 151, 152n, 156
Satisfiability, 49
    and density, 57
    and domain size, 53
    and mean constraint checks, 54
Sato, H., 73, 79
Scheduling
    defined, 273
    learning to improve constraint-based, 271–296
Scheines, R., 238
Schevon, C., 162, 199, 282
Search control rule, 279
Search path, 27, 30
Seering, W., 80

Seidel, R., 17, 321
Selman, Bart, 162, 200, 238, 254, 256n, 258n, 260, 265n, 266, 269
Shamir, A., 17
Shapiro, E., 120
Shapiro, L., 22, 40, 42, 47
Shimono, T., 132
Shuttle mission, components of, 284
Sidebottom, G., 14
Simmons, R. G., 162, 200, 292, 379
Simonis, Helmut, 1
    on constraint satisfaction, 113–159
Simpson, R. L., Jr., 200
Simulated annealing, 285
Single Instruction Multiple Data (SIMD), 216–220, 232, 233
    compared, 220–221
SIPE, 363, 380, 383
Skelboe, S., 106, 108
Skolem functions, 9
Slot variables, 141, 224
Smith, S. F., 146, 163, 173, 274, 277, 278, 282, 292
Snow, P., 22
Solution, defined, 24
Solution function localization technique, 109
Solution functions, 81
Song, F., 303
Sosic, R., 162, 173
Soundness, defined, 87
Spacelab-systems-experiment test, 279
Space Shuttle payload processing, 277–278
SPIKE, 173–174
Spirtes, P., 238
Splitting problem, 95
    solving, 96–97
Stark, P. A., 72
Stars, 253–254
Steele, G. L., Jr., 71, 73, 83, 114, 121, 217
Stefik, M., 207, 363
Steiglitz, K., 306
Stone, H. S., 163, 165, 169, 171
Stone, J. M., 163, 165, 169, 171
Strongly connected components (SCCs), 308, 309
Structural identification, in relational data, 237–270
Structural testing, 128
Subdistributivity law, 104
Subgeom, 334
Subgoals, nonserializable, 379
Submaximal solutions, for hard problems, 60–62
Subsumption, usefulness of, 386
Subsumption relation, 370–372
    and redundancy removal, 374–376, 389

Sufficient bound S, 28
Sufficient satisfaction, 23
Sufficient solution, 29, 66
Surrogate constraints, 146
Sussman, G. J., 114, 121, 162, 200, 292, 362
Susswein, S. Y., 210
Sutherland, I. E., 114
Svanaes, D., 130
Swain, Michael J., 2, 221, 222, 224
    on arc consistency, 207–235
Sycara-Cyranski, K., 200
Szező, G., 75

Tarjan, R. E., 308, 311
Task network planning system, 380
Tate, A., 363
Taylor, W. M., 51, 179
Taylor forms, 106–107
Temperature conversion, constraint net for, *72, 77*
Temporal constraints, 273–274
Temporal reasoning, 297
Tenenbaum, M., 379
Tenenberg, Josh, 210, 392
Termination condition, 100–101
Test generation
    controllability and observability of, 135
    defined, 127
    examples of, *136, 137*
    and fault simulation, 128–129
    heuristics for, 135
    labeling, 135
    and limiting backtracking, 135–136
Test pattern generation, 115, 127–139. *See also* Automatic test pattern generation
Teukolsky, S. A., 328
The Linkage Assistant (TLA), 328, 351
    compared with ADAMS, 351–*352*
Theoretical analysis, of GCE, 350–351
Thrashing effect, 374
Tightness, of constraint, 49
Tinkertoy objects, *223, 229*
Tolerance, 75
Tolerance propagation, defined, 75. *See also* Local tolerance propagation
Tolerance propagation approach, for constraint reasoning based on interval arithmetic, 71–112
Tolerance situation, 77
Tolerance solution
    global, 77
    local, 77–78
Topological sort, 306
Transition system, 151–152

Translational DOFs (TDOFs), 334–336
Tree-structured problems, 43–46
    algorithm for, *44*
    defined, 43
Tsang, Jean Patrick, 392
Turner, J. S., 176, 177–178, 225
TWEAK, 363, 364, 365, 378, 380–381
    and WATPLAN, 382–*389, 383, 384*

Ullman, Jeff D., 246, 269, 306, 324
Underconstrained problems, solving, 73

Valdés-Pérez, R. E., 312, 317
Valiant, L. G., 238, 239, 243, 244
Value(s), 27, 30
    inconsistency count for, 41
Value propagation, 72
Value selection, 192, *193*
    heuristic for, 188
    min-conflict, 188–189
    random, 190
    random-conflicts, 189–190
    and variable selection, 192–*195, 194*
van Beek, Peter, 2, 392
    on reasoning about qualitative temporal information, 297–326
Van Caneghem, M., 114, 120
van Emden, M. A., 256
Van Hentenryck, Pascal, 1, 12, 13, 22, 25, 223
    on constraint satisfaction, 113–159
Variable(s), 24, 30, *61*, 71–72
    effect of number of, 58–*59*
    for resource pool, 273
    for task, 273
    types of, 74, 224
Variable depth repair strategy, 287
Variable ordering, in CSP, 377
Variable ordering control knowledge, 272
Variable selection 190–191, *192*
    and value selection, 192–*195, 194*
VC-dimension, 257–258
Vecchi, M. P., 285
Vellino, A., 73, 80, 108, 110
Veloso, M. M., 200
Verma, T., 238
Vetterling, W. T., 328
Vilain, M., 274, 298, 299, 301, 312, 316, 321, 322, 390

Wald, J., 346
Waldrop, M., 115, 120, 163
Wallace, Richard J., 1
    on partial constraint satisfaction, 21–70
Waltz, D., 83, 126, 208, 210, 285

Waltz filtering
  local, 75
  and local TP, 83–84
Wang, B., 352
Ward, A., 80
Warmuth, M. K., 357
WATPLAN, 381–382, *385, 386*
  compared with TWEAK, 382–389, *383, 384*
  problem decomposition with, 386–389
Weinstein, Amir, 269
Welsch, R. E., 37, 58
White knight, 367
Wilk, M. R., 352
Wilkins, D. E., 363
Williams, T. W., 127
Wilson, M., 22, 37, 38
Wolfram, S., 72, 73
Woo, T. C., 333
Wood, D. E., 25
Woolf, M., 22
Work-in-process (WIP), 280–282, *281*
Wos, L., 115

Yang, Qiang, 2
  on conflict resolution in planning, 361–392
Yannakakis, M., 162, 199, 253
Yap, R., 73
Young, Robert, 352, 359
Yun, D. Y. Y., 169
Yung, M., 169

Zachary, J. L., 210
Zhang, Y., 11
Zimmer, L., 121, 127
Zube, S., 79, 106
Zucker, S. W., 22, 209, 211
Zweben, Monte, 2, 162, 174, 200, 202, 282, 284, 291
  on constraint-based scheduling, 271–296